REAL ESTATE

P E R S P E C T I V E S

REAL ESTATE

P E R S P E C T I V E S

Halbert C. Smith, DBA, SREA, CRE, FCA
University of Florida

John B. Corgel, Ph.D.
Georgia State University

1987

Homewood, Illinois 60430

ISBN 0-256-03180-0

Library of Congress Catalog Card No. 86–81795

Printed in the United States of America

3 4 5 6 7 8 9 0 K 4 3 2 1 0 9 8

Contents

Preface

Real estate means different things to different people. To some people real estate means a set of *legal* rights and constraints which allows them to use a portion of the earth's surface within a framework of public controls. To some people real estate is regarded as an *economic* resource; how it is developed, used, and allocated are questions of public concern. To other people real estate is an object of *financial* decision making; it is a valuable product that is bought, sold, leased, improved, and financed. And to still other people real estate means *business;* the marketing, management development, construction, appraisal, and financing of real estate are ways of earning livelihoods.

Real estate as viewed from these four perspectives (legal, economic, financial, and business) is the subject of this book. Thus, the book is divided into four parts—The Legal Perspective, The Economic Perspective, The Financial Perspective, and The Business Perspective. Chapter 1 is an introduction to the entire book, with the remaining 27 chapters being divided among the four parts. The first chapter(s) in each part presents the theory base for the perspective, while the remaining chapters present the institutional, technical, and policy aspects. For example, the legal perspective section begins with chapters about legal property rights and transfer of those rights, while the remaining chapters follow a real estate transaction (i.e., transfer of property rights) from contract to closing. Applications are included where relevant and appropriate.

While other approaches can be taken to the study of real estate, we believe that a multiview approach is more consistent with the needs of beginning students. It recognizes the diverse contexts in which they will be dealing with real estate as voting citizens, homeowners, investors, and business persons. The approach also has a pedagogical advantage. It allows new students of real estate to study and absorb one viewpoint of the subject before becoming immersed in others. Even so, however, one viewpoint builds upon the others; for example, the economic, financial, and business viewpoints build upon and reinforce the legal perspective, and the financial and business perspectives reinforce the legal and economic perspectives. A logical, progressive learning process occurs.

We believe this book will be an effective teaching and learning aid in beginning real estate courses in colleges, universities, and state licensing programs. More than 200 colleges and universities now offer one or more courses in real estate, and some 30 to 40 offer real estate as a major field. Most state license laws require applicants to take one or more courses as a prerequisite to licensure as salespersons or brokers. In all of these courses a multiview approach to real estate is relevant and appropriate.

Finally, we wish to point out that great strides have been made in recent years in the theory, teaching, and practice of real estate. Real estate is now seen as an important asset in the portfolios of communities, business firms, government agencies, and households. Sophisticated analytical tools from the fields of statistics, economics, and finance are applicable to real estate. Knowledge of accounting, taxation, planning, and construction are essential to real estate decision making. Seat-of-the-pants decisions based on back-of-envelope calculations are no longer adequate for obtaining returns competitive with other investment media. Academic training has become increasingly necessary for real estate users and professionals. We believe the book will be an effective aid for those who wish to obtain this education and training.

Halbert C. Smith
John B. Corgel

Contents

Government Survey System Descriptions. Contracts for the
Transfer of Real Property Rights: *Validity and Enforceability of
Contracts. General Categories of Contracts. The Four Basic
Contracts.*

Study. The Process of Real Estate Market Analysis: *Step 1: Define the Problem. Step 2: Evaluate Project Constraints. Step 3: Define the Market Area(s). Step 4: Estimate Demand for the Project. Step 5: Establish Supply Conditions in the Market. Step 6: Correlate Supply and Demand and Make Recommendations.* Market Analysis Case Study: Marquis Square Condominiums: *Background. Step 1: Market Analysis Problem. Step 2: Evaluate Project Constraints. Step 3: Define the Market Area. Step 4: Estimate Demand for the Project. Step 5: Establish Supply Conditions in the Market. Step 6: Correlate Supply and Demand and Make Recommendations.*

REAL ESTATE

PERSPECTIVES

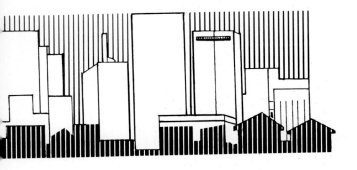

1
Real Estate Perspectives

OUTLINE

INTRODUCTION

Real estate means different things to different people. A large number of people in the United States are engaged in some aspect of the real estate business—real estate brokerage, appraisal, property management, construction, development, or financing—and thus tend to view real estate as a business. Some people serve as managers in large corporations and tend to view real estate as a major corporate asset. Farmers may view real estate in a classical economic sense as one of the three factors of production—land, labor, and capital. Attorneys view real estate as property carrying various rights and responsibilities. Legislators and public officials often view real estate as a source of taxes and as a means of affecting social conditions through housing programs. Each of these viewpoints is somewhat specialized and derives from people's relationships with real estate through their employment or role in society.

Four Perspectives of Real Estate

Since every individual is a consumer of real estate services and since all of the individuals representing the viewpoints mentioned above must interact with others in markets for real estate services, they all share an overriding perspective of real estate as an *economic* good. In accordance with this view, economic relationships exert a powerful influence over every individual's relationship with real estate. Next, since citizens must follow the rules of social order embodied in the law, a second pervasive view of real estate is the *legal* perspective. Third, people usually must borrow funds to purchase and control real estate, and they expect to obtain a return on their use of real estate. Thus we may view real estate from a third encompassing perspective—the *financial* perspective.[1]

---

[1] The theoretical basis for much of the quantitative analysis of real estate problems and issues is derived from the field of corporate finance.

3

Finally, most businesses are involved either directly or indirectly in economic functions, such as management and marketing of real estate. Thus, the fourth perspective is termed the *business* perspective. Within the business perspective are various subdivisions including brokerage, property management, development, and syndication.

Exhibit 1–1 suggests that the production of real estate (i.e., creating valuable improvements on land) is the result of contributions from members of society representing each of the four perspectives of real estate. None of these perspectives, however, is mutually exclusive. Strong interdependencies exist especially between the economic and financial views and the legal and financial contributions. The business perspective represents the application of all the other views to real-world problems and issues.

EXHIBIT 1–1
REAL ESTATE PERSPECTIVES

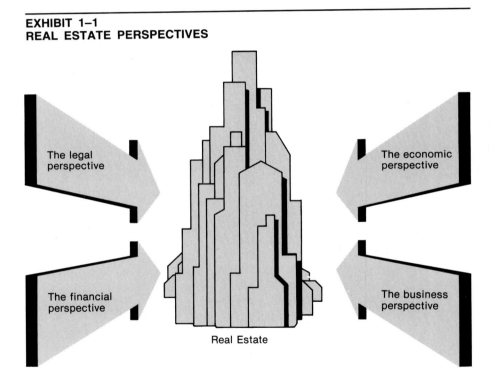

The legal perspective

The economic perspective

The financial perspective

The business perspective

Real Estate

Why Study Real Estate?

Students take a beginning real estate course for a variety of reasons. Some students intend to enter a real estate business or profession and take the beginning course as an introduction to more advanced courses. Other students believe that such a course will be helpful in buying a home or in selecting real estate investments after they leave college. (After all, don't people make a lot of money by investing in real estate?) And some students elect to take the course because they believe it will be an easy A!

While we cannot guarantee that a beginning real estate course will be easy, it should be interesting. In fact, if approached properly, the study of real estate can be fascinating. Investors and businesses regularly make decisions involving millions of dollars' worth of real estate. Home ownership is often a person's largest single lifetime investment. Management of corporate real estate can determine a firm's success. And many people enter real estate as a business or profession.

For students, a beginning course in real estate will:

1. Facilitate better housing decisions.
2. Facilitate better investment decisions.
3. Facilitate better decisions regarding public-policy issues.
4. Serve as an educational base for those wishing to enter one of the professional fields of the real estate business, including brokerage, appraisal, development and construction, investment analysis and counseling, property management, and mortgage financing.

PERSPECTIVES AND PUBLIC AND PRIVATE OBJECTIVES

The four perspectives of real estate provide the analytical framework for studying real estate. Although real estate is viewed differently from each perspective, the objective of real estate analysis remains constant—the wise creation and use of real estate resources. This objective is pursued continually by people who make decisions about real estate including households, corporate managers, investors, developers, financiers, and government officials.

By creating and using real estate wisely, each of these groups maximizes its own private benefits or satisfaction. Households, for example, obtain more housing for the same price, corporate business managers earn higher profits for their firms, investors maximize their wealth, developers meet the demands of those needing new real estate, financiers provide funds for worthwhile projects, legislators create programs beneficial to their constituents, and government officials manage programs competently. Moreover, when each of these private groups creates and uses real estate wisely, social benefits (i.e., the benefits derived by society as a whole) are usually maximized as well.

Not all real estate decisions turn out to be wise. Many mistakes are made. The objective is sometimes lost because of a lack of data, a change in market conditions, or incorrect or inadequate analysis. Nevertheless, optimal decision making on the creation and use of real estate continues to be a dominant goal for the future.

Legal Perspective

Real estate transactions must meet the requirements of contract law and property law. These requirements are designed to promote fairness among the participants and are based on the recognition that a market system could not exist without an organizational base and a set of ground rules. This section deals with these ground rules and the institutional arrangements for carrying them out.

The laws of each state define the property rights and responsibilities associated with various interests in real estate. Each combination of such rights and responsibilities is known as an *estate,* which is the type of entity transferred in a real estate transaction. State laws also prescribe the procedures for transferring the ownership (title) of estates from one party to another. Although there is considerable variation among the state laws governing estates and their transfer, there are also broad similarities that apply to all of the states' property laws. These laws also govern the rights and obligations of lenders and borrowers in financing real estate.

Listing contracts, contracts for purchase and sale, deeds, mortgages, leases, and options are some of the important documents used by real estate investors and business persons. The roles that these documents play in real estate transactions, as well as their legal requirements and characteristics, are part of the environment in which real estate transactions occur. These roles and the financial arrangements can perhaps best be observed at the closing of a transaction, when legal title is conveyed and money changes hands.

Economic Perspective

This section deals with the production and allocation of real estate resources in our economy. From the standpoint of the decision maker, the wise creation and use of real estate is guided by the economic criterion of efficiency. This criterion relates the cost of the property (i.e., purchase price or development and construction cost) to the future benefits (i.e., income) derived from the property. When decision makers believe they are obtaining the most property for the least cost, their actions are consistent with the efficiency criterion.

When decision makers, in general, have adequate and reliable data on which to base their decisions, when their analytical procedures are appropriate and correctly applied, and when their motives concern economic objectives, their decisions lead to efficient solutions. Since the welfare of all decision makers is maximized in such a setting, society's welfare (i.e., the sum of the welfare of all individuals) is also maximized. In this section, the technical conditions for economic efficiency are outlined. One set of conditions requires that markets for real estate be "perfectly competitive," whereas the other set requires that there be no "market failures."

Nevertheless, as shown in this section, real estate markets are imperfect because of a lack of adequate data, inadequate and incorrectly applied analytical tools, disagreements among decision makers about future events, and so forth.

Market failure is also a problem in real estate. To help resolve problems of market imperfections and failures, many laws and institutional arrangements have been developed to control and guide real estate decisions. Generally formulated under the government's police power—the right to enact laws to protect the general health, safety, and welfare of society—laws have been imposed dealing with such aspects as zoning, building standards, licensing of persons in the real estate business, discrimination, and full disclosure of transactional and financial terms.

Additionally, many institutions that serve real estate decision makers, particularly financial institutions, control and guide real estate activity. Lending standards, for example, determine which proposed projects will be financed, and thus constructed, and which will not. Most projects that do not meet such standards are not even proposed. Other institutions such as utility companies, government agencies, planning boards, engineering and permit offices, and architectural control boards also establish standards for real estate projects.

Financial Perspective

The risks and returns associated with real estate transactions must be evaluated. Profitability, financing alternatives, tax impacts, expense relationships, and risk must be assessed by financial, or quantitative, analysis. Financial theory dealing with risk, rates of return, and portfolio effects serves as the basis for this analysis. Quantitative measurement of the desirable and undesirable aspects of real estate decisions is the goal of financial analysis. It is accomplished through the use of such concepts and procedures as compound interest and discounted cash flow analysis, capitalization, capital budgeting, yield estimation, sensitivity analysis, and capital asset pricing.

Decisions hinge on the question of value. After all, sellers do not want to accept a price for their properties that is lower than market value, and buyers do not want to pay a price higher than market value. Thus, appraisal is an important element in the financial perspective of real estate, and real estate entrepreneurs need to be familiar with appraisal theory and procedures. Part Three covers both the appraisal of small residential properties and large income-producing properties.

Nonquantitative objectives must be established for firms or individuals dealing in real estate, risk must be assessed, and returns estimated. Quantitative measures are employed to estimate risks and returns, but subjective analysis is also required to predict whether the objectives are likely to be met. The financial perspective also deals with the interrelationship between overall objectives and quantitative analysis of risks and returns.

The decision-making process for real estate is facilitated by analysis of the legal, economic, and financial aspects of a proposed course of action. The process itself involves the identification of objectives, development of hypotheses (or questions to be answered), collection and analysis of data, specification of alternatives, development of conclusions, and a final decision. The goals of this decision making are to maximize the wealth of individuals in the private sector and to maximize social welfare in the public sector.

Business Perspective

Many businesses deal with real estate directly. They include brokerage, property management, development, construction, appraisal, consulting, financing, and syndication firms. Such firms create, distribute, and finance products and services that include housing, offices, factories, schools, and recreational facilities. When the real estate so produced contributes to people's (society's) welfare, it is worth more than the sum of the value of its components. Thus, real estate is *productive:* It contributes to society's well being and adds to its wealth.

Part Four is concerned with the sources of productivity of real estate and how productivity is released through business activities. The key elements of productivity are shown to be physical, locational, and legal in character. They are created and distributed by development and construction, marketing, management, and syndication firms. Finally, the impact of technological innovation in real estate is analyzed and some ways that technological innovation is expected to affect the future of real estate are noted.

APPLICATIONS OF REAL ESTATE ANALYSIS

One of the objectives of this book is to help students become competent real estate analysts. Real estate analysis has essentially three important applications: (1) problem solving, (2) public policy analysis, and (3) decision making. These applications of real estate analysis lead directly to more efficient utilization of real estate resources.

The first application recognizes that analysis is useful for solving problems. Some of the problems that arise in real estate include (1) how to provide adequate housing for all households, (2) how to anticipate future real estate needs, and (3) how to manage property or a portfolio of real estate investments effectively.

Identifying and helping to resolve issues of public policy is another important application of real estate analysis. Issues of discrimination in housing, concerns about adequate financing for real estate, and the impact of tax legislation on real estate investment are of public concern and are wholly or partially amenable to economic analysis.

Finally, problems in the private sector and issues of public policy result in the need to make decisions for the future. Examples of such decisions include the optimum use of a vacant parcel of land, location and timing of new real estate developments, what rents to charge, and what controls should be placed on real estate development.

APPROACH OF THE BOOK

The book approaches the study of real estate as a combination of the four economic factors of production—land, labor, capital and entrepreneurship. The business activities of real estate are professional in nature because they involve application of several basic disciplines, with the practical goal of enhancing human welfare. The product is created and managed within the economic, legal, financial, and business environments. This book, therefore, approaches the study of real estate from these four major perspectives, recognizing that successful real estate analysis must be undertaken within at least these dimensions.

Students beginning their study of real estate may ask whether the study of real estate would be more interesting or informative if the subject were approached from a particular user's viewpoint. Students aspiring to corporate management may believe that the study of real estate as a corporate asset would be the most relevant approach for them. Students planning to enter the real estate business might prefer to begin their study from a business perspective. A nonbusiness student might prefer to learn about buying a house or leasing an apartment.

The authors prefer a more general approach because most users of real estate enter into more than one relationship with real estate. They are consumers of real estate services, but also voters, investors, attorneys, real estate professionals, corporate managers, farmers, and financiers. With a more general approach, specific as well as general concerns and points of view can be addressed.

The book contains four major sections, in addition to the present introductory chapter. Within each of the sections where one of the four main perspectives of real estate is discussed, the following considerations are addressed: theory, institutional arrangements, and prescriptive analysis (see Exhibit 1–2). The theoretical considerations within each perspective are presented as the foundation for the institutional arrangements that have been devised to facilitate real estate transactions. The theory serves as a justification for institutional organization and as a basis for identifying inefficiencies and measures for improvement.

EXHIBIT 1–2
FUNCTIONAL OUTLINE OF BOOK

Perspective	Considerations	Chapters
Legal	Theory	2 and 3
	Institutional arrangements	4–6
	Prescriptive analysis	7 and 8
Economic	Theory	9 and 10
	Institutional arrangements	11–13
	Prescriptive analysis	14 and 15
Financial	Theory	16
	Institutional arrangements	17–20
	Prescriptive analysis	21–23
Business	Theory	24
	Institutional arrangements	25–27
	Prescriptive analysis	28

The institutional organization is the interface between individual market participants and the general system for resource allocation. From an operational standpoint, "knowledge of the system" means knowledge of institutional arrangements.

Since we intend for this text to serve as a guide for real estate decision makers, we include prescriptive analysis in each perspective. Such prescription includes decision rules and policy directives that follow logically from theory and institutional arrangements.

OVERVIEW

This book approaches the study of real estate from four distinct but overlapping viewpoints—economic, legal, financial, and business. While other viewpoints (e.g., agricultural or sociological viewpoints) may be relevant for some types of analysis, the major viewpoints relevant to most real estate investment decisions are the four perspectives emphasized in this book.

Through use of the analytical approaches and techniques of each viewpoint, a real estate decision maker can expect to make better decisions than without their use. Improved decisions will tend to produce fewer investments that lose money for the investor, more investments that make higher rates of return, and more properties and projects that are desirable in terms of community-wide standards. This type of analysis is also useful for public policy issues, such as whether to increase or decrease public controls to protect the environment, to provide more or fewer subsidies for low- and moderate-income housing, and to change financial policy to make housing more or less affordable.

Along with the analytical approaches and techniques presented within each perspective, the institutional framework is related to the decision-making process. Through institutions such as financial intermediaries and government agencies, market participants command resources for real estate activities and projects. Decision makers must include the characteristics and requirements of these institutions in their decision-making process.

Finally, practical results should derive from proper application of good theory and analysis. Decision rules and policy directives can be formulated from relevant theory and procedure. The development of such rules and directives can be described as a prescriptive approach, which is valid only if based on applicable theory and institutional arrangements.

Part One

The Legal Perspective

The initial section of this book views real estate from a *legal perspective*. We begin with this perspective because of the importance of the legal system in protecting the institution of private property—an institution that is vital to the conduct of business in a free society. Without the legal right to acquire, earn income from, and dispose of property, individuals and firms will not commit resources to the production of real estate or real estate services. An understanding of real property rights and the legal system for protecting those rights therefore is fundamental to understanding the limits of the economic, financial, and business perspectives.

The first two chapters of this section provide basic theories and definitions, including the theory of property rights; definitions of estates in

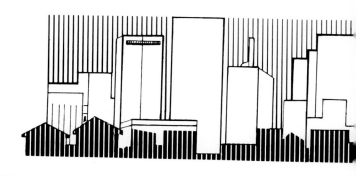

land, real, and personal property and the forms of ownership in real property; the property rights of government; contract law; and the methods of describing real estate.

Since the transfer of real property rights among individuals and firms underlies much of the real estate business (e.g., real estate brokerage, appraising, and mortgage lending), we devote the remaining chapters in this section to the *contractual arrangements* that facilitate the transfer of real property rights. We discuss four basic contractual arrangements—listing contracts, mortgage contracts, contracts for sale, and leases—as well as real estate closings and other contracts, such as options. ■

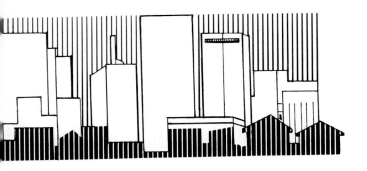

2
Real Property Rights

INTRODUCTION TO REAL PROPERTY RIGHTS

For the purpose of this text, the terms *real estate* and *real property* are synonymous. This is not to say that these terms mean exactly the same thing—they don't. But making a formal distinction in meaning serves no useful purpose for real estate practitioners. What is important to understand is that one acquires a set of distinct and separable *real property rights* when one purchases real estate. Consequently, these real property rights include rights *to* the physical characteristics of real estate and rights *of* legal ownership of real estate. This means that with the purchase of real estate, the owner(s) receive what is traditionally termed a "bundle of rights." This bundle includes a set of rights to the physical characteristics of the real estate and a set of legal rights of ownership. In the following sections, we define the physical and legal rights inherent in real estate ownership, and we discuss how rights are restricted and how they are separated from the main bundle of rights.

Physical Property Rights to Real Estate

Normally, when individuals purchase real estate such as a single-family home, they receive a complete set of physical rights. As shown in Exhibit 2–1, a complete set of physical rights includes surface rights; above-surface rights (known as air rights); and subsurface rights, including mineral, water, oil, and gas rights. The surface rights acquired by the owner encompass the legal rights of ownership (explained below) to the surface of the land and all permanent attachments to the land. These attachments are *improvements on the land* (e.g., a single-family structure and garage) and *improvements to the land,* such as streets, gutters, sewer and water lines, landscaping, grading, and retaining walls.

The air rights of real estate owners *generally* extend above the earth's

EXHIBIT 2–1
PHYSICAL RIGHTS OF REAL ESTATE

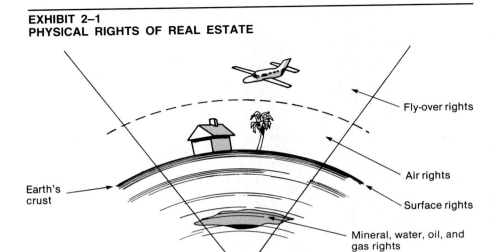

surface to the height of the tallest manmade improvement.[1] Currently, this height is approximately 1,500 feet. The space above this zone of private air rights is public air space, which provides fly-over rights to accommodate air transportation.

The physical rights of real estate owners also extend below the earth's surface—theoretically to the center of the earth in the shape of an inverted pyramid as shown in Exhibit 2–1. As a practical matter, however, these subsurface rights, including the rights to all minerals, water, oil, etc., extend only to the physical limits of man's ability to explore below the surface of the earth (currently to a depth of about 50,000 feet).

This set of physical property rights can be subdivided in a variety of interesting and unusual ways. In most states, any of the physical rights described above can be sold or leased to others independent of all other rights.[2] In urban areas, air rights are frequently bought and sold to facilitate development (see Exhibit 2–2). Also, for example, in some parts of

---

[1]The exception is in the vicinity of airports. Also, this is a general rule. It does not mean, for example, that a developer would be prohibited from putting up a building that is one story higher than the tallest existing building.

[2]Oil and gas rights in some states (California, Louisiana, and Oklahoma) are not considered rights of the landowner until the gas or oil is pumped to the surface. Thus, these rights cannot be sold separately.

the United States it is common to see oil wells operating in the back yards of single-family residences. Typically, the families have sold or leased only the oil rights to their property. Another example is the sale of rights to cut timber from raw land—an arrangement that can yield excellent returns and defer carrying costs (e.g., property taxes) while land is being held for possible future development.

**EXHIBIT 2–2
AIR RIGHTS**

Photo by Jack Corgel

L'Enfant Plaza, Washington, D.C., is constructed over highway and railroad rights of way.

Real versus Personal Property Rights: The Problem of Fixtures

The law recognizes only two basic types of property: personal property (personalty) and real property (realty). Realty is land and all permanent attachments to land (i.e., improvements on and to the land) while personalty is all other tangible property. Making the distinction between personalty and realty has some important implications when real property rights are transferred, valued for property tax purposes, or pledged as security for a mortgage loan.

Assume, for example, that you purchased a home several years ago and in the living room of your home you had a giant-screen television set built into a bookcase. While moving your personal property (i.e., furniture, clothing, and so forth) upon sale of the home, you detach the television set from the bookcase and take it with you. The day after the closing, you receive a telephone call from the buyer's attorney who informs you that you have violated the terms of the contract for sale of house because you removed an item that was permanently attached to the realty (that is, the television). He claims the television rightfully belongs to his client, the buyer. Is the buyer's attorney correct?

This dispute over rights to the television set is typical of the type of problem buyers and sellers have with *fixtures*. A fixture is something that was once personalty, but by reason of its purpose or attachment to real property (land or improvements), has become a part of the realty. In addition to situations involving buyers and sellers, fixtures may present difficulties for landlords and tenants in residential and commercial lease agreements, for tax assessors and taxpayers in the valuation of real estate for property tax purposes, and for lenders and borrowers in determining what property is pledged as security for a loan.

In resolving disputes about fixtures, the courts have relied on a set of four basic tests.

1. *Intent test.* The intention of the parties or what is customary in a particular situation is the most crucial factor in determining whether an item is a fixture. Builders of new homes, for example, install built-in refrigerators. If the property is later sold, the refrigerator would be included as part of the realty as a fixture. Also, it is customary in hotel or motel sales for the furnishings of the rooms to be included with the real property as fixtures.

2. *Annexation test.* If an article cannot be removed without causing physical damage to the adjacent property, the article is usually deemed a fixture. Yet annexation must be considered in relation to other factors, including intent, adaptation, and the relationship of the parties.

3. *Adaptation test.* The use of an item in relation to the real property may help determine whether the item is indeed a fixture. Storm doors and windows especially designed to fit doors and windows of a particular house would qualify as fixtures under the adaptation test. Also, certain industrial equipment is specially designed for use in particular buildings.

4. *Relationship-of-the-parties test.* The courts in recent years have favored purchasers, tenants, or mortgagees (lenders) in disputes over property which might be construed as fixtures. This is essentially a "test of last resort." It is used *exclusively* when the intent of the parties cannot be adequately determined, the significance of the damage to the adjacent property cannot be ascertained, and the adaptation test fails to shed light on the problem. Otherwise,

the relationship of the parties is considered along with other relevant tests in deciding such cases.

In the law related to fixtures (mostly case law), therefore, no universal standard has emerged for resolving such disputes over physical property rights. Usually, the factual evidence of each case and an application of some combination of the four tests govern court decisions regarding fixtures.

The lesson to be learned from this is that all contracts that list real property for sale (i.e., listing contracts) and all contracts for the sale of real property should spell out quite specifically what physical real property rights are being offered or what physical real property rights are being bought and sold.[3]

So who gets the television set? Most likely the buyer, since the intention of the seller is not easily determined, some damage has resulted from removal of the television set from the bookcase, the fact that this particular television set fits into this particular space, and because the courts tend to favor the buyer over the seller.

Fixtures such as the ones just described are different from those referred to in commercial leases as *trade fixtures*. Trade fixtures are items, such as display counters, movable partitions, and cabinets that are used by tenants in shopping centers, office buildings, and other income properties in the production of their income. Unlike ordinary fixtures, these items are personal property and therefore can be removed by tenants at any time. As will be pointed out in Chapter 8, the commercial lease contract should specify clearly those items that are provided by the landlord and those items provided by the tenant—the trade fixtures.

Legal Property Rights of Real Estate Ownership

The notion of the bundle of rights acquired with the purchase of real estate, including (1) a set of physical rights to real property and (2) a set of legal rights of ownership, is analogous to a bundle of sticks that contains two types of sticks. One is thick and sturdy, while the other is very thin, fragile, and more difficult to grasp. The set of legal rights of real estate ownership, in contrast to the physical rights, is intangible, and thus is like the second variety of sticks in the bundle—fragile and somewhat difficult to grasp.

The outright ownership of real estate in a free society carries with it three fundamental legal rights. First, an owner of real estate has the *right of exclusive possession*. This means an owner has the legal right to control entry to the property, to collect damages in case of trespass, and to use the land as collateral for a loan.

---

[3]We will discuss listing contracts in Chapter 4 and contracts for sale in Chapter 6.

━━━━━━━━━━━ *Frame 2–1* ━━━━━━━━━━━

Exclusive Possession and Control of a River

Q. Smith owns a parcel of land bordered by a river. One day Smith finds Corgel
fishing in the river from a small boat. Since the boat is near the bank of the river
on Smith's property, Smith orders Corgel to stop fishing or he will have Corgel
arrested for trespassing. By law, should Corgel move or tell Smith to get lost?

A. In many states, exclusive possession and control of the river adjoining property
depends on whether the river is navigable. Navigability generally depends on
whether the river is capable of transporting boats loaded with freight in the regular course of trade. If the river in question is *not* navigable, then Smith has
exclusive possession and control of his half of the river (i.e., from his property
extending to the center of the main current of the river) and can therefore legally
exclude Corgel. If the river is navigable, then Smith only has possession and
control of the bank to the low-water line and therefore cannot exclude Corgel
from fishing from a boat. Remember, state laws vary on this question.

Second, an owner has the legal *right of quiet enjoyment.*[4] This refers to
the legal right to hold possession without disturbances resulting from defects in the title. With this right, the owner is entitled to the proceeds or
rent from the property, but remains subject to all publicly or privately
imposed limitations on ownership and use of the property (e.g., zoning
regulations).[5]

Finally, owners have *rights of disposition* that allow them to transfer
ownership to others in any way they see fit (e.g., sale, gift, or will), provided that the laws against discrimination are not violated.

In most instances of real estate ownership, this set of fundamental
legal rights (the set of thin sticks) is complete. Like physical real property
rights, however, legal rights can be separated and each right can be significantly altered by private contract. In the next section, we consider the
ways in which legal rights of real estate ownership are subdivided and
altered.

ESTATES IN REAL ESTATE

The term *estate* refers to the degree of interest a party has in land. The
degree of interest is defined by the extent of the legal rights contained in
the main bundle of rights. Thus, each particular type of estate discussed
below is a label that, when used in writing or conversation, conveys a

---

[4]Noise pollution is *not* the issue here.
[5]This and other limitations are discussed later in this chapter.

mental image of the set of legal rights that a party has acquired in real estate.

The tree diagram in Exhibit 2–3 presents the more common estates in land. In most instances, the estates shown in Exhibit 2–3 involve only current interests (i.e., legal rights which begin upon acquisition), but in some cases one or more parties to the estate have future interests (i.e., legal rights that may begin at some future time).

EXHIBIT 2–3
ESTATES IN LAND: CURRENT AND FUTURE INTERESTS
(Future Interests in Parentheses)

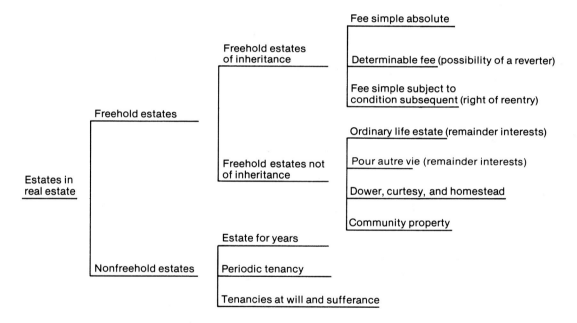

The initial separation of the branches on the tree diagram divides the estates in land into *freehold* and *nonfreehold* categories. A freehold estate is an estate with an *indefinite duration*. The parties to the estate simply do not know when the rights to property will expire. Nonfreehold estates have durations set by private contract. The contract that establishes the estate defines a point when the property rights terminate. Along the freehold estates branch, another separation occurs which divides the freehold estates into freehold estates "of" and "not of" *inheritance*. The term *inheritance* refers to the ability of the party who holds the estate to pass it to his or her heirs.

In the following sections, each of the estates found on the branches of the tree diagram is discussed. We begin with the freehold estates of inheritance and the fee simple absolute.[6]

Freehold Estates

Fee Simple Absolute.   The fee simple absolute estate (or fee simple estate) is the most complete estate in land. This means that, regardless of the physical rights involved, fee simple ownership entitles the owner to the three fundamental legal rights—the right of exclusive possession, the right of quiet enjoyment, and the right of disposition. In a fee simple estate, these legal rights are unabridged and unaltered in any way.[7]

Most owners of land hold fee simple estates. Yet many situations arise in which one or more parties to a contract involving transfer of physical real property rights wishes to limit in some way the set of legal rights. Therefore, each estate shown on the tree diagram in Exhibit 2–3 (except the fee simple estate) describes a set of legal rights that is incomplete or has been altered in some way.

Determinable Fee.   A party with a determinable fee estate has received (for example, through sale, gift, or will) an interest in real property that lasts as long as some stipulation is met. The interest is as complete as in a fee simple estate except that all rights terminate upon the occurrence of the event specified by the party making the grant (grantor). The party receiving the gift (grantee) has a current interest known as a determinable fee, while the grantor has a future interest termed the *possibility of a reverter*. If the event occurs, all physical and legal rights to the property that were granted revert immediately to the grantor.

Assume that a wealthy alumnus and ex-football player of a major university makes a gift to his alma mater of an office building near campus for as long as the university's football team wins at least one game during the season. The university has a determinable fee estate in the building, and the alumnus has a possibility of a reverter estate. Within five years of this gift, croquet replaces football as the nation's premier college spectator and participation sport. After a series of student riots, university officials are forced to drop football to allow the university's croquet team to compete in the stadium on Saturday afternoons. Thus, at the end of the football season, when the football team has not had the opportunity to win one game, the alumnus regains all rights (i.e., a fee simple estate) to the office building. This series of events is displayed in Exhibit 2–4.

---

[6]The word *fee* refers to ownership in land, and the word *simple* suggests that title is held without restrictions.

[7]Fee simple owners are, of course, subject to public and private controls, which are discussed later in this chapter.

EXHIBIT 2–4
DETERMINABLE FEE ESTATE EXAMPLE

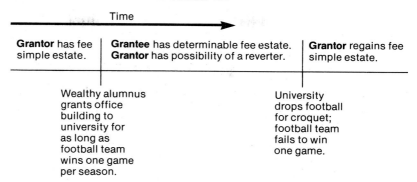

Time

| Grantor has fee simple estate. | Grantee has determinable fee estate. Grantor has possibility of a reverter. | Grantor regains fee simple estate. |

Wealthy alumnus grants office building to university for as long as football team wins one game per season.

University drops football for croquet; football team fails to win one game.

Fee Simple Subject to Condition Subsequent. Suppose the wealthy alumnus in the previous example had made the grant with language stating "on the condition that" the football team fails to win one game, the grantor may repossess the office building instead of the language, "as long as." Now the estate held by the university is a fee simple subject to condition subsequent, and the estate of the alumnus is a right of re-entry estate. The differences between these estates and the estates in the previous situation are demonstrated in Exhibit 2–5.

EXHIBIT 2–5
FEE SIMPLE SUBJECT TO CONDITION SUBSEQUENT EXAMPLE

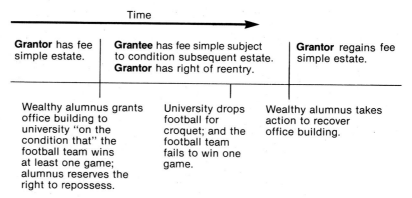

Time

| Grantor has fee simple estate. | Grantee has fee simple subject to condition subsequent estate. Grantor has right of reentry. | Grantor regains fee simple estate. |

Wealthy alumnus grants office building to university "on the condition that" the football team wins at least one game; alumnus reserves the right to repossess.

University drops football for croquet; and the football team fails to win one game.

Wealthy alumnus takes action to recover office building.

The only difference between this and the previous grant arrangement is that, under the language creating the fee simple subject to condition subsequent estate, the reversion to the grantor does not occur immediately upon the occurrence of the event, but rather only after the grantor takes some action to recover the property.[8] Thus, the university has use of the office building until the alumnus takes action to recover the property.

Ordinary Life Estate. The ordinary life estate is the most common of the freehold estates not of inheritance. This type of estate has an uncertain duration and cannot be passed to heirs. The ordinary life estate is an example of what is sometimes termed a *conventional life estate* because the provisions of the estate are imposed by the parties to the contract creating the estate. By contrast, *legal life estates* are estates in which the provisions are imposed by state law.

Suppose that two old friends, Mr. I and Mr. Spry, who are both in their 70s, enter into an ordinary life estate arrangement. Mr. Spry recently married a woman in her 20s, and Mr. I, who owns an exclusive oceanside condominium in Florida, would like Mr. Spry and his wife to have exclusive use of the premises. Mr. I therefore grants (for example, via gift) the condominium to Mr. Spry for as long as Mr. Spry lives. Upon the death of Mr. Spry, the property reverts back to Mr. I. If Mr. I predeceases Mr. Spry, then the property goes to Mr. I's son, Mr. i.

In the case of Mr. I (grantor) and Mr. Spry (grantee), the grantee has an ordinary life estate (current interest) that terminates upon his death. The property cannot be passed in a will to his young wife. Mr. I has a future interest called a *remainder* which is vested in the grantor. If the grantor predeceases the grantee, then the *contingent remainder* interest (i.e., that belonging to Mr. i, the grantor's son) is exercised. Thus, with ordinary life estates, the legal rights of ownership are the same as with a fee simple estate, except the right of disposition is limited.

Pour Autre Vie. The estate pour autre vie ("for the life of another") is a conventional life estate that terminates on the death of a third party. Assume that a wife is forced to have her husband committed to a mental hospital after he loses all his money speculating in agricultural land in Colombia, South America. So that he is adequately taken care of, the wife grants the hospital an estate in a shopping center she owns separately from her husband. This action gives the hospital the right to collect rents from the shopping center for as long as the husband lives.

Thus, the agreement is between the wife and the hospital and terminates upon the death of a third party—the husband. The remainder interests (future interests) in estates pour autre vie operate in much the same way as they do in ordinary life estates.

---

[8]This action can be as simple as a letter or telephone call notifying the grantee to vacate the premises.

Dower, Curtesy, and Homestead. A majority of states have adopted common law provisions (as in the case of dower and curtesy) and enacted statutes (as in the case of homestead) creating legal life estates for surviving partners in marriage. These estates, since they are established by law and give the surviving spouse life estates in certain property upon the death of a spouse, are termed *legal life estates*. Moreover, such estates are freehold (indefinite duration) and cannot be passed on to heirs (not of inheritance).

In *common law property states*, dower refers to the property rights that the wife has upon the death of her husband. Thus, if there is a valid marriage during which the husband predeceases the wife, and real estate is acquired during the marriage that is subject to dower, the wife in common law states typically is entitled to a one-third interest in the real estate.

Once real property is acquired, even if it is bought by the husband acting alone, the wife may be entitled to an inactive ("inchoate") dower right that ripens ("consummates") upon the husband's death. These rights of the wife are superior to all unsecured claims of creditors against the estate of the husband. They are not superior to the claims of mortgage lenders, taxing authorities, and mechanics liens.

Dower rights are an important factor to consider in real estate transactions. Assume, for example, that Mr. Peabody sold property to Mr. Quebody acquired during his (Peabody's) marriage to Mrs. Peabody. If care is not taken to release the dower rights of Mrs. Peabody upon or following the sale, Mrs. Peabody can exercise her dower rights and lay claim to one third of Mr. Quebody's property upon the death of Mr. Peabody.

Curtesy refers to the property rights of the husband in the property of his wife. State laws today involving curtesy rights vary widely. Certain states have abolished curtesy while other states have merged dower and curtesy under dower or a new title.[9]

In some states, dower and curtesy have been abolished in favor of a more limited property right known as homestead.[10] In other states, homestead coexists with dower and curtesy. Homestead refers specifically to rights of spouses, or in the case of unmarried persons living together, to members of the same household. Homestead statutes protect the wife against the husband's selling the family residence against her wishes. These statutes also protect the family against eviction from their home by general creditors (not including tax, mortgage, and mechanics liens).

---

[9]State laws in this area have changed dramatically in recent years to promote sexual equality in state law. For example, Florida law refers to the merged dower and curtesy rights as "elective share." The rights are equal for both spouses.

[10]The term "homestead exemption" has property tax implications. See Chapter 15.

Homestead is established by law—and usually ends upon the death of a surviving spouse. Thus it is often considered a legal life estate.[11]

Community Property.   Several states in the western and southwestern sections of the United States have laws establishing community property rights between spouses.[12] In contrast to common law property states, which operate with dower, curtesy, or homestead, *community property law states* recognize the husband and wife as equal partners in certain community property. *Community property* is any property that is not considered *separate property.* Separate property is defined as property of either spouse that was owned at the time of the marriage or that was acquired during the marriage by gift, will, or inheritance. The rights of a spouse in all community property terminate upon the spouse's death and thus are considered a legal life estate.

Nonfreehold Estates

Nonfreehold estates are interests in real estate that have a definite or certain duration. These include the estate for years, periodic tenancy, and tenancies at will and sufferance.

Estate for Years.   The estate for years describes the typical set of property rights one possesses as a tenant in a lease agreement. Another term for the tenant's interest is a *leasehold estate,* while the landlord's interest is referred to as a *leased fee estate* (i.e., fee simple subject to a lease). The estate for years is a nonfreehold estate (certain duration) because the period over which the tenant can maintain use and possession of the property is limited by the agreement. Agreements of this type are usually measured in periods extending perhaps as long as 99 years as in the case of some leases on land.

The property rights transferred to tenants by landlords are severely restricted. A leasehold interest of a retailer in a shopping mall, for example, will give the tenant the right of exclusive possession, but will *not* give the tenant right of quiet enjoyment with respect to title; and will *not* give the tenant the right of disposition.[13] Leasehold interests therefore only involve rights to use and possession and, in the case of the estate for years, only over a definite period of time.

---

[11]Some states allow the homestead rights to continue for the children in the family until they reach majority.

[12]These states are Arizona, California, Idaho, Louisiana, Nevada, New Mexico, Texas, and Washington.

[13]Tenants may be able to assign the lease, sublet, or sell the leasehold, but cannot sell the property itself. Leases are discussed in more detail in Chapter 8.

Periodic Tenancy. The periodic tenancy constitutes another type of leasehold interest. Under this arrangement, the agreement establishes a set period over which the tenant has rights of use and possession, but at the end of the period these rights are automatically renewed, usually for another period of equal length. The estate is broken when one party gives advanced notice (as stated in the agreement) of its intent to terminate the estate.

Tenancies at Will and Sufferance. Tenancies at will exist when rights of possession are transferred without an agreement. The rights of the tenant can be terminated at any time, without notice, by either the landlord or the tenant. This type of estate is most often created when a tenant retains rights of possession with the consent of the landlord after the term of the lease has expired.

A tenant at sufferance is essentially a trespasser. This type of tenancy occurs without the consent of the landlord and is therefore an illegal tenancy. The tenant at sufferance has few or no legal rights. Thus the courts often must determine whether a tenant is a tenant at will or a tenant at sufferance.

DISTRIBUTION OF PROPERTY RIGHTS AMONG CO-OWNERS

In preceding sections of this chapter we discussed how the bundle of rights inherent in real estate ownership can be divided along physical and legal lines, and how legal rights can be separated by the creation of various estates. In this section, we consider alternative ways in which real estate can be owned by more than one party and discuss how real property rights may be divided among co-owners.

The interrelationship between co-ownership rights, physical rights, and legal rights is encountered in the following example of community property. Suppose that a husband and wife in California (a community property state) acquire air rights to a parcel adjacent to their home for the purpose of maintaining year-round sunlight to operate the solar heating systems in their home. Acquiring these rights will prevent anyone from constructing a building or allowing trees to grow such that the sun cannot reach their solar collection panels. This example demonstrates a three-way interrelationship of subdivided property rights. First, physical rights are separated (i.e., the purchase of air rights). Second, legal rights are separated (i.e., community property as a legal life estate limits the right of disposition). And, finally the ownership of the air rights is divided as community property between the husband and wife co-owners.

The purpose of this section is to examine, in general, how the ownership of real property rights can be divided among various parties under the law. Specific strategies, such as limiting one's personal liability or maximizing one's tax benefits through the selection of an ownership form, are analyzed as part of real estate investment decision making in Chapter 21. Also, the individual form of ownership (i.e., sole proprietorship) is not considered here since this form does not require a division of rights among co-owners.

Joint Tenancy

Joint tenancy is a single estate in which two or more parties own property together and each co-owner has exactly the same property rights as any other co-owner. For a joint tenancy to exist, the ownership rights of all co-owners must begin at the same time (known as *unity of time*), must be conveyed to all co-owners under the same title *(unity of title)*, must be equal among all co-owners *(unity of interest)*, and each co-owner must have equal ability to possess or use the property *(unity of possession)*. If one of these "four unities" is broken, the courts, in disputes over property rights, will likely rule that a joint tenancy does not exist.

Legal disputes over the existence of joint tenancies are usually the result of conflicts involving the *right of survivorship* inherent in joint tenancies. The right of survivorship means that if one co-owner dies, all of his or her rights are then divided among the surviving partners. These rights cannot be passed to the heirs of the deceased co-owner. Assume, for example, that Mr. X and Mr. Y purchase a parcel of land together and decide to own the property as joint tenants. Upon the death of Mr. X, his son, Mr. Xx, discovers that all rights to the parcel of land go to Mr. Y under the right of survivorship. Thus, Mr. Xx, the only heir of Mr. X, has a strong economic incentive to show that a joint tenancy did not exist between his father and Mr. Y. His challenge would be based on the contention that one of the unities was broken in the agreement.

Joint tenancies are most often created between a few close business partners or between family members. In some states, such as Florida, a special form of joint tenancy, known as *tenancy by the entirety,* can be created between husbands and wives.

Tenancy in Common

Tenancy in common is a more conventional form of co-ownership of real property than joint tenancy. Under a tenancy in common arrangement, the co-owners may have unequal interests, they may have separate titles to property, and their rights may begin at different periods. However, each co-owner must have equal rights of use and possession. Perhaps more important, there are no rights of survivorship in a tenancy in common. So, if Mr. X and Mr. Y in the previous example had created a tenancy in common instead of the joint tenancy, Mr. Y would have no claim to Mr. X's share, and Mr. Xx would likely inherit those rights.

Tenancy in Partnership

Under common law, a *partnership* is created by agreement between two or more parties desiring to conduct business together. This traditional partnership is not recognized as a legal entity, however, so any real estate used in the partnership's business must be owned by the individual partners as tenants in common—the usual case—or joint tenants. The partnership business and the real estate used in the partnership business therefore are separate.

With the adoption of the Uniform Partnership Act in 48 states, the partnership itself may hold title to real estate in an estate known as *tenancy in partnership*. Under a tenancy in partnership for real estate, partnership properties are shared equally, partnership interests may not be conveyed without the consent of the other partners, partnership properties are exempt from rights of dower and curtesy, and (unlike a tenancy in common) properties may not be divided among partners until the claims of partnership creditors are satisfied. Moreover, when the partnership is dissolved the real estate must be sold, since it is owned by the partnership.

While the co-ownership rights in real estate owned by a partnership under tenancy in partnership are defined by the Uniform Partnership Act, specific rights and responsibilities of the partners, such as the rights to cash flows and tax losses, management responsibilities, and personal liability for partnership debts, are spelled out by the terms of the partnership agreement. Two types of partnership forms are commonly found. The *general partnership* is created among two or more parties to own real estate, each having personal liability for the partnership's debts. The *limited partnership* has been popular as a vehicle for real estate syndication. In this type of partnership, two classes of partners exist—general partners and limited partners. General partners are the managers of the business, while limited partners provide most of the money and are not personally liable for the debts of the partnership.[14]

---

[14]This means that if the liabilities of the partnership exceed its assets, creditors cannot collect by placing a lien on the assets (e.g., automobile or stereo) of a limited partner. These and other important topics related to partnerships are discussed in Chapters 22 and 27.

Corporations

Real estate corporations, like any other corporation, are chartered under state law and, for federal income tax purposes, must follow certain requirements of the Internal Revenue Code. The traditional corporate form, the *C-corporation*, offers stockholders limited liability (i.e., no personal liability for debts of the corporation), but has some disadvantageous tax features for stockholders. The alternative corporate form, the *S-corporation*, limits shareholders' liability, has excellent tax advantages, but is restricted to smaller operations with fewer than 35 shareholders.[15]

As a legal entity, the corporation can own and operate real estate independently of its shareholders. Thus, except for closely held corporations in which certain shareholders are also officers, shareholders have no legal rights of use and possession, quiet enjoyment, and disposition of the corporation's real estate. The shareholders' co-ownership rights and thus financial claims to the real estate owned by the corporation, however, are proportional to the number of shares they own.

Real Estate Investment Trusts

Real Estate Investment Trusts (REITs) are often referred to as mutual funds for investors who wish to invest in real estate or mortgages. Technically, a trust is an arrangement in which one party holds property for the benefit of others. REITs borrow funds to acquire real estate or to make mortgage loans and then sell shares of the real estate or mortgage portfolio, thus holding the real property or mortgage in trust for shareholders.

The existence of REITs is largely due to a tax law change in the 1960's that gave such trusts tax-exempt status if they meet certain requirements. These include such things as having at least 100 shareholders, maintaining a large proportion (i.e., 75 percent) of their holdings in real estate or mortgages, and distributing most (i.e., 95 percent) of their earnings to shareholders each year. More than one half of the REITs invest in real estate directly and are known as *equity trusts*, whereas the remaining REITs specialize in mortgages (*mortgage trusts*). The ownership and legal rights to the real estate or mortgages are structured in much the same way as they are for corporations.[16]

---

[15]The S-corporation is similar to a limited partnership. See discussion in Chapters 21 and 27.

[16]A student interested in studying the market performance of REITs can consult the Value Line Service publications available in most college libraries.

Condominiums and Cooperatives

The term *condominium*, while almost unheard of 40 years ago, is frequently used today in casual conversation. Yet many people mistakenly think that condominium refers to a multiunit residential development in which people own their units rather than renting them. Actually, condominium is a form of co-ownership of real estate in which individual units are owned *fee simple*, and the common grounds (e.g., elevators, halls, swimming pool, etc.) are owned by the owners of the units as *tenants in common*.

Almost any style of building (e.g., high-rise or garden) and use (e.g., residential, office, retail, industrial) is a candidate for condominium ownership as long as the units can be physically separated. In most areas of the United States, residential condominiums have been constructed or have been converted from apartment houses or complexes. In recent years in some parts of the country, office condominiums have become a popular option particularly for such smaller offices as doctors' offices. (See Exhibit 2–6.)

EXHIBIT 2–6
OFFICE CONDOMINIUMS—AN INCREASINGLY POPULAR OPTION

Photo by Jack Corgel

The offices in this office condominium property in McLean, Virginia, are owned by accountants, lawyers, and an assortment of small businesses.

The owners of individual units are responsible for repairs and maintenance of their units; however, they generally belong to an owners' association that handles the repairs and maintenance of the common areas. To finance this, each owner is assessed a monthly fee by the owners' association.

Co-ownership rights under the condominium form are determined by the contents of the following documents.

1. Declaration—The condominium declaration commits the property to condominium ownership. It defines the rights and responsibilities of individual owners with respect to maintenance and financial liabilities.
2. Bylaws—Similar to corporate bylaws, condominium bylaws outline the structure for administering the association (e.g., composition of the board of directors) and property (e.g., rules and regulations that must be followed by owners).
3. Management agreements—Before all the units are sold, management is performed by the developer. Some time thereafter, the owners' association may negotiate outside contracts for property management.

Time-Share Condominium.   Time sharing of residential condominiums has become extremely popular in recent years especially in resort areas. It represents an interesting and unique way of viewing the separation of co-ownership rights in real estate. Suppose, for example, that Leah Sherwood desires to have a place to stay in Colorado for two weeks every year during the ski season. She has essentially three options. First, she could face the uncertainties of renting every year. Second, she could buy a condominium in the area and face the problem of trying to rent the unit for most of the year. Or, third, she could purchase the two weeks she desires in a time-share condominium near the ski area.

In a time-share condominium, units are owned in fee simple and common elements in tenancy in common, but the fee simple interest is restricted each year to the *time period purchased*. If the ski enthusiast in this example had purchased the first two weeks in February in a one-bedroom unit for $10,000, then each year she has the rights of use, possession, and quiet enjoyment for those two weeks. She must pay her pro rata share of the association fee. She also has the right to sell her period of ownership at any time, to lease the unit for the period, or trade her weeks in Colorado for, say, two weeks in Miami Beach through a time-share exhange.

The purchase of a time-share unit, therefore, represents the acquisition of physical and legal property rights for only the desired period of time and thus avoids uncertainties of renting and the costs of purchasing a traditional fee simple interest. Yet one must be cautious when considering a time-share unit; there are several pitfalls. For example, misman-agement by time-share developers have caused owners to lose their total investment.

Cooperative Ownership.   In most physical respects, cooperative owner-ship is like condominium ownership, but legally they are quite different. Cooperative ownership has been used primarily for co-ownership of multi-unit residential property and is mostly found in a few major met-ropolitan areas of the United States. New York City has many cooperative buildings. In this type of ownership, a nonprofit corporation, the coop-erative, purchases or sponsors the development of an apartment house. Prospective residents purchase shares in the non-profit corporation in proportion to the value of the unit in which they will reside. The pur-chaser is given a proprietary lease by the corporation which entitles the shareholder to use and occupy the unit.

For the following reasons, condominiums are generally thought to be superior to the cooperative form for residential ownership:

1. The co-op project is financed under a single mortgage and share-holders share in the payments and interest deductability of that mortgage. The range of mortgage financing options available to condominium purchasers, therefore, is much broader.
2. The liabilities for maintenance and repairs may be more burden-some for co-op owners than for condominium owners.
3. The rights of disposition of condominium units is usually unre-stricted, while shareholders of co-op corporation may face limita-tions such as a requirement to sell back shares to the corporation at the original purchase price. In New York City, co-op sellers may have to pay a percent of their profits to the co-op corporation.

PUBLIC AND PRIVATE LIMITS ON PROPERTY RIGHTS

Thus far in this chapter, we have concentrated on the ways in which physical, legal, and co-ownership rights to real estate can be assembled and divided. Now we focus on how legal and physical rights of real estate ownership may be limited (i.e., how outside restrictions are imposed). There are two sources of limitations on the rights of real estate owners. First, governments impose limitations on property rights for the purposes of protecting the health, safety, and general public welfare; raising tax revenues; and providing such public facilities as highways. Second, pri-vate contracts, such as those establishing easements and deed restric-tions, create limitations on the rights of real estate owners. Since many of the limitations emanating from governments and private contracts involve rights of use and possession of real estate, they can have a significant effect on real estate values. Therefore, the set of public and private limitations discussed below is an integral part of the analysis of each real estate transaction. A summary of the public and private limitations that can affect the rights of real estate owners is provided in Exhibit 2–7.

EXHIBIT 2–7
PUBLIC AND PRIVATE LIMITATIONS TO OWNERSHIP RIGHTS

Public Limitation	Definition of Right
Police power	The inherent right (i.e., power) of government(s) to limit the activities of private entities to protect the general public's health, safety, and welfare.
Eminent domain	The right of govenment (U.S. Fifth Amendment) to take private real property for a public purpose after paying just compensation to the owners.
Taxation	The right of government to raise revenue through assessments against private property according to constitutional and statutory law.
Escheat	The right of government to take title to the property of a person who dies without a will or legal heirs.
Private Limitations	
Easement	A right transferred by private contract that gives an entity other than the owner of property the ability to make specific use of some part of that property.
Restrictive covenant (deed restrictions)	A limitation on the use of real property created by language in the deed at the time ownership is transferred.
Lien	A legal claim against the property by an entity other than the owner that if not satisfied can be enforced in the courts to force sale of the property (e.g., tax lien, mortgage lien, mechanics lien).

Government's Role in Defining Real Property Rights

The powers of governments to impose limitations on the rights of private property owners emanate from the United States and the various state constitutions. Many of these powers are passed on to local governments (i.e., city and county governments). The powers of government are then used by federal, state, and local agencies to protect the public welfare, raise revenues, provide public facilities, and so on. Disputes between private-property owners and these public agencies are resolved in the federal, state, and municipal courts. Thus, public agencies and the courts play a significant role in defining the real property rights of private entities, since they are primarily responsible for implementing and interpreting the powers of governments.

Police Power. The police power is the inherent right of government to control the activities of private entities for the purpose of protecting the public health, safety, moral character, and general welfare. A city government, as an example of the use of this power to protect public safety, may have an ordinance outlawing the discharge of fire arms within city limits.

The police power extends to real estate in several interrelated ways. Land-use planning and zoning systems in place in the majority of U.S. communities represent the most direct applications of the police-power controls on real estate ownership rights. These systems regulate matters such as the height of buildings, the density of development (i.e., units per acre), the location of shopping areas, and business activities that residents of single-family homes can undertake. Land-use and zoning regulations are imposed to protect public health, safety, morals, and welfare by eliminating the opportunities of owners to use land and improvements in ways that might inflict harm on others. The placement of shopping areas along major highways and away from residential areas, for example, is an attempt to keep traffic volumes low in residential areas and thus minimize potential hazards to children.

Housing codes restrict the number of persons that can inhabit a single housing unit, require that housing units in the community be kept in good repair, and establish minimum lighting and ventilation requirements. These are enforced under the police power to protect the general public from the nuisances and problems resulting from overcrowding and to protect the health and safety of the residents. Similarly, *building codes* set construction standards for the community's buildings, and *subdivision regulations* establish development standards for residential subdivisions. They are applications of police power for the purpose of preventing harm from being inflicted on the general public as a result of builder or developer negligence.

Economists refer to actions of one member of society which inflict physical, psychological, or economic harm on others as an *external cost* or *negative externality*.[17] Thus, in this context, the purpose of the various police power provisions, especially land use and zoning controls, is to prevent or control negative externalities.[18]

Taxation. Another power of the states which is passed on to local governments is the power to levy taxes on real property within their jurisdic-

---

[17]A positive externality would be when the actions of one member of society bestows some benefit on others.

[18]A detailed discussion of externalities is found in Chapter 9. Chapter 14, which is devoted entirely to the subject of land use and zoning controls as well as other police-power provisions, further expands these concepts.

tions. The proceeds from the *ad valorem* ("toward value") real property property tax and personal property tax are used to finance local government operations such as schools, libraries, and street improvements. The power of taxation represents a limitation on real estate ownership rights because if the property owner fails to pay the property tax, the local government may exercise its power to have the property sold at a tax foreclosure sale.[19]

Eminent Domain.   Under the power of eminent domain, governments and their agencies have the right to force private property owners to sell their property for "just compensation" if that property is needed for a public purpose (e.g., highway or recreation area). Usually, the implementing public agency will offer what it considers just compensation for the property being "taken." The property owner has two options—either accept the initial offer or go through formal *condemnation* proceedings in which just compensation will be decided in a court, usually with the aid of at least two professional real estate appraisals.

Escheat.   The system of land tenure in the United States requires that each parcel of property be owned by either a private or public entity. If a property owner dies without a will or any known heirs, after attempts are made to locate all legal heirs the property goes to the owner of last resort—the state—via the power of escheat. When this power is exercised, an infrequent event, a public sale is later conducted to return the property to private ownership.

Private Contracts and Other Limitations on Property Rights

In addition to the set of publicly imposed limitations on the rights of real estate ownership, limitations can be created by the actions of property owners and other parties. Even the actions of previous owners of a property can impose restrictions on the rights of current owners. The main sources of privately created limitations on property rights are easements, restrictive covenants, and liens.

Easements.   If the owner of real estate gives or sells an easement to another, the owner has given up a right to use all or part of the property for a specific purpose. Easements, therefore, generally involve rights of use and are granted for specific purposes. Yet in some instances, the

---

[19]In some states such as Florida, tax certificates are sold at a public auction each year on properties with delinquent taxes. The purchaser of the tax certificate essentially pays the property tax for the owner, and the owner then owes the holder of the certificate this amount plus interest.

holder of an easement possesses the right to convey or transfer the easement as well.

The most common form of easement is the *easement in gross*. This type of easement is said to be personal and *runs with* the party who is granted the right to use land for a specific purpose.

An example of an easement in gross is shown in Exhibit 2–8. The Jones family recently purchased a residence on a one-acre lot and discovered that the previous owners, the Martins, had negotiated an easement in gross with the electric utility company so that wires could be installed along the road. The easement of the utility company is a right to use a particular part of the Joneses' property in a specific manner and technically expires with the sale of the property by the Martins. Usually, however, this type of easement with a utility company is automatically renewed with any new owner of the fee simple estate. Also, the easement in gross, being a personal right, technically cannot be sold or otherwise conveyed to another entity. Yet such easements with utility companies can normally be sold (e.g., to another utility company) as long as the purpose for which the property is used remains unchanged.

EXHIBIT 2–8
ILLUSTRATION OF EASEMENT IN GROSS

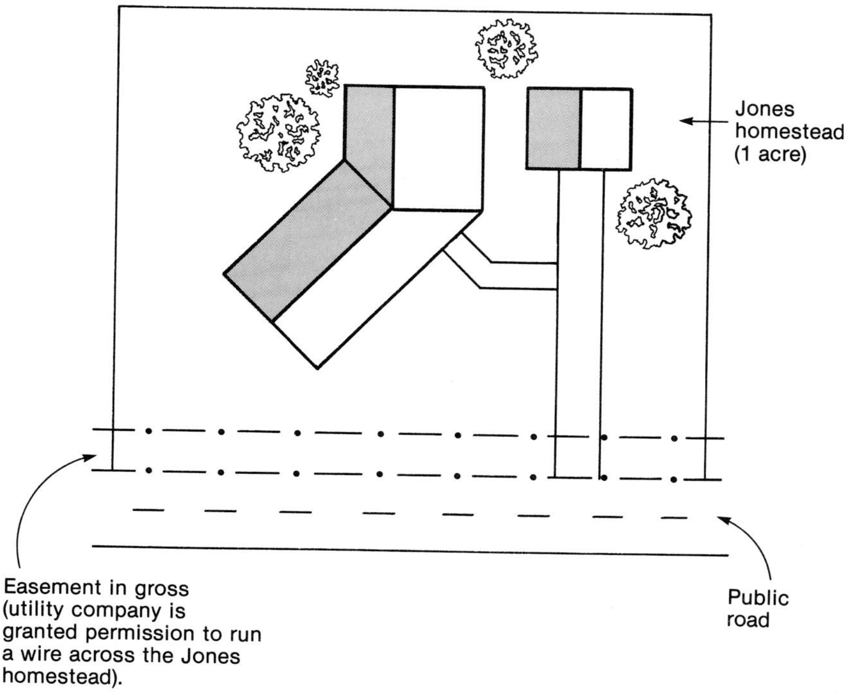

Jones homestead (1 acre)

Easement in gross (utility company is granted permission to run a wire across the Jones homestead).

Public road

Had the Martins sold an easement to an advertising firm to maintain a billboard on the edge of the property, for example, this easement in gross would have to be renegotiated by the advertising firm with the Joneses. In addition, the advertising firm could not sell or otherwise convey their right to use the property for a billboard to any other entity.

The second major type of easement is the *easement appurtenant.* This type of easement is nonpersonal in nature and is said to "run with" the land. Exhibit 2–9 shows the Jones homestead from the previous example and the Smiths' parcel, immediately to the rear, which is on a lake. While examining the property for purchase from the Martins, the Joneses discovered that the Martins had negotiated a 30-foot easement through the property with the Smiths to allow them to use this strip of land for access to the public road.

EXHIBIT 2–9
ILLUSTRATION OF AN EASEMENT APPURTENANT

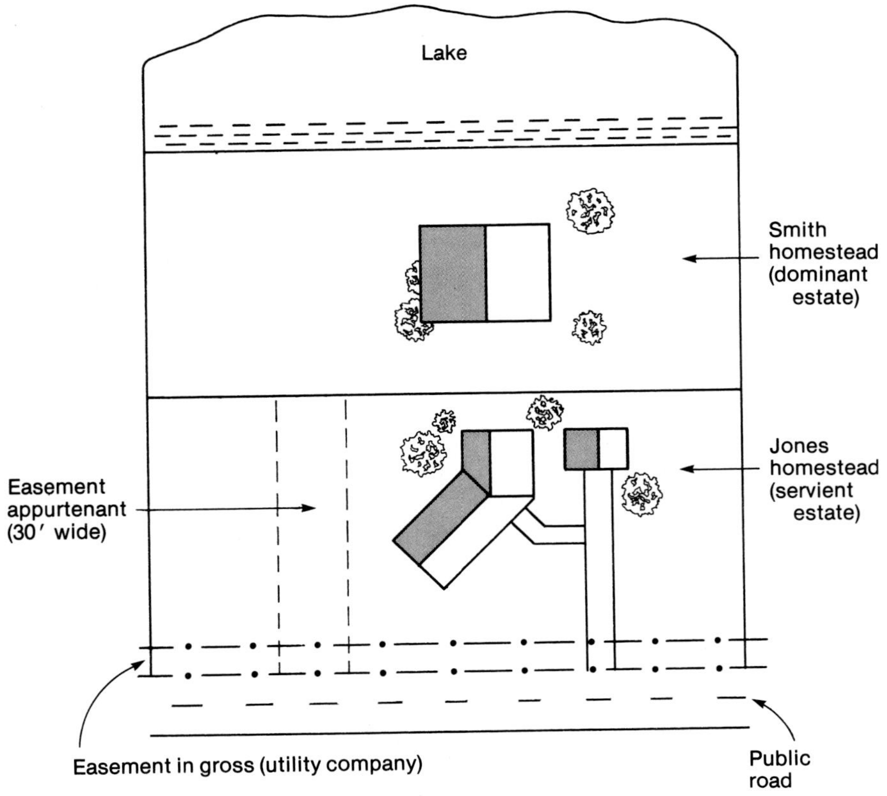

This arrangement established an easement appurtenant where the Jones have the *servient estate* and the Smiths have the *dominant estate*. When the Joneses purchased the fee simple estate from the Martins, this servient estate to the easement was also transferred with the title. This is what is meant by saying that an easement appurtenant "runs with" the land. The easement will always be a limitation on the property rights of owners of the property now owned by the Joneses unless some legal action is taken to remove the easement, the Smiths abandon the easement, or the two properties are merged under one owner.

Easements and related nonpossessory property rights can take on other forms besides the two forms mentioned above. These are outlined in Exhibit 2–10 and include license, easement by implication, easement by necessity, and easement by prescription.

EXHIBIT 2–10
NONPOSSESSIONARY PROPERTY RIGHTS

Right	Example in Use
Easement in gross	See previous example.
Easement appurtenant	See previous example.
License	X gives Y the right to fish in X's pond. This right can be given verbally and can be revoked at any time.
Easement by implication	X and Y own adjoining lots. A drain located on Y's property carries water away from X's property. If Y conveys her property to Z, there is no need to include specified statements about the drain in the transfer of title. The easement is implied.
Easement by necessity	X buys a land-locked parcel from Y who had divided a larger parcel into two parts. One part includes all frontage to the road, and the back parcel, purchased by X, has no frontage. X, therefore, is entitled to an easement by necessity through the front parcel.
Easement by prescription	For seven years X has been using Y's land for a trail to a lake nearby instead of walking around Y's land. X goes to court and is granted an easement by prescription. X had been using the trail privately, the usage was adverse to Y, and a long period of usage had been established (the number of years varies from state to state).

Restrictive Covenants. The deed is a legal instrument that is used to convey title to property. It is recorded in the county courthouse and thus provides evidence of the transfer of title. An owner of real property may, for any number of reasons, want to impose limitations on the use of the property by future owners. The owner can impose these restrictions upon the sale of the property by including restrictive covenants in the deed to the property (also known as *deed restrictions*). To be enforceable by the courts, the restrictions must be reasonable; a covenant cannot state that only a buggy whip factory can operate on the land being deeded—buggy whip factories, of course, no longer exist. It also must not go against public policy—a covenant cannot state that certain minority groups must never own the land being deeded.

While such restrictions are imposed in a wide variety of situations, there are two situations in which they most commonly arise. First, *adjacent property restrictions* might be created in the following instance. Suppose Farmer Brown suddenly finds that the family farm has become quite valuable for residential or commercial development. He subsequently divides his farm into two parcels, as shown in Exhibit 2–11, and sells the parcel closest to the urban area to real estate developers. He plans to retire with his family on the other parcel. To maintain a view of the city and a somewhat tranquil atmosphere for his retirement, Farmer Brown includes a set of restrictive convenants in the deed to the parcel being sold. The most important covenant states that "use of this land is restricted to single-family residences on no less than one-acre lots and of no more than one story in height." These restrictions adversely affect the price that developers will pay for the land, but ensure that the land will not be put to any other use.

EXHIBIT 2–11
ILLUSTRATION OF THE USE OF RESTRICTIVE COVENANTS ON AN ADJACENT PARCEL

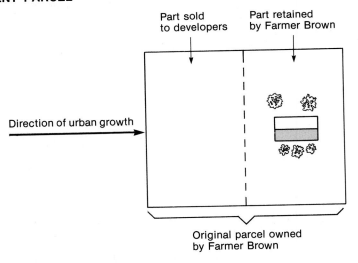

The second situation in which the use of restrictive covenants is common is in the development of new residential subdivisions. These *general plan restrictions* are designed to create a quality residential atmosphere and extend beyond the existing zoning requirements. For example, a developer may deed property with a covenant stating that "trucks or any large vehicles must be parked in a garage and cannot be parked on the street or in a driveway." Once the subdivision is sold out, these covenants are enforced through court actions taken by residents seeking relief through an injunction against the violator.

At least one major city in the United States, Houston, has no formal zoning system. Restrictive covenants and the courts thus play a much larger role in shaping Houston land use patterns than they do in other cities.[20]

Liens. A lien is the right of a creditor to petition the court to force repayment of a debt through foreclosure and sale of real or other property. *Specific liens* are rights of creditors against specific real property; *general liens* are rights of creditors against all assets of the party. Examples of specific liens include (1) tax liens against property, which are present in any jurisdiction that collects property taxes (actually part of the power of taxation, a public limitation), (2) mortgage liens, which are given to lenders on real property by borrowers, and (3) mechanics and materialmans liens, which are rights of those who provide labor and materials for real property improvements (e.g., carpenters, plumbers, and landscape architects).

A purchaser of real property normally should make certain that all prior liens have been satisfied prior to making a commitment to purchase, since such liens are rights to foreclosure against the property. In essence, a lien is a limitation on the ownership of real estate because it represents a property right given up by the owner.

============================== Frame 2–2 ==============================

A Restrictive Covenant Against Building

Q. Five years ago, Smith purchased a parcel of land from Corgel. In the deed that transferred the land to Smith, Corgel included a restrictive covenant saying that "no building shall be constructed on this land." Smith has decided now to sell the land to Irwin. The parties want to know whether this restrictive covenant still applies and whether it should be included in the new deed. What would you tell them?

A. A restrictive covenant runs with the land, so it still applies regardless of whether it is included in the deed transferring the land from Smith to Irwin. Many states, however, limit the number of years such covenants remain in effect in municipalities with zoning laws (e.g., 20 years in Georgia). A court could also rule that such a covenant is unreasonable (for example, if the surrounding area has become developed). Remember, state laws vary on this question.

---

[20]See B. H. Siegan, *Land Use Without Zoning* (Lexington, Mass.: Lexington Books, 1972).

OVERVIEW

In this chapter, we analyzed the rights of real estate owners in four ways. First, we showed that real property rights can be divided and conveyed along *physical* lines. This means, for example, that the rights to use the air space above the land can be sold separately from the land itself.

Second, we discussed the three fundamental and inherent *legal* rights of real estate ownership—the right of use and possession, the right of quiet enjoyment, and the right of disposition. Owners of real estate, through the various estates in land, can take one or more of a wide variety of ownership positions in real estate. The fee simple estate provides an ownership position in which all three of the basic rights are undisturbed, while the other estates contain a less complete bundle of legal rights.

Third, we examined how real property rights can be shared among co-owners. In most instances, a special set of *co-ownership* rights is created to facilitate the joint ownership of real estate. Perhaps the best example of such a right is the right of survivorship in the joint tenancy form.

Finally, we considered the *limitations* on real property rights—physical, legal, and co-ownership. These include a set of limitations imposed by governments to protect the public welfare, raise taxes, and provide public facilities. Also included are a set of limitations created by past and current private contracts. An examination of these limitations is a crucial part of evaluating any real estate transaction.

TEST YOURSELF

Define the following terms and concepts presented in this chapter:

1. Fixtures.
2. Estates in land.
3. "Bundle of rights."
4. Fee simple.
5. Life estate.
6. Leasehold.
7. Joint tenancy versus tenancy in common.
8. Condominium versus cooperative.
9. Police power.
10. Easement.

Answer the following multiple choice questions.

1. An easement-in-gross is said to
   a. Follow a river bed.
   b. Carry no legal rights.
   c. "Run with" the party granted the easement.
   d. "Run with" the land.
   e. "Run with" the wrong crowd.

2. Which of the following is *not* a public limitation on the rights of owners of real estate?
   a. Easement.
   b. Police power.
   c. Eminent domain.
   d. Taxation.
   e. Escheat.

3. With a time-share condominium
   a. Owners pay a pro rata share of the association fee.
   b. Owners may trade ownership rights.
   c. Owners' rights are limited to specific periods of time.
   d. Owners may sell their ownership rights.
   e. All of the above.

4. Mr. Bo Ling grants an estate to his sister Ms. Sa Ling for the life of their father Mr. Weak Ling. What type of estate does Sa Ling have?
   a. Ordinary life estate.
   b. Pour autre vie.
   c. Dower.
   d. Fee simple subject to condition subsequent.
   e. Determinable fee.

5. Which test used by the courts to determine the existence of a fixture is the most important?
   a. Annexation test.
   b. Relation-of-the-parties test.
   c. Intent test.
   d. Adaptation test.
   e. Smoking-gun test.

ADDITIONAL READINGS

Atteberry, William L., Karl G. Pearson, and Michael P. Litka. *Real Estate Law*. New York: John Wiley & Sons, 1984, Chaps. 2–4 and 6.

Corley, Robert N., Peter J. Shedd, and Charles F. Floyd. *Real Estate and the Law*. New York: Random House, 1982, Chaps. 1–3.

French, William B., and Harold F. Lusk. *Law of the Real Estate Business*. Homewood, Ill.: Richard D. Irwin, 1984, Chaps. 2–4 and 6–8.

Jaffe, Austin, J., and C. F. Sirmans. *Real Estate Investment Decision Making*. Englewood Cliffs, N.J.: Prentice-Hall, 1982, Chap. 7.

Jocobus, Charles J., and Donald R. Levi. *Real Estate Law*. Reston, Va.: Reston Publishing, 1980, Chaps. 1–5.

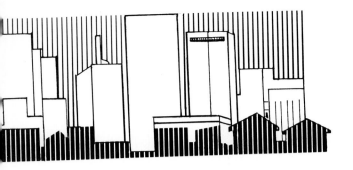

3
Transfer of Real Property Rights

INTRODUCTION

The ability to use the concepts and definitions of real property rights presented in Chapter 2 is the first of two major skills needed to create the legal arrangements for achieving one's objectives in real estate. The second skill involves the ability to use the legal and institutional concepts for the *transfer* of real property rights.

Understanding these concepts is extremely important because much of the real estate industry is devoted to facilitating real property transfers. The most obvious example of this is the real estate brokerage business, which includes hundreds of thousands of real estate salespeople and brokers who serve as intermediaries between the buyers and sellers of real estate.[1] The mortgage lending business (e.g., savings and loan associations and commercial banks) and mortgage banking business exist to provide financing for real property transfers. Most real estate appraisals provide information on property value in real estate transactions. Real estate developers are in the business of selling or leasing their products. Thus, most of the real estate industry revolves around the act of transferring real property rights.

In this chapter we present the various methods of transferring title to real estate. We also include a section on real property descriptions, which has special significance to real estate title transfers as well as other aspects of real estate (e.g., valuation). This chapter includes an outline of the balance of our presentation of the legal perspective of real estate, with a discussion of the four *basic contractual arrangements* for the transfer of real property rights. Each subsequent chapter in the legal perspective section focuses on one of these contracts or on several of them together, as in the chapter on real estate closings.

---

[1]Salespeople and brokers of real estate are licensed separately by the states. Generally, salespeople work for brokers. See Chapter 13.

METHODS OF TRANSFERRING REAL PROPERTY RIGHTS

Property rights to real estate can be transferred, or conveyed, by their owners in several ways. The conveyance of real property rights by the federal government to a private entity, for example, is termed a *public grant*, whereas a voluntary transfer of property rights between private entities (e.g., via a sale, gift, or exchange) is called a *private grant*. Private entities can also obtain real property rights through foreclosure actions, inheritance, legal possession, and even as the result of acts of nature. In this section, the various ways in which real property rights are conveyed and the legal instruments involved in making such transfers are examined.

Evidence and Conveyance of Title to Real Estate

The *title* to real estate evidences the ownership of real property rights.[2] Most people are familiar with titles through buying and selling automobiles. To transfer ownership of an automobile, the seller simply signs the back of the title certificate over to the buyer. The buyer then records the title transfer with the local and state motor vehicle departments.

Evidence and conveyance of title to real estate differs from evidence and conveyance of title to personal property like automobiles in at least two substantial ways. First, there is no actual title certificate to real estate. Owners of real estate evidence their titles in one or more of several ways, which are discussed later—none of which includes a title certificate as such. Second, the transfer of title to real estate, unlike other property, is accomplished through the use of a separate legal instrument called a *deed*. In other words, the existence of a valid deed is evidence of a transfer of title to real estate. It is common to hear people refer to a real estate transfer of ownership by saying, for example, that "Smith deeded property to Corgel." Deeds are utilized in public grants, private grants, and most other types of real estate title transfers.

Why is there a need for this separate legal instrument? The answer is that ownership of land has historically been a measure of political and economic power. In the past, societies have even limited voting rights to landowners. The transfer of ownership of real estate among members of society, therefore, has historically been of great interest to society as a whole. The deed, which is recorded in the name of both the grantor (seller) and grantee (buyer) in a deed book, usually located in the county

---

[2]The terms *title* and *estate* should not be confused. Recall from Chapter 2 that the term *estate* describes the nature or extent of real property rights owned.

court house, provides a convenient means to determine current owner-ship of land and the *chain of title* (that is, the history of ownership). The ability to trace the chain of title to a parcel of land has important impli-cations for evidencing title to that parcel.

Requirements for a Valid Deed.   To substantiate that a transfer of own-ership of real estate has occurred legally, the deed must be a valid legal instrument. The following minimum requirements must be fulfilled in or-der for the deed to be valid:

1. The names of the grantor and grantee must appear on the deed. Both parties must be competent to act, and there must be no bar-riers to mutual assent.[3]
2. A proper description of the property must be included.[4]
3. Words of conveyance (e.g., I, Laina Stephens, hereby transfer all my rights in the subject property to Shelly Stephens . . .) must be included.
4. A statement of consideration must be included.[5] In some states, the words "one dollar plus other valuable considerations" are suf-ficient. In other states, the exact price paid for the property must be included.
5. The grantor must sign the deed and, in some states, a seal must be affixed. The grantee is usually not required to, but most often does, sign the deed.
6. The deed must be properly delivered by the grantor to the grantee. Proper delivery occurs when there is a meeting of the minds. De-livery of the deed typically occurs at the closing, when both parties or their agents are present and the meeting-of-the-minds require-ment is easily satisfied. If, for example, X purchases property from Y and Y delivers the deed to X's office when X isn't there, delivery is improper. If, however, X is in his office and Y shouts to X that he is leaving the deed with X's secretary and X responds by saying "Okay," then delivery is proper—there has been a meeting of the minds.

Other requirements for a deed are imposed by the states (e.g., wit-nessing, dating, and statement of encumbrances), but in most cases if the above requirements are met, the deed is a valid legal instrument. The

---

[3]Mutual assent refers to a meeting of the minds between the parties. An example of a barrier to mutual assent is if one of the parties were under duress when executing the deed.

[4]See the next section of this chapter.

[5]Consideration refers to giving up something of value and receipt of a benefit by both parties.

deed should also be recorded; however, an unrecorded deed is still valid as long as it has been properly delivered to the grantee. The validity of an unrecorded deed is more difficult to prove.

Evidence of Good Title.   As mentioned earlier, establishing a chain of title through the records of recorded deeds is important for evidencing title to real estate. This activity is part of the *title search*, which also includes an investigation of whether all previous liens against the property (e.g., mortgage liens, tax liens) have been satisfied. If no superior claim to title can be found to that being transferred to the grantee and no outstanding liens exist, then the title is said to be "good."

The title search is an integral part of each of the three principal methods for evidencing good title to real estate in use today. These methods are:

═══════════════════════ *Frame 3–1* ═══════════════════════

Proper Delivery of a Deed: You Be the Judge!*

Mrs. Bacon issued a deed to property to her brother for the benefit of his children. When the brother saw that the property was to be owned by his sons and not his daughters, he became angry and tore the deed in half. For some reason, he kept one half of the deed, which was found among his private papers when he died. The plaintiffs in this case are the children of the brother. The defendents are the direct decendants of Mrs. Bacon.

Legal Question: Was there proper delivery of the deed to the brother?

Answer: The courts (trial and appeals) ruled that proper delivery did *not* occur since the brother never accepted the deed. There must be delivery and acceptance for proper delivery of a deed. The brother's action of tearing up the deed, even though he saved one half of the document, was evidence of rejection. Thus the decendants of Mrs. Bacon maintained ownership of the property.

────────────

Underwood v. *Gillespie*, 594 S.W. 2d 372 (Ct. App. 1980) (Missouri).

1. *Abstract and attorney's opinion.* This common method of evidencing good title relies on the development or continuation (i.e., updating) of a property's *abstract*. The abstract is a historical record of the ownership of the property. An attorney prepares or updates the abstract of the property, and once the attorney is satisfied that no prior liens exist on the property or that no prior owner or owner's spouse has an outstanding claim, the attorney issues a letter of opinion regarding the title. Therefore, an updated abstract and a letter of opinion from an attorney constitute evidence of good title.

2. *Title insurance.* Currently, the most common method for evidencing good title in residential transactions is a title-insurance policy. With this method, a title-insurance policy is purchased from a title-insurance company, which guarantees to pay any losses the grantee suffers resulting from a loss of title. Prior to issuing the policy, the title-insurance company performs a title search. The policy premium is paid in full at the closing. Mortgage lenders usually require that title insurance be purchased by the borrower (grantee), because it represents a solid guarantee against any losses due to the claims of previous owners or lien holders. The title-insurance policy is evidence of good title.

3. *Torrens system.* Perhaps the most unusual method of evidencing good title to real estate is the Torrens system. While this system is authorized under the laws of several states, it is only used in a few locations. From the property abstract, a list of all persons and lien holders who might have an interest in the subject property is developed. This list is submitted to the local registrar of Torrens certificates (often the county clerk) with an application for a Torrens certificate on the property. The application results in a law suit filed against all persons on the list requiring them to come forward and make their claims against the property. If no claims are made, a certificate is issued that serves as a good defense against any claims that might be brought in the future. Thus, a Torrens certificate provides evidence of good title to real estate.

Public Grants of Title to Real Estate

Because most of the land in the United States was first owned by the United States government, the original grants of real estate to private entities were public grants.[6] In old western movies, the settlers lined up in wagons loaded with possessions to stake their claims in a "land rush." A public grant such as the one that settlers received is made through the use of a specific type of deed known as a *patent.* Many existing abstracts of title contain references to the patent that originally conveyed title to land to a private entity. In current real estate practice, public grants are quite rare.

Private Grants of Title to Real Estate

Sales, gifts, inheritances, and exchanges between private parties constitute the majority of real estate title transfers. These private grants are

---

[6]This also applies to land granted from state governments, the king of Spain, or American Indian nations.

accomplished with one of several types of deeds. Those most commonly used are the *general warranty deed*, the *special warranty deed*, the *quitclaim deed*, and the *bargain-and-sale deed*.

General Warranty Deed.   From the buyer's perspective, the most desirable type of deed is the general warranty deed. In issuing a general warranty deed, the seller of the property makes several guarantees to the buyer. These guarantees, known as *covenants*, are as follows:

1. *Covenant of seisin.* With this covenant, the seller guarantees that he or she possesses legal (i.e., good) title to the property being conveyed.
2. *Covenant against encumbrances.* The seller guarantees that there are no encumbrances (e.g., liens) against the title other than those disclosed to the buyer.
3. *Covenant for quiet enjoyment.* This covenant means that the seller will protect the buyer against any parties claiming a superior title to the property.

The importance of these covenants is that they provide the grounds for legal action against the seller should the buyer encounter problems related to the title in the future. When title insurance has been purchased, these covenants merely provide added security for the buyer.

Special Warranty Deed.   While the general warranty deed includes guarantees from the seller which carry back in time to the period before the seller owned the property, the special warranty deed contains guarantees that pertain only to events that may have occurred *during* the seller's period of ownership. The same basic covenants apply; however, they are limited to the time period in which they apply. This type of deed is frequently preferred by sellers in situations in which a potential title problem may result from an event occurring before the seller bought the property. For example, the property may have gone through foreclosure proceedings at some time before the seller bought the property.

Quitclaim Deed.   A quitclaim deed does not actually convey rights to real estate, nor does it contain any warranties on the part of the grantor. This instrument simply transfers any rights that a *specific party* has in the property, not rights in the property itself, without covenants to another party. If the grantor has no rights, then no rights are transferred by the quitclaim deed. The quitclaim deed is commonly used to correct defects in titles. For example, if there is uncertainty about the legality of a title because a previous owner's spouse did not sign the general warranty deed and therefore did not release his or her dower rights, a quitclaim deed would be used to facilitate the release of those rights (i.e., the previous owner's spouse must be found and convinced to sign the quitclaim deed).

Bargain-and-Sale Deed. A bargain-and-sale deed, like a quitclaim deed, contains no warranties from the grantor. But unlike the quitclaim deed, the bargain-and-sale deed does convey rights to real estate. In other words, it assumes that the grantor has rights in the property to convey. Thus, this type of deed does not afford grantees as much protection as the general or special warranty deed, but it does provide more protection than the quitclaim deed. Bargain-and-sale deeds are commonly used by corporations in real property transfers as a means of limiting their liability to grantees.

Devise and Descent

Holders of real property rights who die leaving a will indicating which parties will obtain title to real estate have conveyed rights by *devise*. The will itself in such instances serves as the legal instrument that conveys title from the grantor (i.e., the deceased person or *devisor*) to the grantee (i.e., the *devisee*).

When holders of real property rights die without a valid will (intestate), the rights to real property are conveyed to others according to the probate laws of the given state. State probate laws describe the line of succession for inheriting real property from persons who die intestate, usually beginning with the deceased person's spouse and children. In such instances, real property rights are said to be transferred by *descent*. Special types of deeds, known as officer's deeds, executor's deeds, or sheriff's deeds, which contain no warrantees, are used in these cases depending on the specific circumstances.

Foreclosure

A party holding a valid lien on real property (for example, mortgage lender-mortgage lien, roofer-mechanics lien) can force a public sale of real property to receive payments through the process of *foreclosure* when the owner defualts. The deed used in foreclosure actions contains no warrantees and is known as a *referee's deed, sheriff's deed,* or *officer's deed*, depending on where the foreclosure occurs. The process by which real property rights are transferred through foreclosure is discussed in detail in Chapter 5.

Adverse Possession and Prescription

Ownership of real property rights can change from one private party to another by certain legal means designed to ensure that land is used rather than left idle, as in the case of *adverse possession*, or to ensure that parties are not denied rightful access to their properties, as in the case of *prescrip-*

═══════════════════════ Frame 3–2 ═══════════════════════

Acquiring Title by Adverse Possession

The requirements for acquiring title to land by *adverse possession* are not easily met. But in a 1982 Texas case, the court ruled in favor of a farmer (defendant) who had purchased land from an adverse possessor.* In 1941, the plaintiff in this case, Mr. A, leased a farm he owned as an absentee landlord to Mr. B for zero rent so that the farm would be maintained. Mr. B sold the lease to Mr. C who, in 1955, transferred the lease to Mr. D. Mr. D made several improvements to the land including fencing, root plowing, and digging a pond during the 14 years he used the land. In 1969, he sold the land to Mr. E, and in 1977, Mr. A, the original owner of the land, filed suit against Mr. E for trespassing.

Mr. E called several witnesses during the hearing to show that in the late 1950s Mr. D, from whom Mr. E purchased the land, claimed the land against the world and threatened to shoot anyone crossing the farm. The court was convinced that Mr. D had given notice of a constructive nature of his adverse possession of the land and ruled that Mr. D had acquired title as an adverse possessor. Mr. A no longer had any claim to the farm and therefore could not remove Mr. E as a trespasser.

───────────

Dalo v. *Laughlin*, 636 S.W. 2nd 585 (Ct. App. 1982).

───

tion. While state laws vary, a party can gain ownership of another's real property through adverse possession by using the property in a way that is actual, continuous, hostile (to the owner), visible, and exclusive for a period of usually no less than seven years. In other words, owners who fail to use their property or take action against an adverse possessor for the prescribed period stand to lose their property rights to an adverse possessor, if the adverse possessor is making profitable use of the property.

Similarly, the courts will issue prescriptive easements (rights of use) to those who have established a pattern of actual, continuous, hostile, and visible (not exclusive) use of another's property, usually for the purpose of gaining access to another parcel, such as in the case of a roadway through a neighbor's land. Instances of acquiring real property rights through adverse possession and prescription are not common, but are possible (see Frame 3–2).

Title from Nature

Recorded deeds include a physical description of the property, often by describing the natural boundaries of the parcel (e.g., river, lake, and rock formations). When natural landscape features change, a transfer of ownership of part of certain parcels may occur. For example, if a body of water deposits land in a given area, ownership rights to that land are obtained through *accretion*. Where boundary water recedes leaving dry land, ownership rights are acquired through *reliction*. When a body of water, such as a river or stream, changes course, however, no rights are altered between adjacent property owners since the dry bed of the body of water remains as the boundary.

PROPER DESCRIPTIONS OF REAL PROPERTY

A proper description of land is a necessary part of listing contracts, contracts for sale, deeds, mortgage contracts, leases (e.g., long-term ground leases), and any other legal instrument or document that affects the transfer of title to real estate. The purpose of such descriptions is to set the boundaries of the specific *parcel* of land to distinguish it from all other parcels. A *proper description* of land therefore is one that identifies the parcel and distinguishes it from all other parcels. A *legal description* of property is one that will hold up in a court of law and thus provides an exact account of the property boundaries.

Describing a property as 101 Oak Street (its street address), for example, may be a proper description, but is not usually found in legal documents because of the lack of precision it provides in defining boundaries. In general, there are three main types of descriptions of real estate which are both proper and sufficiently precise for legal documents: *metes and bounds*, *recorded plat map*, and the *government survey system*.

───────── Frame 3–3 ─────────

A Boundary Problem: You Be the Judge!*

The Joneses built their home and made other improvements on a lot they had purchased a year earlier. The Joneses believed erroneously that their lot extended 17 feet beyond the point where boundary markers had been placed several years before, when the subdivision was originally surveyed.

Legal Question: Was a *boundary by acquiescence* established when the improvements were made to the lot, or does the original survey line remain as the boundary?

Answer: A lower court held that a boundary by acquiescence had been established, but the appeals court reversed this decision, stating that for a boundary by acquiescence to exist, a clear *boundary line*, such as a fence, must be established between the parcels. Thus, the Joneses were forced to remove the improvements. This case shows the importance of having a survey each time a parcel of land is purchased.

───────

Monroe v. *Harper*, 619 P.2d 323 (1980) (Utah).

To insure the accuracy of the legal description, regardless of its type, a *survey* of the property is frequently undertaken by a licensed (or registered) surveyor at the request of one of the parties to a contract. (See Exhibit 3–1 for some common measurement equivalencies used by surveyors and others dealing in real estate.) The most common example is the case of an ordinary mortgage contract for a single-family residence where the mortgage lender, as part of the underwriting process (i.e., the process of determining what risks the lender is taking in granting the loan), requires a survey of the property. An example of such a survey is shown in Exhibit 3–2. This survey is of a typical residential lot. The dimensions of the lot are stated and the placement of all improvements such as house and driveway are shown. The letter "D" refers to the block and the number "14" is the lot number. These designations are part of the recorded plat description discussed below.

EXHIBIT 3–1
COMMON MEASUREMENT CONVERSIONS

Area Measurements

144 square inches	= 1 square foot
9 square feet	= 1 square yard
30½ square yards	= 1 square rod
43,560 square feet	= 1 acre
160 square rods	= 1 acre
640 acres	= 1 square mile

Linear Measurements

12 inches	= 1 foot
3 feet	= 1 yard
16½ feet	= 1 rod
5½ yards	= 1 rod
660 feet	= 1 furlong (⅛ mile)
220 yards	= 1 furlong (⅛ mile)
40 rods	= 1 furlong (⅛ mile)
5,280 feet	= 1 mile
320 rods	= 1 mile
8 furlongs	= 1 mile

Surveyor's or Chain Measurement

7.92 inches	= 1 link
25 links	= 1 rod
4 rods	= 1 chain
80 chains	= 1 mile

Although the survey is intended to verify the accuracy of the legal description, it also serves to uncover any *encroachments*. As Exhibit 3–3 indicates, an encroachment can occur when the owner of the adjacent parcel constructs a driveway that extends into (i.e., encroaches on) the

EXHIBIT 3–2
SURVEY OF A TYPICAL RESIDENTIAL LOT

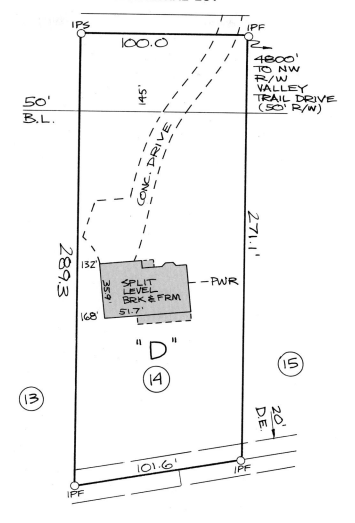

subject parcel. An encroachment is an encumbrance on the title. The owner of the parcel encroached on has the right to force the removal of the encroachment. However, the owners of the two parcels may reach a settlement to adjust the boundary lines. If no action is taken by the owner of the encroached on parcel, the owner of the adjacent parcel ultimately may claim legal title to the affected portion of land through adverse possession or prescriptive easement.

EXHIBIT 3–3
SURVEY SHOWING AN ENCROACHMENT

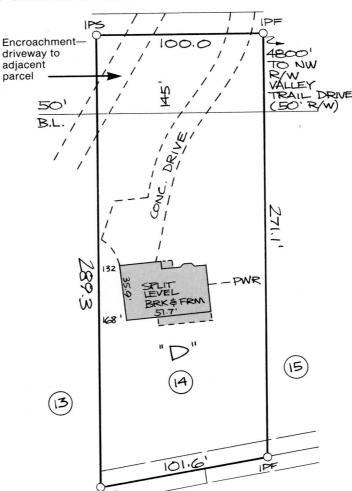

Metes-and-Bounds Description

The oldest of the techniques for describing real estate is the *metes* (distances) *and bounds* (boundaries) description. This technique is based on an ability to identify naturally occurring (e.g., a rock formation) and man-made (e.g., a road intersection) landmarks and then defining the boundaries of the property by measuring the distances and directions between these landmarks.[7] In essence, the reader of a metes-and-bounds description is taken on a tour of the perimeter of the property. This tour begins at a particular landmark known as the *point of beginning.* The following is an example of a metes-and-bounds description that might be found in a deed:

> Beginning at a point 50 feet east of the intersection of Abbey Road and Penny Lane, South 80 degrees, 200 feet to an iron pin (part of the description omitted) . . . returning to the point of beginning.

Before developers began using iron pins and concrete markers, naturally occurring landmarks such as an "old oak tree" were commonly used in metes-and-bounds descriptions. This reliance on natural objects presents a problem when the object is removed by man or nature; thus the need arises to check such descriptions carefully. Many parcels in urban and suburban areas are described by recorded plat maps. Metes-and-bounds descriptions are more commonly encountered when dealing with rural property.

Recorded Plat Map Descriptions

In most cities and counties in the United States, a developer seeking to subdivide a parcel of land must file a detailed map of the subdivision showing the exact location and configuration of the lots, streets, sewers, utility easements, park land, and any other physical features. This map, known as a *plat map,* is considered, along with other relevant information, by the appropriate city or county unit to determine whether the development conforms to local zoning and subdivision regulations. If approval of the plat map and proposal is granted, the plat map is placed in the public record by being recorded in a plat book at the county courthouse or city hall. Since the plat map contains sufficient detail about the boundaries of each lot, the description of the lot as part of a "platted" parcel constitutes a proper and legal description of real estate.

Exhibit 3–4 is a plat map of Heavenly Acres Subdivision. Notice that all of the lots in the subdivision are numbered and all streets are named (details on easements, sewer lines, and measurements have been omitted). The subdivision consists of four *blocks.* A block is a set of lots all of which can be reached without crossing a street. Also, notice that a metes-and-bounds description could be developed for the entire subdivided parcel by referencing the intersections of the surrounding roads. This is usually unnecessary, however, since the name of the subdivision is normally sufficient to identify the subdivided parcel.

---

[7]Landmarks are sometimes referred to as *monuments.* A related technique for describing real estate is also known as the *monuments method.*

EXHIBIT 3–4
HEAVENLY ACRES SUBDIVISION PLAT MAP

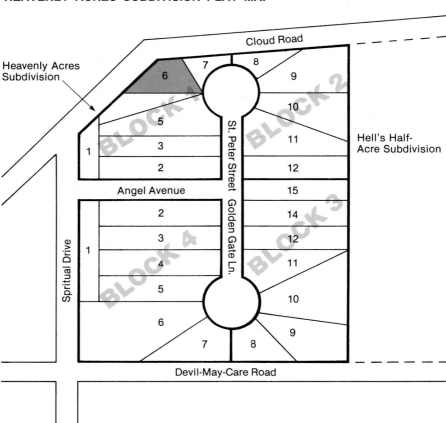

Suppose we are interested in determining a recorded plat map description for the lot shaded on the map. The description would be:

> Lot 6, Block 1 of Heavenly Acres Subdivision according to the plat recorded March 16, 1987, as plat number 5000, page 3000, Almost Heavenly County, State of West Virginia.

Government Survey System Descriptions

The government survey system, formally known as the Government Rectangular Survey System (GRSS), was initiated by Congress under the Land Ordinance of 1785. The purpose of this ordinance was to create a system for describing lands acquired by the United States following the

American Revolution. Thus GRSS, as it is implemented today, is in effect in 30 states, mostly in the midwestern and western United States.[8]

A description of real estate using the government survey system begins with the identification of a point which can be located on a general map of the United States and may end with a parcel as small as one-quarter acre. This system involves a process of continually subdividing larger areas into smaller areas, using a hierarchy of lines on a map. The process begins with the identification of a *principal meridian* and *base line* then, with the aid of *township lines* and *range lines*, one-square-mile *sections* are located. Smaller areas are identified and described by subdividing the appropriate section. To help explain the government survey system, a description of a 10-acre parcel near Orlando, Florida, is developed below along with discussion of each component of the government survey system.

Principal Meridians and Base Lines.   The first step in using the government survey system for a real estate description is to identify the appropriate principal meridian and base line. Principal meridians are survey lines which run north and south throughout the portions of the United States affected by GRSS. Base lines are lines running east and west associated with the principal meridians. Each principal meridian has a corresponding base line. The intersection of a principal meridian and base line, known as the *initial point*, marks the point for beginning the description of a particular parcel.

Exhibit 3–5 is a map showing all of the principal meridians and accompanying base lines in the United States. The different shadings indicate which areas (i.e., states and parts of states) are associated with which meridians and base lines. The initial point in describing the parcel near Orlando, Florida, is the intersection of the Tallahassee principal meridian and its base line (see map).[9]

Township and Range Lines.   Township lines run east and west at six-mile intervals parallel to a base line. Range lines run north and south, also at six-mile intervals, parallel to a principal meridian. Thus, township and range lines create a grid on the map consisting of squares six miles by six miles. These squares are known as *townships*. In addition, a square area consisting of 16 townships (i.e., four townships by four townships) is known as a *check*.

---

[8]The 30 states are Alabama, Alaska, Arizona, Arkansas, California, Colorado, Florida, Idaho, Illinois, Indiana, Iowa, Kansas, Louisiana, Michigan, Minnesota, Mississippi, Missouri, Montana, Nebraska, Nevada, New Mexico, North Dakota, Ohio, Oklahoma, Oregon, South Dakota, Utah, Washington, Wisconsin, and Wyoming.

[9]Note that the placement of principal meridians and base lines was done for expediency; there is no unifying locational principle involved.

Note: Shadings distinguish areas that come under different meridians and base lines (e.g., all of Florida is associated with the Tallahassee principal meridian, whereas Alabama and Louisiana have different shadings, meaning they are associated with different meridians).

Source: Bureau of Land Management, U.S. Department of Interior.

Exhibit 3–6 presents a map of the state of Florida with selected range and township lines superimposed. Notice that these lines are numbered and referenced by direction beginning at the principal meridian and base line. For example, the first township line below the base line is labeled T (township) 1 S (south). Similarly, the first range line to the right of the Tallahassee principal meridian is R (range) 1 E (east). Proceeding south and east, we find that Orlando is located between T22S and T23S and between R28E and R29E. Using the *furthermost township and range line from the initial point*, a description can be developed for the township in which Orlando is located. The correct description is "T23S, R29E of the Tallahassee Principal Meridian and Base Line."

Sections. Each township is 36 square miles in area (i.e., six miles by six miles), and within each township are 36 one-square-mile subdivisions called *sections*. Exhibit 3–7 is a representation of the township in which

EXHIBIT 3–6
MAP OF FLORIDA SHOWING SELECTED RANGE AND TOWNSHIP LINES

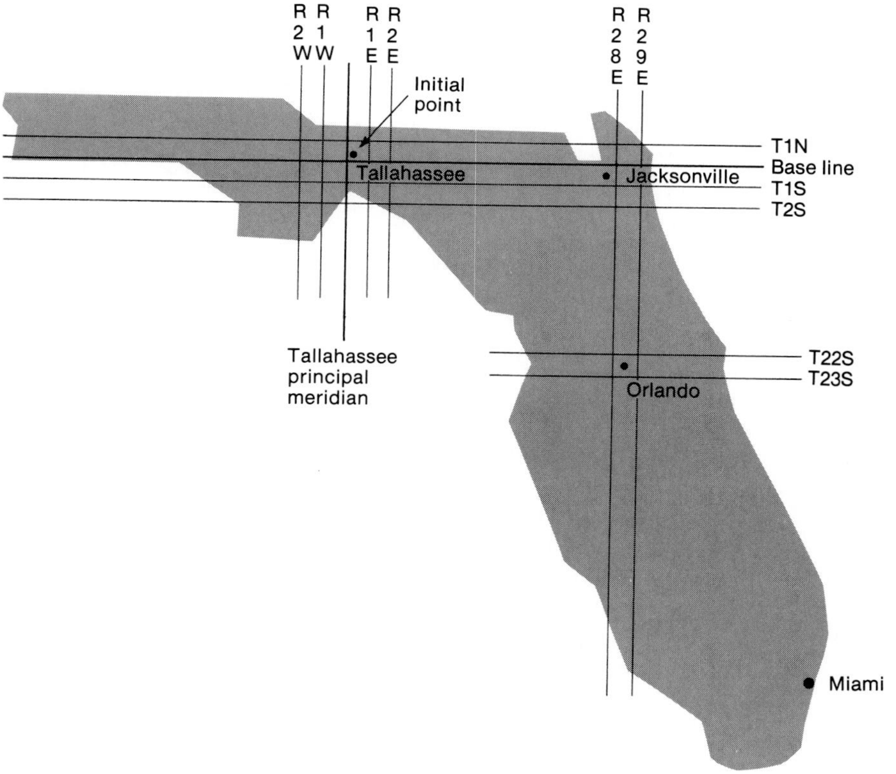

EXHIBIT 3–7
SECTIONS WITHIN A PARTICULAR TOWNSHIP

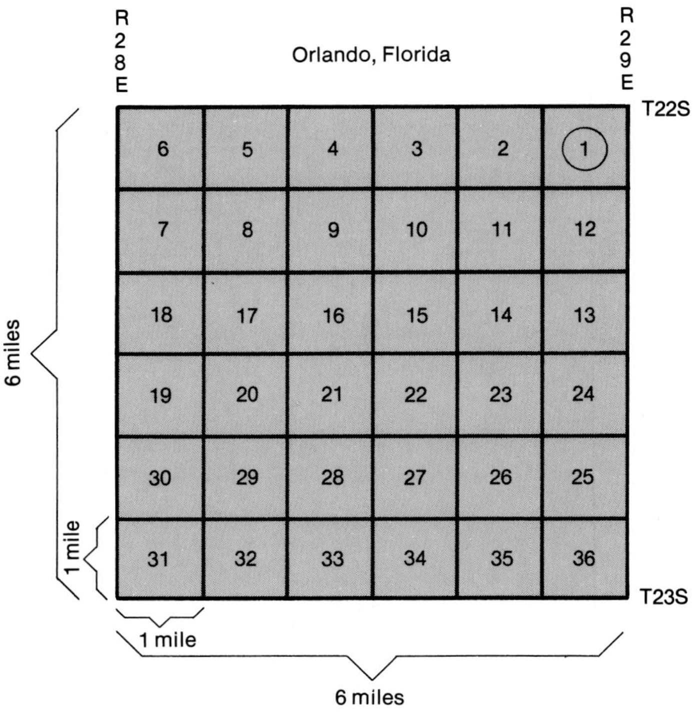

Orlando, Florida, is located. It shows the 36 sections within the township and the numbering system used to designate each section (i.e., section one in the upper right corner, then consecutive numbering in a right-to-left, left-to-right fashion until section 36 is reached in the lower right corner).

Suppose the parcel we want to describe is located in Section One. Then, the GRSS description to this level of detail is "Section One, T23S, R29E of the Tallahassee Principal Meridian and Base Line."

Finer detail in describing parcels under the government survey system comes as a result of subdividing the appropriate section. Exhibit 3–8 shows Section One with subdivision to the 10-acre level. The specific 10-acre parcel we wish to describe is the shaded area in Exhibit 3–8. To begin, we ask the question, in what part of the square, designated as (a), is the shaded parcel located? The answer is the NE ¼. Moving out one dimension, in what part of the square designated as (b) is the shaded area located? The answer is the NE ¼. Now moving out to consider the entire section, in what part of the section is the shaded parcel located? Again,

EXHIBIT 3–8
SUBDIVIDED SECTION
(Section One)

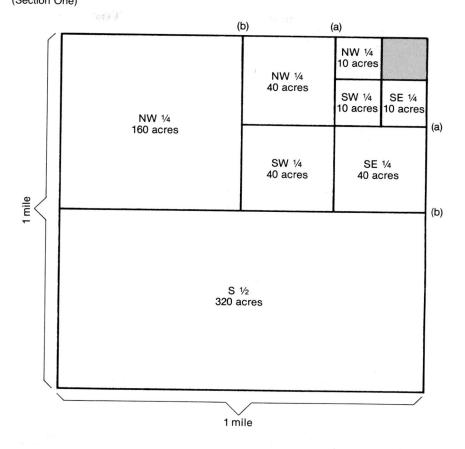

the answer is the NE ¼. Thus, the *complete GRSS description* of the Orlando parcel is the "NE ¼ of the NE ¼ of the NE ¼ of Section One, T23S, R29E of the Tallahassee Principal Meridian and Base Line."

The key to assigning GRSS descriptions is to begin with the subject parcel and then work outward through the successive subdivisions to the section, to the township and range, and, finally, to the principal meridian and base line.

Correction Lines and Government Lots. Description by the GRSS is not as straightforward as described above because the earth is not a flat and featureless plane on which a grid can be placed without distortions. The curvature of the earth is one problem that must be dealt with in a system like the government survey system. To correct for the earth's curvature, *correction lines* are introduced every 24 miles beginning from each principal meridian (called *guide meridians*) and base line (called *standard parallels*). This means that sections along the borders of townships affected by correction lines will not measure exactly 640 acres.[10]

Other problems result from physical features of the earth's surface, such as bodies of water and mountain ranges. While a mountain range can cause distortions in the acreage of a section, bodies of water running through a township can cause fractionalization of sections into smaller pieces known as *government lots*. For numbering purposes, each lot is treated as if it were a separate section. Thus, for example, a township containing a body of water might have 50 subdivisions — 30 complete sections and six fractionalized sections divided into 20 lots.[11]

CONTRACTS FOR THE TRANSFER OF REAL PROPERTY RIGHTS

Contract law is the dominant, underlying rule of social order governing the transfer of real property rights. Because buyers and sellers of real estate rely heavily on the contract law, an understanding of the basic definitions and concepts is a first step in using real estate contracts. Since the law of real estate contracts is an extension of general contract law, we examine in this section some general provisions of contract law and then discuss the specific contracts used in real estate transactions.

Validity and Enforceability of Contracts

A *valid contract* refers to an instrument that satisfies all legal requirements. Specifically, it contains all of the essential elements of a contract discussed later in this section. A *void contract* is nonexistent in the eyes of the law because it does not include one or more of the essential elements of a valid contract. Because such a contract does not exist in the eyes of the law, it cannot be enforced.

A *voidable contract* is a valid contract that is unenforceable against *one of the parties* due to some special set of circumstances. The most common example of a voidable contract is a contract with a minor (i.e., a person under the legally specified age) or an insane person. Because these persons are legally considered incapable to act for themselves, contract provisions cannot be enforced against them.

---

[10]For further discussion, see William M. Shenkel, *Modern Real Estate Principles* (Plano, Tex.: Business Publications, 1980), pp. 112–13.

[11]Ibid., p. 118.

An *enforceable contract* incorporates the essential elements of a valid contract and does not include provisions that are contrary to public policy (such as provisions promoting racial discrimination). Contracts for the sale of real estate have an additional requirement beyond the essential elements of a valid contract: they must be *in writing*. An oral contract for the transfer of real property rights is unenforceable.

General Categories of Contracts

Contracts may be *unilateral* or *bilateral*. A unilateral contract is a *promise for an act;* a bilateral contract is a *promise for a promise.* A real estate contract for sale is an example of a bilateral contract. The seller promises to deliver the deed (and thus title to the property) to the buyer, and the buyer promises to pay the seller money or other property according to the agreed-on terms. Both parties are required to fulfill their promises, and their respective promises are presumably within the power of each party.

The listing contract is an example of a unilateral contract. It carries a promise on the part of the seller of the property for an act on the part of the broker (e.g., "I [seller] will pay 6 percent commission if you [broker] sell my property"). The broker must conduct a search for a willing and able buyer but is not strictly required to find one. Finding a willing and able buyer is not totally within the power of the broker; other factors, such as market conditions, can adversely affect the broker's performance. Thus, an act may be less burdensome than a promise on a party to a contract.

Most contracts are expressed, but sometimes contracts may be created by implication. *Expressed contracts,* either oral or written, reflect explicitly the intentions, terms, and conditions of the parties; an *implied contract* (known as a *contract implied-in-fact*) is an agreement evidenced by acts or conduct.

Suppose that you own an apartment complex and have hired a resident manager to collect rents and show units for rent, but there is no explicit statement in your agreement with the resident manager about making repairs. One day, as you are driving through the complex, you observe the resident manager fixing a broken window for one of the tenants. You slow down, honk your horn, and wave to the resident manager. The next day, the resident manager asks for reimbursement for the window that was replaced. You refuse on the ground that such an act is outside the resident manager's realm of responsibilities. The case eventually goes to court.

How would the court rule? Probably in favor of the resident manager, since an implied contract was created when you acknowledged, and implicitly approved, the actions of the manager in fixing the window while you were driving through the complex.

The Four Basic Contracts

While transfers of real property rights can be accomplished through a number of different types and combinations of agreements, the following general types of contracts are seen most often in practice: (1) listing contracts, (2) contracts for sale, (3) mortgage contracts, and (4) leases. The term *contract* is defined as "a voluntary agreement between two or more competent parties, who for a consideration, agree to do or refrain from doing some legal act." Thus, the terms *contract* and *agreement* are used interchangeably.

Exhibit 3–9 shows the relationships between the parties in each of the four basic contracts. The first three contracts usually apply in situations where all legal rights are being transferred from one party to another through a sale of the property. These contracts can also be used to transfer complete or partial physical rights (e.g., air rights or subsurface

EXHIBIT 3–9
THE FOUR BASIC CONTRACTS FOR TRANSFER OF REAL PROPERTY RIGHTS

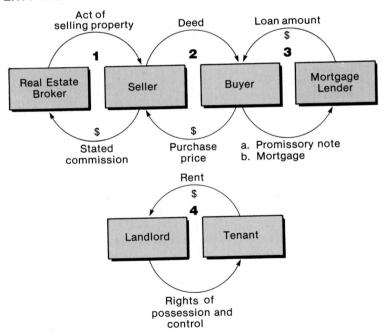

Contracts:
(1) Listing contract
(2) Contract for sale
(3) Mortgage contract
(4) Lease

rights). The lease agreement is used for transactions transferring the legal rights of possession and control.

Listing Contract.   The listing contract is between an owner who wishes to sell real property and a real estate broker. Not all transactions involve listing contracts with brokers because some owners prefer to sell their properties themselves. Nevertheless, because of the somewhat complex legal arrangements in real estate transactions and the characteristics of real estate markets which make the matching of buyers with sellers difficult, contracts with brokers are usually negotiated, especially for the sale of income properties.[12] In such contracts, the seller agrees to pay the broker a fee (usually a percentage of the sale price), if the broker performs the act of finding a willing and able buyer for the property. These contracts are discussed in Chapter 4.

Contract for Sale.   The contract for sale is the agreement between the buyer and seller to transfer the real property rights they have agreed to exchange and includes all the terms of the transaction. In this contract, the seller receives money or its equivalent (e.g., notes or other property), and the buyer receives a deed to the property. The deed is evidence of the transfer of property rights. Contracts for sale are discussed in detail in Chapter 6.

Mortgage Contract.   Most, but not all, transactions involve the use of borrowed funds by the buyer to finance the purchase of real property. When a lender is needed, a mortgage contract is negotiated in which the buyer/borrower receives money and the mortgage lender receives two legal instruments. The first is a promissory note representing the buyer/borrower's promise to repay the loan. The second is a mortgage (in most states) which gives the lender the legal right to foreclose on the property (force a sale) to obtain reimbursement if necessary. Some mortgages or similar contracts (such as land contracts) provide for the seller to help finance the sale for the buyer. Mortgage contracts are the subject of Chapter 5.

Leases.   In a leasing arrangement, the owner/landlord of real property gives up rights of use and possession of the property for a set period of time to a tenant in exchange for rent money. Along with sales agreements, leases are the most common form of contract found in real estate practice and may be considered a substitute for a sale arrangement. Leases and other types of contracts used in real estate are described in Chapter 8.

---

[12]These difficulties are discussed in Chapter 10.

OVERVIEW

Appreciation of the legal perspective of real estate requires both a thorough understanding of the system of property rights in real estate and the methods and mechanisms for transferring property rights among entities in society. In this chapter, we have been concerned with the basic concepts and terminology underlying these methods and mechanisms for transferring real property rights.

Specifically, we discussed the deed, which is the legal instrument that evidences the transfer of real property rights. We described how "good" title to real estate is evidenced. We also discussed various ways that title to real estate can be transferred. These include public grants, private grants (usually sales), devise and descent, foreclosure, adverse possession and prescription, and title transfers as the result of acts of nature.

In the next section of the chapter, we presented the various forms of property descriptions. They include the metes-and-bounds descriptions, which rely on natural and man-made physical features of the land, recorded plat descriptions used for describing parcels in urban areas (especially residential parcels), and the government survey system, which is used in most of the United States except the original 13 states and a few others.

Some basic legal fundamentals of contracts were also presented in this chapter. We emphasized the elements of a valid contract and the elements of a valid and enforceable contract. Finally, we introduced the four types of contracts most commonly found in real estate transactions: listing contracts, contracts for sale, mortgage contracts, and leases. The legal and institutional structure for transferring real property rights is highly dependent on these contracts. Subsequent chapters are devoted to detailed discussions of each of these four common contracts.

TEST YOURSELF

Explain the following terms and concepts presented in this chapter.

1. Title versus deed.
2. Chain of title.
3. Torrens system.
4. Quitclaim deed.
5. Adverse possession.
6. Recorded plat description.
7. GRSS.
8. Valid versus enforceable contract.
9. Expressed versus implied contract.
10. Unilateral versus bilateral contract.

Answer the following multiple choice questions.

1. Special warranty deeds are used if:
   a. Title is not sufficiently secure to qualify for a warranty deed.
   b. The seller wishes to restrict his or her liability to title defects occurring after the seller acquired title.
   c. The seller wishes to transfer only an interest in real estate.
   d. No title insurance is available.
   e. The seller warrants special property rights.

2. Which of the following statements describes a voidable contract?
   a. An instrument that satisfies all legal requirements but lacks one essential element required by law.
   b. Parties to the contract have no legal agreement.
   c. A contract that may be enforced or rejected at the option of one of the parties.
   d. An oral contract conveying interest in real estate.
   e. A contract implied-in-fact.

3. Title is not conveyed until the deed is
   a. Recorded.
   b. Executed by the seller.
   c. Stamped by the county clerk.
   d. Physically handed by the grantee to the grantor.

   e. Delivered by the grantor to the grantee and accepted by the grantee.

4.

Identify NW¼ of the NW¼ of the section shown above.
   a.
   b.
   c.
   d.
   e.

5. A deed that describes the consideration (property) given and conveys title to real property without giving any warranties of title is a
   a. Quitclaim deed.
   b. General warranty deed.
   c. Special warranty deed.
   d. Bargain-and-sale deed.
   e. Private grant deed.

ADDITIONAL READINGS

Atteberry, William L., Karl G. Pearson, and Michael P. Litka. *Real Estate Law.* New York: John Wiley and Sons, 1984, Chaps. 5 and 12.

Corley, Robert N., Peter J. Shedd, and Charles F. Floyd. *Real Estate and the Law.* New York: Random House, 1982, Chaps. 1 and 11.

French, William B. and Harold F. Lusk. *Law of the Real Estate Business.* Homewood, Ill.: Richard D. Irwin, 1984, Chaps. 5 and 16.

Jacobus, Charles J. and Donald R. Levi. *Real Estate Law.* Reston, Va: Reston Publishing Company, 1980, Chap. 7.

Kratovil, Robert and Raymond J. Werner. *Real Estate Law.* Englewood Cliffs, N.J.: Prentice-Hall, 1983, Chaps. 5 and 9.

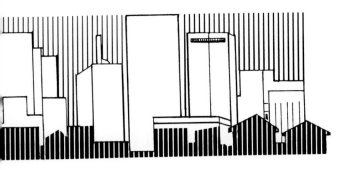

4
Listing Contracts

INTRODUCTION

A *listing contract* as shown in Exhibit 4–1 is an agreement between the owner of real estate and a real estate broker or brokerage firm that requires the broker to *attempt* to sell the property of the owner. If the broker is successful in finding a buyer for the property, the agreement requires the owner to pay the broker a fee or commission. Since this agreement requires a *promise* on the part of the owner to pay a commission if the broker successfully *acts* in selling the property, a listing contract is a *unilateral contract,* as we saw in Chapter 3.

EXHIBIT 4–1
SIMPLE LISTING CONTRACT

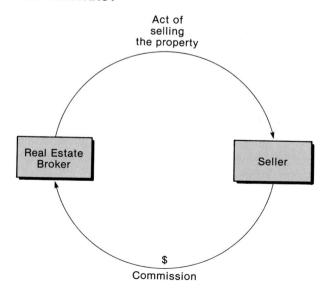

The broker's fee or commission is usually calculated as a percentage of the selling price (e.g., a commission of 6 percent on a selling price of $100,000 is $6,000). The broker need only make a reasonable attempt to find a willing and able buyer to satisfy the terms of the listing contract. If the broker is unsuccessful, the agreement lapses after a specified time period (or reasonable time period, if the time period is not specifically stated), and neither party has any further obligation.

The Agency Relationship

A listing contract creates a relationship of reliance and trust between the parties. The broker becomes the *agent* of the property owner and thus is governed by the *law of agency*. The law of agency in every state establishes the obligations and the duties binding any agent.

The law of agency also governs the relationship between the broker and the sales agents working under the broker. The agency relationship between the broker and the owner is termed a *special agency*, since the broker is not empowered to bind the owner to any agreement. The agency relationship between the broker and the sales agent, known as a *general agency*, carries the power on the part of the sales agent to bind the broker to agreements. (See Exhibit 4–2.)

EXHIBIT 4–2
AGENCY RELATIONSHIPS

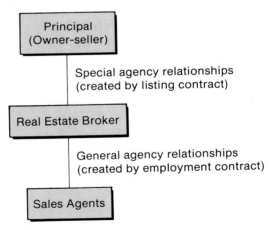

Basically, the law requires an agent to represent the best interests of the *principal* (i.e., the owner)—the other party to the contract. An agent can do nothing to harm the interests of the principal and, positively, must make every reasonable effort to protect and enhance the principal's position. These obligations constitute what is known legally as a *fiduciary relationship*—a relationship in which a principal is entitled to trust the agent and to expect the agent to look out for the principal's best financial interests.

The fiduciary relationship created by a listing contract obligates the broker not to profit at the unknowing expense of the principal. For example, the broker may not purchase the property for himself or herself secretly through a third party. The broker could, of course, purchase the property openly and directly from the principal (owner), provided the complete identity of the broker and his or her relationship to the principal is known by the principal.

The broker-agent cannot withhold information from the principal. The broker must present every offer to purchase the property to the principal. Even if the agent considers an offer too low, the agent must present the offer to the principal, because it may be in the principal's best interest to sell the property quickly, no matter how low the offer.

On the other hand, the broker-agent should not attempt to frighten the principal into accepting a low offer or suggest to a prospective buyer that the seller will accept a price lower than the listed price. (A broker can, of course, state the obvious fact that the seller *might* accept a lower price and that he or she is obligated to present every offer to the seller.)

While a broker-agent may represent a buyer in a transaction, a broker-agent may not represent both buyer and seller without the knowledge and consent of both parties. If, however, both buyer and seller consent to such an agreement, the broker could represent both parties and collect a fee or commission from each.

By signing a listing contract, an owner places his or her property on the list of properties that are available for purchase. Without the authorization of a listing contract, a broker cannot attempt to sell the property by claiming that it is available for sale or that the owner will accept a particular price. Such actions by a broker would cause the state licensing agency (real estate commission) to suspend or revoke the broker's license.

In signing a listing contract, an owner agrees to sell the property at a specified price and under specified terms. If the broker finds a purchaser who is willing to purchase the property at the specified price and terms, the broker is usually entitled to the agreed-on fee or commission. If the owner then refuses to sell the property, the broker is still entitled to the commission and may sue the owner if the owner does not pay. The prospective buyer may also have several legal recourses, which are discussed later in this chapter.

Economic Rationale for Employing a Broker

Brokers are employed to sell properties because they perform a useful service. Brokers have specialized knowledge of the market for properties and have developed expertise in selling such properties. Furthermore, they spend time and effort in finding buyers for listed properties.[1] Brokers have knowledge and expertise in the following areas:

1. Prices and terms of recent market transactions for similar properties.
2. Marketing procedures that have been successful in the past.
3. Legal obligations of buyers and sellers.
4. Similar properties, prices, and terms that are currently listed for sale.
5. Needs of prospective buyers who seek out brokerage firms as sources of properties.
6. Procedures that buyers and sellers should follow in consummating a transaction (e.g., how to obtain a title search, financing, insurance, utility services, and so on).

=== *Frame 4–1* ===

Relationship between Brokers and Buyers

While the relationship between sellers and buyers is well established by the law of agency, the relationship between brokers and the buying public is not as well developed. This relationship is based on the *law of torts*.

Common law dictates that individuals must act so as not to injure innocent individuals. Yet in attempting to gain the highest possible price for the seller, the broker may have an incentive to mislead a buyer by exaggerating claims of quality or by attempting to conceal defects. Such actions could be considered *torts*, thus entitling the prospective buyer to damages.

The courts have traditionally held for plaintiffs (buyers) when torts have been claimed in cases involving personal property, but have followed the doctrine of *caveat emptor* (let the buyer beware) in cases involving real property. Lately, however, the courts have been much more sympathetic to the claims of buyers of real property.

Some property owners sell their properties themselves to avoid the cost of a broker. Often, however, such owners find they are ill-equipped to sell their own properties and end up with less cash than if they had employed a broker. Consider the following two alternative transactions

[1] See G. Donald Jud, "Real Estate Brokers and the Market for Residential Housing," *American Real Estate and Urban Economics Association Journal* 11 (Spring 1983), pp. 69–82.

in Exhibit 4–3 for the same property—one without and the other with a broker:

EXHIBIT 4–3
ALTERNATIVE TRANSACTIONS WITH AND WITHOUT A REAL ESTATE BROKER

		Without Broker	With Broker
Price		$95,000	$100,000
Marketing costs	$1,000		—
Time of owner (60 hrs. @ $50/hr.)	3,000	4,000	—
Commission (6½%)		—	6,500
Proceeds to owner		$91,000	$ 93,500

The gain to the owner by using a broker is the result of a number of factors. While some owners may believe otherwise, buyers tend to negotiate prices downward by at least a portion of the commission when they know a broker is not involved. Furthermore, the offering price may be lower to begin with, because a seller who does not employ a broker does not have access to the number of prospective buyers that a broker usually has. And sellers may waste time with unqualified buyers. In other words, an owner-seller must usually rely on a "thinner" market than a broker.[2] Many owners fail to count the value of their own time and effort, which usually turns out to be considerably greater than anticipated. They also subject themselves to greater legal and financial risks because they are less aware of the pitfalls of selling property than brokers who specialize in this activity.

The net result is that owners who employ brokers often end up better economically than owners who do not employ brokers. If this were not so, most owners would not use brokers, and most brokers would go out of business.

TYPES OF LISTING CONTRACTS

There are four basic types of listing contracts, although only two—the *open listing* and the *exclusive right of sale listing*—are used with much fre-

[2]At least one study has found that brokers do not have an effect on market value but rather on the time it takes to sell property. See Robert Edelstein, "The Determinants of Value in the Philadelphia Housing Market: A Case Study of the Main Line, 1967–1969," *Review of Economics and Statistics* 56 (August, 1974), pp. 319–28. Another study, however, found that the choice of brokers does influence the selling price of the property. See C. T. L. Janssen and J. D. Jobson, "On the Choices of Realtors," *Decision Sciences* 11 (April, 1980), pp. 299–311.

quency. Another term, *multiple listing,* is sometimes confused as a type of listing; however, multiple listing is actually a cooperative arrangement among brokerages to share their listings. It is not a basic type of listing contract between a seller and a broker.

Open Listing

The open listing is a contract between a property owner and a broker that gives the broker the right to market the property. As with any listing contract, if the broker finds a buyer who is *ready, willing, and able* to purchase the property at the price and terms specified in the contract, the broker will be due a fee or commission. The distinguishing characteristic of the open listing is its lack of exclusivity. The property owners are not precluded from listing the property with other brokers. If they do list the property with two or more brokers, only the broker who procures a buyer will be owed a commission. If the owners sell the property themselves, none of the brokers will be owed a commission.

Net Listing

The distinguishing feature of a net listing is the commission arrangement. The broker's commission is the difference between the property's sale price and a specified net amount required by the seller. For example, the contract might state that the sellers require a minimum net amount of $100,000 and that the broker may keep as commission the difference between any higher price obtained and $100,000. Thus, if the broker sells the property for $110,000, the commission would be $10,000. A net listing can be an open listing or one of the types of listings discussed below—an exclusive agency or exclusive right of sale listing.

Exclusive Agency Listing

This type of listing contract requires the sellers to pay a commission to the broker if the property is sold by anyone, including brokers, other than the owners. The owners, however, retain the right to sell the property without incurring liability for a commission. In effect, the sellers agree not to list their property with other brokers but reserve the right to sell the property themselves without owing a commission.

Exclusive Right of Sale Listing

With this type of listing contract, the sellers list their property with one broker and agree to pay the broker a commission if the property is sold within a specified or, if not specified, a reasonable period of time. Thus,

===== Frame 4–2 =====

A Ready, Willing, and Able Buyer*

Lloyd and Edna Evans desired to sell their property. They employed the services of Fleming Realty and Insurance, Inc., a corporation engaged in providing real estate brokerage services. These parties entered into an exclusive right of sale listing agreement, which contained a procurement clause that required the Evanses to pay a commission if Fleming obtained a ready, willing, and able purchaser. The broker located Neal Hasselbach, who signed a standardized purchase agreement offering to buy the Evanses' property on the terms specified in the listing agreement. In essence, in this document Mr. Hasselbach offered to pay the asking price to the Evans. Based on their fears that Mr. Hasselbach was not financially able to purchase their property, Mr. and Mrs. Evans refused to sign a sales contract with this buyer.

Issue:

Did Fleming Realty procure a ready, willing, and able buyer, and was it therefore entitled to the agreed-on commission?

Decision:

Yes.

Reasons:

The evidence at the trial court showed that Hasselbach had a net worth, in cash and property, in excess of $250,000. The proposed contract for the Evanses' land totaled $155,840, to be paid by a down payment of $35,000 and 10 annual installments of $12,184 each. The jury's conclusion that Hasselbach was financially able to perform this sale contract was reasonable. Since the buyer fulfilled the requirements of the listing agreement's procuring clause, the broker was entitled to collect the commission established even though the sale was not closed.

Fleming Realty and Insurance Inc. v. Evans, 259 NW 2d 604 (Neb. 1977).

---

the broker will be owed a commission if any other brokers, or even the owner, sells the property during the contract period. A typical exclusive right of sale listing contract form is shown in Exhibit 4–4. Note the operative words, "I . . . authorize and give to Broker the exclusive right and power . . . to sell . . . the real property herein described" (line 2 of Exhibit 4–4).

Market Acceptance and Use of Listing Contracts

Exclusive Right of Sale Listings.
The exclusive right of sale feature is included in the vast majority of brokerage arrangements. Although one might think at first that such a feature would create an unfair burden on sellers, the exclusivity provision has produced faster sales. Brokers are

EXHIBIT 4—4
SAMPLE LISTING FORM

EXCLUSIVE LISTING CONTRACT
For Filing Property With

FIRST MULTIPLE LISTING SERVICE, INC.
ATLANTA, GEORGIA

LISTING COMPANY

NAME

BRANCH

Dated_____

In consideration of the Undersigned Broker's agreement to use its best efforts to sell the property within the terms of this contract, I, the undersigned Owner or Legal Agent, do hereby authorize and give to Broker the Exclusive right and power from this date and until 12 o'clock midnight the _____ day of_____, 19 _____, to sell at a price of _____ ☐ All Cash at Closing

$_____
☐ To Be Refinanced ☐ To be Sold on Loan Assumption ☐ Other _____
or any other lesser price acceptable to Owner, the real property herein described.

Broker is a member of FIRST MULTIPLE LISTING SERVICE, INC., of Atlanta and Broker binds himself that he will file this listing with said service within 48 hours after owner signs same. Owner agrees that members of FMLS may act in association with Broker in procuring or attempting to procure a purchaser. Owner agrees to pay to Broker a sales commission of _____ of the sales price, in the event that during the terms of this contract: (1) Broker or any member of said FMLS procures a person ready, willing and able to purchase said property at the price and on terms stated above; or (2) Owner enters into an enforceable contract for the sale or exchange of said property with any purchaser, whether by or through the efforts of Broker or any other person, including Owner. Owner agrees to pay to Broker such commission as stated above, if, within 90 days after the termination of this agreement, said property be sold, exchanged or conveyed to any person to whom the property had been submitted during the life of this agreement, unless the property is sold to such purchaser during said 90 day period by or through another licensed real estate broker with whom Owner has made an exclusive listing contract. Owner agrees to refer all inquiries concerning the sale of the property to Broker during the term hereof.

This agreement shall be binding upon, and shall inure to the benefit of the parties hereto, their heirs, successors, legal representatives, administrators, executors and assigns.

Owner hereby grants permission for the property to be photographed and for said photograph to be used in promoting the sale. Broker is also hereby authorized to place his "For Sale" sign upon said property.

If a sales contract on this property is accepted by Seller and Buyer and if this sales contract later becomes void or impossible to consummate, then the terms of this listing contract shall be automatically extended for a period of time, not to exceed 60 days, equal to the length of time that the sales contract was in effect.

Owner hereby releases and discharges FMLS and Broker and its employees and salespersons, from all claims, suits, or causes of action, whenever asserted, for any and all bodily and personal injuries, damages to or loss of property, and the consequences thereof, which result from any acts of persons who are not employees or salespersons of Broker, or which result from any negligent acts of persons who are employees or salespersons of Broker, whenever said acts occur during the period of this agreement (or any extension thereof).

Owner warrants that it has title to the property described herein, and/or has full authority to enter into this agreement.

Owner warrants that the information with respect to the property as set out in this agreement is true and correct, that there are no defects in the house adversely affecting its value, that all appliances, if any, remaining with the dwelling, heating and air conditioning systems, septic tank (if applicable) and all plumbing and electrical systems are in normal operating condition (except
_____),
that Owner has fully revealed to Broker all pertinent information with respect to the house, including defects therein, if any, and that Broker is authorized to convey all such information to prospective purchasers.

Owner acknowledges that Broker intends to rely upon the accuracy of the information furnished by Seller and Owner agrees to hold Broker harmless from any cost, expense of damage incurred by Broker as a result of Owner's withholding any information from Broker or as a result of Owner's giving Broker any information which is incorrect.

LEGAL DESCRIPTION

All that tract or parcel of land lying and being in LAND LOT _____ of the _____ DISTRICT, _____

COUNTY, and being known as LOT _____, BLOCK _____ of the _____SUBDIVISION,

according to plat recorded in PLAT BOOK _____, PAGE _____, _____ COUNTY RECORDS, and
                                                                        (county)

being improved property known as _____ STREET, _____,
                                          (number & name)   (city)

GEORGIA, _____. The full legal description of said property is the same as is recorded with the Clerk of the Superior
           (zip code)
Court of the County in which the property is located and is made a part of this agreement by reference.

Owner hereby acknowledges receipt of a copy of this contract.

Profile Sheet is attached to and made a part of this agreement by reference.

In witness whereof, the parties have this _____ day of _____, 19 _____, duly executed and sealed this Contract.

OWNER (DOES/DOES NOT) REQUEST BROKER TO FURNISH FREE RELOCATION INFORMATION ABOUT _____

_____ (CITY) _____ (STATE).

Rev: 7/15/83   Broker   Agent   Owner more willing to commit their firms to engage in thorough marketing programs for properties and to spend whatever time is necessary to sell them. Under this arrangement, brokers usually advertise in public media, prepare photographs and brochures about listed properties, and work long hours to obtain buyers. Brokers are protected no matter how or by whom the properties are sold. Without this protection, brokers may not spend enough time, effort, and money to sell the properties.

Second, brokers have realized that to justify their best efforts, they must have the protection provided by the exclusive right of sale provision. Thus, most brokers require sellers to accept this feature. Owners may, of course, refuse and attempt to find a broker who will accept an open or exclusive agency listing. But most do not, because most brokers will not accept other types of listings for residential properties.

Finally, multiple listing services (MLS) accept only exclusive right of sale listings.[3] Other types of listings would undermine the workings of an MLS. For example, if an MLS property were sold by an owner or a broker who was not an MLS member, the MLS broker would probably lose the commission. It would not take many such sales to put the MLS out of business. Thus, to obtain the advantages of having their properties listed by an MLS, owners must agree to an exclusive right of sale listing contract with their broker.

Open Listings. The open listing is sometimes used with large, special-purpose, or otherwise difficult-to-sell properties. The owners may not be willing to tie up the property with one broker. A single brokerage firm may not operate in a wide enough geographic area or have sufficient expertise, so the owners may list with several brokers to obtain a wider market for their property. A broker may be willing to accept such a listing because he or she believes that (1) there is a good chance of selling the property, and the owner will not accept an exclusive agency or exclusive right of sale listing or (2) there is not a good chance of selling the property, but there is little to lose in accepting the listing (there is *some* chance the property will sell, and it would yield a large commission).

Other Types of Listings. The net listing and exclusive agency listings are used infrequently. They have the disadvantages, but none of the advantages, of the other two. Both types of listings provide less protection for brokers, who in turn are usually less willing to spend time and effort to market properties. With a net listing, the property's selling price may not yield an adequate commission; an exclusive agency listing may result in the broker's earning no commission if the sale is made by the owner.

---

[3] A multiple listing service is a group or organization of brokers who agree to pool listings and split commissions from transactions, according to an agreed schedule.

Additionally, the net listing produces a disincentive for brokers to live up to their fiduciary responsibilities. For example, if a broker knows that a highway is going to be built or expanded, he or she might attempt to obtain net listings of properties from owners who are not aware of the highway plans. For this reason, professional standards discourage the use of net listing.

LISTING CONTRACT PROVISIONS

While most brokers use standard, preprinted listing contract forms (Exhibit 4–4) and most property owners are willing to sign such forms, both parties to such a contract should be certain that their interests are protected.

Protective Provisions for Property Owners

When signing a listing contract, property owners may want to assure themselves about the following matters:

1. The brokerage firm will put forth its best efforts to find prospective buyers.

   The firm should be willing to advertise frequently in local newspapers, and perhaps in other publications or on television. It should take photographs of the property, prepare a brochure about the property, conduct group inspections by other brokers and sales personnel, and hold open houses.

2. The brokerage firm should indicate its intention to place the listing in a multiple listing service.

   As discussed above, this will require the property owner to sign an exclusive right of sale listing contract.

3. The real estate broker should agree to report every offer promptly.

   This procedure is a legal and ethical requirement of all brokers.

4. The owners and broker should reach understanding and agreement about access to the property.

   Is the broker allowed to place a lock box on the door, allowing all brokers and sales personnel access to the property at all times? Will access be limited to specified times? Or must any broker or sales person call for an appointment to show the property?

5. The listing agreement should be limited to a reasonable period.

   A reasonable period may vary from a month to a year, depending on the type of property, the circumstances, and the conditions of the market. A typical listing period for a residential property is approximately three months; for an industrial property, it may be six months to one year. If the owner must make a business or personal decision within a month, that depends on selling the property, the listing might be limited to one month. If no period is specified in the contract and the issue becomes the subject of a lawsuit, courts will specify a reasonable and typical period that is consistent with local practice.

6. The broker should agree to provide periodic reports about the marketing program and specific steps taken to attract prospective buyers. Such reports should be made at least monthly.

Protective Provisions for the Broker

Since the brokerage firm usually prepares the contract or decides which standard form to use, its interests are usually adequately protected. Thus, the following matters are usually covered in a listing contract:

1. The property owner agrees to pay a commission or fee to the broker upon the broker's finding a buyer who is ready, willing, and able to buy the property at the specified price and terms, or at whatever price and terms are acceptable to the property owner.

    While the brokerage commission is usually payable at the time of closing, the broker may be due a commission even if the transaction is not closed. The sellers, for example, might decide not to go through with the sale. The broker would still be owed the commission because he or she procured a ready, willing, and able buyer. Occasionally, sellers insist that the commission-due clause be stated so that the broker is not owed a commission until the transaction is closed. Obviously, this provision is less favorable to the broker than the ready, willing, and able buyer provision.

    The commission or fee is usually (but not necessarily) based on a percentage of the selling price. While this percentage must be negotiable between sellers and broker, there is a tendency for commission rates to converge around a common number, such as 6 or 7 percent, in most communities. Below these rates brokers cannot earn a reasonable profit and tend to go out of business. Strong competition usually limits commission rates above these levels for single-family homes. Commission rates on commercial, industrial, and unimproved properties are more varied, usually ranging between 3 and 15 percent.

2. The broker attempts to obtain a listing agreement for a sufficient period of time to allow a reasonable chance to sell the property.

    Short time periods are not in the broker's interest (and not necessarily in the seller's interest, either) because a broker's time, effort, and expenditures can easily be wasted. For single-family residences, brokers usually like to obtain listings for at least three months. For larger, more specialized properties, longer listing periods—up to six months or longer—are not uncommon.

3. The broker wants adequate access to the property to allow brokers and sales personnel to show the property without undue limitations and hassle.

   A lock box arrangement provides the greatest access, and many listing contracts give the broker the right to place a lock box on the property. The house key is placed inside the box, which is a heavy metal container usually attached to the front door knob. MLS brokers have a key for the lock box, so brokers and sales agents can show the house to prospective buyers even when the owners are not home or the house is unoccupied. If the owners do not want the device placed on the property, they should strike out that clause.

4. Brokers usually insist on a provision protecting their right to a commission after the listing period expires if the property is sold to someone who learned about the property from the broker.

   Such a provision reduces the opportunity for a seller and buyer to conspire to wait until after the listing expires to complete a transaction and avoid liability for a commission. This provision should have a time limit that is no longer than the specified listing period. Thus, if the listing period is three months, the broker should not require this protection for more than an additional three months.

Termination

A listing contract terminates under any of three circumstances: the specified period expires; the property is sold; or one of the parties abrogates the terms of the contract. The first two courses of termination are straightforward, and there is usually little question about the result.

Abrogation of terms is less clear and usually more difficult to prove. On the owners' part, the most clear-cut abrogation would be their unwillingness to sign a sale contract with a ready, willing, and able purchaser. While such a refusal happens rarely, it may result in legal action against the owners by both the broker and the buyers. The owners may be legally compelled to pay the broker's commission, since the broker fulfilled his or her part of the contract. In cases in which the owners abrogate the terms by refusing to show the property or by otherwise discouraging prospective buyers, the broker usually refuses to make any further efforts to sell the property.[4]

---

[4]Buyers also have legal rights and remedies when sellers abrogate a listing contract. These rights and remedies will be discussed in Chapter 6.

The broker may abrogate the terms of the contract by failing to market the property effectively. The broker may not advertise sufficiently or make enough effort to sell the property. While in some cases owners may have good legal grounds for terminating the contract, their usual remedy is to wait for the listing to expire. Such contentions are both difficult to prove and costly to pursue legally.

The Form Listing Contract

Form listing contracts are prepared forms that have blank spaces for filling in the specific information for each transaction.

Exhibit 4–4 is a form listing contract used by members of First Multiple Listing Service of Atlanta, Georgia. Note the following elements contained in the form:

Provision	Location
Date, company name, and office	Upper right-hand corner
Broker to use best efforts to sell property	Paragraph 1
Termination date of contract	Paragraph 1
Financing arrangements	Paragraph 1
Listing to be filed with the MLS	Paragraph 2
Owner agrees to pay commission when broker (or any member of the MLS) finds a buyer who is ready, willing, and able to purchase	Paragraph 2
Exclusive right of sale agreement	Paragraph 2
Extension period of 90 days	Paragraph 2
Owner authorizes use of photograph and for sale sign	Paragraph 4
Extension due to inability to close transaction	Paragraph 5
Release of liability for any acts of nonemployees and from negligent acts of employees or salespersons	Paragraph 6
Owner warrants (s)he has title	Paragraph 7
Owner warrants veracity of information and condition of appliances and systems	Paragraph 8
Owner agrees to hold broker harmless from any cost incurred from use of any incorrect information withheld by owner	Paragraph 9
Legal description	Paragraph 10
Profile sheet considered part of the contract	Paragraph 10
Owner requests or does not request relocation information	Paragraph 10

Since the owner agrees and warrants more provisions than a broker, the listing contract form may appear to favor the broker. Such a one-sided result may be expected when one party to a transaction prepares the contract. On the other hand, brokers feel that they must be protected in a wide variety of situations involving many different owners and properties. By being in business, brokers open themselves to various legal actions if these protective provisions are not agreed to by owners.

Most owners are mainly concerned with selling their property. However, the listing contract form does not guarantee that the broker will take specific steps or actions to sell the property—it only promises that the broker will use his or her "best efforts." For this reason, owners often must rely on a broker's reputation and track record. Thus, owners wishing to sell their properties should inquire about brokerage firms before signing a listing contract. How has the firm marketed similar properties? What specific procedures has the firm followed and with what degree of success? How much advertising has the firm done for each property?

An owner should talk to other sellers to find out how various firms have performed. What marketing and advertising efforts are made by the firms? How often and what types of reports do they make to owners? What is their reputation in the community? Would the sellers use the firms again?

Choosing a real estate brokerage firm is much like choosing any other professional service. How does one choose a doctor, lawyer, or accountant? Reputation, track record, and personal integrity are the hallmarks of quality and reliability. A property owner should be no less careful in choosing a real estate broker than in selecting other professionals.

LISTING SITUATION—EXAMPLE

Fred and Louise Johnson decide to sell their home in Gainesville, Florida, because they want to move to Fort Myers. They contact William Heath, a salesman with Town and Country Realtors®, who sold them the house five years ago. They like Bill. He was courteous and efficient when he helped them find a home, and he has stayed in touch with them since.

Bill comes to the Johnsons' house, which is located at 1822 NW 40th Avenue. After some discussion, they agree that the listing price should be $85,000, which will include the kitchen stove and refrigerator, two window air conditioners, and one picnic table as well as the real estate. The property is free of encumbrances except for an existing mortgage with a remaining balance of approximately $45,000. The Johnsons prefer not to give a second mortgage or other financing terms. The existing mortgage has a "due on sale" clause (i.e., it cannot be *assumed*—taken over—by the buyer at the same interest rate).

The house has four bedrooms, two baths, living room, dining room, a screened porch, a double carport, and outside storage room. It has central heating, but not central air conditioning. It was built in 1956 with CBS[5]-on-slab construction. The entire house, except for the kitchen, was

---

[5]Concrete block and stucco.

EXHIBIT 4–5

Gainesville Board of REALTORS®

EXCLUSIVE RIGHT OF SALE LISTING AGREEMENT

In consideration of the agreement contained herein, the sufficiency of which is hereby acknowledged by **Town and Country Realtors** hereinafter called REALTOR® and **Fred and Louise Johnson** hereinafter called OWNER, we hereby jointly agree to the following:

1. The Owner hereby gives to the REALTOR® for a period of ___**6**___ from the date hereof, the EXCLUSIVE right and authority to find a purchaser for the below described property, upon the following price and terms or any price and terms acceptable to OWNER.

   Price ___**$85,000.00**_____ Terms ___**Cash**_____

   Legal Description ___**Parcel #3, Block 2 of Spring Meadow Estates, recorded in Plot Book 12,**___
   page 28, Alachua County Courthouse, Florida_____

   All taxes for the current year, rentals, monthly insurance premiums, hazard insurance premiums and interest on existing mortgages (if any) shall be prorated as of the date of closing.

   Personal property to be included in the purchase price: All fixed equipment including drapery hardware, light fixtures, carpeting, and plants and shrubbery now installed on said property, and such additional personal property as may be listed on the attached profile sheet.

2. Owner warrants to the REALTOR® that the representations of the property furnished to the REALTOR® by the Owner on the attached Profile Sheet are true and correct, and that there are no mis-statements of any said representation which would have any material effect on the property value. Owner agrees to indemnify and save REALTOR® harmless of and from any and all loss, damage, suits and claims including reasonable attorneys fees and costs of defense incurred by REALTOR® on account of any representations made by REALTOR® in reliance on the owner's representations. There is attached to this Agreement a Gainesville Board of REALTORS® Profile Sheet which is by reference included in and made a part of this exclusive right of sale listing agreement.

3. The REALTOR® agrees to use due care in the installation, use, maintenance, and operation of the lock box. The owner agrees to hold the REALTOR® harmless from all claims, demands, costs, judgements and liability which seller may suffer as a result of losses or damages arising out of the use, maintenance or operation of the lock box during the term of this agreement. Gross negligence on the part of the REALTOR® or agents acting through him are expressly excluded from this covenant. Owner will allow REALTOR® to use the owner's name when necessary or desirable in marketing the property and will make the property available for the REALTORS® to show during reasonable hours to prospective purchasers. Owner is to initial one of the following: 1. Owner agrees to permit use of lockbox ___**X**___. 2. Owner does not agree to permit use of lockbox ___.

4. The Owner agrees, at his expense, to provide for: (a) preparation of and delivery to the purchaser of a good and sufficient warranty deed (unless otherwise required) conveying an insurable title free and clear of all liens, except encumbrances of record, to be assumed by the Purchaser as part of the purchase price and taxes for the year of sale; (b) binder and policy for fee title insurance or abstract from earliest records; (c) state documentary stamps on the deed; (d) Seller's attorney fee; (e) recording fees for satisfactions of liens of record, if same are paid off; (f) Mortgage discount and mortgage warehouse fees as relates to FHA or VA sales; and (g) evidence from a licensed pest control firm that property is visibly free from infestation or damage by termites or powder post beetles. Treatment and/or repair, not to exceed **$500.00**_____, if infestation or damage is found.

5. The Owner agrees that REALTOR® has the right, at the REALTOR'S® discretion, to order and obtain on behalf of the owner all items necessary to consummate a closing on subject property, such as, but not limited to, pest control report, title insurance, and survey, as may be agreed to in a subsequent purchase and sales agreement.

6. (a) For finding a purchaser ready, willing and able to purchase the above described property, Owner agrees to pay REALTOR® a compensation of ___**six (6)**___% of the total purchase price on the terms herein mentioned, or at any price and upon terms acceptable to Owner, whether the Purchaser be secured by REALTOR® or Owner, or by ANY OTHER PERSON, or, if the property is afterwards sold within ___**3**___ months from the termination of this agreement, or any written extension thereof signed by the REALTOR® and the owner, to any person to whom the said property has been shown by the REALTOR® or his representatives or by cooperating brokers; provided, nevertheless, that the REALTOR® shall not receive a commission on such a subsequent sale if the Owner re-listed the property with another Licensed Real Estate Broker. In the event this Agreement is terminated for any reason other than expiration of the term of this listing, the Owner agrees to reimburse the REALTOR® for all customary documented costs incurred by the REALTOR® in marketing the property up to the date of termination; in no event shall the amount of such reimbursement exceed the full amount of the commission anticipated by this Agreement.
   (b) In any exchange of this property, permission is given REALTOR® to represent and receive compensation from both parties.
   (c) In the event the property is rented or leased by the Owner in lieu of sale or in connection with a lease/option agreement, the Owner will pay the listing REALTOR® a rental or leasing fee equal to ___**10**___% of the rent to be received, except in cases of occupancy agreements between the Owner and the buyer to accommodate the surrender and delivery of possession in connection with closing.

7. In consideration of this EXCLUSIVE right of sale, the REALTOR® agrees to (a) process the property through the Gainesville Multiple Listing Service; (b) advertise the property as REALTOR® deems advisable; (c) furnish information in response to all inquiries related to a possible purchase of the property; and (d) devote the resources of the REALTOR's firm in a diligent effort to market the property throughout the duration of the listing agreement.

8. In consideration of the above, the Owner agrees to immediately refer to REALTOR® all inquiries relative to purchase of his property.

9. Owner authorizes REALTOR® or cooperating Broker to accept in escrow and hold all money paid or deposited as a binder on the subject property and if such deposit is later forfeited by the purchaser to disburse the deposit as follows: (1) all loan application fees, and other costs advanced on behalf of either the Buyer or the Seller shall be reimbursed to the REALTOR® (2) one-half of the remaining net deposit or the total commission the REALTOR® would have received, whichever is less, shall be disbursed to the REALTOR® as compensation for his services and marketing expenses, (3) the remainder of the deposit, if any, shall be disbursed to the Owner as liquidated damages.

10. Owner and REALTOR® acknowledge that this agreement does not guarantee a sale and that there are no other agreements, promises or understandings either expressed or implied between them other than specifically set forth herein, and that there can be no alterations or changes to this contract except in writing and signed by each of them. They also agree that this agreement supersedes any prior agreement regarding the marketing of this property. They each agree that this property is offered to any person without regard to race, color, creed, national origin, sex, handicap or religion.

11. In connection with any litigation arising out of this agreement, the prevailing party shall be entitled to recover all costs incurred including reasonable attorney's fees.

12. THIS IS A LEGAL AND BINDING CONTRACT ON ALL PARTIES HERETO, INCLUDING THEIR HEIRS, LEGAL REPRESENTATIVES, SUCCESSORS AND ASSIGNS. IF NOT FULLY UNDERSTOOD, OWNER SHOULD SEEK COMPETENT LEGAL ADVICE.

13. The Owner and REALTOR® acknowledge that this listing shall be withdrawn from the Gainesville Multiple Listing Service upon the REALTORS® withdrawal, suspension or termination from MLS.

REALTOR® _**Town and Country Realtors**_____ Owner _**Fred Johnson**_____

By: _**William Heath**_____ Owner _**Louise Johnson**_____

Owner's Address _**1822 NW 40th Avenue, Gainesville, Florida 32601**_ DATE _**May 15, 1986**_

WHITE—REALTOR®   YELLOW—MLS   PINK—Owner   2M-985-11260   REV. 12/83 carpeted about eight years ago. The house is in reasonably good condition, although the interior and exterior paint is beginning to look dull and the carpet is becoming worn in heavy traffic areas. The lot is approximately one-half acre and is nicely landscaped. The neighborhood contains similar houses, and property values have been stable over the past 10 years. According to the Johnsons' deed in the Alachua County Courthouse, the property description is: Parcel No. 3, Block 2 of Spring Meadow Estates, recorded in Plat Book 12, page 28. Bill Heath and the Johnsons agree on a commission rate of 6 percent.

Exhibit 4–5 shows the completed listing form for the Johnsons' property. In following chapters, we will follow the sale of the Johnson's house through negotiation of the sale contract, obtaining a mortgage loan (buyers), and closing the transaction.

OVERVIEW

Listing contracts create an agency relationship between a real estate broker and the owners of real estate. A fiduciary relationship between brokers and owners is created by a listing contract. Such a relationship requires honesty, trust, and openness between the broker and the owner. An owner lists a property with a broker to obtain the convenience and expertise of the broker in selling the property.

There are four types of listing contracts: open, exclusive agency, exclusive right of sale, or net. The exclusive right of sale listing is the predominant type of contract used, especially for residential properties. This type of contract is required when the property is to be filed with a multiple listing service.

A multiple listing service is a cooperative arrangement among brokerage firms in which all member firms pool their listings. All sales personnel of the members can then attempt to sell the listed property. Upon sale of the property, the commission is split among the listing and selling firms according to a predetermined schedule.

In signing a listing contract, both broker and owner obtain rights and responsibilities. The brokerage firm has the right to collect a commission if the property is sold within a specified or reasonable period and agrees to exert its best efforts to sell the property. The owner can expect the firm to try to sell the property through a marketing program. The owner can also expect an MLS member firm to file the listing with the MLS and for other member firms' sales personnel to work on the sale. The owner is obligated not to impede the selling effort and to pay a commission if the property is sold.

TEST YOURSELF

Explain the following terms and concepts presented in this chapter.

1. Agency relationship.
2. Special agency.
3. Principal.
4. Fiduciary relationship.
5. Open listing versus exclusive agency listing versus exclusive right of sale listing.
6. Methods of terminating a listing contract.
7. Net listing.
8. Ready, willing, and able buyer.

Answer the following multiple-choice questions.

1. A real estate broker is what type of agent for his or her principal?
   a. General agent.
   b. Special agent.
   c. Limited agent.
   d. Designated agent.
   e. All of the above.

2. If a seller refuses to complete a transaction after a broker has obtained a buyer who is ready, willing, and able to purchase the property on the terms specified by the seller, the seller may be liable to the broker for
   a. The commission.
   b. The market value of the property.
   c. The broker's expenses.
   d. Damages.
   e. The commission plus the broker's expenses.

3. How are commission rates charged by real estate brokers determined?
   a. By agreement among local Realtors.
   b. By rule of the local Board of Realtors.
   c. By state real estate commissions.
   d. By agreement between broker and principal.
   e. By state law.

4. The main reason that real estate brokers prefer exclusive right of sale listings over other types of listings is that
   a. Such listings normally carry a higher commission rate.
   b. There is greater assurance the property will be sold.
   c. There is greater assurance they will receive a commission if the property is sold.
   d. Sellers prefer them.
   e. All of the above.

5. An agent has what type of relationship with his or her principal?
   a. Personal.
   b. Public.
   c. Caveat emptor.
   d. Fiduciary.
   e. Friendly.

ADDITIONAL READINGS

Corley, Robert N., Peter J. Shedd, and Charles J. Floyd. *Real Estate and the Law.* New York: Random House, 1982, Chap. 10.

Lindeman, Bruce. *Real Estate Brokerage Management.* Reston, Va.: Reston Publishing, 1981, Chap. 8.

Wigginton, F. Peter. *The Complete Guide to Profitable Real Estate Listings: Programs of the Pros.* Homewood, Ill.: Dow Jones-Irwin, 1977.

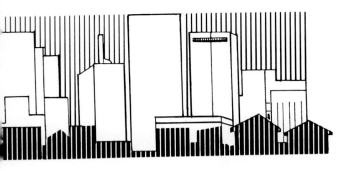

5
Mortgage Contracts

INTRODUCTION

The mortgage contract is one of the three basic contracts found in most transactions to transfer real property rights. The study of mortgage contracts typically comes under the general heading of mortgage finance, which encompasses (1) the *legal agreements* between mortgage lenders and borrowers (mortgage contracts), (2) the *financial aspects* of mortgage lending (the evaluation of mortgage terms and deal structuring), and (3) the *institutional arrangements* for mortgage lending (the characteristics and regulation of mortgage lenders). While there is some overlap among these three areas of mortgage finance—especially between certain mortgage contract provisions and the financial aspects of mortgages—we will defer discussion of financial and institutional matters until Chapters 19 and 20. This chapter, therefore, as part of the legal perspective of real estate, focuses on the law governing the contractual relationships between mortgage lenders and borrowers.

The laws governing the contractual relationships between mortgage lenders and borrowers, like so many other areas of real estate law, differ markedly between states. The legal instruments and provisions found in mortgage contracts also differ, depending on whether the loan is for single-family residential property or for commercial property (e.g., hotels, office buildings, and shopping centers) and whether the loan is for a new development (construction) venture or for an existing property. Throughout this chapter we will point out differences in state mortgage laws and describe how contract provisions vary according to the type of property being mortgaged.

FUNDAMENTALS OF MORTGAGE CONTRACTS
AND MORTGAGE THEORIES

Since real estate is such a high-priced economic good, most investors must borrow funds to secure real property rights. Therefore the mortgage contract, which contains all of the specific elements of the agreement between borrowers and lenders, is an integral part of most real estate transactions.

The simple mortgage contract arrangement shown in Exhibit 5–1 shows that the mortgage lender promises to lend the borrower funds if the borrower promises[1] to give the lender two legal instruments: a *mortgage* and a *promissory note* (also known as the mortgage note or just "the note").

EXHIBIT 5–1
SIMPLE MORTGAGE CONTRACT

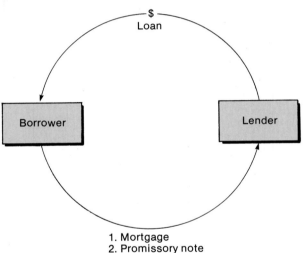

1. Mortgage
2. Promissory note

The mortgage is a legal instrument giving the lender a contingent claim against the *property*. The contingency arises when the borrower defaults on the loan—for example, by not making payments in accordance with the provisions of the contract for repayment of the debt. In other words, if the borrower defaults on the loan, the lender may establish a claim to the property, usually through a procedure known as *foreclosure*, to force a public sale of the property. The property therefore is the pri-

---

[1]Note: this is a bilateral contract because both parties agree to perform.

mary security for the loan. Mortgages—like deeds—are recorded, usually at the county courthouse following the closing. Thus, there is a public record of the borrower's pledge of the property as security for the loan.

The promissory note is usually the second line of security for the loan. In some states, the promissory note is called a *bond*, but there is no substantive difference between this instrument and a note. The borrower, on issuing the promissory note, makes a *personal promise* to repay the loan. This promise may be enforced if the lender decides not to claim the property in the case of default or when the proceeds from sale of the property do not cover the outstanding balance of the loan at foreclosure. When the proceeds from a foreclosure sale are not sufficient to repay the lender, the lender may seek a separate court action against the borrower on the promise in the note.[2]

Title and Lien Theories of Mortgage Security

One of the major differences in state mortgage law concerns the type of security interest the lender obtains in the mortgage instrument. Historically,[3] when a landowner sought to borrow money from a lender, title to real property was deeded by the borrower to the lender, who received interest payments in the form of the profits generated by the land during the period that the loan principal was outstanding. Since then, law-making and law-interpreting bodies, including state legislatures and the courts, have modified this practice of transferring most property rights to lenders in mortgage contracts. Today, mortgage interest payments are paid independently of the profits from the land, and the states have adopted modern theories of mortgage security that allow borrowers to retain most of the property rights in the real property pledged as security for mortgage loans.

Under current state laws, mortgages given by borrowers *(mortgagors)* bestow on lenders *(mortgagees)* either *title* to or a *lien* on property. In so-called *lien-theory* states, the mortgage instrument gives the lender the right to bring legal action forcing the sale of the real property to settle the loan in the event of borrower default. This foreclosure action, discussed

---

[2]The lender may also seek a *deficiency judgment* against the borrower in such instances. The theory behind the deficiency judgment is that the borrower's responsibilities under the mortgage contract do not end with the foreclosure sale. Deficiency judgments, however, are difficult to obtain, especially in cases involving defaults by owners of single-family homes, because courts tend to favor the consumer (e.g., borrowers over lenders, tenants over landlords, and buyers over sellers).

[3]Perhaps beginning as early as the 14th century in England, contracts were negotiated between lenders and borrowers in which the borrower's real property was used as security for the loan.

later in this chapter, may take from one to several months after the borrower has had a reasonable time to pay any overdue installments.[4]

In so-called *title-theory* states, the lender, as in earlier times, technically receives title to the property in the mortgage contract.[5] Yet the law and the courts in these states have modified the property rights given to lenders in mortgage contracts so that the lender can exercise these rights only if the borrower defaults. In practice, mortgage contracts in some title-theory states carry a special clause or clauses, called a *power-of-sale clause*, that allows the lender, upon borrower default, to cut short the foreclosure process. Thus, the title-theory arrangement may save time and money for the lender by bypassing certain foreclosure procedures.

Deed-of-Trust States

A variation of title theory occurs in states that use *deeds of trust* (also known as trust deeds) instead of mortgages.[6] In these states, a third party known as a trustee(s) (e.g., a trust company or bank) receives title to the property via a trust deed issued by the borrower. This relationship is shown in Exhibit 5–2. The trust deed is essentially a mortgage with a power-of-sale clause. In case of borrower default, the lender informs the trustee, and the trustee then takes action to force a sale of the property.

BORROWER AND LENDER RELATIONSHIPS FOR FINANCING REAL ESTATE

The simple mortgage contract in Exhibit 5–1 illustrates one of the many types of contractual relationships between lenders and borrowers in real estate finance. In this section, we will build on this simple mortgage contract concept by extending the scope of the borrower and lender relationship. We will discuss junior mortgages, the introduction of a third party to take over the borrower's responsibilities in the mortgage contract, contractual relationships that fall outside the limits of traditional mortgage contracts, and various financing relationships commonly used in both single-family and income-property transactions.

---

[4]The right to pay overdue payments is called *equity of redemption* and is discussed later in this chapter.

[5]In some title-theory states, the mortgage instrument carries a name other than a mortgage. In Georgia, for example, the instrument that transfers title to the lender in a mortgage contract is called a *security deed*. In other title-theory states it is called a *mortgage deed*.

[6]The following states use deeds of trust: Alabama, Alaska, California, Colorado, District of Columbia, Mississippi, Missouri, Montana, Nebraska, Nevada, New Mexico, North Carolina, Oregon, South Carolina, Tennessee, Texas, Virginia, Washington, and West Virginia.

EXHIBIT 5–2
MORTGAGE CONTRACT WITH A TRUST DEED

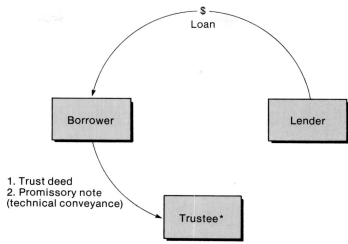

*The trustee may be the agent of the lender but is usually an independent third party.

Some Extensions of the Simple Mortgage Contract

Suppose the mortgage contract in Exhibit 5–1 has the following characteristics:

1. The lender (Lender A) is a lending institution, such as a savings and loan association.
2. The borrower (Borrower A) has not pledged the property to any other lender as security for another loan and plans to own the property until the loan is paid off.

   Since Borrower A has not pledged the property as security for any other loan, the contract constitutes a *first mortgage*. This means that, in the case of default by Borrower A, Lender A stands first in line (has a first-priority lien) to collect the unpaid balance of the loan following a foreclosure sale.
3. The transaction occurs in a lien-theory state.

To extend the concept of the simple mortgage contract, we can vary one or more of these assumptions.

Junior Mortgage.   Suppose Borrower A contacts Lender B to request another loan and pledges the same real property as security. Lender B considers the market value of the property and the remaining balance of the first mortgage loan. Since the market value is significantly higher than the balance of the first mortgage loan and Borrower A is a good credit risk, Lender B grants the loan.

Borrower A and Lender B have contracted to create a *junior mortgage*—in this case, a *second mortgage*. Consequently, in the case of a default, Lender B must stand in line behind Lender A to be repaid from the proceeds of a foreclosure sale. Obviously, junior mortgages have greater risk of losses due to default than first mortgages on the same property and thus typically include more restrictive terms (e.g., higher interest rates and shorter terms to maturity). Some additional implications of junior mortgages in foreclosure actions are discussed later in this chapter.

Wrap-around Mortgage. Suppose Buyer X offers to buy the property from Borrower A but does not have enough cash to make a down payment. Borrower A agrees to provide financing to Buyer X, and, because the mortgage loan with Lender A has such an attractive interest rate, Borrower A decides to keep the original loan.[7]

Therefore, under the *wrap-around mortgage* contract between Borrower A and Buyer X, Buyer X obtains all property rights by making one large payment to Borrower A for the two loans (i.e., the original loan and the loan for the down payment). Borrower A keeps part of this payment and sends the payment as usual each period to Lender A. In the event of default and foreclosure, Borrower A has a second-mortgage position behind Lender A, whose position is unaffected by the wrap-around loan.

Wrap-around financing is popular both in residential and commercial property deals and takes many forms. The term *wrap-around* is used because the new loan wraps around an existing loan while creating additional financing.

Assumption of an Existing Mortgage. Assume Buyer X does not require financing from Borrower A but will simply take over Borrower A's loan with Lender A. Whether Buyer X can be substituted for Borrower A in the original mortgage contract without the permission of Lender A depends on whether there is a *due-on-sale clause* in the contract.[8]

Buyer X may enter the contract either *subject to* the mortgage or by *assumption* of the mortgage. If Buyer X takes title to the property subject to the existing mortgage, Buyer X is not obligated personally for repayment of the mortgage in case of default. That is, the promissory note between Borrower A and Lender A remains in effect, and Borrower A

---

[7]The first mortgage lender's permission is almost always required to undertake this form of financing.

[8]The due-on-sale clause is discussed in more detail later in this chapter.

would be personally liable in the event of a default by Buyer X. Buyer X would *not* be personally liable. The mortgage part of the contract, however, is redrafted—reflecting the change in the name of the borrower—between Buyer X and Lender A so that Buyer X's property is the first line of security for the loan.

If Buyer X takes title to the property by *assuming* the existing mortgage, then both the mortgage and the note are redrafted and Buyer X becomes personally liable in case of default.

Purchase-Money Mortgage. Suppose Buyer X obtains first mortgage financing from Borrower A and Lender A is not a party to the agreement. Borrower A, therefore, is the seller of the property and becomes the first mortgage lender to Buyer X. Such an agreement is known as a *purchase-money mortgage.*

A purchase-money mortgage arrangement is shown in Exhibit 5–3, Panel A. The seller receives a down payment and gives up the deed to the property under the contract for sale; the seller receives the mortgage documentation for providing a loan to the buyer. The seller thus has a first mortgage lien and follows the normal procedures of foreclosure in case of default.

Land Contract. Borrower A, as the seller of the property, provides all financing needed by Buyer X. As shown in Exhibit 5–3 Panel B, Borrower A receives a down payment and gives a loan to Buyer X for the balance of the purchase price. However, there is no mortgage created as in the case of the purchase-money mortgage. Instead, in a *land contract* the seller retains title to the property usually until some percentage (e.g., 50 percent) of the loan is repaid.[9] Should Buyer X miss a payment on the loan as required in the land contract, Borrower A has the right to reclaim possession of the property almost immediately. This is called *strict foreclosure.*

Land contracts have a long history as instruments for transfering rights to real property. They have traditionally been used in rural areas (e.g., the sale of farm land) where the parties know one another and deals can be consummated with relatively small down payments. In recent years, land contracts have been used more frequently in transactions involving urban parcels, especially single-family residences.

Contracts for Single-Family Residential Financing

Contractual relationships between borrowers and lenders differ when the property being financed is single-family residential or income-producing

---

[9]Once this point is reached, the land contract converts to a purchase-money mortgage.

EXHIBIT 5–3
DISTINCTIONS BETWEEN PURCHASE MONEY MORTGAGE
AND LAND CONTRACT

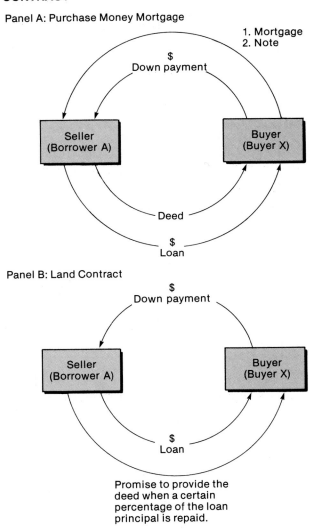

Panel A: Purchase Money Mortgage

1. Mortgage
2. Note

$
Down payment

Seller
(Borrower A)

Buyer
(Buyer X)

Deed

$
Loan

Panel B: Land Contract

$
Down payment

Seller
(Borrower A)

Buyer
(Buyer X)

$
Loan

Promise to provide the
deed when a certain
percentage of the loan
principal is repaid.

and when the property is already operating or is a new development. There are several reasons why lender-borrower relationships are different for single-family residential and income properties. Most important, the trend in single-family residential finance has been toward greater standardization of the mortgage contract, not only because many single-family residential loans are alike, but also because most single-family mortgages with institutional lenders are bought and sold in a secondary mortgage market (see Chapter 12).[10] The secondary mortgage market has encouraged standardization of the mortgage contract to make mortgages more easily tradable. Income-property mortgage contracts, in contrast, have probably become less standardized in recent years. Very little trading occurs in these mortgages.

The reason why new developments have different contractual arrangements can be summed up in one word—risk. Since new developments do not have a track record, they are inherently more risky to finance.[11] Existing properties have a track record and thus their risk can be more easily assessed.

Existing Properties.   Contracts between borrowers and lenders for financing existing single-family homes fall into three general categories:

1. *Conventional mortgages.* The conventional mortgage loan arrangement (shown in Exhibit 5–1) is a straightforward loan agreement in which the borrower gives a note and a mortgage in exchange for the loan.
2. *Government-supported mortgages.* As shown in Exhibit 5–4, the government can act as a third party in the residential mortgage contract. The government may supply an insurance policy against borrower default, as in Federal Housing Administration (FHA) loans. The government may guarantee the loan against default for veterans, as in Veteran Administration (VA) loans. And, in some instances, the government supplies subsidies to help borrowers buy their own homes.[12]
3. *Owner (seller) financing.* Owner financing has traditionally represented a small portion of residential financing in the United States. However, during recent periods of high interest rates contracts between buyers and sellers have at times represented as much as 75 percent of all residential loan contracts. These contracts are mostly purchase-money mortgages and assumptions with second mortgages, although some land contracts have been negotiated between buyers and sellers of single-family homes.

---

[10]The principal secondary-market purchasers of mortgages are the Federal National Mortgage Corporation (FNMA, or "Fannie Mae"), the Federal Home Loan Mortgage Corporation (FHLMC, or "Freddie Mac"), and to some extent the Government National Mortgage Association (GNMA, or "Ginnie Mae").

[11]The risk lies in the possibility that the developer (borrower) will fail some time before the completion of the project, and the lender will be forced to take over. Lenders are not in business to complete partially developed real estate.

[12]On average, conventional loans comprise about 85 percent of all residential loans from institutional lenders, while government-supported loans make up the balance.

EXHIBIT 5–4
GOVERNMENT SUPPORTED MORTGAGE CONTRACT

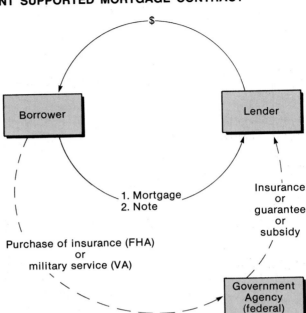

New-Construction Financing.   Because of the inherent risks in new-con-struction and development financing,[13] builders of single-family homes often must establish contractual relationships for two loans, sometimes with two different lenders. The *construction loan* finances the development and construction of the improvements for the construction period only; the second, the *permanent loan*, is long-term and is essentially like a nor-mal first mortgage loan for existing property.

Exhibit 5–5 shows the relationships between builders of single-family residential properties and lenders. There are two types of residential con-struction activities. The first, in which some builders specialize, involves the construction of *spec* (*spec*ulation or *spec*ification) homes. The builder buys or develops residential lots, builds houses (usually of similar style, size, and quality), and sells the houses on the open market. The second involves *custom* homes. The builder is hired by the owner of a lot to build a house according to the owner's specifications. Some builders perform a

---

[13]Development refers to the activity of putting improvements *to* the land in place (for example, putting in streets, gutters, utilities) while construction refers to the activity of put-ting improvements *on* the land (i.e., buildings). Sometimes the two activities are combined and referred to as development.

EXHIBIT 5–5
FINANCING RELATIONSHIPS FOR NEW CONSTRUCTION OF SINGLE-FAMILY HOMES

Panel A: Spec Homes

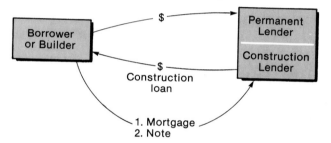

Panel B: Custom Homes (or Spec Homes)

hybrid of spec and custom home building by selling lots on the open market, but making it a condition of the sale that the builder who sold the lot receives the contract to build a custom home.

Panel A of Exhibit 5–5 presents one common financing arrangement for the construction of spec homes. This arrangement involves an agreement among the builder, the construction lender, and the permanent lender in which the permanent lender agrees to pay off the construction lender when the project is completed.

Initially, the builder prepares plans and studies for presentation to a permanent lender, such as a bank or savings and loan association. If the permanent lender likes the deal, a *forward* (or *advance*) *commitment* is issued to the builder. This is a contract with special clauses and provisions that is binding only on the lender. The builder does not have to "take down" (use) the funds committed.

The builder, nevertheless, usually needs the forward commitment to secure construction financing from a construction lender, such as a commercial bank. Recently, construction lenders have been making loans without a permanent loan commitment *(open-end construction loans).* The forward commitment is a binding promise by the permanent lender to pay off the construction loan once construction is completed and, therefore, is security for the construction loan. The construction lender also has additional security provided by the mortgage on the land and any notes given. Once construction is completed, the permanent lender pays off the construction lender, the mortgage documentation is transferred to the permanent lender, and the builder begins to pay back the permanent lender, often as a result of the sale of houses.[14]

For custom homes and for some spec-home ventures, usually two loans are involved but only one lender, such as a savings and loan institution, as shown in Exhibit 5–5 Panel B. Once construction is completed, the construction loan is converted to a permanent loan, and the owner makes payments to the lender as in any mortgage loan arrangement. Construction loans, because they are riskier, generally carry higher interest rates than permanent loans; this explains the dual loan structure. The builder of custom homes is usually not liable for the construction loan. The owner of the land arranges financing and gives the mortgage and note to the financial institution.

Contracts for Income-Property Financing

As with contracts for single-family residential financing, we first examine the arrangements for existing income-property transactions, and then new-construction deals.

Existing Properties. The contractual relationships between borrowers and lenders for the financing of existing income properties can become highly complex, but they often begin with the simple mortgage contract shown in Exhibit 5–1. Two of the most common extensions in mortgage contracts for existing income properties are *income participation* and *equity participation.*

Over the past two decades, lenders have become increasingly aware of how profitable the income-producing properties they finance can be. Thus, lenders have sought to share in this profitability by including income- and equity-participation features in mortgage contracts. As the names imply, income- and equity-participation provisions give the lender

---

[14]With each sale, the lender gets a certain percentage of the sale price and the builder is *released* from that part of the mortgage obligation. Usually, the buyer of the house takes over the loan at that point. See Chapter 26.

a share of the income from the property and a share of the property's appreciation, respectively.

New-Construction Financing. Financing the construction of income properties is similar to financing spec-home construction. One major difference in income-property financing is the *rental-achievement* clause that is inserted by the permanent lender in the forward commitment. The rental-achievement clause might specify that the builder have 75 percent of the space rented by the month following the completion of construction in order for the permanent lender to lend the full value of the forward commitment. If only 60 percent of the space is rented by that time, the permanent lender will pay out, say, 80 percent of the construction loan. This leaves the builder in the position of having to find some additional short-term financing (known as a *gap* loan) to pay off the balance of the construction loan.

━━━━━━━━━━━━━━━━━━━━ *Frame 5–1* ━━━━━━━━━━━━━━━━━━━━

A Permanent-Loan Commitment Dispute: You Be the Judge!*

The builder (plaintiff) received a permanent loan commitment from the lender (defendant) in March to build an apartment complex. The commitment would lapse if the loan was not closed by January 1 of the following year. In November the builder proposed to the lender that the loan be closed with a small "hold back" of funds until minor work was completed on some of the apartments. The lender led the borrower to believe that such an arrangement would be possible. On December 24, the lender notified the builder that the project would have to be totally completed, ready for occupancy, and the loan closed by January 1 or the commitment would be canceled. The builder could not comply with these terms and filed suit against the lender to force the issue of the commitment. Was the lender required to make good on the commitment?

Answer: Since the commitment document stated that the project be substantially—not necessarily 100 percent—complete, the lender was required by the court to honor the commitment and to pay damages.

Selective Builders, Inc. v. Hudson City Savings Bank, 349 A. 2d 564 (N.J. 1975).

Another common arrangement for financing the development of income properties is the *joint venture*. Here, the lender supplies all funds needed for the project, while the developer undertakes the project in exchange for a share in the ownership. Such agreements have resulted in very successful and continuing relationships between some lenders and developers in recent years.

CLAUSES IN MORTGAGE DOCUMENTATION

The term *mortgage documentation* refers to the set of legal instruments that constitute the mortgage contract. In the typical single-family residential mortgage contract, the mortgage documentation is simply the promissory note and the mortgage (or trust deed, etc.). In an income-property mortgage, the documentation might include the forward commitment letter, or the lender/developer partnership agreement, in addition to the note and mortgage(s). This section begins by presenting the requirements for a valid and enforceable mortgage contract and some of the clauses found in the mortgage and related documents. Subsequently, the clauses in the note and mortgage of a standard single-family residential loan agreement are presented. Finally, several of the clauses that often appear in construction-loan mortgages and forward commitments are described.

Requirements of a Valid and Enforceable Mortgage

Like any other contract, a valid mortgage contract must have an offer and acceptance, competent parties, legal objectives, consideration, and no barriers to mutual assent. Also, as in a valid and enforceable real estate contract for sale, mortgage contracts should be in writing, and the property being mortgaged should be properly and adequately described. Beyond these requirements, valid and enforceable mortgage contracts should:

1. Identify the set of property rights (e.g., leasehold or fee simple) being mortgaged.
2. Include words of conveyance or words of grant (e.g., "Grantor hereby grants, bargains, sells, and conveys to Grantee . . .") when the borrower is granting title (title-theory states).
3. Include signatures of the mortgagor (borrower) and the mortgagor's spouse.
4. Are delivered to the mortgagee and recorded.[15]
5. Contain a description of the note, since a mortgage is not valid unless an actual debt exists.

The final requirement brings up an important point about the relationship between the mortgage and the note. Since mortgages are recorded in the public records (usually in the county clerk's office following the closing) and notes, as personal pledges to repay debts, are not recorded, the financial terms of the loan, such as interest rate and maturity, are included

---

[15]The topic of how an instrument is legally delivered was discussed in conjunction with the delivery of the deed in Chapter 3.

in the note but not in the mortgage. This protects the privacy of the contract. Thus, the note evidences the debt and contains the essential details for repayment of the debt.

Clauses Commonly Found in Mortgage Documents

While no attempt is made here to describe all of the clauses found in mortgage contracts for various types of transactions, the discussions that follow are directed at some of the more common provisions contained in mortgage contracts.

1. *Acceleration clause.* As a result of this clause, which appears in the note and also sometimes in the mortgage, the lender (or the holder of the note) has the right to all remaining payments on the loan should the borrower default. It allows the lender to avoid the technicality of having to bring a separate law suit for each and every remaining payment when the borrower defaults on the payments currently due. Thus, the payments are accelerated for the purpose of allowing the lender to bring one foreclosure action.

2. *Prepayment and late-payment clause.* The note often contains a clause that imposes a penalty (e.g., three percent of the outstanding balance) on the borrower for making early payments on the amount borrowed. Lenders include such clauses to avoid having to reinvest funds unexpectedly. How strictly lenders enforce the prepayment penalty (or whether they include such clauses in notes) depends on the prevailing interest rate and whether it is above or below the contract rate. Lenders also may include a late-payment penalty to discourage borrowers from paying after the due date each month (e.g., a $20 penalty may be assessed if payment is received after the 15th day of the month).

3. *Due-on-sale clause.* Found in most residential mortgages today, this is an acceleration clause that is enforceable when the property is sold. It does not apply to defaults. Thus, if the property is transferred to a new owner, the new owner may *not* assume the mortgage under the prevailing terms. These clauses were originally designed to protect lenders against properties being transferred to persons of higher security risk. More recently, due-on-sale clauses have been used to prevent low-interest-rate loans from being assumed. A public debate over whether due-on-sale clauses can be enforced by lenders was settled in favor of lender in a 1982 U.S. Supreme Court case.[16]

---

[16]*Fidelity Federal Savings* v. *de la Cuesta*, 102 S. Ct. 3014 (1982).

4. *Insurance clause.* Lenders usually insist that borrowers carry hazard and fire insurance on the mortgaged property to protect their investments. Frequently, the lender will also insist on collecting the premium for this insurance along with the payment of interest and principal. This is called escrowing.[17] Escrowing of property tax payments is also common.[18] Such escrowing protects the lender against the borrower's neglecting to make such payments. These clauses are part of the mortgage.

5. *Estoppel clause.* If the mortgage is assigned (sold) to a third party by the lender, the new holder of the mortgage will be interested in knowing the exact amount of the balance remaining on the loan. The estoppel clause gives any new holder of the mortgage the right to request an estoppel letter from the borrower, declaring the amount of the remaining balance of the loan.

6. *Interest escalation* and *adjustment clause.* The note in some mortgage contracts contains a clause that allows the lender to make changes in the interest rate. An escalation clause, often found in land-development and construction loans, gives the lender the right to *increase but not decrease* the rate of interest (i.e., changes are tied to upward movements in the prime rate). Interest adjustment clauses common in residential mortgages today allow for adjustments in the interest rate strictly in accordance with the movement, up or down, of some general interest-rate index.[19]

7. *Defeasance clause.* This simply states that the borrower will gain unencumbered title to the mortgaged property once the terms of the loan agreement have been satisfied.

Residential Mortgage Documents: Continuing Saga of a Sale

In Chapter 4, Fred and Louise Johnson listed their house in Gainesville, Florida, with Town and Country Realtors for $85,000. As will be described in Chapter 6, George and Linda Jones sign a sale contract to purchase the house for $83,000. The contract states that the sale is contingent on the Joneses' obtaining an adjustable-rate mortgage starting at 9.75 percent for 30 years with a loan-to-value ratio of 80 percent. The Joneses are able to arrange financing at these terms with Mid-State Savings and Loan Association. Exhibit 5–6 shows the note.

---

[17]An escrow account is set up by the lender to make the insurance payments to the insurance company when they are due.

[18]Thus, the term PITI to describe a mortgage payment, where *P* is principal, *I* is interest, *T* is taxes, and the second *I* is insurance.

[19]A sizable percentage of the residential mortgages originated today have adjustable-rate features. More discussion of this topic is found in Chapter 19.

EXHIBIT 5–6

PROMISSORY NOTE

$ 66,400.00   Gainesville, Florida,   June 1,   ,19 87

For value received, the undersigned, agree   and promise   to pay to the order of
Midstate Savings and Loan Association   the principal sum of
Sixty six thousand, four hundred and   no /100 Dollars
($ 66,400.00   ) with interest thereon at the rate of   9 3/4   per centum per annum from
June 1, 1986 until maturity, said interest being payable
both principal and interest being payable in lawful money of the United States of America at
3711 NW 13th Street, Gainesville, Florida,
or at such other address as the holder from time to time may specify by written notice to the maker, said
principal and interest to be paid at the date specfied and in the manner following:

Payments consisting of principal and interest shall be paid monthly for 30 years.
Payments are due on the first of each month and are considered late if paid on the
21st of the month or later.

This is a variable rate loan, with the interest rate to be adjustable annually.
Payments will be adjusted annually to reflect the interest rate.

If default be made in the payment of any said sums or interest or in the performance of any agreements contained herein, then, at the option of the holder of the same, the principal sum then remaining unpaid with accrued interest shall immediately become due and collectible without notice, time being of the essence of this contract, and said principal sum and said accrued interest shall both bear interest at the rate of eighteen per centum per annum, from such time until paid. All sums paid hereunder shall be credited first to accrued interest and then to principal.

Each maker and endorser waives presentment, protest, notice of protest and notice of dishonor and agrees to pay all costs, including a reasonable attorney's fee, whether suit be brought or not, and including, without limitation, attorney's fees on appeal, if counsel shall after maturity of this note or default hereunder, be employed to collect this note.

This note is secured by real estate mortgage of even date herewith.

Maker's Address   *George Jones*   (SEAL)
1822 NW 40th Avenue
Gainesville, Florida 32605   *Helen Jones*   (SEAL)
CHARLES A. WILLIAMS, JR.
Attorney-at-Law   (SEAL)

1M 185 BP   (SEAL)

The note used in standard residential contracts, such as the one in Exhibit 5–6, is a fairly short and simple instrument.[20] The standard mortgage note contains the following elements:

1. The date the note is executed.
2. The name of the mortgagor and mortgagee.
3. An acceleration clause.
4. The terms of the debt including the interest rate, manner of payment (i.e., type of amortization), frequency of payment (usually monthly), and the maturity date.
5. Prepayment penalty.
6. Escalation clause on delinquent payments.

---

[20]The forms for notes and mortgages or trust deeds are standardized to meet the needs of FNMA (Federal National Mortgage Association) and FHLMC (Federal Home Loan Mortgage Corporation), which buy and sell mortgages in the secondary mortgage market.

The standard residential mortgage form used in the agreement between the Joneses and Mid-State, as shown in Exhibit 5–7, is somewhat longer and involved than the note. The clauses in the mortgage are separated into two categories: *uniform clauses* or covenants that apply in all states and *nonuniform clauses* or convenants that conform to the laws of a particular state.[21]

EXHIBIT 5–7

This instrument was prepared by:

Name _Charles A. Williams, Jr._

Address _2727 North Main Street_

Gainesville, Florida

MORTGAGE DEED

WHEREAS _George and Helen Jones_

hereinafter called the MORTGAGOR (whether one or more, which term shall include the heirs, legal representatives, successors and assigns of said Mortgagor, wherever the context so requires or admits), is justly indebted

unto _Midstate Savings and Loan Association_
hereinafter called the MORTGAGEE (whether one or more, which term shall include the heirs, legal representatives, successors and assigns of said Mortgagee, wherever the context so requires or admits), in the sum of

Sixty six thousand, four hundred and no/100

_____ DOLLARS ($66,400.00), as evidenced by _one_
certain promissory note(s) hereinafter described, and;

WHEREAS, the said Mortgagor is desirous of better and more fully securing the payment of the said sums together with interest to accrue thereon according to the legal tenor and effect of the said Promissory Note(s), and to secure all future advances made by the Mortgagee to the Mortgagor, within twenty years from the date hereof, which said future advances together with the existing indebtedness herein secured shall not exceed at any one time the above amount.

KNOW ALL MEN BY THESE PRESENTS, That the said Mortgagor for and in consideration of the premises hereinbefore mentioned and the sum of One Dollar to said Mortgagee in hand paid, has granted, bargained, sold and conveyed, and by these presents does grant, bargain, sell and convey unto the said Mortgagee and said Mortgagee's heirs, successors, legal representatives and assigns, all the following described piece, parcel or tract of land, situated, lying and being in the County of _Alachua_ , State of Florida, to-wit:

Parcel #3, Block 2 of Spring Meadow Estates, Recorded in Plat Book 12, page 28, in the office of the Clerk of the County Court, Gainesville, Florida

Tax Parcel No.
6029-040-03

---

[21]The term *covenant* means a promise.

EXHIBIT 5–7 (continued)

TOGETHER with all rents, revenues, issue, profit or income derived or to be derived therefrom.

TO HAVE AND TO HOLD the same, together with all and singular the tenaments, hereditaments and appurtenances to the same belonging or in anywise appertaining, unto the said Mortgagee and said Mortgagee's heirs, legal representatives, successors and assigns forever. PROVIDED, however, and these presents are upon this express condition, that if the said Mortgagor shall well and truly pay, or cause to be paid, the said sum of money covenanted to be paid by said promissory note(s) according to the legal tenor and effect thereof together with other notes for such further, other and future advances, or any renewals of the indebtedness evidenced thereby as may be made by said Mortgagee to said Mortgagor and shall fully keep and perform all of the other covenants, conditions and stipulations in this mortgage and said note(s) contained, then this obligation shall be null and void, otherwise to remain in full force and virtue.

The sum of money mentioned in this mortgage is evidenced by Promissory Note(s), the payment of which is secured by this mortgage, said note(s) being substantially in the following words and figures, to-wit:

George and Helen Jones, for value received, agree and promise to pay to the order of Midstate Savings and Loan Association the principal sum of $66,400.00 with interest thereon at the rate of 9 3/4 percentum per annum from June 1, 1986, until maturity, said interest being paid monthly, both principal and interest to be in the following manner:

Payments consisting of principal and interest shall be paid monthly for 30 years. Payments are due on the first of each month and are considered late if paid on the 21st of the month or later.

This is a variable rate loan, with the interest rate to be adjustable annually. Payments will be adjusted annually to reflect the interest rate.

It is further covenanted and agreed by the mortgagor to and with the Mortgagee as follows, to-wit:

1. To pay the sums of money evidenced by said note(s) above described and this mortgage according to the legal tenor and effect thereof, together with other notes for such further, other and future advances, or any renewals of the indebtedness evidenced thereby as may be made by said Mortgagee to said Mortgagor.

2. To pay all and singular the taxes and assessments, levies, liabilities, obligations and encumbrances of every nature on said described property, and if the same be not promptly paid, the said Mortgagee, or said Mortgagee's heirs, legal representatives or assigns may at any time pay the same, and every payment so made shall bear interest from the date thereof at the highest interest rate allowed by law, and said payments together with such interest shall be secured by the lien of this mortgage. In the event the lien of this mortgage is junior or inferior to any other encumbrance, a default in such prior encumbrance shall be a default in this Mortgage entitling the Mortgagee to all remedies allowed by law and contained herein, including, without limitation, the right to declare all sums secured hereby immediately due and payable.

EXHIBIT 5–7 *(continued)*

3. To continuously keep all buildings now and hereafter placed upon said lands fully insured against direct loss by fire, windstorm, hail, explosion, riot, riot attending a strike, civil commotion, aircraft, vehicles, and smoke by an insurance company or companies authorized to do business with the State of Florida, acceptable to the Mortgagee, in an amount of not less than the full insurable value, of same, with a loss payable clause to the Mortgagee as his interests shall appear, and in the event of a breach of this covenant to insure, said Mortgagee shall have the right to place and pay for such insurance and each and every such payment shall bear interest from the date of such payment until paid at the highest interest rate allowed by law, and such payment together with such interest shall be secured by the lien on this mortgage.

4. To permit, commit or suffer no waste, impairment or deterioration of said property or any part thereof, and to keep said buildings and premises in good repair and condition throughout the life of this mortgage.

5. In the event, however, the Mortgagor shall fail to keep and perform fully any of said covenants or agreements set forth in this mortgage or in said note for a period of _____15_____ days the mortgagor shall and does hereby give unto the Mortgagee the right and option of declaring said note(s) and any other notes for future advances secured hereby immediately due and payable, and all rights of the Mortgagor under this mortgage immediately forfeited, and institute such proceedings as may be advised, whether by foreclosure or otherwise, for the collection of said note(s) and enforcing the lien of said mortgage, and any failure to exercise said option shall not constitute a waiver of the right to exercise the same at any other time.

6. In the event it should become necessary in the opinion of the holder of said note(s) and this mortgage to place same in the hands of an attorney for collection or suit is brought on same, the Mortgagor agrees to pay all costs, charges and expenses of the same, including all court costs, a reasonable attorney's fee and abstract charges.

7. The Mortgagee may, at any time while a suit is pending to foreclose or to reform this mortgage, or to enforce any claims arising hereunder, apply to the Court having jurisdiction thereof for the appointment of a receiver, and such court shall forthwith appoint a receiver of the premises covered hereby, including all and singular the income, profits, issues and revenues from whatever source derived, each and every of which, it being expressly understood, is hereby mortgaged as if specifically set forth and described in the granting and habendum clauses hereof, and such receiver shall have all the broad and effective functions and powers in anywise entrusted by a court to a receiver, and such appointment shall be made by such court as an admitted equity and a matter of absolute right to said Mortgagee, and without reference to the adequacy or inadequacy of the value of the property mortgaged or to the solvency or insolvency of said Mortgagor or the defendants, and such rents, profits, income, issues and revenue shall be applied by such receiver according to the lien of this mortgage and the practice of such court.

The Mortgagor hereby fully warrants the title to said lands and will defend the same against the lawful claims of all persons whomsoever.

IN WITNESS WHEREOF, the Mortgagor has hereunto set _____their_____ hand _____ and seal

_____ the ___1st___ day of ___June___ , A.D. 19__87__ .

Signed, sealed and delivered in our presence
as witnesses:

George Jones (SEAL)

Helen Jones (SEAL)

Lynette Snyder _____ (SEAL)

John B. Segal _____ (SEAL)

IN WITNESS WHEREOF, the Mortgagor has caused these presents to be executed in its name and its

corporate seal to be affixed hereto by its undersigned duly elected and constituted officers on this __1st__

day of ___June___ , 19__87__ .

(Corporate Seal)

Attest: _Joe T. Tuff_

By _Dexter B. Burkdale_

Signed, sealed and delivered in our presence
as witnesses:

Joseph L. Schmoe

Henry B. Aaron

EXHIBIT 5–7 *(concluded)*

STATE OF

COUNTY OF

Personally came before me

who being to me well known and known by me to be the individual   described in and who executed the above and foregoing mortgage and   acknowledged before me that signed, sealed and delivered the same at the time and place, in the manner, and for the uses and purposes as therein set forth and contained.

WITNESS my hand and official seal on this   day of   A.D. 19

_____

Notary Public, State of   at Large
My commission expires:

STATE OF

COUNTY OF

I HEREBY CERTIFY, That on this day before me, an officer duly qualified to administer oaths and take acknowledgments, personally appeared
and
and   of   , respectively
a corporation under the laws of the State of   ,
known to be the persons described in and who executed the foregoing mortgage to   to me

and severally acknowledged the execution thereof to be their free act and deed as such officers, for the uses and purposes therein mentioned; and that they affixed thereto the official seal of said corporation and that the said instrument is the act and deed of said corporation.

WITNESS my hand and official seal this   day of
A.D. 19

_____

Notary Public, State of   at Large
My commission expires:

Mortgage Deed

The uniform convenants in these documents require the following:

1. Payment of principal and interest in accordance with the note.[22]
2. Escrowing of insurance and taxes.
3. Application of payments first to taxes and insurance, then to interest, and then to principal.
4. Notice by borrower of all changes and liens affecting the property.
5. Maintenance of hazard insurance.
6. Maintenance of the property in good repair.
7. If the borrower breaks any covenants, the lender can take necessary action to protect the lender's security interest in the property.
8. The lender may enter the property for inspection by giving reasonable notice.
9. In the event of condemnation of the property, the lender is to be paid first.
10. Any changes in the original terms of the contract do not release the borrower from the contract in general.
11. Any lack of action by the lender should not be considered abandonment of the contract or debt.
12. All remedies in the contract can be exercised by the lender concurrently or successively.
13. Successors to the lender (i.e., new holders of the mortgage) are bound by the contract with the borrower.
14. If any part of the mortgage contract conflicts with state law, the remainder of the contract remains in effect.
15. The borrower shall be given a copy of the mortgage.
16. The due-on-sale clause.

Since nonuniform covenants in mortgages comply with state law, readers should examine a copy of the standard mortgage or trust-deed document used in their state. Some typical nonuniform mortgage covenants include:

1. Specific acceleration remedies available to the lender upon borrower default. These include power-of-sale provisions giving the lender or trustee (in trust-deed states) certain powers to expedite the foreclosure sale in title-theory or trust-deed states.
2. Assignment of rents to the lender as additional security for the loan (i.e., the lender may collect any rents from the property on default).
3. Advances of additional funds to the borrower may be made under the same contract.

---

[22]This covenant satisfies the general requirement that the mortgage must reference the note to establish the existence of the debt.

4. The borrower is released from the contract upon satisfying the terms of the contract.
5. The borrower waives all dower, homestead, and redemption (statutory) rights under the contract.[23]

The standard trust deed for residential lending is similar to the standard mortgage both in appearance and in its convenants. Some notable differences between the standard trust deed and the mortgage document are:

1. Three parties are named in the contract instead of two (i.e., a trustee also is named).
2. The lender is given a nonpossessionary security interest, while the trustee is given the possessionary security interest.
3. The trustee is given the power of sale.
4. Lender releases all nonpossessionary security interests upon satisfaction of the contract terms.
5. Provisions are made for an alternate trustee.

Important Clauses in Construction, Development, and Permanent Loan Documents

Mortgage contracts for income-property lending are not standardized and can be quite complex. The lack of standardization, as mentioned earlier, is due to the absence of a secondary market in these mortgages and to the many points of negotiation often present in these transactions, any of which contribute to the complexity of these agreements.

Construction loans and real estate development loans are good examples of nonresidential loan agreements.[24] They have many similarities, since both are designed to provide borrowers with funds that will be used to make new improvements to land. From the lender's viewpoint, the flow of funds in construction loans and development loans is said to be "slow out and fast in." Under the *advance clause* in these contracts, the borrower draws funds from the lender when needed to complete the next phase of the project ("slow out"). Usually, the borrower must show reasonable progress toward completing prior phases to obtain draws. As we discussed, these loans have historically been repaid by permanent loans, either from the same lender or another lender ("fast in").

Construction loans, in addition to having an advance clause, may also include a *subordination clause*. To illustrate, assume that a landowner

---

[23]See the section in this chapter on foreclosure.

[24]Construction loans are for adding improvements *on* land (i.e., the construction of buildings) while development loans are for improvements *to* land (i.e., streets and gutters, utilities, etc.). Development loans are frequently granted for the preparation of residential lots and may also be for the acquisition of the undivided parcel. They are sometimes referred to as *A and D loans,* for acquisition and development.

wants a building constructed on a parcel he or she recently acquired. The landowner has no expertise in construction, so a deal is made with a builder/developer to execute the project. As part of this agreement, the landowner allows the builder/developer to give the construction lender a mortgage on the land. The construction mortgage includes a clause stating that the owner of the land *subordinates* his or her interest in the land to the lender. Thus, the lender gets a security interest in the land.

The permanent-loan mortgage contract contains many of the same clauses as the single-family residential mortgage contract, such as the insurance clause, release clause, and defeasance clause. One major difference is in the additional compensation available to the lender. Many permanent-loan contracts for income-property mortgages contain an *equity* or *income participation clause*, which gives the lender the right to some of the value appreciation or income from the property in addition to the regular mortgage payment. This participation feature (also known as an *equity kicker* or *contingent interest*) is examined more closely in Chapter 20.

ADJUSTMENTS IN BORROWER AND LENDER RELATIONSHIPS

During the course of the long-term relationship between the borrower and lender in a mortgage contract, events can occur that require adjustments to, or even termination of, the relationship before the maturity date of the mortgage. By selling the property, for example, the borrower might repay the outstanding loan balance early. In another situation, the borrower might default on the payment, thus forcing the lender to take legal action to recover the remaining balance of the loan. A third party, for another example, might assume the loan in conjunction with a sale of the property. Also, the borrower and lender could renegotiate the terms of the original mortgage contract, or the lender could sell the mortgage to an investor. In this section, reasons for adjustment or termination of mortgage contract relationships are discussed and some of their consequences examined.

Satisfactory Payment in Full

Whether full repayment of the mortgage debt occurs before or on the maturity date, the terms of the contract can be satisfied if the borrower pays any prepayment penalties. Repayment terminates the mortgage contract. The lender returns the note to the borrower marked "paid" and executes a legal document called a *release*, which eliminates the mortgage lien held by the lender. Like the mortgage, the release is recorded so the public record shows that the lien has been extinguished.

Default and Foreclosure

Exhibit 5–8 presents the typical sequence of events surrounding a mortgage default and property foreclosure. A mortgage is in default when the borrower fails to meet some obligation in the mortgage contract. Mortgage defaults usually result from the borrower's failure to make timely payments of principal and interest, as well as escrowed taxes and insurance premiums. A *technical default,* although rare, might be declared by the lender if, for example, the borrower fails to maintain the property. Defaults resulting from the borrower's failure to make timely payments can be declared on the date specified in the mortgage contract. For example, monthly payments may be due on the first day of the month and considered late on the seventh day of the month.

EXHIBIT 5–8
SEQUENCE OF EVENTS IN A DEFAULT AND FORECLOSURE

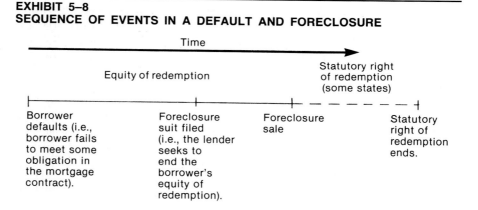

Courts have established a legal right of borrowers in default, called the *equity of redemption.* This right gives borrowers a certain period of time to make up overdue payments (i.e., to redeem their equity in the property). While the period is not always specified in the law, thus being left to the discretion of the court, it is typically two to three months.

Lenders exercise their right to force the sale of properties to gain repayment of mortgage debts by filing foreclosure suits against the properties of delinquent borrowers. A foreclosure suit, in essence, constitutes a motion before the court to end the borrower's equity of redemption and to fix a date for the sale of the property. The courts often seek an alternative solution by attempting to find a way to reestablish a good relationship between borrower and lender. However, if such a solution cannot be found, the lender's motions are heard, and the time, date, and location of the foreclosure sale are set (e.g., two weeks from the current date, 12 noon at the county court house).[25]

The foreclosure sale is a public sale offering properties to the highest bidder. Frequently, the highest bidder is the first mortgage lender, since the lender needs to produce the least cash to buy the property. For example, assume that a lender originally loaned $40,000 to a borrower for a property purchased for $50,000. Later, the borrower defaults and leaves a remaining balance of $39,700. At the foreclosure sale, the lender could start the bidding at $39,700 for the property. Any other bidder would have to pay more than that amount in cash to outbid the first-mortgage lender.[26]

In states such as Colorado, borrowers' rights in a mortgage contract do not end with the foreclosure sale. A period of *statutory redemption* (e.g., one year) is set by state law and gives borrowers the right to regain full ownership rights in foreclosed property, simply by buying the property back from the purchaser for the price paid at the foreclosure sale. Thus, instead of a sheriff's deed, the purchaser of foreclosed property obtains a certificate of sale immediately and a sheriff's deed at the end of the period of statutory redemption. Given the uncertainty surrounding such sales in these states, prices of foreclosed property tend to be somewhat depressed.

Assumption and "Subject to" Transactions

Situations may arise in the life of a mortgage in which the sale of the property does not mark the end of the original mortgage contract. The mortgage contract for example, may not include a due-on-sale clause, as in an FHA or VA loan, so the buyer of the property can "step into" the original mortgage contract in place of the seller who was the original borrower.

A mortgage *assumption* occurs when the new borrower in the contract gives a note to the lender to replace the note of the former borrower, and the mortgage otherwise remains unchanged. While this is the usual course, another type of arrangement is sometimes found in the market. A buyer can also purchase a property *subject to* the original mortgage, meaning that the note of the original borrower remains in effect. The

---

[25]Lenders have several strong incentives to have the foreclosure proceeding completed within the shortest possible time. First, they want to prevent the borrower from letting the property deteriorate. Second, they want to minimize the costs of foreclosure, in terms of both legal fees and lost interest. Many of these costs, however, are reimbursable from the foreclosure sale proceeds.

[26]The foreclosure process becomes much more complex when junior mortgages exist. See William B. Brueggeman and Leo Stone, *Real Estate Finance* (Homewood, Ill: Richard D. Irwin, 1981), pp. 44–50.

buyer makes no personal pledges for the debt. Obviously, such an arrangement is good for the buyer and risky for the seller (original borrower), who continues to have a personal obligation for the debt, even though he or she no longer has any property rights.

Recasting the Mortgage

The exact terms of the relationship between a mortgage lender and borrower may change over time. For example, the two parties may agree to recast the mortgage as the result of a foreclosure action. In such cases, the lender agrees to add the delinquent interest and foreclosure costs to the principal owed if the borrower agrees to pay a slightly higher rate of interest on the loan. Recasting can often be accomplished without changing the public record.

Sale of the Mortgage

As discussed in Chapter 19, mortgages, especially single-family residential mortgages, are bought and sold in an active secondary market. This means that the mortgage lender with whom a borrower contracted may sell the mortgage documents (and thus the rights to the borrower's payments) to a third party. Since the original lender usually continues to service the mortgage by collecting payments, borrowers often are unaware that their mortgage has been sold. Thus, from the borrower's perspective, the sale of a mortgage usually has no effect on the mortgage contract relationship.

OVERVIEW

Since the purchase of real estate requires substantial funds, buyers enter into mortgage contracts with lenders to obtain some portion of the funds needed. The basic mortgage contract comprises two legal documents: a mortgage note, which contains the financial terms of the contract and the personal pledge of the borrower to repay the debt, and the mortgage, which gives the lender a legal claim against the property. Depending on state law, the lender's security interest can take different forms. It can be a specific lien; title to the property with restricted rights; or interest in a title, with restricted rights vested in a trustee.

The simple mortgage contract can be extended and modified in a variety of ways. Such arrangements include junior mortgages, wrap-around mortgages, mortgage assumptions, purchase-money mortgages, and land contracts. These and other arrangements serve as the basis for the financing contracts found today in the single-family residential and income-property markets. As discussed in this chapter, mortgage agreements differ not only by property type, but also by whether the property is already developed or is to be developed with the funds being borrowed.

The building blocks of the mortgage contract are the clauses in the note and mortgage. These clauses are fairly universal and straightforward in single-family residential mortgage contracts, but can be quite diverse and complex in income-property contracts.

The relationship between the mortgage lender and borrower can change or end as the result of any number of events during the life of the mortgage contract. Perhaps the most legally, financially, and emotionally troublesome of these events is a borrower default and lender foreclosure. This process, often culminating in a foreclosure sale of the property, can result in financial losses for both parties as well as termination of the mortgage contract.

TEST YOURSELF

Identify the following terms and concepts presented in this chapter.

1. Lien theory versus title theory.
2. Wrap-around mortgage.
3. Land contract.
4. Forward commitment.
5. Acceleration clause.
6. Due-on-sale clause.
7. Advance clause.
8. Equity of redemption versus statutory redemption.
9. Assumption versus subject to.
10. Trust deed.

Answer the following multiple choice questions.

1. In states in which trust deeds are used the trustee can be a
   a. Bank (other than the lender).
   b. Savings and loan (other than the lender).
   c. Lawyer.
   d. Trust company.
   e. All of the above.

2. A mortgage loan between the buyer and seller of the property in which the buyer gets title to the property in exchange for a mortgage is a (an)
   a. Wrap-around mortgage.
   b. Land contract.
   c. Adjustable-rate mortgage.
   d. Purchase-money mortgage.
   e. None of the above.

3. To increase their yields on loans, for income-producing properties, lenders have included
   a. Income- and equity-participation features.
   b. Subordination clauses.
   c. Rental-achievement clauses.
   d. Yield-enhancement clauses.
   e. None of the above.

4. When the lender sells the mortgage to a third party
   a. The lender must have the permission of the borrower.
   b. The borrower frequently doesn't know the mortgage has been sold.
   c. The mortgage must be a first mortgage.
   d. The mortgage must be in foreclosure.
   e. None of the above.

5. Due-on-sale clauses
   a. Are found in most conventional residential mortgages.

b. Are not found in FHA and VA mortgages.
c. Are fully enforceable by lenders according to recent court rulings.

d. Apply when the property is sold but not when a default occurs.
e. All of the above.

ADDITIONAL READINGS

Atteberry, William L., Karl G. Pearson, Michael P. Litka. *Real Estate Law.* New York: John Wiley & Sons, 1984. Chap. 14.

Brueggeman, William B., and Leo D. Stone. *Real Estate Finance.* Homewood, Ill.: Richard D. Irwin, 1981. Chaps. 1–3.

Dennis, Marshall W. *Mortgage Lending Fundamentals and Practices.* Reston, Va.: Reston Publishing Company, 1983. Chaps. 5 and 14.

French, William B., and Harold F. Lusk. *Law of the Real Estate Business.* Homewood, Ill.: Richard D. Irwin, 1984. Chaps. 12–14.

Kratovil, Robert, and Raymond J. Werner. *Real Estate Law.* Englewood Cliffs, N.J.: Prentice-Hall, 1983. Chap. 15.

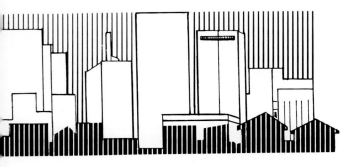

6
Contracts for Sale

INTRODUCTION

Buyers and sellers of real estate usually express the details of their agreement in a written document called a *contract for sale*. The principal provisions of a contract for sale, as shown in Exhibit 6–1, require the seller to deliver a deed to the property to the seller in exchange for payment of the purchase price by the buyer. The contract is signed when a buyer and seller decide to commit themselves to the transaction under terms and conditions worked out between them. *Terms* refers to the arrangements agreed to by the parties, such as price and date of closing, while *conditions* refers to the circumstances that must prevail, such as mechanical equipment being in good condition and title being unencumbered. Thus, real estate transactions differ from personal property transactions in that realty sales almost always involve a two-step process. The parties reach agreement first; sometime later (for example, one month) they consummate the sale at a meeting called the *closing*. In a personal property transaction the parties usually close the transaction at the same time they reach agreement.

A contract for sale of real estate, like any contract, is a legal, enforceable document. If its provisions are not carried out, financial penalties (damages) may be imposed on the party unwilling or unable to fulfill the contract. Thus, a contract for sale is the most important document in a real estate transaction. Whereas most contracts are legal and enforceable whether they are written or oral, the laws of every state (called statutes of frauds) require that contracts for the sale and purchase of real estate be in writing to be enforceable.[1] The many provisions in such a contract leave too much room for both legitimate misunderstandings and purposeful disagreements (fraud) when the agreements are oral. While disagree-

---

[1]This rule of law is known as the *parol evidence rule*.

EXHIBIT 6–1
CONTRACT FOR SALE

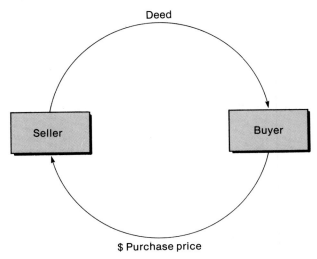

ments may arise with written contracts as well, there is definite language that the courts can interpret and enforce.

RIGHTS AND OBLIGATIONS OF SELLERS AND BUYERS

A contract for the sale of real estate creates certain rights and obligations for both sellers and buyers.

Rights and Obligations of Sellers

The following rights and obligations typically are created for sellers:

Rights of Sellers
1. To receive the sale price specified in the contract at the specified date.
2. To obtain the specified terms of the sale price, such as all cash or part secondary financing.
3. To obtain reimbursement for any property expenses that have been paid for the period during which the property will be occupied by the buyers.

Obligations of Sellers
1. To deliver clear title to the buyers on the specified date by the specified type of instrument, such as a warranty deed.

2. To maintain the property in good repair until title is conveyed to the buyers.
3. To maintain major appliances and subsystems, such as heating, cooling, and electrical, in good condition and to turn them over to the buyers in a condition no worse than when the contract was signed.
4. To allow the buyers or their representative to inspect the property just before closing to determine its condition.
5. To provide the type of evidence of title specified in the contract (e.g., abstract or title insurance).
6. To pay operating expenses of the property until closing and to reimburse the buyers for property expenses, such as property taxes, they may pay for the period during which the property is occupied by the sellers.
7. To pay the agreed-on brokerage commission at closing.

Rights and Obligations of Buyers

The following rights and obligations typically are created for buyers:

Rights of Buyers
1. To obtain clear legal title to the property on the date specified in the contract for sale.
2. To obtain the property in the same condition as when the contract was signed.
3. To obtain the appliances and subsystems in the same condition as when the contract was signed.
4. To have title conveyed by the type of instrument specified in the contract.
5. To back out of the transaction if the property is substantially damaged or destroyed by fire, earthquake, or other hazard.
6. To obtain reimbursement for any property expenses paid for the period during which the property was occupied by the sellers (e.g., property taxes).

Obligations of Buyers
1. To pay the specified price on the terms in the contract on the date of closing.
2. To reimburse the sellers for property operating expenses they have paid that cover the period of occupancy by the buyers.

REQUIREMENTS OF A CONTRACT FOR SALE

A legally binding contract for sale can take many forms. It can be a short, handwritten note, a preprinted form containing several standard paragraphs, or a lengthy document prepared by attorneys to cover many points in a complex transaction. Whatever the form, any contract, whether it be for the sale of real estate or for some other purpose, must contain the following elements:

1. Competent parties.
2. Legal objective.
3. Offer and acceptance.
4. Consideration.
5. No defects to mutual assent.

Two additional requirements must be part of any contract for the sale of real estate:

1. Written form.
2. Proper description of the property.

The Parties Must Be Competent to Act

The principal parties to a transaction must be legally competent. In the case of individuals, such parties must have reached a minimum age (18 years in most states) and be of sound mind. While minors may be legally competent to participate in real estate transactions, a contract with a minor is *voidable:* the minor may legally declare the contract invalid and refuse to carry out its provisions.

In the case of corporations, a party acting on behalf of the corporation must be legally empowered to do so. For example, if a corporation sells property, its president or some other officer must be authorized by a board of directors resolution or bylaw to act in this capacity. Similarly, personal representatives (e.g., executors, administrators, agents, and attorneys-in-fact) and trustees must be authorized to act on behalf of their principals by a legal instrument or order, such as a *power of attorney.* Their powers are defined and limited by the instrument. Real estate purchasers or professionals should always assure themselves that personal representatives and trustees have legal authority to sell properties.

The Parties Must Have Lawful Intent

The objective of a contract must not be illegal or against public policy. For example, a contract to commit a crime for payment is not enforceable in the courts. Similarly, a contract to sell property for the purpose of growing marijuana or for storing illegal weapons is legally invalid. A contract to sell property to members of a certain race, or to exclude members of a certain race, would be counter to public policy against racial discrimination, and would be void.

There Must Be an Offer and an Acceptance

An offer and acceptance indicate that the parties to a contract have a meeting of the minds, or *mutual assent*. The contract binds the parties to specified actions in the future—for the seller to deliver marketable legal title to the buyer and for the buyer to pay the stipulated price for a property. In a real estate contract for sale, the buyer normally offers a specified price under specific terms for specific property rights. The seller has three options—to reject the offer outright, to accept the offer outright, or, as frequently occurs, to reject the offer and present a counteroffer. A series of offers and counteroffers often will ensue until an agreement is reached (i.e., there is a successful offer and acceptance) or one party rejects an offer outright.

The basic agreement ultimately reached between buyer and seller may be simple and straightforward. However, it usually creates many other issues on which agreement must be reached, including the closing date, prorating of expenses, type of title evidence, liability for property damage, and condition of the property. The purpose of a contract for sale is to specify these agreements and to make them legally binding.

There Must Be Consideration

The value given up, or promise made, by each party to a contract is the *consideration*. Both parties to a valid and enforceable contract must provide consideration. In a contract for the sale and purchase of real estate, the seller's consideration is the property to be given up. The buyer's consideration is the money or other goods that constitute the purchase price. Mere promise of consideration by one party does not constitute a contract and cannot be enforced. For example, I. M. Rich promises to deed a property to his friend, B. Weiser and even writes this promise on a piece of paper. Such a promise cannot be enforced because Mr. Weiser did not promise anything in return. Mutual obligations of the parties are necessary to create a legally binding contract.

There Must Be No Defects to Mutual Assent

In certain circumstances, mutual assent—the meeting of the minds—between the contracting parties may be broken, thus invalidating the contract. The following constitute defects to mutual assent:

1. One party attempts to perpetrate a fraud on the other party or makes a misrepresentation.[2]

---

[2]Fraud is intentional misrepresentation, whereas a misrepresentation per se is unintentional. They have the same effect.

2. A substantial error is made (e.g., the name of one of the parties to a written contract is incorrect).
3. One of the parties is under duress, undue influence, or menace.[3]

In addition to the elements described above for any contract, an enforceable contract for the *sale of real estate* must fulfill two additional requirements.

The Contract for Sale of Real Estate Must Be in Writing

The first is that the contract must be in writing. The statute of frauds, the old English law that serves as the basis for contract law in most states, imposed the requirement of writing on some types of contract in order for them to be enforceable.[4] Many agreements involving real estate are subject to this requirement, including contracts for sale, installment sales contracts, option contracts, exchange contracts, and in many states, leases, listing contracts, and mortgage contracts.[5] In most states the *parol evidence rule* is in effect, which prohibits the admission of oral evidence in disputes involving written contracts.

As we noted, most real estate contracts contain many technicalities and points of agreement. Legitimate misunderstandings could easily arise over any of these points in an oral contract. Even more important, unscrupulous parties to an oral contract could gain an unfair advantage by later claiming that protective provisions were not agreed to. For example, most written contracts contain a provision that allows a buyer to back out of a transaction if the building is destroyed by fire or other hazard prior to the closing. A seller could easily claim that such a provision was not part of an oral contract; it would be his or her word against the buyer's.

To satisfy the writing requirement, the contract must usually include adequate identification of the parties, the subject matter, and the terms of agreement, as well as the signatures of the parties or their legally empowered agents. It is essential that both principal parties to a transaction—buyers and sellers—sign the contract. The signatures are legal evidence that the parties understand and agree to the provisions in the contract. They cannot later claim that they did not agree to a provision in the contract or did not understand its meaning.

---

[3]Undue influence involves an abuse of the influence that one person (usually a relative) has over another. Duress involves compelling a person to act by the use of force, while menace is the use of the threat of force to compel a person to act.

[4]The statute of frauds was intended to prevent fraudulent practices in contracting; thus, the writing requirement was imposed for situations where substantial sums of money would normally be involved.

[5]Leases for less than one year normally are not required to be in writing to be enforceable.

In addition to the principals' signatures, the statute of frauds may require a spouse's signature to release his or her marital rights such as homestead rights, dower rights, or community-property rights. Technically, a spouse's signature on a contract indicates his or her agreement to sign the deed, where these rights are actually waived. Also, as we noted, legal written authorization must accompany a contract that is signed by an agent, personal representative, or trustee.

The Property Must Be Properly Described

Satisfying the written-form requirement is fairly straightforward. But the second requirement—identification of the contract's subject matter—means that the legal rights being sold must be identified, and the physical boundaries of the property must be delineated precisely and unambiguously. The importance of proper description of the physical assets and the accompanying property rights in a real estate contract cannot be overstated. The specific purpose of the property description is to ensure that buyer and seller understand exactly what real estate is being transferred. Boundary lines, easements, air rights, mineral rights, and other types of partial interests create a situation, unlike that for personal property, in which it is essential that the sale contract contain a proper and adequate description.

The term *proper and adequate description* means that the description in a contract must enable a knowledgeable person to determine the boundaries or limits of the property. In Chapter 3, we explained several popular forms of description, including the recorded plat description and the government survey system. Each form is acceptable for contracts for sale. However, some forms are preferable to others because they provide more precise identification. The recorded plat description, for example, is generally preferred to the metes-and-bounds description or the government survey system in urban areas. Also, recorded plat descriptions are generally preferred over street addresses. The government survey and metes-and-bounds systems are used in rural areas.

TITLE

Legal Title

As we discussed in Chapter 2, *legal title* means the ownership of an estate (a bundle of rights) in real estate. Legal title passes from seller to buyer at the time of closing, when the deed is delivered by the seller and accepted by the buyer. Legal title gives the owner all of the rights and obligations of the estate. For example, the owners of a fee simple estate can occupy and use the property in any legal manner. They can also convey title to someone else, and by their wills, they can designate to whom title will transfer at the time of their deaths. The owners of a life estate generally have the same rights as the owners of a fee simple estate, except that their rights of occupancy and use are for a specified period. Legal title is neither created nor conveyed by the contract for sale.

Equitable Title

Equitable title is a legal concept that gives buyers the right to obtain legal title to real estate. It is created and conveyed by the contract for sale. With equitable title, buyers can be assured that they will obtain full legal title at the time of closing if they perform their obligations under the contract.

Equitable title places a limitation on sellers: they may not sell their property to another buyer, no matter how attractive the other offer may be. This limitation is more severe than the normal penalty for breach of contract—liability for damages. Thus, if it were not for equitable title, sellers could sell to someone else and let the buyers sue for damages.

Sellers may negotiate with other potential buyers so long as the buyers' equitable title is not violated. For example, another buyer may agree to purchase the property if the original buyers fail to close the transaction. The original buyers' equitable title is not disturbed, since the second contract is contingent on default by the original buyers.

THE FORM OF THE CONTRACT FOR SALE

While the contract for sale may take a variety of forms, the important question to be answered is whether all essential ingredients of a valid and enforceable contract for sale are present. Most transactions today, especially residential transactions, are completed with the use of standard forms, which force the parties to consider all of the necessary elements.

Simple Contract

The following paragraph constitutes a simple real estate contract.

> I, Ben Byer, agree to buy and pay $20,000, and I, Cecil Celler, agree to sell the parcel of real estate at 1013 NE Seventh Road in Nowhere, Nebraska.
>
> Signed: Ben Byer
> Signed: Cecil Celler

In the real world, such a brief contract would not be sufficient; however, it contains the seven essential elements, and therefore it would be legal. Mr. Byer and Mr. Celler are competent. Mr. Byer offers $20,000, and Mr. Celler accepts by agreeing to sell. Consideration is stated for both—$20,000 for the buyer and the property for the seller. The objective is legal, the property is identified, and there are no defects to mutual assent. The contract is written and is signed by both parties.

But several important points are omitted. These could be subject to disagreement later, and they could cause the transaction to be delayed or even aborted. The missing points are:

1. Date of the contract.
2. Date and place of closing.
3. The parties' marital status.
4. Financing terms, if any.
5. Prorating of costs and expenses.
6. Condition of any buildings.
7. Condition of subsystems and appliances.
8. Right of occupancy (or rents) until closing.
9. Liability for major damage to buildings prior to closing.
10. Remedies by each party for breach of contract by the other party.
11. Exact dimensions and location of the property.
12. Brokerage commission, if any.
13. Earnest-money deposit.

Since these points are not covered in the contract, misunderstandings and severe losses for both parties can result. For example, the seller may need the money and count on closing within two weeks. The buyer, however, may be in no hurry and not want to close for three months. Since the contract does not specify the date of closing, the courts will interpret the time between contract and closing as a reasonable time—which could easily be three months. As another example, consider the buyer's problem if the building burns down before closing. Without the contract specifying otherwise, the buyer must complete the transaction even if the building is destroyed. For these reasons, a longer contract form is usually used.

Standard Form Contracts

Since the issues in many transactions are similar, standard preprinted forms are often used. In such forms, all or most of the normal issues requiring agreement are addressed in a way that protects both buyers and sellers. These standard forms are typically used by brokers. For small residential properties in straightforward transactions, a standard form contract is usually adequate to protect the interests of both parties. Even so, buyers and sellers should read such contracts carefully; once they sign such a contract, they can be held to its provisions, no matter how deleterious to their interests.

Both parties can achieve maximum protection by having a competent attorney examine the document *before* signing. Having an attorney examine a contract after it has been signed or to represent one at a closing is like locking the barn door after the horse has run away. While many buyers and sellers of single-family homes do not hire an attorney to draft or examine the contract and do not suffer severe financial losses, small disagreements and losses are relatively common (see Frame 6–1).

Frame 6–1

A Contract Dispute

A new marketing professor, Dr. David Dennis, was hired by a large midwestern university. After looking at a number of houses, he and his wife Marie decided to purchase a large, older home in a pleasant section of town. When they looked at the house, Marie noted that the master bedroom was carpeted, with the carpet fastened to the floor. After the transaction was closed and they began moving in, however, they discovered the carpet in the master bedroom had been removed.

The Dennises immediately protested to the broker who had sold them the house, Ms. Jan Dancy. She contacted the former owners, Mr. and Mrs. Jim Rockledge, who had moved several hundred miles to another city, to inquire why they had removed the carpet. They told Jan they had every right to remove the carpet. It was not part of the house, since it was not tacked to the floor.

When told that Marie had noticed the carpet was fastened to the floor, Mrs. Rockledge replied that the carpet had been tacked down only at the doorway to prevent its being kicked up. It was not fastened down in other places and was not permanently installed. The contract did not mention the carpet, and it was not intended to be sold as part of the house.

The Dennises were deprived of carpet they believed should have belonged to them, the Rockledges refused to pay, and the broker suffered customer dissatisfaction.

Note: To keep their good will, Jan bought the Dennises new bedroom carpet.

Contracts for the purchase and sale of larger, more complex, income-producing properties are usually drafted by attorneys. Typically, the sellers or buyers will have their attorneys draft the instrument, sign it, and then submit it to the other parties and their attorneys. The instrument tends to protect the parties that have drafted the instrument, to the detriment of the other side. Thus, acceptance of the first draft of a contract drawn by the other parties' attorneys is rare. Usually, objections will be raised, new drafts will be prepared, and a bargaining process will occur before a contract is acceptable to both sides.

For most straightforward transactions, standard contract forms are usually prepared and approved by Boards of Realtors® in various communities or states. Use of these forms has some advantages. First, they usually contain provisions that address common issues such as prorations, closing, financing terms, liability for property damage, easements, condition of fixtures and appliances, real estate commission, and so on. Second, such forms tend to treat both parties fairly. They are not inherently biased toward one party or the other, as tends to be the case with contracts drawn by one party.

The main disadvantage in using standard form contracts is that the form cannot fit every situation. For example, most standard contract forms state that the buyer agrees to take the property subject to any easements of record. Since easements do not affect most properties' usefulness, many buyers, especially of single-family residential properties, do not check the public records for easements. Sometimes, however, an easement that could cause severe damage to the property is accepted by a buyer who is unaware of its existence. A house, for example, could be constructed over a utility easement which gives the utility company the right to service the utility line—by destroying part or all of the house, if necessary. If buyers did not check the public records showing the platting of the property and utility easements, they would be unaware of the utility easement.

A standard form contract for the purchase and sale of real estate is presented in Exhibit 6–2. This form contract has been developed and approved by the Florida Association of Realtors and the Florida Bar Association.

Hence, it is called the FAR-BAR form. This form contract is relatively comprehensive and fair to both parties. It contains ten paragraphs or sections covering common issues to be agreed upon in most transactions. An eleventh paragraph provides space for special clauses used to tailor the form to any special aspect of the transaction. Furthermore, the contract is accompanied by 25 "Standards for Real Estate Transactions." The standards explain and interpret the provisions of the contract and are explicitly included in it.

Components of Form Contract

Notice that the FAR-BAR form contract in Exhibit 6–2 contains the elements of any valid contract. The parties to the transaction are identified at the top of the form. There is an offer and acceptance, stated as an agreement that the seller shall sell and the buyer shall buy. Consideration is stated as the purchase price for the buyer and the property for the seller. The conveyance of title to the property is the legal objective, and the property is adequately identified. The contract is in writing, and the buyers and sellers sign in the spaces provided.

In addition to the elements, the contract form also covers other matters. It explicitly incorporates the Standards for Real Estate Transactions, which provide further explanation and interpretation of the contract pro-

EXHIBIT 6–2

CONTRACT FOR SALE AND PURCHASE

PARTIES: _____ , ("Seller"),

of _____ (Phone _____),

and _____ , ("Buyer"),

of _____ (Phone _____),

hereby agree that the Seller shall sell and Buyer shall buy the following property ("Property") upon the following terms and conditions which INCLUDE the Standards For Real Estate Transactions set forth on the reverse side hereof or attached hereto ("Standard(s)").

I. DESCRIPTION:

   (a) Legal description of Property located in _____ County, Florida:

   (b) Street address, if any, of the Property being conveyed is _____

   (c) Personal property ("Personalty") included:

II. PURCHASE PRICE: . . . . $_____

   PAYMENT:

   (a) Deposit(s) to be held in escrow by _____ in the amount of . . . . $_____

   (b) Subject to AND assumption of Mortgage in favor of _____ having an approximate present principal balance of . . . . $_____

   (c) Purchase money mortgage and note bearing interest at _____ % on terms set forth herein below, in the principal amount of . . . . $_____

   (d) Other _____ $_____

   (e) Balance to close, (U.S. cash, LOCALLY DRAWN certified or cashier's check) subject to adjustments and prorations . . . $_____

III. TIME FOR ACCEPTANCE; EFFECTIVE DATE: If this offer is not executed by all parties, and the FACT OF EXECUTION communicated in writing or telegraphically between the parties on or before _____ , the aforesaid deposit(s) shall be, at option of Buyer, returned to Buyer and the offer withdrawn and null and void. The date of Contract ("Effective Date") shall be the date when the last one of Seller and Buyer has signed this offer.

IV. FINANCING:

   (a) If the purchase price or any part thereof is to be financed by a third party loan, this Contract for Sale and Purchase ("Contract") is conditioned upon the Buyer obtaining a firm commitment for said loan within _____ days from Effective Date, at an interest rate not to exceed _____ %; term of _____ years; and in the principal amount of $_____ . Buyer will make application within _____ days from Effective Date, and use reasonable diligence to obtain said loan. Should Buyer fail to obtain same or to waive Buyer's rights hereunder within said time, either party may cancel Contract.

   (b) The existing mortgage described in Paragraph II(b) above has (CHECK (1) or (2)): (1) ☐ a variable interest rate OR (2) ☐ a fixed interest rate of _____ % per annum. At time of title transfer some fixed interest rates are subject to increase. If increased, the rate shall not exceed _____ % per annum. Seller shall, within _____ days from Effective Date, furnish a statement from all mortgagees stating principal balances, method of payment, interest rate and status of mortgages. If Buyer has agreed to assume a mortgage which requires approval of Buyer by the mortgagee for assumption, then Seller shall promptly obtain and deliver to Buyer all required applications and Buyer shall diligently complete and return same to the mortgagee. Any mortgagee charge not to exceed $_____ shall be paid 1/2 by Seller and 1/2 by Buyer. If the Buyer is not accepted by mortgagee or the requirements for assumption are not in accordance with the terms of the Contract or mortgagee makes a charge in excess of the stated amount, Seller or Buyer may rescind this Contract by prompt written notice to the other party unless either party elects to pay any increase in interest rate or excess mortgage charge. The amount of any escrow deposits held by mortgagee shall be credited to Seller at closing.

V. TITLE EVIDENCE: Within _____ days from Effective Date, Seller shall, at Seller's expense, deliver to Buyer or Buyer's attorney, in accordance with Standard A, (CHECK (1) or (2)): (1) ☐ abstract of title OR (2) ☐ title insurance commitment with fee owner's title policy premium to be paid by Seller at closing.

VI. CLOSING DATE: This transaction shall be closed and the deed and other closing papers delivered on the _____ day of _____ 19 _____ , unless extended by other provisions of the Contract.

VII. RESTRICTIONS; EASEMENTS; LIMITATIONS: The Buyer shall take title subject to: zoning, restrictions, prohibitions and other requirements imposed by governmental authority; restrictions and matters appearing on the plat or otherwise common to the subdivision; public utility easements of record (easements are to be located contiguous to the Property lines and are not more than 10 feet in width as to the rear or front lines and 7½ feet in width as to the side lines, unless otherwise specified herein); taxes for year of closing and subsequent years; assumed mortgages and purchase money mortgages, if any; other: _____ ; provided, however, that there exists at closing no violation of the foregoing and same does not prevent use of the Property for _____ purpose(s).

VIII. OCCUPANCY: Seller represents that there are no parties in occupancy other than Seller, but if Property is intended to be rented or occupied beyond closing, the fact and terms thereof shall be stated herein, and the tenant(s) shall be disclosed pursuant to Standard F. Seller agrees to deliver occupancy of Property at time of closing unless otherwise stated herein. If occupancy is to be delivered prior to closing, Buyer assumes all risk of loss to Property and Personalty from date of occupancy, shall be responsible and liable for maintenance thereof from said date, and shall be deemed to have accepted the Property and Personalty in their existing condition as of time of taking occupancy unless otherwise stated herein or in separate writing.

EXHIBIT 6–2 *(continued)*

IX. ASSIGNABILITY: (CHECK (1) or (2)): Buyer (1) ☐ may assign OR (2) ☐ may not assign, Contract.

X. TYPEWRITTEN OR HANDWRITTEN PROVISIONS: Typewritten or handwritten provisions inserted herein or attached hereto as addenda shall control all printed provisions of Contract in conflict therewith.

XI. INSULATION RIDER: If Contract is utilized for the sale of a new residence, the Insulation Rider shall be attached hereto and made part hereof.

XII. SPECIAL CLAUSES: (utilize space below)

THIS IS INTENDED TO BE A LEGALLY BINDING CONTRACT.
IF NOT FULLY UNDERSTOOD, SEEK THE ADVICE OF AN ATTORNEY PRIOR TO SIGNING.
THIS FORM HAS BEEN APPROVED BY THE FLORIDA ASSOCIATION OF REALTORS AND THE FLORIDA BAR.

Approval does not constitute an opinion that any of the terms and conditions in this Contract should be accepted by the parties in a particular transaction. Terms and conditions should be negotiated based upon the respective interests, objectives and bargaining positions of all interested persons.

Copyright 1985 by The Florida Bar and the Florida Association of REALTORS, Inc.

WITNESSES: (Two recommended but NOT required)   Executed by Buyer on_____

_____   _____
                                                                                              (Buyer)

_____   _____
                                                                                              (Buyer)

                                                                    Executed by Seller on_____

WITNESSES: (Two recommended but NOT required)

_____   _____
                                                                                              (Seller)

_____   _____
                                                                                              (Seller)

Deposit(s) under Paragraph II received; if other than cash, then subject to clearance.

By: _____ (Escrow Agent)

BROKER'S FEE: (CHECK & COMPLETE THE ONE APPLICABLE)

☐ (IF A LISTING AGREEMENT IS CURRENTLY IN EFFECT):
    Seller agrees to pay the Broker named below, including cooperating sub-agents named, according to the terms of an existing, separate listing agreement;
OR

☐ (IF NO LISTING AGREEMENT IS CURRENTLY IN EFFECT):
    Seller agrees to pay the Broker named below, at time of closing, from the disbursements of the proceeds of sale, compensation in the amount of (COMPLETE ONLY ONE)_____% of gross purchase price OR $_____, for Broker's services in effecting the sale by finding a Buyer ready, willing and able to purchase pursuant to the foregoing Contract. In the event Buyer fails to perform and deposit(s) is retained, 50% thereof, but not exceeding the Broker's fee above provided, shall be paid to the Broker, as full consideration for Broker's services including costs expended by Broker, and the balance shall be paid to Seller. If the transaction shall not be closed because of refusal or failure of Seller to perform, the Seller shall pay said fee in full to Broker on demand. In any litigation arising out of this Contract, concerning the Broker's fee, the prevailing party shall be entitled to recover reasonable attorney fees and costs.

_____
(firm name of Broker)

By: _____   _____
(authorized signatory)   (Seller)

_____
(name of cooperating sub-agent)   _____
                                                                                              (Seller)

SPECIAL CLAUSES:

Rev. 1/85

EXHIBIT 6–2 *(continued)*

STANDARDS FOR REAL ESTATE TRANSACTIONS

A.   EVIDENCE OF TITLE: (1) An <u>abstract of title</u> prepared or brought current by a reputable and existing abstract firm (if not existing then certified as correct by an existing firm) purporting to be an accurate synopsis of the instruments affecting title to the Property recorded in the public records of the county wherein the Property is located, through Effective Date and which shall commence with the earliest public records, or such later date as may be customary in the county. Seller shall convey a marketable title, subject only to liens, encumbrances, exceptions or qualifications set forth in this Contract and those which shall be discharged by Seller at or before closing. Marketable title shall be determined according to applicable Title Standards adopted by authority of The Florida Bar and in accordance with law. Upon closing of this transaction the abstract shall become the property of Buyer, subject to the right of retention thereof by first mortgagee until fully paid; or (2) a <u>title insurance commitment</u> issued by a Florida licensed title insuror agreeing to issue to Buyer, upon recording of the deed to Buyer, an owner's policy of title insurance in the amount of the purchase price, insuring Buyer's title to the Property, subject only to liens, encumbrances, exceptions or qualifications set forth in this Contract and those which shall be discharged by Seller at or before closing. Buyer shall have 30 days, if abstract, or 5 days, if title commitment, from date of receiving evidence of title to examine same. If title is found defective, Buyer shall within three (3) days thereafter, notify Seller in writing specifying defect(s). If said defect(s) render title unmarketable, as to item (1) hereinabove or uninsurable as to item (2), Seller will have 120 days from receipt of notice within which to remove said defect(s), and if Seller is unsuccessful in removing them within said time, Buyer shall have the option of either accepting the title as it then is, or demanding a refund of all monies paid hereunder which shall forthwith be returned to Buyer and thereupon Buyer and Seller shall be released, as to one another, of all further obligations under this Contract; however, Seller agrees that Seller will, if title is found to be unmarketable or uninsurable, use diligent effort to correct the defect(s) in title within the time provided therefor, including the bringing of necessary suits. If a title policy is being furnished, Buyer has the right to require the Seller to deliver an owner's marketability title policy provided Buyer pays any additional charges and makes request therefor within seven (7) days after Effective Date.

B.   PURCHASE MONEY MORTGAGE; SECURITY AGREEMENT; TO SELLER: The purchase money note and mortgage, if any, shall provide for a 30 day grace period in the event of default if it is a first mortgage and a 15 day grace period if a second or lesser mortgage; shall provide for right of prepayment in whole or in part without penalty; shall not permit acceleration or interest adjustment in event of resale of the Property; and the mortgage, note and security agreement shall be otherwise in form and content required by Seller's attorney; provided, however, Seller may only require clauses customarily found in mortgages, mortgage notes, and security agreements generally utilized by savings and loan institutions, or state or national banks located in the county wherein the Property is located. The mortgage shall require all prior liens and encumbrances to be kept in good standing and forbid modifications of or future advances under prior mortgage(s). All Personalty being conveyed will, at option of Seller, be subject to the lien of a security agreement and evidenced by recorded financing statements.

C.   SURVEY: Buyer, at Buyer's expense, within time allowed for delivery of evidence of title and examination thereof, may have the Property surveyed and certified by a registered Florida surveyor. If the survey shows any encroachment on the Property or that improvements intended to be located on the Property in fact encroach on setback lines, easements, lands of others, or violate any restrictions, Contract covenants or applicable governmental regulations, the same shall be treated as a title defect.

D.   TERMITES: Buyer, at Buyer's expense, within time allowed to deliver evidence of title and examination thereof, may have the Property inspected by a Florida Certified Pest Control Operator to determine whether there is any visible active termite infestation or visible existing damage from termite infestation in the improvements. If Buyer is informed of either or both of the foregoing, Buyer will have four (4) days from date of written notice thereof or two (2) days after selection of a contractor, whichever occurs first, within which to have all damages, whether visible or not, inspected and estimated by a licensed building or general contractor. Seller shall pay valid costs of treatment and repair of all damage up to 2% of purchase price. Should such costs exceed that amount, Buyer shall have the option of cancelling Contract within five (5) days after receipt of contractor's repair estimate by giving written notice to Seller or Buyer may elect to proceed with the transaction, in which event Buyer shall receive a credit at closing of an amount equal to the total of the treatment and repair estimate not in excess of two (2%) percent of the purchase price. "Termites" shall be deemed to include all wood destroying organisms required to be reported under the Florida Pest Control Act.

E.   INGRESS AND EGRESS: Seller warrants that there is ingress and egress to the Property sufficient for the intended use as described in Paragraph VII hereof, title to which is in accordance with Standard A.

F.   LEASES: Seller shall, not less than 15 days prior to closing, furnish to Buyer copies of all written leases and estoppel letters from each tenant specifying the nature and duration of the tenant's occupancy, rental rates, advanced rent and security deposits paid by tenant. In the event Seller is unable to obtain such letter from each tenant, the same information shall be furnished by Seller to Buyer within said time period in the form of a Seller's affidavit, and Buyer may thereafter contact tenants to confirm such information. Seller shall, at closing, deliver and assign all original leases to Buyer.

G.   LIENS: Seller shall, both as to the Property and Personalty being sold hereunder, furnish to Buyer at time of closing an affidavit attesting to the absence, unless otherwise provided for herein, of any financing statements, claims of lien or potential lienors known to Seller and further attesting that there have been no improvements or repairs to the Property for 90 days immediately preceding date of closing. If the Property has been improved, or repaired within said time, Seller shall deliver releases or waivers of mechanic's liens, executed by all general contractors, subcontractors, suppliers, and materialmen, in addition to Seller's lien affidavit setting forth the names of all such general contractors, subcontractors, suppliers and materialmen and further reciting that in fact all bills for work to the Property or Personalty which could serve as a basis for a mechanic's lien or a claim for damages have been paid or will be paid at closing.

H.   PLACE OF CLOSING: Closing shall be held in county wherein Property is located, at the office of the attorney or other closing agent designated by Seller.

I.   TIME: Time is of the essence of this Contract. Any reference herein to time periods of less than six (6) days shall in the computation thereof exclude Saturdays, Sundays and legal holidays, and any time period provided for herein which shall end on a Saturday, Sunday or legal holiday shall extend to 5:00 p.m. of the next full business day.

J.   DOCUMENTS FOR CLOSING: Seller shall furnish deed, bill of sale, mechanic's lien affidavit, assignments of leases, and any corrective instruments that may be required in connection with perfecting the title. Buyer shall furnish closing statement, mortgage, mortgage note, security agreement, and financing statements.

K.   EXPENSES: State documentary stamps which are required to be affixed to the instrument of conveyance, intangible tax on and recording of purchase money mortgage to Seller, and cost of recording any corrective instruments shall be paid by Seller. Documentary stamps to be affixed to the purchase money mortgage, cost of recording the deed and financing statements shall be paid by Buyer.

L.   PRORATIONS: Taxes, assessments, rent, interest, insurance and other expenses and revenue of the Property shall be prorated through day prior to closing. Buyer shall have the option of taking over any existing policies of insurance on the Property, if assumable, in which event premiums shall be prorated. Cash at closing shall be increased or decreased as may be required by said prorations. All prorations will be made through day prior to occupancy if occupancy occurs before closing. Taxes shall be prorated based on the current year's tax with due allowance made for maximum allowable discount and homestead or other exemptions if allowed for said year. If closing occurs at a date when the current year's millage is not fixed, and current year's assessment is available, taxes will be prorated based upon such assessment and the prior year's millage. If current year's assessment is not available, then taxes will be prorated on the prior year's tax; provided,

EXHIBIT 6–2 *(concluded)*

however, if there are completed improvements on the Property by January 1st of year of closing, which improvements were not in existence on January 1st of the prior year, then taxes shall be prorated based upon the prior year's millage and at an equitable assessment to be agreed upon between the parties, failing which, request will be made to the County Property Appraiser for an informal assessment taking into consideration homestead exemption, if any. However, any tax proration based on an estimate may at request of either Buyer or Seller be subsequently readjusted upon receipt of tax bill on condition that a statement to that effect is set forth in the closing statement.

M.   SPECIAL ASSESSMENT LIENS: Certified, confirmed and ratified special assessment liens as of date of closing (and not as of Effective Date) are to be paid by Seller. Pending liens as of date of closing shall be assumed by Buyer, provided, however, that if the improvement has been substantially completed as of Effective Date, such pending lien shall be considered as certified, confirmed or ratified and Seller shall, at closing, be charged an amount equal to the last estimate by the public body of assessment for the improvement.

N.   INSPECTION; REPAIR AND MAINTENANCE: Seller represents that, as of ten (10) days prior to closing, the roof, (including the fascia and soffits), and walls do not have any visible evidence of leaks or damage and that the septic tank, pool, all major appliances, heating, cooling, electrical, plumbing systems and machinery are in working condition. Buyer may, at Buyer's expense, have inspection made of said items by an appropriately licensed person dealing in the construction, repair and maintenance thereof and shall report in writing to Seller such items that do not meet the above representations, together with the cost of correcting same, prior to occupancy or not less than ten (10) days prior to closing, whichever occurs first. Unless Buyer reports such deficiencies within said period Buyer shall be deemed to have waived Seller's representations as to deficiencies not reported. In the event repairs or replacements are required, Seller shall pay up to 3% of the purchase price for such repairs or replacements by an appropriately licensed person. However, if the cost for such repairs or replacements exceed 3% of the purchase price, Buyer or Seller may elect to pay such excess, failing which either party may cancel this Contract. In the event Seller is unable to correct the deficiencies prior to closing, the cost thereof shall be paid into escrow at closing. Seller agrees to provide utilities service for inspections upon reasonable notice. Between the Effective Date and the closing, Seller shall maintain the Property and Personalty including but not limited to the lawn and shrubbery, in the condition herein represented, ordinary wear and tear excepted. Buyer shall be permitted access for inspection of the Property prior to closing in order to confirm compliance with the foregoing.

O.   RISK OF LOSS: If the improvements are damaged, by fire or other casualty prior to closing, and costs of restoring same does not exceed 3% of the assessed valuation of the improvements so damaged, cost of restoration shall be an obligation of the Seller and closing shall proceed pursuant to the terms of Contract with cost therefor escrowed at closing. In the event the cost of repair or restoration exceeds 3% of the assessed valuation of the improvements so damaged, Buyer shall have the option of either taking the Property as is, together with either the said 3% or any insurance proceeds payable by virtue of such loss or damage, or of cancelling Contract and receiving return of deposit(s) made hereunder.

P.   PROCEEDS OF SALE; CLOSING PROCEDURE: The deed shall be recorded upon clearance of funds and evidence of title continued at Buyer's expense, to show title in Buyer, without any encumbrances or change which would render Seller's title unmarketable from the date of the last evidence, and the proceeds of the sale shall be held in escrow by Seller's attorney or by such other escrow agent as may be mutually agreed upon for a period of not longer than five (5) days from and after closing date. If Seller's title is rendered unmarketable, Buyer shall within said five (5) day period, notify Seller in writing of the defect and Seller shall have 30 days from date of receipt of such notification to cure said defect. In the event Seller fails to timely cure said defect, all monies paid hereunder shall, upon written demand therefor and within five (5) days thereafter, be returned to Buyer and, simultaneously with such repayment, Buyer shall vacate the Property and reconvey same to the Seller by special warranty deed and return the Personalty. In the event Buyer fails to make timely demand for refund, Buyer shall take title as is, waiving all rights against Seller as to such intervening defect except as may be available to Buyer by virtue of warranties, if any, contained in the deed. In the event a portion of the purchase price is to be derived from institutional financing or refinancing, the requirements of the lending institution as to place, time of day and procedures for closing, and for disbursement of mortgage proceeds, shall control, anything in this Contract to the contrary notwithstanding. Provided, however, that the Seller shall have the right to require from such lending institution at closing a commitment that it will not withhold disbursement of mortgage proceeds as a result of any title defect attributable to Buyer-mortgagor. The escrow and closing procedure required by this Standard may be waived in the event the attorney, title agent or closing agent insures against adverse matters pursuant to Section 627.7841, F.S. (1983), as amended.

Q.   ESCROW: Any escrow agent receiving funds or equivalent is authorized and agrees by acceptance thereof to deposit promptly and to hold same in escrow and subject to clearance thereof to disburse same in accordance with terms and conditions of the Contract. Failure of clearance of funds shall not excuse performance by the Buyer. In the event of doubt as to escrow agent's duties or liabilities under the provisions of this Contract, the escrow agent may in agent's sole discretion, continue to hold the subject matter of this escrow until the parties mutually agree to the disbursement thereof, or until a judgment of a court of competent jurisdiction shall determine the rights of the parties thereto, or escrow agent may deposit same with the clerk of the circuit court having jurisdiction of the dispute, and upon notifying all parties concerned of such action, all liability on the part of the escrow agent shall fully terminate, except to the extent of accounting for any items theretofore delivered out of escrow. If a licensed real estate broker, the escrow agent will comply with provisions of Chapter 475, F.S. (1983), as amended. In the event of any suit between Buyer and Seller wherein the escrow agent is made a party by virtue of acting as an escrow agent hereunder, or in the event of any suit wherein escrow agent interpleads the subject matter of this escrow, the agent shall be entitled to recover reasonable attorney's fee and costs incurred, said fees and costs to be charged and assessed as court costs in favor of the prevailing party. All parties agree that the escrow agent shall not be liable to any party or person whomsoever for misdelivery to Buyer or Seller of items subject to this escrow, unless such misdelivery shall be due to willful breach of this Contract or gross negligence on the part of the agent.

R.   ATTORNEY FEES; COSTS: In connection with any litigation arising out of this Contract, the prevailing party shall be entitled to recover reasonable attorney's fees and costs.

S.   FAILURE OF PERFORMANCE: If Buyer fails to perform this Contract within the time specified, (including payment of all deposits hereunder), the deposit(s) paid by the Buyer may be retained by or for the account of Seller as liquidated damages, consideration for the execution of this Contract and in full settlement of any claims; whereupon Buyer and Seller shall be relieved of all obligations under the Contract; or Seller, at Seller's option, may proceed at law or in equity to enforce Seller's legal rights under this Contract. If, for any reason other than failure of Seller to make Seller's title marketable after diligent effort, Seller fails, neglects or refuses to perform this Contract, the Buyer may seek specific performance or elect to receive the return of Buyer's deposit(s) without thereby waiving any action for damages resulting from Seller's breach.

T.   CONTRACT NOT RECORDABLE; PERSONS BOUND; NOTICE: Neither this Contract nor any notice thereof shall be recorded in any public records. This Contract shall bind and inure to the benefit of the parties hereto and their successors in interest. Whenever the context permits, singular shall include plural and one gender shall include all. Notice given by or to the attorney for any party shall be as effective as if given by or to said party.

U.   CONVEYANCE: Seller shall convey title to the Property by statutory warranty, trustee, personal representative or guardian deed, as appropriate to the status of Seller, subject only to matters contained in Paragraph VII hereof and those otherwise accepted by Buyer. Personalty shall, at request of Buyer, be conveyed by an absolute bill of sale with warranty of title, subject to such matters as may be otherwise provided for herein.

V.   OTHER AGREEMENTS: No prior or present agreements or representations shall be binding upon Buyer or Seller unless included in this Contract. No modification or change in this Contract shall be valid or binding upon the parties unless in writing and executed by the party or parties to be bound thereby.

Rev. 1/85

visions and are thereby agreed to by the parties. The contract also includes a space to specify items of personal property and questionable items (such as the carpet described in Frame 6–1) as property to which title is being conveyed. The purchase price and form of payment are listed in paragraph II, and a financing contingency clause is provided in III.

Buyers normally pay a deposit (known as escrow money, earnest money, or a binder) at the time they make an offer to show that they are serious and to indemnify the sellers in the event they (the buyers) fail to perform. The broker holds the deposit in a segregated account called an *escrow account* until closing or until other arrangements are made for its disposition.

The contract form also covers type of title evidence, time for acceptance by the parties, closing date, restrictions, easements, limitations, occupancy, assignability, priority of handwritten or typewritten provisions, an insulation rider, and special clauses. Spaces are provided for signatures of witnesses, as well as for those of the principals.

A section is provided for a separate agreement between the sellers and the broker. The sellers agree to pay the broker a commission at time of closing from the disbursement of proceeds. If the buyers fail to perform, the broker and sellers agree to split any deposits, with the broker's share not to exceed the amount of the commission. If the sellers fail to perform, they agree to pay the full commission to the broker.

PRELIMINARY CONTRACTS

Many real estate transactions are quite complex and must be consummated in several stages. Therefore, when preliminary agreement is reached or when one step of a transaction must be completed before proceeding to the next, the parties may use a preliminary contract. Such contracts precede a contract for sale and purchase and are of three types— *binders, letters of intent,* and *options.*

Binder

A binder is an agreement between a potential buyer and seller that commits both parties to sign a contract for sale and purchase after certain details are worked out. The binder contains some of the essential elements to which both parties have already agreed (such as sale price, financing terms, and closing date), but it omits many details. Matters typically excluded from the binder are items to be prorated, repairs, insurance coverage, tenants' fixtures and appliances, termite protection, and warranties about the physical condition of the property.

Buyers usually use binders to tie up a property quickly so it can't be sold to someone else. Such buyers may believe the property is uniquely suitable to their needs or that the price is quite favorable. In effect, they gamble that no significant defects to the property or to the terms of the transaction will arise. Since the binder obligates both parties to negotiate a contract for sale, buyers may have to accept a defect or disadvantage that becomes known after execution of the binder.

Letter of Intent

This type of preliminary contract obligates potential parties to a transaction to negotiate seriously, but it does not require them to effect a transaction. Thus, a letter of intent is less binding than a binder. The letter of intent is used in complex transactions that require long and detailed negotiations. It indicates the good faith and intention of both parties and thus gives them confidence that negotiations will be fruitful and that the time and effort necessary to effect a transaction will not be wasted. Even so, there is the risk that the seller may sell the property to another party who better meets the seller's conditions and terms.

Option

An option is an agreement between a property owner and a potential buyer in which, for agreed payment(s), the owner will sell the property at a specified price and under specified terms and conditions. An option exists for a limited period. If the potential buyer *(optionee)* does not exercise the right to purchase the property during this time, the right expires, and the owner *(optioner)* retains both the property and the option payment(s). If the optionee exercises the right of purchase, the property is conveyed to the buyer under the terms, conditions, and price agreed to in the option.

Options are typically used in large development projects to tie up part of the needed land while negotiations continue for adjacent tracts of land. Owners are often willing to grant options in such circumstances because the developers offer a price considerably higher than the property's market value. Of course, the higher price is made possible by the projected success of the completed project, which may involve assembling several parcels of land. The enhanced value of two or more parcels of land assembled into a single unit is termed *plattage*. The assembled land is worth more than the sum of the individual parcels.

A developer uses options to limit potential losses. If the developer successfully assembles the needed properties, the project can proceed. If, however, some of the needed parcels cannot be obtained, the developer does not exercise the option. The losses are limited to the amounts paid for options—usually a much smaller amount than that required to purchase the parcels.

Options for Disney World

In the 1960s, Disney Productions, Inc., used options to acquire the vast tract of land for Disney World and Epcot Center in Florida. Options were purchased from many land owners while negotiations continued on other parcels. In some cases, "straw men" were used as optionees to conceal the connection with Disney Productions. In this way, owners would not know that one developer was attempting to assemble the land (owners tend to inflate prices when they know their land is crucial to a single development project). When the land was finally assembled—a process that took more than five years—Disney owned 3 million acres in central Florida.

ASSIGNMENT

In general, most contracts—including real estate contracts—can be assigned. Assignment means that one party's contractual rights and obligations are transferred to someone else. If buyers of real estate assign the contract, new buyers, in effect, take their place. The new buyers may pay the agreed price and obtain title to the property.

But any type of *personal performance* contracted by one party cannot be assigned without that party's permission. For example, if the seller has agreed to take a purchase-money mortgage as part of the payment for the property, the buyer cannot assign this right to someone else unless he or she remains personally liable to the seller for payment of the loan. Similarly, land (installment sale) contracts are not assignable without the owner's permission. In these situations, the seller relies on the buyer's qualifications, and the assignee may not be as well qualified.

Note that even though buyers assign their rights to someone else, they do not escape liability under the contract. They are still obligated to the seller and, should the assignees not fulfill the contract's requirements, the seller can look to the assignors for satisfaction. In effect, assignment is an agreement by the assignee to carry out the obligations of the assignor; the assignor's contract with the other party is not affected.

Of course, the other party can agree to an assignment and relieve the assignor of all obligations. When this occurs, a contract is created between the third party and the assignee which absolves the assignor of further responsibility under the contract.

A contract can also prohibit assignment. Such a prohibition would be contained in an *assignment clause.*

REMEDIES FOR NONPERFORMANCE

Buyers and sellers sometimes fail to live up to a contract's provisions. They may change their minds for a number of reasons. For example, if one spouse dies, the other may not want to move. Or, if their financial circumstances change, they may decide they cannot afford a new home.

When a party fails to perform (*breach of contract, nonperformance,* or *default),* the other party may have one or more remedies.

Remedies for a Seller

If a buyer defaults, a seller may take one of the following actions:

1. *Rescind the contract.* The contract is cancelled, and any deposits are returned to the buyer.
2. *Sue for specific performance.* The seller asks a court to require the buyer to complete the transaction and to live up to all other provisions of the contract.
3. *Sue for damages.* The seller may sue the buyer for any loss of financial advantage. Damages are measured as the difference between the purchase price and the market value of the property. If no difference can be shown, the seller is not able to collect.

Remedies for a Buyer

If a seller defaults, the buyer may:

1. *Rescind the contract.* The contract is cancelled, and any earnest-money deposits are returned to the buyer.
2. *Sue for specific performance.* The buyer asks a court to require the seller to convey title to the property to him or her and to live up to all other provisions of the contract.
3. *Sue for damages.* The buyer may sue the seller for any loss of financial advantage. Damages are measured as the difference between the market value of the property and the purchase price. If no difference can be shown, the buyer is not able to collect.

Suits for damages and specific performance by buyers or sellers are costly and time-consuming. Therefore, in most instances of nonperformance, particularly for properties of relatively modest value (say, under $500,000), such suits are uncommon. Most form contracts contain a provision awarding all or a portion of earnest-money deposits to a seller if a buyer defaults, and this remedy is most often followed. Contracts can also provide for *liquidated damages* of a specified amount in the event of seller nonperformance. Under such a provision, the sellers would have to put a specified amount of cash in escrow which would be given to the buyers if the sellers back out of the sale. However, sellers are usually unwilling to put up earnest money for this purpose. They have, in effect, put up their property, and a suit for specific performance would be effective in most cases.

Escrow

To lessen the chances for nonperformance, real estate contracts are often placed in escrow. An escrow agent is a third party who is instructed to carry out the provisions of the contract by means of a separate escrow agreement. The escrow agent must be impartial and may not benefit from the provisions of the purchase and sale contract. The escrow agent is allowed, of course, to collect a fee for services rendered.

Escrow agents are usually attorneys, financial institutions, or title companies. They hold the documents and funds relevant to a transaction and distribute them according to the written instructions at time of closing.

For example, a buyer would give a deposit or full purchase price to the escrow agent, while the seller would deliver a deed and evidence of title (such as an abstract or a title insurance policy) to the escrow agent. Insurance policies, mortgage financing information, and any other documents would also be provided. When all the documents have been assembled, title has been searched, funds have been obtained, and all other conditions met, the escrow agent delivers the deed to the buyer and the funds to the seller.

When escrow agents are not used, attorneys or financial institutions usually provide closing services. Although they assemble the necessary documents and arrange for the title search and evidence of title, the real estate broker may hold the earnest-money deposit until closing. The broker, however, must hold the deposit for the benefit of the principal, cannot commingle deposits with personal funds, and must not disburse deposits except as provided in the contract.

━━━━━━━━━━━━━━━━━━━━━━━━━ *Frame 6–3* ━━━━━━━━━━━━━━━━━━━━━━━━━

Cases on Real Estate Contracts

Case No. 1

Lach paid a deposit of $1,000 to Cahill for the purchase of a house. The sales contract recited that, "This agreement is contingent upon buyer (Lach) being able to obtain a mortgage . . . on the premises." Lach applied to a bank for a mortgage, but his application was denied. Thereafter, his application was denied by five other lending institutions. Cahill was unwilling to finance the house himself, and Lach notified Cahill that he was unable to secure a mortgage and that he wanted his deposit returned. When Cahill refused to return the $1,000 deposit, Lach brought legal action to recover the deposit.

Issue:

Was Lach entitled to the return of his deposit?

Decision:

Yes. Lach had no duty to buy Cahill's house.

Reasons:

To recover his deposit, Lach was required to show (1) that his ability to secure a mortgage was a *condition precedent* to his duty to perform under the terms of the sales contract; and (2) that he had made a reasonable effort to secure financing. A condition precedent is a factor or event which the parties intend must exist or take place before the duty of performance arises. If the condition is not fulfilled, the right to enforce the contract does not come into existence. The language of the contract clearly showed that Lach's ability to secure a mortgage was a condition precedent to his performance. The condition, in addition, implies a promise by Lach that he would make reasonable efforts to secure a suitable mortgage. His attempts to find financing were reasonable under the circumstances, and Lach should accordingly recover his deposit.

Lach v. *Cahill*, 85 A.2d 481 (Conn. 1951).

Case No. 2

This is an appeal from an order granting a motion by the defendants Paul and Catherine Cooper to dismiss the complaint for specific performance of a purported real estate sales contract due to unenforceability under the statute of frauds . . . .

The complaint alleges that on February 16, 1978, plaintiff, William Jones, presented defendants with an unsigned form contract in writing for the purchase of certain real estate . . . . The complaint also alleges that plaintiff delivered a $12,000 check to defendants, payable to Paul and Catherine Cooper, the check stating on its face that it was earnest money for the purchase of 029 Lakeview, Mundelein. Defendants endorsed the check and negotiated it on or about February 25, 1978, but never signed the form sales contract. The transaction was not closed, the $12,000 was not returned, and plaintiff brought suit for specific performance of the contract. The contract was not signed by any of the parties, nor did the names of the seller or purchaser appear on the contract; nor did it contain a legal description, but it did include the address 029 Lakeview, Mundelein, with a lot size of "150 × 150"; it further provided for $12,000 earnest money in the form of a check, payable to sellers and to be deposited by sellers on acceptance of the contract, and that the contract was to be void if not accepted by February 28, 1978. The contract also contained the purchase price, method of payment, terms and conditions of sale.

Trial Court

In granting the motion to dismiss, the trial court ruled that the contract violates the statute of frauds for lack of signatures; that the check does not satisfy the signature requirement because it does not express the terms and conditions of sale;

that the letter does not express the terms and conditions of sale; and that the letter from the law firm regarding the policy of title insurance does not satisfy the signature requirement because it was not signed by defendants or their authorized agent.

The Statute of Frauds requires that a contract for the sale of land must be in writing and be signed by the parties to be charged. . . . It is true, as both sides state, that a contract may consist of several documents. . . . However, where such a situation occurs it is necessary that the signed writing refer expressly to the unsigned writing or writings, or that the several writings be so connected, either physically or otherwise, that it may be determined by internal evidence that they relate to the same contract. . . . In the present cause, the signed writing (the check) does not state the price or the conditions of sale, nor does it refer specifically to the unsigned written contract. The check was in fact signed by plaintiff and both defendants. However, the form contract specifically calls for the purchaser of 029 Lakeview, Mundelein, to deliver to the "Owner of Record" a $12,000 check as an earnest-money deposit, to be deposited by seller on acceptance of the contract; it further provides that the earnest money shall be returned and the contract rendered void if not accepted on or before February 28, 1978.

Appelate Court

In light of the above, it is our opinion that the form contract and the check are, by their own terms, sufficiently connected as to allow them to be read together. Both documents refer to the same common address in the same amount as the earnest money specified in the contract; the check and the contract are dated with the same date; and defendants endorsed and cashed the check prior to February 28, 1978, as required by the contract. In reading the contract and the check together, it is apparent that the requirements of the Statute of Frauds were met, and that the trial court erred in ruling otherwise. In so holding, we do not comment on the enforceability of the contract by specific performance, nor on any of the requirements to obtain such relief. . . .

Reversed and remanded.

Jones v. *Olsen* 400 NE 2d 665 (Ill. App. 1980).

CONTINUING SAGA OF A SALE

Recall from Chapter 4 that Fred and Louise Johnson have listed their house with Town and Country Realtors® through William Heath, a salesman with the firm. The listing price is $85,000. Another salesperson, Linda Lavin, shows the Johnson home to George and Helen Jones, who are moving to Gainesville from Ohio. They like the house and believe it would suit their needs, but they note several maintenance and replacement items. They believe they would have to paint the interior and exterior, install new carpeting, and purchase drapes. Also, they would like to obtain some second financing from the Johnsons at a lower-than-market interest rate, if possible. Thus, they decide to make the following offer:

Price	$80,000
Financing	New ARM loan of $64,000 from a local lending institution at 9.75 percent (adjusted annually); $10,000 second mortgage from the Johnsons at 10 percent for five years; $5,000 cash equity.
Closing	30 days
Binder deposit	$1,000

George and Linda present the offer to the Johnsons, who reject it and counter with a price of $83,000 with no second financing. The counteroffer is then presented to the Joneses. They accept this offer contingent on their obtaining a 30-year 80-percent ARM loan commitment at an initial rate not to exceed 9.75 percent for 30 years. They also want the sellers to furnish a title insurance policy and a termite inspection report. This offer/counteroffer process is reflected in the sale contract form shown in Exhibit 6–3.

OVERVIEW

The contract for sale is the most important document in real estate. It contains the rights and obligations to which the principals in a transaction—buyers and sellers—commit themselves. The contract governs all elements of a transaction; a court can enforce its provisions.

Contracts for sale can be simple or complex. They may be typed, handwritten, or prepared on preprinted forms. No matter what the form, however, an agreement is valid and enforceable if it contains the seven elements required of real estate contracts—(1) competent parties, (2) offer and acceptance, (3) consideration, (4) legal objective, (5) no defects to mutual assent, (6) written form, and (7) a proper description of the property.

Since a contract is a legally binding document, buyers and sellers can protect themselves by having a competent attorney examine the contract before signing; after the contract has been signed is too late—any changes would have to be agreed to by both parties.

When one party breaks the provisions of a contract, the other party may have one or more remedies. Either buyer or seller may (1) rescind the contract, (2) sue for specific performance, or (3) sue for damages. Additionally, some contracts may specify actions that can be taken by one party in the event of default by the other party. For example, the seller

EXHIBIT 6-3

GAINESVILLE BOARD OF REALTORS® , INC.

DEPOSIT RECEIPT AND
PURCHASE AND SALE AGREEMENT
CONVENTIONAL FINANCING

REALTOR®

Date __May 1,__ _____ 19 _87_

Receipt is hereby acknowledged by __William Heath, Town and Country Realtors__, hereinafter called REALTOR, of the sum of __one thousand dollars__ ($1,000.00) (by check) from __George and Helen Jones__, hereinafter called BUYER, as a deposit and as a part of the purchase price on account of an offer to purchase the property of __Fred and Louise Johnson__, hereinafter called SELLER, said property being in __Alachua__ County, Florida, and described as follows:

Tax Parcel No. 6029-040-03

Parcel #3, Block 2 of Spring Meadow Estates, Gainesville, Alachua County, Florida

Also known as: __1822 NW 40th Avenue__

Together with the following personal property:

1 Range, 1 Refrigerator, 2 Window Air Conditioners, and 1 Picnic Table

The SELLER hereby agrees to sell said property to the BUYER and the BUYER hereby agrees to purchase said property from the SELLER upon the following terms and conditions: $83,000.00 GJ. F.J. $80,000.00 H.J. L.J.

1. PURCHASE AND SALES PRICE

   Payable as follows:

   (a) Deposit paid herewith .... $ 1,000.00

   (b) Additional Deposit .... ------------

   (c) Cash at Closing (U.S. cash, certified or cashiers check) 69,000.00

   (d) Balance payable .... -10,000.00 $83,000.00 GJ. F.J. $80,000.00 H.J. L.J.

   ~~(e) second mortgage from sellers at 10%, 10 years, amort monthly~~

   TOTAL PURCHASE AND SALES PRICE

2. TERMS AND CONDITIONS:

   a. Contingent upon buyer's obtaining a commitment of an ARM loan with initial interest rate of 9.75 percent, with a 30 year term in the amount of ~~$64,000.00.~~ $66,400.00 H.J.

   b. ~~Contingent upon seller's providing a second mortgage of $10,000 for 10 years at 10 percent, amortized monthly.~~   F.J. L.J.

   c. Contingent upon seller's providing a title insurance policy, as described in 3 below.

3. ABSTRACT-TITLE INSURANCE POLICY: (Check one) The SELLER shall furnish either ☐ an abstract from earliest records to date, showing his title to be marketable or insurable, or ☐ SELLER shall furnish an ALTA Owner's Title Insurance Binder Form A and Policy insuring title from a recognized Title Insurance Company doing business in this area, said Abstract or Title Insurance Binder to be delivered to the BUYER, or his Attorney or Agent, whose name is __James Henry__ within __20__ days from __May 1, 1987__.

4. EXAMINATION OF TITLE: The BUYER or his Attorney shall have __10__ days within which to examine said Abstract of Title or Title Binder and to signify his willingness to accept the same, whereupon the transaction shall be concluded on __June 1, 1987__ or such earlier date as may be mutually agreeable.

   If the title is unmarketable, the SELLER shall have __10__ days or a reasonable period of time within which to cure the designated defects in the title that render same unmarketable or uninsurable in the opinion of the BUYER or his said Agent, and the SELLER hereby agrees to use reasonable diligence in curing said defects, and upon the defects being cured and notice of that fact being given to the BUYER or his said Agent, this transaction shall be closed within __10__ days of delivery of such notice. At the option of the BUYER, upon SELLER's failure or inability to correct the marketability of the title within the time limit or a reasonable period of time, the SELLER shall deliver the title in its existing condition, otherwise the earnest money deposit shall be returned to the BUYER upon demand therefor, and all rights and liabilities on the part of the BUYER arising hereunder shall terminate. Provided, however, that in the event of disagreement between the SELLER and the BUYER as to the marketability of the title, the SELLER may offer a binder for an ALTA Form A or equivalent policy issued by a recognized title insurance company doing business in this area, agreeing to insure said title against all exceptions other than those mentioned in this agreement and the standard printed exceptions, which binder shall be conclusive that said title is marketable, said Binder and policies pursuant thereto shall be paid for by the BUYER.

5. KIND OF CONVEYANCE. Conveyance of title shall be by full WARRANTY DEED to __George and Helen Jones__ __as joint tenants with right of survivorship__ and clear of all encumbrances and liens of whatsoever nature, except taxes for the current year, and except as herein otherwise provided. The SELLER shall also deliver to the BUYER a lien and possession affidavit at closing.

6. RESTRICTIONS, EASEMENTS, LIMITATIONS: The BUYER shall take title subject to: zoning, restrictions, prohibitions and other requirements imposed by governmental authority; restrictions and matters appearing on the plat or otherwise common to the subdivision; public utility easements of record; taxes for year of closing and subsequent years, assumed mortgages and purchase money mortgages, if any; other: __none__ provided, however, that there exists at closing no violation of the foregoing and that the foregoing do not affect the marketability of title, and they do not prevent the use of the Property for __single-family residential__ purpose(s).

7. EXPENSES: BUYER shall pay for the following expenses: (a) Title examination and title opinion; (b) Recording of deed; (c) All expenses relative to all Notes and Mortgages or Contract for Deed, and transfer of existing mortgages; (d) Survey, if any; (e) BUYER's Attorney's fee. SELLER shall pay for: (a) Real Estate Compensation; (b) Abstract or Title Insurance; (c) Preparation of Instruments of Conveyance; (d) Documentary Stamps on Deed; (e) Termite Inspection Fee; (f) SELLER's Attorney's Fee.

8. PRORATIONS: All taxes for the current year, rentals, insurance premiums, association assessments and interest on existing mortgages (if any) shall be prorated as of the date of closing with BUYER paying for the day of closing. If part of the purchase price is to be evidenced by the assumption of a mortgage requiring deposit of funds in escrow for payment of taxes, insurance or other charges, the BUYER agrees to reimburse the SELLER for escrowed funds assigned to BUYER at closing, with all mortgage payments to be current at the time of closing.

9. SURVEY: If the BUYER desires a survey of the property, he may have the property surveyed at his expense prior to the closing date. If the survey shows any encroachments on the land herein described, or that the improvements located on the land herein described encroach on other lands, or any shortages, written notice to that effect along with a copy of the survey shall be given to the SELLER and the same shall be treated as defects in title to be eliminated by SELLER.

This form is for the exclusive use of members in good standing of the Gainesville Board of REALTORS® unless its use by another person is authorized in writing by the Board of Directors.

REVISED 4/85, © 1984 Gainesville Board of REALTORS®, Inc. All Rights Reserved

EXHIBIT 6–3 *(concluded)*

10. PURCHASE MONEY MORTGAGES TO SELLER: The purchase money note and mortgage, if any, shall provide for a 30 day grace period in the event of default if it is a first mortgage and a 15 day grace period if a second mortgage; shall provide for right of prepayment in whole or in part without penalty; and shall not provide for acceleration or interest adjustment in event of resale of the property; and shall be otherwise in form and content in accordance with covenants established by the Eighth Judicial Circuit Bar Association. Said mortgage shall require all prior liens and encumbrances to be kept in good standing and shall forbid modifications of or future advances under prior mortgage(s).

11. VARIANCE IN AMOUNT OF FINANCING TO BE ASSUMED: Any variance in amount of financing to be assumed from the amount stated herein shall be added to or deducted from: purchase money financing if such is contemplated by this Agreement, otherwise, said variance shall be added to or deducted from the cash at closing, provided that if such procedure results in an increase in cash due at closing in excess of $500.00 or _____ BUYER shall not be obligated to perform unless Seller reduces the purchase price by the amount of the excess over the herein specified sum.

12. TERMITES, OR OTHER INFESTATION: SELLER shall furnish to BUYER or his attorney or his agent at least 5 days prior to closing a certificate of a locally licensed entomologist dated within thirty days prior to closing, showing any improvements on the premises, exclusive of fences and _____ _____ to be apparently free from active infestation (other than infestation by wood destroying fungi) or visible damage (including that caused by wood destroying fungi) by termites or other wood destroying organisms as required to be disclosed by Florida law. In the event active infestation or visible damage is found to be present, the SELLER shall bear the costs of remedying such active infestation and damage. Should the cost of such treatment and repair exceed $_____, the SELLER may elect to terminate this agreement and all rights and liabilities of all parties shall be at an end and the deposit shall be returned to BUYER, unless the BUYER elects to proceed with the transaction, having the above amount deducted from the purchase price. "Damage" as used in this paragraph shall mean only damage that affects the structural integrity of the structure and its components.

13. PAVING, SEWER AND SIMILAR LIENS, ASSESSMENTS AND FRONT FOOTAGE CHARGES: SELLER shall be responsible for payment of all charges relating to paving, sidewalk and other assessments whether in place or under construction as of the date of this Contract. Public utility fees, assessments, or front footage charges shall be paid as follows:
Check one (1):
(X) SELLER shall pay (or has paid) all costs of utilities including sewer and water frontage charges, sewer and water capital facilities charges and water meter charges.
( ) SELLER shall pay (or has paid) sewer and water front footage charges only.
( ) The subject property is presently not served with central water or sewer or SELLER shall not pay any cost of utilities.

14. DESTRUCTION OF PREMISES: If any improvements located on the above described premises at the time of the execution of this binder are damaged by fire or other casualty prior to closing, and can be restored to substantially the same condition within a period of thirty (30) days after such destruction occurs, SELLER shall so restore the improvements, and the closing date shall be extended accordingly. If such restoration cannot be completed within said period of time, this Contract, at the option of the BUYER, shall terminate and the deposit shall be returned to BUYER. All risk of loss prior to closing shall be borne by SELLER.

15. FAILURE OF PERFORMANCE: If BUYER fails to perform this Contract within the time specified, (INCLUDING PAYMENT OF ALL DEPOSITS HEREUNDER), the deposit(s) paid by the BUYER aforesaid may be retained by or for the account of SELLER as liquidated damages, consideration for the execution of this Contract and in full settlement of any claims; whereupon all parties shall be relieved of all obligations under the Contract; or SELLER, at SELLER's option, may proceed at law or in equity to enforce SELLER's legal rights under this Contract. If, for any reason other than failure of SELLER to render SELLER's title marketable after diligent effort, SELLER fails, neglects or refuses to perform this Contract, the BUYER may seek specific performance or elect to receive the return of BUYER's deposit(s) without thereby waiving any action for damage resulting from SELLER's breach.

16. INSPECTION, REPAIR AND MAINTENANCE: Unless otherwise stated in this Agreement, SELLER warrants that: (a) the roof, (excluding the facia and soffit does not have any visible evidence of leaks or structural damage. In the event repairs or replacements are required, SELLER shall pay up to $ 100.00 for such repairs or replacements by an appropriately licensed person. However, if the cost for such repairs or replacements exceeds $ 5----/-- BUYER or SELLER may elect to pay such excess, failing which either party may cancel this Contract, (b) SELLER further warrants that the septic tank, pool, all major appliances, heating, cooling, electrical, plumbing systems and machinery are in good working condition. In the event repairs or replacements are required, SELLER shall pay up to $ 100.00 for such repairs or replacements by an appropriately licensed person. However, if the cost for such repairs or replacements exceeds $ 500.00 BUYER or SELLER may elect to pay such excess, failing which either party may cancel this Contract. BUYER may, at BUYER's expense, have inspections made of the roof and said items by an appropriately licensed person dealing in the construction, repair and maintenance thereof and shall report in writing to SELLER such items that do not meet the above warranty prior to possession or not less than ten (10) days prior to closing, whichever is first. Unless BUYER reports such deficiencies within said period, BUYER shall be deemed to have waived SELLER's warranties as to deficiencies not reported. In the event SELLER is unable to correct the failures prior to closing, the sums may be paid into escrow at closing to cover the cost of repairs or replacements. SELLER agrees to provide availability of utilities for inspection upon a reasonable notice. Notwithstanding the provisions hereof, between the date of this Contract and the closing, SELLER shall maintain the real and personal property in the condition herein warranted, reasonable wear and tear excepted, and shall maintain the lawn and shrubbery, in substantially the same condition as exists upon the date of execution of this Contract. BUYER's designee shall be permitted reasonable access for inspection prior to closing in order to confirm the compliance with the maintenance requirements.

17. POSSESSION: BUYER shall be given possession of said property upon closing

18. ATTORNEY'S FEES AND COSTS: If any litigation arises under this agreement between BUYER and SELLER, the prevailing party shall be entitled to recover from the non prevailing party all reasonable costs incurred in the trial court and on appeal by the prevailing party including a reasonable attorney's fee.

19. OTHER AGREEMENTS: This Contract constitutes the entire agreement between the parties, and any changes, amendments, or modifications hereof shall be void unless the same are reduced to writing and signed by the parties hereto.

20. TIME FOR ACCEPTANCE: If this Contract is not executed by all parties hereto on or before May 3, 19 87 the aforesaid deposit shall be, at the option of the BUYER, returned to him, and the Contract shall be null and void. The date of the Contract for purposes of performance shall be regarded as the date of execution by the last party to the Contract.

21. Disbursement of closing proceeds shall be made as soon after closing as final title certification and examination have been made, but which shall be no later than five (5) business days after closing. The binder deposits referred to herein shall be held in accordance with applicable statutes.

22. Typewritten or handwritten provisions inserted in this form shall control all printed provisions in conflict therewith.

23. THIS IS A LEGALLY BINDING CONTRACT AND SHALL NOT BE RECORDED UNLESS OTHERWISE AGREED TO BETWEEN THE PARTIES. IF NOT FULLY UNDERSTOOD, SEEK COMPETENT LEGAL ADVICE. DO NOT SIGN UNTIL ALL BLANKS ARE COMPLETED. YOUR REALTOR RECOMMENDS THAT YOU OBTAIN TITLE INSURANCE OR A TITLE OPINION FROM YOUR ATTORNEY.

By: Town and Country Realtors, William Heath   By: _____
    REALTOR

I, or we, agree to purchase the above described property on the terms and conditions stated in the foregoing instrument.

Dated this day of May 1, 19 87

WITNESSES: BUYER:

William Heath   George Jones

Linda Larvin   Helen Jones

I, or we, agree to sell the above mentioned property to the BUYER, or his nominee, on the terms and conditions stated in the above instrument, and by the signatures attached on the 3 day of May , 19 87 signify our acceptance and approval of the proposed sale.

WITNESSES: SELLER:

William Heath   Fred Johnson

Annette Griffin   Louise Johnson

SELLER agrees to pay the licensed real estate Broker (REALTOR*) named below, at time of closing, from the disbursements of the proceeds of sale, compensation in the amount of $4,980.00 for his services in effecting the sale by finding a BUYER ready, willing and able to purchase pursuant to the foregoing Contract. In the event BUYER fails to perform and the deposit(s) is retained, 50% thereof, but not exceeding the REALTOR's fee above computed, shall be paid to the REALTOR, as full consideration for REALTOR's services including costs expended by REALTOR, and the balance shall be paid to SELLER. If the transaction shall not be closed because of refusal or failure of SELLER to perform, the SELLER shall pay said fee in full to REALTOR on demand. In any litigation concerning the brokerage fee, the prevailing party shall be entitled to recover reasonable attorney fees and costs.

By: Town and Country Realtors, Gainesville, Fla.   Fred Johnson
    (Name & Address of Selling REALTOR)   (Seller)

same   Louise Johnson
    (Name of Listing REALTOR)   (Seller)

This form is for the exclusive use of members in good standing of the Gainesville Board of REALTORS* unless its use by another person is authorized in writing by the Board of Directors.

may be able to retain all or a portion of any deposits if the buyer fails to complete the transaction. Escrow agents often assist in carrying out the provisions of a contract and lessen the chances of default by either party.

TEST YOURSELF

Explain the following concepts and procedures presented in this chapter.

1. Contract for sale—requirements.
2. Elements of a contract for the sale of real estate.
3. Fraud versus misrepresentation.
4. Parol evidence rule.
5. Statute of frauds.
6. Legal title versus equitable title.
7. Binder.
8. Letter of intent.
9. Option.
10. Assignment.

Answer the following multiple-choice questions.

1. If a buyer defaults on a contract to purchase real property, which of the following is *not* a remedy that the seller can pursue?
   a. Rescind the contract.
   b. Sue for damages.
   c. Sue for assignment.
   d. Return all or part of the binder deposit.
   e. Sue for specific performance.

2. When contracts for the sale of real property are placed with a disinterested third party for executing and closing, they are said to be placed in:
   a. Safe keeping.
   b. A title company or financial institution.
   c. Option.
   d. Escrow.
   e. Assignment.

3. Which of the following conditions would be a defect to mutual assent in a contract for the sale of real property?
   a. One party attempts to perpetrate fraud on the other.
   b. The contract is in written form.
   c. The contract contains an inadequate description of the property.
   d. One of the parties is legally incompetent.
   e. The contract does not specify a time for closing.

4. If some of the terms and/or conditions of a contract are inferred from the acts or conduct of the parties, rather than expressly stated, the contract is known as a(n):
   a. Parol contract.
   b. Executory contract.
   c. Inferred contract.
   d. Unspecified contract.
   e. Implied contract.

5. Which of the following is a unilateral contract?
   a. Contract for the sale of land.
   b. Contract for deed.
   c. Listing contract.
   d. Option contract.
   e. Parol contract.

ADDITIONAL READINGS

Atteberry, William L., Karl G. Pearson, and Michael P. Litka. *Real Estate Law.* New York: John Wiley & Sons, 1984, Chap. 12.

Bergfield, Philip B. *Principles of Real Estate Law.* New York: McGraw-Hill, 1979, Chap. 17.

Corley, Robert N., Peter J. Shedd, and Charles F. Floyd. *Real Estate and the Law.* New York: Random House, 1982, Chap. 11.

Kratovil, Robert, and Raymond J. Werner. *Real Estate Law.* 8th ed. Englewood Cliffs, N.J.: Prentice Hall, 1983, Chap. 9.

Lindeman, Bruce. *Real Estate Brokerage Management.* Reston, Va.: Reston Publishing, 1981, Chap. 9.

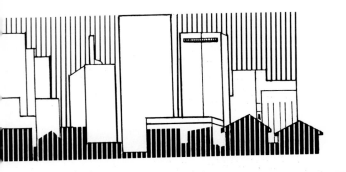

7
Closing Real Estate Transactions

OUTLINE

CONTINUING SAGA OF A SALE

The saga of the sale of Fred and Louise Johnson's house to George and Helen Jones continues. Recall from Chapter 6 (Contracts for Sale) that the contract for sale signed by the Johnsons and Joneses specifies that "The transaction shall be concluded on June 1, 1987, or such earlier date as may be mutually agreeable." It is now June 1, 1987.

The Johnsons, the Joneses, the Joneses' attorney, James Henry, and William Heath, the real estate salesman, arrive at the offices of Last Federal Savings and Loan Association, where closing is to take place. The Joneses' application for a 9.75-percent, 30-year adjustable-rate mortgage (ARM) was approved by Last Federal. Last Federal's attorney, Joe Jenkins, is there to handle the closing.

Steps before Closing

After signing the contract for sale on May 1, 1987, and before arriving for closing on June 1, 1987, the Joneses and their attorney took the following steps:

1. Had the property surveyed for possible encroachments.
2. Reviewed an abstract of documents in the public records to make certain there are no violations of private restrictions.
3. Reviewed the zoning ordinance to make certain that the property is used as legally permitted.
4. Examined the list of estimated closing costs to make certain they are correct and reasonable.
5. Examined the abstract to identify any encumbrances to which the buyers would be subject. Since there were none, except the existing mortgage to the Johnsons, the attorney needed only to obtain a *satisfaction of mortgage* at the closing, which would be recorded and show that the Johnsons' mortgage was paid off in full.

6. If the Joneses were assuming any mortgages, the attorney would obtain an *estoppel certificate* from the mortgagee that would show the amount being assumed, interest rate, length of debt period, periodic payments, and frequency of amortization.
7. Inspected the property to verify condition and vacancy for possession.
8. Reviewed the contract to make certain that other terms of the contract have been met by the sellers, such as having the property inspected for termites.
9. Made arrangements to have hazard insurance coverage, utilities, telephone, and other services begin on the date of closing.

The Johnsons also took some steps between the signing of the contract and the closing. They have:

1. Ordered the abstract brought up to date. Any defects in title or encroachments on the property have been remedied.
2. Had the abstract delivered to the buyers' attorney, Mr. Henry, for examination.
3. Ordered a termite inspection and had the certificate showing the improvements to be free of active infestation or visible damage delivered to the Joneses' attorney.
4. Ordered their hazard insurance coverage, utilities, and other services to be stopped on the closing date.

As closing agent and representative of Last Federal, Mr. Jenkins has obtained or prepared the following documents and legal instruments:

1. General warranty deed in proper form, to be signed by the Johnsons at closing.
2. Mortgage and note, to be signed by the Joneses at closing.
3. Leases, if any (none in this sale), to which title is subject.
4. Assignments of instruments, if any (none in this sale), which are being transferred to the buyers.
5. Check from the lender made payable to the seller.
6. Closing statement showing the expenses and obligations incurred by both parties. Real estate taxes for 1987, as specified in the contract for sale, are prorated between buyers and sellers as of the date of closing.

Steps at Closing

The Johnsons, the Joneses, Mr. Heath, Mr. Henry, and Mr. Jenkins go to a small conference room for the closing. They take seats around a rectangular table, with Mr. Jenkins sitting at the head of the table. He informs everyone that he is closing the transaction on behalf of Last Federal and is also serving as the Johnsons' attorney. He introduces Mr. Henry as the Joneses' attorney. Mr. Jenkins states that he has prepared all documents in accordance with the terms of the contract for sale, the loan application and approval, and applicable state and federal laws. He also states that he has coordinated title matters, inspections, and documents with Mr. Henry and Mr. Heath.

Mr. Jenkins presents copies of the composite closing statement shown in Exhibit 7–1 to the Johnsons and Joneses and explains it as follows: Debits are charges, or amounts due from each party. In this transaction the sellers are owed, or credited, the total purchase price of $83,000, and the buyers are debited this amount. The buyers are credited the binder deposit, since it has already been paid. There is no corresponding entry on the seller's statement because it is included in the total purchase price. The buyers are also credited with the amount of the new mortgage they are obtaining from Last Federal Savings and Loan. In effect, they are responsible for bringing these funds into the transaction and are committed to paying off the loan, with interest, over the next 30 years.

EXHIBIT 7–1
COMPOSITE CLOSING STATEMENT
JOHNSON SALE TO THE JONESES

Seller's Statement		Item	Buyer's Statement	
Debit	Credit		Debit	Credit
	$83,000.00	Purchase price	$83,000.00	
		Binder deposit		$ 1,000.00
		New mortgage		66,400.00
$ 220.00		Prorated taxes		220.00
		Expenses:		
		Loan origination fee	1,992.00	
		Lender's closing fee	150.00	
		Appraisal fee	200.00	
		Credit report	35.00	
		Prepaid items (taxes)	180.00	
527.50		Abstract continuation		
125.00		Attorney's fee	125.00	
		Documentary stamps:		
373.50		Deed		
		Mortgage note	99.60	
		Intangible tax-mortgage	132.80	
		Recording:		
		Mortgage	10.00	
		Deed	10.00	
4,980.00		Broker's commission		
35.00		Deed preparation		
25.00		Termite clearance		
		Survey	175.00	
6,286.00	83,000.00		86,109.40	67,620.00
76,714.00		To Seller—Amounts Due		
		—From Buyer		18,489.40
$83,000.00	$83,000.00	Grand Totals	$86,109.40	$86,109.40

Property taxes are the only item *prorated* in this transaction. Prorating means dividing an expense between buyers and sellers proportionately on the basis of the time the property is occupied by each party. Since property taxes are paid in arrears (after the period for which they are incurred), the *buyers* will have to pay the tax bill for the entire year of 1987. Therefore, they are given credit for the amount of time the property was occupied by the sellers—151 out of 365 days. Since the total tax bill for 1987 was estimated to be $531.79, the credit of $220 to the buyers (and debit of the same amount to the sellers) is calculated as follows:

$$\frac{151}{365} \times \$531.79 = \$220.00$$

The buyers are charged for various expenses incurred to obtain the loan and to purchase the property. The lender charged a fee of 3 points (3 percent of the loan amount) to originate (make) the loan, a closing fee of $150, an appraisal fee of $200, and a credit report fee of $35. The lender also requires the borrowers (buyers) to pay four months of estimated 1987 taxes into escrow (a segregated account). Mr. Henry is charging $125 for his services.

Documentary stamp taxes are required on the loan documents in the amounts shown, and the lender requires borrowers to pay these amounts. The calculation of these items is discussed further in the section on preparation of closing statements. It should be noted, however, that such taxes vary from state to state.

The borrowers must also pay to have both the mortgage and the deed recorded. Recording documents in the public records provides *constructive notice* of an interest in real property. It informs anyone who may have a potential interest in the property of both the owner's and the lender's interests.

The final expense charged to the buyers is for a survey of the property. Most lenders require that borrowers have property serving as security for a loan surveyed. A survey enables the lenders (and owners) to know the exact boundaries of the property so that any encroachments can be detected. Without a survey, lenders and owners run the risk that buildings and other improvements, such as driveways, have been constructed on someone else's property. Needless to say, such encroachments can drastically affect the value of the property.

The sellers' first expense is for continuation of the abstract. An abstract is a summary of documents recorded in the public records that affect the title to the property. It would be very time-consuming and expensive for the buyers' attorney to find and review every document recorded. Thus, abstract (or title) companies perform this service. If an entirely new abstract is required, the cost is relatively high; in most cases, however, an abstract already exists and can simply be brought up to date. After the abstract has been updated, it can be examined by the buyers' attorney to determine whether the buyers will obtain clear title.

The sellers are also responsible for paying the attorney's fee charged by Mr. Jenkins, the brokerage commission of 6 percent of the sale price, and the costs of preparing the deed and a termite inspection. These amounts, together with the debit for prorated taxes, are deducted from the sale price of $83,000. The sellers will thus receive a check for $76,714.00. The buyers must write a personal check for $18,489.40, which together with the binder deposit, borrowed funds, and prorated tax credit will cover all the amounts owed.

To assure that the amounts received fully cover amounts owed, a cash reconciliation statement (Exhibit 7–2) has been prepared. All of the cash inflows and outflows are listed and tested for balance. The prorated property tax credit is not included since it is not a cash item.

EXHIBIT 7–2
CASH RECONCILIATION STATEMENT

	Receipts	Disbursements
Binder deposit	$ 1,000.00	
Check from buyer	18,489.40	
Check from lender	66,400.00	
Brokerage fee		$ 4,980.00
Check to seller		76,714.00
Seller's expenses (less brokerage)		1,086.00
Buyer's expenses		3,109.40
Grand Totals	$85,889.40	$85,889.40

After explaining the various items on the closing statement, Mr. Jenkins asks the Joneses to write a check to Last Federal in the amount of $18,489.40 and to sign the note and mortgage. He asks the Johnsons to sign the deed and to hand it to the Joneses. He than hands a check for $76,714.00 to the Johnsons and states that all of the expenses have either been paid or will be paid immediately. He gives a check for $4,980.00 payable to Town and Country Realtors® to Mr. Heath. The closing is now completed, and all parties in the room rise, shake hands, and leave.

CLOSING AND CLOSING STATEMENTS

The Johnson-Jones closing was relatively simple and straightforward. Closings for large commercial properties can be very complex and lengthy. Particularly burdensome are closings for properties subject to many leases having a variety of terms and durations, properties being purchased by trusts and partnerships, and properties in probate or litigation. Such transactions can take days or even weeks to close.

Closing practices vary from state to state depending on state laws and local customs. In some states, for example, closings are usually handled by *escrow agents*. These are people or companies that perform the closing function for a fee. They prepare or obtain the deed, abstract or title insurance policy, mortgage certificates and satisfactions, lease assignments, mortgages and notes, and any other documents needed in a transaction. They collect the funds from the buyers and lender and at the closing disburse them to the sellers. They deliver the deed to the buyers, have the loan documents signed, deliver all documents to the appropriate parties, and record the deed and mortgage.

In other states, closings are handled primarily by attorneys or financial institutions. In all states, however, real estate brokers who are involved in a transaction are responsible to their principals to make certain that closings are handled properly and that monies are properly accounted for. Thus, even if they do not handle a closing, brokers are responsible and must check the closing statement to assure that it is prepared properly. Therefore, brokers as well as anyone involved in real estate transactions should understand the mechanics of a transaction and how closing statements are prepared.

Estimated Closing Expense Statements

The laws of some states require that real estate brokers provide buyers and sellers with a list of *estimated closing costs* before signing a contract for sale. Also, the Federal Real Estate Settlement Procedures Act (RESPA) requires lenders to provide borrowers with an estimate of the settlement expenses that are likely to occur. Such estimates must be provided when the borrower applies for a loan or within three business days. Exhibits 7–3 and 7–4 show the estimated closing expenses in the sale of the Johnson property. Note that the various costs and expenses closely approximate the final amounts on the final closing statement (Exhibit 7–1). The final amounts due from buyer and due to seller, however, differ because the prorated taxes are not included in the estimated figures.

Preparation of Closing Statements

Normally, when a buyer signs an offer to purchase, the broker receives a *binder* from the purchaser amounting to 5 or 10 percent of the purchase price. This amount should immediately be placed in an account with a title company or financial institution. Most states have laws requiring brokers to maintain a separate account for earnest-money deposits and to be able to account for all such monies at any time. Failure to do so may result in a broker's license being suspended or revoked.

EXHIBIT 7–3

A MEMBER OF THE SEARS FINANCIAL NETWORK

COLDWELL BANKER □

Conventional
Seller's Estimated Closing Costs

M. M. PARRISH AND ASSOCIATES, INC., REALTORS®

An Independently Owned and Operated Member of Coldwell Banker Residential Affiliates, Inc.

SELLER Fred and Louise Johnson   BUYER George and Helen Jones

PROPERTY ADDRESS 1022 NW 40th Avenue   ASSOCIATE William Heath

PURCHASE PRICE:	$ 83,000.00	
Less Mortgage(s)	66,400.00	
		$ 16,600.00

CLOSING COSTS:

Home Warranty Ins.	$ -0-	
Doc. Stamps (50¢/$100)	415.00	
Abstract Recertification or Title Insurance	527.50	
Preparation of Deed	35.00	
Termite Clearance	25.00	
Record Satisfaction Previous Mortgage	----	
Mortgage Prepayment Penalty	----	
Attorney's Fee	125.00	
Brokerage Fee	4,980.00	
TOTAL CLOSING COSTS:	$ 6,107.50	

PRORATIONS:

Taxes	$ 220.00	
Interest		
Insurance		
TOTAL PRORATIONS:	$ 220.00	
TOTAL CASH DUE:	$10,272.50	

It is understood that the above cost figures are an estimate only and prorations will be determined by the attorneys or closing agents.

Dated: May 15, 1987   SELLER: *Fred Johnson*
                                                 Louise Johnson

WHITE File Copy   CANARY Seller's Copy   PINK Listing Broker's Copy   1M-286-13026

EXHIBIT 7–4

A MEMBER OF THE SEARS FINANCIAL NETWORK

COLDWELL BANKER ▢

Conventional
Buyer's Estimated Closing Costs

M. M. PARRISH AND ASSOCIATES, INC., REALTORS®
An Independently Owned and Operated Member of Coldwell Banker Residential Affiliates, Inc.

BUYER George and Helen Jones   SELLER Fred and Louise Johnson

PROPERTY ADDRESS 1822 NW 40th Avenue   ASSOCIATE William Heath

PURCHASE PRICE:	$ 83,000.00	
Less Binder	1,000.00	
Less Mortgage(s)	66,400.00	
		$ 15,600.00

CLOSING COSTS:

Doc. Stamps (15¢/100 Mortgage)	$ 99.60	
Intangible Tax (.002 x Mtg.)	132.80	
Title Opinion/Title Insurance	-------------------	
Attorney's Fee	125.00	
Assumption Fee	-------------------	
Preparation of Note & Mortgage	35.00	
Record Note and Mortgage	10.00	
Record Deed	10.00	
Survey	175.00	
Home Warranty	-------------------	

★NEW FINANCING COSTS:

Discount Points (_____)	$ 1,328.00	
Origination Fee (1%)	664.00	
Application Fee	50.00	
Lender's Closing Fee	150.00	
Credit Report	35.00	
M.I.P. (_____% 1st year)	-------------------	
Review Fee		
Appraisal Fee	150.00	
Tax Service Fee	-------------------	
Underwriting Fee	25.00	
Amortization Schedule	-------------------	

★ Check with lender for fees and rates which
are applicable to that mortgage company.

	TOTAL CLOSING COSTS:	$ 2,989.40

PRORATIONS:

Interests	$ -------------------	
Taxes	-------------------	
Insurance		
	TOTAL PRORATIONS:	$ -0-

PREPAID ITEMS:

M.I.P. (_____ after 1st year)	$ -------------------	
14 mos. Hazard Insurance	-------------------	
3 mos. Estimated Taxes	132.00	
Prepaid Interest	-------------------	
	TOTAL PREPAIDS:	$ 132.00

TOTAL AMOUNT NEEDED AT CLOSING	$ 18,721.40

It is understood that the above cost figures are an estimate only and prorations will be determined by the attorneys at closing. It is further understood that M.M. PARRISH AND ASSOCIATES, INC., REALTORS® is the agent for the Seller and will be paid by the Seller. Buyer acknowledges that this instrument has been read and signed before any Contract for Sale and Purchase of the real estate here in question has been signed.

Dated this ___15th___ day of __May_____, 19_87_.

WITNESSES: BUYER:

William Heath   _George Jones_____ (SEAL)

Lester Farris   _Helen Jones_____ (SEAL)

WHITE—File   CANARY—Buyer   1M-985-11255

The seller must sign the offer to signify acceptance. The accepted offer is then a contract for sale (and purchase). Expenses incurred by the closing agent for the buyer and seller must be strictly accounted for and accurately disclosed in separate statements prepared for the buyer and seller at closing. The broker must also keep a copy of the closing statement and a summary of receipts and disbursements of all monies involved in the transaction.

A closing statement comprises three parts:

1. Buyer's statement.
2. Seller's statement.
3. Cash reconciliation statement.

These three statements may be presented in a composite form, as in the Johnson-Jones Transaction (Exhibits 7–1 and 7–2). Whether shown in composite form or separately, each statement must be accurate. Buyers, sellers, their attorneys, and their real estate brokers should check the accuracy of the statements and their consistency with the contract for sale.

Listed in Exhibit 7–5 are the typical expenses that are paid in full at

EXHIBIT 7–5
CLOSING EXPENSES AND ALLOCATIONS

Item	Debit	Credit
1. Purchase price	Buyer	Seller
2. Binder deposit	—	Buyer
3. First mortgage balance (when assumed by buyer)	Seller	Buyer
4. Second mortgage (to seller)	Seller	Buyer
Prorations and Prepayments:		
5. Rent (when paid in advance)	Seller	Buyer
6. Interest on mortgage (when existing mortgage is assumed by buyer)	Seller	Buyer
7. Prepayment on mortgage (when existing mortgage is assumed by buyer)	Buyer	Seller
8. Insurance (for unexpired term)	Buyer	Seller
9. Property taxes	Seller	Buyer
Expenses:		
10. Abstract continuation	Seller	—
11. Attorney's fee (buyer)	Buyer	—
12. Attorney's fee (seller)	Seller	—
13. State documentary stamp tax on new mortgage and note	Buyer	—
14. State documentary stamp tax on deed	Seller	—
15. State intangible tax on new mortgage and note	Buyer	—
16. Recording of new mortgage	Buyer	—
17. Recording of deed	Buyer	—
18. Title insurance	Buyer	—
19. Brokerage commission	Seller	—

time of closing or prorated between buyer and seller. These latter expenses have been paid by the seller for the time during which the buyer will occupy the property or will be paid by the buyer for the time during which the seller occupied the property. All expenses must be accounted for on the closing statement. Each item is shown as either a debit (charge) or credit to each party. Payment of closing expenses should be governed by the contract for sale; if they are not covered by the contract, local custom should be followed in charging and crediting each expense. The logic leading to the allocations in Exhibit 7–5 is as follows:

1. The purchase price is the principal charge to the buyer. It is the ultimate closing cost, for without its payment there would be no closing. The seller is credited for receiving it, and the buyer is debited for owing it.

2. The binder has already been paid by the buyer before the closing. Thus, the buyer is not charged for this amount. It is contained in the purchase price already credited to the seller in 1; however, the seller has not yet received it.

3 & 4. An assumed first mortgage and a purchase-money second mortgage are long-term obligations taken on by the buyer that reduce the amount of cash the buyer must pay the seller at closing. The buyer is thus credited for assuming these obligations, and the seller is debited for being relieved of them.

5. When rent is paid to the seller in advance by the lessee (renter), the seller owes the buyer the amount proportionate to the time the buyer will own the property for the rental period. Thus, the seller is debited this amount, and the buyer receives an offsetting credit.

6. Interest on a mortgage is paid at the end of the period. Thus, the buyer will make a payment on an assumed mortgage, part of which represents the seller's ownership period and part of which represents the new owner's period. The seller will therefore be debited the amount representing his or her ownership period, and the buyer will be credited.

7. A prepayment by the seller on an assumed mortgage is for at least a portion of the buyer's ownership period. Thus, the buyer must "pay" the proportionate amount by being debited. The seller will receive a credit for this amount.

8. When a buyer takes over the seller's insurance policy, the seller will already have paid for the entire period. The seller is credited the amount proportionate to the time the buyer will use the insurance, and the buyer is debited this amount.

9. Property taxes are paid in arrears (after the tax year) by the buyer. Thus, the estimated tax bill must be allocated between the time the property is owned by the respective parties. The seller is debited for the amount the buyer will pay on behalf of the seller's ownership period. The buyer receives a credit for this amount.

10. It is logical for the seller to provide evidence of title. An abstract is such evidence, and its continuance is thus a seller's expense. The buyer is not involved in obtaining the abstract.

11. Buyers should hire an attorney to examine the seller's evidence of title and to represent them at the closing. The seller is not involved.

12. Sellers usually hire an attorney to prepare the deed and represent their interests at closing. Most states levy taxes on deeds, mortgages, notes, and contracts. They are discussed in items 13–15.

13. A state documentary stamp tax on mortgages, notes, and contracts may be required on any new loans used to finance the transaction.

14. A state documentary stamp tax on deeds also may be required. It is considered an expense of delivering title to the buyer and is therefore paid by the seller, unless there is an agreement to the contrary.

15. A state intangible tax on mortgages and notes may be imposed. Since the buyers are obtaining such mortgages to finance the purchase, the tax is usually charged to them.

16 & 17. Recording of both the mortgage and the deed is usually the buyer's burden. Recording of the deed is necessary to protect the buyer's interest, whereas the lender requires the borrower (buyer) to pay the mortgage recording charges.

18. Title insurance premium is normally paid by the buyer, since the buyer will receive the benefit of the protection.

19. Usually the seller has hired the broker and therefore owes the commission.

The procedures for prorating should reflect the actual number of days in the period, the number of days during the period that the property was owned by the seller, and the number of days it will be owned by the buyer. The date for dividing the financial responsibilities of buyers and sellers is subject to agreement between the parties. Often the day of closing is counted as a day of seller ownership, although many transactions specify the day of closing as "belonging" to the buyer. If the contract does not cover this matter, local custom will prevail.

For example, if a transaction is scheduled to close on May 14 of a 365-day year, taxes for the year would be allocated between buyers and sellers as shown below (day of closing belongs to buyer):

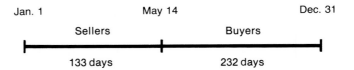

If the estimated tax for the year is $500, the sellers would be debited $182.19, thus:

$$133/365 \times \$500 = \$182.19$$

The buyers would be credited with this amount, since they will pay the tax for the present calendar year.

As another example, consider the insurance proration for a transaction scheduled to close on March 16 of a 365-day year. The premium in the amount of $250 was paid by the sellers for the policy commencing on December 15 of the previous year and ending on December 14 at midnight of the current year. The premium is prorated between buyers and sellers as shown below, with day of closing belonging to buyers:

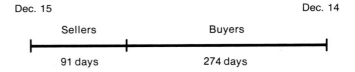

Since the sellers have already paid the premium, they are credited with the portion of the policy period that the buyers will own the property, thus:

$$274/365 \times \$250 = \$187.67$$

The buyers would be debited this amount.

OVERVIEW

Closing is the consummation of a real estate transaction. At closing, title is conveyed and the purchase price is paid. Expenses are paid by each party, and prorations between the parties are made. A document summarizing the financial flows that occur at closing is known as the closing statement.

It comprises three statements—the buyer's statement, the seller's statement, and the cash reconciliation statement. Various money flows are debited or credited to the buyer or seller reflecting the charges and credits to each party. Each party incurs expenses in connection with the closing, and these are debited to the appropriate party, with no corresponding credit to the other party.

Perhaps the most difficult aspect of closing statements is the prorating process. Prorating is required when an expense has been prepaid by the seller, or will be paid subsequently by the buyer, and covers a time period during which both buyer and seller own the property. The procedure involves crediting the party that pays the expense with the proportionate amount covering the period during which the other party owns the property. Typical items to be prorated are prepaid rent, insurance, real estate taxes, mortgage interest (either prepaid or paid in arrears), and prepaid mortgage principal.

TEST YOURSELF

Explain the following concepts and procedures presented in this chapter.

1. Closing a transaction.
2. Estoppel certificate.
3. Composite closing statement.
4. Prorating.
5. Documentary stamp tax.
6. Cash reconciliation statement.
7. Escrow agent.
8. Real Estate Settlement Procedures Act.

Answer the following multiple-choice questions.

1. The purpose of a closing statement is to
   a. Determine who pays the brokerage commission.
   b. Allocate expenses and receipts of buyer and seller.
   c. Prorate expenses between buyer and seller.
   d. Account for monies in a transaction.
   e. All but a above.

2. If a closing occurs on September 1 of a 365-day year, how will the year's property tax of $900 be prorated? (Note: the taxes will be due on January 2 of the following year.)
   a. Seller credits buyer with $300.80.
   b. Seller credits buyer with $599.20.
   c. Buyer credits seller with $300.80.
   d. Buyer credits seller with $599.20.
   e. None of the above.

3. An estoppel certificate is usually obtained by the buyer's attorney or broker from the
   a. Public records.
   b. Seller.
   c. Mortgagor.
   d. Mortgagee.
   e. State licensing board.

4. The document that governs closing arrangements is the
   a. Deed.
   b. Contract for sale.
   c. Mortgage.
   d. Listing contract.
   e. Estoppel certificate.

5. Which of the following expenses does the seller usually *not* pay?
   a. Documentary stamp tax on deed.
   b. Recording of new mortgage.
   c. Brokerage commission.
   d. Abstract continuation.
   e. Seller's attorney fees.

ADDITIONAL READINGS

Floyd, Charles J. *Real Estate Principles.* New York: Random House, 1981, Chap. 10.

Kratovil, Robert, and Raymond J. Werner. *Real Estate Law.* 8th ed. Englewood Cliffs, N.J.: Prentice-Hall, 1983, Chap. 10.

Semenow, Robert W. *Questions and Answers on Real Estate.* 9th ed. Englewood Cliffs, N.J.: Prentice-Hall, 1978, pp. 679–87.

Unger, Maurice A., and George R. Karvel. *Real Estate Principles and Practices.* 7th ed. Cincinnati: South-Western Publishing, 1983, Chap. 11.

U.S. Department of Housing and Urban Development. *Settlement Costs and You: A HUD Guide for Homebuyers.* Washington, D.C.: U.S. Government Printing Office, 1977.

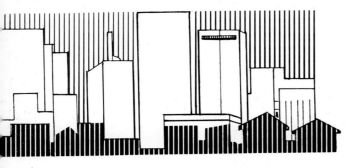

8
The Lease Contract

OUTLINE

NATURE OF A LEASE
Oral versus Written Leases
A Contract versus a Conveyance
General Rights and Obligations

REQUIREMENTS OF A VALID LEASE
Names of Lessors and Lessees
Description of Property
Consideration
Legality of Objective
Offer and Acceptance
Written Form

RESIDENTIAL LEASES
Typical Issues and Provisions
Residential Landlord-Tenant Laws
Other Typical Lease Provisions

COMMERCIAL LEASES
Types of Commercial Leases

Important Considerations for Commercial Lessors
Important Considerations for Commercial Lessees

SHOPPING-CENTER LEASES
Signs and Displays
Business Hours
Cancellation
Merchandise Inventory
Utilities
Fixtures and Trade Fixtures
Relocation
Tenant Improvements

GROUND LEASES

OVERVIEW

TEST YOURSELF

ADDITIONAL READINGS

NATURE OF A LEASE

A lease is an arrangement between the owners of a parcel or unit of real estate and the users of the parcel or unit. It is usually reflected in a document that specifies the rights and obligations of both the owners and users; the document itself is often called the lease. The lease, in effect, divides the bundle of rights in real estate into two legal interests, or estates. The owners' estate is termed the *leased fee* estate, and the owners are called *lessors*. The users' estate is termed the *leasehold* estate, and the users are called *lessees*.[1] Basically, as shown in Exhibit 8–1, lessors have the rights to collect rent for the term of the lease and to obtain the property back at the end of the lease in the same condition, except for reasonable wear and tear. The lessees have the right to use the property for the term of the lease.

Oral versus Written Leases

While a lease is usually thought of as a written document, certain leases do not have to be written. State laws specify which circumstances require written leases, but generally, leases of more than one year must be written to be enforceable in court. Oral leases for less than a year are generally valid but are difficult to enforce by the lessee. For example, if the lessor fails to maintain the property in habitable condition, the lessee's most efficient remedy is usually to move out and not pay the rent. On the other side, if the lessee fails to pay the rent, the lessor can, through legal procedures, have the tenant evicted. *Eviction* terminates the rights of the lessee to the property. The lessor could sue the lessee for unpaid

---

[1]We prefer to use the more precise legal terms *lessor* and *lessee* rather than the terms *landlord* and *tenant*. However, we use *landlord* and *tenant* when discussing state laws specifically titled "residential landlord-tenant laws."

163

EXHIBIT 8–1
LEASE CONTRACT

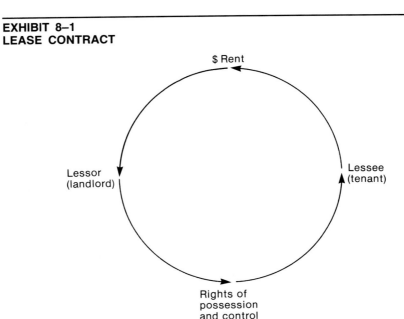

rent but would have to be able to show that an oral lease existed and that certain amounts were due periodically. In most cases, the cost of pursuing legal action to recover unpaid rent would outweigh any amounts that might be recovered.

A Contract versus a Conveyance

We refer to a lease as a contract; however, a lease is both a contract and a conveyance. It is sometimes legally regarded as a conveyance because it transfers a major right of property ownership—the exclusive right of occupancy and use (i.e., possession and control)—to a lessee.

The practical significance of whether a lease is regarded as a contract or a conveyance lies in the legal remedies for disputes that may arise between lessor and lessee. If the lease is considered a contract and either party claims the lease has been violated, the legal remedies include the rights to sue for damages and/or specific performance, as well as the right to abrogate the lease. If the lease is regarded as a conveyance, the remedy for either party is termination of the lease and return of the property to the lessor.

Courts in different states vary considerably in their interpretations of leases, but the modern trend is to regard leases more as contracts than as conveyances. This interpretation gives more flexibility to courts, with remedies more adjustable to fit the nature of the violation. Some remedies, for example, have allowed both the return of the property to the lessor and the right to sue for damages. For real estate decision-making purposes, we will regard the lease essentially as a contract.

General Rights and Obligations

A lease creates rights and obligations for both the lessor and lessee. As we noted, any lease gives the lessor the right to obtain rent and to receive the property back at the end of the lease. This latter right is termed *reversion*. A residential lessor's obligations include keeping the property in a safe and habitable condition. The lessee's basic rights are to occupy and use the property during the lease period. A residential lessee must maintain the property in a safe and habitable condition.

These rights are created in the simplest leases; in their absence, a lease would not exist. Most leases, however, are longer and more complex. They may create many additional rights and obligations for both parties. Some of these potential rights and obligations are discussed below in the sections describing typical residential and commercial leases.

While almost any combination of rights and obligations can be created in a lease, some rights of a lessee cannot be removed or limited by a residential lease. These rights have been created by common law court decisions and by statute in order to protect tenants who have sometimes been at the mercy of landlords. The essence of these rights is that even if the lease stipulated that the lessee waived certain rights, the lessee could still have them enforced. These nonwaivable rights of a residential lessee are

1. To have the property maintained in a safe and habitable condition.
2. To privacy from unreasonable entry by the lessor.
3. To cancellation of the lease if the property is destroyed by fire or other hazard.

"Safe and habitable condition" is usually defined in local housing codes and interpreted by community authorities. The courts consider these local standards in determining whether a tenant's rights have been violated. Nevertheless, the courts are leery of making a ruling adverse to the lessor if the lessee has not tried to get the lessor to make necessary repairs or if the lessee has renewed the lease while the condition exists. In some cases, tenants have been successful in withholding rents from the landlord, if they place the rents in a trust or escrow account until the unsafe or uninhabitable condition has been remedied.

Unreasonable entry by the lessor is also a matter of judgment. Clearly, frequent entry (say, more than once a month) or entry at inconvenient times (such as during the night) for nonemergency reasons would be regarded as harassment. Some leases permit entry during the last month of a lease to show the property to prospective tenants. Even under this provision, entry would have to be at reasonable times and in acceptable frequency.

While most residential leases contain provisions regarding the tenant's obligations in the event the property is destroyed, a tenant cannot be forced to pay for services not received. If the lessor provides equally acceptable substitute quarters while the property is being replaced or repaired, the lessee may be obligated to continue paying rent. In the absence of such arrangements, however, the lease could be cancelled.

REQUIREMENTS OF A VALID LEASE

The requirements of a valid lease are similar to the requirements of a valid contract and a valid conveyance (deed). As with other contracts, no particular form is required. If the required elements are contained in a lease, it is valid; therefore, leases can be very simple or highly complex. Most residential leases are relatively short (one or two pages), while many commercial leases are long, complex documents of 50 pages or more.

Names of Lessors and Lessees

As a practical matter, the lessors and lessees should be named in a lease, and both parties should sign the document. If the lessors prepared the lease document but failed to insert their own names or to sign it, the lease would probably be enforceable against them. If, on the other hand, the lessees were not named and did not sign the document, the lease could not be enforced against them.

Description of Property

The property must be described adequately for it to be identified, but no particular type of description is required. A street address is often sufficient if the property is situated in an urban area. The type of description could also be by recorded plat. Rural descriptions could be made by the government rectangular survey system or by metes and bounds.

Consideration

Consideration is required in a valid lease. On the lessor's side, giving up the use of the property, or the promise to give up its use, is the consideration. On the lessee's side, the promise to pay rent is consideration. Without specification of consideration by *both* parties, the lease is not a valid contract and is unenforceable.

Legality of Objective

Owners have the right to lease their properties. Issues sometimes arise, however, about the lessors' responsibility and liability when lessees use the property illegally. For example, do the lessors have any responsibility if they lease their property to tenants who process and store illegal drugs?

Generally, the answer depends on whether the lessors knew or should have known about the illegal operation. If they knowingly leased the property for an illegal use, they probably could not enforce the lease. They would also, of course, be subject to prosecution for criminal conspiracy or other charges. If they had no knowledge of the illegal use, they could probably enforce the lease.

Similarly, if the lessees use the property in a manner that does not conform to the zoning laws, the lease is still valid. The lessees and the local government may dispute the permitted use of the property, but such a dispute does not affect the lessors' right to lease the property and collect rent. If the lessees continue to use the property illegally after ordered to stop, they may be prosecuted. If the lessors were not a party to the prohibited use, their rights in the lease would continue.

Offer and Acceptance

Offer and acceptance indicate a meeting of the minds between the lessors and lessees. Statements to the effect that the lessors agree to lease the property for a specified period and that the lessees agree to lease the property and pay a certain amount of rent periodically are adequate to meet this requirment.

Written Form

As pointed out previously, many leases must be in writing to be valid. State laws specify which ones must be in writing and which ones need not be. In most states, however, leases for longer than one year must be in writing to be valid.

RESIDENTIAL LEASES

All leases that contain the required elements of a contract are valid, and therefore a simple statement such as the following would constitute a valid lease:

> I, James Henry Tutweiler, do hereby agree to lease my property at 725 Maple Street in Hogtown, Missouri, from January 1, 1987, through December 31, 1987, to John D. and Mary Boscowitz, who do hereby agree to pay rent in the amount of $500 on the first day of each month.

S/James Henry Tutweiler, Lessor
S/John D. Boscowitz, Lessee
S/Mary Boscowitz, Lessee

Nevertheless, most written leases contain additional provisions that create various rights and obligations of both lessors and lessees. In this section, we discuss some of the additional provisions typically included in residential leases; leases for commercial properties are discussed in the following section. Generally, a good lease should create an equitable balance of rights and responsibilities between lessors and lessees. If either party is burdened unfairly, he or she may attempt to abrogate the lease or to compensate for the inequity in some other way. For example, tenants who feel they are being treated unfairly may inflict a high level of "wear and tear" on the property.

Typical Issues and Provisions

Possession of the Property.   A lease should identify the period during which the lessees may occupy the property. If a definite period is not specified, a *tenancy at will* (See Chapter 2) is created, and the period of occupancy is determined by the frequency of rental payments (month to month, quarter to quarter, etc.). In any event, a beginning date must be specified.

Usually there is no problem. The property is vacant, and the lessees move in. Occasionally, however, the property is not vacant; a previous tenant refuses to vacate. The lessees may already have paid the rent. What are their rights?

In most states the lessees would be entitled to void the lease and have their rent and security deposit returned because they could not take actual possession of the property. In some states, however, they would not be entitled to void the lease because they have the *right of possession*. It would be their responsibility to have the holdover tenants evicted.

Lessors sometimes insert a provision in a lease that the lease period does not begin until the property is vacant and the lessors can take actual possession. Such a clause eliminates the possibility that the lessees will void the lease if actual possession cannot be delivered on the specified date. It creates the risk for the lessees, however, that they may not obtain possession for some time while subject to the lease. They would prefer a clause stating that the lease could be voided if they cannot obtain possession on the date specified. A compromise provision that may be acceptable to both parties states that the beginning date of the lease commences upon actual delivery of possession to the lessors, which must be by, say, the 10th of the month.

Use of the Property.   Unless restricted by the lease, the lessees may use a property in any legal manner. Often, however, lessors want to ensure that the property is used only in specified ways. For example, they may limit the property to residential use or to occupancy by no more than three persons. Or they may exclude pets. Lessees should read such restrictions carefully before signing a lease.

Maintenance and Repairs.   Lessors of agricultural, commercial, and industrial properties usually have no obligation to maintain and repair those properties, unless required by the lease document to do so. Even lessors of detached, single-family homes usually have no such obligation. In these situations, lessees are required to make needed repairs and maintenance and to return the property to the lessors in the same condition it was in as at the beginning of the lease (except for normal wear and tear).

This rule, however, does not apply to the leasing of multiunit apartment buildings. In recent years, court decisions and state statutes have imposed an obligation on lessors of apartments in multiunit structures to maintain the properties in a safe and habitable condition in accordance with community housing codes.

Leases should identify as precisely as possible the obligations of each party for maintenance and repairs. If lessees abuse a property or do not meet the lease requirements for maintenance and repairs, lessors can pursue the legal remedy of eviction. They can also sue for damages or retain all or a portion of a security deposit as liquidated damages. If lessors fail to maintain a property in a safe and habitable condition or to live up to the obligations created in the lease, the lessees may (1) declare the lease voided and move out, (2) continue to occupy the property and pay the rent but sue the lessors for damages to the leasehold through lack of proper maintenance and repairs, or (3) continue to occupy the property, but reduce the rent proportionally to the deteriorated condition. Obviously, any of these remedies may result in disagreements with and counteractions by the lessors. Since lessors are usually financially stronger than lessees, lessees should not undertake any of these remedies without legal advice.

Lessor's Right of Entry.   Lessors usually have no right of entry to agricultural, commercial, industrial, or detached, single-family properties. As we pointed out above, lessees have complete responsibility for maintenance and repairs, and a lease grants them exclusive right of occupancy and use. The only exceptions are the right of entry by lessors to collect rent and to prevent *waste*—lessees' physical abuse of a property or damage that may result when repairs are not made. For example, if a water pipe breaks and is not repaired by the lessees, the lessors could enter the property to fix the pipe and repair any resulting damage.

With respect to apartment properties, lessors often have a greater right of entry because they are obligated to maintain the property in a safe and habitable condition. To do so, they must be able to enter a property to perform maintenance and repairs. This right, however, is limited to reasonable frequency and times. Without a specific lease provision, lessors of such properties usually cannot enter for normal maintenance and repairs more often than once a month.

Most apartment leases contain provisions about the lessor's right of entry—usually they give lessors the right to enter for monthly inspections and at other reasonable times for maintenance and repairs.

Lessee's Right to Assign and Sublet.   Unless prohibited or limited by the lease, lessees have the right to assign or sublet their leasehold. An assignment transfers the lessees' rights to new lessees, who buy the original lessees' total package of rights. Nevertheless, if the new lessees do not live up to the provisions of the lease (such as paying the rent), the lessors can sue the original lessees as well as the new lessees.

A sublet is the sale of part of the lessees' rights. It could involve the partitioning of space, with the new lessees occupying part of the original lessees' space. It could involve a sublease of the entire property for a portion of the original lessees' term (say, five years out of the original lessees' 10-year term). In either situation, the original lessees also become lessors, and they have what is known as a *sandwich leasehold*, as shown in Exhibit 8–2. Their interests are "sandwiched" between the property owners' and the sublet leasehold's interests; that is, the original lessees are still subject to the terms of the original lease and are also subject to the terms of the lease with their tenants (the sublet leasehold).

In a subleasehold, the original lessees continue to be completely liable for rental payments and other lease provisions to the lessors. (In many cases, the lessors would not even be aware of the subleasehold.) In an

**EXHIBIT 8–2
SANDWICH LEASEHOLD**

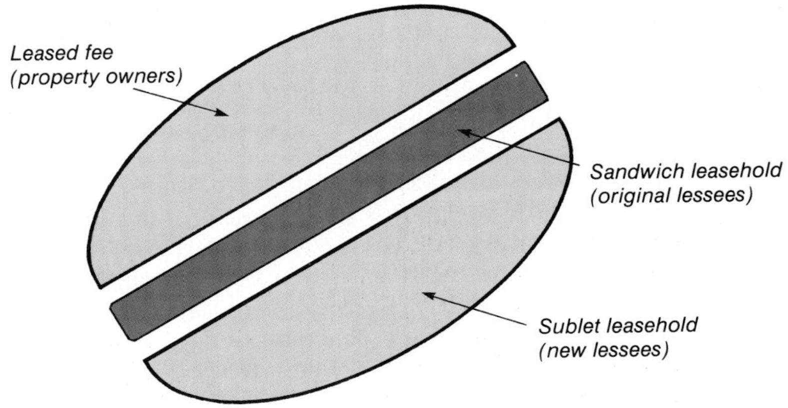

Leased fee
(property owners)

Sandwich leasehold
(original lessees)

Sublet leasehold
(new lessees)

assignment, the assignees become primarily liable for rent and other lease provisions. The lessors can go back to the original lessees only after attempting and failing to obtain satisfaction from the assignees. Consequently, in the lease document, most lessors attempt to limit the right of lessees to assign or sublet.

Many leases state that the lessees cannot assign or sublet the property without the lessor's written permission. The lessors could then check the potential assignees' or sublettors' credit history and rental experience in previous apartments. Lessees may be protected by a clause stating that the lessors must have a valid reason for refusing permission to assign or sublet. In other words, failure to give permission would have to be based on a poor credit rating, a history of delinquent rental payments, or a record of destructive behavior in prior apartments.

Residential Landlord-Tenant Laws

Most states in recent years have enacted landlord-tenant laws to address many of the issues that arise between lessors and lessees. These laws have become necessary because neither contract law nor common law spells out the relationships between owners or managers of large buildings and apartment dwellers. Landlord-tenant laws vary from state to state, but they generally cover application fees, security deposits, advance rents, defects, landlords' right of entry, maintenance and repairs, and rule changes. Apartment buildings with four or fewer units are usually exempt from such laws.

Application Fees. Most landlord-tenant laws state that landlords may charge an application fee to cover the costs of checking a prospective tenant's references and creditworthiness. Such fees must be reasonable, and any excess over costs must be returned to applicants or credited to their security deposits or advance rent. Uses of the fee must be itemized and accounted for or returned to the applicant within a specified number of days.

Security Deposits. Landlords may require tenants to pay a security deposit to cover any breach of the lease. State landlord-tenant laws generally allow such deposits, but limit the amount and govern how they must be held, accounted for, and returned on termination of the lease. They usually limit the amount of security deposits landlords can have in separate accounts and/or require landlords to post surety bonds for the total amount of such deposits held.

If security deposit funds are used by the landlords and not kept in a separate account, the laws generally require the landlord to pay interest on the amounts so used. If the funds are placed in an interest-bearing account, the tenant may be entitled to some portion, (e.g., 75 percent) of the earnings. Landlords are required to inform tenants of how their deposits are being held or used and the address of the financial institution in which the funds are deposited. Security deposits must be returned to tenants within several days (usually 15) after they have vacated the premises, unless the landlord makes a claim for damages against the tenants. If the landlord intends to withhold part or all of the security deposit, he must so inform the terminated tenant, who may then object. Any irreconcilable differences must be settled in court.

Advance Rents. Landlords sometimes require tenants to pay the final month's rent in advance. This protects the landlord if the tenant refuses to pay the last month's rent and moves out.

Generally, advance rents are treated similarly to security deposits. They must be accounted for, held in a separate account and/or have a surety bond posted for them, and, if placed in an interest-bearing account or used by the landlord, have interest paid on them.

Defects. Tenants must be given a written list of defects when they move in; they are allowed to add any defective items they may find. This protects both parties later if claims are made against security deposits. Tenants should prepare such a list if they do not receive one from the landlord. Failure of either party to object or add to a list is regarded as acceptance of the list.

Maintenance and Repairs. The residential landlord-tenant laws require landlords to maintain the property in safe and habitable condition. Going beyond the common law minimum standards, however, the laws specify some of the components of such a condition. For example, landlords must (1) provide hot and cold running water and sufficient heat to meet seasonal needs, (2) keep common areas clean and provide waste receptacles, (3) maintain in safe and working order all plumbing, electrical, heating, air conditioning, and other major equipment and appliances, and (4) maintain the property in conformity with all applicable housing, zoning, and fire codes.

Right of Entry. The landlord-tenant laws give landlords the right of entry to inspect for maintenance and repairs. They usually require the landlord to give written notice prior to an inspection and except in emergency, to conduct it at a reasonable time. Landlords cannot use right of entry to harass tenants.

Landlords must also inspect the property being vacated by a tenant to determine its condition and to itemize any damage. If the tenant wants to be present at the inspection, he or she must notify the landlord. The

━━━━━━━━━━━━━━━━━━━━━ *Frame 8–1* ━━━━━━━━━━━━━━━━━━━━━

Flooding from Frozen Water Pipes

In December 1983, the worst cold snap of the century hit the southeastern United States. In Gainesville, Florida, the water pipes in a large apartment complex froze and flooded many apartments, most of which were rented by students who were out of town for the holiday. At first, the landlord—one of the largest corporate developers and property owners in the area—claimed it was not responsible. A clause in the lease stated that the landlord would not be liable for damage caused by tenants' neglect. The landlord claimed that because the tenants left town and turned down their thermostats, they were the cause of the damage.

The tenants claimed they were not aware that the pipes would freeze and that it was not their responsibility to provide the heat to keep them from freezing.

The issue was resolved within a few days in the face of unfavorable publicity toward the landlord's position. An editorial in the local newspaper opined that the tenants deserved prompt and equitable repairs and replacements. The landlord dropped its claims against the tenants and began repairing the damage and replacing damaged goods.

---

landlord must then inform the tenant of the time and date of the inspection.

Other Typical Lease Provisions

In addition to the rights and responsibilities imposed by landlord-tenant laws, many other provisions are contained in a typical residential lease. While such leases should not become overly complex, they should cover common points that otherwise might lead to disagreements and litigation. Exhibit 8–3 is an example of a typical residential lease. In addition to the provisions already discussed, note that it covers (1) disclosure of the owner's agent, (2) joint liability of multiple tenants, (3) house rules, (4) compliance with ordinances and statutes, (5) furnishings provided, (6) indemnification for damage or injury, and (7) options under default.

COMMERCIAL LEASES

Commercial leases are used for all types of income-producing nonresidential properties (e.g., offices, small stores, restaurants, specialty shops, department stores, fast food outlets, hotels and motels, service stations, manufacturing plants, and so forth). Even leases on small commercial properties are usually longer and more complex than residential leases,

EXHIBIT 8–3

LEASE APPLICATION

NAME _____ SOCIAL SECURITY NO. _____ BIRTHDATE _____
      Last   First   Middle

SPOUSE _____ SOCIAL SECURITY NO. _____ BIRTHDATE _____

TOTAL NO. OF OCCUPANTS _____ NAMES AND AGES OF CHILDREN _____

PRESENT ADDRESS _____ PHONE NO. _____
                  St. No. Street   Apt. No.   City   State   Zip

PRESENT LANDLORD OR MORTGAGE HOLDER _____ PHONE NO. _____

LENGTH OF RESIDENCE YRS. ____ MOS. ____   MONTHLY RENT OR MORTGAGE PAYMENT _____

PREVIOUS ADDRESS _____ LENGTH OF RESIDENCE _____
                  St. No. Street   Apt. No.   City   State   Zip

PREVIOUS LANDLORD OR MORTGAGE CO. _____ PHONE NO. _____

EMPLOYMENT

PRESENT EMPLOYER _____ CITY & STATE _____ PHONE NO. _____

POSITION _____ LENGTH OF EMPLOY. _____ YRS. ____ MOS. INCOME _____ PER ____ SUPERVISOR _____

PREVIOUS EMPLOYER _____ CITY & STATE _____ PHONE NO. _____

POSITION _____ LENGTH OF EMPLOY. _____ YRS. ____ MOS. INCOME _____ PER ____ SUPERVISOR _____

SPOUSE'S EMPLOYER _____ CITY & STATE _____ PHONE NO. _____

POSITION _____ LENGTH OF EMPLOY. _____ YRS. ____ MOS. INCOME _____ PER ____ SUPERVISOR _____

BANK AND CREDIT REFERENCES

BANK NAME _____ CITY & STATE _____ CKING. ACCT. NO. _____

BANK NAME _____ CITY & STATE _____ LOAN NO. _____

CREDITOR _____ CITY & STATE _____ ACCT. NO. _____

CREDITOR _____ CITY & STATE _____ ACCT. NO. _____

CREDITOR _____ CITY & STATE _____ ACCT. NO. _____

AUTOMOBILES

FIRST CAR _____ SECOND CAR _____
           Year Make Model Tag No. State   Year Make Model Tag No. State

DRIVERS LICENSE NO. _____ STATE _____ ADDRESS SHOWN _____

IN CASE OF EMERGENCY, NOTIFY _____ ADDRESS _____ PHONE NO. _____

NEAREST RELATIVE NOT LIVING WITH YOU: _____ ADDRESS _____ PHONE NO. _____

HAVE YOU EVER BEEN EVICTED FROM A RENTAL RESIDENCE FOR NONPAYMENT OF RENT ____ YES ____ NO.

IF YES, LANDLORD NAME _____ PHONE _____

Applicant represents that all of the above information is true and complete and authorizes the verification of same by reasonable means. Applicant understands that false information given herein may constitute grounds for rejection of this application and/or forfeiture of any deposits.

Applicant has deposited the sum of $ _____ in partial payment of the first month's rent with the understanding that this application is subject to approval and acceptance by the Landlord. Upon approval and acceptance, the applicant agrees to execute the Landlord's standard lease agreement before possession of residence is given and to pay any balance due on the first month's rent and security deposit within five days after the approval of application or the deposit will be forfeited to the Landlord. If this application is not approved or if applicant cancels within five days, the deposit will be refunded, the applicant hereby waiving any claim for damages by reason of non-acceptance. This application is for information only and does not obligate Landlord to execute a lease or deliver possession of the proposed residence.

Applicant understands that he is being charged a NON-REFUNDABLE Application Processing Fee of $ _____

I, the undersigned Applicant, have read and agree to all provisions of this application.

_____
Applicant's Signature

_____
Spouse's Signature

APT. TYPE _____ APT. NO. _____ MOVE IN DATE _____

FIRST MONTH'S RENT $ _____
SECURITY DEPOSIT _____
APP. FEE _____
TOTAL _____
LESS DEPOSIT ABOVE _____
TOTAL DUE PRIOR MOVE IN _____

EXHIBIT 8–3 *(concluded)*

LEASE-RENTAL AGREEMENT AND DEPOSIT RECEIPT

RECEIVED FROM ....

....hereinafter referred to as Tenant.

the sum of $ .... (....DOLLARS),

evidenced by , as a deposit which, upon acceptance of this rental agreement, shall belong to the Owner of the premises, hereinafter referred to as Owner and shall be applied as follows:

	RECEIVED	PAYABLE PRIOR TO OCCUPANCY
Rent for the period from .... to	$	$ ....
Last .... month's rent....	$	$ ....
Security Deposit	$	$ ....
Other..	$	$ ....
TOTAL	$	$ ....

In the event that this agreement is not accepted by the Owner, within........days, the total deposit received shall be refunded. Tenant hereby offers to rent from the Owner the premises situated in the City of,......................................, County of,...........................

State of **Florida**, described as .... consisting of ....

upon the following TERMS and CONDITIONS:

TERM: The term hereof shall commence on ....,19......, and continue (check one of the two following alternatives);

☐ Until 19

☐ on a month-to-month basis, until either party shall terminate the same by giving the other party.....days written notice delivered by certified mail, provided that Tenant agrees not to terminate prior to the expiration of ....months.

RENT: Rent shall be $...............per month, payable in advance, upon the..............day of each calandar month to Owner or his authorized agent, at the following address ....

or at such other places as may be designated by Ow..er from time to time. In the event rent is not paid by the 2nd of each month, Tenant agrees to pay a late charge of $10.00. Tenant agrees further to pay for each dishonored bank check.

DISCLOSURE: The Owner hereby designates ....

as the agent to receive any and all rent, notices and demands in his behalf made by the Tenant.

MULTIPLE OCCUPANCY: It is expressly understood that this agreement is between the Owner and each signatory individually and severally. In the event of default by any one signatory each and every remaining signatory shall be responsible for timely payment of rent and all other provisions of this agreement.

UTILITIES: Tenant shall be responsible for the payment of all utilities and services, except: ....

which shall be paid by the Owner.

USE: The premises shall be used as a residence with no more than ....adults and.........................

children, and for no other purpose, without the prior written consent of the Owner. Occupancy by guests staying over 7 days will be considered to be in violation of this provision.

PETS: No pets shall be brought on the premises.

HOUSE RULES: In the event that the premises are a portion of a building containing more than one unit, Tenant agrees to abide by any and all house rules, whether promulgated before or after the execution hereof, including but not limited to, rules with respect to noise, odors, disposal of refuse, pets, parking, and use of common areas. Tenant shall not have a waterbed on the premises. All such house rules shall constitute a part of this lease.

ORDINANCES AND STATUTES: Tenant shall comply with all statutes, ordinances and requirements of all municipal, state and federal authorites now in force, or which may hereafter be in force, pertaining to the use of the premises.

ASSIGNMENT AND SUBLETTING: Tenant shall not assign this agreement or sublet any portion of the premises without prior written consent of the Owner which may not be unreasonably withheld. Should the owner agree to such subletting or assignment, a minimum service fee of $45.00 shall be charged to the tenant.

FURNISHINGS: The owner shall provide the Tenant with the furnishings as set forth in schedule_____ if applicable. The furnishings shall at all times remain the sole exclusive property of the Owner.

MAINTENANCE, REPAIRS OR ALTERATIONS: Tenant acknowledges that the premises are in good order and repair, unless otherwise indicated herein. Owner may at any time give Tenant a written inventory of furniture and furnishings on the premises and Tenant shall be deemed to have possession of all said furniture and furnishings in good condition and repair, unless the objects thereto in writing within five days after receipt of such inventory. Tenant shall, at his own expense, and at all times maintain the premises in a clean and sanitary manner including all equipment, appliances, furniture, and furnishings therein and shall surrender the same, at termination hereof, in as good condition as received, normal wear and tear excepted. Tenant shall be responsible for all repairs required for damages caused by his negligence and that of his family or invitees or guests. Tenant shall not paint, paper or otherwise redecorate or make alterations to the premises without the prior written consent of the Owner.

ENTRY AND INSPECTION: Tenant shall permit Owner or Owner's agents to enter the premises at reasonable times and upon reasonable notice, except in case of an emergency, for the purpose of inspecting the premises, showing the same to prospective tenants or purchasers, or for making necessary repairs.

INDEMNIFICATION: Owner shall not be liable for any damage or injury to Tenant, or any other person, or to any property, occurring on the premises, or any part thereof, or in common areas thereof, and shall hold the Owner or agents harmless from all damages sustained during the lease term.

POSSESSION: If Owner is unable to deliver possession of the premises at the commencement hereof, Owner shall not be liable for any damage caused thereby, nor shall this agreement be void or voidable, but Tenant shall not be liable for any rent until possession is delivered. Tenant may terminate this agreement if possession is not delivered within .... days of the commencement of the term hereof.

DEFAULT: In the event of a default by Tenant, Owner may elect to (a) continue the lease in effect and enforce all his rights and remedies hereunder, including the right to recover the rent as it becomes due, or (b) at any time, terminate all of Tenant's rights hereunder and recover from Tenant all damages he may incur by reason of the breach of the lease, including the cost of recovering the premises, and including the worth at the time of such termination, or at the time of an award if suit be instituted to enforce this provision, of the amount by which the unpaid rent for the balance of the term exceeds the amount of such rental loss which the tenant proves could be reasonably avoided.

SECURITY: The security deposit set forth above, if any shall secure the performance of Tenant's obligations hereunder. Owner may, but shall not be obligated to, apply all or portions of said deposit on account of Tenant's obligations hereunder. Any balance remaining upon termination shall be returned to Tenant. Tenant shall not have the right to apply the Security Deposit in payment of last month's rent. Security Deposits and/or last month's rents are deposited in the......................................of.........................

DEPOSIT REFUNDS: Any returnable deposits shall be refunded within fifteen days from date possession is delivered to Owner or his authorized Agent.

WAIVER: No failure of Owner to enforce any term hereof shall be deemed a waiver, nor shall any acceptance of a partial payment of rent be deemed a waiver of Owner's rights to the full amount thereof.

NOTICES: Any notice which either party may or is required to give, may be given by mailing the same, postage prepaid, to Tenant at the premises or to Owner at the address shown below or at such other places as may be designated by the parties from time to time. It is expressly understood that this lease is for the dates listed and the hold over of one (1) day shall constitute a full month's rent becoming due and payable. Move-out time is by 12:00 noon the last day of the lease period.

ADDITIONAL TERMS AND CONDITIONS:

The undersigned **Tenant hereby acknowledges receipt of a copy hereof:** DATED ....

Agent ....

Address/Phone ....by ....

Tenant .... Tenant ....

Tenant .... Tenant ....

The Tenants do hereby designate ....

to act as their official representative when dealing with the Owner for any reason whatsoever. All communications between Owner and Tenants shall be through and with said designated individual, including, but not necessarily limited to, the person responsible for delivery of rental payments to the Owner, communications regarding maintenance problems and complaints, and the person upon who all notices received under this Lease or the Florida Landlord Tenant Act shall be served. Anything contained in this provision to the contrary notwithstanding, all parties to this Lease shall be jointly and severally liable for all duties and obligations of the Tenants under the terms of this Lease.

and leases on larger commercial and industrial properties may be as long as 50 pages.

Commercial leases are usually quite complicated because they govern the payment of large amounts of rent over relatively long periods of time. Most commercial leases have terms of three to 50 years or longer. Thus, they need to cover possible circumstances and happenings that are less likely to occur during shorter-term residential lease periods.

Commercial leases create business relationships between lessors and lessees. The lease document determines which parties pay which expenses, what happens when expenses increase, and how the rents are calculated. The lease also affects the parties' income tax liabilities in terms of gross income and deductibility of expenses.

Fewer laws govern commercial lease arrangements. The parties tend to be more knowledgeable than typical apartment tenants and usually seek competent legal advice. Exhibit 8–4 is an example of a relatively simple commercial lease.

EXHIBIT 8–4

RAMCO'S FORM 28-B

Business Property Lease

To

Expires_____, 19_____

EXHIBIT 8–4 *(continued)*

𝔅𝔲𝔰𝔦𝔫𝔢𝔰𝔰 𝔏𝔢𝔞𝔰𝔢

THIS AGREEMENT, entered into this   day of   , 19

between

, hereinafter called the lessor,

party of the first part, and

of the County of   and State of

hereinafter called the lessee or tenant, party of the second part:

WITNESSETH, That the said lessor does this day lease unto said lessee, and said lessee does hereby hire and take as tenant   under said lessor Room   or Space

No.

situate in   Florida, to be used and occupied by the lessee as
and for no other purposes or uses whatsoever, for
the term of   , subject and conditioned on the provisions of
clause ten of this lease beginning the   day of
19   , and ending the   day of   , 19   ,
at and for the agreed total rental of
Dollars, payable as follows:

all payments to be made to the lessor on the first day of each and every month in advance without demand at the office of   in the City of
or at such other place and to such other person, as the lessor may from time to time designate in writing.

The following express stipulations and conditions are made a part of this lease and are hereby assented to by the lessee:

FIRST: The lessee shall not assign this lease, nor sub-let the premises, or any part thereof nor use the same, or any part thereof, nor permit the same, or any part thereof, to be used for any other purpose than as above stipulated, nor make any alterations therein, and all additions thereto, without the written consent of the lessor, and all additions, fixtures or improvements which may be made by lessee, except movable office furniture, shall become the property of the lessor and remain upon the premises as a part thereof, and be surrendered with the premises at the termination of this lease.

SECOND: All personal property placed or moved in the premises above described shall be at the risk of the lessee or owner thereof, and lessor shall not be liable for any damage to said personal property, or to the lessee arising from the bursting or leaking of water pipes, or from any act of negligence of any co-tenant or occupants of the building or or any other person whomsoever.

THIRD: That the tenant_____shall promptly execute and comply with all statutes, ordinances, rules, orders, regulations and requirements of the Federal, State and City Government and of any and all their Departments and Bureaus applicable to said premises, for the correction, prevention, and abatement of nuisances or other grievances, in, upon, or connected with said premises during said term; and shall also promptly comply with and execute all rules, orders and regulations of the Southeastern Underwriters Association for the prevention of fires, at_____own cost and expense.

FOURTH: In the event the premises shall be destroyed or so damaged or injured by fire or other casualty during the life of this agreement, whereby the same shall be rendered untenantable, then the lessor shall have the right to render said premises tenantable by repairs within ninety days therefrom. If said premises are not rendered tenantable within said time, it shall be optional with either party hereto to cancel this lease, and in the event of such cancellation the rent shall be paid only to the date of such fire or casualty. The cancellation herein mentioned shall be evidenced in writing.

FIFTH: The prompt payment of the rent for said premises upon the dates named, and the faithful observance of the rules and regulations printed upon this lease, and which are hereby made a part of this covenant, and of such other and further rules or regulations as may be hereafter made by the lessor, are the conditions upon which the lease is made and accepted and any failure on the part of the lessee to comply with the terms of said lease, or any of said rules and regulations now in existence, or which may be hereafter prescribed by the lessor, shall at the option of the lessor, work a forfeiture of this contract, and all of the rights of the lessee hereunder, and thereupon the lessor, his agents or attorneys, shall have the right to enter said premises, and remove all per-

EXHIBIT 8–4 *(continued)*

sons therefrom forcibly or otherwise, and the lessee thereby expressly waives any and all notice required by law to terminate tenancy, and also waives any and all legal proceedings to recover possession of said premises, and expressly agrees that in the event of a violation of any of the terms of this lease, or of said rules and regulations, now in existence, or which may hereafter be made, said lessor, his agent or attorneys, may immediately re-enter said premises and dispossess lessee without legal notice or the institution of any legal proceedings whatsoever.

SIXTH: If the lessee shall abandon or vacate said premises before the end of the term of this lease, or shall suffer the rent to be in arrears, the lessor may, at his option, forthwith cancel this lease or he may enter said premises as the agent of the lessee, by force or otherwise, without being liable in any way therefor, and relet the premises with or without any furniture that may be therein, as the agent of the lessee, at such price and upon such terms and for such duration of time as the lessor may determine, and receive the rent therefor, applying the same to the payment of the rent due by these presents, and if the full rental herein provided shall not be realized by lessor over and above the expenses to lessor in such re-letting, the said lessee shall pay any deficiency, and if more than the full rental is realized lessor will pay over to said lessee the excess of demand.

SEVENTH: Lessee agrees to pay the cost of collection and ten per cent attorney's fee on any part of said rental that may be collected by suit or by attorney, after the same is past due.

EIGHTH: The lessee agrees that he will pay all charges for rent, gas, electricity or other illumination, and for all water used on said premises, and should said charges for rent, light or water herein provided for at any time remain due and unpaid for the space of five days after the same shall have become due, the lessor may at its option consider the said lessee tenant at sufferance and immediately re-enter upon said premises and the entire rent for the rental period then next ensuing shall at once be due and payable and may forthwith be collected by distress or otherwise.

NINTH: The said lessee hereby pledges and assigns to the lessor all the furniture, fixtures, goods and chattels of said lessee, which shall or may be brought or put on said premises as security for the payment of the rent herein reserved, and the lessee agrees that the said lien may be enforced by distress foreclosure or otherwise at the election of the said lessor, and does hereby agree to pay attorney's fees of ten percent of the amount so collected or found to be due, together with all costs and charges therefore incurred or paid by the lessor.

TENTH: It is hereby agreed and understood between lessor and lessee that in the event the lessor decides to remodel, alter or demolish all or any part of the premises leased hereunder, or in the event of the sale or long term lease of all or any part of the_____; requiring this space, the lessee hereby agrees to vacate same upon receipt of sixty (60) days' written notice and the return of any advance rental paid on account of this lease.

It being further understod and agreed that the lessee will not be required to vacate said premises during the winter season: namely, November first to May first, by reason of the above paragraph.

ELEVENTH: The lessor, or any of his agents, shall have the right to enter said premises during all reasonable hours, to examine the same to make such repairs, additions or alterations as may be deemed necessary for the safety, comfort, or preservation thereof, or of said building, or to exhibit said premises, and to put or keep upon the doors or windows thereof a notice "FOR RENT" at any time within thirty (30) days before the expiration of this lease. The right of entry shall likewise exist for the purpose of removing placards, signs, fixtures, alterations, or additions, which do not conform to this agreement, or to the rules and regulations of the building.

TWELFTH: Lessee hereby accepts the premises in the condition they are in at the beginning of this lease and agrees to maintain said premises in the same condition, order and repair as they are at the commencement of said term, excepting only reasonable wear and tear arising from the use thereof under this agreement, and to make good to said lessor immediately upon demand, any damage to water apparatus, or electric lights or any fixture, appliances or appurtenances of said premises, or of the building, caused by any act or neglect of lessee, or of any person or persons in the employ or under the control of the lessee.

THIRTEENTH: It is expressly agreed and understood by and between the parties to this agreement, that the landlord shall not be liable for any damage or injury by water, which may be sustained by the said tenant or other person or for any other damage or injury resulting from the carelessness, negligence, or improper conduct on the part of any other tenant or agents, or employees, or by reason of the breakage, leakage, or obstruction of the water, sewer or soil pipes, or other leakage in or about the said building.

FOURTEENTH: If the lessee shall become insolvent or if bankruptcy proceedings shall be begun by or against the lessee, before the end of said term the lessor is hereby irrevocably authorized at its option, to forthwith cancel this lease, as for a default. Lessor may elect to accept rent from such receiver, trustee, or other judicial officer during the term of their occupancy in their fiduciary capacity without effecting lessor's rights as contained in this contract, but no receiver, trustee or other judicial officer shall ever have any right, title or interest in or to the above described property by virtue of this contract.

FIFTEENTH: Lessee hereby waives and renounces for himself and family any and all homestead and exemption rights he may have now, or hereafter, under or by virtue of the constitution and laws of the State of Florida, or of any other State, or of the United States, as against the payment of said rental or any portion hereof, or any other obligation or damage that may accrue under the terms of this agreement.

SIXTEENTH: This contract shall bind the lessor and its assigns or successors, and the heirs, assigns, administrators, legal representatives, executors or successors as the case may be, of the lessee.

SEVENTEENTH: It is understood and agreed between the parties hereto that time is of the essence of this contract and this applies to all terms and conditions contained herein.

EIGHTEENTH: It is understood and agreed between the parties hereto that written notice mailed or delivered to the premises leased hereunder shall constitute sufficient notice to the lessee and written notice mailed or delivered to the office of the lessor shall constitute sufficient notice to the Lessor, to comply with the terms of this contract.

NINETEENTH: The rights of the lessor under the foregoing shall be cumulative, and failure on the part of the lessor to exercise promptly any rights given hereunder shall not operate to forfeit any of the said rights.

TWENTIETH: It is further understood and agreed between the parties hereto that any charges against the lessee by the lessor for services or for work done on the premises by order of the lessee or otherwise accruing under this contract shall be considered as rent due and shall be included in any lien for rent due and unpaid.

TWENTY-FIRST: It is hereby understood and agreed that any signs or advertising to be used, including awnings, in connection with the premises leased hereunder shall be first submitted to the lessor for approval before installation of same.

EXHIBIT 8–4 *(concluded)*

IN WITNESS WHEREOF, the parties hereto have hereunto executed this instrument for the purpose herein expressed, the day and year above written.

Signed, sealed and delivered in the presence of:

_____   _____ (Seal

_____   _____ (Seal

As to Lessor   Lessor

_____   _____ (Seal

_____   _____ (Seal

As to Lessee   Lessee

STATE OF FLORIDA,

County of_____

Before me, a Notary Public in and for said State and County, personally came_____

_____to me

well known and known to be the person_____ named in the foregoing lease, and_____

acknowledged that_____executed the same for the purpose therein expressed.

IN WITNESS WHEREOF, I have hereunto set my hand and affixed my official seal the_____

day of_____, 19_____.

_____

My commission expires_____

Notary Public, State of Florida at Large.

This Instrument prepared by:

Address

Types of Commercial Leases

Commercial leases are classified in several ways—(1) by the extent to which the lessor pays operating expenses, (2) by the basis for determining rental payments, (3) by the timing of rental payments, and (4) by the terms of the leases. These types are not mutually exclusive; they are simply different ways of analyzing the most important provisions of typical commercial leases.

Extent to Which Lessor Pays Operating Expenses. Lessors may pay all, some, or none of the operating expenses. In a *gross* lease, lessors pay all operating expenses. From the lessors' viewpoint, the rental payment is gross income; it must be large enough to cover the operating expenses. (Gross leases are rare.)

In a *net, net-net,* or *partially net* lease, lessors pay some of the operating expenses and lessees pay some. The first "net" provision usually obligates lessees to pay property taxes, while the second "net" obligates them to pay insurance premiums.

When the lessees are obligated to pay all operating expenses, including repairs and maintenance, the lease is termed an *absolutely net* or a *net-net-net* lease (i.e., triple-net lease). Rental payments to lessors are truly net; lessors have no property expenses to pay. Such leases are commonly used for long-term rentals of special-purpose properties, such as manufacturing or assembly plants, large retail stores, and entire office buildings.

The extent to which lessors and lessees share the payment of operating expenses depends on the relative bargaining power of both parties and on market conditions for the type of property involved. Today, most commercial leases require lessees to pay all or some operating expenses. Medium and shorter-term leases on small- and medium-size properties tend to involve a sharing of expenses between lessors and lessees.

Some leases involve a compromise—they contain "stop" clauses or "escalator" clauses that require lessors or lessees to pay operating expenses up to a given amount, up to a specified portion of the expenses, or a specified portion of any increase.

Basis for Determining Rental Payments. A lease may require fixed amount of rent, a variable amount based on a percentage of the lessees' gross receipts, an amount subject to periodic renegotiation, or an amount determined by an index. The following is a list of the common forms of leases based on rental:

1. *Fixed rental.* Rental payments can be fixed for the term of the lease. The lease can also specify increases or decreases by a certain amount or percentage at given dates. These are termed *step-up* and *step-down leases*. Note that the amount of rent is determined at the beginning of the lease agreement.
2. *Percentage rental.* Percentage rentals are based on gross receipts of the lessees' business. In other words, the lessors' rental income is determined by the amount of business done by the lessees. It allows lessors to share in the profits and the risk. Net receipts are seldom used as a basis for determining rent because of the accounting difficulties and judgment involved in determining net receipts.

    A variation of the percentage rental basis is used when a base rental is specified—an amount that must be paid regardless of the gross receipts, with a percentage of gross receipts over and above the base rental level or some other specified level. The rental amount in excess of the base rental is termed *overage rental*.
3. *Renegotiation rental.* A renegotiation provision is sometimes used to determine rent. In it, the rental may be determined as a percentage

of the property's market value or as a function of the rental on other competing properties in the market. At periodic intervals (such as every two years or every five years), the lessors and lessees agree to renegotiate rental payments based on a reappraisal of the property's value or of market rents.

4. *Indexed rental.* Sometimes commercial lease rentals are tied to an index such as the consumer price index, the producers price index, the GNP implicit price deflator, or a local building-cost index. As the index changes up or down, the rent is adjusted up or down by a specified amount or percentage.

While indexes have been widely used, they may not provide a relevant basis for rent payments. For example, one study showed that, during inflationary periods, the consumer price index increases at a faster rate than commercial real estate expenses. The study compared several other indexes with an index of commercial real estate operating costs and found greater accuracy and reliability with both the *Engineering News Record* building-cost index (BCI) and the GNP implicit price deflator (GNPIPD).[2]

Timing of Rental Payments. Leases are often classified according to when and how frequently rental payments must be made. Whereas residential leases (and some commercial leases) usually require payments to be made at the beginning of the periods, most commercial leases call for payments to be made at the end of the period so the period's gross receipts can be determined. Variations require that a base rental be paid at the beginning of a period, and an overage rental be paid after the period is completed.

Frequency of rental payments may also be specified (monthly, quarterly, semiannually, or annually). Most commercial leases, just like residential leases, call for monthly payments.

Term of Leases. A lease is often classified as *short-term* or *long-term* depending on the length of its term. While the distinction is somewhat arbitrary and subjective, short-term leases usually cover three to five years or less. A more meaningful classification would be: short-term, 3 years or less; medium-term, 3 to 10 years; long-term, 10 years or longer.

Important Considerations for Commercial Lessors

Commercial lessors have the same concerns as residential lessors. They want reliable lessees who will pay the rent on time, take care of the prop-

---

[2]Michael J. Kazen, *The Consumer Price Index as a Basis for the Escalation of Long Term Commercial Real Estate Leases: A Critical Analysis,* unpublished M.A. thesis, University of Florida, 1982.

erty, cooperate in allowing reasonable access for inspections, and use the property compatibly with other uses in the area. Yet commercial lessors have additional considerations and may need to investigate potential lessees more intensively.

Creditworthiness. The creditworthiness of commercial lessees usually depends on their ability to operate a business profitably. Thus, commercial lessors usually must analyze the need for the lessees' business in the community and the lessees' ability to operate the business. A market analysis may be useful in determining the need for the business. Lessors may require lessees to review such studies performed by independent consultants.

Lessors often analyze a lessee's track record and managerial abilities. Additionally, lessors may analyze lessees' management structure, financial strength, and competitive market position.

Compatibility. A lessee's ability to run a profitable business may depend on the nature of the business relative to other businesses in the area. For example, in shopping centers, retail stores complement each other by helping to attract customers and by selling a variety of goods and services. Certain types of firms are compatible with each other, while others are neutral or detract from each other.[3] For example, dress shops and shoe stores help attract customers to each other, but mortuaries repel customers of most retail stores. Lessors may want to assure themselves that a proposed lessee's business will be compatible with other nearby businesses.

Reputation and Prestige. A lessee's reputation and prestige affect surrounding businesses and, ultimately, land values. Highly regarded tenants contribute to the desirability of a building, a shopping center, a neighborhood, or an entire community. A lessee's undesirable reputation can have the opposite effects. Owners usually avoid such lessees, except in an area of similar establishments.

Specialized Space and Equipment Requirements. Many tenants require specialized space or equipment. For example, physicians and dentists require small rooms and specialized plumbing. Usually, lessees provide any special equipment, but they expect lessors to install items regarded as part of the real estate (plumbing, electrical service, sinks, stoves, and cabinets).

---

[3]See Richard L. Nelson, *The Selection of Retail Locations* (New York: McGraw-Hill Book Co., 1958).

Important Considerations for Commercial Lessees

Commercial lessees have concerns similar to those of lessors: They want properties that are compatible for their uses, that are well located for their businesses and well maintained, and that will enable them to operate their businesses profitably. For lessors to obtain and retain lessees who will pay rent on time, maintain the property, and contribute positively to neighborhood properties, they need lessees who can use the property profitably. Lessees, however, must analyze competing properties from their own point of view. They must seek appropriate properties at fair rental rates and negotiate lease terms that provide the necessary degree of flexibility. Some of the important general concerns of lessees are discussed below:

Appropriateness of the Property. The property's location and physical characteristics should meet the lessees' needs. Commercial establishments rely on traffic and access appropriate to their use. A good location for a shoe store, for example, might not be good for a physician's office.

The physical characteristics of the site and building must be considered. Is the size and type of space appropriate? Is there ample parking? Is the building in good repair and well maintained? Is it adequately heated and cooled? Are special facilities provided, such as plumbing, electrical service, elevators, security, and so forth? Is the property attractive for its intended use? Is the property compatible with surrounding properties?

Potential for Expansion. Most businesses seek growth. Will the property accommodate expansion? Is the space currently large enough, or can the building be expanded? Is the interior space flexible? Will the lease agreement address expansion satisfactorily? For the firm that expects to expand, the lease should give the lessee the right to occupy additional space, after a specified notice period, at market rental rates. If additional space is not available, the lease should provide for cancellation, after reasonable notice.

Cooperation of Lessors. An important consideration for lessees is whether the lessor will cooperate to meet their current and future needs. One good indication is the lessor's willingness to include clauses pertaining to expansion, periodic rehabilitation or remodeling, and cancellation in the event of business reverses.

While lessees cannot expect one-sided or unfair terms, they can negotiate. In short, lessees need to decide what is important and what provisions they can give up to accommodate the lessor's concerns.

SHOPPING-CENTER LEASES

Shopping-center leases are usually quite complex because of the relationships among the particular tenant, the owner, and the other tenants in the center. The center's owner and management want compatible tenants who will contribute to the effectiveness of the entire center. Consequently, lease provisions and tenants' association rules are established to govern these relationships, and membership in a tenants' association and agreement to abide by its rules are important clauses in such leases. Other important clauses in shopping-center leases are discussed below.

Signs and Displays

Usually, only *anchor* or key tenants (e.g., major department stores) are allowed to place signs on the exterior of an enclosed shopping mall. These signs are regulated in the lease as to size, shape, position, and so forth. Interior signs in enclosed malls and exterior signs in unenclosed centers are also regulated by provisions in shopping center leases. Generally, signs must conform to the size, shape, and placement standards for the center. Other types of advertising and displays in individual stores are also regulated to conform to standards of attractiveness and good taste.

Business Hours

Shopping center leases normally require tenants to be open during specified hours—usually the hours preferred by anchor tenants. While smaller ones might otherwise prefer not to stay open during evenings or on Sundays or holidays, consistency among tenants is important to the shopping center's overall success.

Cancellation

Shopping center leases often contain a clause allowing the lessors to cancel the lease of a tenant whose business falls below a specified level for a specified time. When the lease is canceled, the tenant must vacate the space without penalty. The management is then free to lease the space to a more viable tenant.

Merchandise Inventory

Tenants are usually required by the lease to maintain a level of inventory comparable to that carried in other branch stores of the same company or comparable to that carried by competing firms. The purpose of such a clause, of course, is to require firms to make a reasonable effort to be successful. A company may wish to retrench or move its store from the shopping center to another location. In order to abrogate the lease, it might attempt to have the lessors cancel the lease because of low business volume. The merchandise inventory provision seeks to prevent a deliberately low business volume caused by lack of inventory.

Utilities

Shopping center leases usually specify that tenants pay their own utilities, either to the utility companies or to the center management (which makes a profit on the sale of power). Lessors usually agree to pay utility expenses for common areas, such as a mall. Often mall managements try to limit common-area expenses by agreeing to pay for a specified amount of heating, cooling, and lighting. Beyond this level, the expense is prorated among the tenants.

Fixtures and Trade Fixtures

Fixtures are real estate and cannot be removed by tenants (see Chapter 2). *Trade fixtures*, on the other hand, are specialized equipment used by commercial tenants in their businesses and are personal property. They can be removed by the tenants. Examples are counters, showcases, cabinets, and movable partitions. The lease should specify items regarded as trade fixtures.

Relocation

Lessors may require the right to relocate tenants to alternative space equal in size and quality. Such a provision gives added flexibility to management in dealing with prospective tenants who may want space already occupied. Lessees in a shopping center should be leery of a relocation clause and, if possible, hold out for voluntary compliance with a relocation request.

Tenant Improvements

Most shopping center leases require that tenants contract with the center's management to ensure that improvements conform with the center's standards; to ensure that management knows the location of plumbing, electrical lines, and so on; and to avoid mechanics and materialmans liens in case the tenant does not pay for labor or materials. While tenants may want the right to have improvements made, they should not object to this arrangement provided there are adequate assurances the job will be completed according to the tenant's specifications and without an unreasonable markup by the center management. Tenants, of course, may attempt to have the lessor pay for any improvements.

GROUND LEASES

Leases of vacant land or of the land portion of an improved parcel of real estate are called *ground leases*. They are long-term leases, ranging from 20 to 99 years or longer, and usually call for absolutely net rental payments to the landowners. In addition to property taxes and maintenance expenses, lessees usually agree to pay for any construction costs, insurance expenses, property assessments, and liability awards to injured parties. In short, lessors are relieved of all expenses and liabilities for the property, and receive a periodic rent.

Ground leases are used to convey the rights of occupancy and use to lessees who expect to use properties for many different purposes, from single-family residential to large commercial and industrial uses. Single-family homes are built on leased land in areas where land costs are very high—notably Hawaii and some areas of Southern California and Florida—while major commercial and industrial complexes are built on leased land in many areas. The Empire State Building in New York City was built on leased land, although currently both the building and land are owned by the Prudential Insurance Company of America. Also, in New York City, the huge Rockefeller Center complex was built on land leased for 99 years from Columbia University.

Whether the use of leased land for residential purposes is a cause or effect of high land values is debatable. The U.S. Supreme Court recently upheld a 1967 Hawaii law enabling homeowners to purchase leased land on which their homes were built (see Frame 8–2). Since almost half of the state's land is owned by a few large owners, the legislature believed that land could be made more affordable for individual homeowners by breaking up the large holdings.

Ground lessees usually construct buildings on the land. In fact, many ground leases *require* lessees to construct buildings so that the land will support higher lease payments. In addition to periodic lease payments, lessors obtain the entire property—land and buildings—at the termination of the lease.

Whether the lessors are obligated to pay for the value of the buildings, or any part thereof, at the termination of the lease is a matter for negotiation when the lease agreement is prepared. Many ground leases, particularly longer-term leases of 50 to 99 years, require no such payment, while shorter-term leases sometimes require lessors to pay the current market value of the buildings at the end of the lease term; one or more appraisers determine the value. Occasionally, a predetermined amount is specified in the lease.

━━━━━━━━━━━━━━━━━━━━━━━ *Frame 8–2* ━━━━━━━━━━━━━━━━━━━━━━━

State's Right—Hawaii's Land Reform Is Upheld*

The ruling sounded more fitting for El Salvador than the United States. Indeed, last week's Supreme Court decision upholding Hawaii's right to break up large privately held estates and redistribute ownership to the tenants seemed downright radical. But the unanimous 8–0 ruling† was made for the most conservative of reasons. Said Hawaii's Deputy Attorney General Michael Lilly: "It's a classic states' rights case."

The decision grew out of a suit challenging the constitutionality of the Land Reform Act passed by Hawaii's legislature in 1967. This law was designed to put an end to the remnants of Hawaii's feudal tenure system, a holdover from the islands' settlement by Polynesian immigrants who allowed only high chiefs to own land. The challenge was brought by trustees of the Bishop estate, Hawaii's largest private landowner (340,000 acres). The estate is the legacy of Princess Bernice Pauahi Bishop, a member of one of Hawaii's royal families, who died in 1884.

The Bishop estate and about 70 other large landholders own 47 percent of Hawaii's 4 million acres; the local and federal governments hold 42 percent. Less than 11 percent is held by small property owners. The state argued that this concentration of land in a few hands has sharply inflated housing costs for Hawaii's homeowners. Says Congressman Cecil Heftel, a Honolulu Democrat: "The ruling protects a lot of people who otherwise would have been unable to maintain their homes."

In upholding the land-reform law, the court cited the Fifth Amendment, which allows the government to acquire property for "public use" after paying "just compensation." Typically, this right of eminent domain is invoked to permit the purchase of land for roads and public projects. The court affirmed that a state could exercise this right for other purposes, such as land reform, as determined by its legislators. "The people of Hawaii have attempted, much as the settlers of the original 13 colonies did, to reduce the perceived social and economic evils of a land oligopoly traceable to their monarchs," wrote Justice Sandra Day O'Connor.

Unless Hawaii's state supreme court invalidates the program, the lines of the volcanic islands will be redrawn. Prospective buyers and sellers must now go to court to haggle over prices on about 5,700 lots in 39 tracts of land, most of them owned by the Bishop estate. Myron Thompson, a trustee of the Bishop estate, calls the process perhaps "the greatest rip-off of this nation in the 20th century." But Mike Morita, who owns a home near Honolulu but not the land beneath it, is predictably pleased. Said he: "I have three kids, and I'd like to turn property over to them."

---

*Time, June 11, 1984, p. 27.

†Justice Thurgood Marshall, who is married to a Hawaiian, exempted himself from the case.

Whether stated or not, lessees have the right to borrow on a mortgage against their leasehold interest. Nevertheless, ground lessees usually insist that this right be stated in the lease. Such a provision precludes any misunderstanding and recognizes the need of most ground lessees to borrow funds in order to construct buildings. It also recognizes the requirement of most lenders for the right to assign or sublet the property if the lessees default on either the mortgage or the lease agreement. Lenders insist that lessors notify them of any default so they can remedy the default and either operate the property or assign or sublet the leasehold.

Lessors in ground leases do not give up their right to sell their leased fee interest, and this right is not a problem for most lessees. Any purchasers, of course, take title to the property subject to the lease, provided the lessees gave adequate public notice by recording the lease or by physically possessing the property. Nevertheless, lessees usually insist that a provision be included in the lease document requiring the lessors to sell their leased fee interest only to purchasers who recognize and take title subject to the lease. Any later misunderstandings give the lessees right of action against the lessors.

Ground leases are employed by landowners who do not want to operate a property or construct buildings but who want a steady, secure income from the property, who want to preserve ownership rights for themselves or future generations, and who want some control over the way a property is used.

Through good leases, lessees are able to occupy and use a property without the capital outlay that would be required to purchase the land. They often expect to have no use for the property at termination of the lease and thus place no premium on ownership rights. Lessees can construct buildings specifically designed for their use and can pay more for construction than they could if they also had to purchase the land. They also may receive favorable income tax treatment through the deductibility of lease payments, interest on a leasehold mortgage, and depreciation allowances.

OVERVIEW

Lease contracts are used to separate the rights of occupancy and use of real estate from the other rights of ownership. While some leases of less than one year's duration can be oral, most leases must be written in form. A lease is primarily a contract, but also a conveyance. In the event of default, it gives both parties the same legal remedies as with other contracts in event of default (the right to sue for damages or specific performance, or the right to void the lease and return the property to the lessors).

Residential leases typically are written documents that include a number of provisions. They are regulated and limited, however, by state or local landlord-tenant laws, which give both parties certain unwaivable rights and obligations. Such laws typically require tenants to use the property in a safe and reasonable manner, to obey housing and zoning codes, not to damage the property, and not to deny reasonable access by landlords. They require landlords to maintain the property in a safe and habitable condition, to respect the lessee's right of privacy, and to inform lessees about the disposition of security deposits and advance rents.

Since most residential leases are prepared by lessors, lessees should read leases carefully and be prepared to abide by their provisions. Failure to do so can result in default, forefeiture of security deposits and advance rents, and eviction. Lessees should also know their rights to receive information about their security deposits and advance rents, to safe and habitable living conditions, and to privacy from intrusion by landlords.

Commercial and ground leases are usually lengthier, more complex documents than residential leases. They are less regulated by law because both parties are assumed to be knowledgeable. In addition to term and rental payments, they usually cover such matters as use of the property, operating expenses, fixtures and tenant's fixtures, renewal and expansion, assignment and subletting, security for rent payments, liability to third parties, abandonment, and subordination of the lease to mortgage financing. Shopping-center leases are a specialized type of commercial lease, often containing even more detailed and complex provisions. They recognize the interrelationships between the operation of a store in a shopping center and the overall operation of the entire center. Ground leases are long-term conveyances of the use and occupancy rights of land. They give lessees time to construct buildings in order to use the property most efficiently and provide lessors with stable, secure income.

TEST YOURSELF

Explain the following concepts and procedures presented in this chapter.

1. Leased fee estate versus leasehold estate.
2. Contract versus a conveyance.
3. Reversion.
4. Lessor versus lessee.
5. Consideration.
6. Offer and acceptance.
7. Assignment versus subletting of a leasehold.
8. Sandwich leasehold.
9. Net versus net-net versus net-net-net lease.
10. Renegotiation versus indexed rental.
11. Fixtures versus trade fixtures.
12. Ground lease.

Answer the following multiple-choice questions.

1. The requirements for a valid lease are
   a. Names, description, consideration, legality, offer and acceptance, and written form.
   b. Name of lessor, description, legality, offer, and acceptance, and written form.
   c. Names, consideration, written form, offer and acceptance, and legality.

     d. Description, proper form, legality, consideration, seal of lessor, and signatures.

     e. None of the above.

2. An oral lease usually creates a(n)
   a. Estate for years.
   b. Tenancy at sufferance.
   c. Tenancy from year to year.
   d. Tenancy at will.
   e. Joint tenancy.

3. In most states, residential landlord-tenant laws have been enacted to
   a. Protect tenants from landlords.
   b. Protect landlords from tenants.
   c. Govern landlord-tenant relationships in apartment buildings having four or fewer units.
   d. Establish standard provisions in residential leases.
   e. Establish equitable and balanced rights and obligations of both landlords and tenants.

4. When leasing a commercial property, a lessor makes what representation regarding the condition of the property?
   a. That the property is in sound, safe condition.
   b. That the property meets housing and safety code standards.
   c. That the property either meets housing and safety code standards or will be brought up to code requirements.
   d. All of the above.
   e. None of the above.

5. Lessors tend to obtain rents that increase faster than the rate of inflation by having lease payments determined by what method?
   a. Percentage of rental based on gross receipts.
   b. Fixed rental.
   c. Renegotiation rental at two-year intervals.
   d. CPI-indexed rental.
   e. GNPIPD-indexed rental.

ADDITIONAL READINGS

Ferguson, Jerry T. *Fundamentals of Real Estate Investing.* Glenview, Ill.: Scott, Foresman, 1984, Chap. 11.

French, William, and Harold Lusk. *Law of the Real Estate Business.* 5th ed. Homewood, Ill.: Richard D. Irwin, 1984, Chap. 19.

Frome, Richard M. "Critical Provisions in Commercial Leases." *Real Estate Outlook* 4 (Spring 1982).

Kratovil, Robert, and Raymond J. Werner. *Real Estate Law.* 8th ed. Englewood Cliffs, N.J.: Prentice-Hall, 1983, Chap. 37.

Stamaugh, David R., Alan R. Bullock, R. L. Greer, Peter H. Larson III, and Elliot I. Young. "Leasing Space for Success." *Real Estate Today,* August 1978.

Part Two

The Economic Perspective

In this section of the text, we view real estate from an economic perspective. As analysts, we recognize that real estate is an economic good for which people will pay money or other valuable consideration. As an economic good, real estate is similar to other economic goods. This means that analysts need not "reinvent the wheel" to understand how people behave toward real estate. People buy it, lease it, use it, rehabilitate it, and sell it in conformity with economic principles. These principles allow analysts to understand why and how decisions are made about real estate—and more important, to help predict how real estate markets will behave.

If we understand and can predict how real estate markets behave, we can make intelligent decisions about how people use real estate. Each of us can, as economists would say, maximize its productivity—which means using real estate to obtain the most satisfaction per dollar

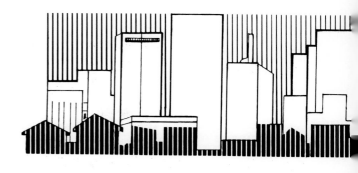

spent. The more participants in the market who maximize the productivity of real estate, the greater the national welfare.

This section of the text begins with two somewhat conceptual chapters. These chapters explain the motivating forces behind real estate decisions and the resulting patterns of market behavior. We introduce the goals of efficiency and equity and examine the consequences of market failures that sometimes impede our attainment of satisfaction. We discuss the operation of real estate markets and the applied analysis of those markets in Chapters 10 and 11. In Chapters 12 through 15, we discuss various types of governmental activity in regulating real estate markets to promote economic efficiency and equity and correct market failures. These activities include housing policy and programs at the federal level; licensing of real estate practitioners at the state level; and land use, zoning, and property taxation at the local level. ▪

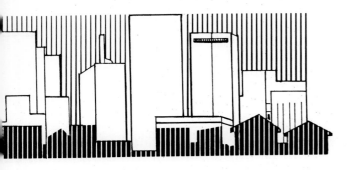

OUTLINE

INTRODUCTION

While sometimes jokingly called "the dismal science,"[1] economics is more appropriately defined as the study of how society accomplishes its goals through the management of its scarce resources. Since society includes all of us, economics is simply the study of how we behave (as individuals and as groups) in exchanging goods and services that have money value. In order to determine goals, members of society must make decisions about four types of economic activity: (1) resource allocation, (2) income distribution, (3) economic growth, and (4) economic stability.

Resource allocation refers to the commitment of basic resources such as land, labor, and capital to various uses such as consumer goods, national defense, education, and housing. *Income distribution* concerns the level of wealth obtained by people of different occupations such as laborers, skilled workers, executives, and professionals. *Economic growth* concerns policies designed to achieve an expanding level of output so that the general welfare improves. Finally, *economic stability* concerns policies to prevent wide swings (up or down) in the rate of growth.[2]

Though all four areas of economics are important on a national level, resource allocation is also important to individual persons and organizations. In fact, we, as individuals and as real estate decision makers, must usually regard the last three areas as givens, or part of the economic environment in which decisions are made. We influence policies on income distribution, economic growth, and economic stability by voting for public officials. As individuals, however, we can make *resource allocation decisions* in our roles as consumers, investors, professionals, or business ex-

---

[1]Thomas Carlyle, a Scottish essayist and historian, is blamed for attaching this stigma to economics. He once referred to the famous economists, Malthus and Ricardo, as "the respectable professors of the dismal science."

[2]Although large upswings are nice, they may lead to unbearably large downswings.

ecutives. These decisions determine how much real estate is devoted to various uses including farms, homes, offices, manufacturing plants, stores, schools, hotels, golf courses, tennis courts, parks, used-car lots, etc.

The principal goal of this system of resource-allocation decisions is the achievement of economic *efficiency*. The economic system in a free society enables individual decision makers to allocate their resources to uses that maximize their satisfaction. Thus, efficiency is achieved when all people or decision-making units, such as business firms, maximize their satisfactions with the resources at their command. In effect, when resources are allocated efficiently, we all obtain the most or best (as each of us defines these terms) for what we have available to pay.

Although the efficiency criterion is basic, it will not always guide decisions in our less-than-perfect, private market economy. In at least three situations, the private market economy may fail, resulting in less-than-optimal outcomes to real estate allocation decisions. Markets may fail because of what economists call externalities, public goods, and adverse selection. A conceptual analysis of these problems is presented in this chapter, while later chapters deal with specific applications.

Finally, we argue that the efficiency criterion must be modified by the *equity* criterion. Real estate resources that are allocated efficiently may not necessarily be distributed equitably—that is, fairly—to all members of society. For example, there may be an adequate supply of housing to shelter all members of society, yet some families live in 200-room mansions while others share one room. If society, through its elected representatives, decides this is not an equitable situation, it will devise policies and programs to rectify it.

The equity criterion, therefore, directly affects the issue of income distribution. According to many economists, governments in private market economies should promote economic efficiency by removing the causes of market failure, while at the same time not promote an inequitable shift in the distribution of income or wealth.

THE EFFICIENCY GOAL

Technical Efficiency

We can define economic efficiency in two ways. First, efficiency refers to the relationship between inputs and outputs in the production of a product or service. In this context, a manager or entrepreneur decides on the best methods and resources to be incorporated in producing a product or providing a service. For example, a home builder must decide on materials and construction methods, financing, and marketing channels. Since these types of decisions involve technical questions of how to best produce a product or service, this type of efficiency is termed *technical efficiency*.

Allocative Efficiency

The second definition of efficiency is more general. It states that the desired goods and services in an economy are best produced by the combination of resources having the *lowest total value.* This optimal combination is decided by the total number of dollars that consumers are willing to pay for goods and services. Since this criterion concerns what resources are allocated to produce the proper combination of goods and services, it is called *allocative efficiency.* Questions of allocative efficiency include how much of what types of real estate should be constructed. For example, how many apartments, condominiums, single-family houses, commercial buildings, industrial properties, and so on are needed in the nation or in a local market?

From the economic perspective of real estate, we are concerned primarily with allocative efficiency because it deals with questions that consumers, investors, and business executives can act on to achieve their goals. Technical efficiency involves questions of how best to produce something *after the decision to produce it has been made.* Allocative efficiency involves questions of what and how many to produce.

Exhibit 9–1 illustrates a simple problem in allocative efficiency. Assume that the economy produces and consumes only two goods, housing and video games. In any given period, a household (i.e., a family or sin-

---

EXHIBIT 9–1
PRODUCTION POSSIBILITIES FOR HOUSING AND VIDEO GAMES

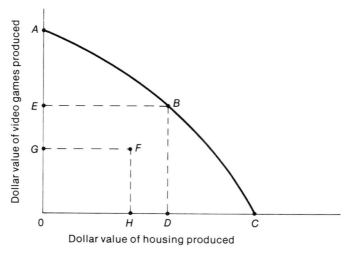

gle person) seeks to expand either its quantity of housing or its quantity of video games but cannot expand both simultaneously. Rather than allocating all of their resources to either video games (point *A*) or housing (point *C*), households presumably would decide to allocate resources to both.

Points *A*, *B*, *C*, and all points on the curve represent efficient solutions because consumers will pay the total value of any combination of both goods produced. That is, society desires only these two goods, and all of the resources available to society are being used to produce them. No moral judgment is made, however, about the *best* combination of the two goods.[3]

Point *F* represents an inefficient solution because some of the resources available to society are not being used to produce the two products society desires. Since consumers are willing to pay for the total value of the goods produced, economic incentives will allocate resources toward production combinations at some point along the curve.

Later in this chapter, we examine a few of the reasons why real estate production and consumption may occur at point *F* rather than at an efficient level on the curve. Such instances represent *market failures*. Market failures in real estate involve such situations as those in which home buyers cannot obtain adequate information to make intelligent decisions among houses, owners of real estate are burdened by the pollution generated by other owners, and citizens are incorrectly advised by dishonest or incompetent real estate professionals. In some cases, government should intervene to correct or offset the causes of market failure; in other cases, intervention may be inappropriate.

An Efficiently Allocated Resource

The production of housing benefits society in the form of shelter, prestige, and as a stock of wealth. Housing production also results in costs from the use of scarce resources (land, labor, and capital) that could be used to produce other goods. These costs are referred to as *opportunity costs*—the costs of lost opportunities to produce something other than, in this example, housing.

The efficient allocation of resources to housing occurs when the total benefits to society of producing a certain level of housing exceed the total costs to society by the greatest amount. Since total social benefits (SB) minus total social costs (SC) equals net social benefits (NSB), *allocative efficiency occurs when NSB is maximized.*

---

[3]Allocative efficiency, therefore, is a *descriptive* ("what is" efficient) rather than a *normative* ("what should be" efficient) rule. Because goods and services are represented by dollar value (or prices), resource allocation decisions are made through the price mechanism.

Frame 9–1

Why Shouldn't the Goal of Society Be to Maximize Total Benefits?

The efficiency criterion of maximizing *net* social benefits is often misinterpreted to mean maximizing *total* social benefits. The criterion of maximizing total social benefits usually takes the form of a "needs" approach to resolving public policy issues—"We need more land-use control in this community," or "We need more industrial development."

Unfortunately, the costs to society of more land-use control or more industrial development are frequently and unjustly subordinated to the benefits of such actions. What is important are the *net* benefits (total benefits minus total costs) to society of a particular policy initiative—not simply total benefits.

INEFFICIENT ALLOCATION OF RESOURCES: MARKET FAILURE

General Nature of Market Failure

Members of society can change their spending behavior if they dislike the existing allocation of resources. The ability to change to an efficient allocation of resources, however, assumes that consumers have adequate and accurate information about the benefits and costs of various goods. It also assumes that such decisions can be implemented immediately and that political realities conform to economic rationale (e.g., that special-interest groups will not oppose changes that would improve the general welfare even if such changes hurt their own position).

Obviously, these ideal conditions do not exist in reality. Consumers often lack adequate information about product characteristics and substitutes. Long time lags may intervene between the recognition of an inefficient mix and its correction. And consumers may lack the power to effect political or economic change.

In all of these cases, the private costs or benefits connected with the production and consumption of a good or product are disconnected from private decisions. An inefficient allocation of resources occurs when producers or consumers fail to incur all of the costs of their actions or inadvertently receive undeserved benefits from the actions of others. Such situations violate two conditions for allocative efficiency: (1) the sum of all private benefits (PB) equals social benefits (SB), and (2) the sum of all private costs (PC) equals social costs (SC). Therefore, markets fail when $PB \neq SB$ or when $PC \neq SC$. The consequence of market failure is the production of a good or service at a level other than that where NSB is at a maximum (i.e., Point *F* in Exhibit 9–1 rather than along curve *ABC*).

In this section, we analyze three types of private market failure. Market failures occur when the problems of externalities, public goods, or adverse selection are present. In each case, government responds by enacting laws, regulations, and programs to deal with the misallocation of resources resulting from market failure. In essence, market failure explains why such laws, regulations, and programs exist.

Externalities

There are two types of externalities—negative and positive. The first results in value losses; the second results in value increases. While negative externalities create hardships and are therefore more noticeable, both types of externalities produce inefficient allocation of resources.

Negative Externalities.   Negative externalities, sometimes referred to as *indirect costs*, arise from the actions of producers or consumers who do not pay the full costs of their activities.

Suppose there are two communities, Dumpsberg and Cleansville. As shown in Exhibit 9–2, Cleansville is located downstream from Dumpsberg. Housing developers in Dumpsberg increase their profits by dumping all wastes in the Joan River rather than providing proper sewage treatment. In order for the residents of Cleansville to use the river as a water supply, they must pay to construct an otherwise unnecessary water-purification plant north of the city. While developers' profits are higher and prices are lower in Dumpsberg, some of the costs of development in Dumpsberg are actually being borne by the residents of Cleansville. *Indirect costs* are imposed on members of society who do not benefit from the action creating the externality. The residents of Cleansville are powerless to change the situation, which results in an inefficient allocation of resources: Private costs are not equal to social costs (PC $\neq$ SC). For the residents of Dumpsberg, PC is less than SC and, for the residents of Cleansville, PC is greater than SC.

Other examples of negative externalities are pollution and acid rain from manufacturing plants, noise and unsightliness from highways and shopping centers, lack of upkeep of one or several houses in an otherwise attractive neighborhood, and crime and litter. In each case, those incurring the indirect costs have little power to effect a change.

Positive Externalities.   Assume that a physician, Dr. Gentrification,[4] has decided to purchase a row house in a severely run-down, inner-city neighborhood. She buys the property for $50,000 and invests $100,000 in rehabilitating the structure. Sensing that a neighborhood revival is taking

---

[4]*Gentrification* is a term that has become associated with the rehabilitation of some inner-city neighborhoods.

EXHIBIT 9–2
NEGATIVE EXTERNALITIES: THE CASE OF DUMPSBERG AND CLEANSVILLE

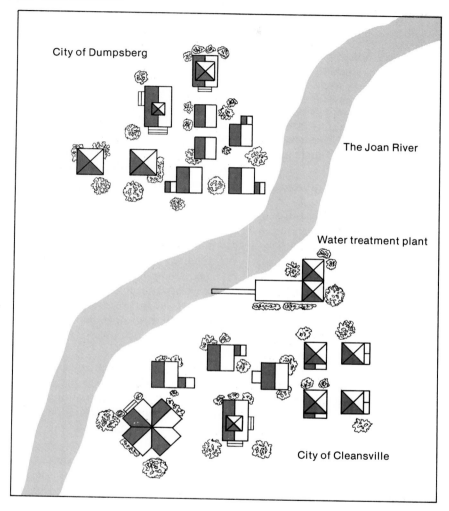

place, a real estate speculator (a market participant seeking a quick and profitable resale) purchases identical row houses on either side of the doctor's property for $75,000 each. Thus, even though the owners of the neighboring row houses had no part in the investment and consumption decisions of Dr. Gentrification, they received indirect benefits from her actions in the form of increased property values ($75,000 instead of $50,000).

The case of Dr. Gentrification is an example of positive externalities, since someone benefits indirectly without incurring the costs of the action that created the externality. Even though a benefit is created, this situation represents an inefficient solution because private benefits (PB) exceed social benefits (SB). That is, the net worth (PB) of the owners of the adjacent rowhouses increases by $25,000 each without any additional improvement in general housing conditions (SB). The efficient solution in this case is one sale at $50,000, but due to the indirect benefits generated by the doctor's investment, two sales occurred at $75,000 each.

Other examples of positive externalities are the construction of new or improved highways adjacent to commercial establishments, the establishment of a new park close to a residential subdivision, and the superior upkeep of one or several houses in an otherwise average neighborhood. In all such cases, the value to the recipients of the indirect benefits is greater than the value to society.

The Case for Government Intervention. Because they impose indirect costs on others rather than indirect benefits, negative externalities are far more serious than positive externalities. Assume, for example, that the efficient level of housing production in Cleansville is 500 units per year at $60,000 per unit. Yet, the actual level of production is 450 units per year at $65,000 per unit. The actual level is inefficient because private costs are higher than social costs, and those paying the difference in private costs are paying them indirectly and not sharing in the benefits.

Governments may have a legitimate role in correcting such market failures. To prevent the sort of negative externality imposed by Dumpsberg, many state governments require communities to have their own sewage treatment systems, and homes outside of urban areas to have septic tanks. In general, negative externalities are controlled by nuisance laws, public planning, zoning, building codes, hazardous waste laws, and so forth. These laws and regulations are examined in Chapter 14.

Government intervention has its costs as well in administration, enforcement, and perhaps some loss of freedom. The ultimate test, therefore, is whether the benefits of government intervention outweigh its costs. Allocative efficiency results when NSB is maximized.

Public Goods

Public goods are products and services that are consumed *collectively* by members of society. This means that no members of society can be excluded from consumption of public goods, irrespective of who incurs the cost of supplying those goods. In addition, one individual's consumption of the goods or services usually does not affect another's.

While purely public goods are provided exclusively by the government, some goods traded in the private market have public good characteristics. Magazines, for example, are available in public libraries; thus, no individual can be excluded from consuming (reading) magazines, and an individual's consumption does not (in the short run) alter another's consumption of magazines. Yet enough people enjoy the convenience of having their own copies of magazines that sales in the private market continue to grow.

National defense is a classic example of a pure public good. What differentiates national defense and other pure public goods from private goods that have public-goods characteristics is the fact that consumers have difficulty evaluating the benefits of public goods to themselves and others. And even if they can evaluate the benefits, they may be unwilling to *reveal their preferences*—and thus unwilling to pay individually—for pure public goods.

To demonstrate this market failure, let's consider the case of open space and parks—a good that private real estate markets generally do not provide. A family, the Greens, recently moved to Parkless, a medium-size community without (you guessed it) parks or public open spaces. Real estate developers considered constructing private parks in the community, but found that the cost of excluding citizens who do not pay an admission fee makes the price of admission excessive for most Parkless residents.

Mrs. Green recognizes the need for parks. Children are playing in the streets, people are picnicking in the Sears parking lot, and the crime rate on Sundays has reached astronomic proportions. Believing that everyone would benefit from having parks, she embarks on a campaign to raise private funds for public park development. Mrs. Green visits many residents and asks them "How much would you value a new park for Parkless?" and "How much would you be willing to pay to obtain a park?"

Many residents respond that the community would benefit greatly, that their neighbors would benefit individually, but that they themselves would not realize much benefit. They are therefore unwilling to pay for park development. These residents believe that their replies would have little effect on the ultimate decision to build the park. Furthermore, they know that if a park is built, they could not be excluded from using it.

Because she believes that residents either do not see the benefits they would receive from a park or are unwilling to reveal their true preferences, Mrs. Green decides to lobby the city council to impose additional taxes for park development. She contends that a park is a public good that benefits all citizens. Eventually, taxes are raised, a park is built, and the community changes its name to Parkland.

The inability of the market to produce an efficient quantity of pure public goods is a form of market failure. This occurs because individuals either cannot evaluate the benefits or are unwilling to pay for them. Without government intervention, a lower-than-efficient quantity of the public good is produced. The provision of pure public goods to correct a market failure, therefore, is a legitimate form of government involvement in private markets. National defense; public parks; roads; bridges; sewage systems; airports; and police, fire, and public-health services are all examples of public goods provided by government.

Adverse Selection

Economists have long recognized that consumers make decisions on the basis of the *quality* of goods and services as well as their *price*. However, in some markets, especially real estate markets, there is wide disparity between suppliers' and purchasers' knowledge of product quality. In other words, sellers know more about the quality of their products than buyers can discover without incurring unreasonable expenses. This form of market failure leads to what economists label *adverse selection.*[5]

The classic example of this information disparity is the used-car market. Used-car salesmen frequently have better information about the defects of their products than the average buyer can determine in a test drive. A similar situation often occurs in the market for existing houses. Sellers usually know of defects that potential buyers cannot easily detect. Other examples include markets for the services of professionals such as physicians, dentists, attorneys, accountants, real estate brokers, appraisers, managers, consultants, and so on. Is your doctor, for example, any better at medical diagnosis and treatment than other doctors who might charge less? Are some real estate professionals more competent than others? Is their competence related to the fees they charge? Such questions are difficult to answer without costly research.

The market's failure to provide relevant information quickly and easily may have one of two possible outcomes: the consumer (1) selects less-than-the-best product or service for a given price, or (2) pays too much for a product or service. In other words, private benefits are lower than social benefits. Not only will some consumers suffer from incompetent professional services or pay too much, some competent professionals will not be compensated adequately to reflect the high quality of their services. They will tend to drop out of the profession, leaving only suppliers of average or below-average competence. In other words, the *selection* of suppliers in the market that remains is poor or *adverse.*

These potential market results from adverse selection provide the economic justification for the licensing of various professionals, including

---

[5]This problem is recognized in an important article by George Akerlof, "The Market for Lemons: Quality Uncertainty and the Market Mechanism," *Quarterly Journal of Economics* 84 (August 1970), pp. 488–500.

real estate brokers and appraisers. Licensing of real estate professionals prevents incompetent suppliers from entering the market and keeps competent suppliers from dropping out of the market. In Chapter 13, we discuss the regulation of real estate occupations and other possible methods of dealing with the problem of adverse selection.

THE EQUITY CRITERION

The equity criterion concerns the question of fairness. As an economic principle, it is unlike the efficiency criterion in at least two ways. First, equity issues involve the distribution of income in society rather than the allocation of resources to the production and consumption of goods. Second, the equity criterion, because it relates directly to the elusive question of what is fair, cannot be strictly defined, unlike the efficiency criterion (i.e., the maximization of NSB).

Consider the continuum in Exhibit 9–3. At one extreme is the income distribution under an unregulated market system, and at the other extreme is a distribution in which all members of society receive equal incomes. Neither solution is completely satisfactory. An entirely unregulated market will not produce an equitable distribution of income. Discrimination and the use of monopoly power in certain markets leave some people with not enough income to survive. On the other hand, an equal distribution of income would be unfair to those who work harder or who have special skills, such as inventors and professional football players. Thus, society must decide, through its governments, what constitutes an equitable distribution of income. Total agreement is impossible; only a consensus can be achieved. Today, many people feel free societies have gone too far toward equality of income, while many others feel they have not gone far enough.

EXHIBIT 9–3
CONTINUUM OF POSSIBLE INCOME DISTRIBUTIONS

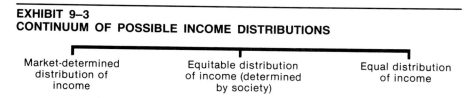

Market-determined distribution of income   Equitable distribution of income (determined by society)   Equal distribution of income

Horizontal and Vertical Equity

Because the notion of fairness varies widely among individuals, the criteria by which public policies and programs are judged are as elusive as the idea of equity itself. Yet two general standards are applied to help resolve questions of equity. The *horizontal equity* standard requires equal treatment of equals. More specifically, it requires that members of society in the same economic circumstances pay the same costs to receive the same benefits. The horizontal equity standard would be violated if, for example, two taxpayers having equal taxable incomes paid different amounts of income taxes, or if the owners of two properties of equal value and with equal exemptions paid different amounts of property tax. The standard would also be violated if a local government decided to levy a property tax based on construction material of homes in the community. For example, owners of brick houses pay twice what owners of frame houses pay. This particular characteristic may have little relation to the value of the houses or the economic circumstances of their owners.

Vertical equity requires unequal treatment of unequals. It involves the question of how much individuals in different economic circumstances should pay in taxes or receive in benefits. Vertical equity would be violated, for example, if the owners of $100,000 homes paid the same amount of taxes as the owners of $50,000 homes. Vertical equity would also be violated if city firemen extinguished a fire in only half of a $100,000 house, while saving an entire $50,000 house.

Equity considerations are especially important in two areas of real estate. First, since housing is a basic human need, equity has always been the basis for the development and evaluation of subsidized housing programs. Some citizens cannot afford housing that meets socially acceptable standards, so government programs are instituted to increase these citizens' housing quality or effective incomes. Second, the equity criterion is applied in the evaluation of tax policies. Tax laws should be revised periodically in an attempt to keep them fair or make them more fair. Federal housing programs and the local property tax are examined in Chapters 14 and 15, respectively.

OVERVIEW

This chapter deals with the economic concepts of real estate resource allocation and income distribution. Two basic criteria operate in economic decisions pertaining to real estate—efficiency and equity. Resources are allocated efficiently when net social benefits are maximized. Net social benefits are the difference between total social benefits and total social costs.

The chapter also describes three types of market failure pertaining to real estate—externalities, public goods, and adverse selection. Externalities result in market failure when real estate consumers do not take into account the total benefits or total costs of their decisions. The market's inability to produce public goods is a form of market failure. This occurs because real estate owners cannot evaluate benefits and costs of some goods or are unwilling to pay their fair share for them. Adverse selection is a type of market failure that results when consumers do not have enough information to distinguish between different qualities of products or services.

Government regulations and programs attempt to correct these market failures. Many of these government activities, such as land-use control and zoning, public-works projects (i.e., highway construction), local and federal taxation, and licensing have a direct bearing on the behavior of participants in real estate markets. They are considered in much greater detail in subsequent chapters.

Finally, the equity criterion recognizes that economically efficient solutions in an unregulated market economy may not produce equitable results for everyone. A certain distribution of income (or the rights to goods and services) may make some members of society so disparate as to be regarded as unfair. If equals are treated unequally, the standard of horizontal equity is violated; if unequals are treated equally, the standard of vertical equity is violated. Government programs redistribute income or wealth to those considered to be treated unfairly. In real estate, such programs are exemplified by government subsidies that allow moderate- and low-income families to afford better housing.

TEST YOURSELF

Identify the following terms and concepts discussed in this chapter.

1. Technical efficiency versus allocative efficiency.
2. Opportunity costs.
3. Market failure.
4. Negative externalities versus positive externalities.
5. Indirect costs versus negative externalities.
6. Public goods.
7. Adverse selection.
8. Equity versus efficiency.
9. Horizontal equity.
10. Vertical equity.

Answer the following multiple choice questions.

1. Members of society must make decisions about four types of economic activity. Which of the following is *not* included among these four?

    a. Economic efficiency.
    b. Income distribution.
    c. Resource allocation.
    d. Economic stability.
    e. Economic standards.

2. Economic efficiency in real estate markets is not achieved when there are
    a. Problems with equity.
    b. Market failures.
    c. Too many market participants.
    d. Opportunity costs.
    e. None of the above.

3. If someone indirectly benefits from the actions of others without incurring the costs,
    a. A negative externality has been created.
    b. An efficient solution results.
    c. Adverse selection has taken place.
    d. A public good has been created.
    e. None of the above.

4. Which of the following is the best example of a pure public good?
    a. Magazines.
    b. Disney World.

c. A public toll road.
d. Police protection.
e. All of the above.

5. Corgel owns a house worth $100,000 and a lot worth $30,000. Smith owns a lot worth $100,000 and a house worth $300,000. Corgel pays $2,000 per year in property taxes, while Smith pays only $200 per year. What economic concept is at issue here?
a. Horizontal equity.
b. Vertical equity.
c. Efficiency.
d. Adverse selection.
e. Public goods problem.

ADDITIONAL READINGS

Alchian, Armen A., and William R. Allen. *University Economics*. Belmont, Calif.: Wadsworth, 1972, Chaps. 12 and 14.

Heilbroner, Robert L., and Lester C. Thurow. *The Economic Problem*. Englewood Cliffs, N.J.: Prentice-Hall, 1978, Chap. 19.

Schreiber, Arthur F., Paul K. Gatons, and Richard B. Clemmer. *Economics of Urban Problems*. Boston: Houghton Mifflin, 1971, Chap. 2.

Spencer, Milton H. *Contemporary Microeconomics*. New York: Worth Publishers, 1980, Chap. 1.

Wonnacott, Paul, and Ronald Wonnacott. *Economics*. New York: McGraw-Hill, 1979, Chaps. 21 and 31.

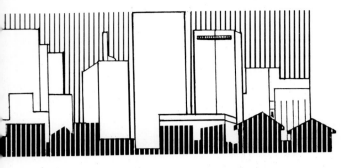

10
Operations of Real Estate Markets

INTRODUCTION

In Chapter 9 we stated that in an efficient market the greatest quantity of goods and services are produced per dollar's worth of resources. The efficiency criterion is, in reality, an ideal since no market is perfectly competitive. Yet the goal of market efficiency is closer to being achieved in some markets than in others because the conditions for perfect competition are more nearly satisfied there. In this chapter, the characteristics of a perfectly competitive market are identified and then compared to the characteristics of real estate markets. We will find that real estate markets are less competitive, and thus tend to be less efficient than many other markets, such as those for stocks and bonds.

The overriding objective of this chapter is to establish a foundation for understanding and analyzing the markets for various types of real property. In Chapter 11 we will describe the process used by real estate professionals to analyze real estate markets.

THE NATURE OF REAL ESTATE MARKETS

A discussion of real estate markets logically begins with the definition of a market. For our purposes, a *market* is the setting or environment in which buyers and sellers come together to exchange goods and services and in which price-determining forces operate. Real estate transactions, however, do not take place in a single, universal market. The real estate market is segmented, and therefore its parts are distinguishable.

One important and obvious segmentation involves *property type.* For example, buyer and seller behavior in establishing prices for single-family homes in an area may be affected by a new regional shopping center planned nearby. Yet buyers and sellers do not look to sales of shopping centers for information about possible selling prices for single-family homes; they look to sales of other single-family homes in the area.

Another segmentation involves *geographic scope.* In general, real estate markets are highly localized. Thus, the market for single-family homes in Hawaii is unimportant to buyers and sellers in Maine. On the other hand, markets for other types of property, such as industrial plants or regional shopping centers, can be regional, national, or international in scope. While the supply of these properties is localized, the demand may be international. As we examine the economic characteristics of real estate and real estate markets, the difficulties in establishing a successful national or international market for real estate will be apparent.

Functions of Real Estate Markets

In general, real estate markets perform three functions:

1. Allocate existing space among those who demand space.
2. Expand or contract space to meet changing conditions.
3. Determine land uses.

Note that each is accomplished through the *price mechanism.*

To demonstrate the three functions of real estate markets, consider the case of a hypothetical Texas city. The city has been growing, and a new computer-manufacturing plant is being constructed nearby. The new plant will have some rather dramatic short- and long-term effects on the city's rental housing market, as shown in Exhibit 10–1. Panel A shows that the supply curve for rental housing is inelastic (see Frame 10–1 for a refresher on supply-and-demand curve analysis and Frame 10–2 for a refresher on the concept of elasticity). This means that even though demand increases from D_1 to D_2, apartment developers or those who can convert their units to rental uses have insufficient time to add to the supply of rental units in the short run. The increase in demand caused by the influx of new workers to the area therefore causes the rental rates for existing properties to increase from R_1 to R_2. This rent increase results in a reallocation of space in the market. Tenants who cannot afford the higher rent move to lower-quality rental housing, and new tenants who can afford the higher rents move in. The market is working to carry out the first function—to allocate existing space among those who demand it.

As shown in Panel B, the long-run supply curve for rental housing is more elastic. Over a period of three to six months, existing space expands to meet the increase in demand from new residents. Apartments are built in the upstairs and attics of single-family homes, and other existing build-

EXHIBIT 10–1
FUNCTIONS OF THE REAL ESTATE MARKET: THE CASE OF A NEW MANUFACTURING PLANT

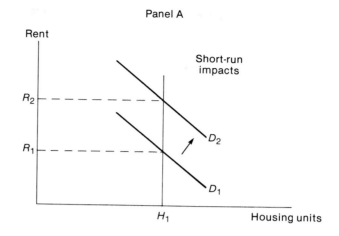

Panel A

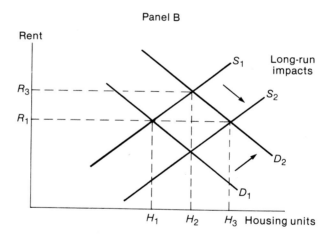

Panel B

ings are converted into apartments. The market is now working to carry out the second function—to expand or contract space to meet changing conditions.

Eventually, new rental units will be constructed on the outskirts of the city to accommodate the in-migration of households. This conversion of agricultural land to urban use is an example of the third function—to determine land uses.

Frame 10–1

A Refresher on Supply and Demand

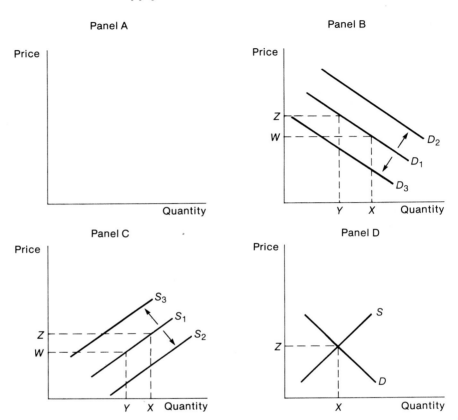

Panel A   Panel B

Panel C   Panel D

Panel A illustrates supply-and-demand relationships. Price is measured along the vertical axis and quantity along the horizontal axis. Panel B shows a set of demand curves. Consider D_1; it has a downward slope, indicating that when the price of a good increases from, say, W to Z the quantity demanded by consumers falls from X to Y. If something occurs that affects demand, such as an increase or decrease in income, the demand curve will shift. The movement from D_1 to D_2 (i.e., to the right) represents an increase in demand—perhaps from an increase in income. The movement from D_1 to D_3 (i.e., to the left) indicates a decrease in demand.

Panel C shows supply curves. Consider S_1; it has an upward slope indicating that when the price increases, again from W to Z, producers will supply more. If something happens that affects supply, such as an increase or decrease in the costs of materials, then the curve will shift. As with the demand curve, an increase is represented by a shift to the right (S_1 to S_2) and a decrease by a shift to the left (S_1 to S_3).

In panel D, the market is in *equilibrium* at price *Z* and quantity *X* (i.e., where the supply and demand curves intersect). If demand were to increase, the demand curve would shift to the right, and the market would be in short-run disequilibrium. This would be a signal that the quantity supplied is not adequate to satisfy the quantity demanded. Suppliers would move to increase supply, thus bringing the market back into equilibrium.

Frame 10–2

A Refresher on the Concept of Elasticity

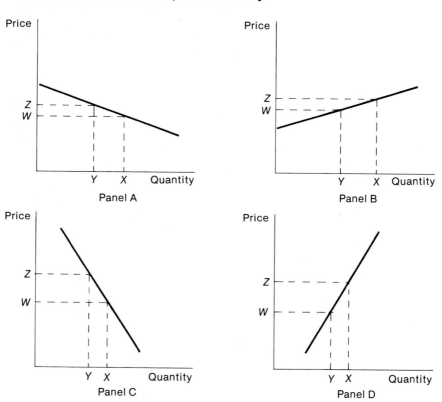

The elasticities of supply and of demand represent degrees of response in quantity to changes in price. Panel A shows a *relatively elastic* demand curve. A small change in price from *W* to *Z* results in a relatively large change in quantity demanded, from *Y* to *X*. Vacation trips have relatively elastic demand. Panel B shows a *relatively elastic* supply curve. Panels C and D present *relatively inelastic* demand and supply curves. In these cases, it takes a large change in price to effect a relatively small change in quantity demanded or supplied. One of the most important characteristics of real estate is that supply is relatively inelastic in the short run because of inherent time lags in development and construction. Suppliers of real estate are not able to respond in the short run to changes in price.

Conditions for a Perfectly Competitive Market

The following conditions are necessary for a perfectly competitive market:

1. *Free markets.* A perfectly competitive market operates freely—that is, with no significant external (government) control.
2. *Perfect knowledge.* All participants possess perfect knowledge about all competing goods and their prices and share the same expectations for the future.
3. *Product homogeneity.* The products traded are identical.
4. *Size and control.* There are many buyers and sellers, yet no individual buyer or seller is large enough to influence the operation of the market or its prices.
5. *Mobility and divisibility.* Products can be divided into smaller units for sale. Products are also mobile; they can be transported immediately to satisfy excess demand conditions wherever they occur.

Imperfections in Real Estate Markets

The nature of a market often reflects the character of the good traded in that market. Real estate markets are highly imperfect because real estate itself has an unusual set of characteristics. Most important, every parcel of real estate is different from every other parcel in at least one essential respect: *location.* Each parcel has a "locational monopoly," meaning that it has its own market and that the suppliers of parcels have significant control over their prices. Real estate, therefore is *not* a homogeneous product. Furthermore, perfect knowledge is unattainable in real estate markets because the costs of acquiring information about every competing parcel are prohibitive.

Real estate has other idiosyncrasies that may lead to market imperfections: fixity of location, long economic life, and large economic size.

Fixity of Location. Even though conditions become unfavorable at a given location, real property normally cannot be moved to a more advantageous market or location.

This unique feature of real estate has several implications. First, real estate is more susceptible to externalities than other goods. Recall the example from the previous chapter about the waste-treatment problems of two communities. One community used the river between the two communities for waste disposal, forcing the residents of the other community to incur the cost of building a water-treatment facility. If the real estate in the affected community were mobile, it could be relocated to avoid the pollution and therefore the costs of pollution control. Since such moves are physically impossible, the residents of the affected community must either accept the full costs of the treatment facility or lobby for pollution control by state or federal governments.

Second, the fixed location of real estate significantly raises the information costs of market participants. Market participants not only must acquire information about national and regional market factors (e.g., interest rates and population migration patterns) but also about local and site-specific factors.

Long Economic Life. The economic life of land is infinite. The economic lives of improvements on land, however, are finite but generally indeterminable.[1] Because it is difficult to estimate the lives of improvements, market participants disagree on the longevity of the benefits from owning real estate, thus making perfect knowledge even less attainable.

Large Economic Size. Economic size has more far-reaching implications for market imperfections than long economic life. First, because real estate is high-priced, real estate markets are "thin" (i.e., few buyers are seeking properties and few sellers are offering them at any given time). The breadth of real estate markets is usually proportional to the prices asked. For example, the market for residential property, in which the average price may be $80,000, is far more active than the market for million-dollar office buildings. This absence of a large number of buyers and sellers violates one of the conditions for the perfectly competitive market mentioned earlier.

Second, because of large economic size, developers are unable to place properties into service quickly enough to satisfy new demand immediately. This characteristic, as we have seen, is the inelasticity of supply of real estate. Recall that inelasticity of supply results from both a lack of mobility of existing units and from the lengthy time required for new construction.

Finally, large economic size raises the information requirements of market participants. Because financing is usually necessary when buying real estate, market participants must acquire information about financing options as well as the economic, physical, legal, and social aspects of properties.

The notion of *market inefficiency* is related to the notion of market imperfection. Market inefficiency involves lapses of time before new information about products in a market are captured in the prices of those prod-

---

[1]For a more detailed discussion of economic life determination, see John B. Corgel and Halbert C. Smith, "The Concept and Estimation of Economic Life in the Residential Appraisal Process: A Summary of Findings," *Real Estate Appraiser and Analyst* 48 (Winter 1982), pp. 4–11.

ucts. In an inefficient market, participants have an opportunity to capitalize on the information they acquire and sometimes make large profits. Because of certain market imperfections (e.g., nonhomogeneous product) information about real estate is thought to be costly, and therefore real estate markets are believed to be inefficient. Recent research has shown that real estate markets may be more efficient than previously believed.[2]

THE MONOPOLISTIC COMPETITION MODEL

The preceding section describes the conditions for a perfectly competitive market and discusses the reasons real estate markets do not meet these conditions. In an imperfect market setting, participants must engage in extensive market analysis to make decisions about real estate. When analyzing an imperfect market, it would be helpful to have a realistic model of market behavior to explain and predict how markets behave in various situations. Many believe that such a model exists—the *monopolistic competition* model.

We can view the range of all possible market models as a continuum, as shown in Exhibit 10–2. At one extreme is the perfect-competition model; at the other is the pure-monopoly model, in which only one producer is able to choose the level of production. The level chosen tends to be where profits are maximized, given the extent of market demand for the product. Like perfect competition, there are no examples of pure monopolies—both are polar cases.[3]

EXHIBIT 10–2
CONTINUUM OF MARKET MODELS

Pure monopoly	Monopolistic competition	Perfect competition

Because of the fixed location of each parcel of real estate, owners of real estate are monopolists. Yet adjacent parcels can have similar locational characteristics. So if the owners of Parcel A offer their property at an exorbitant (monopoly) price, the owners of adjacent Parcel B may offer theirs at a slightly lower price to attract buyers away from Parcel A. A significant element of competition is thus present in real estate markets because of the *substitutability* of parcels with similar locational characteristics.

---

[2]George W. Gau, "Public Information and Abnormal Returns in Real Estate Investment," *Journal of the American Real Estate and Urban Economics Association* 13 (Spring 1985), pp. 15–31.

[3]Some public utility companies have near-monopoly power in limited areas; however, even in those areas, there are usually alternative sources of service. Nevertheless, government usually regulates the rates utilities can charge. Until a decade ago, the major automobile producers in the United States held significant market power, but they attracted intense competition from foreign producers.

In the late 1930s, economist Edward Chamberlin presented a model of market behavior known as *monopolistic competition*.[4] This model combines elements of perfect competition with elements of pure monopoly. Monopolistic competition is like pure monopoly in that a producer, not competition in the market, decides the level of output to be produced. However, the model differs from pure monopoly in that there is no true market demand for the "product"—only demand for individual variations of the product.

Individual producers differentiate their products through brand names, small physical variations, or by providing special services. Product differentiation, nevertheless, does not fully compensate for the fact that products traded in this type of market are close substitutes. Moreover, the monopolistically competitive producer, unlike the pure monopolist, cannot entirely satisfy the market demand for the product. The presence of excess or economic profits in the short run will induce producers of substitute products to enter the market until excess profits are eliminated.

The monopolistic competition model is fairly well suited to explain the operations of real estate markets. Each property has a locational monopoly, yet close substitutes tend to keep prices reasonably competitive. How high a price buyers will pay for superior location, and the length of time excess profits occur before the owners of substitute properties enter the market, depend on many factors. Whereas these factors vary among specific properties, market prices are strongly influenced by both locational monopoly power and inherent competitive market forces. As we will discuss in Chapter 11, which deals with market analysis, both forces must be considered when estimating market needs at a specific site.

THE SPATIAL ECONOMICS OF REAL ESTATE MARKETS

Since monopoly profits can be earned at least in the short run from a locational advantage, the operation of real estate markets is largely determined by participants' location decisions. This spatial perspective of real estate markets involves the interrelationship between prices (or rent) for real estate and the uses to which the property may be put. Whereas classical economists believed that prices determine land uses, modern economic theory suggests that prices are determined by market participants bidding for the use of land. Thus, land uses in an urban economy depend on the factors that motivate participants in the market to bid for the right to use locations.

---

[4]Edward Chamberlin, *Monopolistic Competition* (Cambridge, Mass.: Harvard University Press, 1939).

Classical Location Theory

The classical view of land values, originated in the early 1800s, was formulated for an agrarian economy.[5] The English economist and social philosopher David Ricardo argued that land rents, or the bids made for the use of land, are partially a function of location, but primarily a function of the fertility of the land for agricultural production. The most fertile land would command the highest rent.

A few years later a German economist, von Thunen, expanded the theory of land rent based on locational advantage. Von Thunen argued that rent is primarily a function of the accessibility of a parcel of land to a market center. Good access creates value because it results in lower transportation costs for producers. The arrangement of land uses around a market center, therefore, arises from the bids for land made by producers. Producers with the greatest transportation costs per unit of distance to the center would make the highest bids for close-in locations because they would save the most in transportation costs.

Exhibit 10–3 presents the *bid-rent curve* in one direction from a market center for three agricultural producers. All economic activity is assumed

EXHIBIT 10–3
BID-RENT CURVE IN AN AGRICULTURAL ECONOMY

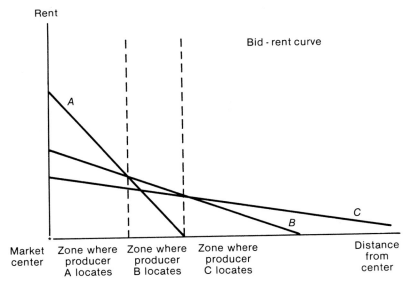

[5]See William Alonso, *Location and Land Use* (Cambridge, Mass.: Harvard University Press, 1964), Chap. 1, for a more complete review.

to occur at the market center, all land is equally productive, and each producer produces only one commodity. Producer A raises cattle, which are extremely costly to transport. This producer's *bid-rent line* is quite steep because Producer A will make relatively high bids for locations close to the center; Producers B and C grow avocados and radishes, respectively. The slopes of their bid-rent functions are not as steep, indicating that they would be willing to accept locations farther from the center because their transportation costs are lower. The bids shown by the market bid-rent curve result in a pattern of agricultural land uses in which Producer A, who makes the highest bid, secures the location closest to the center, and Producers B and C settle for locations farther out. Thus, classical location theory is based on the relationship between transportation costs and the productivity of land. It explains market behavior when these two factors are the only ones buyers and sellers consider.

Neoclassical Location Theory: Capital/Land Substitution

During the latter part of the 20th century, Alonso and other economists extended von Thunen's ideas to an urban spatial economy.[6] In this theory, the single market center becomes the city's central business district instead of the agricultural market center. Land is used for office buildings, apartment complexes, industrial plants, and single-family residences rather than farming. Bidding, based on the need to avoid transportation costs, determines the allocation of land to different uses as before; however, the presence of buildings adds a new dimension to location decisions.

In classical location theory the payment of rent for land was treated as a residual after payments were made to the other factors of production (i.e., labor and capital).[7] Thus, land was not considered to be a factor of production. Consider the following equation for determining excess profits for a given producer:

$$\text{Profit} = PQ - W - TQ(u) - R(u) \qquad (10\text{--}1)$$

where

P = Price
Q = Quantity
T = Transportation costs per unit (therefore, TQ = Total transportation costs)

---

[6] Ibid.

[7] Entrepreneural skill is not treated as a factor of production in classical theory.

u = Distance from the center
R = Rent on land
W = Labor costs

This equation states that excess profits result from total revenues *(PQ)* less the costs of labor *(W)*, transportation *(TQ)*, and rent *(R)*. When excess profits are zero, and therefore only normal profits exist, Equation (10–1) becomes

$$R(u) = PQ - W - TQ(u) \qquad (10\text{--}2)$$

since the payments to land owners are treated as a residual.

The neoclassical view also recognizes that land is a factor of production, along with labor and capital, and that each input costs the producer the value of its contribution to the product or service being produced. This means that producers pay for the factors of production based on their relative contribution to the production of the good. This relative contribution is referred to as the marginal product of the factors of production. The following equation incorporates the neoclassical view of rent:

$$PQ = P_N MP_N + P_K MP_K + P_L MP_L \qquad (10\text{--}3)$$

Equation 10–3 says that total revenue from production is consumed by the payments required to acquire the factors of production—labor *(N)*, capital *(K)*, and land *(L)*—in accordance with their prices *(P)* and marginal products *(MP)*. The equation implicitly recognizes that to some extent factors may be substituted for each other if one factor becomes too expensive. Such *factor substitution* is relevant to the economic analysis of any production process. The use of robots in the manufacture of automobiles, for example, involves the substitution of capital for high-cost labor. But when energy prices increase dramatically, the cost of operating capital becomes expensive relative to other inputs, thus resulting in a substitution of labor for capital.

The concept of factor substitution is fundamental to land-use decisions in the real estate market. It states that when the price to land as a factor of production becomes excessive, improvements to land (i.e., capital), may be substituted for land. This explains why multistory buildings are found in and around central business districts and other important centers (e.g., shopping centers) in major cities (see Exhibit 10–4.) We already know that rents are high in and around central locations because producers make high bids for such locations to avoid transportation costs. Not every producer, however, can readily substitute capital for land. Some production processes, such as those requiring assembly lines, cannot be altered from a horizontal to a vertical direction. Thus, land-use patterns are affected by the *ability* of individual producers to substitute capital for land effectively.

EXHIBIT 10–4
CBD Buildings

Photo by John R. Disney

Multistory buildings are found in central business districts and around major nodes in the city, such as shopping centers, because developers substitute capital (buildings) for expensive land. Land prices are high in these areas because people make high bids for centrally located sites to avoid transportation costs. (Photo is of downtown Atlanta.)

In summary, two economic principles have a pervasive influence on the determination of land uses:

1. The pattern of transportation costs in the city and the need or desire of firms and individuals to avoid such costs.
2. Capital/land substitution and the ability or desire of firms and individuals to substitute capital for land.

Frame 10–3

Trains, Trucks, and the Decentralization of American Cities

Economists Leon Moses and Harold F. Williamson* investigated the location and relocation behavior of 2,000 Chicago industrial and commercial firms during 1950–1964. They hypothesized that firms located near the center of the city instead of suburban sites before the early 1900s because of (1) the high cost of moving goods relative to moving people within cities and (2) the high cost of moving goods between cities. Center-city locations afforded firms accessibility to the main train depot, allowing them to avoid costs of moving goods to and from this point of transfer. Many firms, however, desired more and cheaper land and could reduce their labor costs by moving closer to the locations of households.

According to Moses and Williamson, the beginning of the exodus of industrial and commercial firms from the center of Chicago during the early 1900s correlated closely with the introduction of the truck. The availability of trucks (along with better roads) served to break the transportation tie between many firms and center-city locations. The truck reduced the cost of moving goods dramatically and gave firms the freedom to locate farther from such central points of transfer as train depots. The truck, therefore, may have been the single most important invention to shape the landscape of American cities.

---

*Leon Moses and Harold F. Williamson, "The Location of Economic Activity," *American Economic Review* 57 (May 1967), pp. 211–22.

Residential Location Decisions

The location behavior of households is important in real estate market analysis for two reasons. First, suppliers of residential housing must predict which sites will be acceptable for new residential developments. Second, the location decisions of commercial real estate developers are based on residential location since products and services tend to follow consumers.

Early studies of household location behavior between 1900 and 1940 provided models to explain the internal growth of urban areas. These models of urban growth describe the expansion of urban areas as (1) a series of rings around a single center (concentric-circle model), (2) pie-shaped wedges emanating from a center (sector model), (3) development along transportation lines (axial model), and (4) development around multiple centers (multiple-nuclei model).[8] While these models have some value in describing how households locate within urban areas, they fail to offer much predictive insight. Moreover, they focus on the aggregate pattern of household location decisions rather than the individual house-

---

[8]A more complete discussion of these and other models is found in Truman A. Hartshorn, *Interpreting the City: An Urban Geography* (New York: John Wiley & Sons, 1980), Chap. 11.

hold's decision-making process. An understanding of individual house-hold decisions is necessary to predict future residential locations.

Alonso,[9] Muth,[10] and others recognized that the same economic factors that affect location decisions in general—the need to avoid transportation costs and the need for land—also influence the location decisions of individual households. Thus, two fundamental principles underlie the household location decision models developed in recent decades:

1. Households, like firms, seek to avoid transportation costs and thus have an incentive to locate as close to an economic center as possible. Transportation costs, especially for wage earners, involve both the actual outlays for travel and the cost of forgone wages due to time lost during travel. Transportation costs, therefore, *increase* with distance from a center.

2. Households demand varying quantities of land. It is usually assumed that household demand for land increases as incomes increase. Since businesses and households bid for central locations, the price of land *decreases* with distance from economic centers of cities.

The trade-off decision facing each household involves how far from the center the household should purchase or rent housing, given that transportation costs increase and land prices (i.e., housing prices) decline with distance. In other words, at some location (the *household equilibrium location*), each household will feel it is not spending too much on commuting costs while satisfying its desire for housing.

Trade-off models of household location decisions provide insights about important urban policy questions concerning population density and expansion of cities. By examining what would happen to household equilibrium locations if, for example, bonds[11] are issued to spur new housing construction or the fare structure of a mass transportation system is altered, urban decision makers can judge how such policies might affect future land-use in cities. These models predict that any policy that lowers the cost of housing relative to other goods will lead to an outward expansion of the city. A policy of lower transportation costs (e.g., a new highway system) will also lead to an outward expansion of the city. According to this theory, people prefer to avoid transportation costs and live on more land rather than less.

---

[9]Alonso, *Location*.

[10]Richard F. Muth, *Cities and Housing* (Chicago: University of Chicago Press, 1969).

[11]Housing-bond programs have been popular throughout the United States in recent years. Under such programs, cities sell bonds and use the proceeds to offer mortgage loans to residents at below-market rates.

Why Do the Lowest-Income Households Live on the Highest-Value Land in the Center of Cities?

Location theory suggests that the highest-income households would outbid other households for central locations. Yet as a general rule, high-income households have chosen to live considerable distances from the economic centers of American cities, while low-income households occupy dwellings on the highest-value residential land close to these centers. Why? What role does accessibility play in household location decisions?

Three hypotheses have been proposed to explain this apparent paradox.

1. The Speculation Hypothesis—Close-in residential property is speculative property that is allowed to deteriorate rapidly so that landlords can extract the maximum income by not expending funds on maintenance. As lower-income households move into these deteriorating dwellings, higher-income households move farther out to avoid living near low-income households.

2. The Tiebout or "vote with their feet" Hypothesis*—Households locate in political jurisdictions that maximize their investments in local government. High-income households locate in suburban communities, since the tax base is strong due to the high proportion of industrial and commercial enterprises. They avoid communities such as central cities where expenditures are high for services to low-income households. By the same logic, low-income households choose political jurisdictions where services are greater.

3. The Land Preference Hypothesis†—As household income rises, demand for land increases at an even faster rate (i.e., households have a high elasticity of demand for land). Thus, their demand for land outweighs their desire to avoid transportation costs and they move farther out to reside on more land.

A long debate has occurred in the academic literature on whether the second or third hypothesis is the correct explanation for the paradox. Research has discredited both propositions, as well as shown that both have merit. It is fair to conclude that both the desire of households to maximize their investments in local governments and their ability (i.e., income) to reside on more land have contributed to the phenomenon.

---

*Charles M. Tiebout, "A Pure Theory of Public Expenditures," *Journal of Political Economy* 64 (October, 1956), pp. 416–24.

†Alonso, *Location*.

Commercial/Industrial Firm Location Decisions

Transportation costs and land requirements also affect the location decisions of most commercial and industrial firms. In addition to minimizing their own transportation costs, firms also want to cut transportation costs for their customers and suppliers, who would otherwise buy elsewhere or increase prices to cover such costs. Therefore, good locational relationships with the firm's customers and suppliers minimize costs. Such relationships or interactions between land uses are termed *linkages*.

Two types of linkages are important in the location decisions of commercial and industrial firms. *Input linkage* refers to the locational relationship between a firm and its suppliers of goods or production materials. *Output linkage* refers to the locational relationship between a firm and its retail markets (i.e., customers) or wholesalers. To demonstrate these concepts, assume a hypothetical automobile manufacturer is seeking a location for a plant in a Third World country. As shown in Exhibit 10–5, the raw materials (input) for the manufacturing process are located in the northeastern and north central regions of the country. A concentration of skilled labor (input) for the company's production is located in the main university city in the north central region of the country. The markets (output) for automobiles are all in the equatorial cities in the southern and western regions. Thus, if transportation costs are equal in all directions, the logical location for the plant is near the center of the country. The location of the plant in Exhibit 10–5 establishes optimal input and output linkages (i.e., the plant location minimizes transportation costs from and to the input and product markets).

The plant location is altered when the assumption of equal transportation costs in all directions is relaxed. If, for example, the transportation system is not as well developed in the northern region as in the southern region, transportation costs will be higher from the north, and the optimal location of the plant moves somewhat north of its location in Exhibit 10–5.

Frame 10–5

Do Market Rents Actually Decline with Distance from Important Urban Centers?

Most research confirms that rents do decline with distance from important urban centers. Austin J. Jaffe and Robert G. Bussa,* for example, collected data on apartment rents paid by 600 students living at various distances from the University of Illinois campus in Urbana–Champaign to determine the relationship between rents and distance from campus. After adjusting rents for size and age differences among apartments, the researchers discovered that rental rates declined noticeably with distance from campus.

---

*Austin J. Jaffe and Robert G. Bussa, "Using a Simple Model to Estimate Market Rents: A Case Study," *Appraisal Journal* 45 (January 1977), pp. 7–11.

EXHIBIT 10–5
INPUT AND OUTPUT LINKAGES FOR A MANUFACTURING FIRM IN A HYPOTHETICAL COUNTRY

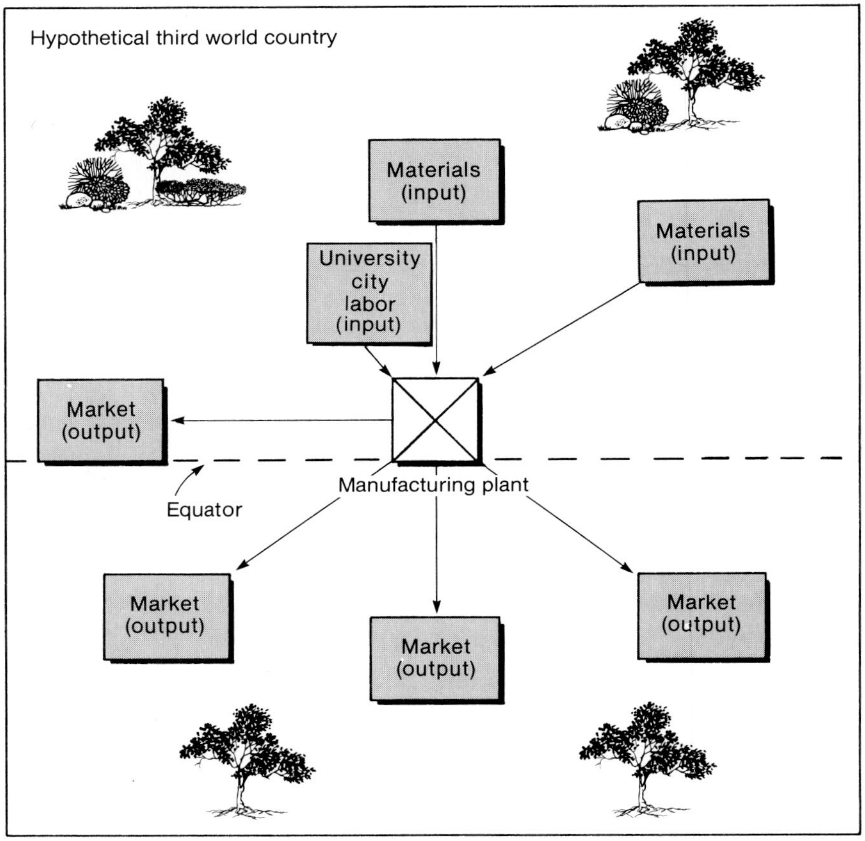

The firm's type of manufacturing operation also influences location decisions because it dictates the transportation costs for the input and output linkages. Some firms such as beer and soft drink bottling companies are *weight-gaining* operations, since they add water at the point of operation. Exhibit 10–6, Panel A shows that the transportation-cost curve is steeper to the market than from the source of materials for the weight-gaining firm. Thus, the optimal location for a weight-gaining firm is close to the market, where total transportation costs are minimized as seen in Panel A. The opposite is true for a *weight-losing* operation, such as steel production, in which large amounts of iron ore, coke, and limestone are needed to make a relatively small amount of steel. Thus, the optimal lo-

EXHIBIT 10–6
TRANSPORTATION COST STRUCTURE FOR WEIGHT-GAINING AND WEIGHT-LOSING FIRMS

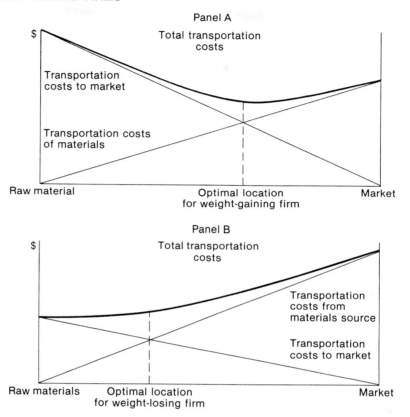

cation for the weight-losing operation is close to the source of materials, as indicated in Panel B.

Most commercial firms, especially retail firms, seek locations that provide optimal linkages with their markets. They attempt to minimize the transportation costs of their customers. As in the cases of weight-gaining and weight-losing firms, the location decisions of retail firms are strongly influenced by the type of good they sell. If the good has a *high density of demand*, meaning that the good is purchased frequently (e.g., convenience groceries), the establishment needs a relatively small surrounding trade area to be profitable. Such an outlet may locate almost anywhere not prohibited by zoning, where some population exists, and where competition has not made that location undesirable. (See Exhibit 10–7.)

An establishment selling goods with a *low density of demand* (i.e., in-

EXHIBIT 10–7
DOWNTOWN AND HIGHWAY ESTABLISHMENTS

Photo by Jack Corgel

Retail establishments that sell infrequently purchased goods or services tend to locate in downtown areas or shopping malls to be situated centrally within the large market area they require. (Photo is of bookstore in Georgetown, Washington, D.C.)

frequently purchased items such as antique books) requires a relatively large trade area to be profitable. Such establishments must locate centrally in relation to the population to minimize the transportation costs of their customers.

The Location of Cities

Have you ever wondered why cities are located where they are? Undoubtedly, access to cheap water transportation helps explain the location of major port cities such as New York, Boston, San Francisco, and San Diego. But what about Atlanta, Denver, and Dallas? From what you know about location behavior, you may suspect that cities' locations must be related to the avoidance of transportation costs. They are.

Aside from a few resort communities, the American city was founded on an industrial base. Through their location decisions, industrial firms

EXHIBIT 10–7 (concluded)

Photo by Jack Corgel

Commercial, especially retail, firms that sell frequently purchased goods, such as groceries and fast foods, locate their establishments along major highways to provide a good linkage between their establishment and their customers. (Photo is of major highway in northern Virginia near Washington, D.C.)

seek to avoid transportation costs to and from sources of materials and markets. Industrial firms also seek to avoid the *terminal costs* associated with transferring materials or products from one mode of transportation to another. These points of transfer are called *breaks in transportation*.[12] The most obvious break in transportation occurs along the coast line.

Exhibit 10–8 illustrates a firm's location decision given a break in transportation between the source of materials and the market. Assume that transportation costs are the same in all directions and the firm is neither a weight-gaining nor weight-losing operation. Breaks in transportation involve the terminal costs of loading and unloading raw materials or finished goods. If the plant is constructed on a site somewhere other than *at* the break in transportation, as in Panel A, the firm faces two sets of terminal costs—one at the break in transportation and one at the plant location. The logical decision, then, is to locate the plant at the break in transportation, as in Panel B, to avoid one set of terminal costs.

Many large cities in the United States are situated on the coasts largely because industrial firms sought to avoid additional terminal costs.

---

[12]Richard F. Muth, *Urban Economics* (New York: Harper & Row, 1975).

EXHIBIT 10–8
THE LOCATION OF FIRMS AT BREAKS IN TRANSPORTATION

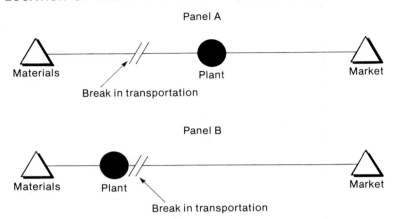

Denver is also located at a break in transportation: before the development of modern transportation systems, crossing the Rocky Mountains
required a change in transportation modes. The old name of Atlanta was
Terminus because for many years the city was located at the end of railroad systems in the southeastern portion of the United States. Dallas has
a similar railroad heritage.

The benefits and costs associated with transportation have had a major impact on the location of cities. Although the "avoidance of terminal
(or transportation) costs" theory does not completely explain the location
of all cities, it does provide an economic rationale for the location of
many. Cities, in essence, develop from the economic location decisions of
firms and households.

OVERVIEW

This chapter focused on the functions and imperfections of real estate
markets. It also considered the monopolistic-competition market model as
an alternative to the perfect-competition or monopoly models, and presented the fundamentals of location theory. The central point of the chapter was that *location* is the most important factor in real estate decision
making. The locational monopoly of each parcel of real estate makes each
parcel unique. This monopoly power represents a serious imperfection in
the markets for real estate because it results in the trading of nonhomogeneous goods.

This chapter also provided the theoretical background for location
analysis and decision making for residential and commercial/industrial

properties. Relative locations (or linkages) and transportation costs between the locations of related land uses are the crucial decision factors. Firms and households locate based on their need to avoid transportation costs between them and other land uses and on their need or desire for land.

TEST YOURSELF

Identify the following terms and concepts presented in this chapter.

1. Functions of real estate market.
2. Real estate market imperfections.
3. Monopolistic competition.
4. Bid-rent curve.
5. Neoclassical location theory.
6. Factor substitution.
7. Determinants of household equilibrium locations.
8. Linkages.
9. Location decisions of firms in weight-gaining versus weight-losing industries.
10. Breaks in transportation.

Answer the following multiple choice questions.

1. The optimal location for a soft drink bottling plant is
   a. Near the source of raw materials (other than water).
   b. Midway between the sources of raw materials and customers.
   c. Near the markets for the product.
   d. At the edge of a mountain range.
   e. It doesn't matter; the plant could be located anywhere.

2. Which is not a function of real estate markets?
   a. To allocate existing space.
   b. To expand or contract space to meet changing conditions.
   c. To determine land uses.
   d. To delineate market boundaries.
   e. All of the above.

3. Which characteristic of real estate is primarily responsible for the imperfect nature of real estate markets?
   a. Locational monopoly.
   b. Fixity of location.
   c. Large economic size.
   d. Long economic life.
   e. Diversity of demand.

4. According to one popular theory, households locate where they do to avoid transportation costs and
   a. Because they want to be near relatives.
   b. Because they want to be near shopping.
   c. Because they want to be near work locations.
   d. Because of their preferences for land.
   e. All of the above.

5. Where would convenience stores selling groceries tend to locate?
   a. In a shopping mall or other central location.
   b. On the first floor of office buildings.
   c. Any place where there is some concentration of households.
   d. In and around hospitals and airports.
   e. In and around industrial parks.

ADDITIONAL READINGS

American Institute of Real Estate Appraisers. *The Appraisal of Real Estate.* Chicago: AIREA, 1983, Chap. 4.

Hartshorn, Truman A. *Interpreting the City: An Urban Geography.* New York: John Wiley & Sons, 1980, Chap. 11.

Hirsch, Werner Z. *Urban Economics.* New York: Macmillan, Publishing Co., 1984.

Muth, Richard F. *Urban Economics.* New York: Harper & Row, 1975, Chaps. 2 and 3.

Ratcliff, Richard U. *Real Estate Analysis.* New York: McGraw-Hill, 1961, Chap. 10.

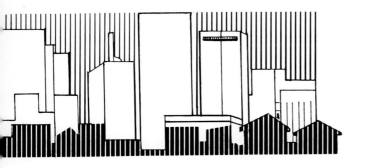

11
Applied Real Estate Market Analysis

OUTLINE

INTRODUCTION

The principles and practice of real estate market analysis are important to the study of real estate for several reasons. First, as we noted in Chapter 10, real estate markets are highly imperfect, especially with respect to locational differences. For this reason, they require specialized knowledge by developers, builders, buyers, and other market participants that only market studies can provide.

Second, market analysis is an important component of a larger decision-making framework known as *feasibility analysis.* The title of an article on this subject best expresses the relationship: "Market Study + Financial Analysis = Feasibility Report."[1] As the source of essential inputs to the financial analysis in which the decisions are actually made on whether to invest, the market study is a critical first step for determining project feasibility. These inputs include the expected rents and occupancy rates in future periods for rental properties such as office buildings and shopping centers, or the expected levels of sales and prices for salable properties such as residential and office condominiums.

Third, since most market studies are undertaken for land-development and new-construction ventures, the market study is a source of information for the preparation of architectural plans. Market studies answer such design-related questions as how many bedrooms buyers of residential condominiums are demanding in today's market and what amenities (e.g., recreation facilities) are required by purchasers of office condominiums.

Finally, market studies are usually required by mortgage lenders for large commercial-property deals. An analysis of the market normally must be included in the package of information known as the loan sub-

---

[1] John B. Bailey, Peter F. Spies, and Marilyn K. Weitzman, "Market Study + Financial Analysis = Feasibility Report," *Appraisal Journal* 45 (October 1977), pp. 550–77.

mission package that is supplied to lenders by borrowers wishing to secure construction or long-term mortgage financing.

Types of Market Studies

Market studies fall into two broad categories. *General market studies* are commissioned to determine the potential for a particular type of development in a large geographic area, without reference to any specific parcel of land. A shopping-center developer who has developed retail centers successfully in the eastern United States, for example, may wish to consider opportunities in Texas. General market studies would discover the potential for new shopping-center developments in Texas cities such as Houston, Dallas, and Austin. The objective is to select the city or cities with the greatest market potential. Additional studies will lead to site selection and eventually to development.

The second category is *site-specific market studies*. As the name implies, these studies are performed after specific parcels of land have been identified for development or redevelopment. The use of the land (e.g., residential condominium, office park, or retail center) has either been predetermined or will be determined by the study. If the study is to determine the use of the land, it is called a *highest-and-best use study*. But site-specific studies in which the use of the land has been predetermined are more prevalent. Thus, the discussions to follow concern this form of market study. Exhibit 11–1 provides a quick reference to the various types of market studies.

EXHIBIT 11–1
SUMMARY OF TYPES OF MARKET STUDIES

Categories	Objectives
1. General market study	To determine market potential, usually for a particular type of development in a large geographic area such as a metropolitan area. There is no reference to specific sites.
2. Site-specific market study *a.* Highest-and-best use	To determine the most profitable development alternatives for a specific site (see Chapter 16 for further discussion).
b. Predetermined use	To provide essential information for the development of preliminary architectural plans and the financial analysis to determine project feasibility.

Market Analysis in the Development Process

The conceptual scheme for land development in Exhibit 11–2 places the market study between the land acquisition and planning phase (Phase 1)

EXHIBIT 11–2
CONCEPTUAL SCHEME FOR LAND DEVELOPMENT

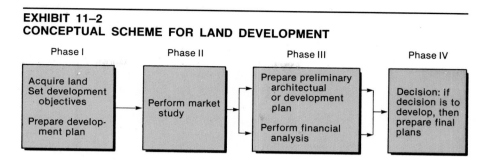

and the final analytical phase (Phase 3), in which preliminary architectural plans are prepared and the financial analysis is performed. The market study has two functions. First, it is a screening mechanism for determining whether developmental constraints, such as severe zoning or access problems, preclude or hinder a project. Second, the market study provides essential inputs for the preparation of preliminary architectural and development plans and for the financial analysis.

Six Questions to Be Answered by a Market Study

The real estate market study should answer the following six fundamental questions.[2]

1. *Are there any constraints on the development of the project?* Severe problems in zoning, utilities, access, environmental protection, community relations, or soil and topography can lead to an early decision to abort the project. Even if these considerations are not found to be severe constraints on development, information gathered on their possible effects may be useful in preparing cost estimates for the financial calculations.

2. *How large will the market be in future periods and what proportion can be attracted to the subject site?* This question involves the *quantity* of space—whether the number of units that can be sold (as in a residential condominium) or the number of square feet that can be leased (as in an office building)—and the *timing* of the transactions. The interaction between quantity and time in the sale or lease of property is called *absorption*. If for example the market for residential condominiums is sufficiently strong that the developer can sell 10 of a possible 50 units in the first three months of mar-

[2]Vincent G. Barrett, "Appraisal Should be Market Study: Techniques of Analysis," *Appraisal Journal* 47 (October 1979), pp. 538–55.

keting, the initial *quarterly absorption rate* is 20 percent (10/50 units). If the remaining units are sold the next four quarters, the overall absorption rate for the project is ten percent per quarter (5 quarters/50 units).

3. *How much can be charged in the market?* This relates to the prices when the units are to be sold or to rents when they are to be leased.

4. *What types of units are demanded in the market?* For residential developments, type refers to building styles, such as garden or high rise. For shopping centers, this question refers to the types of retail outlets that might be appropriate for the center (i.e., drug store or fashion garments).

5. *What sizes should the units be?* For both residential and commercial developments, size refers to the square footage required for each unit.

6. *What amenities or special facilities should be provided?* To market residential condominiums effectively, for example, it is often necessary to incorporate such amenities as tennis courts and swimming pools in the development plan. In hotel developments, it may be essential or desirable to include meeting or convention facilities.

THE PROCESS OF REAL ESTATE MARKET ANALYSIS

We may divide the step-by-step process of developing a real estate market study into three phases. The initial phase, which includes the first two steps described below, considers all project constraints and defines the market area for the study. The next phase involves collecting demand-and-supply data and processing these data. The final phase covers correlation of supply and demand data and reaching conclusions from the study. Those conclusions should be formulated as explicit answers to the six questions presented above.

Step 1: Define the Problem

Definition of the problem is a prerequisite to any investigative study or research project. In the case of a site-specific market study in which the use is predetermined, the problem involves finding answers to the six fundamental questions presented above. Once this is recognized, the market analyst sets forth a plan for examining the questions. The plan may take the form of a proposal to a client or an actual plan of work (time and budget) that considers work items for subsequent steps.

Step 2: Evaluate Project Constraints

Although demand-and-supply conditions may appear quite favorable for development in a particular market, any of several factors can cause a project to be aborted or unduly delayed. Obviously, the sooner these factors are identified and evaluated the better. The following is a checklist of factors that should be considered at this point.

1. Zoning problems (e.g., obtaining a zoning change to allow for development at the desired density).
2. Utility problems (e.g., obtaining cooperation of a municipality for extending services to the site).
3. Parking problems (e.g., inadequate space for both employee and customer parking).
4. Negative community reactions (e.g., organized opposition by neighborhood residents).
5. Access problems (e.g., inability to secure enough curb cuts for the driveways needed).
6. Environmental impact problems (e.g., noise problems necessitating noise barriers).
7. Topographic or soil problems (e.g., severe slopes or poor soil drainage).

Step 3: Define the Market Area(s)

The geographic limits of the market area are determined in general by the density of demand (e.g., potential buyers per square mile) for the products or services to be offered at the site. Therefore, the market area for residential condominiums, since they are purchased infrequently, would be much larger than the market area for convenience groceries. Establishing precise market-area boundaries involves considerable judgment. Precision is often sacrificed for convenience. Political jurisdictions or census tracts, for example, are sometimes chosen in the specification of market areas to facilitate collecting supply and demand data. As a general rule, the lower the density of demand for the commodity to be offered at the site, the less precision is required in setting market-area boundaries.

Travel time and distance are also critical factors. One method for setting the boundaries of a market area for residential developments relies heavily on travel time. It begins by defining the market or "competitive area" as the area within which dwelling units are substitutable for one another.[3] As shown in Exhibit 11–3, the market area is determined by (1)

---

[3]John McMahan, *Property Development* (New York: McGraw-Hill, 1976), pp. 131–51.

EXHIBIT 11–3
MARKET AREA DETERMINATION FOR A PROPOSED RESIDENTIAL DEVELOPMENT

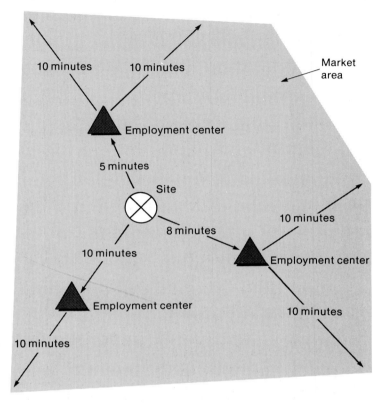

finding the major employment centers within, say, 10 minutes' driving time from the subject site and (2) defining a geographic area which has limits indicated by a 10-minute drive in all directions from each employment center. Any residential development with similar units for sale and located in this area would be viewed as a competitor that may draw customers away from the subject development. The boundaries of this market should be adjusted for the presence of such physical barriers as swamp areas or flood plains, and for demographic characteristics such as a high concentration of apartments. Also, the critical travel time (e.g., 10 minutes or 15 minutes) depends on the size of the urban area and the capacity of the highway network.

Step 4: Estimate Demand for the Project

The estimation of demand is the most crucial step in preparing a market study. The demand for real estate is a *derived demand*, meaning that demand for properties is derived from consumers' demands for the goods and services supplied at particular locations. For example, the demand for a retail outlet in a shopping center that sells personal computers is derived from the local demand for the outlet's product—personal computers. Similarly, the demand for residential condominiums is derived from the local demand for the type of housing service a condominium provides. Housing services might include low maintenance responsibility for the owner, amenities such as a pool and tennis courts, and smaller living space than is usually found in traditional single-family detached homes.

The ultimate concern in a market analysis is *excess demand*. Excess demand exists when the demand for space for a given type of property is estimated to exceed its supply at a given price in a future period. As shown in Exhibit 11–4, the supply of real estate is fixed in the short run (i.e., the supply curve in Panel A is vertical, meaning supply is inelastic).[4] A shift in demand from D_1 to D_2 causes prices or rents to increase above the old equilibrium level (PR_E) to a new equilibrium level (PR_1). This signals that more units are demanded at PR_E than are available; thus, excess demand exists and developers begin planning new projects. In the long run, as the supply curve shifts incrementally (i.e., to S_2 and S_3) with each new development, the supply of real estate eventually satisfies the excess demand and PR_1 is driven back to its old equilibrium level.

If a developer's project helps shift the market supply curve from S_1 to S_2, rather than from S_2 to S_3, he or she should be able to sell or rent units at higher prices or rents (i.e., PR_2 instead of PR_E) over a short absorption period. This requires an ability to "read the market" both in determining when the most units will be demanded in excess of current supply, and in identifying what locations will best satisfy consumer demands. The ability to read the market is partly instinctive, but also comes from an understanding of how and why urban areas grow. The latter understanding is also useful in forecasting which cities will grow most rapidly—a critical input for general market studies. The concepts of urban growth, therefore, provide a theoretical foundation for demand analysis—and to a large extent for market analysis.

---

[4]This example is similar to the example of the functions of real estate markets in Chapter 10. See Exhibit 10–1, Frame 10–2, and accompanying discussions.

EXHIBIT 11–4
EXCESS DEMAND FOR REAL ESTATE AND DEVELOPER RESPONSES

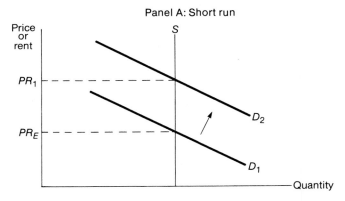

Panel A: Short run

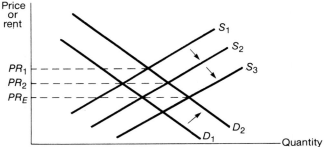

Panel B: Long run

Urban Growth: The Conceptual Basis for Demand Analysis. Urban economists and other social scientists have offered several explanations of why cities have grown during the past century (see Frame 11–1). But they have been unable to agree on a theory that allows accurate prediction of the future growth of cities.

Some economists believe a *general demand theory* of city growth should guide predictions of future urban expansion. According to this theory, the wage-rate differential between two areas determines which will grow faster in the short run. Assume that a golf pro living in Tuscon, Arizona, earns $40 for a one-hour lesson but could earn $60 per hour by moving to Birmingham, Alabama. This wage-rate differential could exist only in the short run, because wage rates would tend to equalize as golf pros moved from Arizona to Alabama. Yet Birmingham would experience an increase in population while a new equilibrium wage was being set.

Why Have Cities Grown in the United States?

City growth in the past century can be traced to a variety of supply and demand factors. The principal supply-side explanation lies in the concept of *specialization of labor.* Assume an agrarian economy in which each farmer is self-sufficient. One day farmer Wiser decides that he can quit farming and produce beer (can you guess Wiser's first name?) for all other farmers more economically than each farm family can produce beer for itself. This results from spreading the fixed cost of production (e.g., equipment purchases) over a larger number of units.

Wiser sells his farm and establishes a brewery in the middle of the region to minimize transportation costs to all other farmers. In a short time another farmer decides that the same thing that Wiser did with beer can be done with pretzels. The second farmer moves next to the brewery to produce pretzels. Eventually, other people move closer to these producers to work at the brewery and pretzel factory, and a city begins to grow.

A demand-side argument is used to explain why the producers of beer, pretzels, and other nonagricultural products expand and hire additional workers. During the past century the price and income elasticities of nonagricultural products have exceeded those for agricultural products. Consumers, for example, have been much more willing to increase their expenditures as a proportion of their incomes on televisions and washing machines than on milk and eggs. Thus, as incomes rise and prices fall due to specialization of labor, the demand for employees in nonagricultural sectors of the economy grows faster than the demand for farmers. These nonagricultural industries are the economic bases on which cities are built and grow.

The transition from an agrarian to a nonagrarian economy in the United States may be largely complete; thus, such explanations of past urban growth are not relevant for predicting the future growth of most cities in the United States, either in terms of how much a particular area will grow or which areas will grow relative to others. These economic concepts may be useful, however, for understanding events occurring in developing countries.

One popular theory of wage rate differentials is *economic base theory* (EBT). Developed in the 1930s by Homer Hoyt, EBT involves the equation

$$\Delta TE = \Delta BE + \Delta NBE \qquad (11–1)$$

where ΔTE is the change in total employment in a particular area during a given period ΔBE is the change in basic employment, and ΔNBE is the change in nonbasic employment. *Basic employment* includes employees in industries that sell goods or services mainly outside their areas (called *export industries*), whereas *nonbasic employment* includes employees in industries that sell goods and services within their areas (called *service industries*).

We require two assumptions for an *economic base analysis* using this theory. First, we assume that the change in nonbasic employment is equal to the change in total employment multiplied by some constant g. In symbols, $\Delta NB = \Delta TE(g)$. Therefore, we can also say that $g = \Delta NB/\Delta TE$. This assumption is similar to stating that people spend a constant proportion of their income on consumption items (e.g., approximately 85 percent).

Second, we assume that the change in basic employment in the area equals the changes in employment occurring outside the area as the result of goods and services imported to the area (i.e., inputs equal exports).

To derive the final form of the economic base model, divide both sides of Equation 11–1 by ΔTE:

$$\frac{\Delta TE}{\Delta TE} = \frac{\Delta BE}{\Delta TE} + \frac{\Delta NBE}{\Delta TE} \qquad (11\text{–}2)$$

which simplifies to

$$1 = \frac{\Delta BE}{\Delta TE} + \frac{\Delta NBE}{\Delta TE} \qquad (11\text{–}3)$$

Since $g = \Delta NBE/\Delta TE$, Equation 11–3 becomes

$$1 = \frac{\Delta BE}{\Delta TE} + g \qquad (11\text{–}4)$$

Solving for ΔTE, we obtain the final form

$$\Delta TE = \Delta BE[1/(1 - g)] \qquad (11\text{–}5)$$

Equation (11–5) says that the change in total employment in an area is equal to the change in basic employment multiplied by $[1/(1 - g)]$, which is called the *employment multiplier*. The problem of determining the change in total employment in the next period has been reduced to one variable—the change in basic employment.

As an example, assume that Birmingham has one basic industry, golf/tourism, and that the change in employment in the golf/tourism industry next year is expected to be 1,000 persons. Also, the ratio of nonbasic employment to total employment (i.e., g) is a constant 80 percent. The EBT model, therefore, predicts a change in total employment of 5,000 persons.

$$\begin{aligned} \Delta TE &= 1{,}000\ [1/(1 - .80)] \\ &= 1{,}000\ (5) \\ &= \underline{5{,}000} \end{aligned}$$

It is easy to convert the change in employment to changes in area population or in area income, if those measures of urban growth are needed.

If the change in area population is required and the historic ratio of population to employment is 2:1, then in the example above the expected change in population is 10,000 persons.

Although economic base analysis is widely used in market studies and real estate appraisals, it has received much criticism. Some of the more serious objections include:

1. *Difficulty in estimating* ΔBE. Two methods are commonly used. The first relies on a survey of local industries to determine how many employees will be hired during the next period. The second method is a mathematical procedure designed to find relationships between local basic employment and national basic employment.

2. *Instability of g.* Studies show that g changes as population grows or declines. This is due to the failure of EBT to consider the effects of change in local wage rates and prices. Thus, there is tendency to import cheaper goods and services instead of relying on local non-basic industries.

Moreover, the general demand theory of urban growth itself has come under strong criticism. The more serious of these criticisms include:

1. Hourly wages have been shown to be fairly constant geographically in the long run. Therefore, if a golf pro moved from Tucson to Birmingham, as in an earlier example, he or she may not be better off in the long run and presumably would not move.

2. Migration studies show that people do not necessarily move because they are attracted by wage differentials. This implies that even short-run wage differences are not important in explaining why one area grows and another does not.

Because of these problems with the general demand theory of urban growth, and with EBT as a special case of that theory, some economists believe a *general supply theory* of city growth should guide predictions of future urban expansion. According to this theory, employment growth is not dependent on wage-rate differentials, but rather on a variety of factors such as climate, lifestyle, and expectations of future well being. From the practical standpoint of predicting urban growth, this theory of externally caused shifts in labor supply is unwieldly, since predictions cannot be based on a single variable such as wage differentials, as it can in demand-oriented theories. Therefore the critical task of predicting population growth in a market analysis is done by extrapolations that rely on past trends as predictors of the future. Such approaches, although not grounded in economic theory, are consistent with the general supply theory of urban growth.

Population-Projection Techniques.   Until now we have used the term *prediction* to mean obtaining estimates of population in future periods. Prediction implies that estimation is subject to some error that can be specified. The use of extrapolative methods by themselves is called *projection*. Usually estimates of future population, however, are termed *forecasts*. These are projections adjusted by forecasters for expected future events, such as a major corporation's moving to the area. Population projections, for example, may indicate that by 1990 the area population will be one million, but because of a recent announcement that two Fortune 500 companies plan to move to the area in the next few years, the population forecast is 1.1 million.

Since population projections and forecasts are available to market analysts from local planning agencies or chambers of commerce, there is a tendency for analysts to rely exclusively on these sources and not to perform their own analyses.

This is a mistake! Analysts should make their own forecasts, if only to compare their estimates to those of others. The following techniques represent some of the simpler methods for projecting population.[5] This does not mean, however, that they are always less accurate than more complicated techniques. These techniques are demonstrated with the data in Exhibit 11–5.

EXHIBIT 11–5
POPULATION DATA FOR DEMONSTRATING PROJECTION TECHNIQUE

Period	Year	Population	Percent Change*
1	1982	145,000	—
2	1983	150,000	0.034
3	1984	153,000	0.020
4	1985	155,000	0.013
5	1986	160,000	0.032

Note: Hypothetical data for City of Kingston, used in case study at end of chapter.
*From previous period.

1. *Simple Linear Projection*

   The simple linear technique is based on the equation for a straight line,

$$Y = a + bx \qquad (11\text{–}6)$$

   where Y is population, a is the Y-axis intercept, b is the slope of the line (or $\Delta Y/\Delta X$), and x is the period.

---

[5]For a more detailed discussion of population projection techniques, see Donald A. Krueckeberg and Arthur L. Silvers, *Urban Planning Analysis: Methods and Models* (New York: John Wiley & Sons, 1974), chap. 8.

Example: Using data from Exhibit 11–5, the population for Period 6 (1987) can be projected. First, calculate b as

$$b = \frac{\Delta Y}{\Delta x} = \frac{160,000 - 145,000}{(6 - 1)} = 3,000.$$

Since a is 145,000, the beginning-period population, the equation for Period 6 population becomes

$$Y = 145,000 + (3,000)(6)$$
$$= \underline{163,000}$$

2. *Nonlinear Projection*

When the relationship between population and time is not believed to be linear, a nonlinear projection technique may give better estimates. The nonlinear technique is based on the equation

$$P_{t+n} = P_t (1 + r)^n \qquad (11\text{–}7)$$

where

P_{t+n} = population for forecast period
t = current period
n = future period
P_t = population in current period
r = rate of population growth in past periods, defined as

$$r = \frac{1}{m} \sum_{t=2}^{N} \frac{P_t - P_{t-1}}{P_t} \qquad (11\text{–}8)$$

(i.e., the sum of percentage changes divided by the number of intervals) where

m = number of intervals
N = last period of historic data.

Example: Using data from Exhibit 11–5, the population for Period 6 (1987) can be projected. First calculate r as

$$r = \left(\frac{1}{4}\right)(.034 + .020 + .013 + .032)$$
$$= .0248.$$

Then P_{t+n} is calculated as

$$P_{t+n} = (160,000)(1 + .0248)^1$$
$$= \underline{163,968}.$$

3. *Weighted-Average Projection*

For this technique the percentage change is weighted to obtain a weighted average growth rate. Using the data in Exhibit 11–5, the simplest weighting scheme would be to weight the growth rate between Periods 1 and 2 (i.e., .034) by one, the next growth rate by two and so on. Once the weighted average is obtained, the following equation is used to project population

$$P_{t+n} = P_t (1 + r) \qquad\qquad (11\text{–}9)$$

where

$$r = \frac{1}{x}\left[\sum_{t=2}^{N} (P_t - P_{t-1})w\right] \qquad\qquad (11\text{–}10)$$

w = weighting factor
x = sum of the weighting factors.

Example: By weighting the growth rates in Exhibit 11–5 progressively (as described above) we obtain

$$r = [1/(1 + 2 + 3 + 4)] [(.034)(1)$$
$$+ (.020)(2) + (.013)(3) + (.032)(4)]$$
$$= .0241.$$

Then P_{t+n} can be calculated as

$$P_{t+n} = (160{,}000)(1 + .0241)$$
$$= \underline{163{,}856}$$

An attempt is usually made to find the weighting scheme that best predicts past population.

4. *Moving-Average Projection*
   This technique requires the calculation of an average growth rate for a recent set of periods. For example, we might select a two- or three-year moving average. Once the moving-average growth rate is calculated, the procedure becomes identical to that for the weighted-average technique.
   Example: Using a two-year moving average and data from Exhibit 11–5, the average growth rate over the last two intervals is obtained

$$r = \left(\frac{1}{2}\right)(.013 + .032)$$
$$= .0225$$

Then

$$P_{t+n} = (160{,}000)(1 + .0225)$$
$$= \underline{163{,}600}.$$

The rationale for this approach is that growth rates in future periods should be related closely to growth rates in the most recent periods. Again, experimentation with how well various moving averages predict past population would help in selecting the appropriate moving average for the series.

5. *Ratio Projection*

   The ratio method is founded on the premise that the larger the area, the more reliable the projections of population. Thus, we may project the population of an urban area by assuming it to be a constant ratio of the state's population. The following equation applies

$$UP_{t+n} = (UP_t/SP_t)(SP_{t+n}) \qquad (11\text{--}11)$$

where

$$UP_t, UP_{t+n} = \text{urban population in the}$$
$$\text{current and projection periods}$$
$$SP_t, SP_{t+n} = \text{state population in the current}$$
$$\text{and projection periods}$$

Example: Assume the state population is 10,000,000 in 1986 and is expected to be 10,500,000 in 1987. The equation for UP_{t+n} then becomes (again using data from Exhibit 11–5)

$$UP_{t+n} = (160,000/10,000,000)(10,500,000)$$
$$= \underline{168,000}$$

Applied Demand Analysis.   As a practical matter, the demand for real estate is related to the number of potential purchasers of goods and services, their incomes and employment characteristics, other demographic factors (e.g., household size), prices, taxes, interest rates, and expectations. Before introducing a model that considers these factors in estimating demand for a particular project, we shall discuss the data requirements. Although data for demand analyses may come from several sources, these data may be broadly classified into two categories.

Primary data are obtained directly from face-to-face or telephone interviews and written questionnaires. These data are important for establishing buyer or renter attitudes, opinions, and preferences at one point in time. Due to the tremendous expense of collecting primary data, there is seldom a time series of interview studies available from which trends in buyer or renter behavior can be determined.

Secondary data come from such published sources as U.S. census reports, local planning commission documents, and state departments of transportation traffic counts. Since these data are collected and tabulated by others, they are usually less expensive than primary data. Thus, market analysts attempt to substitute secondary for primary data whenever possible. One advantage of secondary data is that trends in consumer behavior can be examined. Their major disadvantage is that they are usually aggregated and therefore do not yield individualized information on buyer or renter attitudes, opinions, and preferences that comes from primary data. If their resources were unlimited, market analysts would always use primary data.

The demand model in Exhibit 11–6 is one of many conceptual approaches to estimating real estate demand. This model is customized to fit the case of a new residential condominium project, but could be adapted quite easily to other real estate market analyses. The last section of this chapter presents a case study in which the model is applied, along with the entire market-analysis process.

EXHIBIT 11–6
A CONCEPTUAL APPROACH FOR MARKET ANALYSIS: RESIDENTIAL CONDOMINIUM EXAMPLE

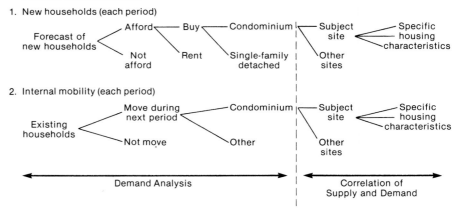

As shown by the tree diagram in Exhibit 11–6, the potential demand for new residential condominiums comes from two sources: *new households* and *internal mobility*. The first step in estimating new household demand for the next period is to project and then forecast the population. To obtain the number of households, the forecast population for the next period is divided by the appropriate person-per-household ratio. This ratio has declined in the United States from slightly over four persons per household in the late 1700s to approximately 2.5 today. However, the ratio remains fairly stable in a given area over the relatively short span of a normal forecasting period.

A reliable estimate of the next-period ratio of persons per household should be available from recently published demographic data for the area (i.e., secondary data). Finally, we note that, in many areas, most new households result from immigration, whereas fewer result from new-household formation.

Not all new households are able to afford a new condominium unit. Thus, an affordability analysis segments the total number of new households into those households that can afford a new condominium unit and those that cannot. Two pieces of information are needed for an affordability analysis. First, the expected financing conditions for the next period must be specified, including the mortgage interest rate, loan-to-value ratio (i.e., percentage down payment required), and term.[6] Second, the analyst must estimate the incomes new households in the area will have. Several techniques are available for such estimates.[7]

With these data, we can estimate the number of households that can afford the mortgage payments on a new condominium unit.[8]

A certain proportion of the households that can afford to purchase housing will choose to rent instead. The most accurate method for determining this proportion is to collect primary data on current buy-versus-rent behavior; however, discussions with real estate brokers or property managers usually will produce good estimates.

The final segmentation performed in the demand analysis is to ascertain the proportion of buyers that will purchase condominium units and the proportion that will purchase traditional single-family detached houses. Again, the most accurate estimates come from primary data (i.e., interviews with new households to determine current buyer behavior), but it is easier to assume that the current distribution of condominiums versus single-family detached houses will persist into the next period.

Once we obtain an estimate of the expected number of households that will purchase condominiums, we must make an allocation of sales to the specific site. This is a crucial step, because the allocation establishes the absorption rate for the project. Allocation of demand to the site and specification of housing characteristics, such as the number of bedrooms and the amenities, depend on competitive conditions in the market. Therefore, we shall defer discussion of these steps to our later discussion of correlating demand and supply.

Internal mobility (i.e., the number of households moving in the same market area) is the second potential source of residential condominium sales. To estimate internal mobility, the number of existing households must be segmented into those that expect to move during the next period and those that do not. As in segmenting the new-household portion of the market, the best approach is to survey households. This survey queries existing households on their moving plans. Alternatively, real estate brokers can usually provide accurate estimates of the proportion of all

---

[6]See Chapter 19 for details on residential finance.

[7]See, for example, Bruce S. Singer, "A Systematic Approach to Housing Market Analysis," *Appraisal Journal* 35 (October 1967), pp. 527–49.

[8]Assumptions could also be made about the proportion of new households with the necessary wealth to make the required downpayment.

households that move during a given period. The remaining steps in the analysis of demand from internal mobility are identical to those for estimating new household demand, as shown in Exhibit 11–6.

Step 5: Establish Supply Conditions in the Market

We estimate the supply of competing units in the market by consulting two sources of information: (1) building permits; and (2) existing and recently completed projects of competitors. The compilation of data on competitors' projects is known as the *competitive market survey.*

Since real estate developers must obtain building permits from local governments before beginning construction, it is possible to project additions to supply that will occur in the next month or year. A number of methods are available for projecting housing starts from housing permits,[9] but for most market studies on commercial properties we can make reliable estimates of additional supply simply by having good building permit data and knowing (1) the probability that the permitted project will be completed (usually in excess of 90 percent) and (2) the average length of construction period for the type of development planned.

Although the analysis of building permits provides information on the number of units or amount of square footage to be added to the existing supply, such an analysis does not reveal much about market acceptance, amenities, pricing, and other specific information about the current market. We can obtain these data, however, on existing and recently completed projects through a competitive market survey. This survey contains the following information about competing properties already on the market:

1. Number and type of units (e.g., 10 one-bedroom, 30 two-bedroom, etc.).
2. Size (square footage) of the units (e.g., one-bedroom—900 square feet).
3. Rents or sale prices.
4. Acreage and density per acre (e.g., 15 acres, 12 units per acre).
5. Number of units rented or sold and the amount of time required. From this we can calculate an *absorption rate.*
6. Number of units remaining on the market.
7. Amenities offered and parking provided.

An example of a competitive market survey is shown in the case study at the end of this chapter.

---

[9]Singer, "A Systematic Approach."

Step 6: Correlate Supply and Demand and Make Recommendations

As the final step in the market analysis, the correlation of supply and demand is designed to answer the six questions posed earlier (actually, Question 1 on project constraints should be answered before beginning the demand analysis). The segmentation of total demand for condominiums between the subject site and other sites shown in Exhibit 11–6 is the direct result of correlating supply and demand. This correlation answers Question 2—how large will the market be in future periods and what proportion can be attracted to the subject site? This is the same as asking what will be the excess demand for this type of property at this particular site. The proportional allocation of future market demand to the site is often termed the *capture rate*.

Assignment of a capture rate to the subject property is more judgmental or subjective than scientific or objective. The analyst, after estimating total market demand for the next period, incorporates the information from building permits and the competitive market survey.

Sometimes too much emphasis is placed on building permits alone. For example, if total demand for residential condominiums is 200 units next year, and building-permit information indicates that 200 units will be constructed next year, a naive interpretation is that there will be no excess demand for residential condominiums next year. Does this mean that no units can be sold?

Not necessarily! The determination of sales depends on how competitive the project will be. The critical determination of potential sales, therefore, is the result partially of building-permit analysis and partially of the judgment of the market analyst on how well the subject property will compete against other projects.

The competitive market-survey data are essential for answering the four remaining questions on prices (or rents), types of units, sizes of units, and amenities. The usual assumption is that the combination of prices, types, sizes, and amenities that has been successful in the past will be successful in the future. If primary data were available, however, less emphasis would be placed on the competitive market survey.

--- Frame 11–2 ---

How Important Are Market Studies? Where Have Market Studies Failed?

The problems of foreclosures, bankruptcies, capital losses, and the failure of many real estate investment trusts during the recession of the mid-1970s are traced to "deliberate negligence" on the part of developers, lenders, appraisers, and market analysts in not maintaining the quality of real estate feasibility studies. John

White, the prominent real estate analyst who made this accusation,* cites 10 reasons for inadequate feasibility studies. Several of these relate directly to the market-study component of the feasibility analysis, including:

1. Failure to show probable ranges for inputs such as rents and sales. Most studies simply use a single estimate for each input.
2. Overstatement of local and regional economic growth.
3. Overallocation of the market shares that would be attracted by the projects (i.e., the capture rates).
4. Insufficient use of primary data from questionnaires and interviews. Too much reliance was placed on secondary data.

White's conclusion is that the market study, which is too often viewed by developers as merely a necessary prerequisite to obtaining financing, can be insurance against economic or financial disaster of the project. White sees the lender as the key to maintaining the quality of market studies and feasibility reports.

In a similar evaluation, Eldred and Zerbst examined 45 typical feasibility reports and noted deficiencies in ten areas.† The following table presents their results:

Deficiency	Portion of Feasibility Study	Percent of Time Found
1. Statistics without explanations	Market study	82%
2. Faulty financial analysis	Financial analysis	82
3. Inattention to economic indicators	Market study	76
4. Unspecified research direction	General	73
5. Misspecification of supply and demand	Market study	67
6. Unwarranted recommendations	General	62
7. Failure to correlate supply and demand	Market study	60
8. Poor citation and presentation of data	Market study	51
9. Omission of primary data	Market study	49
10. Avoidance of responsibility	General	44

---

*John R. White, "Nonfeasance with Feasibility = Failure," *Urban Land* (October 1976), pp. 5–9.
†Gary W. Eldred and Robert H. Zerbst, "A Critique of Real Estate Market and Investment Analysis," *Appraisal Journal* 46 (July 1978), pp. 443–52.

Final recommendations from the market analysis will be used both in the financial-analysis component of the feasibility study and in the development of architectural plans. For the financial analysis, the analyst needs the following information from the market analysis:

1. The number of units of each type expected to be sold over the absorption period.
2. The prices of the units expected to be sold.

To prepare architectural plans, the architect requires the following information from the market analysis:

1. The number of units of each type expected to be sold over the absorption period.
2. The sizes of the units.
3. The amenities required for the project.

Thus, if the market analysis is designed and implemented to answer the six fundamental questions, the process will proceed smoothly toward yielding answers to the larger questions of whether to develop the project and what features to include, if the project is developed.

MARKET ANALYSIS CASE STUDY: MARQUIS SQUARE CONDOMINIUMS

(Note to students: The case of Marquis Square Condominiums is based on an actual real estate development. The following section contains a basic market analysis of the project.)

Background

Arthur Knight is a 45-year-old real estate developer in the city of Kingston (1986 metropolitan population of 160,000). Mr. Knight developed Round Table, the largest apartment complex in Kingston and Court Jester, a successful condominium project. Recently, he purchased an option on a site near the central business district of Kingston (shown in Exhibit 11–7) for possible development as condominiums (or fee simple townhouses).

The site, shown in Exhibit 11–8, covers approximately 2.06 acres[10] and is situated at the intersection of two minor city streets, Fifth Avenue and Second Street. The site is located in an historic and once-prestigious close-in residential area of Kingston called Courtyard. Like similar older residential areas in other cities, Courtyard is characterized by a wide range of lifestyles, including a large number of elderly residents who have owned their homes for many years, young single and married professional people with few or no children, a low-income population, and a significant proportion of Kingston's gay community.

Market Setting. Kingston has grown substantially in recent years. Much of this growth has occurred because Kingston is in the southern United States and the development of Interstate Highway 1000 has greatly improved access to the city. Largely because of I-1000, most of Kingston's growth has occurred in the northern part of the metropolitan area.

---

[10]The site measures 360 feet by 250 feet, which is equal to 90,000 square feet. One acre is 43,560 square feet; 90,000/43,560 = 2.06 acres.

EXHIBIT 11–7
LOCATION MAP OF COMPARABLE CONDOMINIUMS: CASE STUDY
MARQUIS SQUARE

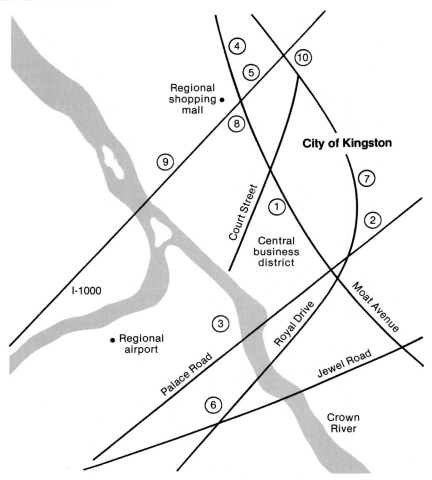

Comparable Condominiums S. Marquis Square (subject)

1. Kingsborough	6. Princess Walk
2. Prince Place	7. Royal Run
3. Queen's Rise	8. Palace Guard
4. The Dukes	9. Court Jester
5. Earl of Kingstown	10. Kingston Arms

Seven years ago, a regional shopping mall (see Exhibit 11–7) was built in the northern section of Kingston along I-1000. This had a devastating effect on the remaining retail business in the central business district. During the five years following the construction of the regional mall, the central business district and surrounding areas (including Courtyard) ex-

EXHIBIT 11–8
LOCATION MAP OF SUBJECT PROPERTY: CASE STUDY
MARQUIS SQUARE

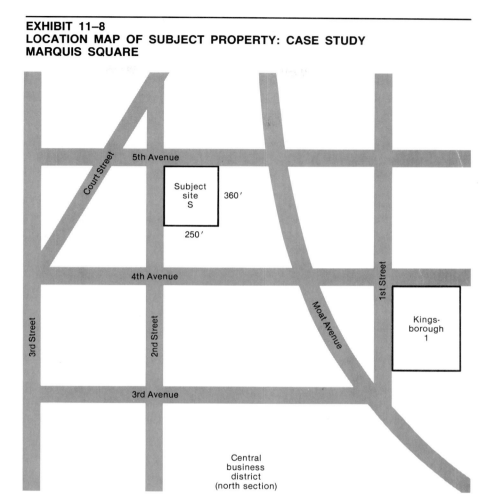

perienced rapid decline. In the past two years, however, some public (i.e., city- and state-government) and private office developments have occurred in downtown Kingston. These developments have stimulated a renewed interest in Courtyard for residential development and redevelopment. One condominium project, Kingsborough (see Exhibits 11–7 and 8), was recently completed, and a few older homes have been rehabilitated in the past year.

Step 1: Market Analysis Problem

As the first step of a feasibility analysis, Mr. Knight requires a market study for a condominium project at the subject site. Thus, the study will be a site-specific market study in which the use is predetermined. This study will confirm or refute his suspicions about the viability of the project and will satisfy the mortgage lender's concerns about financing the project. Mr. Knight hired us to conduct the market study. Our assignment is to answer the six fundamental questions of market studies by following the step-by-step process outlined in this chapter. By defining the problem the developer needs to solve, we have already completed the initial step (problem definition) in this process.

Step 2: Evaluate Project Constraints

A preliminary analysis of the site yields the following information:

1. *Zoning.* To encourage higher-density residential development in Courtyard, much of the area has been zoned R-2 (medium-density residential) by the Kingston Planning and Zoning Commission. This means that a condominium project of 15 units per acre could be developed on this site.
2. *Topography and soils.* The site is flat and the soil conditions are excellent for development.
3. *Utilities and access.* Public utility and transportation authorities have given preliminary approval for the necessary utility hookups and curb cuts.
4. *Parking.* Parking is a potential, but not necessarily insurmountable, problem. Much will depend on the number of units to be constructed and the design. The city currently allows on-street parking on one side of the adjoining streets.
5. *Neighborhood and Environmental.* No negative neighborhood reaction was encountered with the Kingsborough project. Some residents near the subject site have been contacted and seem unconcerned about the project's impact. No special environmental regulations directly affect a project of this size.

Step 3: Define the Market Area

The market area for this project is the entire Kingston metropolitan area, since the density of demand for in-town condominiums is expected to be relatively low and driving times to all employment centers are 15 minutes or less.

Step 4: Estimate Demand for the Project

To estimate the demand for the Marquis Square condominiums, we follow the process in Exhibit 11–6.

New Households. The process begins with an estimate of the number of new households that will move into Kingston during, say, the next three years.[11] The population data in Exhibit 11–5 are for Kingston; thus, the 1987 population estimates using the five techniques described earlier in this chapter range from 163,000 to 168,000 persons.

Since the simple linear regression method has worked well in predicting population for earlier periods and provides a relatively conservative estimate, we use it to estimate Kingston's 1987, 1988, and 1989 populations (Equation 11–6). They are 163,000, 166,000, and 169,000, respectively. Assuming a persons-per-household ratio of 2.6 (the current ratio for Kingston), the estimated number of new households per year is 1,154 (i.e., 3,000/2.60).

The incomes of the new households moving to Kingston in recent years have been quite high. Assume that about 65 percent of these households will earn $30,000 or more. With a constant interest rate of 12 percent for the next three years, the annual payments on an average mortgage loan of $70,000 will be $8,640 (this assumes the condominiums in Marquis Square will sell for $80,000 to $100,000).[12] Using a ratio of mortgage payment (principal and interest only) to gross income of 30 percent, an income of $28,800 (i.e., $8,640/.30) will be required to qualify for a loan on an average Marquis Square condominium. Therefore, approximately 60 to 65 percent of the new households will be able to afford a Marquis Square condominium. Assuming 60 percent, this means that each year 692 households (1154 × .60) have the financial capacity to purchase a condominium in the $80,000–$100,000 range.

The next question is how many of the new households that can afford to buy will rent instead. Several real estate brokers were contacted, and estimated that the proportion is 20 percent. So, of the 692 households that can afford to buy, only 553 (692 × .80) actually will buy each year. The real estate brokers also estimate that 10 percent of the new households that will buy will select a condominium. This leaves a potential new demand each year of 55 condominiums.

Internal Mobility. Recent surveys by real estate brokers in Kingston show that 10 percent of existing households move each year but remain in Kingston. This translates into 6,292 households [(163,000/2.60) × .10] that will move in 1987, 6,385 in 1988, and 6,500 in 1989. Brokers also estimate that a larger percentage of these households will choose single-family detached homes than the new households (i.e., approximately 96 percent). So if only four percent buy condominiums, the number of po-

---

[11] Assume a three-year absorption period. Construction will begin early in 1987.

[12] See Chapter 16 for details on how to calculate mortgage payments.

tential buyers decreases to 252 (6,292 × .04), 255, and 260 in 1987, 1988, and 1989, respectively.

Step 5: Establish Supply Conditions in the Market

For the supply side of the Kingston condominium market, it is important to know the number and characteristics of the supply of existing condominiums and of any planned condominium projects. Exhibit 11–7 shows the locations of all existing condominium developments in the area. Most units are located in the north suburban section of Kingston. Only one other is located in the in-town (i.e., Courtyard) area.

Exhibit 11–9 shows a competitive market survey of the condominium developments in Kingston. The results of this survey indicate that:

1. Most developments occurred in the late 1970s and early- to mid-1980s.
2. The suburban developments tend to be larger and have three- and four-bedroom units.
3. Prices of new units in recent developments have been mostly in the $70,000–$90,000 range.
4. The northside suburban developments have been absorbed fastest and have the best resale record.
5. The only other in-town development experienced slow-to-moderate absorption and a fair resale record. It offered two amenities, whereas other, more land-intensive developments, offered more.

A survey of building-permit records and discussions with brokers and mortgage lenders revealed that two other new condominium projects and one apartment conversion are planned. One of the new condominium projects is near the Courtyard area and has 10 units, whereas the other is near I-1000 and has 75 units. The apartment conversion will involve 40 units and is in the northeast section. The Kingston Arms Development will also complete with the subject development, especially in 1987.

Step 6: Correlate Supply and Demand and Make Recommendations

Having established the supply-and-demand conditions in the market area for the next three years, we need to correlate supply and demand to make specific estimates of potential sales. This important activity results in an allocation of excess market demand (i.e., demand greater than supply) to the subject site in each of the three years of the expected absorption period.

The critical question to be answered in this market study is how fast in-town property will sell, both to new households and to households

EXHIBIT 11–9
COMPETITIVE SURVEY OF COMPARATIVE CONDOMINIUM PROJECTS: CASE STUDY MARQUIS SQUARE

Project	Type of Units	Bedroom/Bath Sizes	Square Feet	Number of Units	Year Constructed	Sale Prices*	Absorption Rate per Month	Recent Resale Prices*	Amenities†
Kingsborough (1)	Townhouses	1/1	975	15	7(1979); 8(1981)	$52–68k	1(1979), 1/2 (1981)	$54–72k	CP
Prince Palace (2)	Garden apts.	2/2	1150	15	7(1979); 8(1981)	$70–88.5k	1.5	71–91k	P, T, CH
		1/1	1020	7	1981	$46,500		$46.5k	
		2/2	1200	35		62–66k		61–66k	
		3/2½	1650	25		78–84		79–85k	
Queen's Rise (3)	Midrise (eight-story)	1/1	895	20	1978	$88.5k	1/2	$88.5–89.5k	P, CP
		2/2	1125	20		105.5k		100–106k	
		3/2	1500	10		122–140k		125–127k	
The Dukes (4)	Garden apts.	2/2	1300	20	1984	$75k	4	$80k	P, T, CH, WO,R
	Duplexes	3/2	1650	40		80–82.5k		—	
	Townhouses	3/2½	1750	40		82.5–85k		95–97k	
		4/2½	2000	20		105–110k			
Earl of Kingston (5)	Low-rise	2/2	1275	30	1980	$73–75k	2	$82.5–84k	P, T, CH
	Garden apts.	3/2½	1700	40		82.5–84.5k		96–99.5k	
Princess Walk (6)	Garden apts.	2/2	1350	20	1977	$56.5–60k	1	$62.5–64k	P, CH
		3/2	1650	25		69.5–71.5k		71.5–73k	
Royal Run (7)	Townhouse	1/1	975	10	5(1975); 5(1977)	$36.5–38.5k	1/2	$40–43k	P, CH
	Garden apts.	2/2	1200	18	8(1977)	40–42k		46–54k	
Palace Guard (8)	Garden apts.	2/2	1200	20	1977	$62–65k	3	$69–71k	P, T, CH
	Low-rise	2/2	1650	30		70–75k		79–82k	
	Townhouse	3/2½	1900	20		85–88k		98–99.5k	
Court Jester (9)	Garden apts.	2/2	1300	10	1982	$69.5–71.50k	5	$82.5k	P, T, CH
		3/2½	1700	40		76–78k			
		4/2½	2100	15		90k			
Kingston Arms (10)	Garden apts.	2/2	1300	10	Under construction	$90k	} Good presales	N/A	P, T, CH, R, WO
	Cluster	3/2½	1800	20		100–110k			
	Homes	4/2½	2200	20		125k			

*Note on prices: k = $1,000.

†P - Pool, T - Tennis, CH - Clubhouse, WO - Workout facilities, CP - Covered parking, R - Racketball

moving within the area. We collected primary data on the attitudes of Kingston residents about living in the in-town part and other parts of the community. The survey consisted of 110 telephone interviews. Respondents were selected at random, and the interview included 15 questions about residential location preferences, demographic characteristics (e.g., age, income, occupation), and length of residency in Kingston.

Exhibit 11–10, which provides information about the residential attractiveness of areas of Kingston, indicates that the in-town area is perceived as desirable or better only by about 18 percent of Kingston's residents. Yet further results indicate that this proportion differs between residents who have lived in Kingston more than two years (14 percent) and recent residents (25 percent). Also, young, single professionals and white-collar workers with relatively high incomes showed a much stronger preference for living in the in-town areas of Kingston.

EXHIBIT 11–10
DISTRIBUTION OF RATINGS OF RESIDENTIAL ATTRACTIVENESS BY AREAS OF KINGSTOWN (Percent of Respondents)

Area	Extremely Desirable	Desirable	Undesirable	Extremely Undesirable	Not Recorded
In town	1.8	16.1	35.1	46.4	.5
NW section	28.0	54.3	16.1	5.0	.6
NE section	5.2	43.3	33.6	12.3	.5
SW section	13.5	51.2	24.0	10.2	1.1
SE section	4.3	15.7	46.5	32.7	.9

Given the information from the supply analysis and the telephone interviews, the subject site *in our judgment* will attract an estimated 8 to 12 percent of new households and 2 to 4 percent of internal movers. These *capture rates* are derived judgmentally and are influenced by the following factors:

1. Competition is expected to be formidable during the next three years, both from resales and from other new developments.
2. The development is located in an area of Kingston that most residents, especially those of longer tenure, find undesirable.
3. New households, consisting mainly of young, single professional and white-collar workers, are expected to be the largest market for Marquis Square condominiums.

Exhibit 11–11 presents estimates over three years for the absorption of the Marquis Square condominium development. These estimates show that, even if the pessimistic demand scenario is realized (i.e., only 8 percent of new households and 2 percent of internal movers), 27 units can be sold over the three-year period.

EXHIBIT 11–11
THREE-YEAR ABSORPTION ESTIMATES FOR MARQUIS SQUARE CONDOMINIUMS

Source	Absorption (sales of units)			
	1987†	1988	1989	Total
New households (total)*	55	55	55	
Optimistic (12%)	7	7	7	21
Pessimistic (8%)	4	4	4	12
Internal mobility (total)*	252	255	260	
Optimistic (4%)	10	10	10	30
Pessimistic (2%)	5	5	5	15

*Total number of potential purchasers of condominium units per period.
†Year of construction.

Recommendations. Recommendations following the market analysis for the Marquis Square condominium project can be summarized as answers to the six fundamental questions a market study should address.

1. *Constraints on development.* There do not appear to be any significant constraints on the development of this project. Zoning regulations will limit the development to a maximum of 30 units.
2. *Size of the market.* The market for this project is expected to be between 27 and 51 units, according to the information in Exhibit 11–11.
3. *Prices of units.* Since the target market is financially strong and there are few units in the upper price levels of the market, we feel that the units in Marquis Square should be priced in the upper 80s to low 100s. These prices set the tone for Marquis Square a high-quality development.
4. *Types of units.* Given the size of the site and the past history of the Kingston market (see Exhibit 11–9), we suggest either a townhouse or well-designed low-rise development. The bedroom mix should be 30 percent one-bedroom and 70 percent two-bedroom units.
5. *Sizes of units.* The units should be rather spacious. We suggest approximately 1,050 square feet for the one-bedroom units and 1,200 square feet for the two-bedroom units.
6. *Amenities.* Amenities will be important to the success of this development but, of course, the size of the site imposes limitations. We suggest, as a minimum, a small pool, a work-out room, and covered parking. Space requirements for these amenities may dictate, however, that slightly fewer than 30 units be constructed.

Development Concept. The development concept for Marquis Square condominiums calls for relatively high-priced, high-quality, and spacious one- and two-bedroom units, with amenities aimed at young professional and white-collar households. A minimum of 27 units can be sold over a three-year period. It is likely, however, that faster absorption will occur, given the fairly optimistic two-year outlook for demand and the possibility of sales to investors. This latter source of sales has not been incorporated directly into this analysis due to the difficulty of making demand estimates for this segment of the condominium market.

OVERVIEW

Market analysis plays an important role in determining the feasibility of a real estate project. As a result of a market study, important inputs to the financial analysis are generated such as rent levels, vacancy rates, and absorption periods. With these inputs, financial calculations are made to determine whether to build or whether to invest. A market study also provides information for the development of architectural plans in conjunction with new construction projects.

A market study should answer six basic questions for the decision maker: (1) Are there any constraints on development of this project? (2) How large will the market be in future periods and what proportion can be attracted to this site? (3) How much can be charged? (4) What types of units are demanded? (5) What sizes should the units be? and (6) What amenities or special feature should be provided?

Much of the process for a market analysis involves the question of the size of the future market. After the problem in the market study is defined, the possible project constraints are evaluated and the market area(s) is determined. Much of the work that remains is confined to estimating the demand for the project. This requires an understanding of urban growth and some intuition on the part of the analyst. Such specific tools as economic base analysis and population projection techniques are useful for estimating demand. The analyst must also be able to obtain and analyze both primary and secondary data.

To answer the remaining questions, estimates of future supply conditions are developed from data on building permits and the competitive market survey. Finally, supply-and-demand considerations are jointly evaluated.

This process is demonstrated in a case study in this chapter.

TEST YOURSELF

Identify the following terms and concepts discussed in this chapter.

1. Feasibility analysis versus market analysis.
2. General market studies versus site-specific market studies.
3. Highest-and-best use study.
4. Absorption rate.
5. Capture rate.
6. Economic base analysis.
7. General demand theory of urban growth.
8. General supply theory of urban growth.
9. Forecasting versus prediction versus projection.
10. Weighted-average projection technique.

Answer the following multiple-choice questions.

1. A developer has a parcel of land near a metropolitan rail transit station. What type of study does the developer need to indicate the market potential for this parcel?
   a. General market study.
   b. Site specific study where the use is predetermined.
   c. Financial analysis.
   d. Highest-and-best use study.
   e. None of the above.
2. In the conceptual scheme for the development of a parcel of land, what role does the market study play?
   a. It provides essential information for the financial analysis.
   b. It provides essential information for the architectural plans.
   c. It helps the developer obtain mortgage financing.
   d. All of the above (a, b, and c).
   e. None of the above (a, b, and c).
3. Which is *not* one of the fundamental questions that a market study should answer?
   a. What type of financing is being offered in the market?
   b. What size of units are purchasers or renters demanding?
   c. What amenities are typical in the market?
   d. What prices or rents are being asked in the market?
   e. All of the above are fundamental questions.
4. The purpose of economic base theory is to
   a. Project population.
   b. Reduce the problem of estimating employment growth to one variable, basic employment.
   c. Forecast household size.
   d. Extropolate past levels of basic employment.
   e. Separate the effects of basic and nonbasic employment on population change to obtain a better understanding of how urban areas grow.
5. For analyzing the supply side of the market, analysts rely on
   a. Competitive market surveys and building-permit data.
   b. Primary data.
   c. Secondary data with primary data.
   d. Construction cost estimates.
   e. All of the above.

ADDITIONAL READINGS

Barrett, G. Vincent, and John P. Blair. *How to Conduct and Analyze Real Estate Market and Feasibility Studies.* New York: Van Nostrand Reinhold, 1982.

Detoy, Charles J., and Sol L. Rabin. "Office Space: Calculating the Demand." *Urban Land* 31 (June 1972), pp. 4–13.

Eldred, Gary W., and Robert H. Zerbst. "Consumer Research and the Real Estate Appraiser." *Appraisal Journal* 44 (October 1976), pp. 510–22.

Graaskamp, James A. *A Guide to Feasibility Analysis.* Chicago: Society of Real Estate Appraisers, 1970.

Messner, Stephen D.; Byrl N. Boyce; Harold G. Trimble; and Robert L. Ward. *Analyzing Real Estate Opportunities: Market and Feasibility Studies.* Chicago; Realtors National Marketing Institute, National Association of Realtors, 1977.

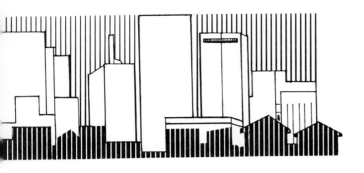

12
Housing Policy and Programs

OUTLINE

INTRODUCTION

We noted in previous chapters that an efficient market may not result in a completely equitable distribution of income or of the goods and services that income commands. Further, markets that are less than perfectly competitive may produce an even less equitable distribution, since market imperfections may place certain groups of people at a disadvantage. For example, lower-income, poorly educated consumers may have greater difficulty in obtaining market information than higher-income, better-educated consumers. And discrimination on the basis of race, sex, religion, or other grounds may result in lower incomes for groups who are discriminated against. The search for equity, or fairness, is a legitimate and ongoing concern of government.

In the field of real estate, the search for equity has led to government programs to help various groups obtain better housing than they could otherwise afford. Over the past 50 years, these programs have ranged from the direct provision of housing for low-income households to subsidies for middle-income households in private housing. On an experimental basis, the government also has supplemented the incomes of some people to enable them to upgrade their housing in the private market.

Whether government should provide housing subsidies for some groups, and the proper scope and depth of such programs, are the key issues facing housing policy makers. Such issues primarily concern equity. The government, however, has enacted many programs aimed at promoting efficiency in housing markets. The majority of these programs involve assisting people in financing home purchases. One noted economist, Allan Meltzer, has argued that "housing policy" in the United States has been essentially "mortgage policy," the purpose of which is to stimulate housing production—unsuccessfully, according to Meltzer—by increasing the availability of mortgage credit.[1] Thus, we will dedicate much of this chapter to discussing the institutional arrangements and instruments underlying housing or mortgage policy in the United States today. In Chapter 19, Residential Mortgage Finance, we extend the analysis to include the role of debt arrangements in making financial decisions.

The Need for Government Intervention

Identification of housing as an area in need of government intervention is a social and political decision. One point of view is that housing markets should be left alone and allowed to function without efforts by government to improve efficiency or equity. Another point of view endorses efforts to improve efficiency but disagrees with efforts to improve equity. Nevertheless, the prevailing mood of the U.S. government and voters over the past 50 years has been to seek achievement of both goals through a variety of government programs.

There are a number of reasons for the positive attitude toward such government intervention. First, housing has great social significance. It has perhaps a greater impact on individual people and families than any other physical good. It provides the environment in which people live the greatest part of their lives. The shelter aspect of housing is a physical necessity, while its luxury aspect has become an indicator of social status and prestige. A good housing environment is probably the most highly desired physical good for most American families.

Second, housing has great economic significance. The construction of new housing in the United States constitutes about 4 to 5 percent of the annual gross national product (GNP). Personal consumption expenditures for housing average about 10 percent of GNP, and approximately 3.5 million persons are employed directly in the residential construction industry. Moreover, housing is highly sensitive to national monetary policy, changes in which result in the large fluctuations in new construction. When interest rates are high or rising, housing starts decline rapidly; when rates are low or declining, housing starts tend to increase rapidly. Thus, the state of the housing industry is usually a good indicator of the state of the general economy.

Third, the physical nature of housing allows policy makers to establish indexes or indicators of physical adequacy. Characteristics can be identified that indicate whether housing is adequate. For example, the absence of plumbing, electrical wiring, or central heating could determine whether a house is substandard. Some other valuable goods and services,

---

[1] Allan H. Meltzer, "Credit Availability and Economic Decisions: Some Evidence from Mortgage and Housing Markets," *Journal of Finance* 29 (June 1974), pp. 763–77.

such as education and health care, may be less susceptible to such objective analysis.

Finally, access to vast amounts of developable land has enabled many moderate-income households to seek new, modern housing in outlying areas. Highway construction in general, and the interstate highway system in particular, have made suburban living by city workers feasible in most communities. The demand for housing has been an important source of government concern for promoting housing accessibility.

Given the social and economic importance of housing, analysts and policy makers recognized the inability of the private market to function during the Great Depression of the 1930s. Many families lost their homes because of stringent financing requirements. Consequently, the Federal Housing Administration was created to facilitate financing for housing on much more liberal terms than had previously been available. Many more families were able to purchase their own homes, which stimulated the construction of additional new housing. The result was improved market efficiency.

It was also recognized during the 1930s that many low-income families could not afford safe, sanitary housing even with more liberal financing. Consequently, programs were established in which the federal and local governments together constructed housing for low-income households. These programs marked the beginning of the government's efforts to promote equity in housing.

Although the United States is often regarded as having one of the highest standards of living and housing quality of any country, there is great variation in housing quality. Today, after 50 years of government intervention and billions of dollars spent on housing programs, approximately 3 percent of year-round housing units lack some or all plumbing. Approximately 3 percent of all occupied housing units have at least some exposed wiring. Water leakage occurs in about 6 percent, and there are cracks or holes in walls in about 11 percent of occupied units.

Nevertheless, significant strides have been made in improving housing quality. For example, in 1960 approximately 16 percent of year-round housing units lacked some or all plumbing, compared with 3 percent today.

Many analysts regard government intervention in the housing market as successful. Few people today are truly homeless or without shelter of some type. Besides, a realistic housing policy probably cannot overcome all other social problems such as inadequate education and discrimination. Still, a continuing need is recognized. Many families occupy substandard housing, and high interest rates make home ownership unaffordable for others. Without continuing government involvement, the differential in housing standards between high- and low-income households might widen.

PROGRAMS TO PROMOTE EFFICIENCY

The general perception among many United States economists and policy makers has been that an inefficient level of housing production would occur if government policies and programs were not in place to help middle- and lower-middle-income households purchase homes. In terms of the efficiency criterion we discussed in Chapter 9, an inefficient solution would result without these policies and programs because private costs would exceed private benefits. Government policies and programs therefore promote economic efficiency by lowering the cost of home ownership to a large number of people. They remove a major impediment to satisfying the demand for housing—financing. Although it might be argued that federal income tax policies that are beneficial to homeowners[2] also lower the cost of home ownership, these devices are generally regarded as economic stimulants, rather than promoters of efficiency. The reason for this view is that tax policies do not function directly to remove an impediment to the purchase decision.

In this section of the chapter we discuss the major institutions and instruments for implementing housing policy intended to promote economic efficiency.

Mortgage Insurance and Guaranty Programs

One policy initiative to promote efficiency has been to make loan insurance and guarantees available through the Federal Housing Administration and the Veterans Administration. The effect of these programs has been to lower the costs of financing for qualifying households.

Federal Housing Administration. The FHA was established in 1934. Before that, the typical home loan was relatively short term (5 to 15 years) and required principal repayment in full at the end of the term of the loan (i.e., loans were nonamortizing). With the decline in incomes during the Great Depression, many people could not repay their mortgage loans and lost their homes through foreclosure. Policy makers reasoned that if the terms for home loans were extended to 25 to 30 years, if the principal could be repaid a little at a time (i.e., fully amortized) over the term of the loan, and if a government agency provided insurance against losses,

---

[2]See Chapter 22.

the possibilities for home ownership would be greatly enhanced. First, lenders would be encouraged to make home-mortgage loans because of the insurance feature. Second, many more families could afford homes because of the longer maturities of loans. Third, fewer defaults would occur because of the amortization feature.

Thus, the FHA was organized to demonstrate the feasibility of home lending with long-term, amortized loans and to provide the insurance premiums for such loans. Borrowers of FHA-insured loans pay a one-time *mortgage insurance premium* (MIP) based on the amount of the loan and its maturity. The MIP may be paid in a lump sum at closing, or by including all or part of the premium in the loan amount, thus financing it over the life of the loan. As an example, the MIP on a $40,000, 30-year loan is $1,520, as calculated from FHA tables. If the MIP is totally financed, it would be added to the loan, making the loan amount $41,520. The monthly payments would be based on this amount. FHA-insured loans have experienced relatively low default rates, and this success has made lenders more willing to grant long-term, low-down-payment, uninsured (conventional) loans.

Today, the FHA is an agency of the U.S. Department of Housing and Urban Development. It continues to have the same basic purposes as when it was founded—to promote home ownership, to improve housing, and to provide opportunities for mortgage-loan financing. The FHA's principal loan insurance programs are mandated by Sections 203 and 207 of the National Housing Act. Section 203 authorizes insurance of loans on one-to-four-family properties, while Section 207 authorizes insurance of loans for the construction of rental apartment buildings of five units or more. Another important section of the act, Title I, authorizes insurance for loans to repair or improve existing housing.

The standard limits for FHA insurance on one-to-four-family dwellings currently are $67,500 for one-family units, $76,000 for two-family units, $92,000 for three-family units, and $107,000 for four-family units. However, the secretary of Housing and Urban Development may increase the insurable amounts on an area-by-area basis to meet local differences in the cost of housing. The maximum term for these loans is 30 years. For owner-occupied units, a borrower must make a minimum down payment of 3 percent of the first $50,000 of the property's value and closing costs plus 5 percent of the amount exceeding $50,000. See Chapter 19 for an example of how this program operates.

Today, the FHA administers some 37 HUD housing programs (see Exhibit 12–1). These programs include insurance of loans on multifamily housing projects; mobile homes; residential condominiums; land development projects; urban renewal projects; experimental housing; and housing for the elderly and handicapped, servicemen, and disaster vic-

EXHIBIT 12–1
FHA HOUSING PROGRAMS

One-to-four family home mortgage insurance
   (Section 203[b] and [i])
Home ownership assistance for low- and moderate-income families
   (Revised Section 235)
Home ownership assistance for low- and moderate-income families
   (Section 221[d] [2])
Housing in declining neighborhoods
Special credit risks
Condominium housing
Cooperative housing
Mobile homes (Title I)
Mobile home courts
Multifamily rental housing
Existing multifamily rental housing
Multifamily rental housing for low- and moderate-income families
   (Section 221[d] [3] & [4])
Assistance to nonprofit sponsors of low- and moderate-income housing
Rent supplements
Lower-income rental assistance (Section 8)
Low-income leased public housing (Section 23)
Low-income public housing
Public housing modernization
Public housing operating subsidies
Direct loans for housing for the elderly or handicapped
   (Section 202)
Mortgage insurance for housing for the elderly
Nursing homes and intermediate care facilities (Section 232)
Hospitals
Group practice medical facilities
Home improvement loan insurance (Title I)
Rehabilitation mortgage insurance (Revised) Section 203(k)
Supplemental loans for multifamily projects and health-care facilities
Single-family home mortgage coinsurance
Graduated payment mortgage
Indian housing
College housing
Armed services housing for civilian employees
Housing in military-impacted areas
Homes for servicemen
Flexible subsidy
The Office of Independent Living for the Disabled

tims. In addition to its level-payment loan program for single-family residences, the FHA also has a graduated-payment loan program. Under this program borrowers can make lower payments than under a level-payment plan, but these payments increase over the early years. At the end of the graduated increase period, the monthly payments will be higher than for a level-payment loan having the same maturity and interest rate.[3]

Veterans Administration.   Among its various programs for helping veterans adjust to civilian life, the Veterans Administration has two programs to facilitate the purchase of housing. First, VA can partially guarantee loans made by qualified lenders to eligible veterans. Second, VA can make direct loans to veterans to buy housing in areas where mortgage credit is not available from regular institutional lenders. But because of the wide dispersal of financial institutions and the general availability of mortgage credit, this second program has not been used often in recent years.

Under the guaranty program, the VA will guarantee up to 60 percent of a loan or $27,500, whichever is less, for a period of 30 years and 32 days. (See Chapter 19 for an example.) Such a loan can be made for the construction or purchase of a home (including a mobile home) by the veteran. Although the home may contain up to four living units, it or one of its units must be occupied by the veteran as his or her place of residence. The full guaranty eligibility of $27,500 need not be used in a single transaction, but can be spread over two or more loans. For example, if a veteran has used a guaranty of $18,000 to purchase a home, the home could be sold and the veteran would still have $9,500 of guaranty left with which to obtain another loan to purchase another home.

The administrator of the Veterans Administration sets the maximum interest rate on VA-guaranteed loans. Although this rate is often below market rates for conventional loans, veterans are precluded by law from paying any premium or charge for obtaining a loan (known as *points* or *discount points*). A seller could pay such a premium, but cannot raise the price of the house to cover the premium above the appraised value.

The mortgage insurance and guaranty programs of FHA and VA remain in place to help overcome a perceived imperfection in the housing market—that many families want to own their own houses but cannot qualify for conventional mortgage loans. Although these programs have been successful in making housing available to moderate-income households, it is possible that they also have assisted in *creating*, not simply serving, demand for owner-occupied housing. If the FHA and VA programs are functioning to stimulate rather than facilitate housing programs, then it is appropriate to ask how these programs interact with federal government attempts to manage the economy.

---

[3]We will discuss graduated-payment mortgages in depth in Chapter 19.

Regulation of Interest Rates and Mortgage Credit

The U.S. government attempts to promote stability and growth in the general economy and in individual sectors by regulating the supply of funds and interest rates. The government's *fiscal policy* and *debt-management policy,* together with *monetary policy* carried out by the Federal Reserve System, are the means to accomplish this regulation.

Fiscal policy involves the taxing and spending activities of the government. Increases or decreases in taxes affect all citizens' abilities to purchase goods and services. Similarly, the spending patterns of government determine, at least partially, how much of the national income will be consumed by government versus the private sector, and which sectors will benefit from the government spending. For example, spending on a large-scale military buildup will divert resources from other sectors into the defense industry.

Because of the mammoth national debt (currently in excess of $2 trillion), the government's financing of new debt and refinancing of maturing debt (i.e., Treasury bonds, notes, and bills) can have an important impact on private-sector financing. When the government borrows funds, it competes with private borrowers. If the government's budget deficit is large, the U.S. Treasury must borrow large amounts in the money and capital markets to finance the deficit. Such amounts, together with the refinancing of maturing debt, can deplete the supply of funds available to private borrowers and possibly drive up interest rates, a phenomenon sometimes called "crowding out." Relatively small government financing requirements can leave relatively large amounts available at more favorable interest rates for private borrowers.

Federal Reserve System. Fiscal and debt-management policies do not have the goal of directly regulating the supply of funds and interest rates in the economy; the Federal Reserve System is charged with this responsibility. As shown in Exhibit 12–2, the Federal Reserve System ("the Fed") has two main components: a policy body and a system for implementation. The Board of Governors, which comprises seven members appointed by the President and confirmed by the Senate for 14-year terms, is responsible for monetary policy in the United States and for the supervision and regulation of member commercial banks (e.g., First National Bank of Younameit). Policy is implemented through the Fed Open Market Committee, which is responsible for certain key monetary-policy tools, and through the 12 regional Federal Reserve Banks, which are responsible for the regulation and supervision of the member commercial banks and for the remaining monetary-policy tools. The member banks are the only part of the system that interfaces with the market; thus, they ultimately carry out most of the Fed's policies.

By controlling the money supply and interest rates, the Fed attempts

---

EXHIBIT 12–2
FEDERAL RESERVE SYSTEM

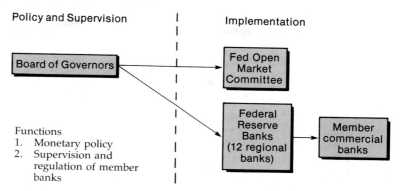

to promote moderate, sustainable economic growth and stability. Its means of carrying out monetary policy are (1) *reserve requirements* for commercial banks, (2) the *discount rate,* and (3) *open-market operations.*

Reserve requirements determine the percentage of deposits that a bank must maintain in reserve. By increasing or decreasing the reserve requirement, the Fed decreases or increases, respectively, the funds that would otherwise be available to the general economy. A small change in the reserve requirements has a large effect on available funds, so the Fed uses this tool very sparingly.

The discount rate is the interest rate the Fed charges banks and other financial institutions to borrow funds from it. Banks sometimes need to borrow from the Fed to meet reserve requirements, and the interest rate charged determines how burdensome this borrowing is. A low discount rate encourages banks to borrow to meet reserves and to lend more money to private borrowers; a high discount rate has the opposite effect. The discount rate is adjusted periodically, largely to reflect the general level of interest rates in the economy. By itself, it is a weak tool for regulating the money supply and interest rates.

The Fed's primary tool for fine tuning the economy is its purchase and sale of securities in the open market. Because of these open-market operations, the Fed owns and manages an enormous portfolio of assets—mostly U.S. Treasury securities. By purchasing securities, the Fed injects funds into the banking system, making money and credit easier to obtain by private borrowers. By selling securities, the Fed absorbs funds from the banking system, making money and credit more expensive and difficult to obtain. Because the Fed can vary the dollar volume of its purchases and sales of securities from very small to very large amounts, open-market operations are the most flexible tool in the Fed's kit. It uses this tool almost on a daily basis to implement monetary policy. The Open Market Committee has primary responsibility for setting the limits on the purchase and sale of securities from the Fed's portfolio.

────────────────── *Frame 12–1* ──────────────────

Monetary Policy During the Early 1980s

During the early 1980s, the Fed's primary monetary goal was to control inflation. The rate of inflation had increased during the late 1970s and 1980 to 14 percent per year. Inflation and people's expectations of future inflation were destabilizing the economy: Consumers were borrowing at record high levels to buy large-ticket items, with loans to be repaid later with cheaper dollars. Consumer savings and investment were at record low rates. People on fixed incomes found it virtually impossible to maintain their standards of living, and in some cases to survive. And U.S. industry was losing its competitiveness with foreign manufacturers.

The Fed instituted a tight money policy to bring the rate of inflation under control. The policy was successful, as the rate of inflation dropped from about 14 percent in 1980 to less than 4 percent in 1985. The cost was a major, two-year recession from 1981 to 1983 and the highest unemployment rate (10.6 percent) since the Great Depression of the 1930s.

──

Monetary policy has great significance for real estate and housing. Because almost all real estate transactions are financed, a tight-money policy by the Fed affects real estate activity more than any other segment of the economy. For example, during 1980–82, the Fed's tight-money policy caused the fewest new housing starts since World War II. All real estate activity was greatly reduced, and single-family homes lost real value of 15 to 20 percent as housing demand was dampened by the high interest rates.

Clearly, housing policy must be examined in relation to general economic activity and the responses of fiscal, debt-management, and monetary authorities. A policy to improve the country's housing cannot be effective in the face of tight monetary policy and a large demand for funds by government and other sectors of the economy. A policy to lower the priority of housing can best be effected during periods of monetary restraint and high demand for funds. A policy to improve housing therefore can best be implemented during periods of monetary ease and reduced demand for funds by government and other sectors.

Federal Home Loan Bank System. The Federal Home Loan Bank System (FHLBS) also plays a role in determining interest rates and the availability of funds for housing. The system is a source of credit for savings and loan associations (S&Ls) and mutual savings banks (MSBs), the na-

======================================= *Frame 12–2* =======================================

Has the National Priority for Housing Decreased?

During the early 1980s the financial institutions that provide most of the funds for housing in the United States, savings and loan associations, were restructured into less specialized, more bank-like financing firms. Savings and loans historically concentrated their lending in long-term, fixed-interest mortgages for homes. Laws and regulations required them to invest the vast majority of their deposits in home loans.

In the early 1980s, however, S&Ls became financially pinched between the high interest rates they had to pay for deposits and borrowed money and the rates they were receiving on old, long-term, fixed-rate loans. New certificate accounts required S&Ls to pay much higher interest rates to savers, almost doubling the cost of money to S&Ls. Many went out of business (725 in 1981 and 1982), and the remaining institutions were given greatly expanded investment powers. The new, bank-like powers and adjustable loans were designed to make S&Ls competitive with other financial institutions and to increase the S&Ls' investment yields. No longer would S&Ls have such large concentrations of home loans.

Some critics contended that the Reagan Administration used the period of high interest rates and financial stress to reduce the national priority for housing. Secretary of Treasury Donald Regan and Chairman of the Council of Economic Advisers Martin Feldstein were not known as friends of housing. In fact, Dr. Feldstein stated during his confirmation hearings before the U.S. Senate that housing had received too much of the national income and that other sectors of the economy should receive more. Such statements, the restructuring of S&Ls, high interest rates, and reduced funds for subsidized housing led many observers to believe that indeed a reordering of the nation's priorities for housing had occurred.

---

tion's primary suppliers of mortgage credit. As shown in Exhibit 12–3, the FHLBS is organized much like the Fed. The Federal Home Loan Bank Board (FHLBB), with three members appointed by the President and confirmed by the Senate for four-year terms, sets policy for the system. Twelve district banks, as well as the Federal Home Loan Mortgage Corporation and the Federal Savings and Loan Insurance Corporation, implement policy, which is eventually carried out by the member institutions, mostly federally chartered S&Ls and MSBs (e.g., First Federal Savings and Loan of Mostanywhere).

The FHLBS is the nation's second largest borrower of funds after the U.S. Treasury. Because of its size, the system can have a substantial impact on credit markets and interest rates when it borrows funds. Funds that it borrows by issuing bonds and notes backed by the federal government are allocated to the 12 district banks, which in turn lend the funds to member institutions, sometimes at favorable interest rates. The amount

EXHIBIT 12–3
FEDERAL HOME LOAN BANK SYSTEM

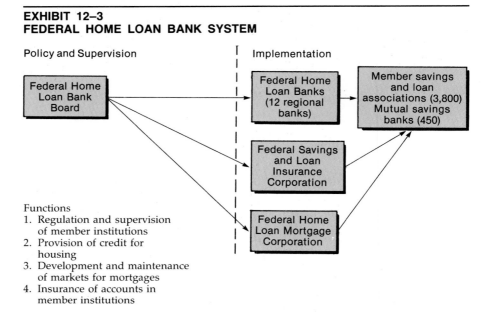

Policy and Supervision | Implementation

Federal Home Loan Bank Board

Federal Home Loan Banks (12 regional banks)

Member savings and loan associations (3,800) Mutual savings banks (450)

Federal Savings and Loan Insurance Corporation

Federal Home Loan Mortgage Corporation

Functions
1. Regulation and supervision of member institutions
2. Provision of credit for housing
3. Development and maintenance of markets for mortgages
4. Insurance of accounts in member institutions

of borrowings, timing, interest rates, and priorities established by the FHLBB influence the amount and cost of funds available for housing.

Under a broad interpretation of market efficiency, the Fed and the FHLBS promote efficiency in the housing market by facilitating the flow of funds into the mortgage markets. However, the fundamental concern of these government-authorized participants in the mortgage markets may be to promote market *stability*. Wide variations in housing production resulting from fluctuations in interest rates and the availability of mortgage funds have created much hardship and uncertainty for those employed in construction and related industries. Most economists agree, however, that the Fed and the FHLSB should be maintained, perhaps with modification, in an attempt to improve market stability. For without them, housing markets presumably would be far more volatile.

Development of Secondary Markets for Mortgages

When mortgage loans are granted by a financial institution, it may keep the loans in its portfolio or sell the loans in the secondary mortgage market. A secondary market involves the sale and purchase of existing assets—such as stocks, bonds, or mortgages—while a primary market involves the creation and sale of new assets. Existence of a secondary market makes a primary market more efficient. If mortgage lenders can sell their mortgages, they can obtain funds to make more loans. A secondary market means that mortgage lenders have a choice of whether to keep their loans or sell them. This business decision is based on yields, timing, availability of funds, portfolio diversification, and the demand for funds.

The relationship between the primary and secondary mortgage markets is shown in Exhibit 12–4. In the primary market, mortgage lenders provide funds to assist home buyers in making their purchases. In exchange, lenders receive security in the form of a mortgage that gives lenders a lien to foreclose on borrowers who default (see Chapter 5) and a note that gives lenders the right to seek judgments against borrowers' personal assets. Lenders have the option of keeping these mortgages in their portfolios or selling them in large packages to one of the secondary mortgage market agencies discussed below. The second option allows mortgage lenders to have the proceeds available to make more mortgage loans. Sometimes the secondary mortgage-market agencies hold the mortgage documents; at other times the documents are sold to mortage investors such as corporations, life insurance companies, pension funds, and college endowment funds.

EXHIBIT 12–4
THE TWO MORTGAGE MARKETS

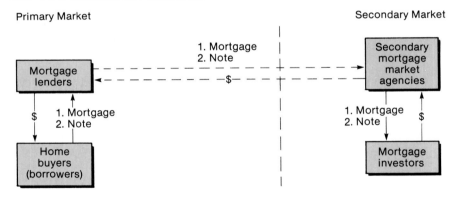

Well-developed private secondary markets exist for most securities (stocks and bonds) and some physical assets. However, the secondary market for mortgages prior to government involvement was fragmented and poorly developed. Financial institutions sometimes traded whole loans, especially financial institutions in capital-surplus regions that bought loans from institutions in capital-deficit areas. Nevertheless, this activity was sporadic and unorganized.

The reasons for a weak private secondary mortgage market include mortgage instruments and laws that vary greatly among states, the differences among properties that serve as mortgage security, differing appraisal practices, and varying loan standards and underwriting practices of lending institutions (i.e., the process and policies for evaluating the risks of mortgage loan default). This lack of standardization resulted in government action to promote efficiency by organizing secondary markets.

Federal National Mortgage Association. The FNMA (also known as Fannie Mae) was organized in 1938 to serve as a secondary market for FHA-insured mortgages. Its funds were provided by the U.S. Treasury. In 1948 its authority was expanded to include the purchase of VA-guaranteed mortgages, and in 1954 the agency received a new charter with a more private orientation. Its functions were to:

1. Provide a secondary market through private financing (selling bonds in the private capital market) instead of borrowing from the U.S. Treasury.
2. Provide special assistance to housing subsidy programs enacted by Congress.
3. Manage and liquidate its existing portfolio of mortgages.

In 1970, the FNMA was authorized to purchase conventional mortgages. Also in that year, the FNMA, under authority of the National Housing Act of 1968, became a semiprivate organization. It was authorized to sell one-third of its capital stock to private owners and to have two-thirds of its board of directors elected by its private owners. However, one-third of its board of directors would be appointed by the President, and it could continue to borrow from the Treasury. It also continued to be obligated to help attain the national goal of safe and decent housing for low- and moderate-income families.

Today, FNMA has well-developed plans for the purchase of both conventional and government-underwritten mortgages. It obtains its funds for purchases by selling securities (listed on the New York Stock Exchange) in the private capital market, by selling mortgages and interests in mortgage pools from its portfolio, by obtaining commitment fees for loan purchases, and by earning interest on its mortgage portfolio and other investments.

Government National Mortgage Association. The National Housing act of 1968 also created the Government National Mortgage Association (GNMA also known as Ginnie Mae). Two of FNMA's functions—the special-assistance function and the management-and-liquidation function—were transferred to GNMA. FNMA was thus freed of its governmental functions so it could concentrate on private secondary-market activities. GNMA became the government agency to help housing programs that promote equity. Thus, GNMA's special-assistance activities are discussed later in this chapter under equity programs.

GNMA's management-and-liquidation function required it to manage and liquidate all mortgage loans that had been acquired by FNMA since 1938. GNMA was to convert these old loans to private financing media as quickly as possible and at minimum cost to the federal government. GNMA was authorized to guarantee mortgage-backed securities issued by GNMA or other approved issuers (e.g., mortgage bankers). Under this authority, GNMA sells securities (like bonds) backed by pools of FHA- or Farmers Home Administration (FmHA)-insured and VA-guaranteed mortgages, which are also backed by the full faith and credit of the U.S. government. Needless to say, these securities are virtually risk-free and trade at relatively low yields. This program has produced vast sums of capital from an otherwise static and unproductive portfolio of mortgages.

Federal Home Loan Mortgage Corporation. Congress created the Federal Home Mortgage Corporation (FHLMC also known as Freddie Mac) in 1970 under control of the FHLBB. FHLMC's purpose, like that of FNMA, is to develop the private secondary mortgage market. However, it was originally designed to serve savings and loan associations. The S&Ls had not found FNMA particularly helpful because they primarily made conventional loans, whereas before 1970 FNMA was not even authorized to purchase conventional loans. Thus, original capital of $100 million was contributed by the 12 district federal home loan banks. Today, FHLMC buys mortgages from other lenders, as well as from S&Ls. However, its board of directors still consists of the members of the FHLBB.

FHLMC currently buys government-underwritten, as well as conventional, loans. It may also buy participations (or shares) in pools of mortgage loans. FHLMC attempts to balance its purchases with sales of loans and interests in pools of loans. It also earns a return from commitment fees[4] and from interest on its mortgage portfolio.

In developing and facilitating the secondary market in mortgages, FNMA and FHLMC have developed standardized documents and procedures for loans submitted to them for purchase. Standard forms for notes, mortgages, and appraisals, together with standard underwriting criteria, have brought a much greater degree of conformity to the primary, as well as the secondary, mortgage market. Investors today are much better able to buy and sell mortgages because their risk characteristics are more amenable to analysis than a few years ago. The government and government-related institutions of the secondary mortgage market have truly improved its efficiency by making more information available in usable form

---

[4]Commitment fees are charges for agreeing to purchase loans at a future date.

and by enabling more investors to purchase mortgage loans. GNMA has performed similar functions for government-assisted housing loans.

PROGRAMS TO PROMOTE EQUITY

Through the goal of "a decent home and suitable living environment for every American family" contained in the National Housing Act of 1949, Congress established the standard for equity in the distribution of housing services in the United States. Since at that time many Americans were not living in what Congress considered decent homes and suitable environments, policies and programs were instituted to shift the distribution of housing services away from a market-determined distribution to what was considered an equitable distribution. In this section, we will first examine how changes in the distribution of housing services occur in the market and then consider the specific federal policies and programs designed to facilitate such changes.

Filtering in Housing Markets

A local housing market can be envisioned as an interrelated set of several submarkets. These submarkets are based on quality and price, and range from the highest-priced, highest-quality housing to the lowest-priced, lowest-quality units. Since housing units are long-lived assets, several families typically occupy a unit over its useful life. As a housing unit ages, it generally becomes less desirable and less valuable, thus enabling lower-income households to occupy it. If lower-income households are able to move into better units formerly occupied by higher-income households, they improve their housing condition by the market process of *filtering*.

Exhibit 12–5 shows a local housing market as a set of interrelated submarkets. Each submarket is self-contained, in that prices and vacancy rates can vary greatly among them. Nevertheless, the submarkets are linked directly or indirectly. The households in Submarket C would prefer units in B, but cannot afford them, unless their incomes go up or prices in B come down. Prices in B might come down if an excess of new construction occurs there. Residents in C could then move up to B, and those in D could move up to C and so on. There is only one problem: The introduction of a significant excess is unlikely at any level. Builders will discontinue construction of new units if they cannot expect to sell the units at a reasonable profit. Note also that some submarkets may be directly related to two or more submarkets.

The concept of filtering is attractive to those who contend that the

EXHIBIT 12–5
HOUSING SUBMARKETS AND FILTERING

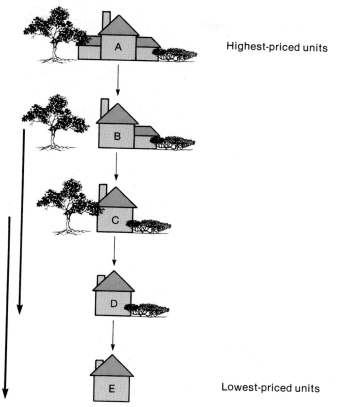

Highest-priced units

Lowest-priced units

government should not provide aid to low- or moderate-income households for better housing. Just as virtually everyone can afford to buy a second-hand automobile, even the lowest-income households should be able to acquire decent housing that was formerly owned by higher-income households. Yet as we noted earlier in this chapter, many American families continue to occupy housing that is fundamentally deficient.

Filtering alone has not improved the housing condition of many moderate- and low-income households—at least not sufficiently to obviate government intervention. There are several reasons for failure of the filtering process to provide adequate housing. First, housing is a big-ticket item, even at the low end of the price/quality spectrum. It is the single largest component of most families' budgets. Some households simply do not have adequate income to afford even minimal quality in housing.

From this viewpoint, the housing problem is a demand issue and should be attacked by programs to improve the incomes of those who are inadequately housed.

Second, filtering is at best slow and uncertain. It relies on the housing suppliers to produce excess new units in submarkets above the lowest levels. However, as we noted, builders are not apt to construct excess units, since their returns would not justify their efforts.

Nevertheless, despite the inadequacies of the filtering process, the average quality of housing for most American families has improved over the years. This improvement has generally occurred in the moderate-to-upper-level price categories of housing, leaving unacceptably wide gaps between these and lower levels. This need for programs to promote equity in housing at the lower price levels is therefore at least partially the result both of success at the higher levels in upgrading housing quality and of the failure of filtering.

Subsidized Housing Programs

The federal government, through decisions by Congress and the President, has provided programs for many years to help poorly housed households obtain decent housing. In 1937 the government embarked on the public housing program that was to supply many units over the next 30 years. This program subsidized the cost of constructing new housing by local housing authorities, which in turn rented the units to low-income households at below-market rates. While the number of new units constructed under this program has declined greatly in recent years, public housing projects in almost every city continue to house many families.

In addition to articulating the goal of "a decent home and suitable living environment for every American family,"[5] in 1949, Congress established a program of governmental assistance to privately constructed housing and began a program for slum clearance and urban redevelopment. In 1954 it added programs for conservation and rehabilitation in renewal areas.

In the 1960s, the emphasis shifted to aid for moderate-income families. Interest-rate subsidies, rent supplements, blighted-area FHA loans, model cities grants, home counseling service, special credit-risk insurance, displaced families insurance, and subsidies for nonprofit sponsors of subsidized housing are some of the principal programs begun in the decade. Most are no longer operative.

---

[5]This goal has the dual emphasis of setting the policy standard for improving (1) housing quality in the United States and (2) the neighborhood environment of American families. The programs and housing acts that followed over the next three decades reflected either the emphasis on housing quality, neighborhood living environment, or both.

The Housing and Community Development Act of 1974 was the major housing legislation of the 1970s and remains the basic applicable housing law. This act is particularly important because it shifted emphasis to include the objective of a suitable living environment (i.e., neighborhood quality) along with the objective of decent housing. Title I of the act consolidated a number of programs into a single block-grant program. Title IV provided funds for comprehensive planning by communities to determine community and housing needs. Title VIII authorized urban homesteading, an experimental housing allowance program, and national flood insurance. It also outlawed discrimination on the basis of sex and encouraged the formation of state housing and development agencies.

Title II (Section 8) of the 1974 act authorized the leasing of new, existing, and rehabilitated private housing, not in ghetto areas, to low-income families. Families must contribute at least 15 but not more than 30 percent of the family income to rent.

As an example of how the Section 8 program works, take a family with an income of $6,500 per year ($541.66 per month) that is seeking assistance in acquiring rental housing through the Section 8 program (families who qualify cannot have incomes in excess of 80 percent of the average family income in the area). Based on their income and the disability of the principal wage earner, the local housing authority approves them for the program; they are required to pay 25 percent of their monthly income for rent.

Concurrently, a landlord in the family's neighborhood decides to convert his apartment house to Section 8 use. The local housing authority inspects the landlord's property, using FHA standards. The authority approves the property and landlord, with only minor repairs to the property required. Also, FHA assigns a fair market rent to the property of $385 per month. This is based on rentals charged by landlords on competitive properties in the area ($350) plus ten percent ($35) to induce the landlord to participate in the program; this incentive amount can go as high as 20 percent.

The housing authority notifies the family of the availability of a unit in the landlord's building and the family decides to rent the unit. Each month the landlord receives $385 in rent. The family pays 25 percent of its monthly income, or $135 ($541.66 × .25). FHA pays the remainder of the rent, $250, as part of its annual budget from Congress. This low-income family, therefore, receives a $250 subsidy each month for the purpose of renting decent housing that is being provided by a private landlord.

The Title II (Section 8) program described above is the principal subsidized-housing program currently in effect for *rental housing*. A modified Section 235 program for moderate-income households also helps those households purchase new housing. The FHA must preapprove the unit purchased, and the builder is allowed a maximum cost that includes reasonable overhead and profit.

To demonstrate how the modified Section 235 program operates, assume that the family in the example of the Section 8 program has improved their financial condition to the point where they can make a down payment on a home under FHA Section 235. Since they live in a high-cost area as defined by FHA, the maximum price they can pay is $38,000. The program requires a minimum down payment of three percent or $1,140 ($38,000 × .03).

The FHA mortgage payment subsidy paid to the mortgage lender is somewhat more complicated to compute than the rental subsidy paid to the landlord under Section 8. FHA will pay the lower of (1) the difference between the mortgage payment and 20 percent of the family's income, or (2) the difference between the actual mortgage payment and what the payment would be at a 4-percent interest rate.

If, for example, interest rates are currently 12 percent, then the family's payment would be $379.15.[6] Twenty percent of the family's income is $108.33 ($541.66 × .2); thus, the subsidy with subsidy option No. 1 is $271.05 ($379.15 − $108.33). At a 4-percent rate of interest the mortgage payment would be $175.98; thus, the subsidy with subsidy option No. 2 is $203.17 ($379.15 − $175.98). Since this second option results in a lower subsidy, the family would pay $175.98 each month to the mortgage lender, and FHA would pay the lender $203.17.

An experimental housing-allowance program was instituted during the latter 1970s. In this program, families were given a dollar allowance, or voucher, to spend on housing. While the allowance had to be spent on housing, the families could select housing from the private market. The results of the experiment were mixed. While some families improved their housing, others elected to continue living in below-standard housing and to increase their purchases of other goods and services.[7] For some families the allowance appeared to provide a disincentive for employment. Disagreement continues over the efficiency of a housing-allowance program compared with other subsidy programs.

Role of GNMA.   Recall from our discussion of GNMA that one of its principal functions is to provide special assistance in the granting of subsidized and other special-purpose loans. It carries out this function by purchasing such loans at their face value, when these loans otherwise would be less salable or could be sold only at a large discount. Without

---

[6]See Chapter 19 for a discussion of the calculation of mortgage payments.

[7]In theory, the households receiving the subsidy should spend an increasing amount on housing. This additional expenditure on housing should encourage landlords of higher-quality housing to allow their units to filter down more quickly to these households, or allow the households to purchase higher-quality housing.

being able to sell these loans, lenders would not make them, since they are usually risky and may carry below-market yields. GNMA may also use this power to help stimulate construction of certain types of housing that are needed.

After purchasing such loans, GNMA often resells them to FNMA at a discount sufficiently high to give them a favorable yield. This is called the *Tandem Plan* and allows GNMA to recover most of the funds spent for any single special-assistance purchase. These funds are then available for additional purchases.

For example, assume that government housing authorities recognize a need for multifamily housing for moderate-income households. Assume that the mortgage interest rate on loans for such developments is 15 percent and thus not feasible for most multifamily projects. To initiate a Tandem Plan program to stimulate the development of multifamily housing, GNMA notifies mortgage lenders that if they make 10-percent loans to developers of multifamily housing for moderate-income households, GNMA will buy these mortgages from the lenders as though they were 15-percent loans. GNMA would therefore pay above-market prices for the mortgages.

The tandem part of the program involves GNMA's subsequent sale of these mortgages to FNMA. The mortgages are sold as 10-percent mortgages; thus, GNMA receives the market price for the mortgages, but less than it paid for them. The loss is absorbed as part of the GNMA's budget. Whereas in this example the purpose of implementing the Tandem Plan program was to stimulate the construction of multifamily housing for moderate-income households, the program can also be used to buy mortgages, such as Section 235 mortgages, that lenders otherwise would not make unless they knew these mortgages could be sold without a discount.

Community Development and Block Grants

Recognizing that properties in blighted and slum areas are subject to adverse neighborhood effects (negative externalities) imposed by surrounding properties, the federal government has provided funds for communities to upgrade public facilities and services. Conservation and rehabilitation programs begun in the 1950s and grant programs under the model cities legislation of the 1960s were efforts in this direction. In 1974, several community-development programs, such as urban renewal, public-facility loans, model cities grants, and rehabilitation loans, were combined into a single program of block grants. Cities, counties, and nonurban areas received grants for use in eliminating slums and blight, increasing public services, improving land use, and preserving property values.

POLICY ISSUES IN HOUSING

From the brief overview of housing programs presented in this chapter, the reader can begin to appreciate the diversity of the government's attempts to improve the housing of moderate- and low-income American families. Many programs have been tried and abandoned. No single program seems able to accomplish the goal of improving housing-market efficiency and equity without serious drawbacks. Billions of dollars in taxpayers' money have been spent on these programs, still without a consensus on the proper objectives, much less the best approach. It may be helpful to review some of the policy issues that continue to be relevant in the search for the proper role of government in housing matters.

The issue of whether the government should be directly involved in programs to improve housing today involves questions of equity. Are some households unfairly restricted from obtaining minimally acceptable housing in the private market? If the answer is yes, clearly the government must act; if not, the government should not be involved in housing markets. While economists can obtain and analyze the data about housing conditions, they are no better qualified than other citizens to make a judgment about equity. It is a decision that only the American public can make, democratically through its elected representatives. The view at this time seems to be that the government should continue to have a role, albeit a smaller, more selective one, aimed primarily at moderate-income households.

Questions continue about the proper form of government activity in housing. If poor housing stems from inadequate income, perhaps the government could improve housing more effectively by subsidizing families' incomes. The housing-allowance program is one plan to increase incomes and continues to be advocated by some housing analysts. The negative income tax, in which individuals having incomes below a specified level would receive payments from the government, is another such plan.

On the other hand, if programs to supply housing are to be used, what form should they take? Should only low-income households be subsidized, or should moderate-income households be included—or subsidized exclusively? Here economists can provide useful analysis, but again without answering the ultimate questions of who should be helped and by how much.

For example, one study showed that the housing condition of low-income families is improved more through the direct provision of housing in a public-housing program, but that the subsidy cost per household is higher than with subsidies aimed at moderate-income households.[8] Sub-

---

[8]Ronald L. Racster, Halbert C. Smith, and William B. Brueggeman, "Federal Housing Programs in the Local Housing Market," *Appraisal Journal* 39 no. 3 (July 1971), pp. 402–6.

sidy programs for moderate-income households help more households at a lower cost per household, but the most needy—low-income households—do not obtain as much benefit. Moderate-income subsidy programs rely on filtering to help low-income families by stimulating their movement to housing in higher-priced submarkets—a process which at best is slow and uncertain.

We should also realize that subsidized housing programs result in a redistribution of income. When determining policy it is useful to know who must pay the cost and who will benefit from a government subsidy program. Nourse, in a study of the potential shifts in income from a public-housing program, found that although the most important shift of income is from the taxpayers to public-housing tenants, other important shifts may also occur.[9] For example, national income would be increased and construction workers would benefit if they were otherwise unemployed. If, without the program, they could be employed on nonsubsidized construction projects, there would be a shift in employment from other real estate development to public housing. During periods of full employment, additional construction would contribute to increasing costs and prices in the construction industry. The sale of bonds to finance public housing would shift capital away from other investments and into housing. A local government may or may not benefit, depending on how much tax revenue was being obtained from the property before development and how much is obtained after development for public housing. Property owners whose land is used for the project may or may not benefit, depending on the price they obtain in relation to its value for other purposes. All of these questions of income redistribution simply add to the burden of economists in evaluating the effects of housing policy and programs to promote efficiency and equity.

OVERVIEW

The federal government plays an important role in housing, primarily through financing. Whether people can afford housing depends on the availability and price of borrowed funds. By establishing financial institutions, government regulatory agencies, secondary sources of credit, deposit insurance, and by regulating interest rates the government carries out its national housing policy.

To improve the housing condition of American families, the government has attempted to increase both the efficiency and fairness of the housing and mortgage markets. It has increased competitive pressures by enabling more people and institutions to participate in the market, and it

---

[9]Hugh O. Nourse, "Redistribution of Income from Public Housing," *National Tax Journal* 19 no. 1 (March 1966); pp. 27–37.

has improved equity by outlawing discrimination and providing lower-income households access to the mortgage market. Perhaps the program that has affected the largest number of families and had the greatest impact on financing practices is the FHA-insured mortgage loan program. It enables moderate-income families to obtain loans at reasonable interest rates.

Other government programs have been designed to aid specific groups of people. Subsidy programs for low-income families have taken several forms, including public housing, interest-rate subsidies, rent supplements, and builder subsidies. The main program currently operating is the Title II Section 8 program that subsidizes families' rents in approved private housing outside of ghetto areas. The emerging intent of subsidy programs is to encourage private enterprise to construct, own, and operate the needed housing. Subsidies permit below-market rents and housing expense to be charged, while providing adequate profits to developers and builders. Although studied experimentally, a housing-allowance program has not been adopted for general use. Proposals for unrestricted income supplements have encountered political opposition.

TEST YOURSELF

Explain the following terms and concepts presented in this chapter.

1. Mortgage insurance.

2. Graduated payment loan.

3. Points.

4. Secondary mortgage market.

5. Commitment fees.

6. Filtering.

7. "Section 8" housing program.

8. Tandem Plan.

Answer the following multiple-choice questions.

1. The Federal Housing Administration is part of which federal agency?
   a. Federal Home Loan Bank Board.
   b. Department of Housing and Urban Development.
   c. Federal Reserve System.
   d. Government National Mortgage Association.
   e. Office of Management and Budget.

2. The arrangement by which the GNMA multiplies the effect of its funds in carrying out its special-assistance function is known as
   a. Section 202 BMIR.
   b. Section 8.
   c. Tandem plan.
   d. Secondary-market operations.
   e. Block grants.

3. Providing and creating sound patterns for mortgage-loan financing, upgrading and improving housing standards, and promoting home ownership are basic purposes of the
   a. FHA.
   b. FHLBS.
   c. FHLMC.
   d. FNMA.
   e. VA.

4. The process used by the federal government to accomplish goals through taxation and spending is known as
   a. Secondary-market assistance.
   b. Oversight and review.
   c. Monetary policy.
   d. Fiscal policy.
   e. Debt-management policy.

5. The Federal Home Loan Bank System comprises which of the following?
   a. Federal Home Loan Bank Board.
   b. Federal Home Loan Banks.
   c. Federal Savings and Loan Insurance Corporation.
   d. Member savings and loan associations and mutual savings banks.
   e. All of the above.

ADDITIONAL READINGS

Bendick, Marc, Jr., and James P. Zais. *Income and Housing: Lessons From Experiments with Housing Allowances.* Washington, D.C.: The Urban Institute, 1978.

Burns, Leland S., and Leo Grebler. *The Housing of Nations.* New York: John Wiley & Sons, 1977.

Congressional Budget Office. *Federal Housing Policy: Current Problems and Recurring Issues.* Washington, D.C.: U.S. Government Printing Office, 1978.

————— *Federal Housing Assistance: Alternative Approaches.* Washington, D.C.: U.S. Government Printing Office, 1982.

Downs, Anthony. *Neighborhoods and Urban Development.* Washington, D.C.: Brookings Institution, 1981.

Heilbrun, James. *Urban Economics and Public Policy.* New York: St. Martin's Press, 1981, Chaps. 12–13.

Lowry, Ira S. *Housing Allowances: Lessons From the Supply Experiment,* Document P–6455. Santa Monica, Calif.: The Rand Corporation, 1980.

Housing, President's Commission on. *The Report of the President's Commission on Housing.* Washington, D.C.: U.S. Government Printing Office, 1982.

Wallace, James E., et al. *Participation and Benefits in the Urban Section 8 Program: New Construction and Existing Housing.* Cambridge, Mass.: Abt Associates, 1981.

Weicher, John C. *Housing: Federal Policies and Programs.* Washington, D.C.: American Enterprise Institute for Public Policy Research, 1980.

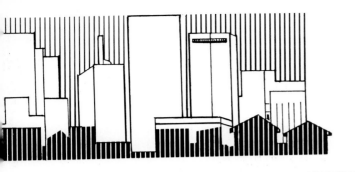

13
Regulation of Real Estate Occupations

OUTLINE

INTRODUCTION

Occupational regulation of one form or another affects every segment of the real estate business, including brokerage, real estate appraisal, property management, syndication, investment counseling, and construction. In certain segments, such as brokerage, construction, and to some extent appraisal, the behavior of persons providing real estate services is influenced by state licensing laws. The legal basis of licensure emanates from the police power of the state, as we discussed in Chapter 3.[1]

In other segments such as property management, syndication, investment counseling, and appraisal, trade groups representing that particular segment self-impose regulation. The Society of Real Estate Appraisers (SREA), for example, has no affiliation with any government, but offers training and designations (i.e., certificates of accomplishment) to real estate appraisers or analysts who become members. Member appraisers control the standards set by the organization. As in the case of licensed occupations in which the right to practice is evidenced by a license, trade groups offer designations to members of nonlicensed occupations who have passed examinations and accomplished other specified activities (e.g., one or more demonstration appraisal reports in the case of appraisers). We will refer to this process as *certification*. The principal distinction between state regulation via licensure and self-regulation via certification is that licenses are *required* to practice in a state, whereas designations are obtained on a *voluntary* basis.

Traditional Reasons for Occupational Regulation

Since obtaining a license is required by law for certain occupations, most discussions of occupational regulation focus on whether licensing is nec-

---

[1]Also, see Donald R. Epley and Carolyn Armbust, "Legal Limitations on Real Estate Prelicensing Requirements," *Real Estate Law Journal* 7 (Summer 1978), pp. 15–25.

essary or not. Real estate brokers were first licensed in 1919 in California, and the reason then (and still today) for such regulation was consumer protection. Simply stated, many people view licensing as a means of protecting the public against incompetent or dishonest practitioners. Their inability to pass licensing examinations and to abide by the code of ethics imposed by the states bars incompetent or dishonest practitioners from practicing.[2]

Usually, however, licensing laws are not the result of a public outcry for protection, but are initiated by the affected industry group. There have been two reasons for this behavior. First, the public associates licensing with professionalism: Only professionals have licenses. Thus, if an occupational group wants to upgrade its professional standing or prestige, it has an incentive to support licensing laws.

Second, some occupational groups have seen licensing as an opportunity to increase their incomes. If current licensees set the standards or requirements high enough, only a limited number of new licensees will be able to enter the occupation; fees will remain high. In other words, this restricts supply, and any demand increases will result in higher prices for that service.

The reasons for certification, like licensing, are consumer protection and professionalism. To a lesser degree, it is also based on monopoly power. Professional groups may tend to set designation requirements high to limit competition. However, due to the voluntary nature of certification, those professional groups do not control the supply of nondesignated practitioners. Certified practitioners face competition from noncertified practitioners, and therefore monopoly power is diminished.

THE ECONOMICS OF OCCUPATIONAL REGULATION

Recent developments in the economic theory of information have led to an enlightened perspective on regulation of occupations. The economics of information concerns how well purchasers of goods and services are informed about the quality of what they buy. Typically, in markets for real estate services (e.g., brokerage or appraisal services), the seller of the service is better informed about the *quality* of service he or she can provide than is the buyer. This is because information about quality of services is costly for buyers to obtain. Most buyers will not take the time to read *Consumer Reports*, to comparison shop among many products, or to

---

[2]These standards are usually set by state licensing boards or commissions, which are comprised mainly of licensed practitioners.

obtain testimonials from previous customers. Thus there is said to be an information imbalance or "asymmetry" in many markets for services.

The consequence of this information asymmetry is that buyers cannot easily differentiate high-quality from low-quality sellers. Therefore, the prices buyers are willing to pay will converge toward an average price for the service across all quality levels in the market. As a result of this averaging, high-quality sellers will not be adequately compensated and will either drop out of the market or lower the quality of the services they offer. This breakdown of the market, resulting from a lack of information about the quality of services, is an example of a market-failure problem known as adverse selection. It was described in Chapter 9.

When markets fail, some form of regulation, either self-regulation or government regulation, may be appropriate to eliminate the causes of the failure. In the case of the markets for real estate services, licensing has been imposed in some, whereas certification prevails in others. A license or a designation informs buyers that the person holding that credential has achieved a certain level of education and experience. Thus, the market will adequately compensate higher-quality sellers (i.e., those with credentials) for higher-quality services because they can be identified by buyers. This overcomes the problem of adverse selection.

Objectives of Occupational Regulation

Whether the states impose regulation on an occupational group as in the case of licensing, or an industry group self-imposes regulations as in the case of certification, two objectives are sought. First, occupational regulation seeks to induce practitioners to obtain education and training in their respective fields. Anyone seeking a real estate broker's license in the United States, for example, must satisfy the educational requirements of the state where he or she will practice.[3] Also, persons seeking a professional designation, such as the MAI (Member of Appraisal Institute), must pass a series of exams, obtain specified experience, and demonstrate competence through written reports.

The second objective of occupational regulation is to screen out incompetent or dishonest practitioners. Licensing and certification represent two distinctly different approaches to achieving this objective. Under a licensing system, the law bars incompetent or dishonest practitioners from practicing. In an unregulated occupation with certification, incompetent and dishonest practitioners can practice. But those who have earned a designation or certificate essentially signal buyers that they are

---

[3]The appendix at the end of this chapter contains a summary of the license requirements for salespersons and brokers in each state.

competent and honest. Thus, buyers are on their own in deciding whether to do business with designated practitioners and perhaps pay higher prices—or take their chances with undesignated and potentially incompetent or dishonest practitioners and probably pay lower prices.

The philosophies of licensing and certification, therefore, are markedly different. Licensing is *mandatory,* in that practitioners must meet educational and other requirements in order to practice. Certification is *voluntary,* in that practitioners are free to seek or not to seek education leading to an occupational designation. Buyers make their own choices between certified and uncertified practitioners.

Effectiveness and Market Implications

Because of its mandatory nature, licensing is considered the most effective means of inducing practitioners to obtain education and training, and of screening out incompetent or dishonest practitioners. Licensing, however, also has some adverse effects on the markets for occupational services that certification does not have.

First, licensing does not allow freedom of choice for consumers. Some consumers would be perfectly willing to accept the risks of dealing with unlicensed practitioners in exchange for lower prices. Thus, licensing may lead to inefficiency in the allocation of resources to education and training of practitioners, as well as to inefficiencies in the market for the service. Note that in some occupations, such as medicine and law, the need to protect the public may override the need for freedom of choice. Some argue that the need to protect the public from incompetent and dishonest real estate salespersons and brokers overrides the need for freedom of choice because of the large amount of money involved in a typical real estate transaction.

Secondly, licensing creates the problem of already-licensed practitioners' raising requirements to restrict supply and thus maintain or raise their incomes. Carroll and Gaston have studied the issue of monopoly power in the real estate brokerage business.[4] They examined the pass rates for real estate licensing exams nationwide and found that the higher the income level of the real estate practitioners who were already licensed in the state the lower the pass rates in that state. They concluded that income protection (i.e., monopoly motives) has had a strong effect on how many real estate brokerage licenses are issued.

To conclude, any economic evaluation of occupational regulation must consider the market implications of the regulation, as well as its effectiveness in eliminating the problem of market failure. Too often these

---

[4]Sidney L. Carroll and Robert J. Gaston, "State Occupational Licensing Provisions and Quality of Service: The Real Estate Business," *Research in Law and Economics,* vol. 1 (Greenwich, Conn.: JAI Press, 1979), pp. 1–13.

market effects are not recognized when occupational regulation of real estate practitioners is established.

STATE LICENSING OF THE REAL ESTATE BUSINESS

Each of the 50 states and the District of Columbia has a licensing law regulating practitioners in at least one area of the real estate business. In all of them, licenses are required to conduct real estate brokerage activities, which include the purchase or sale of real estate and the renting or leasing of real estate for others. Some states include property management and appraisal among the functions requiring a broker license. One state, Nebraska, requires a separate license for those who appraise real estate.[5]

State licensing laws generally prescribe two levels of real estate brokerage licensing. The most complete license is the *broker license,* since only a broker is permitted to own and operate a real estate brokerage business in the state. Brokers are totally responsible for the completion of documents used in sales and leases negotiated by people in their business, for handling money held in trust for clients (e.g., earnest-money deposits or rent collected), and for the actions of their employees. Each real estate sales office, therefore, must have at least one licensed broker.

To enter the brokerage business, one must first obtain a *salesperson* license.[6] The salesperson is an employee of a broker, and thus the broker is said to hold the salesperson license. The salesperson may perform activities such as negotiating listing contracts or contracts for sale, but must perform them *in the name of* the broker. Also, laws and regulations usually strictly forbid salespersons to hold client monies in trust; these funds must be delivered to the broker or the broker's trust account on receipt.

In addition to brokerage and sometimes appraisal activities, the states also license the practices of *construction contractors.* A brief discussion of these licensing requirements will follow a detailed discussion of brokerage licensing.

Brokerage Licensing Administration

As shown in Exhibit 13–1, the line of authority for real estate brokerage licensing begins with the legislative branch of state government, which originates licensing laws and amendments. Interpretations of state licen-

---

[5]See Richard P. Koch, "State Licensure Requirements and the Practice of Real Estate Appraising," *Real Estate Appraiser and Analyst* 48 (Spring 1982), pp. 13–20.

[6]The terms salesman license and associate broker license are also used.

EXHIBIT 13–1
ORGANIZATIONAL STRUCTURE FOR ADMINISTERING REAL ESTATE LICENSING LAWS

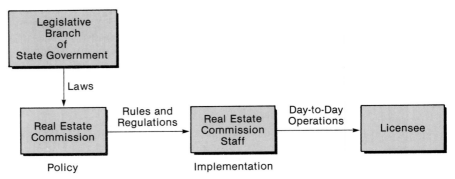

sing laws take the form of rules and regulations set by the real estate commission. The commission is usually a board (i.e., like a board of directors in a corporation) comprised of prominent brokers or other business people. In some states, the commission or board is part of the department of state government that is responsible for licensing many occupations (e.g., barbers and morticians).

The commission or department board has several functions. First, it specifies educational requirements for applicants and licensees. It may also prescribe courses and determine whether other courses, usually offered outside the state, are equivalent to those prescribed. The second function is to provide examinations. Passing the state license examination is the determining factor in obtaining a real estate license. Finally, the commission or board enforces the licensing law and regulations implementing the law. The commission or board must hold hearings for licensees accused of violations of the state's licensing law and has the right to suspend or revoke licenses.

The commission or department staff carries out the day-to-day relationships with licensees. The real estate commissioner, secretary, or department chief heads this group, depending on the state, and is responsible for developing educational materials, record keeping, collecting license fees, and researching complaints against licensees.

How to Obtain a Real Estate License

Unlike a driver's license, a real estate license obtained in one state does not automatically qualify one to practice real estate brokerage in another state. The requirements for obtaining brokerage licenses, however, generally have become more uniform among the states in recent years; thus, a greater degree of reciprocity exists today than in the past, especially with respect to education and examination requirements. To answer the question of how to obtain brokerage licenses in the states, we will examine the various licensing requirements, which include exemptions, general requirements, education, examinations, and experience.

Exemptions. Some persons who buy, sell, rent, or lease real estate for others are exempt from the licensing law. Usually attorneys, because of their extensive legal training, are exempt. Other exempt categories may include resident managers, government employees (e.g., state transportation department employees), trustees, executors, and those with power of attorney. These exemptions either involve public employees or persons who have a special relationship with the parties for whom they perform brokerage services.

General Requirements. Anyone interested in obtaining a salesperson license must apply to take the salesperson license examination. On the application, the individual must demonstrate that he or she has completed the real estate educational requirement discussed below, and has satisfied a set of general requirements. These include such things as minimum age (usually 18 years old for a salesperson license and 21 years old for a broker license), general education (usually a high school diploma), and reputation. Some states require references.

Once the applicant satisfies these general and educational requirements and pays a fee, he or she may sit for the state examination. If he or she earns a passing grade, the applicant may apply for a license from the real estate commission. Another fee may be required at that time. Commonly, the applicant for a license must choose a broker (sponsor) with whom the license will be placed.

Traditionally, applicants for brokerage licenses had to demonstrate their financial capacity to cover damage judgments brought against them by clients. The trend in recent years, however, has been for the real estate commission to establish a *recovery fund* from license fees. Monies from this fund are used to pay judgments against licensees in the state.

Education Requirements. The appendix at the end of this chapter provides real estate education prelicensing requirements for the various states. They range from zero to 180 hours of real estate training. Postlicensing and continuing-education requirements are also common.

Examination Requirements. Most states today contract with independent, professional testing services to develop and administer the examinations for broker licenses. In more than 30 states, the Educational Testing Service (ETS)[7] administers these exams; in several others American College Testing (ACT)[8] provides this service.

Usually, real estate brokerage exams have two parts. The first part, known as the "multistate section", includes approximately 100 questions on general real estate principles that are applicable throughout the United States. Exhibit 13–2 shows the typical distribution of questions found on this part of the examinations.

EXHIBIT 13–2
TYPICAL DISTRIBUTION OF REAL ESTATE EXAMINATION QUESTIONS: MULTISTATE SECTION

	Examination	
Topic	**Salesperson**	**Broker**
Real estate law and contracts	50%	50%
Real estate finance	15	10
Real estate valuation	17	15
Special fields (e.g., public land-use controls, real estate math, and federal laws affecting real estate)	18	25

Source: 1983 ACT Candidate Information Booklet.

The second part includes approximately 30 questions on various aspects of real estate that are specific to the state. This "state section" contains queries on such areas as the state's licensing law and the state real estate commission's rules and regulations. The minimum passing grade for the entire examination is usually 70 to 75 percent.

Experience Requirements. Generally, the states do not impose a brokerage experience requirement (i.e., apprenticeship) for obtaining a salesperson license. For a brokerage license, however, in addition to having to take further course work in real estate, an applicant must have had actual experience as a salesperson. This experience is at least one year, but does not exceed five years.

Licensing Law Infractions

State licensing laws prescribe both general and very specific behavioral requirements of licensees for them to keep their licenses. Most such laws specify that licensees must not behave in an unethical, fraudulent, or dishonest manner toward their clients and prospective buyers. Licensing laws generally prescribe the following activities:

---

[7]Box 2837, Princeton, N.J. 08541.
[8]Box 1009, Iowa City, Iowa 52243.

1. *Mishandling trust money*, including practices such as commingling trust money with personal funds and accepting noncash payments in trust.
2. *Improper handling of fees*, including paying commissions to licensees not in the broker's employ and paying commissions to unlicensed persons.
3. *Failure to provide required information*, including failure to provide copies of contracts to all relevant parties and failure to inform buyers of closing costs.
4. *Misrepresentation and fraud*, including taking kickbacks without the employer's knowledge, false advertising, and intentionally misleading clients or prospective buyers.
5. *Improper business practices*, including offering property at terms other than those specified by the client or failure to submit all purchase offers to the client.

One additional control over the business practices of salespersons and brokers is federal legislation to guarantee equal, or fair, housing opportunities. Title VIII of the Civil Rights Act of 1968 and subsequent amendments make it illegal to discriminate against persons in housing transactions when such transactions occur with the aid of a third party (i.e., a salesperson or broker).

Specifically, under the provisions of this law, a salesperson or broker cannot refuse to sell or rent to anyone on the basis of sex, creed, race, color, or national origin. He or she may not discriminate on terms or conditions in a sale or rental, advertise preferences or discrimination, or falsely claim that a property is unavailable. Also, a salesperson or broker cannot practice "steering," which is showing buyers properties only in certain areas, or "blockbusting," which involves spreading rumors to homeowners about a change in the racial or socioeconomic composition of the neighborhood just to secure a listing.

Construction Contractor Licensing

About one half of the states impose some form of regulation on contractors (i.e., builders and remodelers) that reside within the state.[9] The requirements for contractors among the states are far more diverse than for brokers. Traditional licensing requirements, including examinations, ex-

---

[9]States with contractor licensing for *resident* contractors are Colorado, Connecticut, Georgia, Idaho, Illinois, Indiana, Iowa, Kansas, Kentucky, Maine, Minnesota, Missouri, Montana, Nebraska, New Hampshire, New York, Ohio, Oklahoma, Pennsylvania, Rhode Island, South Dakota, Texas, Vermont, West Virginia, Wisconsin, and Wyoming. See National Association of Home Builders, *Analysis of State Builder Licensing Laws* (Washington D.C.: 1984).

perience or education requirements, and fees, are found only in about ten states. Other states simply require the contractor to pay a fee and register as a contractor operating in the state. Some states require a bond to be posted as a public-protection device, or require the contractor to submit an annual financial statement, or both.

In several of the states with contractor regulations, builders and remodelers of single-family residences and condominiums are exempt from contractor requirements. While licensing and registration of building contractors has for many years been labeled as merely a revenue-raising device for the states, the current trend is for more education and testing in more states.

CERTIFICATION OF REAL ESTATE OCCUPATIONS

In the real estate business there is an expanding number of certification or designation programs. Some of these credentials serve as *primary* signaling devices (i.e., certificates that take the place of licenses) and some are purely *secondary* (i.e., certificates for a particular specialization). Most of these programs are affiliated with the National Association of REALTORS® (NAR).[10]

Practitioners voluntarily seek designations and certificates from trade organizations because they want to differentiate themselves from less competent or dishonest undesignated practitioners. These credentials, therefore, are signals to buyers of the holder's competence and honesty; in return, designated practitioners expect higher fees. Sometimes licensed practitioners seek certification in a specialty (e.g., industrial property brokerage) to signal buyers that they have expertise beyond other licensed brokers in a particular segment of the market. Such credentials are secondary, rather than primary, signaling devices.

National Association of REALTORS Designations

Brokerage licensees may choose to become affiliated with the National Association of REALTORS as a REALTOR (broker) or REALTOR-Associate (salesperson).[11] Such affiliations are secondary signals to the public that the licensee abides by the NAR code of ethics, in addition to the state licensing requirements.

---

[10] 430 North Michigan Ave., Chicago, Ill. 60611, or 777 - 14th Street N.W., Washington, D.C. 20005.

[11] REALTOR® is a federally registered collective trademark. Only active brokers who are members of state and local NAR boards are permitted to use this trademark.

Are Salesperson and Broker Rates for Services Set by State Licensing Laws?*

The answer is no! Brokerage commissions are, by practice, a certain percentage of the sale price of the property, but they could be a flat fee. In the usual case, the salesperson must split with the broker (e.g., 50% each) any commission earned from the sale of a property the salesperson listed or from the sale of a property by the salesperson. This is because the broker essentially speculates in salespersons, in that he or she provides training, office space, telephones, and secretarial support in the hope that the salesperson will produce listings and sales.

Brokerage commissions are established in a competitive market. Yet, because many brokers in the same area are members of multiple listing services and charge the same commission rates, claims have been made that brokers engage in price fixing (collusion to fix prices). This is still being debated in the courts. For some additional readings on this subject, see the references below.

---

*George J. Siedel III, "Antitrust Implications of Trends to National Real Estate Firms," *Real Estate Review* 12 (Spring 1982), pp. 88–92; Semoon, Chang, "Multiple Listing Services: The Antitrust Issues," *Real Estate Law Journal* 10 (1982), pp. 228–46. Bruce M. Owen, "Kickbacks, Specialization, Price Fixing, and Efficiency in Residential Real Estate Markets," *Stanford Law Review* 29 (May 1977), pp. 931–67.

The national association is organized as a set of state associations and local boards. The various state associations are authorized to issue certificates for the GRI (Graduate REALTORS Institute) designation, a credential earned by members who take courses to complete the GRI program. These programs are concentrated in the area of residential sales, with some treatment of leasing, property management, and commercial property investment analysis.

Beyond this basic organizational structure of national and state associations and local boards, NAR, through its various institutes, societies, and councils, offers a wide variety of specialized designations across the real estate business. Many of these designations are primary signaling devices within a particular segment of the real estate business. Exhibit 13–3 provides a summary of NAR affiliations, including their purpose, the designations offered, and some general requirements for earning designations.

Appraisal Designations

The largest real estate appraisal organization in the United States is the Society of Real Estate Appraisers (SREA or "the society," as it is fre-

EXHIBIT 13–3
AFFILIATES OF THE NATIONAL ASSOCIATION OF REALTORS®

Affiliate	Purpose	Designation	Requirements
American Institute of Real Estate Appraisers (AIREA)	To provide educational programs, sponsor research, and publish materials on real estate appraisal.	Member of Appraisal Institute (MAI); Residential Member (RM)	Experience, education examinations, and demonstration appraisals, MAI requirements are more rigorous.
American Society of Real Estate Counselors (ASREC)	Same as AIREA but for individuals involved in sophisticated real estate consulting.	Counselor of Real Estate (CRE)	Very selective; by invitation only to those with extensive education and experience.
Farm and Land Institute (FLI)	To provide educational programs and publish materials to assist those in land sales, development, management, and syndication.	Accredited Farm and Land Member (AFLM)	Experience, education, written exam, and oral exam.
International Real Estate Federation (IREF)	To promote an understanding of real estate practices throughout the world.	None	Invitation to join as a member based on membership in a local Board of REALTORS®
Institute of Real Estate Management (IREM)	To provide educational programs, publish materials, and to promote professionalism among real-property managers.	Certified Property Manager (CPM); Accredited Resident Manager (ARM); Accredited Management Organization (AMO)	All designations awarded on the basis of education, experience, and examinations.
Realtors National Marketing Institute (RNMI)	To provide educational programs, publish materials, and promote professionalism among REALTORS® in areas of commercial/investment property analysis, residential sales, and office administration.	Certified Commercial and Investment Member (CCIM); Certified Residential Broker (CRB); Certified Residential Specialist (CRS)	Completion of GRI program plus experience, education, and examinations.
Society of Industrial Realtors (SIR)	To provide educational programs, publish materials, and promote professionalism among REALTORS® involved with industrial property.	Society of Industrial Realtors (SIR)	Education, experience, exams, and ethical practice.
Real Estate Securities and Syndication Institute (RESSI)	To provide educational programs, publish materials, and promote professionalism among those marketing real estate securities and syndication shares.	Certified Real Estate Securities Sponsor (CRSS); Certified Real Estate Securities Marketer (CRSM)	Education, exams, and REALTOR® status.
Women's Council of REALTORS®	To provide educational programs, training, and publications for women REALTORS® primarily involved in residential sales.	None	An interest in furthering the role of women in real estate brokerage.

quently called). The society offers three designations: Senior Real Estate Analyst (SREA), Senior Real Property Appraiser (SRPA), and Senior Residential Appraiser (SRA). To obtain an SRA designation, which indicates a specialization in residential appraisal, or an SRPA designation, which signals a specialization in income-property and residential appraisal, a person must successfully complete a series of courses, pass examinations, and complete demonstration appraisal reports. Only those who perform activities beyond the normal appraisal functions (e.g., market analysis or real estate investment analysis) can earn the SREA designation.

The American Institute of Real Estate Appraisers (AIREA or "the institute," as it is often called) is an affiliate of NAR and the second largest real estate appraisal organization in the United States. As shown in Exhibit 13–3, the Institute offers two designations: the MAI (Member of the Appraisal Institute), which is an income-property designation, and the RM (Residential Member), which is a residential designation. The MAI designation is probably the most widely known and prestigious of the real estate certifications. Frequently, buyers in contracts for sale and mortgage lenders will specify that an "MAI appraisal" must be performed.

In Canada, the primary professional appraisal organization is the Appraisal Institute of Canada. It awards the AACI (Accredited Appraiser, Canadian Institute) designation.

Other professional appraisal organizations include the National Association of Independent Fee Appraisers, which awards the designations IFA (Member), IFAS (Senior Member), and IFAC (Appraiser-Counselor); the American Society of Farm Managers and Rural Appraisers, which awards the designations AFM (Accredited Farm Manager) and ARA (Accredited Rural Appraiser); and the American Society of Appraisers, which awards the ASA designation to senior members. Its membership includes appraisers of both real property and personal property (e.g., art objects, jewelry, machinery, and oriental rugs). Other real estate appraisal organizations have memberships that specialize, for example, in property tax assessment practices and review appraising.

OVERVIEW

The regulation of real estate occupations includes both state-imposed mandatory standards, as in the case of licensing of real estate brokers and construction contractors, and industry-imposed voluntary standards, such as those for real estate appraisers and syndicators. Both forms of regulation provide information to purchasers about the quality of services offered by sellers. A broker license, for example, informs buyers that the individual holding the license is competent and ethical, since state law bars incompetent or unethical practitioners from practicing. Similarly, an appraisal designation informs buyers that the designated appraiser has been educated in real estate appraisal, has experience in the area of appraisal, has passed industry-imposed exams, and abides by the ethical standards of the industry organization. The designated appraiser, therefore, should be competent and ethical.

State licensure of real estate salespersons and brokers is by far the most well-developed regulatory system for real estate occupations. Each state sets its own requirements for exemptions, general qualifications, real estate education, examinations, and experience. Licensees in all states jeopardize their licenses when they mishandle trust money, mishandle brokerage fees, fail to provide required information, perpetrate fraud, or carry on improper business practices.

Certification among real estate practitioners is also well developed, mainly because of efforts of the National Association of REALTORS. The designations offered through the various institutes, societies and councils of the NAR include those for such specialists as appraisers, syndicators, industrial REALTORS, and investment analysts.

In recent years, the trend has been toward more certification of specialists in the real estate business. Certification serves as a secondary signaling device by informing buyers that the individual is honest and competent in a particular specialty. It is difficult to determine at this time whether there is a trend toward more licensing or more certification as the primary signaling device to buyers of real estate services.

TEST YOURSELF

Identify the following terms and concepts discussed in this chapter.

1. Licensure versus certification.
2. Information asymmetry and adverse selection.
3. Salesperson versus broker.
4. Salesperson versus associate broker.
5. Real estate commission or board.
6. Recovery fund.
7. Educational Testing Service.
8. Title VIII of the 1968 Civil Rights Act.
9. Resident contractor.
10. National Association of REALTORS.

Answer the following multiple choice questions.

1. Which of the following practitioners may *not* be exempt from real estate licensing laws?
   a. Attorneys.
   b. Those with power of attorney.
   c. Resident managers.
   d. Government employees.
   e. All may be exempt.

2. Which of the following is considered a secondary signaling device to the purchasers of real estate services?
   a. A designation from the Society of Industrial REALTORS.
   b. An MAI designation.
   c. Salesperson license.
   d. Brokers license.
   e. None of the above.

3. About one half of the state licensing exams for salespersons cover the area(s) of real estate
   a. Sales techniques.
   b. Investment.
   c. Valuation.
   d. Law and contracts.
   e. Finance.
4. Real estate salespersons can lose their licenses for
   a. Using aggressive sales techniques.
   b. Not showing buyers all available properties in an area.
   c. Commingling escrow (trust) money with personal funds.
   d. Not using modern sales methods.
   e. All of the above.
5. The state real estate commission is responsible for
   a. Setting fees for brokerage services.
   b. Marketing data on real estate transactions.
   c. Establishing education requirements for licensees.
   d. Overseeing the activities of mortgage lenders.
   e. Setting up multiple listing systems.

ADDITIONAL READINGS

Carroll, Sidney L., and Robert J. Gaston. "State Occupational Licensing Provisions and Quality of Service: The Real Estate Business." *Research in Law and Economics*, vol. 1. Greenwich, Conn.: JAI Press, 1979, pp. 1–13.

Corgel, John B., and Austin J. Jaffe. "Should Real Estate Appraisers Be Licensed?" *Real Estate Appraiser and Analyst* 50 (Fall 1984), pp. 21–32.

Kratovil, Robert, and Raymond J. Werner. *Real Estate Law.* (Englewood Cliffs, N.J.: Prentice-Hall, 1983, Chap. 8.

Lindeman, Bruce. *Real Estate Brokerage Management.* Reston, Va.: Reston Publishing, 1981, Chap. 3.

National Association of Real Estate License Law Officials. *Guide to Examinations and Careers in Real Estate.* Reston, Va.: Reston Publishing, 1979.

APPENDIX: TABLE OF STATE REQUIREMENTS FOR SALESPERSON AND BROKER LICENSING

Note: All states require applicants to take real estate broker examinations. The exams are developed in one of four ways: (1) American College Testing (ACT) Program, (2) Educational Testing Service (ETS), (3) state real estate commissions or departments, and (4) state universities. The table that follows indicates the educational and experience requirements, and types of examination used for broker and salesperson licenses in each state.

State	Education Requirements for Broker Applicants	Education Requirements for Salesperson Applicants	Experience Requirements for Broker Applicants	Exam Type	Required Continuing Education
Alabama	45-hour course, college major in RE, or 15 semester hours in RE at accredited college or university, if applicant does not meet experience requirement.	45-hour course taught over eight-week period	Two years as full-time salesperson	ACT	None
Alaska	None	None	Two years continuously active as salesperson	ETS	None
Arizona	Classroom hours in addition to salesperson requirements	45 classroom hours pre-license	Three years as salesperson	Staff	12 classroom hours per year
Arkansas	90 classroom hours or six semester-hour course in RE from college or university, Arkansas Business School, or Arkansas REALTORs® Institute, or two years RE sales and 30 hours or three-semester-hour course in RE from college or university, Arkansas Business School, or Arkansas REALTORs® Institute	None to take exam, 30-hour course completed within one year of passing exam	None, except as an alternative to the extra education requirements	ASI	None
California	270 classroom hours	None	Two years full-time as a salesperson; or college graduate	Staff	45 classroom hours every four years
Colorado	96 classroom hours	48 classroom hours	Two years as duly licensed salesperson or experience that commission finds to be equivalent	ETS	None
Connecticut	90 classroom hours	30 hours approved RE principles and practices course	Two years as licensed RE salesperson	ETS	12 hours every two years
Delaware	126 classroom hours	201 classroom-hour course approved by Commission, or equivalent	Five years RE sales	ETS	15 hours every two years
Florida	63 classroom hours	72 classroom hours	12 months RE sales	Staff	14 classroom hours every two years

State	Broker Education	Salesperson Education	Experience	Exam	Continuing Education
Georgia	164 classroom hours or 15 quarter hours in RE subject at college or university	24 classroom hours or five quarter hours at college or university in RE subject	Three years as active salesperson	ACT	Salesperson: 80 classroom hours first two years, then six hours every two years Broker: six hours every two years
Hawaii	40 classroom hours at accredited school or equivalent experience	46 classroom hours at accredited school or equivalent experience	Two years as RE state. May be reduced based on other experience	ETS	None
Idaho	135 classroom hours or equivalent correspondence hours in designated RE courses	45 classroom hours or equivalent correspondence hours in designated RE courses	Two years as salesperson in state. May be reduced based on educational background or experience in related field	ACT	None
Illinois	90 hours of instruction from approved school, B.A. degree with minor in RE, or license to practice law in state	30 classroom hours of instruction from approved RE school	One-year sales	ACT	None
Indiana	64 classroom hours	40-classroom-hour approved course	One year	ETS	None
Iowa	During first year must complete 30-hour course. Then issued sales license and one year later may apply for broker license	30 hours	12 months after securing or completing the 30-hour course while holding an apprentice sale license	ACT	12 classroom hours annually
Kansas	None	30 hours	2 years' RE experience	ETS	Eight hours every two years
Kentucky	336 classroom hours	96 classroom hours	Two years RE sales (apprenticeship reduced to one year if applicant holds degree in RE)	ETS	None
Louisiana	150 classroom hours or 15 semester hours	90 classroom hours or 15 semester hours	Two years as licensed RE salesperson	ETS	15 classroom hours every two years
Maine	90 classroom hours of study or one year of experience	None	May quality for exam in lieu of education requirements by being licensed on a full-time basis for one year	Staff	12 classroom hours every two years
Maryland	135 classroom hours of approved RE education	45 classroom hours of approved RE education	Three years as licensed salesperson	ASI	12 classroom hours every two years
Massachusetts	30 classroom hours	24 classroom hours	One year as licensed salesperson	ACT	None

State	Education Requirements for *Broker* Applicants	Education Requirements for Salesperson Applicants	Experience Requirements for *Broker* Applicants	Exam Type	Required Continuing Education
Michigan	90 classroom hours	30 classroom hours if applicant fails first exam	Three years sales	ETS	None
Minnesota	Sales current	60 classroom hours prelicense; 30 classroom hours in first year of license, or six semester hours	Two years RE sales in state or state with similar qualifications	ETS	45 classroom hours every three years
Mississippi	12 semester hours college credit in RE courses or nine semester hours and one year's experience	Six semester hours college credit courses in RE	One year as salesperson	Staff	Salesperson: None
Missouri	40 classroom hours in commission-approved school	54 classroom hours in commission-approved school	None	ETS	12 hours
Montana	None	None	Two years actively engaged as salesperson or equivalent	ETS	None
Nebraska	120 classroom hours plus two years' experience or 180 classroom hours in RE courses	Minimum of 60 classroom hours	Two years' active licensed experience or 120 classroom hours of RE education	ETS	None
Nevada	24 semester hours of college-level credits	90 classroom hours	Two years' active licensed experience	ACT	20 classroom hours first two years; then 10 classroom hours every two years
New Hampshire	None	None	One year sales or 2,000 hours part-time	ETS	None
New Jersey	135 classroom hours RE instruction	45 classroom hours	One year immediately before application	ASI	None
New Mexico	180 classroom hours of accredited course in RE or 90 classroom hours plus two years as salesperson	60 classroom hours of accredited RE instruction	One year full-time or 2,000 hours part-time	ETS	Three credit hours every two years
New York	Approved 90-hour RE course	45 classroom hours	One year active sales or two years' equivalent experience	ACT	45 classroom hours
North Carolina	90 classroom hours at approved RE school	30 classroom hours at approved RE school or equivalent experience	Two years sales or equivalent or 90 hours of education	ETS	None
North Dakota	90 classroom hours	30 classroom hours of RE education in first year of license	Two years sales or equivalent experience as determined by commission	ETS	24 classroom hours every three years

State					
Ohio	180 classroom hours	60 classroom hours plus 60 hours within two years of license	Two years	Staff	30 hours every three years
Oklahoma	90 clock hours	45 hours	One year sales	Staff	21 classroom hours every three years
Oregon	150 clock hours in RE principles, law, and finance	90 classroom hours	Three years sales within last five years	Staff	24 classroom hours every two years
Pennsylvania	240 classroom hours of courses approved by RE commission	60 classroom hours in approved RE courses	Three years sales within last five years	ETS	None
Rhode Island	90 hours' approved study at licensed schools	None	One year sales	ETS	None
South Carolina	90 classroom hours	30 classroom hours plus another 30 hours within first year of licensing	Three years sales or equivalent experience	University of South Carolina	None
South Dakota	90 classroom hours	30 classroom hours	Two years sales	ETS	24 classroom hours every two years
Tennessee	90 hours	30 hours	Two years sales or one year experience and B.A. degree in RE	ETS	Sales: 30 hours within two years of license. Broker: 60 contact hours within three years of license
Texas	720 classroom hours	180 classroom hours plus 90 hours over first three years of licensure	Two years sales	Staff	None
Utah	210 classroom hours	90 classroom hours of RE Principles and Practices	Three years	ACT	12 classroom hours per year
Vermont	High school diploma	High school diploma	One year sales	ASI	None
Virginia	180 classroom hours of RE education	45 classroom hours	Three years	ACT	None
Washington	90 classroom hours prior to exam	630 classroom hours prior to second renewal	Two years or equivalent experience in past five years	ACT	None
West Virginia	180 classroom hours	90 classroom hours	Two years sales	Staff	None
Wisconsin	60 classroom hours of education program approved by Examining Board or 20 credits in law or RE at accredited institution	30 classroom hours	None	ACT	10 classroom hours every two years
Wyoming	60 hours	30 hours	Two years full-time sales or RE degree	ETS	60 hours every three years

Source: National Association of Real Estate License Law Officials, Annual Report of the Interstate Cooperation Committee, 1983 NARELLO Annual Report, Orlando, Florida, 1983.

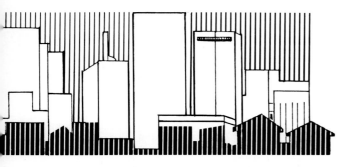

14
Land Use, Planning, and Zoning

INTRODUCTION

In a private enterprise economy, individuals, businesses, and institutions own much of the nation's property. These entities make decisions about how land is used, usually with the objective of maximizing the individual owner's wealth or rate of return. In the absence of legal limitations, they may give little or no concern to how a particular land use will affect neighboring owners or the larger community.

Recognizing the impact that land uses may have on a neighborhood and community, governmental jurisdictions (such as cities and counties) typically regulate how land may be used through *zoning*. Acceptable land uses are specified for various areas, or zones. A general, or comprehensive, plan for the community determines the acceptable land uses.

In Chapter 10 we noted that real estate markets perform the important functions of allocating existing space among those who demand space, expanding or contracting space to meet changing needs, and determining land uses. We showed that this third function of land-use determination operates primarily through two economic principles:

1. As transportation costs increase, the values of parcels of land tend to decrease relative to similar parcels with lower transportation costs.
2. As land prices increase, capital investment (i.e., improvements) on individual parcels of land is intensified, in effect substituting capital for additional land.

The operation of these economic principles of real estate markets helps determine how individual parcels of real estate are used. Land uses are usually identified in relatively broad categories such as single-family residential, multifamily residential, commercial, shopping center, office, light-industrial, and heavy-industrial uses. And, as we discussed in Chapter 10, similar land uses tend to occupy similar locations and thus to form patterns of land uses. For example, single-family residential uses tend to occupy large sections of an urban area. Similarly, commercial, office, and industrial uses tend to be grouped in the same or similar geographic areas. This occurs because economic principles tend to have similar effects on similar users of real estate. If one manufacturing firm finds economic advantage in terms of transportation cost savings and capital requirements at one location, other manufacturing firms may find similar advantage at adjacent or similar sites. This tendency for similar land uses to agglomerate has been termed *economic zoning.*

Although there is a tendency for market forces to produce groups or patterns of land uses, economic advantage may also accrue to competing and inharmonious land uses. Such uses, if not precluded by private or public restrictions, may obtain a monopoly position and enable their owners to profit at the expense of long-run social benefits. For example, a convenience store located in the center of a high-class residential subdivision would undoubtedly generate a great deal of business. Such a use, however, might lower the attractiveness of the subdivision to the extent that lowered land values would more than offset the value of the commercial use. Furthermore, the same motivation would lead other commercial firms to purchase other sites for commercial use to capture at least a portion of the potential business. This eventually could destroy the uniform nature of the subdivision, and reduce residential land values greatly.

The Market Solution

Economic theory suggests that, in the absence of transaction costs, market participants tend to negotiate away the economic advantage of land-use decisions that lower net social benefits. In the convenience-store example, the residential owners, recognizing that their property values would be reduced by a convenience store, would try to purchase the rights of the commercial firm to construct and operate the store.

Transaction costs, however, may inhibit this process. Such costs include the cost of gathering information about property values, attorneys' fees and court costs (or the anticipation of these costs) if there is any significant probability that the negotiation would end up in court, and the participants' time and effort in the negotiations. The market solution also assumes that both parties could measure and agree on the impact of the inharmonious use on both the user and the neighboring property owners.

Another problem arises in the market solution. The adverse influence may affect several or many parties, but some affected parties may not participate in the negotiations. Some property owners, for example, may not be willing to bear their fair share of the costs of purchasing the convenience store's rights or to spend the time and effort in the negotiations, hire attorneys, or forgo the convenience of shopping at the store. Although they might like to see the convenience store removed from the neighborhood, they are willing to let others fight the battle. This unwillingness of some parties to participate in a common course of action is known as the "free-rider" problem. The result is to inhibit market processes from negotiating solutions to externally imposed negative influences.

Externalities

As we discussed in Chapter 9, externally imposed influences, positive or negative, are termed externalities. They are particularly important in real estate analysis because of fixity of location; a parcel of real estate cannot be moved to escape negative externalities. There are many examples of potential negative externalities: A factory may spew smoke and dirt on neighboring properties; a supermarket may generate odors that are wafted to adjacent properties; occupants of a house may keep an unmowed and littered yard that detracts from the neighborhood; college fraternity members may throw wild parties, producing unwanted noise for neighbors; and fast-food stores or other commercial establishments may generate noise, litter, and visual pollution that detract from neighboring residential properties. In recent years, crime or the threat of crime has become a particularly burdensome negative externality to many urban residents.

Positive externalities also may be important influences on property values. Residents who maintain attractive yards and keep their houses painted, for example, enhance the values of neighboring properties. Similarly, owners of office buildings, commercial buildings, or even industrial properties who maintain their properties attractively contribute to property values in the general area. Both public and private facilities may provide positive externalities. Public parks, swimming pools, and other recreational facilities may have an important positive effect on area properties. Private developers often build housing units near major recreational facilities such as swimming pools, tennis courts, and golf courses to attract buyers and enhance property values.

While positive externalities have the opposite effects on property values as negative externalities, they do not offset each other. A negative externality is usually more capable of destroying a property's value than a positive externality is capable of enhancing value. For example, it is unlikely that a public park on one side of a single-family residence could offset the adverse effect of a garbage dump on the other side. Builders or buyers can probably find other sites adjacent to the park, but not adjacent to the garbage dump, thus placing the site subject to the negative influence at a disadvantage. Increasing the number or size of parks adjacent to the site will not offset the damage done by the negative influence.

Property owners thus attempt to protect their property values from negative externalities by two means—*private restrictions* and *public restrictions.*

PRIVATE RESTRICTIONS

Landowners create private restrictions on land use. These restrictions generally take the form of *restrictive covenants* and *easements* in deeds or subdivision plats. The limitations include such aspects as architectural style, size, and quality of improvements; the purpose for which the improvements may be used; outbuildings; external attachments such as vapor stacks, TV antennas, porches, and other protrusions; sheltering of automobiles and animals; and activities that might create nuisances such as burning, operating a business, or creating noise. An owner creates private restrictions by recording them in the platting documents for a new subdivision, by including them in deeds given to purchasers of the land, or both. For example, Exhibit 14–1 contains the deed restrictions for Oak Crest Estates. Any purchasers of property in the subdivision are subject to the restrictions, which any owner of property in the subdivision can enforce through a court action seeking injunctive relief.

EXHIBIT 14–1
DECLARATION OF RESTRICTIONS, OAK CREST ESTATES

This indenture entered into this 23rd day of May, A.D 1967, by Fletcher Land & Cattle
Co., a Florida corporation, as the owner of the fee simple title to the following described
real property, situate, lying and being in Alachua County, Florida:
Lots, parcels or tracts of land, being serially numbered from One (1) to Fifty-three (53),
both inclusive, known as OAK CREST ESTATES, as same are identified, surveyed, and
set apart on the survey plat of Harris H. Green, Registered Land Surveyor, under date
of March 10, 1966, as per Plat Book "G", page 45, of the Public Records of Alachua
County, Florida,
and such owner being desirous of selling and conveying various and sundry lots, parcels,
or tracts of lands, surveyed as aforesaid, and to provide for restrictions and convenants
to run with the title of each of said lots for the joint and mutual benefit of this owner
and its several respective grantees, successors in title, and their respective heirs and
assigns;
IT IS, THEREUPON, BY THESE PRESENTS, hereby stipulated, covenanted, and agreed by
and between the undersigned owner of the above described lands, and its several and
respective grantees and successors in title, each of whom, by the acceptance of the
delivery of a deed of conveyance from said undersigned owner, hereafter, to any lot,
tract, or portion of the lands above described and referred to herein and on said survey
plat of OAK CREST ESTATES, as aforesaid hereby agree and obligate themselves to
comply with and abide by each and every of the following restrictions, conditions and
covenants hereafter set forth, as follows:

1. The following restrictive covenants shall run with the title of each of the lots or parcels
   in said survey plat and be binding upon all parties, firms, corporations and any other
   persons claiming title thereto until January 1, 2010 A.D.
2. Each of said lots or parcels shall constitute and remain a single home site and none of
   them shall be sold in part, or resubdivided by these owners or any of their successors
   in title.
3. Each lot or home site herein referred to shall be used for residential purposes only and
   no commercial enterprises shall be conducted thereon; and there shall be constructed

EXHIBIT 14–1 *(concluded)*

thereon only one building for residential use, exactly as hereafter provided, which shall contain a minimum of One Thousand Five Hundred square feet of ground floor space for living area, exclusive of garage, car ports or porches attached thereto; except that there may be constructed on each of said lots or home sites a single service building for use as a pump house or tool storage building, provided that such second allowed building shall be constructed at a location no closer than 100 feet from the front lot lines, or 20 feet from the rear lot lines. For the purpose of determining the front lot lines of the various building sites herein referred to same shall be and are hereby specified as the lines of such lots contiguous to and facing east on the street area designated as N.W. 91st Terrace; those facing north and facing south on the street area designated as N.W. 9th Avenue, N.W. 10th Place (including the cul-de-sac area) and N.W. 11th Place (including the cul-de-sac area); also those lots facing east and west on the street area designated as N.W. 94th Street.

4. No residence or building shall be placed upon any of the lots in such subdivision except in conformity with the setback and side lot provisions as fixed by the zoning regulations of Alachua County, Florida, provided that no such residence of building shall be constructed closer than 25 feet from the front lot lines or 15 feet from the side lot lines.

5. Each home shall be designed and planned as a single-family dwelling unit and there shall be no apartment buildings, duplexes, or temporary residences of any kind whatsoever, constructed upon either of said lots other than a single-family dwelling unit.

6. No house trailers, temporary construction, or dwellings may be moved to either of said lots from other sites; no dwelling having tin roofs shall be placed, erected, or constructed upon either of said lots.

7. No detached garage or other outbuildings shall be constructed upon any of the lots in such subdivision excepting only one additional building for use as a pump house, for the storage of tools and equipment as herein provided.

8. Except for unforseen circumstances beyond the control of the owner, no residence shall remain uncompleted for more than nine months from the start of construction.

9. No poultry, cattle, horses, or swine shall be kept, housed, or maintained upon either of the lots in said subdivision.

10. Before commencing the construction of any improvements to be placed upon any of the lots or parcels contained in said survey plat, adequate plans and specifications therefor shall be submitted to and approved by an officer or director of Fletcher Land & Cattle Co., a Florida corporation, provided that approval shall not be unreasonably withheld or refused. All plans so submitted shall require, and all residences constructed in accordance therewith shall be so designed and constructed that the interior of all garages, car ports, or outbuildings shall be so constructed and placed that the interior thereof shall not be visible from the street area or areas upon which the residence served thereby is built; it shall be further required that the front elevation and each of the side elevations of all residences to be constructed in this subdivision shall be of identical materials, except where the front elevation contains only a portion of brick or concrete block or other masonry materials.

11. Any of the owners of either of the lots in said subdivision who shall be hereafter guilty of violating any one or more of the foregoing restrictive covenants shall be required to respond in damages to anyone or all other owners of lots in said subdivision and, in addition, be required to remove and correct such violation, and in addition to such damages and such action shall pay to any party or parties who shall successfully conclude a suit for the purpose of obtaining damages and the removal of such violation a reasonable fee for the services of their attorneys in that behalf, together with any and all other costs lawfully taxed in such proceedings.

12. All persons, firms and corporations who may hereafter succeed to the title, or acquire any lien or interest against or in the above described real property and improvements situated thereon, do hereby jointly and severally agree to keep and maintain the said improvements in a good state of repair and to properly care for and maintain all lawns and shrubbery in a neat and attractive condition.

Commercial easements are usually created in the same way: An owner-developer reserves the right for utility companies to install and maintain utility lines across individual properties. The easements are identified and recorded in the subdivision plat, and they bind all future purchasers by references in deeds to restrictions and easements of record. Utility easements usually enhance values by providing access to essential public services; however, they can also be negative influences. Utility easements have been discovered under buildings, gardens, patios, and other inconvenient places. Needless to say, the value of such improvements is impaired if they must be totally or partially destroyed to service the utility.[1]

Restrictive covenants and easements are generally effective devices for controlling land uses and dealing with nuisances within subdivisions. Nevertheless, they carry two important drawbacks—enforcement procedure and geographic scope. With respect to the first, we noted earlier that owners in a subdivision carry the responsibility of enforcement. They must take the initiative by instituting court action to stop any violations of the restrictive covenants. If owners are unaware of violations or lack the motivation or resources to institute court action, the violations may continue.

The second drawback—limited geographic scope—obviously renders private restrictions ineffective in most cases as a device to control land uses beyond the boundaries of the subdivision. In a few cases in which a single developer creates an entire community, this drawback does not apply. Examples are the new towns and communities of Columbia, Maryland; Reston, Virginia; and Palm Coast, Florida. Such communities have an extensive list of restrictive covenants which owners agree to abide by when they purchase properties. Since the restrictive covenants apply to the entire community, the private restrictions have the force of public controls.

PUBLIC PLANNING FOR LAND-USE CONTROL

We may define public planning, or public land-use planning/zoning, as the development of guidelines and criteria for the determination and control of future land uses in a community or geographic area. Public planning is carried on by cities, counties, and regional planning agencies, usually through a planning commission of elected or appointed officials. The authority to control land uses is vested in cities and counties by the states through the police power. City or county governments often appoint members of planning commissions. The planning commissions usually

---

[1]For a general discussion of the property rights affected by easements, see Chapter 2.

serve in an advisory capacity to the elected bodies that appoint them; all major plans and decisions are subject to the elected body's discretion. In order to carry out its work, the planning commission employs a staff of professional planners. A typical planning organizational structure is shown in Exhibit 14–2.

EXHIBIT 14–2
TYPICAL PLANNING ORGANIZATION

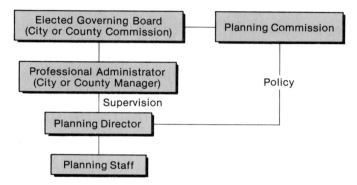

The planning commission and staff normally have several functions. These include developing a comprehensive plan, recommending action on rezoning, approving site plans, and controlling commercial signs.

Exhibit 14–3 provides an overview of the public planning process from the establishment of community goals and objectives through implementation of a comprehensive plan via zoning. We discuss the specifics of the land-use planning/zoning process in the remaining section of this chapter.

Development of a Comprehensive Plan

A comprehensive plan is a general guide to a community's future growth and development. It involves projecting a community's future population growth, its requirements for water and other natural resources, its physical characteristics (e.g., existing development, terrain, and soil conditions), its need for public services (e.g., schools, police and fire protection, utilities, and recreation), its need for various types of land use (e.g., single-family residential, multifamily residential, office, commercial, and industrial), financial resources, and political constraints. Thus, a comprehensive plan contains a number of major elements, or studies of a community's future needs. It attempts to guide future growth and development to accomodate the various needs of the community.

EXHIBIT 14–3
OVERVIEW OF LAND-USE PLANNING/ZONING PROCESS

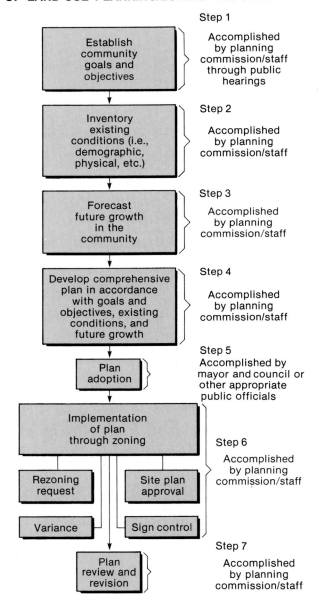

Step 1
Accomplished by planning commission/staff through public hearings

Establish community goals and objectives

Step 2
Accomplished by planning commission/staff

Inventory existing conditions (i.e., demographic, physical, etc.)

Step 3
Accomplished by planning commission/staff

Forecast future growth in the community

Step 4
Accomplished by planning commission/staff

Develop comprehensive plan in accordance with goals and objectives, existing conditions, and future growth

Step 5
Accomplished by mayor and council or other appropriate public officials

Plan adoption

Step 6
Accomplished by planning commission/staff

Implementation of plan through zoning

Rezoning request

Site plan approval

Variance

Sign control

Step 7
Accomplished by planning commission/staff

Plan review and revision

Objectives. In preparing and maintaining a comprehensive plan, a planning commission must identify objectives based on community goals. Although such goals are by necessity general in nature, they provide direction to the planning process. Goals may not be stated explicitly but may be implied from decisions made in public hearings and by elected governing bodies. For example, decisions regarding expansion of a utility or transportation system, imposition of impact fees, subdivision approvals, and rezoning requests may indicate whether a community favors or wishes to limit growth. Such decisions may also indicate the types of growth that are favored or discouraged. Zoning regulations and utility-expansion decisions, for example, may indicate clearly that certain types of industries are favored, while others are not. In recent years, many communities have rejected potentially dirty, noisy, and unattractive industrial plants, although those plants would contribute to the economic base of the communities by paying taxes and employing residents. In many cases, these communities have attempted to entice clean, attractive businesses (e.g., computer assembly plants) to locate or to expand their operations in the communities.

Similarly, communities can direct and regulate the volume of residential growth. An aggressive utility-expansion policy will encourage residential development at the urban fringe, whereas a limited expansion policy or one that requires developers to pay service charges and impact fees will have the opposite effect. The permit process that builders and developers must follow (e.g., building permits) can also be streamlined or onerous. Onerous processes will encourage builders and developers to prefer other communities or areas. Often builders and developers change operations from a central city to outlying communities and county areas when the central city imposes significantly more burdensome procedures.

Governing boards may identify policies to guide the planning effort. For example, a city commission may state that the community should attempt to rejuvenate commercial activity in the central business district, or that it should avoid six-lane streets. The comprehensive plan must then be formulated with these goals in mind. Sometimes the goals are contradictory. A goal to develop an adequate street system for a community's expected traffic growth, for example, may conflict with the desire of residents not to have streets widened to accommodate additional traffic. The comprehensive plan, therefore, must take into account diverse points of view and attempt to balance potential conflicts.

Existing and Future Conditions. Also in the early stages of the public planning process, the planning staff takes an inventory of the existing conditions in the community and forecasts future growth. The inventory of existing conditions, which provides the base on which forecasts are made, includes such items as total population, total employment, household income, household size, number of miles of highways, topography, retail sales, and water usage. Several key measures, such as total population, are forecast to establish future conditions in, say, 1990, 1995, 2000, 2005 and 2010.[2] The comprehensive plan, therefore, shows where and how the expected growth should be accommodated. For example, the plan will outline districts for new residential, commercial, and industrial development and describe how additional water resources will be allocated to these districts.

Alternative Approaches.   After identifying objectives and forecasting future growth, planners must consider various ways of accomodating both. There are usually many directions a plan can take. For example, the provision of adequate land for industrial development might be accomplished in one or several areas. The planners would have to identify and evaluate the advantages and disadvantages of each possibility. The evaluation process considers such matters as existing land-use patterns and plans for the provision of utilities, community facilities, transportation, and housing. Similar evaluations would be required for alternative plans for residential, commercial, industrial, and office development. Explicitly or implicitly, this evaluation involves a direct trade-off between the overall costs and benefits to the community of a particular alternative, compared to the costs and benefits of another.

Different plans have different cost implications, and these cost differences may be an important determining factor in choosing among alternative plans. Funding sources include the property tax and other local revenue generators, federal and state aid plans, and utility and other business operations of the local government. Additional revenue may be available through special taxing districts, bond issues, new taxes, and increases in existing taxes. The benefits comparisons involve determinations of how much better off the community will be with one alternative as opposed to another. Thus, the analysis of benefits is far more subjective than the analysis of costs.

Political Process.   Selection of a final comprehensive plan is usually a lengthy—and perhaps ongoing—process. The jurisdiction's governing board must adopt the plan, which usually requires significant public input through public meetings. Politics normally plays an important role in the process. A united stand by a large number of voters against the designation of a street as a major traffic artery or of a particular area as commercial development, for example, may provide enough political pressure for a governing body to change that portion of a plan.

---

[2]We presented methods of population forecasting in Chapter 11.

━━━━━━━━━━━━━━━━━━━━━━ Frame 14–1 ━━━━━━━━━━━━━━━━━━━━━━

Limits on Growth through Local Land-use Controls: The Case of Petaluma, California*

During the past two decades, several communities in the United States have instituted provisions in their land-use/zoning regulations to limit growth. These communities include Ramapo, N.Y.; Boca Raton, Fla.; and Boulder, Col. One of the most interesting court cases involving limits on growth occurred in Petaluma, Calif. This rapidly growing community south of San Francisco instituted a number of provisions to control its growth during the early 1970s. One of these measures was the placing of a cap on the number of housing units that could be provided in the city in any year (approximately six percent of the total stock, or about 500 units).

The Construction Industry Association of Sonoma County (builders) challenged the regulation, asserting that it violated the constitutional right to travel. The Federal District Court agreed with the builders and struck down the regulation. The Court of Appeals overturned the ruling, thus allowing the plan to stand as a legitimate use of the city's police power. The U.S. Supreme Court refused to hear the case, so the Court of Appeals' ruling stands.

The higher courts have universally upheld the right of a community to use the police power to control land use. The Petaluma case is one example.

---

*Source: *Construction Industry Association of Sonoma County* v. *City of Petaluma*, 275 F. Supp. 574 (1974); *Construction Industry Association of Sonoma County* v. *City of Petaluma*, 522 F. 2nd 897 (9th cir. 1975).

Innovation and Flexibility in Comprehensive Planning

A comprehensive plan usually must undergo continued scrutiny and thus needs to be sufficiently flexible to accommodate periodic modifications. Ideally, a comprehensive plan should guide, yet be consistent with, market forces and activity. When market forces are inconsistent with a plan, pressures will mount to change the plan. Yet repeated modifications will cause loss of confidence in the plan. It can also be rendered ineffective through legal actions and political pressures. In such cases, the planning process usually must begin again.

To provide adequate flexibility, modern plans allow for many types of nontraditional development and encourage an overall, or composite, approach by developers. Plans may encourage the use of such innovations as *planned unit developments* (PUDs), in which variances from traditional requirements for such matters as setback lines (distance of buildings from lot lines), minimum areas per lot, and curbs and gutters are allowed in exchange for larger areas of open space, public facilities, and attractive layouts and designs. Also, PUDs often integrate residential and commercial developments, which traditionally have been separated to eliminate externalities. Condominiums, attached single-family houses, and zero-lot-line layouts (in which houses are built up to the lot line on one side) add flexibility to traditional residential development. Additionally, some modern comprehensive plans are formulated with a *point system*. In these plans, new developments must accumulate a specified minimum number of points, which may be obtained by a variety of layouts and designs. For example, points would be awarded for open space, recreational facilities, streets, curbs, sewers, adequate private restrictions, and a demonstration that the existing infrastructure can accommodate the additional residents. A developer might obtain the required points by a traditional subdivision layout, a condominium development, or a PUD. Flexibility would be granted the developers' specific plans as long as they generate the required points.

Finally, some communities use *performance standards* to allow such facilities as light-industrial plants (e.g., a computer plant) to locate in commercial districts. These standards are based on the extent to which operations impose negative externalities on surrounding parcels. Performance standards, like PUD regulations, represent attempts to reduce the emphasis on the traditional land-use/zoning theory that strict separation of land uses is required to control externalities. Economists have argued for years that such strict separation is inefficient. The benefits of controlling externalities in many cases are insufficient to justify the costs imposed on society by separating land uses. For example, if all of the employment centers are on one side of the community and all residential areas are on the other, large public expenditures for roads and public transportation will be required.

Implementation and Review of the Comprehensive Plan

A comprehensive plan is usually general in nature. It identifies land uses in categories such as single-family residential, commercial, and industrial. These categories must be subdivided further by types, sizes, and permitted activities. For example, a residential district might be divided into R–1, where only ½ acre lots for single-family homes are allowed, and R–2, where apartments are allowed. A commercial district might be divided into BP (business and professional), BR (retail sales and services), and BH (highway oriented business services). The process of dividing the comprehensive plan's general land use categories into more specific districts is known as zoning. Since the characteristics of zones are defined rather precisely, the intent of the comprehensive plan can be enforced. Zoning, therefore, is usually the principal device for carrying out the comprehensive plan.

After formulation and implementation of a comprehensive plan, the plan must be monitored continually. Few plans stand the test of time without modification, and comprehensive plans especially are buffeted by many sources. Conflicts inevitably arise among developers, builders, environmentalists, and public interest groups.

The plan should contain enough rigidity to preclude most changes for individual parcels, but enough flexibility to allow more general changes when conditions warrant. For example, a change to allow commercial development of a parcel planned for residential development should not be allowed without proof that the landowner otherwise would suffer significant and unrecoverable damage that was unforeseen when the land was purchased. On the other hand, if development patterns indicate that an area should be allowed to develop in ways inconsistent with the plan, the plan should be modified. Thus, a comprehensive plan should be regarded as a guide to future growth and development, not as a straitjacket that constricts growth and development to undesirable or unrealistic patterns. The process requires continual review, analysis, and modifications.

PUBLIC ZONING FOR LAND-USE CONTROL

From our previous description, we may define *zoning* as the regulation of land uses, population densities, and building types and sizes by districts or zones. It involves the categorization of each parcel of land in a community according to a system of differentiated land uses. Such a system usually contains 10–15 broad categories of land use, with a number of subcategories in each broad category. For example, in the residential category may be subcategories for single-family detached, single-family attached, multifamily up to four or eight units, multifamily high rise, and so on. Chapter 14's appendix provides a condensed version of a typical set of zoning regulations. The zoning categories also may limit building heights and sizes and the number of unrelated occupants living in the same unit. The number of unrelated occupants, as well as various other requirements, such as adequate plumbing facilities in dwelling units, is for many communities governed by a separate set of regulations known as the *housing code*.

Purpose of Zoning

Zoning is intended to control negative externalities through the implementation of the comprehensive plan. As we pointed out above, externalities are difficult to control in the private market because of impediments to efficient land-use determination by the market system. When these impediments (i.e., transaction costs) do not exist, market participants bid away less-than-optimium land uses. They realize they have more to gain by protecting their property values than by permitting the detracting uses to occur.

High transaction costs in the real estate market, however, make an efficient market solution impossible. These costs consist of the time and effort required to assess property-value impacts, the inaccuracies of those assessments and lack of agreement about the impacts, legal fees, capital costs, and free-rider costs. Since an efficient market solution cannot occur, negative externalities arise and result in reduced property values. Zoning is thus an attempt to preclude or limit negative externalities through public or community action, with the objective of enhancing and preserving property values.

Legality of Zoning

As we discussed in Chapter 2, real property refers to the exclusive right of owners to use and dispose of real estate (the tangible good) as they desire. Property rights, however, are not total and absolute; they are subject to the inherent constraints imposed by governments: taxation, police power, eminent domain, and escheat. Zoning is an exercise of police power—the right of a government to enact and enforce laws to protect the health and welfare of its citizens. Since zoning may greatly limit the use of property, some citizens may not agree that zoning protects their health and welfare. Increasingly numerous and severe land-use regulations have led some observers to contend that land is becoming more of a public resource than private property.[3] For this reason, zoning laws in general, and specific applications of them, have been attacked on both constitutional and applied grounds. Indeed, zoning laws have been attacked in courts as confiscation of property without compensation—an act prohibited by the U.S. Constitution! On applied grounds, they have been attacked as ambiguous, discriminatory, and arbitrary.

Although some zoning laws have been declared unconstitutional, most have met constitutional tests, and zoning as a general practice has been legally acceptable in the United States for over 50 years. Almost all cities of any size have zoning laws, as do many counties. Some states require counties to engage in comprehensive planning, which normally results in zoning as an implementing device. For example, in Florida the

---

[3]See Halbert C. Smith, "Developable Land: Private Property or Public Resource?" *The Real Estate Appraiser,* vol. 42, no. 6 (November–December 1976), pp. 5–12.

Local Government Comprehensive Planning Act requires all counties and all communities of significant size to have comprehensive plans. Absent such a plan, the state may impose one of its own on a local jurisdiction.

The general thrust of court decisions on zoning laws is that zoning is constitutional and will be upheld when zoning ordinances are reasonable, are based on a comprehensive plan, and provide for all types of housing. Courts have overturned zoning ordinances that do not provide for low- and moderate-income housing on the ground that they are *exclusionary*—i.e., they exclude certain types of people from living in the community. Similarly, zoning ordinances that have attempted to limit the number of housing units and thus population have been overturned on the grounds that they are arbitrary and exclusionary.

A number of zoning ordinances have been challenged on the basis of *inverse condemnation*—the confiscation of development rights without condemnation proceedings or payment for the rights taken. (Under the U.S. Constitution, property rights may not be taken without due process and compensation.) Most of these challenges have not been successful, except in certain instances when allowable use intensities were reduced. The lowering of land-use density is known as *downzoning*. Downzoning has generally been upheld on the grounds that property values in general, including that of the affected parcel, may be preserved or enhanced by lowered use intensities. However, when landowners have shown that a

======= *Frame 14–2* =======

The Landmark Decision on the Legality of Land-Use Control/Zoning Regulations*

The Ambler Realty Company intended to sell the 68-acre tract of land it owned in the village of Euclid, Ohio, to an industrial developer. However, in 1922 Euclid enacted a land-use/zoning ordinance that set aside part of this tract for residential development. Ambler Realty sued Euclid, claiming that the ordinance resulted in a "taking" of Ambler's property without payment of just compensation, as prescribed by the U.S. Constitution.

The District Court agreed with Ambler Realty, but in a landmark decision the U.S. Supreme Court ruled that Euclid was not taking any part of the tract for a public purpose and that this ordinance was a legitimate use of the village's police power to control land uses.

This Supreme Court ruling has withstood the test of time in that it has served as an important precedent in virtually all subsequent disputes involving inverse condemnation. The ruling legitimized both land-use control as a police-power exercise and the separation of land uses into districts and zones for land-use control.

---

*Source: *Village of Euclid, Ohio* v. *Ambler Realty Co.* 272 U.S. 365, 47 S. Ct. 1/4, 71 L. Ed. 303 (1926).

community intended to buy land, but instead downzoned it, the courts have ruled against downzoning on the basis that the community had already recognized the value of the land. The downzoning was simply a way to avoid the expense of purchasing the land.

With the constitutionality of zoning established, the courts in recent years have been concerned with the fair and impartial application of zoning. They have disallowed changes in permitted uses that clearly reduce property values and unreasonable denials of rezoning requests. Although communities might wish to prevent development or preserve open spaces, they cannot do so at the expense of private owners and developers. Communities must achieve a delicate balancing of private property rights and public goals. If communities have the right to plan and to limit negative externalities by zoning, they also have an obligation not to confiscate private property and the values created by reasonable, conforming development.

Zoning Administration

Often property owners seek to have the zoning classification of their property changed. A developer may want to construct a residential subdivision on land currently zoned for agriculture. An apartment building owner may wish to increase the size of the project to accommodate more units. Or an individual parcel owner may wish to have the zoning changed from multifamily to commercial or light industrial. The planning and zoning commission and staff normally review all such *rezoning requests*.

In considering rezoning requests, the planning commission and staff use the following criteria:

1. Will the new zoning be consistent with the comprehensive plan?
2. Should the comprehensive plan be modified?
3. What effect will the new zoning have on surrounding land uses and on the larger community?

A request for rezoning that is consistent with the comprehensive plan is much easier to justify than one that varies from the comprehensive plan. If the request is inconsistent with the comprehensive plan, the question of whether the comprehensive plan should be modified must be considered. If the plan is still viable and realistic, the rezoning request should be denied. But if the rezoning request is reasonable, realistic, and consistent with current and expected development patterns, the plan should be modified to accommodate the changed zoning.

Finally, if either of the first two criteria justify the request, its impact on surrounding land uses and the community should be evaluated. Will the change lead to more intensive use of other parcels? What effect will these changes have on neighboring property values? Will the change stimulate other rezoning requests?

Unlike a rezoning request that involves a proposal to change the zoning classification of a parcel, a *variance* request usually involves a minor change in the rules in an existing zone. Consider the situation presented in Exhibit 14–4. The Stephens family has purchased a lot in a residential subdivision and plans to build a home with a pool and a detached garage on the lot. The local zoning regulation states that for property zoned R–1, any improvements must be set back at least 50 feet from the road. Since the owners are planning a garage that violates the setback regulation, they must obtain a zoning variance. Thus, the variance would involve only an adjustment in the setback requirement for this specific case, not a change in the R–1 classification.

EXHIBIT 14–4
VARIANCE REQUEST: STEPHENS' RESIDENCE

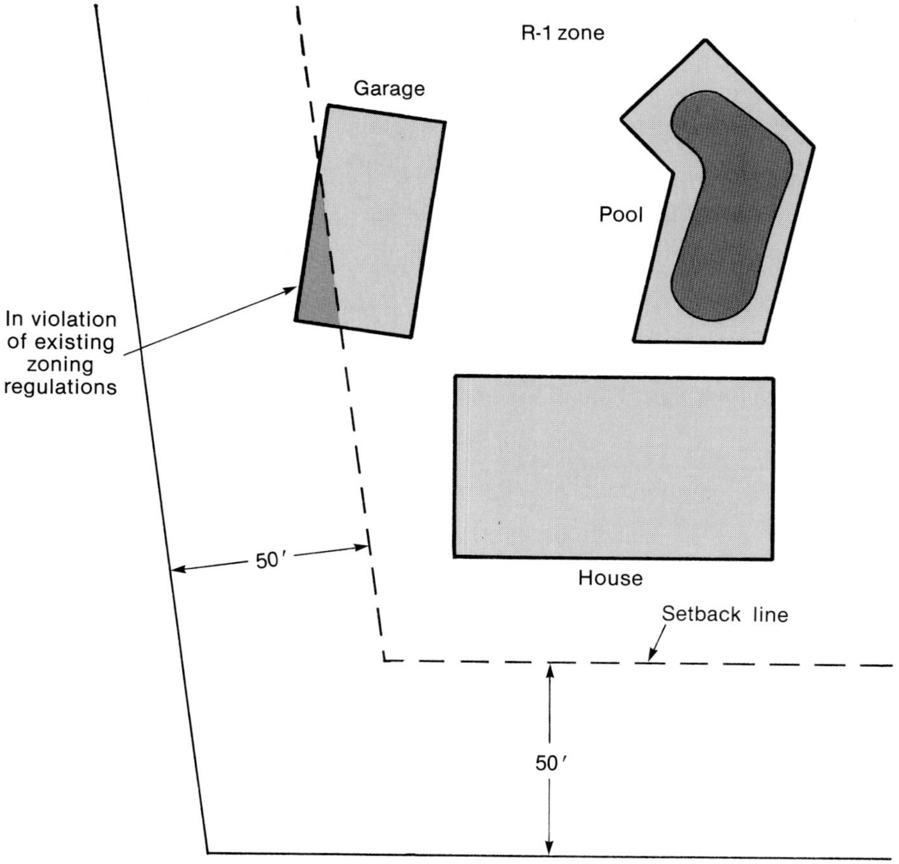

Planning and zoning commissions are also charged with the responsibility of reviewing and approving site plans for large projects such as shopping centers, apartment complexes, and office developments. A *site plan* is a map of a project on its site. It identifies the building arrangement on the site and normally includes several views, or *elevations*, for the planned development. Such matters as parking, traffic circulation, ingress and egress, and landscaping are also specified.

The planning commission also approves residential subdivision plats. It will consider the design of the subdivision, adequacy of streets, drainage and other utilities, and compliance with the city's *subdivision ordinance*. After approval, the plan can be recorded and the developer can proceed. The subdivision ordinance establishes a specific set of controls for the development of residential subdivisions in the community. In the past some communities experienced a poor quality of subdivision development, which imposed costs on the entire community. The county or city usually takes over the maintenance of streets and gutters in a subdivision, for example, shortly after completion of the development. If poor-quality materials and designs are permitted, the taxpayers in the community will soon bear a heavy financial burden to maintain these improvements to the land. Therefore, to ensure high-quality subdivision development, the subdivision ordinance sets forth engineering standards (e.g., the type of pavement that must be used for streets).

The planning staff reviews site plans both from the point of view of the developer's efficient utilization of the site and also with regard to the public's concerns. For example, ingress and egress may be planned at an undesirable location in terms of safety or convenience. The commission would require the developer to change this before granting approval. Or the commission might require a vegetation buffer between the development and adjacent properties to make the new project less objectionable to its neighbors. Usually approval of the site plan is required before a developer is granted a building permit. The authority to review and approve these plans helps ensure the wise and efficient use of land.

Many communities have enacted *sign ordinances* that limit the size, location, and lighting of signs in commercial districts and shopping centers. The planning and zoning commission's function is usually similar to that of site-plan approval. It reviews proposed signs to ensure that they comply with all relevant ordinances and regulations. Approval of a proposed sign allows the applicant to proceed with its construction.

PROBLEMS WITH PLANNING AND ZONING

The legal attacks and controversies surrounding planning and zoning are rooted in fundamental problems that people experience who are subject to zoning laws. The attempt to overcome some market inefficiencies inevitably creates others; perpetuation of the status quo may be good for some but inequitable for others. Whether the problems created by planning and zoning are less significant than the problems alleviated is a matter of judgment. Since judgment has been in favor of planning and zoning in most jurisdictions, the primary effort must be directed toward overcoming and minimizing the difficulties created. The main problem areas involve inconsistency with private market outcomes, discrimination, and administrative bias.

Inconsistency with Private Market Outcomes

Inherently, planning and zoning substitute nonmarket for market decisions. When the results of the two types of decisions differ, frictions will occur. The plan may zone too much land for one purpose and too little for another. It may extend utilities in one direction where development does not occur, but not to areas where development would otherwise occur. By limiting densities, zoning may contribute to urban sprawl; by allowing high densities, zoning may contribute to congestion and negative externalities. Such results lead to legal actions claiming unfair and capricious decision making and inverse condemnation of property rights.

Although widely supported in concept, some analysts advocate the elimination of zoning. Siegan has concluded that the land-use pattern obtained without zoning in Houston (the only major U.S. city not having zoning) is as desirable as the pattern obtained in other cities having zoning.[4] Although such a conclusion is based on many value judgments, it illustrates the fact that the private market, using the device of private restrictions may produce a reasonable pattern of uses. Also, it should be pointed out that Houston *does* engage in traditional land-use planning—a development-guiding process.

Planning and zoning probably can never be totally consistent with market activity. There may be too much land zoned for some uses and not enough for other uses. Or the land zoned may not be in the best location. Nevertheless, planning and zoning should be formulated in recognition of market realities and in response to forecasts of *future* market activity. Sufficient flexibility to allow periodic revisions and fair and impartial administration are perhaps the keys to an acceptable system of guided land use.

Discrimination

Some communities have enacted zoning laws that do not provide for high-density, low-cost housing. Consequently, low-income households,

---

[4]Bernard H. Siegan, *Land Use Without Zoning* (Lexington, Mass.: D.C. Heath, 1972).

many of whom may be blacks or other minorities, have been precluded from obtaining housing in these communities. Although the courts have overturned such laws, similar but less blatant practices also may have exclusionary effects. For example, zoning categories that prescribe minimum lot sizes and maximum densities tend to maintain high costs and prices for residential properties, thus excluding low-income households. In general, the courts have overturned unreasonable requirements (e.g., three-acre lots in urban areas).

Administrative Bias

Planning and zoning officials and staffs may not be adequately educated and trained to carry out their functions. If trained as planners, they may not understand the decision-making process of the private market. If trained in real estate or economics, they may not understand public concerns and the political process. Obviously, education in these areas and competence in understanding and synthesizing various points of view are desirable attributes of technical and administrative personnel working in this highly sensitive area.

It is often contended that developers and wealthy landowners are able to exert undue influence over the planning and zoning process. The lure of jobs and economic activity that development creates may focus attention on short-term benefits without adequate consideration of the longer-term costs of utilities, roads, recreational facilities, other public services, and environmental damage. On the other hand, aversion to growth and development may result in stagnation and inadequately planned facilities for present and future residents. Again, the necessity for balancing public concerns and private property rights is evident.

Strong, politically independent planning commissions and well-trained, competent planning staffs appear to provide the best response to the possibility of incompetence or biased decision making. The planning commissions can serve as a political buffer for both the planning and zoning staff professionals and the elected governing body. If planning and zoning are to be effective, they must have the confidence of the vast majority of citizens. Incompetence, favoritism, and bias will result in a loss of confidence that can lead to the downfall of the system.

TRANSFERABLE DEVELOPMENT RIGHTS

A relatively new method of regulating land uses is through the use of transferable development rights (TDRs). With this method the right to develop some properties to their maximum potential is taken away or reduced, but the development rights given up may be sold to the owners of other properties. Development rights of some property owners are reduced, but the owners are provided a means of obtaining compensation for their lost rights. Thus those who receive the rights pay the owners of rights taken or reduced.

For this method to work, there must be a *sending* area of development rights and a *receiving* area, in which property owners are eligible to purchase the rights. By purchasing development rights, property owners in the receiving area are allowed to develop their properties beyond the limit allowed by zoning. The allowable additional density is known as a *bonus maximum*.

Frame 14–3

TDRs from Grand Central Station

Although the Penn Central Transportation Co., Inc., owner of Grand Central Terminal in New York City, wanted to construct a 56-story office building above the terminal, the application was rejected by the New York City Landmarks Preservation Commission; the station is an historic landmark, and its character would be substantially changed. Penn Central sued the city. The litigation took nearly 10 years, and was decided by the U.S. Supreme Court in 1972 in favor of the city.

Penn Central then decided to sell a portion of its development rights. The Philip Morris Corporation had planned to build its world headquarters on a small (20,000-square-feet) lot on 42nd Street across from the terminal, but needed more space than zoning allowed. Thus, in 1978 Philip Morris purchased development rights from Penn Central that allowed construction of approximately 75,000 additional square feet of floor space for $2,240,000. This price was about double the market value of land in the area, but it allowed Philip Morris to construct an additional three and one half floors in the building.

The TDR system protects and preserves threatened areas or properties by limiting further development. TDR programs have been implemented in New York, Chicago, Denver, and San Francisco primarily to preserve historic districts and landmarks; in Montgomery and Calvert Counties, Md., and the Pinelands of New Jersey primarily to preserve agricultural land and open space; in Palm Beach and Dade Counties, Fla., to preserve environmentally sensitive areas; and in Hollywood, Fla., to preserve access to the beachfront.[5] As Exhibit 14–5 shows, the intensity of use allowed under normal zoning is reduced in the sending areas and increased in the receiving areas. In urban areas the intensity of use can be specified in terms of numbers of floors or floor-area ratios (square feet per floor ÷ lot size), while in rural areas intensity can be specified in terms of the number of structures or units per acre.

---

[5]David E. Levy, *Transferable Development Rights,* unpublished master's thesis, Graduate School, University of Florida, 1985.

EXHIBIT 14–5
OPERATION OF TDR SYSTEMS

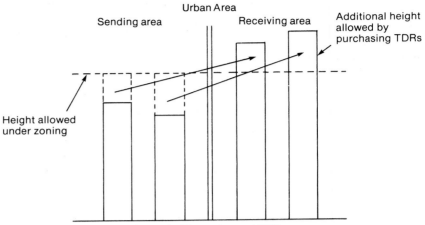

Heights allowed under zoning and with purchase of TDRs

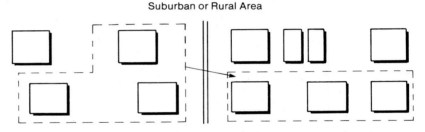

Density allowed under zoning: 4 units per acre

Development rights for three units per acre transferred to receiving area.

The use of TDRs is not a substitute for zoning, but instead is a complementary tool for land-use regulation. Although courts might find that zoning laws that attempt to differentiate among small areas and types of structures are discriminatory, TDRs provide compensation to landowners whose development rights are restricted. They also rely more on market forces in determining the value of development rights than do condemnation proceedings in which a landowner's rights are simply taken.

There are, however, some problems with TDRs. Unless demand is matched with the supply of TDRs, they cannot be sold immediately to private recipients. To remedy this difficulty, some plans have established a TDR "bank," in which TDRs are deposited after being purchased by the jurisdiction or a private institution, such as a commercial bank. They are then available for purchase when the demand increases. Such a bank requires capital and leads to further problems of determining which TDRs to buy and sell, the value of the TDRs, and the tax liability for the TDRs. The Chicago TDR plan failed to become active because of a lack of demand for the TDRs.

Another problem with TDR plans is that they usually apply only to a few properties having historic, environmental, or recreational significance. For example, in the Palm Beach plan, development rights may be transferred only from properties in "reserve" or "conservation" areas in the unincorporated portion of the county. The TDRs may be used only as bonuses in planned unit developments (PUDs) within the urban service area of the unincorporated portion of the county. Only one transaction has occurred there, and relatively few transactions have occurred in other plans.

TDRs appear to be a viable tool for land-use regulation in conjunction with zoning. Their use seems limited to a few socially significant properties in small areas in which there is strong development demand. Variations of the basic concept may be devised that will extend its usefulness to larger areas; however, it seems likely that greater flexibility could be built into traditional zoning and accomplish the same objectives.

OVERVIEW

Planning and zoning are devices to control land use. Communities use these tools because the land uses that might otherwise result are sometimes detrimental to long-term property values and community standards. Decisions made in a market that is inefficient due to high transaction costs produce these undesirable land uses. These costs include information gathering, legal fees, negotiating time, and the free-rider problem.

Planning is the process of developing guidelines for controlling growth and development. A community's comprehensive plan, while providing constraining bounds to development, must also contain provisions for flexibility to accommodate changing conditions. A comprehensive plan therefore must be broad in scope, long range in outlook, and flexible in application. Zoning is the assigning of specific permitted uses to individual parcels of land to carry out the comprehensive plan.

An appointed commission assisted by a professional staff typically carry out planning and zoning. A community's elected governing body (city council or city commission) has the final authority over planning and zoning matters. Typically, it delegates planning commissions the final authority in variance requests, approval of site plans, and sign control.

Private restrictions and easements also control land use. Individual property owners may control the future use of the property through restrictions in deeds or recorded plats. These restrictions bind subsequent owners, so long as the restrictions do not violate public policy. Private restrictions and easements, however, are not effective devices for wide-scale land-use control. Enforcement is limited to affected property owners, and application is limited to an individual parcel, tract, or subdivision.

Law suits have attacked zoning from a variety of standpoints. However, the courts have upheld its constitutionality, and ruled that specific applications are valid when they are reasonable, nonexclusionary, and comprehensive. Courts have overturned specific applications that were arbitrary, did not provide for low-income housing (and thus were discriminatory against low-income groups), or that resulted in the confiscation of property rights without compensation.

Transferable development rights (TDRs) have gained limited use in large cities and other urbanized areas. The TDR system limits development of some properties, but allows the owners of those properties to sell the development rights to owners of other properties, who are then allowed to develop beyond the intensity permitted by zoning. While the use of TDRs may be effective in guiding development in areas of intensive growth, the system has important drawbacks that will likely limit its more widespread adoption.

It seems apparent that planning and zoning are here to stay. Real estate owners, investors, developers, and users must be prepared to work within the system of public land use controls. Familiarity with a community's comprehensive plan, zoning categories, administrative structure, and appeals process are crucial to successful real estate operations.

TEST YOURSELF

Explain the following terms and concepts presented in this chapter.

1. Comprehensive plan.
2. Zoning.
3. Private restrictions.
4. Planned unit developments.
5. Inverse condemnation.
6. Downzoning.
7. Variance.
8. Site plan.
9. Transferable development rights.
10. Sending area versus receiving area.

Answer the following multiple choice questions.

1. Zoning is an exercise of which type of general limitation on property rights?
   a. Eminent domain.
   b. Taxation.
   c. Police power.
   d. Escheat.
   e. All of the above.

2. A comprehensive plan usually deals with which of the following elements?
   a. Land uses.
   b. Population.

c. Public services.
d. Natural resources.
e. All of the above.

3. The reason(s) why a market solution is claimed not to be adequate for land-use control is (are)
   I. The effects of transaction costs
   II. The contention that markets are too efficient
   III. Lack of full participation by affected parties
   IV. Inequity of market decisions
   a. I
   b. II
   c. I and II
   d. III and IV
   e. I and III

4. In cities the authority for approving site plans for large projects usually rests with the
   a. City council or commission.
   b. Mayor or city manager.
   c. Planning board or commission.
   d. Planning board or commission staff.
   e. Zoning review board.

5. Downzoning has generally been upheld by the courts *except* when it has been shown that
   a. Property values would be affected.
   b. The community intended to buy the land.
   c. The downzoning was not in accordance with the comprehensive plan.
   d. Public rights would be reduced.
   e. The public objected.

ADDITIONAL READINGS

Cartwright, Timothy J. "Problems, Solutions, and Strategies: A Contribution to the Theory and Practice of Planning." *Journal of the American Institute of Planners*, May 1973, pp. 179–87.

Hendon, Williams S. *Economics for Urban Social Planning*. Salt Lake City: University of Utah Press, 1975.

Mandelker, Daniel R., and Roger A. Cunningham. *Planning and Control of Land Development*. Indianapolis, Ind.: Bobbs-Merrill, 1979.

Natural Resources Defense Council. *Land Use Controls in the United States*, ed. Elaine Moss. New York: Dial Press/James Wade, 1977.

Urban Land Institute. *Management and Control of Growth*, vols. 1, 2, and 3. Washington, D.C.: Urban Land Institute, 1975.

APPENDIX: TYPICAL ZONING REGULATIONS (Condensed)

Condensed version of uses permitted within various zone classifications.

Agriculture A–1: Single-family dwellings on basis of one dwelling per acre. Public parks and recreation areas, golf courses, game preserves, historical areas, churches, and private schools. General agricultural uses.

Agriculture: Single-family dwellings and mobile homes on basis of one dwelling per acre. Public parks and recreation areas, golf courses, game preserves, historical areas, churches, and private schools. General agricultural uses.

RE (Single-family—low density): Single-family dwellings and related accessory buildings on basis of one dwelling per 40,500 sq. ft., if lot is served by central water and sanitary-sewer systems.

R–1aa (Single-family—low density): Single-family dwellings and related accessory buildings on basis of one dwelling per 20,000 sq. ft., if lot is served by central water and sanitary-sewer systems.

R–1a (Single-family—low density): Single-family dwellings and related accessory buildings on basis of one dwelling per 10,000 sq. ft., if lot is served by central water and sanitary-sewer systems.

R–1b (Single-family—medium density): Single-family dwellings and related accessory buildings on basis of one dwelling per 8,500 sq. ft., if lot is served by central water and sanitary-sewer systems.

R–1c (Single-family—mobile home): Single-family dwellings, mobile homes for living purposes, and related accessory buildings on basis of one dwelling or mobile home per 10,000 sq. ft., or per 8,500 sq. ft. if lot is served by central water and sanitary-sewer systems.

R–2 (Multiple-family—low density): Single-family detached dwellings, single-family attached dwellings up to and including four units per building, multiple-family dwellings up to and including four units per building, and customary accessory buildings incidental thereto.

R–2a (Multiple-family—medium density): Single-family detached dwellings, single-family attached dwellings up to and including eight units per building, and multiple-family dwellings up to and including eight units per building, and customary accessory buildings incidental thereto.

R–3 (Multiple-family—high density): Single-family attached dwellings, single-family detached dwellings, multiple-family dwellings, rooming houses, fraternities, sororities, dormitories, and customary accessory buildings incidental to these uses.

RP (Residential—professional district): Single-family dwellings, business and professional services, excluding the retail sales of goods and commodities and excluding personal services. Additional permitted uses shall include churches; schools; clubs; lodges; fraternities; sororities; dormitories; rooming houses; studios including dance, music, and art; and customary buildings incidental thereto. Off-street parking shall be permitted in all required yards.

RM (Mobile home park district): Mobile home parks and customary accessory uses, buildings, and structures incidental thereto.

RM–1 (Travel trailer park and campground): Transient parking of trailers and campers and the placing of tents on individual sites.

Planned unit development district: Residential units, including single-family attached and detached dwellings, two-family dwellings and multiple-family dwellings. Churches, schools, community or club buildings and similar public and semipublic facilities. Nonresidential uses, including commercial or retail uses, industrial uses and offices, clinics and professional uses.

HM (Hospital—medical district): Single-family dwellings, rooming houses, and hotels and motels. Hospitals for human care, nursing homes, medical or dental offices, clinics for medical or dental practice, and clinical laboratories. Churches, schools, and dormitories. Pharmacies devoted exclusively to the preparation and retailing of drugs.

AP (Administrative and professional): Offices of physicians, dentists, osteopaths, chiropractors, opticians or other professional persons concerned with improving personal or community health. Offices of architects, engineers, artists or other persons employed in the graphic arts. Offices in which personnel will be employed for work in one or more of the following fields.

Executive, administrative, legal, writing, clerical, stenographic, accounting, insurance, real estate, mortgage loan service or other similar enterprises but not commercial banks.

Offices for veterinarians, veterinary hospitals or clinics conducted wholly within a soundproof structure, and their customary accessory uses.

BP (Business and professional): Professional services, business services, personal services, public and private institutions, parks, government and community buildings, studios, clubs and lodges, hospitals, veterinarians, churches, funeral homes, and nursing homes.

BR (Retail sales and services): Professional services, personal services, business services, financial institutions including commercial banks, retail sales and services, Type "A" restaurants, cocktail lounges, bars, taverns, hotels and motels, and nightclubs within the principal building; and excluding automotive sales and services and service stations. Special exceptions, such as drive-in windows, commercial recreation and entertainment, and self-service gasoline pumps after public hearings and approval by the board of county commissioners.

BH (Highway-oriented business services): Professional services, personal services, retail sales and services, hotels and motels, cocktail lounges and nightclubs within the principal building and accessory to hotels and motels; types "A," "B," and "C" restaurants, service stations, and financial institutions including commercial banks; but excluding major repairs, paint-and-body works. Special exceptions—commercial recreation and entertainment, after public hearings and approval by the board of county commissioners.

BA (Automotive oriented business): Business services, professional services, personal services, retail sales and services. Type "A," "B," and "C" restaurants, cocktail lounges, bars, taverns, nightclubs, drive-in theaters, service stations, sale of new and used automobiles, truck sales, trailer rental and sales, motels, hotels, and auto repair facilities including overhauling, major repairs, paint-and-body works, commercial recreation and entertainment uses, but excluding mobile home sales and rental.

BA–1 (Automotive oriented business): All uses as outlined in the "BA" district, provided, however, that the storage or display of goods and commodities shall be contained within a completely enclosed building.

BW (Wholesale and warehousing): Professional services, business services, personal services, retail sales and services, hotels and motels, nightclubs, bars, taverns, cocktail lounges, recreation and entertainment, drive-in establishments, Type "A," "B," and "C" restaurants, service stations, automotive sales and services, mobile homes rental and sales, wholesale, warehousing, trucking facilities, freight terminals, moving and storage uses.

MA (Marine business): All uses permitted in the BR district, and in addition boat sales and services including the sale of fuel and lubricants to boats only, boat storage and repair, fish camps.

MS (Local service industrial district): Establishments engaged in manufacturing, processing, storage and warehousing, wholesaling, and distribution. Institutional and residential uses are prohibited in this district. Service and commercial activities relating to the character of the district and supporting its activities are permitted. Certain commercial uses relating to automotive and heavy-equipment sales and repair are permitted but this district is not to be deemed commercial in character.

MP (Manufacturing and industrial district): Establishments engaged in manufacturing, processing, storage and warehousing, wholesaling, and distribution, where such primary activities require districts five acres or more in size. Service and commercial activities relating to the character of the district and supporting its activities are permitted, but this district is not to be deemed commercial in character.

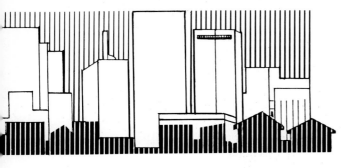

15
Property Taxation

OUTLINE

INTRODUCTION

The largest single source of revenue for most local governments is the tax on real estate. Cities, counties, school districts, and other special taxing jurisdictions, such as urban service districts and water management districts, levy real property taxes. It is levied on the owners of real estate in the jurisdiction based on the assessed value of the property owned. Thus, it is called *ad valorem* taxation.

While the tax liability imposed on owners of real estate may seem burdensome, the revenue raised by the tax generally provides important benefits to the owners. The revenue pays for police and fire protection, schools, streets, curbs, sewers, street lighting, parks, and a number of social services. Without these services, the properties would be worth much less; thus, we may view the property tax as the price of higher property values. Nevertheless, the property tax, as other taxes, may be levied unfairly or unwisely, which tends to lower property values.

The property tax is popular with local governments because it is capable of raising large amounts of revenue and may not be used by the federal government. The U.S. Constitution (Section 9) effectively prohibits a federal property tax by the following requirement: "No capitation or other direct tax shall be laid, unless in proportion to the census or enumeration herein before directed to be taken."

In other words, the federal government may not levy a tax that is not borne equally by every person. Although taxes on incomes were specifically exempted from this requirement by the 16th Amendment, ratified in 1913, the requirement applies to all other taxes. The property tax does not meet this criterion because each property owner pays a different amount based on his or her property's value.

MECHANICS OF THE PROPERTY TAX

Several jurisdictions within which a property is located simultaneously may levy property taxes. A property owner, for example, may pay property taxes to support the budget of a city, a county, a school district, and a special taxing district (e.g., a downtown redevelopment area). Determining a property owner's tax liability requires a general understanding of property-tax mechanics such as tax rates, exemptions, and special assessments, as well as the requirements for each jurisdiction.

Determining the Rate of Taxation

A jurisdiction's tax rate is established by the percentage of budgeted expenditures to the jurisdiction's *tax base*. The tax base consists of all the jurisdiction's taxable properties. Thus, the formula is:

$$R_T = \frac{E_B - I_O}{V_T - V_X}$$

where

R_T = Tax rate
E_B = Budgeted expenditures
I_O = Income from sources other than the property tax
V_T = Total assessed value of all properties
V_X = Value of exempt properties.

As an example, consider a community's budget, which forecasts expenditures for the coming year of $50 million. Nonproperty-tax income is forecast to be $10 million, and the community contains properties with a total value of $2.5 billion. There are also properties worth $500 million that are exempt from the property tax. The tax rate would be established by the following calculation:

$$R_T = \frac{\$50,000,000 - \$10,000,000}{\$2,500,000,000 - \$500,000,000}$$

$$R_T = 0.020 \text{ or } 2.0 \text{ percent}$$

In other words, two percent of the value of all taxable properties in the community is required in taxes to pay for the community's expenditures during the coming year. Instead of percentages, however, tax rates are usually stated in *mills*, or dollars per $1,000 of value. Converted to mills, the tax rate, or *millage rate*, for the above community would be 20 mills. (To obtain mills, the decimal point is moved one place to the right to convert from percent or three places to the right to convert from decimals.)

"What do you suggest for someone who's just had his property reassessed?"

From *The Wall Street Journal*, with permission of Cartoon Features Syndicate.

Tax-Exempt Properties

Most communities contain a number of tax-exempt properties. Such properties include government-owned properties and others exempted by state law or the state constitution. This category typically includes schools, hospitals, and places of worship.

Exempt properties lower the tax base of the community, thus raising the taxes of other property owners. Tax-exempt properties require public services, such as police and fire protection, and sometimes house families that use schools, roads, sewers, and all other public services. When military bases have an impact on a local community, the federal government makes payments in lieu of taxes to the community to defray the costs of such services. Similarly, housing agencies may make such payments for public-housing projects.

While public opinion generally favors tax exemption for churches and synagogues, their related enterprises sometimes create controversy over a claimed tax exemption. How much business activity should a church or synagogue be allowed before losing its tax exemption? Ongoing profit-making ventures will probably subject a religious organization to demands that its property be taxed.

Homestead and Other Exemptions

Some states allow certain homeowners to deduct a specified amount from their assessed valuations before calculating their property tax bills. The largest of these exemptions is for *homestead*. In these states, if the property owner occupies a home as the family's principal residence and has lived in the state for a required period (usually one year), the property is regarded as the family's homestead. For example, in Florida, homeowners who have lived in the state for at least one year may apply for the homestead tax exemption for their principal residences. If they qualify, $25,000 will be deducted from the assessed valuation before their taxes are calculated.

Many states also allow tax exemptions for disabled persons, veterans, widows, and blind persons. The value of all such exemptions must be subtracted from the total value of properties in calculating a community's tax base.

Calculating an Individual's Tax Liability

The tax assessor (or county property appraiser) appraises all taxable properties in a jurisdiction for property tax assessment. The value for taxation, or *assessed value*, is always related to market value, with the percentage usually ranging from 50 to 100 percent, as established by state law. After the property value for tax purposes is determined, the tax rate is multiplied times the value, less any applicable exemptions, to determine the amount of tax owed.

Take the case of a property appraised for $100,000 in a state that requires tax assessments to be 80 percent of market value. Thus, the assessed value for tax purposes is $80,000. The owner qualifies for a $5,000 homestead exemption. The principal taxing jurisdictions where the property is located have established tax rates as follows:

County	.0075	(7.5 mills)
City	.0080	(8.0 mills)
School district . .	.0064	(6.4 mills)
Total	.0219	(21.9 mills)

The property owner's tax bill would be:

$$(80,000 - \$5,000) \times .0219 = \$1,642.50$$

If the property owner did not qualify for the homestead exemption, the tax liability would be:

$$\$80,000 \times .0219 = \$1,752.00$$

Thus, the value of the homestead exemption in terms of property taxes saved is $1,752.00 − $1,642.50 = $109.50, or .0219 × $5,000 = $109.50.

Special Assessments

Another form of the property tax is sometimes levied to finance public improvements. Properties adjacent to the improvements may be charged a portion of the total cost (e.g., 50 or 75 percent), with the community paying the remainder of the cost. Such taxes are termed special assessments and are typically used to finance streets, gutters, sewers, and sidewalks.

Special assessments will not be upheld by the courts if the improvements do not increase the value of the properties. For example, homeowners cannot be required to pay for the widening of a street when it results in increased traffic and decreases the properties' desirability for residential purposes. The same special assessment would probably be legal for commercial properties where increased traffic would be desirable.

Another form of special assessment occurs when a property is located in a special taxing jurisdiction. Suppose, a city decides to redevelop its downtown area through substantial investment of public funds for street improvements and parks. Since the property owners in the downtown area will benefit directly from such investments, city administrators establish a special taxing district in the downtown area. Property owners within this district are assessed additional taxes to help pay for these improvements.

Special assessments, just as other property taxes, must be paid, or the taxing jurisdiction can foreclose on the property to obtain the unpaid taxes. In other words, property taxes, including special assessments, constitute a lien against private property, specifically, a *tax lien*. Large special assessments may be divided into installments, allowing the property owners to pay for them over several years. For this reason, purchasers of property should always check to determine whether there are any special assessments, as well as unpaid taxes, outstanding against the property.

Nonpayment of Taxes

Foreclosure for nonpayment of property taxes takes several forms among various states. Typically, lists of delinquent taxpayers are published in a newspaper of general circulation, and the delinquents are given a grace period to pay the taxes plus interest and penalties. This right to pay unpaid taxes plus interest and penalties before public sale and to reclaim full title to the property is, as with overdue mortgage payments (see Chapter 5), known as the *equity of redemption*. If the taxes are not paid, the properties may be sold at public auction, with the proceeds first used to pay back taxes. In some states the original owner has a period of time (up to two years) after the sale to pay all back taxes, interest, and penalties and to reclaim the property. This right is known as *statutory redemption.* In some states the purchaser obtains title without this liability at time of the public sale.

In other states (e.g., Florida) taxing jurisdictions sell tax certificates for unpaid taxes. The certificates carry a rate of interest determined by public bidding. In order to avoid losing the property, the owner must pay back the owner of the tax certificate both the amount advanced to pay the tax and the interest. If the owner does not pay the certificate holder within a certain period (usually two years), the certificate holder may force a public sale of the property. The sale proceeds must be used first to pay off the certificate holder. Of course, the certificate holder may bid for the property, the amount of the certificate plus interest constituting part of the purchase price.

CRITERIA FOR EVALUATING THE PROPERTY TAX

As with all taxes, we may evaluate the property tax on the basis of two criteria—efficiency and equity (fairness). Efficiency pertains to the ability to raise large amounts of revenue quickly and at relatively low cost through a tax. Equity refers to the equal taxation of property owners who are in comparable ownership positions.

Efficiency of the Property Tax

Several characteristics of the property tax contribute to its efficiency as a source of revenue for local governments.

1. The property tax is capable of raising large amounts of revenue; the tax base is large.
2. The object of the tax is fixed in location; it cannot be moved or hidden to avoid taxation.
3. Owners of private property can be identified relatively easily; if the owners of a parcel of real estate cannot be found, title to the property reverts to the state.
4. The value of properties for tax purposes can be established relatively easily by common appraisal procedures.
5. The federal government is effectively precluded from levying a property tax, and state governments rely primarily on such other taxes as sales and income taxes.
6. The amount of revenue raised tends to keep up with inflation, since property values generally increase with inflation.

The efficiency criterion can also be applied to the *effect* of the tax on the property tax base—property values. From this standpoint, two main disadvantages of the property tax have been cited.

Property Taxation of Improvements Inhibits New Construction. Perhaps if owners did not have to pay taxes on newly constructed buildings and other improvements, they would tend to construct more improvements. In order to raise needed revenue in adequate amounts, much of the tax burden would presumably be shifted to the land portion of real estate. The economic effect would be to encourage much quicker and more intensive utilization of land in order to absorb the land-tax burden.

Studies by economists have generally concluded that not enough revenue could be raised by a single property tax on land to provide the current level of local governmental services. One tax economist, however, has suggested that a relatively larger share of the tax should be levied against the land portion of real estate,[1] while another tax economist has suggested combining a land tax with user charges, especially for congestion and pollution.[2] Given the entrenched practice of taxing both improvements and land at the same percentage of value, it seems unlikely that a major shift away from the taxation of improvements will occur in the foreseeable future.

Property Taxation Inhibits Maintenance and Rehabilitation of Existing Improvements. This criticism is similar to the previous argument against the taxation of improvements: If owners did not anticipate higher taxes resulting from more valuable improvements, they would tend to maintain them in better condition and to rehabilitate them earlier in their economic lives. It is doubtful that this contention has merit for the vast majority of commercial, industrial, office, and middle-to-upper-class residential properties. To the owners of such properties, the tax incidence is a relatively minor consideration,[3] and the value lost by inadequate maintenance or untimely rehabilitation more than offsets increases in property taxes incurred with adequate maintenance and timely rehabilitation.

For the owners of low-income residential properties, however, the property tax is usually a relatively more important annual expense. Rental

---

[1]James Heilbrum, *Real Estate Taxes and Urban Housing* (New York: Columbia University Press, 1966), p. 169.

[2]Dick Netzer, "Is There Too Much Reliance on the Local Property Tax?" in *Property Tax Reform*, ed. George E. Peterson (Washington, D.C.: John C. Lincoln Institute and Urban Institute, 1973), p. 23.

[3]A study by Helene A. Cameron showed that property tax levels have relatively little impact on locational choices for new industrial plants. Other factors such as labor costs and nearness to raw materials and product markets were shown to be much more important. See "The Effects of the Property Tax on Location of Industrial Plants," *Bulletin of Business Research,* Center for Business and Economic Research, Ohio State University (April 1969).

rates usually cannot be increased to cover increased tax rates, and owner-occupants cannot usually afford any increased housing expenses. A program of tax abatement on the *additional* values created by rehabilitation of low-income housing might alleviate a significant part of the problem of providing adequate housing for low-income households. Such a program would require owners to spend the tax dollars saved on upgraded maintenance or rehabilitation. While additional revenue to the local community would not be obtained, the original tax base would be maintained and revenue would not be lost, as it has been under the existing system.

Given the advantages of the property tax for raising revenue for local jurisdictions and the limited disadvantages, we conclude that the property tax is a relatively *efficient* tax. While some economic disincentives for new construction, adequate maintenance, and timely rehabilitation are created, they are not sufficient to warrant abandonment of the property tax. For most types of properties, investment considerations can accommodate the tax burden. The property tax can raise large amounts of revenue to provide services that offset the disincentives, and the costs of raising the revenue are relatively low.

Fairness, or Equity, of the Property Tax

In Chapter 9 we pointed out that two equity standards can be analyzed to judge fairness. *Horizontal equity* requires that members of society in the same economic circumstances pay the same costs and/or receive the same benefits. *Vertical equity* requires that members of society in different economic circumstances pay different costs; they should also receive different levels of benefits. According to these standards of equity, the property tax burden should be higher for those who can afford to pay more and lower for those who can afford to pay less. The benefits, or services received, should also vary according to the contributions of each taxpayer. Several major criticisms of the property tax have been based on horizontal and vertical equity.

Property Taxation Is Regressive. This criticism holds that lower-income households pay higher property taxes than higher-income households *relative to their incomes*. Higher-income households do not tend to occupy housing that is proportionately more valuable than lower-income households. For example, households with $500,000 annual incomes do not own houses that are ten times as valuable as households with $50,000 annual incomes. The higher income households might have houses averaging $1,000,000 in value, while the $50,000 households might have houses averaging $200,000 in value—only five times as valuable. Since the property tax is based on property values, the lower-income households would be paying approximately twice the property taxes per dollar of income as higher-income households.

Additionally, some studies show that low-income residential properties are taxed at a *higher rate of value* than higher-income residential properties.[4] Higher-value properties may tend to be discounted more in the tax appraisal process. Presumably this results from poor appraisal practices and could be corrected by improved appraisal procedures and tax rate studies.

In his landmark study, Netzer concluded that property tax payments tend to be regressive.[5] However, he also found that lower-income taxpayers use locally provided services to a greater extent than higher-income households. Relative to the taxes paid, lower-income households required more police and fire protection and used more school facilities, public health, and public welfare benefits. Netzer concluded that the net result of the property tax, when benefits received are taken into account, is that it is *not* regressive. While lower-income households may pay higher taxes relative to their incomes, they receive more benefits than higher-income households.

Property Taxes Are Not Related to Ability to Pay. This criticism suggests that the criterion of vertical equity is violated. High-income households may elect to live in modest housing, escaping high levels of the property tax. Other forms of wealth such as securities, savings accounts, and personal property are typically taxed at lower rates than real estate. Lower-income households, on the other hand, may be required by their large families or personal desires to live in larger, relatively more valuable housing. To the extent that real estate is taxed at a higher rate than other forms of property, these lower-income owners are placed at a disadvantage.

On the other side, we should point out that homeowners enjoy various tax advantages. Although the earnings of most assets are taxed by the federal government, homeowner-occupants are not required to pay income taxes on "rent" saved. They may also deduct mortgage interest and real estate taxes in calculating their federal income tax liability.

Our conclusion on this criticism is that, whereas it may be valid in individual cases, overall the property tax is not a major violation of vertical equity. Higher-income households tend to live in higher-value housing and pay higher taxes. Although the relationship between the tax and ability to pay may be indirect, it exists nevertheless.

Property Taxes Vary among Geographic Areas. Because of the local nature of the property tax and its administration, the incidence of the tax may vary from property to property, county to county, and state to state.

---

[4]See George E. Peterson, Arthur P. Solomon, Hadi Madjid, and William C. Apgar, Jr., *Property Taxes, Housing, and the Cities* (Lexington, Mass.: Lexington Books, 1973).

[5]Netzer, "Is There Too Much Reliance?" pp. 45–62.

Within a taxing jurisdiction, tax appraisers attempt to appraise properties consistently. Yet similar properties may be appraised for tax purposes at different values. In evaluating tax consistency among properties, a *tax burden study* is often useful. This study compares the percentages of tax liability to recent sale prices of similar properties. Suppose that Joe Hotchkiss was thinking about purchasing a house for $100,000. He found several similar properties in the same neighborhood that had sold recently and calculated their tax burdens to compare them with the tax burden of the property he was considering (the subject property). The tax liability, sale price or value, and ratio of tax liability to sale price for the subject and comparable properties are shown in Exhibit 15–1.

EXHIBIT 15–1
TAX BURDEN ANALYSIS

	Property				
	A	**B**	**C**	**D**	**Subject**
Tax liability, 1987	$ 1,000	$ 1,150	$ 975	$ 1,050	$ 1,200
Recent sale price or value	92,500	112,000	98,000	105,000	100,000
Tax liability $\div$ SP (or V)	1.08%	1.03%	.99%	1.00%	1.20%
	Average of A,B,C,D = 1.03%				

This analysis shows that the tax burden for the subject property is higher than that for similar properties, which is 1.03%. Thus, Joe would probably have a good chance of getting his tax reduced to about $1,030.

Taxpayers who wish to contest their tax assessments should first appeal to the county tax assessor or appraiser. If they are not satisfied with the decision of the assessor, they may appeal to a tax or property-appraisal appeals board. Finally, appeals can be carried to the court system, if the taxpayers are not satisfied with decisions by the administrative agencies.

Since each county has a different tax assessor or property tax appraiser, wide differences often occur among counties. For example, a study conducted several years ago in one state showed that tax appraisals in the counties varied from an average of about 55 percent to about 75 percent of market value. Because of such variations, many states have undertaken programs to equalize the percentage of tax appraisals to market value among their counties.

While states may attempt to equalize tax burdens among counties, no such attempts have been made among states. Thus, similar properties in different states may bear highly different tax liabilities. While the typical tax burden ranges between 1 and 3 percent of market value, properties in some states have been taxed at considerably higher rates. Some states have enacted constitutional provisions or laws to limit property taxes. The most famous of these was Proposition 13 in California, which limited the property tax rate to one percent of property values. (See Frame 15–1.) Similar efforts to reduce and limit property taxes have occurred in a number of other states. With the federal government's policy of shifting the responsibility and costs of some social programs from the federal level to the state and local levels, the budgets of local governments have become severely strained.

Benson et al. suggest that the property tax should be administered on a regional basis.[6] This would combine groups of states into a large region for tax assessment, with the country divided into six to eight such regions. Regional administration would enable assessment officials to strive for uniformity in tax burdens within these large areas. The goals of vertical and horizontal equity presumably would be advanced. At this time, however, the prospect of regional administration in the foreseeable future seems remote.

Frame 15–1

California's Proposition 13

Probably the most famous property tax revolt in recent times occurred in California in 1978, when voters approved Proposition 13. This voter-initiated statute limited the property tax rate to one percent of "full cash value" and rolled back assessed values to 1975–76 levels. Assessments could increase by only two percent annually after 1978, and reassessments to market value could occur only when a property is sold. The proposition also prohibited the legislature from imposing new property taxes, and local governments were required to obtain approval by two-thirds of voters to enact "special taxes."

The average tax rate in California before Proposition 13 was about 3.2 percent of market value; therefore, local governments were subject to a potential revenue loss of more than two thirds of previous levels. Fortunately, at the time of the enactment of Proposition 13, the state government had a large surplus and was able to channel funds to local governments to offset revenue losses. Thus, local governments had about two years to adjust. They adjusted by trimming expenditures, cutting some services, increasing user fees, and charging for many services that previously had been free to users. Much of the increase in fees and new charges was imposed on builders, who increased prices and rents to cover these additional costs. The decrease in taxes to property owners was less than the full amount of cuts, since property taxes are deductible in computing federal income tax liability.

---

[6]George C. S. Benson, Sumner Benson, Harold McClelland, and Procter Thompson, *The American Property Tax: Its History, Administration, and Economic Impact* (Claremont, Calif.: Claremont Men's College, Institute for Studies in Federalism and the Lincoln School of Public Finance, 1965).

The Property Tax Is Poorly Administered. In most states county tax assessors or appraisers are elected officials. Special qualifications are not required; they need no special knowledge about appraisal procedures or other matters related to taxation. Given this lack of required qualifications and the large number of asessing officials, the quality and uniformity of assessing procedures are likely to be less than ideal. While the assessors in most large counties are usually quite competent, assessors in small counties typically have little education or background in property appraisal. Poor and unfair administration of the taxing process is bound to occur in these counties.

Assessors are also often subject to political pressures. Political supporters and large financial contributors may be able to exert considerable influence for favorable appraisals. City or county officials may want favorable treatment for a local industry. Friends and associates may seek special treatment. While most assessors will not consider direct requests for favorable treatment, their general desire not to alienate large groups of voters, financial supporters, government officials, or friends may lead to subtle, but noticeable, efforts to maintain assessments at acceptable levels.

To promote education and competence in tax assessing, the International Association of Assessing Officials (IAAO) sponsors courses and other educational programs for members. Many assessors also take courses and seminars sponsored by the leading professional appraisal organizations. And state departments of revenue require that assessors follow prescribed procedures and adhere to minimum appraisal standards.

Taxpayers who believe they have been treated unfairly can always appeal to a review board and to the courts. While tax assessment procedures are far from perfect, it seems clear that assessment administration has improved considerably in recent years and that a viable procedure for redressing injustices provides a safety valve that will enable the system to minimize public hostility.

OVERVIEW

The property tax is the principal source of revenue for local governments and taxing jurisdictions, such as school districts. The tax is levied on the value of all property in the taxing jurisdiction, less exempt property. Additionally, taxpayers may qualify for exemptions such as homestead, disability, and military service. A property's value for tax purposes is usually equal to or a direct function of market value. Special assessments are a form of property taxation for financing public improvements adjacent to private properties.

The property tax, as other taxes, can be evaluated in terms of efficiency and equity. The taxation of real property is an efficient means of raising revenue because large amounts can be generated at a relatively low cost. Some disincentive for new construction, maintenance, and rehabilitation is created by the property tax—a cost that is ultimately borne by all users of real estate.

In terms of equity, the property tax is potentially undesirable. Without exemptions for certain classes of taxpayers, equalization of burdens among tax jurisdictions, and professional administration, the tax is more burdensome to some property owners than to others. Efforts to improve the fairness of the property tax have been undertaken in most states. Yet, since low-income taxpayers may benefit more than high-income taxpayers from the services funded by the property tax, the tax tends to be more fair.

TEST YOURSELF

Explain the following concepts and procedures presented in this chapter.

1. *Ad valorem* taxation.
2. Property tax base.
3. Mill.
4. Procedure for determining a community's tax rate.
5. Tax-exempt properties.
6. Homestead exemption.
7. Assessed value.
8. Procedure for determining a property owner's tax liability.
9. Special assessments.
10. Regressive tax.

Answer the following multiple choice questions.

1. Property taxes are the principal source of revenue for
   a. Federal government.
   b. School districts.
   c. Local governments.
   d. State governments.
   e. Local governments and school districts.

2. County assessors (or property appraisers) determine
   a. The tax rate.
   b. The tax amount.
   c. Property value for taxation.
   d. Homestead and other exemptions.
   e. All or none of the above.

3. A property owner who owes eight mills in school taxes, 10 mills in city taxes, and five mills in county taxes, and who qualifies for a $25,000 homestead exemption, would owe how much tax on a property assessed at $80,000?
   a. $1,840.
   b. $1,725.
   c. $1,265.
   d. $1,500
   e. $1,250.

4. A street is to be paved and gutters installed in front of your property. The city assesses property owners 75 percent of the cost of such improvements, which is estimated to be $60 per running foot. Your property has 100 feet of frontage on one side of the street. How much will be your special assessment?
   a. $4,500.
   b. $6,000.

c. $2,250.
d. $1,000.
e. $5,000.

5. A regressive tax is one in which
   a. Lower-income households pay more taxes relative to their incomes than higher-income households.
   b. Lower-income households pay less taxes relative to their incomes than higher-income households.

c. Higher-income households pay more taxes relative to their incomes than lower-income households.
d. Higher-income households pay the same ratio of taxes to income as lower-income households.
e. There is no relationship between taxes and income.

ADDITIONAL READINGS

Heilbrun, James. *Urban Economics and Public Policy.* New York: St. Martin's Press, 1981. Chap. 14.

King, A. T. *Property Taxes, Amenities and Residential Land Values.* Cambridge, Mass.: Ballinger Books, 1973.

Neltzer, Dick. *Economics of the Property Tax.* Washington, D.C.: Brookings Institution, 1966.

Peterson, George E. *Property Tax Reform.* Washington, D.C.: Urban Institute, 1973.

Peterson, George E.; Arthur P. Solomon; Hadi Madjid; and William C. Apgar. *Property Taxes, Housing and the Cities.* Lexington, Mass.: Lexington Books, 1973.

Segal, David. *Urban Economics.* Homewood, Ill.: Richard D. Irwin, 1977, Chap. 11.

Part Three

The Financial Perspective

The financial perspective of real estate incorporates what most real estate educators agree is the core of real estate studies today. The essential elements of real estate curricula include the study of appraisal (i.e., the valuation of real estate), real estate or mortgage finance, and real estate investment. The difference between real estate finance and real estate investment is that real estate finance emphasizes the borrower and lender relationship, whereas real estate investment emphasizes the real estate investor's relationship with all other entities, including lenders, property managers, government, etc. Although the term financial perspective implies only the study of real estate finance, it actually has a much broader meaning.

What, then, is the common thread running through real estate appraisal, finance, and investment that brings them together in a real estate principles textbook? Although the institutional framework—the characteristics and behavior of firms, professionals, and trade organizations—and terminology of each arena differ markedly, the underlying concepts and techniques for decision making are the same. These concepts and techniques come under the general heading of *financial analysis.*

Specifically, financial analysis refers to the application of valuation theory and concepts of the time value of money in real estate appraisal,

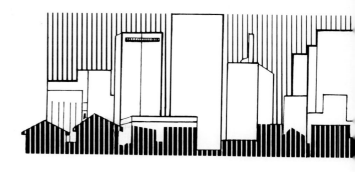

finance, and investment decision making. Financial analysis therefore is a fundamental element of each of these three areas of real estate. Moreover, the three areas within the financial perspective of real estate are bound by a single fundamental equation in valuation theory that relates the value of property rights to the benefits to be received.

Part Three, The Financial Perspective, begins with a chapter describing underlying concepts and theory (i.e., valuation theory and the time value of money). The remaining chapters describe the institutional setting, terminology, and techniques as they are applied in real estate appraisal, finance, and investment. Chapters 17 and 18 are devoted to one-to four-family residential appraisal and income-property appraisal, respectively. The next two chapters cover one-to-four-family residential finance and income-property finance. The last three chapters in this section describe the process of real estate investment decision making, including the effects of federal income taxes and risk analysis.

Note to Students: An essential foundation for a thorough understanding of the financial perspective of real estate is an understanding of valuation theory and time-value-of-money concepts. Thus, students should be especially certain they have a good grasp of the material in the first chapter, Chapter 16, of this section. ■

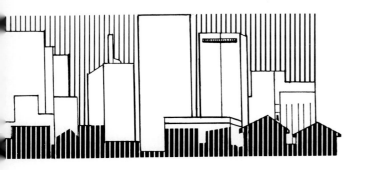

16
Valuation Theory and Financial Analysis

INTRODUCTION

The *valuation* of property rights is a fundamental concern in real estate appraisal, finance, and investment. Real estate appraisers are hired specifically to estimate the values of real property rights, usually fee simple interests in real estate. Their task most often involves estimating market value—the price that a typical buyer would be willing to pay should the property be placed on the market.

In real estate finance, mortgage lenders obtain property rights through the mortgage contract in the form of a claim against the borrower (the note) and the property (the mortgage). Mortgage lenders are entitled to receive a mortgage payment each period. The payment includes interest on the loan and a partial repayment, or amortization, of the principal amount borrowed. The borrower makes a mortgage payment each period to satisfy the claim of the lender. These claims have value and, because mortgages are frequently bought and sold in secondary markets, the valuation of the claims of the lender is a major concern in mortgage finance.[1]

Real estate investors seeking to make investments need to know the value of real property rights so they do not bid too much for these rights. The valuation problem in real estate investment analysis is estimating the price a *particular* investor should pay for a property, given that investor's unique tax situation and financing opportunities. This personalized estimate of value is called *investment value*. It differs from market value in that the concern is with what a particular investor should pay rather than with what a typical investor might pay.

Valuation of property rights is the cornerstone of *financial analysis*, the general framework for analyzing problems in real estate appraisal, fi-

---

[1]The valuation of the claims of the lender (i.e., the debt position) is also a fundamental concern in some approaches to estimating the market value of properties in real estate appraisal.

nance, and investment. Financial analysis involves the use of *time-value-of-money* concepts to provide quantitative information for solving problems and making decisions in appraisal, finance, and investment. An estimate of value is an example of the type of quantitative information real estate decision makers need. In addition to estimates of value, mortgage lenders are interested in their yields on mortgages, and borrowers are concerned about the effective cost of mortgage borrowing. Similarly, real estate investors are interested in knowing their rate of return on their investment. The tools of financial analysis are applied by real estate analysts to supply this information.

We issue a warning here about overreliance on the quantitative information—the "numbers"—provided by financial analysis techniques. As we discussed in Chapter 10, real estate markets are imperfect. This suggests that *qualitative information*, in the form of appraiser, lender, and investor interpretations and judgment, plays a significant role in real estate decision making. Therefore, quantitative information for financial analysis should be viewed as merely one important input into the real estate decision-making process. Judgment and interpretations are also important inputs. Moreover, as a general rule financial analysis techniques tend to become less reliable as markets become less perfect or competitive.

This chapter focuses on the underlying concepts of financial analysis. The chapters that follow show how financial analysis is used to provide quantitative information in specific real estate decision making settings (e.g., residential finance, income property appraisal, etc.). We begin this chapter with a discussion of valuation theory. Then we discuss time-value-of-money concepts. Finally, we present the main financial analysis techniques used in real estate appraisal, finance, and investment.

VALUATION THEORY

A real estate appraisal provides an estimate of the value of real property rights. Depending on the appraisal assignment, the appraiser will rely on one or more of the three basic *approaches to value.* Each of the approaches relies on a different *valuation concept:* The cost concept underlies the *cost-less-depreciation approach* to value; the market concept underlies the *sales-comparison approach;* and the income concept underlies the *income-capitalization approach.*

The Cost-Less-Depreciation Approach

Valuation of a fee simple interest in real estate using the cost-less-depreciation approach can be represented by the following equation:

$$\text{Value} = \text{Land Value} + (\text{Construction Cost} - \text{Accrued Depreciation})$$
$$(16\text{--}1)$$

Several points should be made about this equation. First, notice that the valuation problem approached from a cost point of view requires a separation of the two principal physical components of the real estate—the land and the buildings.[2] This separation of real estate into its physical components for valuation purposes has been one of the main themes in traditional real estate appraisal. The second point is that the value of the land must be estimated separately, using either the sales comparison or income capitalization approach. Land is usually not depreciated, since land does not necessarily lose its ability to produce income.

The essence of the cost-less-depreciation approach, therefore, is the calculation of the current construction cost of the building or its equivalent and the subtraction of monetary penalties for the physical, functional, and economic losses the building has suffered over time. These deductions are based whenever possible, on market information derived from similar buildings. The result is added to the value of the land to obtain an estimate of value. Since these physical, functional, and economic effects are difficult to estimate, the cost approach is sometimes considered the least reliable of the three basic approaches to value.

An estimate of value using the cost-less-depreciation approach is currently required for one-to-four family residential appraisals primarily to check the estimate obtained by the sale-comparison approach.[3] For some appraisal assignments, such as the valuation of government buildings and churches, neither the sales-comparison nor the income-capitalization approach can be used effectively, so the cost-less-depreciation approach is frequently used.

The Sales-Comparison Approach

As the term implies, the sales-comparison approach to estimating real estate value relies on information obtained directly from experiences in the real estate market. Specifically, the idea is to estimate the value of a subject property from recent sale prices of similar or comparable properties.

We obtain estimates of real estate values by the sales-comparison approach in two steps. First, the appraiser must carefully select comparable

---

[2]Construction cost less accrued depreciation refers to the building component of the property.

[3]This requirement is imposed by the institutions that buy and sell mortgages.

properties. These properties should strongly resemble the subject property with respect to the following factors:

1. *Property rights.* If only real property rights are involved in the appraisal of the subject, then comparables should be chosen in which only real property rights were sold (i.e., no personal property was included).
2. *Conditions of sale.* If a comparable property had a buyer and a seller who are related, then the conditions of the sale are not comparable to those assumed for the subject.[4]
3. *Market conditions.* The optimal situation is when the comparable was sold on the day the appraisal assignment began.
4. *Financing terms.* If, for example, the subject property in the current market is expected to sell with conventional fixed-rate financing, the appraiser should strive to find comparables that sold with this same type of financing.
5. *Location.* The optimal situation is where the comparable is next door to the subject property.
6. *Physical characteristics.* Examples include the size of the lot and size of the building (i.e., square feet) and the number of bedrooms and bathrooms, if the property is a one-to-four-family residential property.

The second major step is adjusting the comparables for the differences in these factors between the subject property and each comparable. Suppose that the subject property is a single-family residence and has a new swimming pool, while a particular comparable property does not have a pool. The comparable sold for $172,500. The appraiser knows that a new pool of this design would cost $20,000 to install but that the market will pay only half the cost of a new pool in the purchase price of a residential property. Thus, the appraiser adjusts the comparable by adding $10,000 to the actual sale price, giving an adjusted price of $182,500.[5]

Needless to say, the adjustment process is somewhat subjective and requires much experience and judgment. Some factors are extremely difficult (e.g., locational differences) or impossible (e.g., differences in the conditions of the sale) to adjust for, while others can be handled well by an experienced appraiser (e.g., physical characteristics and market conditions).

---

[4]Sales to relatives would be less than "arms-length transactions."

[5]Frequently, adjustments are made on a percentage basis in which amounts based on percentages are added or subtracted from the transaction price of the comparable. In the former example, the appraiser would add five or six percent to the actual sale price of the comparable because it does not have a pool. The sequence commonly used for making percentage adjustments is as follows: adjustment for financing terms, adjustment for conditions of sale, adjustment for market conditions, adjustment for location, and adjustment for physical characteristics.

Since we require a set of comparables, the types of properties that can be valued using the sales-comparison approach must be traded in a fairly active market. Typically, single-family residences and often residential condominiums are appraised using this approach, while regional shopping malls, for example, are difficult to appraise by this method. Chapter 17 includes a detailed discussion of the sales-comparison approach for valuing real estate.

The Income-Capitalization Approach

The income-capitalization approach to valuing real estate is by a wide margin the most advanced of the three basic valuation approaches. There are literally dozens of variations on the fundamental idea underlying the income-capitalization approach. We discuss many in Chapter 18. It is the accepted approach for appraising income-producing properties such as shopping centers and other retail establishments, hotels, office buildings, apartment buildings, and industrial buildings.

The idea behind the income-capitalization approach is quite simple. The value of income-producing real estate depends on the benefits the property generates for the owner in the future.

The Fundamental Equation.   In more specific terms, we can express the idea behind the income capitalization approach with the following equation:

$$V = f(B) \tag{16-2}$$

where V is value, B refers to the flow of benefits derived from the property, and f is some functional relationship between V and B. While real estate ownership may provide what economists call *psychic benefits* (i.e., the thrill or prestige of owning real property), the benefits referred to in Equation 16–2 are monetary benefits flowing to the owner. Therefore, we can revise Equation 16–2 to

$$V = f(I) \tag{16-3}$$

since $B = I$ and where I is income.

Now, the only remaining question is what functional form is commonly used to express the relationship between V and I. In selecting this functional relationship, we could choose to multiply I by some factor, but instead, the convention is to divide I by a rate R to convert I to V. In symbols,

$$V = \frac{I}{R} \tag{16-4}$$

Equation 16–4 is termed the *fundamental equation* because it embodies the important concepts for much of what goes on in real estate appraisal, finance, and investment. Moreover, this equation is fundamental to valuing other types of assets, including stocks and bonds. The inverse relationship between values (or prices) and rates indicated by this equation is seen every day in the bond market. As interest rates rise, the prices of bonds fall, because an investor could buy a newly issued bond for the same face value as, and at a higher interest rate than, the old bonds.

In the field of income-property appraisal, the process of converting I to V presented in Equation 16–4 is called *capitalization* and thus R is termed the *capitalization rate*. The terms capitalization and capitalization rate stem from the fact that the value of an asset is a reflection, in a single number, of all future income that the asset will generate. The term *capitalization*, therefore, refers to the conversion of an asset's income flows to a *capital* stock amount—the single number or value.

The appraiser's main tasks in applying the income-capitalization approach are to estimate the incomes that will be generated by the property and to estimate the capitalization rate currently being used in the market. By rearranging the terms of the fundamental equation,

$$R = \frac{I}{V} \tag{16–5}$$

we can see that R is simply a rate reflecting the return (income) on the investment (amount paid). Thus, the key to estimating the capitalization rate lies in determining what total rate of return is currently being demanded by investors in the market for this type of property.

Considerable attention is also directed toward the estimation of I for purposes of appraisal, finance, and investment. The fundamental equation contains two important assumptions about I. First, we assume I to be the same at every period in the future (i.e., I is constant). Second, we assume this constant income to extend infinitely into the future. These assumptions are quite restrictive, but they are relaxed in variations that we will add to the formula in Chapter 18. We will be able to value properties in cases in which I varies from period to period and stops at some terminal period.

Market Value and Investment Value

Most real estate appraisals are undertaken for the purpose of estimating the market value of the property. Providing a definition for market value that is consistent with the three approaches to valuation, as summarized in Exhibit 16–1, has been a troublesome problem. In modern valuation theory, market value is a probablistic *prediction* of what a property will sell for in the open market. This concept of a predicted sale price is known as *most-probable sale price.*

To comprehend the concept of most probable sale price, we must ac-

---

EXHIBIT 16–1
SUMMARY OF THE THREE BASIC APPROACHES TO VALUE

Approach	Key Steps in Appraisal Process
Cost less depreciation	1. Estimate land value using sales-comparison or income-capitalization approach.
	2. Estimate cost to reproduce the building.
	3.* Estimate and subtract depreciation from the estimated cost.
	4. Estimate value from the sum of the land value and adjusted building cost.
Sales comparison	1. Select comparable properties based on factors such as physical characteristics and location.
	2.* Adjust sale prices of comparables to the subject property in accordance with the same factors.
	3. Estimate value of the subject from the adjusted sales prices of comparables.
Income capitalization	1. Estimate benefits (i.e., income).
	2.* Determine appropriate capitalization rate.
	3. Divide the income by the rate to obtain estimate of value.

---

*Indicates the most difficult appraisal operation.

cept the notion that real estate is traded in an imperfect market. Specifically, many of the requisite conditions for a perfect market, such as many buyers and sellers, homogenous product (no locational monopoly), and perfectly informed buyers and sellers, do not exist in real estate markets.[6] As a result, the appraiser must be a student of the conditions in the market in which the property is to be traded to judge the market value of the property. This idea is conveyed in the following excerpt:

> The price at which the subject property will sell is strongly influenced by the market conditions under which the transaction will take place. By "market conditions" we mean the totality of factors and forces which have any impact on the transaction. The appraiser, who must predict probable selling price (V_p), must be an assiduous student of the market environment for it is on the basis of his knowledge of past market behavior that he will be able to predict the market reactions to the hypothetical exposure for the sale of the subject property.[7]

Most-Probable Sale Price Defined. The concept of most-probable sale price bears directly on an important distinction between the *market price* and *the market value* of real estate. The market price of real estate is the result of a transaction—an historical fact of an exchange of money or

---

[6]See Chapter 10.

[7]Richard U. Ratcliff, *Valuation for Real Estate Decisions* (Madison, Wis.: Democrat Press, 1972), p. 50.

other consideration for real property rights. It is therefore the result of the intersection of supply and demand at a particular point in time.

Let's assume for now that the real estate market operates without imperfections, such as uninformed buyers and sellers and locational monopoly. In a perfect market, market price and market value are equal because the actual price paid in the market would not deviate from what a well-informed appraiser would estimate the price to be (i.e., the market value). That is, the intersection of supply and demand at any particular point in time is exactly what the appraiser estimates it will be, given his or her evaluation of the prevailing supply and demand conditions in the market. This relationship is shown in Panel A of Exhibit 16–2.

EXHIBIT 16–2
MARKET VALUE, MARKET PRICE, AND THE CONCEPT OF MOST-PROBABLE SALE PRICE

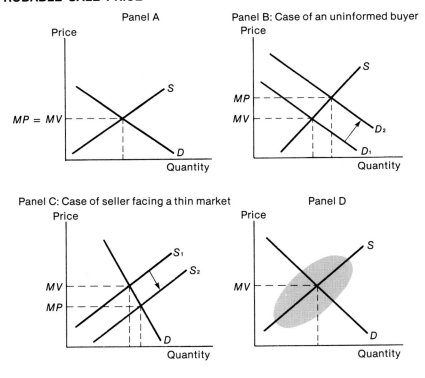

Now assume that a buyer, Mr. Les Informed, makes a bid on a property that is more than he would bid had he known what prices other buyers and sellers were negotiating for similar properties. As shown in Panel B of Exhibit 16–2, this transaction results in a one-time increase in the demand for this type of property (i.e., a shift from D_1 to D_2) and a market price that is higher than the market value in a perfectly competitive market. Since this buyer is the only buyer without perfect information, all subsequent transactions occur where $MP = MV$.

Now take the case of a seller, Ms. I. M. Inahurry, who has been transferred to another city and must sell her condominium. Since the market is thin (fewer buyers and sellers) and she is in a hurry to sell, she offers the property at a price below the market value.[8] As shown in Panel C of Exhibit 16–2, the actions of Ms. Inahurry have temporarily increased the supply of condominiums at a price below the market value.

Panel D of Exhibit 16–2 shows an oval-shaped area of possible demand and supply intersections surrounding the market value in a perfectly competitive market. Given the imperfect nature of real estate markets, the *estimate* of value will likely fall somewhere in this area. That is to say, the most-probable sale price of the property will fall within the band.[9] Thus, the appraiser estimates the most-probable sale price, given the imperfect nature of the real estate market, as the market value of the property.

We can reach two conclusions regarding market price and market value. First, market prices are *actual amounts* resulting from transactions, whereas market values are estimates of where supply and demand intersect. Second, market value is highly dependent on the assumptions made about the market. If an imperfect market is assumed, the most-probable sale price is an estimate of the market value given prevailing market conditions. In a perfect market, the market price and market value are equal.

The Investment-Value Perspective.   Market value is an amount that any typical buyer in the market will pay and a typical seller will accept. Investment value, by contrast, is the *maximum* amount a *particular* buyer will pay (buyer's investment value) or the *minimum* amount a *particular* seller is willing to accept (seller's investment value). We will rely on the investment-value concept heavily in subsequent chapters on real estate investment. The investment value concept also provides an enlightening perspective on the definition of market value and most-probable sale price.

Suppose that Mr. John Celler is offering a rental house for $80,000. The $80,000 asking price represents the minimum amount he is willing to accept—his investment value for the property. Also assume that he has

---

[8]She would allow for a normal time of exposure to the market but realizes that, given current market conditions, the property would probably remain longer than the normal time on the market.

[9]It isn't likely that selling prices would deviate too much from the market value in an imperfect market. Real estate markets are somewhat imperfect, but not highly imperfect.

received three offers for the property—$78,000 from Ms. Alice Byer, $80,500 from Ms. Betty Bieair, and $82,000 from Ms. Connie Buyair.

Exhibit 16–3 presents a hypothetical distribution of all potential bids that could be made for John Celler's property. The investment values of the three known buyers and the seller are also shown. The first question to be answered is why do Alice, Betty, and Connie have different investment values for the same property? The answer is that the characteristics of each potential buyer are different. Connie is in a relatively high tax bracket, and because the property can generate some excellent tax advantages for her, she submits a relatively high bid. Betty's father is a banker and has offered to help her with the financing of the purchase; therefore, she can make a bid for the property that is higher than the asking price. Alice, however, is in a relatively low tax bracket and must use conventional financing, so her bid is relatively low. Other factors that might lead to differences in buyer investment values, in addition to tax advantages and exceptional financing opportunities, include different holding-period expectations, different expectations about the benefits the property will generate in the future, and different information levels about competing properties in the market.

EXHIBIT 16–3
MARKET VALUE/INVESTMENT VALUE EXAMPLE

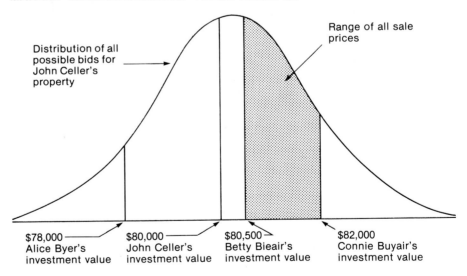

What will be the selling price of the property? If none of the bidders know each other's bids, the price will be the highest bid, $82,000. If, however, Connie knows Betty's bid of $80,500, she might try to obtain the property by bidding only slightly more than $80,500.

The shaded area in Exhibit 16–3 is the range of possible selling prices for this property. This suggests that the investment values of buyers and sellers in the market determine the most probable sale price, or market value, of the property.

While the investment-value perspective of market value reflects how market values are actually determined, appraisal techniques have not yet been developed to yield most-probable selling prices in this fashion. With the gradual convergence of appraisal and investment analysis, however, such a perspective may guide appraisers in the future.

Highest and Best Use

Highest and best use is a widely used term in appraisal. In general, it refers to the most profitable use that can reasonably be expected for a parcel of real estate. Thus, the words *highest and best* usually mean *most profitable*. The word *use* has two different meanings, depending on the type of highest and best use involved. As we will describe, the first type of highest and best use refers to the kind of building or other improvement that should be constructed on a vacant parcel of land (or site). The second type of highest and best use refers to the occupancy that is most profitable for an existing property, including the building.

The important principle of highest and best use in appraisal and investment theory is that sites and properties tend to be placed in their highest and best uses *at the time when decisions can be made about them.* For example, a site will tend to have a building constructed on it that will maximize the site's income and value when the building is new. Obviously, however, a new building will not be constructed on the site every two or three years in order to achieve continual highest and best use.

Similarly, an improved property will tend to be occupied by owners or tenants who can obtain the greatest utility or income from the property. Tenants having long-term leases cannot be evicted, however, to allow the owner to lease the property to higher-paying tenants.

Highest and Best Use of a Site as Though Vacant. A site's value is determined by its *potential* highest and best use. This principle of real estate holds true even for sites having existing buildings on them. Many sites with older buildings, for example, regularly sell for many times the value of the buildings, because the buildings can be demolished and new highest-and-best-use buildings constructed.

The type of analysis employed to determine highest and best use of a site is shown in Exhibit 16–4. Suppose that site could reasonably be expected to be used for an apartment building, an office building, or a commercial (store) building. The analyst estimates the cost, income, and expense information for the three alternative uses presented in Exhibit 16–4.

EXHIBIT 16–4
HIGHEST AND BEST USE ANALYSIS OF A SITE AS THOUGH VACANT

	Use		
	Apartment Building	**Office Building**	**Commercial Building**
Cost of construction	$1,000,000	$900,000	$800,000
Effective gross income	250,000	200,000	180,000
Operating expenses	120,000	80,000	69,000
Net operating income	130,000	120,000	111,000
Income to building at 12 percent (cost × .12)	120,000	108,000	96,000
Income to site	10,000	12,000	15,000
Indicated site value at 10 percent (Income to site/.10)	$ 100,000	$120,000	$150,000

As we can see from these estimates, the site's highest and best use would be the commercial building. It produces the highest site income, after deducting a 12 percent return on the capital invested in the building for all three alternative uses. Note that the highest and best use is not necessarily the most costly building or the building producing the highest gross income or even the highest net operating income. Rather, the relationships among these variables determine the highest and best use; it is the use that maximizes the income (return) to the site.

Highest and Best Use of a Property as Improved. We determine an improved property's highest and best use by comparing rates of return on logical, competing types of occupancies. This type of analysis is shown in Exhibit 16–5. Suppose that an owner of a small building has asked a real estate analyst to determine the type of tenants who would produce the highest return on the investment in the property. Two alternative uses of the existing building are offices and small shops. Another alternative that must be considered, since the building is more than 25 years old, is to demolish the existing building and construct a new building. Exhibit 16–5 shows the three alternatives, with their associated capital, income, and expense requirements.

As shown by this analysis, the highest and best use of the property as improved would be for small shops. It produces the highest return on invested capital. Note that demolition of the existing building is not warranted at this time. If it were, we would proceed to a highest-and-best-use analysis of the site as though vacant to determine the type of new building that should be constructed. This type of highest and best use

EXHIBIT 16–5
HIGHEST AND BEST USE ANALYSIS OF A PROPERTY AS IMPROVED

	Use		
	Offices	Stores	Demolish and Construct New Building
Capital required	$120,000	$100,000	$505,000
Effective gross income	19,000	17,100	58,000
Operating expenses	3,000	1,000	4,000
Net operating income	16,000	16,100	54,000
Rate of return on required capital	13.3%	16.1%	10.7%

analysis (of the site as though vacant) would also be necessary if the purpose of the appraisal is to value the site separately from the value of the building.

TIME VALUE OF MONEY

The importance of time-value-of-money concepts for decision making and the analysis of problems in real estate appraisal, finance, and investment cannot be overemphasized. Time-value-of-money concepts are the cornerstones of most financial analysis techniques described in this and other business texts (e.g., accounting and finance). Time-value-of-money concepts also allow analysts to relax the restrictive assumptions of constant and infinite-duration incomes contained in the fundamental equation. In many real estate appraisals, finance, and investment situation incomes are neither constant nor infinite.

We begin this section with some definitions and then proceed with discussions and applications of the *six functions of a dollar*. An understanding of these basic time-value-of-money concepts provides the necessary preparation for the study of financial analysis tools.

Definitions

Money is an economic good. Like other economic goods such as televisions, people prefer to have more money than less money and they prefer to have it *now rather than later*. If money is received later, say next week instead of today, it isn't worth as much to the party receiving the money, and an adjustment is required. The interest that is lost from not having the money to invest must be deducted. Understanding how to compensate for money received at different times is the essence of the time-value-of-money problem. The adjustment procedures should reflect the preferences of people for money received at different times in the future.

Assume that an investor has $100 to invest and desires a 10 percent return on investment. That is,

$$\text{Rate of return} = \frac{\text{Income from the investment}}{\text{Value of the investment}}$$

$$.10 = \frac{X}{\$100} \qquad\qquad (16\text{--}6)$$

$$X = \$10.$$

To get a $10 return on a $100 investment, the investor investigates three plans that can be purchased, each covering a 10-year period. These plans are:

> Plan A—The investor receives $10 at the end of the first year and no other returns during the remaining nine years.
> Plan B—The investor recieves $1 at the end of each year for ten years.
> Plan C—The investor receives $10 at the end of the tenth year of the plan and no other returns.

Which plan should the investor adopt? A more challenging question is *why* should the investor choose Plan A? The answer lies in the fact that one of two possible uses can be put to money when it is received. First, the investor can spend or consume with the money (e.g., take a friend to a movie). Second, the investor can invest the money. With Plan A, the investor has the greatest opportunity to earn interest on the money throughout the 10-year period from a reinvestment of the $10 received at the end of year one. Therefore, investors who reinvest returns prefer earlier returns to later returns because of the opportunity to earn interest. Investors who consume their money returns have the same time preferences for early returns. Would you want to wait ten years to take your friend to a movie?

The Time Line. The ability to visualize graphically the time pattern of money returns is helpful in working with time-value-of-money concepts. Panel A of Exhibit 16–6 presents a time line, which is simply an aid for visualizing the time pattern of money returns. The line is broken into periods, beginning on the left with the present period, Period Zero, and ending on the right with the terminal period, Period N. Usually annual periods are used, but sometimes monthly periods are appropriate (e.g., when analyzing mortgage payments).

All money inflows are placed on top of the line, and all outflows of money (e.g., the initial investment and deficits) go beneath the line, corresponding to the period in which they occur. The money flows from the investment decision involving the three alternative plans are shown in Panel B of Exhibit 16–6. Note that the $100 investment is located beneath

EXHIBIT 16–6
THE TIME LINE

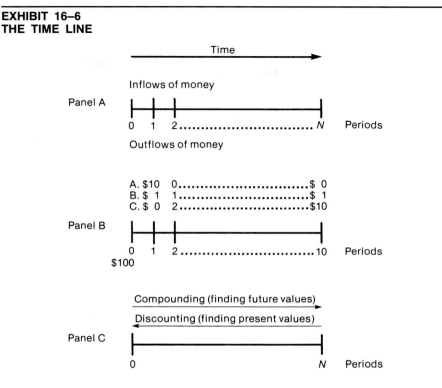

the line at Period Zero, and the three sets of inflows are located on top of the line beginning at the end of Period 1. All future inflows and outflows are assumed to occur at the end of the period in which they are received or paid, respectively.

Terminology.   The following are common terms used in applying time-value-of-money concepts.

1. *Present Value (PV).* The value of money in Period Zero. "Taking the PV of money returns" means converting future money returns to what they would be worth now.
2. *Future Value (FV).* The value of money in some period beyond period zero. "Taking the future value of money returns" means converting money returns received in the current period or some prior period to what they would be worth in the future.
3. *Reversion.* This is a one-time amount of money occurring in a given period. In Panel B of Exhibit 16–6, the $10 received under Plan A is an example of a reversion, as is the $10 received in period ten

under Plan C. Also, the $1 amounts received under Plan B could be considered as a series of reversions.

4. *Annuity.* A common amount of money received in every period (i.e., a series of equal reversions). The series of money returns under Plan B is an example of an annuity.

5. *Compounding.* Calculation of future values, as shown in Panel C of Exhibit 16–6.

6. *Discounting.* Calculation of present values, as shown in Panel C of Exhibit 16–6.

Calculators and Tables.   Various mathematical equations aid in making the critical adjustments for differences in monetary amounts in different periods. It is not necessary, however, that these equations be solved every time an adjustment is required or that the analyst even know the form of the equations. The individual may either know how to operate a financial calculator or refer to a set of tables to make time-value-of-money adjustments.[10]

Many students today own financial calculators. Through the manipulation of the financial functions of these calculators, any problem that can be solved with the equations or compound interest tables can also be solved with a calculator—and usually much faster. Unfortunately, since there are several brands of financial calculators available, it is impossible to demonstrate the keystrokes for time-value-of-money adjustments for all calculators. Because the Hewlett-Packard 12C and the Texas Instruments BA-35 (Student Business Analyst) are among the more popular varieties, and because these calculators are used in some important real estate trade-group courses (e.g., the HP-12C is used in courses offered by the American Institute of Real Estate Appraisers), the HP-12C and BA-35 keystrokes are presented in this book.

Exhibit 16–7 shows the keyboard for the HP-12C calculator. Basically, this machine has three sets of functions. To demonstrate how to access these functions, consider the key in the upper left corner of the keyboard that reads *AMORT, n, 12x*. After turning the calculator on, the user can access the set of functions on the main part of the key (i.e., the symbol in the middle where there are three symbols on a key, or the symbol on top where there are only two symbols on a key). Thus access to the symbol *n* on the subject key can be obtained directly. By pressing the *f* key (second from the left on the bottom row) we may access the top set of functions. Therefore, to access the AMORT function, press *f* then *AMORT*. Similarly, to access the bottom set of functions press the *g* key (third from the left on the bottom row). So, to access *12x*, press *g* then

---

[10]Personal computer programs are also available to perform these tasks.

12x. As we work through the keystrokes of the HP-12C to solve various time-value-of-money problems, we will gain a better feel for how this calculator operates.

EXHIBIT 16–7
HEWLETT-PACKARD 12C CALCULATOR KEYBOARD

DISPLAY

hp
12 C

AMORT	INT	NPV	RND	IRR					
n	i	PV	PMT	FV	CHS	7	8	9	÷
12x	12÷	CFo	CFj	Nj	DATE	BEG	END	MEM	

BOND — DEPRECIATION

PRICE	YTM	SL	SOYD	DB					
y^x	$1/x$	%T	△%	%	EEX	4	5	6	×
$\sqrt{x}$	e^x	LN	FRAC	INTG	ΔDYS	D.MY	M.DY	x̄w	

— CLEAR —

P/R	Σ	PRGM	FIN	REG	PREFIX				
R/S	SST	R↓	x≷y	CLx		1	2	3	−
PSE	BST	GTO	x≷y	x=0	E N T E R	x̂,r	ŷ,r	n!	

| ON | f | g | STO | RCL | | 0 | . | Σ+ | + |
| | | | | | LSTX | x̄ | s | Σ− | |

© Copyright Hewlett-Packard Company 1984. Reproduced with permission.

Exhibit 16–8 shows the keyboard for the BA-35 calculator. This machine has two sets of functions. After turning the calculator on using the *ON/C* key, the user can access the set of functions printed on the face of the keys. The set of functions printed above certain keys is accessed using the *2nd* key in the upper left corner of the calculator.

The BA-35 has two modes of operation, a financial mode and a statistical mode. To enlist the financial mode, the user presses the *2nd* key and then the *N* key. The statistical mode is engaged by pressing the *2nd* key and then the *FRQ* key. Mathematical operations (i.e., addition, percentage, etc.) can be performed in either mode, but statistical procedures can only be undertaken when the statistical mode is engaged. The same rule applies for the financial mode. As we work through the keystrokes for time-value-of-money problems with the BA-35, we will gain a better feel for how this calculator operates.

EXHIBIT 16–8
TEXAS INSTRUMENTS BA–35 (STUDENT BUSINESS ANALYST)
CALCULATOR KEYBOARD

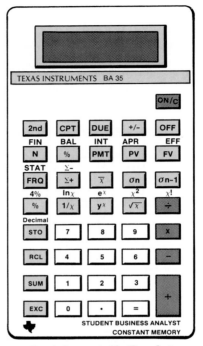

Permission granted by Texas Instruments Incorporated.

Exhibit 16–9 includes examples of the compound interest tables for real estate applications used in making time-value-of-money adjustments. A more complete set of tables is supplied in the appendix to the text. The tables are categorized according to interest rates and periods. Panel A of Exhibit 16–9 is a 10 percent annual table and Panel B is a 10 percent monthly table. The interest rate on an annual basis is shown in the upper left and right hand corners of each table (Note: the effective rate is 10 percent on the annual table and .833 percent, or 10 percent divided by 12 months, on the monthly table). Periods are shown on the extreme left and right margins of the tables. We assume all money flows occur totally at the *end* of each period (except for column one).

The tables have six columns that correspond to the six functions of a dollar needed to make time-value-of-money adjustments. In the section to follow, we will study how to use each of the six columns.

EXHIBIT 16–9
ANNUAL AND MONTHLY COMPOUND INTEREST TABLES FOR REAL ESTATE APPLICATIONS

Panel A

10.00%

ANNUAL COMPOUND INTEREST TABLES
EFFECTIVE RATE 10.00

10.00%

	1 AMOUNT OF $1 AT COMPOUND INTEREST	2 ACCUMULATION OF $1 PER PERIOD	3 SINKING FUND FACTOR	4 PRESENT VALUE REVERSION OF $1	5 PRESENT VALUE ORD. ANNUITY $1 PER PERIOD	6 INSTALMENT TO AMORTIZE $1
YEARS						
1	1.100000	1.000000	1.000000	0.909091	0.909091	1.100000
2	1.210000	2.100000	0.476190	0.826446	1.735537	0.576190
3	1.331000	3.310000	0.302115	0.751315	2.486852	0.402115
4	1.464100	4.641000	0.215471	0.683013	3.169865	0.315471
5	1.610510	6.105100	0.163797	0.620921	3.790787	0.263797
6	1.771561	7.715610	0.129607	0.564474	4.355261	0.229607
7	1.948717	9.487171	0.105405	0.513158	4.868419	0.205405
8	2.143589	11.435888	0.087444	0.466507	5.334926	0.187444
9	2.357948	13.579477	0.073641	0.424098	5.759024	0.173641
10	2.593742	15.937425	0.062745	0.385543	6.144567	0.162745
11	2.853117	18.531167	0.053963	0.350494	6.495061	0.153963
12	3.138428	21.384284	0.046763	0.318631	6.813692	0.146763
13	3.452271	24.522712	0.040779	0.289664	7.103356	0.140779
14	3.797498	27.974983	0.035746	0.263331	7.366687	0.135746
15	4.177248	31.772482	0.031474	0.239392	7.606080	0.131474
16	4.594973	35.949730	0.027817	0.217629	7.823709	0.127817
17	5.054470	40.544703	0.024664	0.197845	8.021553	0.124664
18	5.559917	45.599173	0.021930	0.179859	8.201412	0.121930
19	6.115909	51.159090	0.019547	0.163508	8.364920	0.119547
20	6.727500	57.274999	0.017460	0.148644	8.513564	0.117460
21	7.400250	64.002499	0.015624	0.135131	8.648694	0.115624
22	8.140275	71.402749	0.014005	0.122846	8.771540	0.114005
23	8.954302	79.543024	0.012572	0.111678	8.883218	0.112572
24	9.849733	88.497327	0.011300	0.101526	8.984744	0.111300
25	10.834706	98.347059	0.010168	0.092296	9.077040	0.110168
26	11.918177	109.181765	0.009159	0.083905	9.160945	0.109159
27	13.109994	121.099942	0.008258	0.076278	9.237223	0.108258
28	14.420994	134.209936	0.007451	0.069343	9.306567	0.107451
29	15.863093	148.630930	0.006728	0.063039	9.369606	0.106728
30	17.449402	164.494023	0.006079	0.057309	9.426914	0.106079
31	19.194342	181.943425	0.005496	0.052099	9.479013	0.105496
32	21.113777	201.137767	0.004972	0.047362	9.526376	0.104972
33	23.225154	222.251544	0.004499	0.043057	9.569432	0.104499
34	25.547670	245.476699	0.004074	0.039143	9.608575	0.104074
35	28.102437	271.024368	0.003690	0.035584	9.644159	0.103690
36	30.912681	299.126805	0.003343	0.032349	9.676508	0.103343
37	34.003949	330.039486	0.003030	0.029408	9.705917	0.103030
38	37.404343	364.043434	0.002747	0.026735	9.732651	0.102747
39	41.144778	401.447778	0.002491	0.024304	9.756956	0.102491
40	45.259256	442.592556	0.002259	0.022095	9.779051	0.102259
41	49.785181	487.851811	0.002050	0.020086	9.799137	0.102050
42	54.763699	537.636992	0.001860	0.018260	9.817397	0.101860
43	60.240069	592.400692	0.001688	0.016600	9.833998	0.101688
44	66.264076	652.640761	0.001532	0.015091	9.849089	0.101532
45	72.890484	718.904837	0.001391	0.013719	9.862808	0.101391
46	80.179532	791.795321	0.001263	0.012472	9.875280	0.101263
47	88.197485	871.974853	0.001147	0.011338	9.886618	0.101147
48	97.017234	960.172338	0.001041	0.010307	9.896926	0.101041
49	106.718957	1057.189572	0.000946	0.009370	9.906296	0.100946
50	117.390853	1163.908529	0.000859	0.008519	9.914814	0.100859

(continued)

EXHIBIT 16–9 *(concluded)*

Panel B

10.00%   MONTHLY COMPOUND INTEREST TABLES   10.00%
EFFECTIVE RATE 0.833

	1 AMOUNT OF $1 AT COMPOUND INTEREST	2 ACCUMULATION OF $1 PER PERIOD	3 SINKING FUND FACTOR	4 PRESENT VALUE REVERSION OF $1	5 PRESENT VALUE ORD. ANNUITY $1 PER PERIOD	6 INSTALMENT TO AMORTIZE $1	
MONTHS							
1	1.008333	1.000000	1.000000	0.991736	0.991736	1.008333	
2	1.016736	2.008333	0.497925	0.983539	1.975275	0.506259	
3	1.025209	3.025069	0.330571	0.975411	2.950686	0.338904	
4	1.033752	4.050278	0.246897	0.967350	3.918036	0.255230	
5	1.042367	5.084031	0.196694	0.959355	4.877391	0.205028	
6	1.051053	6.126398	0.163228	0.951427	5.828817	0.171561	
7	1.059812	7.177451	0.139325	0.943563	6.772381	0.147659	
8	1.068644	8.237263	0.121400	0.935765	7.708146	0.129733	
9	1.077549	9.305907	0.107459	0.928032	8.636178	0.115792	
10	1.086529	10.383456	0.096307	0.920362	9.556540	0.104640	
11	1.095583	11.469985	0.087184	0.912756	10.469296	0.095517	
12	1.104713	12.565568	0.079583	0.905212	11.374508	0.087916	
YEARS							**MONTHS**
1	1.104713	12.565568	0.079583	0.905212	11.374508	0.087916	12
2	1.220391	26.446915	0.037812	0.819410	21.670855	0.046145	24
3	1.348182	41.781821	0.023934	0.741740	30.991236	0.032267	36
4	1.489354	58.722492	0.017029	0.671432	39.428160	0.025363	48
5	1.645309	77.437072	0.012914	0.607789	47.065369	0.021247	60
6	1.817594	98.111314	0.010193	0.550178	53.978665	0.018526	72
7	2.007920	120.950418	0.008268	0.498028	60.236667	0.016601	84
8	2.218176	146.181076	0.006841	0.450821	65.901488	0.015174	96
9	2.450448	174.053713	0.005745	0.408089	71.029355	0.014079	108
10	2.707041	204.844979	0.004882	0.369407	75.671163	0.013215	120
11	2.990504	238.860493	0.004187	0.334392	79.872986	0.012520	132
12	3.303649	276.437876	0.003617	0.302696	83.676528	0.011951	144
13	3.649584	317.950102	0.003145	0.274004	87.119542	0.011478	156
14	4.031743	363.809201	0.002749	0.248032	90.236201	0.011082	168
15	4.453920	414.470346	0.002413	0.224521	93.057439	0.010746	180
16	4.920303	470.436376	0.002126	0.203240	95.611259	0.010459	192
17	5.435523	532.262780	0.001879	0.183975	97.923008	0.010212	204
18	6.004693	600.563216	0.001665	0.166536	100.015633	0.009998	216
19	6.633463	676.015601	0.001479	0.150751	101.909902	0.009813	228
20	7.328074	759.368836	0.001317	0.136642	103.624619	0.009650	240
21	8.095419	851.450244	0.001174	0.123527	105.176801	0.009508	252
22	8.943115	953.173779	0.001049	0.111818	106.581656	0.009382	264
23	9.879576	1065.549097	0.000938	0.101219	107.853730	0.009272	276
24	10.914097	1189.691580	0.000841	0.091625	109.005045	0.009174	288
25	12.056945	1326.833403	0.000754	0.082940	110.047230	0.009087	300
26	13.319465	1478.335767	0.000676	0.075078	110.990629	0.009010	312
27	14.714187	1645.702407	0.000608	0.067962	111.844605	0.008941	324
28	16.254954	1830.594523	0.000546	0.061520	112.617635	0.008880	336
29	17.957060	2034.847259	0.000491	0.055688	113.317392	0.008825	348
30	19.837399	2260.487925	0.000442	0.050410	113.950820	0.008776	360
31	21.914634	2509.756117	0.000398	0.045632	114.524207	0.008732	372
32	24.209383	2785.125947	0.000359	0.041306	115.043244	0.008692	384
33	26.744422	3089.330596	0.000324	0.037391	115.513083	0.008657	396
34	29.544912	3425.389448	0.000292	0.033847	115.938387	0.008625	408
35	32.638650	3796.638052	0.000263	0.030639	116.323377	0.008597	420
36	36.056344	4200.761236	0.000238	0.027734	116.671876	0.008571	432
37	39.831914	4659.829677	0.000215	0.025105	116.987340	0.008548	444
38	44.002836	5160.340305	0.000194	0.022726	117.272903	0.008527	456
39	48.610508	5713.260935	0.000175	0.020572	117.531398	0.008508	468
40	53.700663	6324.079581	0.000158	0.018622	117.765391	0.008491	480

Six Functions of a Dollar

The six functions of a dollar correspond to the six columns of the compound interest tables shown in Exhibit 16–9. Some of these columns are more important for real estate decision making than others. The use of Columns 3 through 6 should be mastered.

Columns 1 and 2. Columns 1 and 2 of the compound interest tables are for calculating future values resulting from the compounding of interest. *Compound interest* means the investor earns interest on the principal amount invested plus interest on any previous interest earned.

Suppose that an investor deposits $100 today in an interest-bearing account at a local bank. The account pays 10 percent compounded annually, and the investor expects to withdraw the principal plus compound interest five years from today. We use Column 1 to determine how much the investor will receive at the end of the fifth year.

Panel A of Exhibit 16–10 provides a time-line demonstration of the money flows for this problem. To solve this problem, the present value (PV) amount of $100 is converted to a future value (FV) occurring at the end of five years. We make the conversion by multiplying the PV by a Column 1 table factor (TF) at some interest rate for some period of time. Since the interest rate is 10 percent and the period is five years, the conversion equation and calculator keystrokes are

$$FV = PV \times TF \text{ (Col. 1, 10\%, 5 years)}$$
$$= 100 \times 1.610510$$
$$= \underline{\$161.05}$$

HP-12C: $\boxed{\text{ON}}$, $\boxed{\text{f}}$ $\boxed{\dfrac{\text{REG}}{\text{CLX}}}$ 100 $\boxed{\text{CHS}}$, $\boxed{\text{PV}}$, 5 $\boxed{\text{n}}$, 10 $\boxed{\text{i}}$, $\boxed{\text{FV}}$ = $\underline{161.05}$

BA-35: $\boxed{\text{ON/C}}$ $\boxed{\text{ON/C}}$ $\boxed{\text{2nd}}$ $\boxed{\text{FIN}}$, 100 $\boxed{\text{PV}}$, 5 $\boxed{\text{N}}$, 10 $\boxed{\text{\%i}}$, $\boxed{\text{CPT}}$ $\boxed{\text{FV}}$ = $\underline{161.05}$.

The table factor comes from the first column, fifth row, of the 10 percent annual table (see Exhibit 16–7, Panel A). Thus, the $100 will grow to $161.05 by the end of five years if interest is compounded annually at 10 percent.

To solve this problem using the HP-12C calculator, first the machine should be turned on and all of the registers should be cleared. This is accomplished by pressing the on key followed by the *f* and *REG/CLX* key. Next, the information about the problem should be entered. The $100 present value is entered as a negative number (i.e., the CHS key changes the sign of the number on the display) as it appears (as an outflow) in

EXHIBIT 16–10
TIME-LINE DEMONSTRATION FOR COLUMNS 1 AND 2
EXAMPLE PROBLEMS

Panel A: Column One Problem—
Future Value of Invested Amount

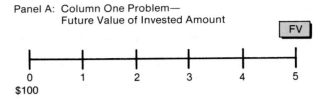

Panel B: Column Two Problem— Future Value of an Annuity

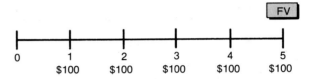

Panel A of Exhibit 16–10. After entering the number of periods and the interest rate, the answer is obtained by pressing the *FV* key.

The operation of the BA-35 for solving this problem is similar, but not identical to that of the HP-12C. The operation begins with the calculator being turned on and cleared. Then, the financial mode is engaged by pressing the *2nd* and *FIN/N* keys. The present value amount is entered as a positive number, and the number of periods and interest rate are entered as they are with the HP-12C. To obtain an answer with the BA-35, however, the *CPT* (compute) key is pressed followed by the FV key.[11]

Now assume that an investor plans to deposit $100 at the end of each year in a 10 percent annually compounded account and wants to know how much these deposits will be worth at the end of five years. As shown in Panel B of Exhibit 16–9, the deposit flows are an annuity (A). Thus, solving this problem involves finding the future value of the annuity. Column 2 table factors are used to convert an accumulation of one per period (i.e., where money flows occur at the end of a period) to future values. The conversion equation and calculator keystrokes are

$$FV\ (A)\ =\ A\ \times\ TF\ (\text{Col. 2, 10\%, 5 years})$$
$$=\ 100\ \times\ 6.105100$$
$$=\ \underline{\underline{\$610.51}}$$

---

[11]Throughout the balance of this book, the keystrokes for the two calculators will be given, but we will not attempt to describe the operations of the calculators. The reader should refer to the calculator instruction manual as needed.

HP-12C: [ON] [f] $\frac{REG}{CLX}$ 100 [CHS][PMT], 5 [n], 10 [i] [FV] = <u>610.51</u>

BA-35: [ON/C] [ON/C] [2nd] [FIN], 100[+/−] [PMT], 5 [N] 10 [%i]

[CPT] [FV] = <u>610.51</u>.

(BA-35 Note: For payments, the sign must be changed to obtain a positive result.)

This table factor comes from the second column in the 10 percent annual table in Exhibit 16–9, Panel A. Thus, the annuity deposits of $100 will grow to $610.51 in five years.

Column Three. The third column of the compound interest tables is called the *sinking fund factor*. It is used to find an annuity amount when the future value is specified. Therefore the sinking fund problem is the mirror image of the Column 2 problem (i.e., the Column 3 factor is the reciprocal of the Column 2 factor).

Suppose, that an investor desires to buy some jewelry for his daughter when she graduates from college five years from now. The investor estimates that the jewelry can be purchased for $610.51 in five years and wants to save an equal amount in each of the next five years so that, with compound interest at 10 percent annually, he will have $610.51 at the end of the fifth year. The money flows for this problem are shown on the time line in Exhibit 16–11. The conversion equation for the problem is similar to previous equations except that now the objective is to solve for the annuity amount. The conversion equation and the calculator keystrokes are

$$A = FV \times TF \text{ (Col. 3, 10\%, 5 years)}$$
$$= 610.51 \times .163797$$
$$= \underline{\$100.00}$$

HP-12C: [ON] [f] $\frac{REG}{CLX}$, 610.51 [FV],5 [n], 10 [i], [PMT] = <u>−100</u>

BA-35: [ON/C] [ON/C] [2nd] [FIN], 610.51[FV], 5 [N], 10 [%i],

[CPT] [PMT] = <u>−100</u>.

The negative result means that the investor must put aside or *pay out* $100 per year to obtain the $610.51 in five years.

The table factor is obtained from the third column, fifth row of the 10 percent annual table in Exhibit 16–9, Panel A. Since this problem is the mirror image of the column 2 problem, it should come as no surprise that the annuity investment is $100.

EXHIBIT 16–11
TIME-LINE DEMONSTRATION FOR SINKING-FUND EXAMPLE PROBLEMS

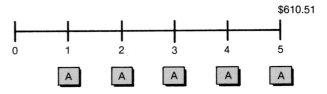

Column 3 has several important applications for real estate analysis. Suppose that the owner of an apartment complex estimates that he will require $50,000 to replace carpets and appliances in seven years. The owner wants to set aside from net income an equal amount at the end of each year for the next seven years so that, with compound interest of 10 percent, the deposits will grow to exactly $50,000. The conversion equation and calculator keystrokes to solve this problem are

$$A = FV \times TF \text{ (Col. 3, 10\%, 7 years)}$$
$$= 50,000 \times .105405$$
$$= \underline{\$5,270.25}$$

HP-12C: [ON], [f] [REG/CLX] 50000 [FV], 7 [n], 10 [i], [PMT] = $\underline{-5270.27}$

BA-35: [ON/C] [ON/C] [2nd] [FIN], 50000 [FV], 7 [N], 10 [%i], [CPT] [PMT] = $\underline{-5270.27}$.

The apartment complex owner should set aside $5,270.25 in an interest-bearing account each year to replace the appliances and carpets. Such accounts are commonly known as *reserve for replacement accounts.*

Columns 4 and 5. Columns 4 and 5 of the compound interest tables are used to convert future dollar amounts to present values. The concept underlying these columns is important for financial analysis because converting future dollar amounts to a present value is the essence of valuation under the income approach to value. Recall that capitalization involves the conversion of future money flows to capital amounts. Also, recall that capitalization using the fundamental equation requires making the assumptions that future flows are constant and are infinite in duration. Columns 4 and 5 allow for valuation via capitalization without these restrictive and unrealistic assumptions. Therein lies their real importance.

Column 4 is used to calculate the present value of a reversion. Thus, it is useful for discounting future cash flows, positive or negative, back to the present.

Assume an investor is offered an investment opportunity that provides $161.05 at the end of five years, as shown in Panel A of Exhibit 16–
12 and, the investor can earn 10 percent on other investments (i.e., he or
she will require at least a 10 percent return on any investment), how
much should the investor pay for this reversion?

This problem calls for the conversion of a future amount to a present
value. We want to find the dollar *value* of this investment opportunity.
The conversion equation and calculator keystrokes are

$$PV = FV \times TF \text{ (Col. 4, 10\%, 5 years.)}$$
$$= 161.05 \times .620721$$
$$= \underline{\$100.00}$$

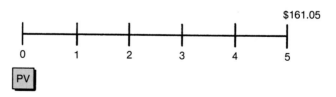

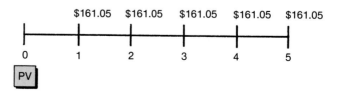

The table factor comes from the 10 percent annual compound interest
table, fourth column, fifth row. This investor should be willing to pay
$100 today for an investment that provides $161.05 at the end of the fifth
year, assuming that the investor's required rate of return is 10 percent.

EXHIBIT 16–12
TIME-LINE DEMONSTRATION FOR COLUMNS 4 AND 5
EXAMPLE PROBLEMS

Panel A: Column Four— Present Value of a Reversion

$161.05

```
 |----+----+----+----+----|
 0    1    2    3    4    5
```

PV

Panel B: Column Five— Present Value of an Annuity

$161.05 $161.05 $161.05 $161.05 $161.05

```
 |----+----+----+----+----|
 0    1    2    3    4    5
```

PV

Column 4 allows for the relaxation of both restrictive assumptions inherent in the fundamental equation. For example, in the above problem there could have been a reversion of $200 at the end of year seven as well as the $161.05 at the end of year five and we could still have found the value of the investment opportunity. The procedure we used in the conversion equation is repeated simply by multiplying the table factor from column four, row seven of the table by $200 and then adding the result to $100. Once money amounts are "brought back" to the same period, they may be added or subtracted.

Now suppose that same investor is confronted with an opportunity to receive $161.05 at the end of *every* year for five years, as shown in Exhibit 16–12 Panel B. As we noted above, this income stream is called an ordinary annuity. The investor requiring a 10 percent return needs to know how much to pay for this annuity. Two options are available for converting this annuity to a present value. One is to apply Column 4 five times, or once for each year. The less time-consuming option is to use Column 5. The conversion equation using column five and the calculator keystrokes are

$$PV\ (A) = A \times TF\ (\text{Col. 5, 10\%, 5 years})$$
$$= \$161.05 \times 3.790787$$
$$= \underline{\$610.51}$$

HP-12C: [ON] [f] $\boxed{\frac{\text{REG}}{\text{CLX}}}$, 161.05 [PMT], 5 [n], 10 [i], [PV] = $\underline{\underline{-610.51}}$

BA-35: [ON/C] [ON/C] [2nd] [FIN], 161.05 [PMT], 5 [N], 10 [%i], [CPT] [PV] = $\underline{610.51}$.

The table factor is obtained from the fifth column, the 10 percent annual table. The investor requiring a percent return would be willing to pay $610.51 for the right to receive this annuity.

Column 6.   Column 6 is another important column for real estate analysis, especially real estate appraisal and mortgage-finance applications. The factors in this column are obtained by adding Column 3 to the interest rate. Also, since Column 6 is the reciprocal of Column 5, the previous annuity problem can be solved as well with the following conversion equation:

$$PV\ (A) = \$161.05/TF\ (\text{Col. 6, 10\%, 5 years})$$
$$= \$161.05/.263797$$
$$= \underline{\$610.51}$$

(The calculator keystrokes are the same as in the previous example.)

The table factor is from the sixth column, fifth row of the 10 percent annual table.

Note that this conversion equation has the form of the fundamental equation (Equation 16–4):

$$V = \frac{I}{R} \qquad (16\text{–}7)$$

only now I is not infinite in length; it terminates at the end of the fifth year. This conversion therefore is a capitalization of income and Column 6 is a *capitalization rate*. The capitalization rate, by definition, is comprised of two components: a rate of return *on* investment or capital and a rate of return *of* capital. In symbols,

$$R = ROI + ROC \qquad (16\text{–}8)$$

where R is the capitalization rate and ROI and ROC are the rates of return on and of capital, respectively.

The notion of a rate of return *on* capital is fairly straightforward. The interest rate in the compound interest tables (e.g., 10 percent) represents the rate of return on capital in the Column 6 capitalization rate. The rate of return *of* capital, represented by Column 3 in the capitalization rate, is conceptually a little more difficult to grasp. To demonstrate, consider an application of Column 3 that we did not discuss previously. Assume that an investor decides to purchase a building worth $500,000 on a parcel of land valued at $200,000. She believes that the building will be sufficiently deteriorated and obsolete by the end of 40 years so that it will be worthless. This represents an economic loss of $500,000 to the investor over the 40 years and does not leave her with any capital to replace the building. The investor wants to avoid such a situation.

One possible approach to solving this problem is to use Column 3 to establish a reserve account for replacement of the building. Assuming the investor has a 10 percent required return *on* investment (the conversion equation and the calculator keystrokes are the same as the previous example of this type).

$$
\begin{aligned}
A &= FV \times TF \text{ (Col. 3, 10\%, 40 years)} \\
&= \$500,000 \times .002259 \\
&= \underline{\$1,259.50}
\end{aligned}
$$

Therefore, if she desires to recover the $500,000 value of the building and have $500,000 available at the end of 40 years, she should withhold $1,259.50 of cash flow from the property each year for 40 years and deposit that amount in a 10 percent account. But would a rational investor actually withhold cash flow to prevent such a loss? Probably not!

The alternative is for the investor to require a higher rate of return than 10 percent. This higher rate would include a rate of return *of* capital to compensate the investor for the loss in the value of the building. In the above example, the additional component of the capitalization rate is .002259, which is the Column 3 factor *(ROC)*. Therefore, the capitalization rate in Column 6 is .102259. It is the sum of the interest rate and the Column 3 factor. Because of the inverse relationship between values and rates, including *ROC* as part of the capitalization rate results in lower value estimates. That investors pay less for properties in which a loss in the value of the building is expected over time, as opposed to other investments (e.g., land only), is consistent with rational economic behavior.

When applied in real estate finance, the Column 6 factor is referred to as the *mortgage constant*. The amount of a mortgage loan *LA*, the mortgage payment known as *debt service DS*, and the mortgage constant R_m are related in the same way as are the value, income, and capitalization rate in the fundamental equation. In symbols,

$$LA = \frac{DS}{R_m} \tag{16--9}$$

To the mortgage lender, the *value* of the mortgage is the amount loaned, the *income* is the debt service received each period, and the *capitalization rate* is the mortgage constant.

Real estate analysts are often interested in calculating the debt service on a mortgage loan for a given set of terms. Suppose that a new home can be purchased for $100,000. A savings and loan association will lend 80 percent of the value or $80,000 at 10 percent interest over 30 years. The borrower's monthly debt service on this loan is

$$\begin{aligned} DS &= LA \times MC \\ &= LA \times TF \text{ (Col. 6, 10\%, 360 periods)} \\ &= \$80,000 \times .008776 \\ &= \underline{\$702.88} \end{aligned}$$

HP-12C: $\boxed{\text{ON}}$ $\boxed{\text{f}}$ $\boxed{\dfrac{\text{REG}}{\text{CLX}}}$, 80000 $\boxed{\text{PV}}$, 30 $\boxed{\text{g}}$, $\boxed{\dfrac{\text{n}}{\text{12x}}}$, 10 $\boxed{\text{g}}$, $\boxed{\dfrac{\text{i}}{12 \div}}$,

$\boxed{\text{PMT}}$ = -702.08

BA-35: $\boxed{\text{ON/C}}$ $\boxed{\text{ON/C}}$ $\boxed{\text{2nd}}$ $\boxed{\text{FIN}}$, 80000 $\boxed{\text{PV}}$, 30 $\boxed{\text{X}}$ 12 $\boxed{=}$ $\boxed{\text{N}}$,

10 $\boxed{\div}$ 12 $\boxed{=}$ $\boxed{\%i}$ $\boxed{\text{CPT}}$ $\boxed{\text{PMT}}$ = $\underline{702.08}$.

The table factor is from the 10 percent monthly table in Exhibit 16–9.

The mortgage constant, like the capitalization rate, comprises a rate of return *on* capital and a rate of return *of* capital. Each time a debt-service payment is made, the lender receives interest and part of the loan amount back. This is known as *amortization of principal*. The rate at which the principal is returned is a function of the number of periods of the loan and the interest rate. The rate of principal amortization is a Column 3 factor. The interest rate is stated in the loan contract. In the previous example, the interest rate *(ROC)* is 10 percent on an annual basis and .833 (10%/12%) percent (.0083333 in decimal terms) on a monthly basis. The sinking-fund factor *(ROC)* is .000442. Thus, the mortgage constant is .008776 (.008333 + .000442).

We include a set of compound interest tables for annual and monthly periods at various interest rates in the appendix to this book, and a tutorial on applying time-value-of-money concepts to real estate in the appendix at the end of this chapter.

FINANCIAL ANALYSIS

The purpose of financial analysis is to provide quantitative information to real estate decision makers. Quantitative information can take on a variety of forms reflecting results from any or all intermediate steps in the financial analysis. The emphasis here is not with the financial analysis or with intermediate results for a particular real estate problem; we develop these subjects in Chapters 17–22. Rather, we are concerned in this chapter with measures of the final results from the financial analysis (i.e., the "bottom line"). These measures fall into two related categories: present-value measures and yield measures.

Present-Value Measures

Many decisions and recommendations in real estate appraisal, finance, and investment involve determining how much certain real property rights are worth today. Thus the present value of a set of real property rights results from converting future incomes generated from controlling these rights to the value of the incomes in the present. The conversion is simply a direct application of time-value-of-money principles, specifically the use of Columns 4, 5, or 6.

Take the case that a pension fund manager wants to purchase an apartment building for the pension fund's portfolio. Two properties are available to the manager, Cedar Ridge and Oak Glen. The manager requests that his real estate acquisitions personnel estimate the *cash flows* for each property during the next five years of operation and estimate the proceeds from the sale of each complex at the end of the fifth year.[12] 16–13 shows these estimates, along with a time-line display of the estimated future cash flows.

---

[12]The process of obtaining such estimates is presented in Chapter 21.

EXHIBIT 16–13
CASH FLOWS FROM TWO ALTERNATIVE APARTMENT
INVESTMENT OPPORTUNITIES

	Cedar Ridge		Oak Glen	
Year	Estimated Cash Flow from Operations	Estimated Sale Proceeds	Estimated Cash Flow from Operations	Estimated Sale Proceeds
1986	$40,000		$30,000	
1987	45,000		40,000	
1988	45,000		50,000	
1989	50,000		50,000	
1990	55,000	$425,000	60,000	$450,000

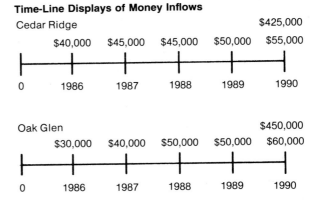

Time-Line Displays of Money Inflows

To find the present values of the benefits of the two properties, the cash flows and sale proceeds are multiplied by the appropriate Column 4 factors. The pension fund manager estimates that the required rate of return for the fund is 10 percent; therefore the 10 percent annual compound interest table is consulted. These conversions are found in Exhibit 16–14. The present value of the returns from the Cedar Ridge investment opportunity is $439,556, while a present value of the Oak Glen alternative is $448,718.

These present values are *investment values* because they incorporate the following investor-specific considerations:

1. The cash flows are estimated as they would come to this pension fund. Pension funds, for example, do not pay federal income taxes; thus, the cash flows would be different for a tax-sensitive investor.
2. Pension funds usually pay all cash (i.e., all equity financing) for their investments. Thus, the investment value does not include any debt, as it normally would for other types of investors.

EXHIBIT 16–14
PRESENT VALUE CALCULATIONS FOR TWO ALTERNATIVE APARTMENT INVESTMENT OPPORTUNITIES

	Cedar Ridge			Oak Glen		
Year	Cash Flows and Sale Proceeds	Column 4 Table Factor (10%)	Present Value	Cash Flows and Sale Proceeds	Column 4 Table Factor (10%)	Present Value
1986	$ 40,000	.909091	$ 36,364	$ 30,000	.909091	$ 27,273
1987	45,000	.826446	37,190	40,000	.826446	33,058
1988	45,000	.751315	33,809	50,000	.751315	37,566
1989	50,000	.683013	34,151	50,000	.683013	34,151
1990	480,000	.620921	298,042	510,000	.620921	316,670
			$439,556			$448,718

HP-12C: ON f REG CLX , 40000 CHS , FV , 1 n ,10 i ,

PV = 36,364; 2 n , 45000 CHS , FV , PV

= 37,190; 3 n . . . etc.

HP-12C and *BA-35:* Same procedure as for the Cedar Ridge present-value calculation.

BA-35: ON/C ON/C 2nd FIN , 40000 FV , 1 N , 10

%i CPT PV = 36364; 45000 FV , 2 N 10

%i CPT PV = 37190; 45000 FV . . . etc

3. The required rate of return of 10 percent is a specific policy requirement of this particular fund.

Apparently, Oak Glen is a better investment for the pension fund because of its higher investment value. However, one important consideration has been omitted—the asking price of each property.

Net Present Value. The net present value, *NPV*, is defined as the difference between the present value of the money inflows, PV_{in}, and the present value of the money outflows, PV_{out}. In symbols,

$$NPV = PV_{in} - PV_{out}. \qquad (16\text{--}10)$$

If, for example, the asking prices are $420,000 for Cedar Ridge and $450,000 for Oak Glen, then the present values of the money outflows for these two investments are $420,000 and $450,000, respectively. The *NPVs* of the two opportunities, therefore, are

$$NPV \text{ (Cedar Ridge)} = \$439,556 - \$420,000$$
$$= \$ 19,556$$
$$NPV \text{ (Oak Glen)} = \$448,718 - \$450,000$$
$$= \$-1,282.$$

The *NPV* simply compares the costs (PV_{out}) with the benefits (PV_{in}) of an investment opportunity. This measure is used in implementing the following very simple, but very important, decision rule: *If the NPV is zero or greater, the property should be purchased, if the investor has adequate resources; if the NPV is negative, the investment should be rejected.* As we will see later, a zero or positive *NPV* means that the investor is receiving exactly the investor's required rate of return or better.

Now that we have incorporated the asking price into the financial analysis, a different picture emerges concerning the pension fund's investment in the two apartment properties. While Oak Glen has the higher investment value, its cost is sufficiently high so as to make the *NPV* negative, $-1,282$. Cedar Ridge is the only acceptable property because of its positive *NPV*. If both properties were acceptable because of their positive *NPVs,* the property with the highest *NPV* would be chosen if only one could be purchased.

Yield Measures

Often it is awkward to express measures of returns or costs in money terms. For example, if the pension fund manager in the previous example were to inform the fund's policy board that the Cedar Ridge investment should provide an *NPV* of $19,556, it would be difficult for policy makers to evaluate how well this investment compares to other investments. If, however, the pension fund portfolio has an overall yield of 10 percent and the Cedar Ridge property yields 12 percent, policy makers are better able to make comparisons. Yield measures are an alternative way of providing quantitative information to decision makers. They are important in investment analysis for evaluating the cost of borrowing in a mortgage contract and for evaluating many other types of real estate problems. Some important applications of yield measurements in real estate financial analysis are demonstrated in the examples in the following section.

Internal Rate of Return.   The most popular yield measure is the internal rate of return *(IRR)*. While there are a number of problems associated with its use, the internal rate of return continues to be the standard, comprehensive measure of effective returns and costs in real estate and other business fields such as corporate finance. The *IRR* is also called the yield-to-maturity, effective yield, or effective cost.

Perhaps the clearest way to view the *IRR* is in its relationship to *NPV*. The *IRR* is the rate of return that equates PV_{in} to PV_{out}. Thus it is the rate of return that results in $NPV = 0$. We recall from the financial analysis of the Cedar Ridge and Oak Glen investment opportunities that the cash flows and sales proceeds were discounted at the required rate of return of 10 percent. In neither case was 10 percent the *IRR*, because the *NPV* was not zero for either. Thus to find the *IRR*, other rates must be tried in discounting these money flows to find the rate that makes *NPV* = 0.

Exhibit 16–15 presents the results of calculating the *IRR* on the Cedar Ridge investment by a trial-and-error method and by the HP-12C procedure.[13] As we determined earlier, the *NPV* using a 10 percent discount rate is $19,559. This means that to drive the *NPV* toward zero (i.e., to make the present value of the inflows equal to $420,000) a *higher* discount rate must be applied. In other words, the higher the rate the lower the present value, as shown in the fundamental equation. At 11 percent the *NPV* is still positive, but only slightly: $3,256. At 12 percent, the *NPV* has turned negative. This means that the *IRR* lies between 11 and 12 percent, because at some rate between 11 and 12 percent (probably closer to 11 percent) *NPV* is zero. Using the HP-12C keystrokes shown at the bottom of Exhibit 16–15, the *IRR* is calculated as 11.21 percent.

EXHIBIT 16–15
CALCULATION OF IRR FOR CEDAR RIDGE APARTMENT INVESTMENT OPPORTUNITY: BY TRIAL AND ERROR AND HP-12C

Year	Cash Flows and Sale Proceeds	10% Table Factor	10% PV	11% Table Factor	11% PV	12% Table Factor	12% PV
1986	$ 40,000	.909091	$ 36,364	.900901	$ 36,036	.892857	$ 35,714
1987	45,000	.826446	37,190	.811622	36,523	.797194	35,874
1988	45,000	.751315.	33,809	.731191	32,904	.711780	32,030
1989	50,000	.683013	34,151	.658731	32,937	.635518	31,776
1990	480,000	.620921	298,042	.593451	284,856	.567427	272,365
PV			$439,556		$423,256		$407,758
NPV (Asking price $420,000)			$ 19,556		$ 3,256		$(12,242)
IRR (exact) = 11.21%							

HP-12C: [ON] [f] [REG/CLX] , 420000 [CHS] [g] [PV/CFo] , 40000 [g] [PMT/CFj] , 45000 [g] [PMT/CFj] , 45000 [g] [PMT/CFj] , 50000

[g] [PMT/CFj] , 480000 [g] [PMT/CFj] , [f] , [IRR] = 11.21%

BA-35: This IRR cannot be computed with this calculator.

---

[13]The trial and error method is used because IRR cannot be easily solved mathematically. Also, the IRR cannot be computed with the BA-35 calculator when the cash flows are variable from one period to the next.

The decision rule for the *IRR* is consistent with that for the *NPV: If the IRR is equal to or greater than the investor's required rate of return, the investment should be accepted; otherwise, it should be rejected.* When the *IRR* is equal to the required rate, the investor is earning exactly the required rate of return. This also means that *NPV* is exactly zero when *IRR* equals the required rate; therefore, when $NPV = 0$ the investment is acceptable.

Lender Yield/Effective Cost of Borrowing. We find other applications of yield measures in the area of mortgage finance. When a mortgage lender makes a loan, it is an investment in expectation of a return. The investment (PV_{out}) is the loan amount, while the present value of the money inflows (PV_{in}) is the present value of the debt-service payments and any other payments to be received by the lender. The *lender's yield* is the *IRR* that equates the loan amount and the present value of the payments to be received by the lender. The mirror image of the lender's yield is the borrower's *effective cost of borrowing.* Lender yield and effective cost of borrowing are found by exactly the same calculation. The only difference is that the money flows on the time lines are reversed (i.e., inflows become outflows and outflows become inflows).

Suppose that a lender offers a borrower the following two options:

1. A $100,000 loan with terms of 12 percent, 30 years, and monthly payments; or
2. A $100,000 loan with terms of 10 percent, 30 years, and monthly payments, and the borrower must make a one-time $4,000 payment of interest when the loan is taken out.[14]

Which is the least costly option for the borrower and most profitable for the lender?

The mortgage payment for each loan is calculated as follows:

Option 1: $DS = LA \times MC$
= $100,000 \times TF$ (Col. 6, 12%, 360 periods)
= $100,000 \times .010286$
= $1,028.60.

Option 2: $DS = LA \times MC$
= $100,000 \times TF$ (Col. 6, 10%, 360 periods)
= $100,000 \times .008776$
= $877.60.

Therefore, for a $4,000 payment when the loan is taken out, the borrower can save $151 ($1,028.60 − $877.60) in payments each period. To judge whether the borrower should accept the second option, we should con-

---

[14]This $4,000 is the value of the discount points charged by the lender (see Chapter 19).

sider the lender yield and effective cost of borrowing. Exhibit 16–16 shows time-line presentations of the lender and borrower perspectives on these two options.

EXHIBIT 16–16
TIME-LINE PRESENTATION FOR LENDER YIELD/EFFECTIVE COST OF BORROWING EXAMPLE

Option One

Lender perspective

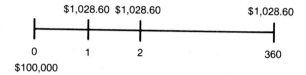

Borrower Perspective

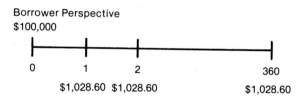

Option Two

Lender perspective

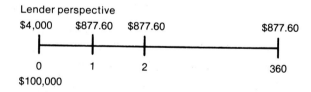

Borrower perspective

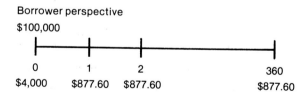

The yield measures are easy to calculate for Option 1. Both the lender yield and the effective cost of borrowing are 12 percent, since the present value of a $1,028.60 annuity over 360 periods at 12 percent is $100,000 (remember that Column 5 is the reciprocal of Column 6). For Option 2, however, the payment is based on $100,000 but the actual *net* loan amount is only $96,000 ($100,000 − $4,000 prepayment of interest). Thus, the lender yield and effective cost of borrowing must be calculated by finding the rate that equates the present value of the $877.60 annuity payment to the $96,000 loan amount.

Since the present value of the $877.60 annuity discounted at 10 percent is $100,000, a higher rate is required to drive the present value toward $96,000. A discount rate of 12 percent is a logical choice, since Option 1 yields/costs 12 percent. This calculation is:

$$PV\ (A) = A \times TF\ \text{(Col. 5, 12\%, 360 periods)}$$
$$= \$877.60 \times 97.218331$$
$$= \$85,319.$$

Because $85,319 is well below $96,000, it can be concluded that the yield/cost with this arrangement is considerably below 12 percent. Therefore, Option 2 should be chosen by the borrower. Using calculator keystrokes to solve for the interest rate,

HP-12C: [ON] [f] [REG/CLX] , 96000 [CHS] [PV] , 877.60 [PMT] , 30 [g]

[n/12x] , [i] = .874362   12 [x] = 10.49

BA-35: [ON/C] [ON/C] [2nd] [FIN] , 96000 [PV] , 877.60 [PMT] 30 [x]

12 [=] [N] [CPT] [%i] [x] 12 [=] 10.49.

We find the yield/cost to be 10.49 percent on an annual basis.
(BA-35 note: The effective yield/cost and IRR can be computed if the future money flows are constant.)

Finding the lender's yield and borrower's effective cost of borrowing involve exactly the same procedures as finding an *IRR*. In the above example, we could have narrowed the rate to between 10 and 11 percent by trial and error, just as we did in calculating the *IRR* by trial and error.

While other financial analysis tools exist, the *PV*, *NPV*, and *IRR* are probably the most important for supplying quantitative information to real estate decision makers. They are, however, summary measures reflecting the results of many intermediate steps.

OVERVIEW

Quantitative evaluations of real estate today involve heavy use of financial analysis techniques. Under the broad heading of real estate financial analysis, we discussed valuation theory, time-value-of-money concepts, and some specific analytical procedures as they apply to real estate.

Valuation theory comprises three separate approaches to value. The cost-less-depreciation approach to value, which is most often used as a secondary approach or an approach of last resort to estimating real estate values. In the sales-comparison approach to value, used mostly in residential valuations, the appraiser studies the prices of comparable properties to obtain an estimate of the value for the subject property. Finally, the income-capitalization approach is based on the notion that the value of real estate is determined by the benefits that the real estate will generate in the future. It is used in estimating the values of income-producing properties, such as office buildings and apartments.

We also explored in this chapter the basic distinctions and relationships between market value and investment value. We can view market value as the most-probable selling price in the market, given the interaction of a set of buyers and sellers. In contrast, investment value is the price that should be acceptable to a particular buyer or a particular seller.

The appraisal principle of highest and best use states that each parcel of land and each property will be put to their most profitable use. Land is always valued as if it were in its highest and best use, since buildings can be demolished and replaced. In practice, land and improved property may or may not be put to their highest and best use.

The discussion of time-value-of-money concepts began with a presentation of some basic terminology and tools. We examined each of the six functions of a dollar through the use of examples. We developed solutions to the problems in these examples both with compound interest tables and financial calculators.

We presented some of the more important financial analysis techniques in the final section of this chapter. These include present value, net present value, and internal rate of return.

The main contribution of this chapter was the demonstration of how valuation theory and time-value-of-money concepts come together in specific financial analysis techniques. These techniques have important applications in real estate appraisal, finance, and investment, as we will see in more detail in later chapters.

TEST YOURSELF

Answer the following practice problems and identify the type of calculation required to answer each.

1. How much will a $50 deposit made today be worth in 20 years if the compound rate of interest is 10%?

2. How much would you pay for the right to receive $80 at the end of 10 years if you can earn 15% compound interest?

3. How much would you pay to receive $50 in one year and $60 in the second year if you can earn 15% compound interest?

4. What amount invested each year at 10% compounded annually will grow to $10,000 at the end of five years?

5. How much would you pay for the right to receive nothing a year for the next 10 years and $300 a year for the following 10 years if you can earn 15% compound interest?

6. What is the present value of $500 received at the end of each of the next three years and $1,000 received at the end of the fourth year, assuming a discount rate of 15%?

7. What is the monthly mortgage constant for a 10 percent, 25-year loan?

8. Using the monthly mortgage constant computed in the previous problem, what are the monthly payments and annual payment on a monthly basis of a $75,000 loan?

9. If an income-producing property is priced at $5,000 and has the following income stream

Year	After-Tax Cash Flow
1	$1,000
2	− 2,000
3	3,000
4	3,000

would an investment with a required rate of return of 15 percent be wise at the current price?

10. If you owned a property that you expected would require a new $2,500 roof at the end of five years from today, how much would you set aside in equal installments from income each month to be assured of having the necessary capital, if you could reinvest your capital at 10 percent annual interest?

11. Dr. Bob Jackson owns a parcel of land that a local farmer has offered to rent for the next 10 years. The farmer has offered to pay $20,000 today or pay an annuity of $3,200 at the end of each of the next 10 years. Which payment method should Dr. Jackson accept if the appropriate rate of interest is 10 percent?

12. What is the present value of an annuity of $1,000 to be received in each of the next three years, if the appropriate rates of interest are 8 percent in the first year, 10 percent in the second, and 12 percent in the third?

13. You can buy a mortgage note for $1,000 that gives you the right to receive $438 in each of the next three years. What is the effective rate of return on this investment?

14. A friend wants to borrow $635 and agrees to return $1,000 at the end of the fourth year from today. What is the effective interest rate?

15. Calculate the *IRRs* for the following investment opportunities:

Project 1		Project 2	
Year	Cash Flow	Year	Cash Flow
0	− $10,000	0	− $10,000
1	1,000	1	1,000
2	2,000	2	12,000
3	12,000	3	1,800

ADDITIONAL READINGS

American Institute of Real Estate Appraisers. *The Appraisal of Real Estate.* Chicago: AIREA, 1983, Chaps. 1–3, 12–20.

Bieman, Harold, and Seymore Smidt. *The Capital Budgeting Decision.* New York: MacMillan, 1980, Chaps. 1–5.

Epley, Donald R., and James A. Millar. *Basic Real Estate Finance and Investment.* New York: John Wiley & Sons, 1984, Chap. 14.

Friedman, Jack P., and Nicholas Ordway. *Income Property Appraisal and Analysis.* Reston, Va: Reston Publishing, 1981, Chaps. 1–5.

Polley, Joseph H. *Applied Real Estate Math.* Reston, Va: Reston Publishing, 1980, Chaps. 17 and 20.

APPENDIX: TUTORIAL ON APPLYING TIME-VALUE-OF-MONEY CONCEPTS TO REAL ESTATE*

Column 1:   *Amount of $1 at Compound Interest*

How much will $1 be worth at some future time if invested at a given interest rate?

Example: If you deposit $1 today at 10 percent interest, it will be worth approximately $2.59 ten years from now.

$1 × 2.593742 = $2.59

HP-12C: ON f REG/CLX , 1 CHS PV , 10 n , 10 i ,

FV = 2.59

BA-35: ON/C ON/C 2nd FIN , 1 PV , 10 N ,

10 %i CPT FV = 2.59.

Example: If you purchase a parcel of land today for $25,000, and you expect it to appreciate 10 percent per year in value, how much will your land be worth ten years from now?

$25,000 × 2.593742 = $64,843.55

HP-12C: ON f REG/CLX , 25000 CHS PV , 10 n , 10 i ,

FV = 64843.55

BA-35: ON/C ON/C 2nd FIN , 25000 PV 10 N ,

10 %i , CPT FV = 64843.56.

Problem: You purchase a piece of real estate today for $15,000. You expect to hold the property for eight years and then sell it. You believe the property will increase in value approximately 15 percent per year. How much should you be able to sell the property for in eight years?

Answer: $45,885.

---

*Solutions given using the compound interest tables in the appendix at the end of the book, and using the HP-12C and BA-35 calculators.

Column 2:   *Accumulation of $1 per Period*

How much will a series of $1 payments invested each period at a given interest rate be worth at some future time?

Example: If you deposit $1 at the end of each of the next 10 years, and these deposits earn interest at 10 percent, the series of deposits will be worth approximately $15.94 at the end of the 10th year.

$1 × 15.937425 = $15.94

HP-12C: [ON] [f] [REG/CLX], 1 [CHS] [PMT], 10 [n], 10 [i],

[FV] = 15.94

BA-35:   [ON/C] [ON/C] [2nd] [FIN], 1 [+/−] [PMT], 10

[N] 10 [%i], [CPT] [FV] = 15.94.

Example: If you deposit $50 per month in a savings and loan association at 10 percent interest, how much will you have in your account at the end of the 12th year?

$50 × 276.437876 = $13,821.89

HP-12C: [ON] [f] [REG/CLX], 50 [CHS] [PMT], 12 [g] [n/12x],

10 [g] [i/12÷], [FV] = 13821.89

BA-35:   [ON/C] [ON/C] [2nd] [FIN], 50 [+/−] [PMT], 12

[x] 12 [=] [N], 10 [÷] 12 [=] [%i],

[CPT] [FV] = 13821.89.

Problem: You purchase a parcel land for $50,000. How much will you have to sell the property for in 15 years to earn a return on both your $50,000 outlay and expected annual payments of $1,000 for taxes and insurance. These funds could be invested at comparable risk to earn a 10 percent return.

Answer: $240,632.

Column 3:   *Sinking Fund Factor*

How much must be deposited each period at a given interest rate to accumulate to $1 at some future time?

Example: If you deposit $.062745 (a little over 6 cents) each year for 10 years at 10 percent interest, you will have $1 at the end of the 10th year.

.062745 × $1 = $.062745

HP-12C: ON f REG/CLX , 1 FV , 10 n , 10 i , PMT =

−.062745

BA-35: ON/C ON/C 2nd FIN , 1 FV , 10 N , 10 %i , CPT PMT = −.062745.

Example: a. If you wish to accumulate $10,000 in a bank account in eight years, and the account will draw 15 percent compounded monthly, you must deposit $54.45 each month for eight years.

$10,000 × .005445 = $54.45

HP-12C: ON f REG/CLX , 10000 FV , 8 g n/12x , 15 g i/12÷ , PMT = −54.45

BA-35: ON/C ON/C 2nd FIN , 10000 FV , 8 x 12 = , 15 ÷ 12 = , CPT PMT = −54.45.

b. *If the amounts were compounded annually,* what annual payments would be required?

$10,000 × .072850 = $728.50

HP-12C: ON f REG/CLX , 10000 FV , 8 n , 15 i , PMT

= −728.50

BA-35: ON/C ON/C 2nd FIN , 10000 FV , 8 N , 15 %i , CPT PMT = −728.50.

Problem: You purchase a building (exclusive of land) for $50,000, which is expected to depreciate to zero over the next 50 years. If amounts to cover each year's depreciation are taken from the building's income and invested at 10 percent, how much must the annual amounts allocated for depreciation be?

Answer: $42.95.

Column 4:   *Present Value Reversion*

How much is $1, due at some time in the future, worth to-day when discounted at a given interest rate?

Example: If someone owes you $1, which is due in five years, and can be discounted at 10 percent, it is worth approximately 62 cents today.

$1 \times .620921 = \$.620921$

HP-12C: $\boxed{\text{ON}}$ $\boxed{\text{f}}$ $\boxed{\dfrac{\text{REG}}{\text{CLX}}}$, 1 $\boxed{\text{FV}}$, 5 $\boxed{\text{n}}$, 10 $\boxed{\text{i}}$, $\boxed{\text{PV}}$

$= -.620921$

BA-35: $\boxed{\text{ON/C}}$ $\boxed{\text{ON/C}}$ $\boxed{\text{2nd}}$ $\boxed{\text{FIN}}$, 1 $\boxed{\text{FV}}$, 5 $\boxed{\text{N}}$, 10 $\boxed{\text{\%i}}$, $\boxed{\text{CPT}}$ $\boxed{\text{PV}}$ $= -.620921$.

Example: If your parents purchased an endowment policy of $10,000 for you and the policy will mature in 12 years, how much is it worth today, discounted at 15 percent?

$10,000 \times .186907 = \$1,869.07$

HP-12C: $\boxed{\text{ON}}$ $\boxed{\text{f}}$ $\boxed{\dfrac{\text{REG}}{\text{CLX}}}$, 10000 $\boxed{\text{FV}}$, 12 $\boxed{\text{n}}$, 15 $\boxed{\text{i}}$, $\boxed{\text{PV}}$

$= -1869.07$

BA-35: $\boxed{\text{ON/C}}$ $\boxed{\text{ON/C}}$ $\boxed{\text{2nd}}$ $\boxed{\text{FIN}}$ 10000 $\boxed{\text{FV}}$, 12 $\boxed{\text{N}}$, 15 $\boxed{\text{\%i}}$, $\boxed{\text{CPT}}$ $\boxed{\text{PV}}$ $= -1869.07$.

Problem: You own a remainder estate in a property, which means you can obtain title and possession at a future time. If the property is expected to be worth $50,000 in 15 years when your remainder interest will ripen, what is the present value of your interest, discounted at 10 percent?

Answer: $11,970.

Problem: You want to buy a house for which the owner is asking $62,500. The only problem is that the house is leased to someone else with five years remaining on the lease. However, you like the house and believe it will be a good investment. How much should you pay for the house today if you could strike a bargain with the owner for him to continue receiving all rental payments until the end of the leasehold, at which time you would obtain title and possession of the property? You believe the property will be worth the same in five years as it is worth today and that this future value should be discounted at a 10 percent annual rate.

Answer: $38,806.

Column 5: *Present Value of an Ordinary Annuity*

How much is $1 per period for a given length of time worth today when discounted at a given interest rate?

Example: If someone pays you $1 per year for 20 years, the value of the series of future payments discounted at 10 percent is approximately $8.51.

$1 × 8.513564 = $8.513564

HP-12C: | ON | | f | | REG CLX |, 1 | PMT |, 20 | n |, 10 | i |, | PV |

= −8.51

BA-35: | ON/C | | ON/C | | 2nd | | FIN |, 1 | PMT |, 20 | N |,

10 | %i |, | CPT | | PV | = −8.51.

Example: If you are at retirement age and one of your benefit options is to accept an annual annuity of $7,500 for 15 years, you could take an equivalent lump-sum settlement of $57,045.60 if the annuity is discounted at 10 percent.

$7,500 × 7.606080 = $57,045.60

HP-12C: | ON | | f | | REG CLX |, 7500 | PMT |, 15 | n |, 10 | i |, | PV |

= −57045.60

BA-35: | ON/C | | ON/C | | 2nd | | FIN |, 7500 | PMT |, 15 | N |,

10 | %i |, | CPT | | PV | = −57045.60.

Problem: a. What price should you pay for the right to receive the annual income of $10,000 for 20 years from a piece of real estate if the series of income payments is discounted at 10 percent? (Note: Assume that the property will be worth zero at the end of the 20-year period; therefore there is no value to your right to sell or con-

tinue owning the real estate beyond 20 years.)
Answer: $85,136.

b. If the property in *a* is forecast to be worth
$50,000 at the end of the 20-year period, what
should you pay for it?
Answer: $92,566.

Column 6:   *Installment to Amortize $1*

How much must be paid each period to pay back (amortize)
a debt of $1, including interest at a given rate?

Example: a. If you borrow $1 for five years and agree to
repay the debt annually with interest at a rate
of 10 percent, you must pay a little over 26
cents each year.
$1 × .263797 = $.263797

HP-12C: $\boxed{\text{ON}}$ $\boxed{\text{f}}$ $\boxed{\dfrac{\text{REG}}{\text{CLX}}}$, 1 $\boxed{\text{PV}}$, 5 $\boxed{\text{n}}$, 10 $\boxed{\text{i}}$, $\boxed{\text{PMT}}$

= − .263797

BA-35: $\boxed{\text{ON/C}}$ $\boxed{\text{ON/C}}$ $\boxed{\text{2nd}}$ $\boxed{\text{FIN}}$ 1 $\boxed{\text{PV}}$, 5 $\boxed{\text{N}}$,
10 $\boxed{\%i}$, $\boxed{\text{CPT}}$ $\boxed{\text{PMT}}$ = − .263797.

b. If you agreed to amortize the loan above in
monthly installments, your payments would
be a little over 2 cents each month.
$1 × .021247 = $.021247

HP-12C: $\boxed{\text{ON}}$ $\boxed{\text{f}}$ $\boxed{\dfrac{\text{REG}}{\text{CLX}}}$, 1 $\boxed{\text{PV}}$, 5 $\boxed{\text{g}}$ $\boxed{\dfrac{\text{n}}{12\text{x}}}$, 10 $\boxed{\text{g}}$ $\boxed{\dfrac{\text{i}}{12}}$,
$\boxed{\text{PMT}}$ = − .021247

BA-35: $\boxed{\text{ON/C}}$ $\boxed{\text{ON/C}}$ $\boxed{\text{2nd}}$ $\boxed{\text{FIN}}$, 1 $\boxed{\text{PV}}$, 5 $\boxed{\text{x}}$ 12 $\boxed{=}$
$\boxed{\text{N}}$, 10 $\boxed{÷}$ 12 $\boxed{=}$ $\boxed{\%i}$, $\boxed{\text{CPT}}$ $\boxed{\text{PMT}}$
= − .021247.

c. The annual total of your monthly payments
would be a little over 25 cents.
12 × .021247 = $.254964.

Problem: a. You want to purchase a house having a price
of $80,000. The real estate salesperson believes
you could obtain an 80% monthly-payment

loan for 29 years at a 15% interest rate. How much would your monthly payments be?

Answer: $810.75.

b. What percentage of the original loan amount is your monthly payment? (Note: This percentage is termed a "monthly loan constant.")

Answer: 1.2668 percent.

c. What percentage of the original loan amount is the annual total amount of your monthly payments? (Note: This percentage is termed an "annual constant for a monthly payment loan.")

Answer: 15.20 percent.

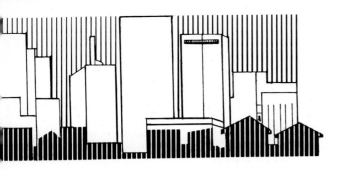

17
Appraising One- to Four-Family Residences

OUTLINE

INTRODUCTION

Appraisal is the process of estimating values of properties. Residential appraisal involves the systematic comparison of important value-determining features among similar properties: lot size, location, financing terms, and so on. Usually, the appraiser compares the features of the *subject property* whose value is being evaluated with the features of several neighboring properties that have sold recently (known as *comparable properties*). Appraisers adjust the sale price of each comparable property to reflect the ways in which the subject property is more or less valuable. Therefore, this comparison involves two steps: (1) selecting comparable properties and (2) making adjustments.

For income-producing properties, the comparisons usually are of the income streams and *capitalization rates* of the subject and comparable properties. Adjusting the net income of each comparable property yields the income that should be produced by the subject property. The capitalization rate is an annual percentage (in decimal form) obtained for each comparable property by dividing its adjusted net income by its sale price. The appraiser then divides a single, overall capitalization rate into the adjusted net income of the subject property to obtain an estimate of value.

Another general comparison method for all types of properties involves the present cost of reproducing the subject property and the amount of depreciation (value loss) that the property has experienced, as judged by the depreciation of comparable properties. The total dollar depreciation is subtracted from the cost of reproducing the building today to obtain an estimate of the building's value. The land value, estimated separately, is added to the building value to obtain the entire property value.

Why Is Real Estate Appraisal Important?

Appraisal is a necessary and important process for all real estate because property values are not readily apparent. The process of evaluating real estate may be contrasted with that for the prices of stocks traded on the New York Stock Exchange. In that market many transactions occur each minute and prices are known almost instantaneously. Each share of a company's stock is like every other share. Unlike stocks, no two properties are exactly alike, and transactions of similar properties may be infrequent, resulting in a scarcity of price data. Appraisers often must make detailed and systematic adjustments among several less-similar properties to estimate values.

Estimates of value are important because they determine the prices that owners ask for their properties and that potential buyers are willing to pay. Most people are unwilling to sell a possession, especially their most valuable possession—real estate—for less than it is worth; most buyers do not want to pay *more* than it is worth. Since real estate values are not readily known, appraisers are employed to estimate values through specialized methods and techniques (see Frame 17–1).

Frame 17–1

Appraisal: A Science or an Art?

Students of appraisal sometimes debate whether it is more science or art. On the side of science we may note that appraisal is based on economics, which is regarded as a social science. There are lengthy formulas, and algebra and statistics are often involved. Also, appraisal uses a problem solving process (called the appraisal process) very much akin to the scientific method.

On the side of art, we realize that a great amount of judgment is required by appraisers to determine such matters as which properties are comparable, how much weight should be accorded each approach, and what capitalization method should be used. Because of the diversity of property types and appraisal problems, experience is very important to the development of a good appraiser. The amount of generalization is less than in many scientific disciplines.

Our conclusion is that appraisal is more of an applied social science than art. Judgment is not limited to artists; even physical scientists must use generous amounts of it. While the data appraisers must use are not as plentiful or reliable as would often be desired, substantial amounts of data are collected and analyzed. The tools of science are applicable—including the scientific method, mathematics, and statistics. In contrast, artists conceive new ideas, forms, and combinations. Their minds create, rather than analyze. Appraisers, as scientists, seek to detect and explain; artists seek more to feel and touch.

Estimating the values of one- to four-family residential properties is especially important for at least three reasons. First, there are many such properties—more than 75 million. The sheer number means that many appraisals are performed to help solve problems of value.

Second, appraisals facilitate transactions by establishing a basis for bidding and asking prices. Sellers often do not know the worth of their properties and therefore seek a professional appraisal. Similarly, buyers often use an appraiser's estimate of value to help them make a bid. More important, since most buyers borrow the funds to purchase properties, lenders require appraisals to help determine maximum loan amounts. Regulatory authorities require that loan amounts be related to the professionally estimated value of properties, so many residential appraisals are done for mortgage lenders.

Third, appraisals of small residential properties help establish the basis for both property and federal income taxes, help resolve legal disputes, and help personal financial planning. Many different problems arise in which questions of value must be answered. The worth of a property for tax purposes is a common issue requiring appraisals. Settlements of estates, divisions of property in divorces, and other disputes often require appraisals. Finally, family and individual financial-planning needs often require knowledge of the approximate value of properties.

Qualifications of Professional Appraisers

While some states impose no formal requirements of education or experience for professional appraisers, a number require appraisers to be licensed as salesmen or brokers.[1] Even this requirement, however, offers little assurance that appraisers have the requisite level of education, training, and experience to conduct truly professional appraisals. Thus appraisers have formed a number of professional appraisal organizations to certify the competence of their members. The organizations award professional designations to those members who meet prescribed educational and experience criteria. The most widely known organizations and the professional designations they award are shown in Frame 17–2.

Consumers of appraisal services should employ only appraisers having one or more professional designations, unless they have personal knowledge of the professional competence of other undesignated appraisers and feel qualified to judge their abilities. Real estate brokers and salespersons are usually neither qualified nor competent to make professional appraisals.

---

[1]We discussed licensing and certification of appraisers in Chapter 13.

Frame 17–2

Appraisal Organizations and Designations

Following is a list of the best-known appraisal organizations and the professional designations they award.

1. American Institute of Real Estate Appraisers
   a. MAI (Member, Appraisal Institute)
      Indicates competence to appraise all real estate.
   b. RM (Residential Member)
      Indicates competence to appraise one- to four-family residential properties. Certified competence does not cover other types of property.
2. Society of Real Estate Appraisers
   a. SREA (Senior Real Estate Analyst)
      Indicates competence to appraise and analyze all real estate.
   b. SRPA (Senior Real Property Appraiser)
      Indicates competence to appraise all real estate.
   c. SRA (Senior Residential Appraiser)
      Indicates competence to appraise one- to four-family residential properties. As with the RM, certified competence does not extend to other types of properties.
3. Appraisal Institute of Canada
   AACI (Accredited Appraiser Canadian Institute)
   Indicates competence to appraise all real estate.
4. American Society of Appraisers
   ASA (Member, ASA)
   Indicates competence to appraise property in the field of the member's specialty.
5. National Association of Independent Fee Appraisers
   a. IFA (Member, IFA)
   b. IFAS (Senior Member, IFA)
   c. IFAC (Appraiser-Counselor Member)
      All indicate general competence to appraise property.
6. International Association of Assessing Officers
   a. CPE (Certified Personalty Evaluator)
      Indicates competence to assess personal property.
   b. AAE (Accredited Assessment Evaluator)
   c. CAE (Certified Assessment Evaluator)
      Indicate competence to assess property.
7. National Association of Review Appraisers
   CRA (Certified Review Appraiser)
   Indicates experience in reviewing appraisals.
8. American Society of Farm Managers and Rural Appraisers
   a. AFM (Accredited Farm Manager)
      Indicates competence to manage farms.
   b. ARA (Accredited Rural Appraiser)
      Indicates competence to appraise rural properties.

Appraisal Procedures

Appraisers usually divide the systematic comparison process in appraisal into three general methods, or approaches: the *sales-comparison approach*, the *cost-less-depreciation approach*, and the *income-capitalization approach*. For one- to four-family residential properties, they use a variant of the income-capitalization approach, known as *gross-rent-multiplier analysis*. Some appraisers occasionally use more sophisticated statistical techniques such as simple and multiple regression analysis, discriminant analysis, and analysis of variance. However, such techniques fall within the three general approaches and are not usually regarded as separate. The three approaches follow the general type of comparative analysis outlined in the introduction section on the nature of appraisal. In this chapter we discuss in depth these approaches applied to small residential properties. We will consider the application of these approaches to income-producing and other types of property in the Chapter 18.

SALES-COMPARISON APPROACH

The sales-comparison approach to value estimation involves the direct comparison of a subject property's value-determining features with those of several comparable properties that sold recently. Ideally, no adjustments would be needed if the comparable properties were exactly like the subject property and the transactional details were the same. As we noted in Chapters 10 and 16, however, the real estate market is imperfect. No two properties are exactly alike, and the motivational and financing aspects of transactions vary greatly. Therefore, appraisers must make adjustments by additions and subtractions to and from the sales prices of comparable properties. All the adjustments result in a final adjusted sale price for each comparable property. Then the appraiser reconciles the final adjusted prices into an indicated value from the sales-comparison approach. Exhibit 17–1 shows these steps.

EXHIBIT 17–1
STEPS IN THE SALES COMPARISON APPROACH

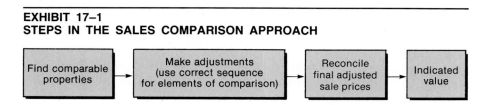

Adjustments

Appraisers must consider five types of adjustments in sales comparison analysis. If the subject property is better than the comparable property with respect to any of these items, the comparable property's sale price would be adjusted upward, and vice versa if the subject property is inferior to the comparable property. The five types of adjustments are:

1. Transactional characteristics
   a. Conditions of sale
   b. Financing terms
   c. Market conditions
2. Property characteristics
   a. Location
   b. Physical characteristics

Note that we label the first three "transactional characteristics." They concern the nature and terms of the transactions; they recognize that matters other than the physical nature and location of a property help determine value. The last two concern the differences between the properties; they recognize that the locational and physical differences between properties help determine differences in values. We will explain in greater depth each of these types of adjustments.

Conditions of Sale. The transaction price of comparable properties may not reflect relative equality in bargaining power between buyers and sellers. Or personal relationships may cause a transaction price to be lower than market value, such as when a parent "sells" real estate to a son or daughter. Appraisers must be aware of these and check each comparable-property transaction to ensure that it truly was an arm's-length bargain between buyers and sellers who have relatively equal bargaining power. If any nonarm's-length bargaining occurred in the transaction, the appraiser should reject the property as a comparable, because market-derived adjustments for such conditions are impossible to obtain. For example, how can an appraiser know how much to adjust a comparable transaction for a sale from a father to his daughter, or from a girl friend to her boy friend?

Financing Terms. Occasionally, properties are sold with nonmarket financing. For example, an owner may grant a below-market interest rate to a buyer or a buyer may assume an existing loan at a below market interest rate. The latter is becoming rare, however, since most lenders have due-on-sale clauses in their mortgage loans. Nevertheless, appraisers must investigate these possibilities and adjust the transaction prices of comparable properties accordingly.

Favorable financing terms can cause buyers to pay a somewhat higher price to get lower mortgage payments. The price between a property having normal market financing and the same property having more favorable financing can be determined by comparing recent sales of similar properties, some having favorable financing and others not having favorable financing. Also, formulas have been devised for estimating the amount of the financing adjustment.[2] In general, however, buyers tend to pay about 10 times the *difference* in monthly mortgage payments more for favorable financing than they do for normal market financing. For example, if the monthly payments on a new mortgage loan are $950, but a buyer can asume a loan having payments of $750, he or she would probably be willing to pay approximately $10 \times 200 = \$2,000$ more for the property. Thus, an appraiser should subtract $2,000 from the actual sale price that buyers would pay with normal market financing.

Market Conditions.   The transaction prices of comparable properties are *historic:* They may have occurred yesterday, last month, or several months ago. The less recent they are, the greater the likelihood that the market has changed; the same comparable property probably would not sell at appraisal time for the same price as a month or several months before. Changes in market conditions result from inflation or deflation, increased or decreased demand, and increased or decreased supply.

Appraisers must be sensitive to changes in market conditions. They can estimate the amount of such changes by tracking sales of properties over time. For example, consider three properties in the same neighborhood that all sold today and at some previous time during the past 18 months. Exhibit 17–2 shows the monthly average and compound rates of increase in the market prices of these properties.

EXHIBIT 17–2
SEQUENTIAL ANALYSIS OF MARKET TRANSACTIONS

Property	Date of Previous Sale	Price at Previous Sale	Price Today	Average Monthly Rate of Increase	Compound Monthly Rate of Increase
A	6 mos. ago	$82,500	$85,000	.0051 ($416.67)	.0050 ($412.00)
B	12 mos. ago	$91,000	$97,500	.0060 ($541.67)	.0058 ($527.80)
C	18 mos. ago	$88,600	$95,000	.0040 ($355.56)	.0039 ($343.97)
			$\bar{x}$ (mean) =	.0050	.0049

[2]For example, see Halbert C. Smith and John B. Corgel, "Adjusting for Nonmarket Financing: A Quick and Easy Method." *Appraisal Journal* 52, no. 1 (January 1984), pp. 75–83.

The mean of the average monthly rate of price increase is about .0050 (.50 percent per month) and the mean of the compound monthly rate of increase is about .0049 (.49 percent per month). Appraisers could then use these rates to adjust the normal sale prices of comparable properties for the number of months since they were sold. The result is the *market-adjusted normal sale price*.

Location.   Location involves the time-distance relationships between a property and all other potential origins and destinations of people coming to and going from the property. We term these relationships *linkages*. Exhibit 17–3 shows linkages for a typical residential property.

EXHIBIT 17–3
LINKAGES FOR A TYPICAL RESIDENTIAL PROPERTY

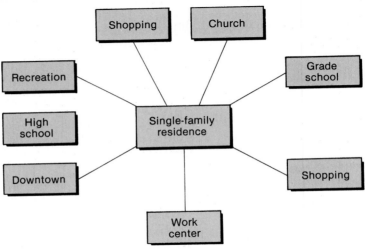

A location adjustment is appropriate only when a comparable property has a set of linkages significantly different from those of the subject property, such as when a comparable is in a different neighborhood. Thus, an appraiser derives location adjustments by comparing the prices of similar properties, some of which are in the subject property's neighborhood and some in the comparable property's neighborhood. The general method of comparison is known as *paired-sales analysis*, as seen in Exhibit 17–4. This exhibit shows the prices of three pairs of very similar properties. One property in each pair is in the subject property's neighborhood (Convenient Acres), while the other property is in the comparable property's neighborhood (Far-Out Hills).

EXHIBIT 17–4
PAIRED SALES ANALYSIS FOR LOCATION ADJUSTMENT

Pair	Property	Neighborhood	Recent Sale Price	Difference	Difference as a Percentage of B
1st	A	Convenient Acres	85,000		
	B	Far-Out Hills	83,000	$2,000	2.41
2nd	A	Convenient Acres	94,300		
	B	Far-Out Hills	90,000	$4,300	4.78
3rd	A	Convenient Acres	87,750		
	B	Far-Out Hills	84,800	$2,950	3.48
			$\bar{x}$ (mean) =		3.56

As calculated in Exhibit 17–4, houses in Convenient Acres sell for an average of 3.56 percent more than similar houses in Far-Out Hills. Thus, a Far-Out Hills comparable property's market-adjusted normal sale price should be increased by about 3.56 percent when appraising a subject property in Convenient Acres. In other words, home buyers appear to be willing to pay about 3.5 percent more for the better location of Convenient Acres compared with Far-Out Hills.

This analysis, of course, assumes that the paired properties are highly similar or that adjustments have been made to their sale prices to reflect any dissimilar property characteristics. It also assumes that the neighborhoods are similar in other respects (such as upkeep and attractiveness) or that sale prices have been adjusted to reflect dissimilar neighborhood characteristics.

Physical Characteristics. Adjustments for physical characteristics cover all the ways that a comparable property differs physically from the subject property. These include such differences as lot size, size of the structure, floor plan, architectural style, condition, type of construction, quality of construction, materials, and the presence or absence of various features such as garage, fireplace, built-in appliances, bookshelves, second or third bathroom, carpet, swimming pool, or patio. Again, appraisers use the paired-sales technique to estimate the value difference these considerations cause. Appraisers compare the sale prices of pairs of recently sold properties that are highly similar except for a particular physical characteristic. The difference in sale prices for each pair is then a good indication of the value of the feature.

As an example of paired sales analysis to determine the value a swimming pool adds to properties, note the differences in sale prices of two pairs of properties in Exhibit 17–5. Properties A have a swimming pool, while Properties B do not.

EXHIBIT 17–5
PAIRED-SALES ANALYSIS FOR PHYSICAL
CHARACTERISTIC ADJUSTMENT

Pair	Property	Recent Sale Price	Difference	Differences as a Percentage of Homes W/O
1st	A (with)	$115,000		
	B (w/o)	$110,000	$5,000	4.5
2nd	A (with)	$137,000		
	B (w/o)	$130,000	$7,500	5.8
				5.2
		$\bar{x} =$		

Thus in this market swimming pools appear to add about 5.2 percent in value to homes. The market-adjusted normal sale price of comparable properties not having a pool should be increased by this percentage if a subject property has a pool.

Subject Property Compared to Each Comparable Property

For percentage adjustments, the subject property is always stated as superior or inferior to a comparable property. For example, if we state that the subject property's location is 10 percent superior to that of the comparable property, and the comparable property sold for $100,000, the location adjustment is $10,000 and is added to the comparable property's price. It would be improper to state that the comparable property is inferior to the subject property by some percentage, since we do not know the value of the subject property.

Types of Adjustments

Appraisers use two types of adjustments—dollars or percentages. If the dollar difference is known, the appraiser simply adds it to or subtracts it from the comparable property's price. Some adjustments lend themselves to, and are usually made in, dollars. They are financing and physical characteristics. Appraisers usually analyze and state market conditions and location in terms of percentages. For example, they say that one location is about 10 percent better than another or that market conditions have resulted in value increases of about 8 percent in the past year.

Sequence of Adjustments

Appraisers should make adjustments in a definite sequence, as Exhibit 17–6 shows. Note that the appraiser calculates prices after Adjustments 2, 3, and 5. He applies Adjustments 1 and 2 to the transaction price,

---

EXHIBIT 17–6
SEQUENCE OF ADJUSTMENTS

1. Conditions of sale
2. Financing terms
    Normal sale price
3. Market conditions
    Market-adjusted normal sale price
4. Location
5. Physical characteristics
    Final adjusted sale price

Adjustment 3 to the normal sale price, and adjustments 4 and 5 to the market-adjusted normal sale price. Although the sequence makes no difference for dollar adjustments, it does make a difference for percentage adjustments. The percentage is multiplied by the next previous price in the sequence, rather than the actual transaction price. The purpose of the sequence is to adjust the comparable property's price, first to reflect the price it would have sold for under normal market terms when it actually sold and then to adjust that price for any changes in market conditions since the actual transaction. When an appraiser obtains a price that reflects normal terms in today's market, he or she can apply adjustments for differences in property characteristics. He or she should *not* apply them, however, to a transaction price that is not applicable to the current market.

Reconciliation

The final step in obtaining an *indicated value* of the subject property from the sales-comparison approach is to reconcile the adjusted sale prices. The appraiser considers which, if any, of the comparable properties' adjusted sale prices are better indications of the subject property's value than the others. More complete data, fewer and smaller adjustments, and more recent transactions would probably cause him to weight the adjusted sale prices for some comparables more than others. On the other hand, if the data are about equally complete, the adjustments are about the same, and the transactions are of about equal vintage, the appraiser probably would weight all adjusted sale prices equally. In this case, the indicated value would be the mean, or average, or the adjusted sale prices.

COST-LESS-DEPRECIATION APPROACH

The second method for estimating the values of one- to four-family residences is the cost-less-depreciation approach. The basic ideas of this approach are that the value of a new building tends to equal the cost of reproducing it today, and that the appraiser can identify and measure any reductions in this value. Reductions in value that occurred in the past are termed *accrued depreciation*. After the appraiser has estimated the building's value by subtracting all elements of accrued depreciation from the building's cost, the site value is estimated separately and added to the building value. This relationship is shown by the following expression:

$$V_m = (\text{Reproduction Cost} - \text{Accrued Depreciation}) + \text{Value of the Site}$$

Exhibit 17–7 shows the steps in the cost-less-depreciation approach. We now consider each element of the cost-less-depreciation approach in greater depth.

EXHIBIT 17–7
STEPS IN THE COST-LESS-DEPRECIATION APPROACH

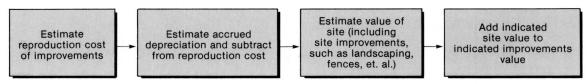

Cost

The estimation of a building's cost can be a long and detailed task. If an appraiser attempts to add up the individual costs of all materials, parts, components, assemblies, labor, and overhead of even a small house, he could easily take several hours or days.[3] Appraisers, however, do not need such a detailed estimate and therefore often rely on alternative methods of obtaining the cost estimates, even though this may cause a loss of some accuracy. Thus appraisers tend to rely on builders' cost figures, to maintain comparative cost data on a square-foot or cubic-foot basis for various types of houses, and to use cost-estimating services. The appraisers' resulting cost figures would not be useful for contractors, but are accurate enough for appraisals.

For appraisal purposes there are two possible types of cost—*reproduction cost* and *replacement cost*. The reproduction cost of a building is the cost to construct the building today, replicating it in exact detail. This includes any outdated functional aspects of the building such as poor room arrangement, better-than-necessary fixtures, or inadequate equipment. It also includes the cost of any outmoded materials such as surface wiring, steel window frames, and steel plumbing.

---

[3]Such a detailed cost estimation procedure is called the *quantity survey method.*

In contrast, replacement cost is the money required to construct a building of *equal utility*.[4] This includes the use of modern construction techniques, materials, and design, and represents the cost of a building for which some or all outdated aspects are eliminated.

Appraisers principally use reproduction cost, since it represents the building as it actually exists except for accrued depreciation. When using replacement cost, appraisers must keep track of any functional obsolescence that is removed from the cost figure so that it is not wrongly subtracted as accrued depreciation. Also, appraisers may be criticized because replacement cost represents only a hypothetical building, not the actual appraised building. Our analysis and discussion will assume that the cost-less-depreciation approach uses reproduction cost.

Accrued Depreciation

Buildings can lose value for three reasons: The physical materials and components wear out; the building becomes functionally less usable and desirable compared with newer buildings; and external forces reduce the building's usefulness within its surroundings. Thus, the three major elements of accrued depreciation are *physical deterioration, functional obsolescence,* and *external obsolescence.* Exhibit 17–8 shows how these elements are further divided.

EXHIBIT 17–8
ELEMENTS AND EXAMPLES OF ACCRUED DEPRECIATION

Elements of Accrued Depreciation	Typical Examples
1. Physical deterioration	
a. Short-lived	
(1) Curable	Completely worn-out items such as paint, roofing, floor cover, appliances, HVAC, and interior decoration.
(2) Incurable	Partially worn-out items such as paint, roofing, floor cover, appliances, HVAC, and interior decoration.
b. Long-lived (always incurable)	The building itself—foundation, walls, roof structure, windows, doors, floors, stairs.
2. Functional obsolescence	
a. Curable	Absence of a bathroom, outdated fixtures, too few electrical outlets, lack of bookcases, too-high ceilings, lack of insulation.
b. Incurable	Architectural design, floor plan, electrical system, plumbing.
3. External obsolescence (always incurable)	Introduction of a nonconforming use in neighborhood; transition from higher to lower uses; odors; unpleasant sights.

Note: HVAC stands for heating, ventilating, and air conditioning.

---

[4]The term *utility* means satisfaction. Therefore, a building of equal utility is a building that provides satisfaction to people who use it equal to that another building would provide.

Physical Deterioration. This is divided into short-lived and long-lived components. Short-lived components last a shorter time than the building itself lasts and must be replaced one or more times during a building's economic life. Long-lived components consist of the main parts of the building itself—foundation, walls, roof, etc. The short-lived components are further divided into curable and incurable elements. Curable elements are those whose cost of replacement will be no greater than the value added by replacing them. For example, if a house needs painting, the value of that house usually will be increased by at least the cost of the paint job.

Incurable elements are those whose cost exceeds the value added when they are are fixed or replaced. For example, if a house does not need painting but is painted anyway, the value increase will be less than the cost of the paint job. Similarly, if the roofing or furnace are only partially worn out but are replaced, the value increase will be less than their cost. Nevertheless, the building is worth less than it would be if the incurable elements were new. Thus the appraiser must estimate the value loss due to partial wearing out of the short-lived components and include it in accrued depreciation.

Similarly, the long-lived components of a building gradually wear out. The appraiser must estimate value loss due to the partial deterioration of the structural components and include it in accrued depreciation. He does this by multiplying the ratio of effective age of the building to its total economic life by the building's reproduction cost minus short-lived items, thus:

$$AD = \frac{\text{Effective age}}{\text{Economic life}} \times (\text{RC} - \text{Short-lived items})$$

Functional Obsolescence. We must compare the usefulness and desirability of an existing building with new buildings, which compete for potential buyers. Newer building materials, construction techniques, and designs, coupled with changing consumer tastes and preferences, generally make older buildings less desirable and thus less valuable than newer buildings. Also, some buildings contain materials and features more expensive than buyers are willing to pay for, and the appraiser must count the excess costs contained in such buildings' reproduction costs as functional obsolescence. Examples are gold-plated faucets and swimming pools on small residential properties.

Note that functional obsolescence is a completely different type of accrued depreciation from physical deterioration. An old-fashioned bathtub, for example, may be in excellent physical condition but probably would not contribute as much value to a house as a less costly, more modern tub.

As with physical deterioration, appraisers also divide functional obsolescence into curable and incurable elements. As the examples in Exhibit 17–8 suggest, items causing curable functional obsolescence are generally those that can be corrected without major modification of the structure. For example, a half bath may be added in an existing clothes closet or similar available space; old fixtures or appliances can be replaced; electrical outlets can be added; ceilings can be lowered; or insulation can be added without major alteration of the structure.

Appraisers calculate the amount of curable functional obsolescence by two procedures.

1. $AD = \dfrac{\text{Cost of installing item}}{\text{in existing structure}} - \dfrac{\text{Cost of installing item}}{\text{if building were new}}$

2. $AD = \text{Cost of replacing item} - \text{Remaining value of existing item}$

Appraisers use the first procedure to estimate the functional obsolescence due to the absence of items they consider functionally appropriate or necessary in a structure being built today (e.g., a second bathroom). Note that the depreciation figure obtained is the *excess* cost of retrofitting the items in the existing building, as compared with the cost of their installation in a building being built today. The excess is the cost of tearing out and modifying the existing structure to accommodate the item, which would not be incurred in a new structure.

Appraisers use the second procedure to estimate the functional obsolescence resulting from items that are partially obsolete but still have some value. For example, if the bath fixtures are outdated but still usable, the functional obsolescence is the difference between the cost of replacing them and the value remaining in the old fixtures.

Incurable functional obsolescence is related to the structural characteristics of the building—floor plan, architectural design, or major system(s)—that would require major remodeling or rehabilitation of the structure. Appraisers estimate the amount of such functional obsolescence by capitalizing the rent loss or increased expense resulting from the unfavorable condition.

$$AD = \dfrac{\text{Rent loss or}}{\text{increased expense}} \times \text{Gross rent multiplier}^5$$

For example, a poor floor plan might result in $10 per month less rent than a more desirable one, or an inefficient heating system in $10 per month higher heating costs. If the appropriate gross rent multiplier is 100, the accrued depreciation would be $1,000 (100 × $10).

External Obsolescence. This is a loss of a *building's* value through influences outside of the property. It is always incurable, since the building

---

[5]We discuss GRMs in the next section.

would have to be moved to cure it. Noxious odors, unpleasant sights, and increased traffic due to more intensive uses (such as commercial or industrial) introduced into a residential neighborhood are examples of this type of accrued depreciation. Since the value of only the building is being estimated at this point, appraisers must allocate the total amount of external obsolescence between building and site on the basis of the approximate ratio of building value to total property value. The formula for external obsolescence thus is

$$AD = \text{Rent loss} \times \text{GRM} \times \frac{\text{Building value}}{\text{Property value}}$$

Consider a single-family house on a major street that is becoming increasingly commercial. The property next door has just been rezoned for a small shopping center, increasing the likelihood of more traffic, noise, trash, and odors. The owners find that they must reduce the rent by $50 per month to attract tenants. The appropriate GRM for the area is 100, and houses typically represent about 80 percent of total property value. Thus the amount of accrued depreciation to the building caused by external obsolescence would be

$$AD = \$50 \times 100 \times .80$$
$$= \$4,000.$$

INCOME CAPITALIZATION APPROACH

Appraisers sometimes use a variant of the income-capitalization approach, known as gross-rent-multiplier (GRM) analysis, to appraise small residential properties. While income capitalization uses *net* operating income, GRM analysis uses *gross* income. A crucial assumption, therefore, is that expenses for comparable small, residential properties are approximately equal.

Another key assumption of GRM analysis is that the subject property is either a rental property or *could be* a rental property; that is, it is similar to other properties that are rented. Appraisers can thus estimate gross rental rates from other similar properties in the market. They may make adjustments to account for differences between the comparable properties and the subject property. For example, if a comparable property's gross rent includes utilities, but the subject property's does not, the expected monthly utility bill would be subtracted from the comparable's rent to obtain an adjusted gross rent. After obtaining adjusted gross rents from several comparable properties, the appraiser can impute a reconciled indicated gross rent to the subject property.

The appraiser obtains a gross rent multiplier from several comparable properties that have sold recently. The formula for a GRM is

$$GRM = \frac{Sale\ Price}{Monthly\ Gross\ Rent}$$

He makes no adjustments either to the sale price or to the monthly gross rent, since any adjustment would have to be made proportionately to both numerator and denominator in the equation. For example, a higher gross rent due to an extra bedroom would also result in a proportionately higher sale price. After obtaining GRMs for the comparables, the appraiser derives a single, reconciled GRM and multiplies it by the indicated rent for the subject property, thus:

$$V_m = GRM \times Indicated\ monthly\ rent$$

Exhibit 17–9 shows the steps in GRM analysis; and Exhibit 17–10 shows an example of the use of GRM analysis in appraising a small rental house.

EXHIBIT 17–9
STEPS IN GROSS-RENT-MULTIPLIER ANALYSIS

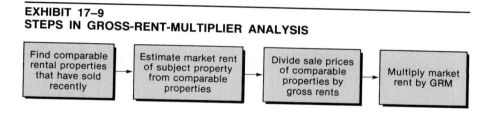

EXHIBIT 17–10
APPRAISAL BY GRM ANALYSIS

An appraiser is appraising a small rental house. She finds five comparable rentals having the monthly rents and recent sales prices below.

Comparable No.	Price	Rent	GRM
1	$49,550	$450	110.11
2	44,820	415	108.00
3	42,500	380	111.84
4	42,950	385	111.56
5	44,000	400	110.00

She concludes from this analysis that the appropriate GRM should be 110.0. The appraiser also finds five rental properties quite similar to the subject property, which she believes provide a good basis for estimating market rent. There are some differences between the comparable properties and the subject property. Currently it is renting for $350 per month, but she believes this rental may not reflect the current market. She identifies the elements of comparison and assigns the following value differences:

(continued)

EXHIBIT 17–10 *(concluded)*

Item	Comparables					Subject
	1	**2**	**3**	**4**	**5**	
Rent	$405	$425	$440	$465	$470	?
Bathrooms	1	2 (−$20)	2 (−$20)	2 (−$20)	1	1
Garage size	Carport (+$10)	One-car	One-car	Two-car (−$15)	One-car	One-car
Basement	Unfinished	Unfinished	Unfinished	Finished (−$15)	Unfinished	Unfinished
Utilities payment	Tenant	Tenant	Tenant	Tenant	Owner (−$55)	Tenant
Adjusted rent	$415	$405	$420	$415	$415	

The appraiser concludes that the indicated market rent is $415.00 per month. She then multiplies this figure by the indicated gross rent multiplier of 110.0.

$$\$415.00 \times 110.0 = \$45,650, \text{ or } \underline{\$45,700} \text{ in round numbers.}$$

Her indicated house value from gross-rent-multiplier analysis is thus $45,700.

APPLICABILITY OF THE THREE APPROACHES

The sales-comparison approach is applicable to almost all one- to four-family residential properties. There are usually a number of recent sales of comparable properties, and appraisers usually can make reasonable adjustments to the sale prices to reflect the subject property. The sales-comparison approach often is the only approach used for single-family homes. It has the additional advantage of being easily understood by buyers and sellers of such properties. They can follow the procedures and check the data to determine whether they agree with the appraiser's value estimate.

The cost-less-depreciation approach is applicable to as many as 50 percent of small residential properties. It is generally appropriate for tract homes less than 15 years old. Such homes usually have a good record of costs, and depreciation is not so extensive that it cannot be measured. For structures older than 15 years, depreciation becomes large and increasingly difficult to estimate. The cost-less-depreciation approach is less applicable for larger, more customized single-family homes. Both costs and depreciation are difficult to estimate and are less accurate.

Gross-rent-multiplier analysis is applicable to the appraisal of rental houses and small apartment houses up to about 16 units. It requires recent sales of similar properties from which GRMs can be calculated. Appraisers can use the same comparables, or others that have not necessarily sold recently, as a basis for deriving market rent. They can use this approach only when there are several comparable properties that have similar rental and expense patterns in the market.

OVERVIEW

Appraisal is the process of estimating the values of parcels of real estate. The process involves the systematic comparison of the sale prices of a subject property and several comparable properties. Appraisers use three general methods, or approaches—sales comparison, cost-less-depreciation, and income capitalization.

The appraisal of one- to four-family residential properties is an important function because of the large number of such properties and the frequent need for appraisals. The sales-comparison approach is usually the most applicable method for estimating values of such properties. It involves the analysis of the five elements of comparison—conditions of sale, financing terms, market conditions, physical characteristics, and location. The appraiser adjusts the sale price of each comparable property to reflect differences between it and the subject property for each element. He follows a sequence of adjustments calculated either as percentages or dollar amounts.

Appraisers sometimes value small residential properties by the cost-less-depreciation and gross-rent-multiplier (a variant of income capitalization) approaches. In the cost-less-depreciation approach, the appraiser subtracts the building's accrued depreciation from its current reproduction cost. Three types of accrued depreciation may exist: physical deterioration, functional obsolescence, and external obsolescence. Reproduction cost of the building minus accrued depreciation equals the building's indicated value. The appraiser adds separately estimated site value to this estimate to obtain total property value.

Appraisers can use gross-rent-multiplier analysis for rental houses and small apartment buildings. They multiply an estimate of the gross income for the subject property by a multiplier obtained by dividing the recent sale prices of similar properties by their gross incomes.

An appraiser should use as many of the three approaches as are appropriate in an appraisal. The sales-comparison approach is almost always appropriate. The cost-less-depreciation approach is appropriate for structures less than 15 years old that have no unusual features or characteristics that would cause unique depreciation patterns. Gross-rent-multiplier analysis is, of course, appropriate for small, income-producing residential properties.

TEST YOURSELF

Explain the following terms and concepts presented in this chapter.

1. Sales-comparison approach.
2. Cost-less-depreciation approach.
3. Transactional characteristics.
4. Property characteristics.

5. Market conditions.

6. Reconciliation.

7. Accrued depreciation.

8. Functional obsolescence.

9. Curable versus incurable items.

10. Sequence of adjustments.

Answer the following multiple-choice questions.

1. To reflect a change in market conditions between the date on which a comparable property sold and the date of appraisal of a subject property, which type of adjustment is made?
   a. Conditions of sale.
   b. Market conditions.
   c. Location.
   d. Financing terms.
   e. Unit.

2. In appraising a single-family home, you find a comparable property very similar to the subject property. One important difference, however, concerns the financing. The comparable property sold one month ago for $120,000 and was financed by the seller, who took back an 80 percent, 30-year mortgage at 9.5 percent interest. If current market financing terms are 80 percent, 30-year mortgages at 13 percent interest, by how much (and in which direction) should you adjust the sale price of the comparable property? The monthly payments on the market financing would be approximately $1,327, while the monthly payments on the financing provided by the seller are approximately $1,009.
   a. Subtract $3,180.
   b. Add $3,180.
   c. Subtract $6,360.
   d. Add $6,360.
   e. None of the above.

3. You find two properties that have sold twice within the last two years. Property A sold 22 months ago for $98,500; it sold last week for $108,000. Property B sold 20 months ago for $105,000; it sold two weeks ago for $113,500. What is the average monthly *compound* rate of change in sale prices?
   a. .0081.
   b. .0050.
   c. .0041.
   d. .0063.
   e. .0391.

4. A comparable property sold 10 months ago for $100,000. This sale price is adjusted to a normal sale price of $98,500. Given the adjustment for market conditions calculated in Problem 3, what would be the market-adjusted normal sale price of the comparable property?
   a. $104,100.
   b. $95,462.
   c. $95,900.
   d. $102,539.
   e. $98,480.

5. A comparable property sold six months ago for $150,000. The adjustments for the various elements of comparison have been calculated as follows:

   Location: −5 percent
   Market conditions: + 8 percent
   Physical characteristics: +$12,500
   Financing terms: −$2,600
   Conditions of sale: −0−

   What is the comparable property's final adjusted sale price?
   a. $163,732.
   b. $164,400.
   c. $169,600.
   d. $162,500.
   e. $167,200.

ADDITIONAL READINGS

American Institute of Real Estate Appraisers. *The Appraisal of Real Estate*, 8th ed. Chicago: 1983.

Bloom, George F., and Henry S. Harrison. *Appraising the Single Family Residence.* Chicago: American Institute of Real Estate Appraisers, 1978.

Boyce, Byrl N., ed. *Real Estate Appraisal Terminology,* rev. ed. Cambridge, Mass.: Ballinger, 1981.

Boyce, Byrl N., and William N. Kinnard, Jr. *Appraising Real Property.* Lexington, Mass.: D. C. Heath, 1984.

Shenkel, William M. *Modern Real Estate Appraisal.* New York: McGraw-Hill, 1978.

Smith, Halbert C. and Jerry D. Belloit *Real Estate Appraisal,* 2d ed. Dayton, Ohio: Century 22, 1987.

APPENDIX: SINGLE-FAMILY RESIDENTIAL APPRAISAL

This appendix contains the heart of a narrative single-family residential appraisal. Readers should note the use of all three major approaches in estimating the value of the subject property. They should also note that each significant adjustment is justified from market data and that the indicated values from each approach are reconciled in a final estimate of value.

THE SUBJECT PROPERTY

The property to be appraised is a small, single-family house in Gainesville, Florida. The property rights involved are those of a fee simple absolute estate. The structure is approximately 23 years old and is of concrete-block construction. Quality of construction and current condition are average. The house contains 974 square feet of finished area, including a living room, dining area, kitchen, three bedrooms, and one bathroom. There is also a 45-square-foot entry porch, a 31-square-foot patio, and a 71-square foot outside utility room.

The house has central heating and gas water heater, but no air conditioning. Utility services are average and adequate. There are no apparent major structural defects.

The site measures 76 feet by 107 feet and covers 8,132 square feet. The surrounding neighborhood comprises similar single-family properties, most of which appear average in appeal and marketability.

"Highest and best use of the site as though vacant" would be a new single-family house. It would contain approximately 1,100 square feet, with the additional area used for a half bath and slightly larger rooms. It would also have air conditioning, and all physical deterioration would be eliminated.

"Highest and best use of the property as improved" is continued single-family residential occupancy. Neither the zoning nor the type of structure would accommodate any other kind of occupancy. The structure appears to have approximately 30 years of economic life remaining.

SALES-COMPARISON APPROACH

The sales-comparison approach involves three similar homes located within four blocks of the subject property; see Exhibits 17A–1 through 17A–4. The three comparables were similar to the subject property with

---

EXHIBIT 17A–1
SALES-COMPARISON APPROACH ADJUSTMENT GRID

Property	Address
Comparable Sale No. 1	2602 N.E. 11 Street Gainesville, FL 32601
Comparable Sale No. 2	2924 N.E. 15 Street Gainesville, FL 32601
Comparable Sale No. 3	2322 N.E. 11 Street Gainesville, FL 32601
Subject property	3024 N.E. 10 Street Gainesville, FL 32601

	Comparable Sale No. 1	Comparable Sale No. 2	Comparable Sale No. 3	Subject Property
Price	$38,000	$39,900	$41,000	?
Financing	Market	Market	Market	N/A
Conditions of sale	Normal	Normal	Normal	No sale
Normal sale price	$38,000	$39,900	$41,000	
Market conditions*	Equal	Equal	Equal	Today
Market-adjusted normal sale price	$38,000	$39,900	$41,000	
Physical:				
Bedroom/bath				3/1
Landscaping				Average
Living area†		−1,644	−1,248	974 sq. ft.
Air conditioning‡			−1,600	None
Carport				Carport
Maintenance				Average
Final adjusted sale price	$38,000	$38,236	$38,152	?

Range of value = $38,236 − $38,000 = $236

$\bar{x}$ (mean) = $38,140 or $38,100

*See Market Conditions Adjustment (Exhibit 17A–2).
†See Gross Living Area Adjustment (Exhibit 17A–3).
‡See Air Conditioning Adjustment (Exhibit 17A–4).

respect to construction quality, age, condition, and the number of bed-rooms and bathrooms. Market-derived adjustments for the differences in gross living area and for air conditioning were made. The appraiser used paired sales analysis to determine the sizes of the adjustments.

Comparable Property No. 1 is three blocks south of the subject prop-erty in Highland Court Manor. It sold in May 1986 for $38,000. It is a concrete block home with approximately 962 square feet of floor space and no central air conditioning.

Comparable Property No. 2 is four blocks east of the subject property and has no central air conditioning. It has approximately 1,078 square feet and sold for $39,900 in January 1986.

Comparable Property No. 3 is a concrete block home with central air conditioning four blocks south of the subject property in Highland Court Manor. It sold for $41,000 in July 1986 and has approximately 1,052 square feet.

The final adjusted selling prices range from $38,000 to $38,236. All three properties are equally comparable and the appraiser gave them equal weights. Therefore the value indicated by the sales-comparison ap-proach is $38,129 or rounded off, $38,100.

EXHIBIT 17A–2
MARKET CONDITIONS ADJUSTMENT

Property	Address
Comparable Sale No. 2	2924 N.E. 15 Street
	Gainesville, FL 32601
Comparable Sale No. 3	2322 N.E. 11 Street
	Gainesville, FL 32601

	Comparable Sale No. 2	Comparable Sale No. 3
Price	$39,900	$41,000
Living area		+ 400*
Central A/C		− 1,600†
Adjusted Sale Price	$39,900	$39,800

*1,078 sq. ft. (Comp. No. 2) − 1,052 sq. ft. (Comp. No. 3) = 26 sq. ft., 26 sq. ft. × 16.00 = $400.00
†See air conditioning adjustment.

Comparables No. 2 and 3 are very similar homes. They have no sig-nificant differences except for central air conditioning and gross living area. The appraiser adjusted comparable No. 3 plus $400 for its smaller size and minus $1,600 for its central air conditioning. The adjusted value of comparable No. 3 is $39,800, or only $100 less than the actual sale price of comparable No. 2. This insignificant difference required no adjustment for market conditions.

EXHIBIT 17A–3
GROSS LIVING AREA ADJUSTMENT

	Property	Address
Comparable Sale No. 1		2602 N.E. 11 Street Gainesville, FL 32601
Comparable Sale No. 2		2924 N.E. 15 Street Gainesville, FL 32601

	Comparable Sale No. 1	Comparable Sale No. 2
Price	$38,000	$39,900
Living area	962 sq. ft.	1,078 sq. ft.

Comparables No. 1 and 2 are very similar homes. There are no significant differences except for gross living area; Comparable No. 2 has 116 square feet more. Comparable No. 2 sold for $1,900 more than Comparable No. 1:

Comparable No. 2	$39,900.00	1,078 sq. ft.
Comparable No. 1	− 38,000.00	− 962 sq. ft.
	$ 1,900.00	116 sq. ft.

$$\frac{\$1,900.00}{116 \text{ sq. ft.}} = \$16.37 \text{ per square foot}$$
or $16.00/sq. ft. rounded off.

EXHIBIT 17A–4
AIR CONDITIONING ADJUSTMENT

	Property	Address
Comparable Sale No. 1		2602 N.E. 11 Street Gainesville, FL 32601
Comparable Sale No. 3		2322 N.E. 11 Street Gainesville, FL 32601

	Comparable Sale No. 1	Comparable Sale No. 3
Price	$38,000	$41,000
Living area	38,000	− 1,400
GLA-Adjusted Price	$38,000	$39,600

Comparable No. 3	$39,600.00
Comparable No. 1	− 38,000.00
Price paid for A/C	$ 1,600.00*

*This implies that the market values air conditioning at approximately $1,600.00.

Comparables No. 1 and 3 are very similar homes. There are no significant differences except for gross living area and air conditioning. The appraiser adjusted the difference in gross living area at $16.00 per square foot, after which the adjusted sale price of comparable No. 3 was $39,600.

GROSS RENT MULTIPLIER ANALYSIS

Although the property is not rented today, it is highly possible that the property will be rented in the future. Therefore the appraiser derives a gross rent multiplier and market rent for the subject property. He found the market rent of the subject property by comparing three rented homes located within 12 blocks of the subject property. He made adjustments for differences in gross living area, air conditioning, and carports. Then he multiplied the estimated market rate by the appropriate gross rent multiplier to get the estimated value of the subject property. (See Exhibits 17A–5 and 17A–6.)

EXHIBIT 17A–5
DERIVATION OF GROSS RENT MULTIPLIER

Property	Address
Sale and Rental No. 1	2602 N.E. 11 Street Gainesville, FL 32601
Sale and Rental No. 2	2924 N.E. 15 Street Gainesville, FL 32601
Sale and Rental No. 3	2322 N.E. 11 Street Gainesville, FL 32601

	Sale/Rental No. 1	Sale/Rental No. 2	Sale/Rental No. 3
Sale price	$38,000	$39,000	$41,000
Monthly rent	310	325	325
GRM*	123	123	126

All properties appear to be equally comparable; hence, the average gross rent multiplier is 124.

*GRM = Sale Price/Monthly Rent.

Comparable rental No. 1 is six blocks east of the subject property in Carol Estates and has monthly rent of $325.00. The structure has 973 square feet, and includes three bedrooms and one bath, central air conditioning, and a carport. The home is of concrete block construction.

Comparable rental No. 2 is 12 blocks south, in Carol Estates, and rents for $325.00. The three-bedroom, one-bath home has 1,236 square feet of living area but has neither central air conditioning nor a carport.

Comparable rental No. 3 is four blocks east of the subject property in Highland Court Manor; it rents for $325.00. No. 3 has 1,052 square feet of living area, central air conditioning, and a carport.

The three properties in this analysis are all within four blocks of the subject property. All three are of concrete block construction and contain three bedrooms, and one bathroom. Two properties have a one-car carport, while comparable No. 2 has none.

EXHIBIT 17A–6
INDICATED MONTHLY MARKET RENT

Property	Address
Comparable Rental No. 1	1619 31 Avenue Gainesville, FL
Comparable Rental No. 2	1441 N.E. 18 Avenue Gainesville, FL
Comparable Rental No. 3	2322 N.E. 11 Street Gainesville, FL
Subject Property	3024 N.E. 10 Street Gainesville, FL

	Comparable Rental No. 1	Comparable Rental No. 2	Comparable Rental No. 3	Subject Property
Monthly Rent	$325	$325	$325	?
Market Condition	9/86	9/86	9/86	
Physical:				
Bedroom/bath	——————	——————	——————	3/1
Landscaping	——————	——————	——————	Average
Living area	——————	−34	−10	974 sq. ft.
Air conditioning	−13	——————	−13	None
Carport	——————	+10	——————	Carport
Maintenance	══════	══════	══════	Average
Adjusted Monthly Market Rent	$312	$301	$302	?

All three rental comparables are small concrete-block homes located within 12 blocks of the subject property. All three have three bedrooms and one bathroom and are equally weighted.

Adjustments were made as follows:

1. The appraiser based adjustments for central air conditioning on the $1,600 value determined by paired sales analysis in Exhibit 17A–4. He divided $1,600 by the gross rent multiplier to determine the adjustment ($1,600/124 = $13.00).
2. The appraiser made adjustments for size by dividing the $16.00 per

square foot difference in gross living area and dividing it by the gross rent multiplier.

Comparable No. 2

$$\frac{(1{,}236 \text{ sq. ft.} - 974 \text{ sq. ft.}) \times 16.00}{124} = \$33.81, \text{ or } \$34.00$$

Comparable No. 3

$$\frac{(1{,}052 \text{ sq. ft.} - 974 \text{ sq. ft.}) \times 16.00}{124} = \$10.6, \text{ or } \$10.00$$

After equally weighting the indicated monthly market rent for each comparable, he obtained an indicated monthly market rental for the subject property of $305.00.

The appraiser calculated the property's indicated value by multiplying this market rent by the gross rent multiplier of 124. The indicated value by this method is $37,820, or $37,800 rounded off.

COST-LESS-DEPRECIATION APPROACH

Using cost less depreciation, the appraiser can derive the market value of a subject property by estimating the reproduction cost of a building, subtracting accrued depreciation (including physical deterioration, functional obsolescence, and external obsolescence), and adding the market value of the site.

Reproduction Cost

The appraiser used *Marshal & Swift's Residential Cost Handbook* and its accompanying procedures to obtain the reproduction costs of the subject property—what it would cost if it were built today. He used rates for a one-story concrete-block house of average construction quality.

Category	Area	Cost/Sq. Ft.	Cost
Living	974 sq. ft.	@ $35.00	$34,090
Open Porch	45 sq. ft.	@ $8.00	360
Patio/Walks	31 sq. ft.	@ $6.45	200
Utility Room	71 sq. ft.	@ $16.00	1,136
Carport	205 sq. ft.	@ $8.00	1,640
Site improvements			
Driveway			500
Total estimated reproduction cost			$37,926

Source: *Residential Cost Handbook* (Los Angeles: Marshall and Swift Company, 1985), p. A-43.

Site Valuation

Comparable Site No. 1 in Highland Estates (Lot 15) is one block west of the subject property in northeast Gainesville. The site sold for $8,500 in October 1985. The topography is level, and the lot size is 143.30 by 76.90 feet. The utilities (electric, sewer, and water) are provided.

Comparable Site No. 2 in Palmetto Woods No. 3 (Lot 16) is 2 ½ miles west of the subject property in northwest Gainesville. It sold for $10,800 in July 1985. The site is level, and the lot size is 86.00 by 100.14 feet. Electric, sewer, and water are all provided.

Comparable Site No. 3 in Palmetto Woods No. 3 (Lot 6) is also 2 ½ miles west of the subject property. It sold for $11,000 in June 1985, and the lot measures 80.00 by 118.56 feet. The site is level; electric, sewer, and water are provided.

EXHIBIT 17A–7
SITE SALES ADJUSTMENTS

	Comparable Site No. 1	Comparable Site No. 2	Comparable Site No. 3	Subject Property
Price	$8,500	$10,800	$11,000	?
Market conditions	10/85	7/85	6/85	
Location	_____	− 2,700	− 2,700	
Size/shape	_____	_____	_____	
Topography	_____	_____	_____	
Utilities	_____	_____	_____	
Final adjusted sale price	$8,500	$ 8,100	$ 8,300	

The adjustments were as follows.

Market Adjustment.   The appraiser made no adjustment for market conditions. Exhibit 17A–2 contains the justification for this.

Locational Adjustments.   Comparable Sites No. 2 and 3 are in the Palmetto Woods subdivision. The average value of the homes in the subject neighborhood is $40,000.00, whereas the average value in Palmetto Woods is $50,000.00 Because homes in Palmetto Woods average 25 percent (or $10,000) more than those in the subject neighborhood, the appraiser made a 25 percent adjustment.

The above three sales range from $8,100 to $8,500. Comparable Site No. 1 was located only one block west of the subject property. The appraiser gave Comparable Site No. 1 the most weight because of its similar location. Comparable Sites Nos. 2 and 3 supported Comparable Site No. 1.

Comparable Site No. 1	70 percent × 8,500 = $5,950
Comparable Site No. 2	15 percent × 8,100 = $1,215
Comparable Site No. 3	15 percent × 8,300 = $1,245
Indicated site value	$8,410, or $8,400

Accrued Depreciation

The appraiser estimated the amounts of various elements of accrued depreciation by the observed-condition-breakdown method. He observed each item and estimated the extent to which the item suffered from deterioration or obsolescence. Then he multiplied the appropriate ratios by the replacement costs of the items.

Physical Deterioration

						Totals
Curable short-lived						
General clean-up	$100					
Replace broken window	20					
Total						$ 120
Incurable short-lived						

Item	Cost	Life	Age	SFF at 10%	Accrued Depreciation	
Hot water heater	$ 150	15	7	.031474	$ 33.05	
Roofing	$1,560	15	7	.031474	$343.70	
Floor covering	$1,440	15	7	.031474	$317.26	
Electrical fixtures	$ 300	20	7	.017460	$ 36.67	
Plumbing fixtures	$1,165	30	7	.006079	$ 49.57	
Appliances	$ 600	15	7	.031474	$ 90.19	
Gas furnace	$ 820	20	7	.017460	$100.22	
Total	$6,035				$970.66, or	971

Incurable long-lived		
Total reproduction cost	$37,926	
Curable deterioration	−120	
Total cost new of incurable short-lived items	−6,035	
Cost to be depreciated	$31,771	

$$\frac{\text{Effective age}}{\text{Economic life}} = \frac{7 \times \$31,771}{50} = \$4,448$$

Total		4,448
Total physical deterioration		$5,539

Functional Obsolescence

Curable: None		
Total	$ –0–	
Incurable	1,600	
Total	$1,600	
Total functional obsolescence		1,600

External Obsolescence

Total external obsolescence		-0-
Total accrued depreciation		$7,139

The subject property has no central air conditioning system. This is a feature that today's market for homes demands in the subject neighborhood. The rent loss due to lack of central air conditioning is $13.00; the appraiser multiplies this by the gross rent multiplier of 124 to obtain the incurable functional obsolescence of $1,600.00 ($13.00 × 124).

External obsolescence stems from forces outside the property that have a negative effect on the property value. As a result of these forces, the property structure is worth less than it would be at a different location. The appraiser believes no external obsolescence exists for the subject property. Hence, the indicated value from the cost-less-depreciation approach, as shown in Exhibit 17A–8, is $39,200 rounded off.

EXHIBIT 17A–8
INDICATED VALUE FROM COST-LESS-DEPRECIATION APPROACH

Reproduction cost	$37,926
Less: Accrued depreciation	7,139
Indicated value of improvements	$30,787
Plus site value	8,400
Value indicated by cost-less-depreciation approach:	$39,187

RECONCILIATION OF THE VALUE INDICATIONS TO A FINAL VALUE ESTIMATE

In the appraisal of single-family residences, the sales-comparison approach is the best approach to estimating market value. The appraiser gave this approach the most weight (60 percent) because it reflects the actions of buyers and sellers.

Since the subject property is twenty years old, he considered the cost-less-depreciation approach less reliable. The estimation of accrued depreciation is difficult in older properties.

Gross rent multiplier analysis seems fairly reliable, but does not reflect the premium owners are usually willing to pay over the value of rental housing. Thus the appraiser relied on GRM analysis less than the sales-comparison approach.

	Weight	Value	Weighted Value
Sales-comparison approach	60 percent	38,100	$22,860
GRM analysis	25 percent	37,800	$ 9,450
Cost-less-depreciation approach	15 percent	39,200	$ 5,880
Final estimated value	100%		$38,190, or $38,200

As a result of his investigation and analysis, the appraiser's opinion is that the market value of the property, as of November 24, 1986, is:

THIRTY-EIGHT THOUSAND TWO HUNDRED DOLLARS
($38,200.00).

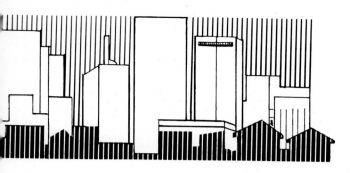

18
Income Property Appraisal

INTRODUCTION

Recall from Chapter 16 that the value of real estate is a function of the income it produces, when that income can be measured. Since income is usually measurable for income-producing properties, appraisers usually estimate the value of these properties by the income-capitalization approach. Although they may also use the sales-comparison and cost-less-depreciation approaches, the income-capitalization approach usually provides the most realistic value estimate for such properties. This approach requires estimation both of the relevant income for appraisal purposes (net operating income) and of an appropriate capitalization rate. The appraiser states a capitalization rate as a percentage (such as 10% or .10) and divides it into the annual income estimate to obtain an indicated value of the property.

Rental Income

Income properties generate income either for owners who use the properties themselves or for owners who lease the properties. For owner-users, the income is usually reflected in the income of a business or profession. For example, an owner may operate a store, a medical office, or a dental office in a property she owns. She measures the amount of income the property generates by the rent she could obtain by leasing the property on the open market. In effect, the income an owner-occupied income property generates is *implicit;* an explicit rent is not specified.

Leased income properties generate explicit rent. Rent is specified in the lease contract; thus it is called *contract rent.* This rent may or may not be equal to the rent that could be obtained by renting the property on the open market—the *market rent.* The lease contract may call for fixed rentals or for some growth in rental that is not necessarily as large as the growth in market rentals. Appraisers work primarily with contract rent if the ap-

443

praisal property is leased long-term to a financially reliable tenant. They work primarily with market rent if the property is leased short-term or if they believe that a longer-term tenant may break the lease or otherwise be unable to pay rent.

Frame 18–1

Types of Income Property

The following is a partial list of the types of income properties. No official classification system for properties exists, so readers may think of some types of properties not listed here. Nevertheless, this list should provide some idea of the range and diversity of income-producing properties.

Apartments	Commercial properties (freestanding)
Hotels and motels	Shopping centers
Restaurants	Office buildings
Warehouses	Farms, orchards, and groves
Service stations	Combination properties
Financial institutions	Specialty properties
Automobile repair shops	Resorts
Automobile dealerships	Grain elevators
Parking lots and garages	Pulp mills
Hospitals	Feed mills
Nursing homes	Log mills
Retirement homes	Lumber yards
Recreational properties	Amusement parks
Rental houses	

Purchasers as Investors

In contrast to purchasers of single-family homes, purchasers of income properties usually have different motivations and objectives. They purchase such properties primarily to receive (1) periodic income, (2) tax shelter, and (3) appreciation (see Chapter 16). While home buyers also seek the income-tax advantages and protection from inflation of home ownership, these objectives are usually secondary to shelter and amenities (e.g., swimming pool, good neighborhood, and scenic site).

When estimating income-property values, appraisers usually attempt to identify the types of purchasers who buy such properties and their financial objectives. High-income investors, for example, often prefer tax shelter and appreciation to periodic income. Lower-income investors and certain institutions such as pension funds typically want periodic income and place less emphasis on tax shelter or appreciation. Other investors may seek all three. Appraisers then find recently sold comparable properties that have these financial benefits to determine how selling price relates to the expected level of benefits. They apply this relationship to the expected level of benefits for the subject property to estimate its market value, or most probable selling price.

Geographic Scope

While housing markets are local, the markets for many income properties are regional, national, or international. When they seek financial benefits, investors are little concerned about the physical location of such benefits. Many real estate investors are large firms or wealthy persons who employ property managers where their properties are. Many large office buildings, shopping centers, and other income properties in the United States are owned partially or wholly by foreign investors from South America, Saudi Arabia, Germany, and Great Britain. Similarly, U.S. individual investors and firms own income properties around the world.

Some income properties, however, tend to be purchased by local investors. Small apartment buildings, shopping centers, commercial buildings, and office buildings offer substantial tax shelters attractive to high-income investors. Since location is relatively important for such properties, local investors are better able to evaluate them than distant investors. Also, personal management and supervision make the ownership of such properties feasible for small investors. In appraising income properties, therefore, appraisers must identify the primary financial benefits they produce and determine the types and geographic scope of potential purchasers.

INCOME CAPITALIZATION

The income capitalization approach is the primary approach that appraisers use to evaluate income properties. It resembles closely the thinking that purchasers go through in evaluating such properties. Income is quite broad in this context. It includes a property's future sale price (reversion), owner's income enhancement from tax shelter, and property operating income. Capitalization means the conversion of expected future income into a lump-sum, capital amount.

Fundamental Equation

From Chapter 16 the fundamental equation for capitalizing income is

$$V = \frac{I}{R} \qquad (18\text{--}1)$$

where

V = value
I = income
R = capitalization rate

In general, an appraiser estimates a property's value by dividing its annual income by the capitalization rate. As with any equation having three variables, if any two are known the third can be calculated. Thus after rearrangement appraisers can use the formula to estimate R if V and I are known:

$$R = \frac{I}{V} \qquad\qquad (18\text{--}2)$$

and they can use it to estimate I if R and V are known:

$$I = RV \qquad\qquad (18\text{--}3)$$

A capitalization rate is thus a percentage ratio of annual income to the value or sale price of a property. There are several ways of estimating capitalization rates and various methods of applying them to a property's income. These, however, are simply variations on the basic formula. In this chapter we present the basic methods of capitalization-rate estimation and application. Although these methods are adequate for the appraisal of almost all property types, the appendix at the end of this chapter contains more sophisticated methods, as do appraisal texts. We now discuss the numerator and denominator of the basic formula.

Income

In appraisals, the income that appraisers capitalize is a specific type—*net operating income (NOI).* Appraisers calculate this by deducting all expenses and allowances from the property's rental income. NOI excludes financing expenses, personal expenses, and other nonproperty expenses. In other words, it focuses on the income produced by the property before debt service and income taxes are paid. These expenses are personal and unique to each owner and not related to the property's income-producing ability.

In estimating expected NOI, appraisers rely on (1) the experience of similar properties in the market and (2) the historic experience of the subject property (if it is an existing property). The owners may not rent the subject property at the going market rate, and its expenses may differ from market averages. Thus appraisers must evaluate all income and expense items in terms of the current market. They place these items in a *reconstructed operating statement* format, as Exhibit 18–1 shows. This format includes some types of income and expense but excludes others that are usually included in accounting statements or reported for income tax purposes. Furthermore, the appraisers forecast income and expenses for the first year, rather than using estimates for a previous year. We discuss each of the major components of such a statement below.

EXHIBIT 18–1
RECONSTRUCTED OPERATING STATEMENT FOR
INCOME-PROPERTY APPRAISAL

Potential gross income (PGI)
    Less: Vacancy and collection allowance (V&C)
    Plus: Other income (OI)
Effective gross income (EGI)
    Less: Fixed expenses ⎫
    Less: Variable expenses ⎬ Operating expenses (OE)
    Less: Reserve for replacements ⎭

Net Operating Income (NOI)

Potential Gross Income. The appraiser's first step in estimating NOI is to forecast potential gross income (PGI). PGI is the total annual income the property would produce if it were fully rented and had no collection losses (tenant always pays the full rent on time). Appraisers forecast PGI by examining the terms of the existing lease(s) and the present tenant(s), if any. From this the appraiser decides whether to forecast PGI as contract rent or market rent. If the property is under a long-term lease to a financially reliable tenant, the basis for PGI is contract rent. Otherwise, the basis should be market rent. Often, of course, contract rent and market rent are approximately equal.

Example. The Suburban Office Building, has four first-floor units with long-term leases, renting for $400 per month. The second floor also contains four units, two of which rent for $400 per month and two for $300, all under short-term leases. The appraiser expects these rental rates to prevail for the next two to three years. He therefore estimates potential gross income to be[1]

First floor:
    4 units × $400 × 12 months   = $19,200
Second floor:
    2 units × $400 × 12 months   = $ 9,600
    2 units × $300 × 12 months   = $ 7,200
    Potential gross income (PGI)   = $36,000

---

[1]This presentation is also known as the "rent roll."

If the market rent for the two $300 units is $400 per month, the appraiser would increase the PGI by $2,400 to reflect the high probability that the owner would raise the rents when the short-term leases expire.

The appraiser also gathers rental data on similar properties to judge whether the contract rents are equal to market rents. For example, to determine the market rents for the second-floor units of the Suburban Office Building, the appraiser obtained the data in Exhibit 18–2 on second-floor units in similar buildings.

EXHIBIT 18–2
RENTS FOR SECOND-FLOOR UNITS

	Comparables			Subject Property
	1	**2**	**3**	
Rent/month (2nd-floor units)	$400	$480	$440	?
Square feet per unit	900	910	940	950
Rent per square foot	.44	.52	.46	?

The appraiser might conclude that the monthly market rent for the second-floor units is about $.48 per square foot:

$$.48 \times 950 \text{ sq. ft.} \times 4 \text{ units} = \$ \ 1,824 \text{ per month}$$
$$\$1,824 \times 12 \quad = \$21,888 \text{ per year}$$

In this case, he estimates PGI for the Suburban Office Building as

First-floor units	$19,200
Second-floor units	21,888
PGI	= $41,088

Effective Gross Income. The second step in estimating NOI is for the appraiser to forecast vacancy and collection (V&C) losses and other income (OI). Again, he forecasts these on the basis of (1) historical experience of the subject property and (2) experiences of competing properties. The normal range for V&C losses is 2 to 10 percent of PGI. He subtracts this normal V&C loss from PGI.

He adds to PGI other income from such sources as garage rentals, parking fees, laundry machines, and vending machines. The net result of these calculations is called *effective gross income* (EGI).

Example. Assuming that normal V&C loss is five percent, and the appraiser expects other income to be $100 per month, the EGI for the Suburban Office Building is

PGI		$36,000
Less: V&C (.05 × $36,000) −		1,800
Plus: Other Income	+	1,200
EGI		$35,400

Operating Expenses. The expenses a typical owner incurs in operating his property are termed *operating expenses* (OE). They are divided into three categories—fixed expenses, variable expenses, and reserve for replacements.

Fixed expenses do not vary with the level of operation (i.e., occupancy) of the property. The most common fixed expenses are real estate taxes and property insurance. Owners must pay them whether the property is vacant or totally occupied.

Variable expenses, as the name implies, vary with the level of operation of the property; they are higher for a higher level of occupancy and lower for a lower level. They include such items as utilities, garbage and trash removal, maintenance, repairs, supplies, and management.

Reserve for replacements is an annual allowance that reduces the property's operating income by an amount sufficient to replace major components periodically. These components wear out faster than the building itself; the owner must replace them several times during the building's expected economic life.

Example. The appraiser expects the components of the Suburban Office Building to wear out over their indicated lives and to have the replacement costs shown in Exhibit 18–3. The reserve for replacements is the sum of the reserves for all of the components.

EXHIBIT 18–3
RESERVE FOR REPLACEMENTS

Component	Life (Years)	Annual Sinking Fund Factor (10%)	Replacement Cost	Reserve
Heating, ventilation, air conditioning	10	.062745	$20,000	$1,255
Roof	15	.031474	7,500	236
Water heaters	10	.062745	3,000	188
Driveway and parking area	10	.062745	6,000	376
Total reserve for replacements				$2,055

Net Operating Income. The appraiser obtains the final estimate of NOI by subtracting all operating expenses from EGI. With assumed operating expenses for the Suburban Office Building, Exhibit 18–4 shows NOI in a Reconstructed Operating Statement.

EXHIBIT 18–4
SUBURBAN OFFICE BUILDING RECONSTRUCTED
OPERATING STATEMENT

Potential gross income			$36,000
Vacancy and collection losses		$ 1,800	
Other income		1,200	− 600
Effective gross income			$35,400
Less: Operating expenses			
Fixed expenses			
Real estate taxes	$3,200		
Insurance	3,000	$ 6,200	
Variable expenses			
Utilities	$3,600		
Garbage and trash collection	200		
Supplies	800		
Repairs	1,200		
Maintenance	3,000		
Management	1,770	$10,570	
Reserve for replacements		$ 2,055	$18,825
Net operating income			$16,575

Evaluating the Estimates

The appraiser should answer some important questions when reconstructing the operating statement. The answers assist the evaluation of the completeness of the statement and the accuracy of its individual items.

Are the Sources of Income and Expenses Appropriate? The appraiser should include only those sources of income and expenses that relate directly and entirely to the productivity of the property. He does not include financing costs and federal income taxes because they are specific to the investor. He should exclude business-related expenses *not* directly attributable to the operation of the property. The appraiser cannot calculate depreciation, although it is a legitimate expense of the property, since depreciation is related to the market value being estimated. He accounts for depreciation, or capital recovery, in the capitalization rate as the following section shows.

Have the Trends for Each Revenue and Expense Item Been Considered? This question is important in evaluating the revenue and expense forecasts. An appraiser should avoid considering only short-term or current events to the detriment of long-term trends. For example, current vacancy rates may be low, although rates for the past ten years have been somewhat higher. Thus current market conditions could easily bias a forecast of vacancies.

What Have Been the Experiences of Comparable Properties Regarding Each Revenue and Expense Item? Considering the experience of the subject property only, regardless of its current status, is often too narrow a perspective. Whenever possible the appraiser should obtain information about revenue and expense items for comparable properties. As an example, property tax trends for frequently reassessed comparable properties may be better for forecasting future property taxes of the subject property than its own past property-tax trends.

Capitalization Rate

The denominator of the basic formula $V = \dfrac{I}{R}$ is the capitalization rate.

There are several types of capitalization rates, depending on whether the appraiser is valuing an entire property or some component of it. These rates and their symbols are

Symbol	Type of Capitalization Rate	Income to Which Applied
R_o	Overall capitalization rate	NOI (entire property)
R_B	Building capitalization rate	Building income
R_L	Land capitalization rate	Land income
R_e	Equity capitalization rate (also equity dividend rate)	Equity income (before tax cash flow)
R_m	Mortgage capitalization rate (also mortgage constant)	Debt income
R_{LF}	Leased fee capitalization rate	Leased fee income
R_{LH}	Leasehold capitalization rate	Leasehold income

In all cases, the appraiser divides the capitalization rate into the income from the property or component to obtain value.

Overall Capitalization Rates. The overall capitalization rate R_o is perhaps the most widely used and useful type of capitalization rate. It is simply the percentage ratio of the NOI produced by properties to their selling prices. As shown in Exhibit 18–5, the most straight-forward method for estimating an R_o is by *direct market extraction*. In evaluating the Suburban Office Building, the appraiser found five comparable properties that sold recently and calculated their R_os.

EXHIBIT 18–5
DIRECT MARKET EXTRACTION OF R_o

Office Building	Forecast NOI	Price	R_o (NOI/Price)
A	$20,000	$170,000	.118
B	$28,500	$235,000	.121
C	$25,000	$220,000	.114
D	$18,000	$150,000	.120
E	$22,500	$175,000	.128
	$\bar{x}$ (mean) = .1202		

The average (mean) of the five R_os is .1202. Thus, the appropriate indicated R_o appears to be 12 percent (.120). Dividing this rate into the property's NOI produces the following indication of market value:

$$\$16,575/.12 = \$138,125, \text{ say } \$138,000$$

The reciprocal of R_o is $1/.12$, or 8.33. Thus, another way of looking at the relationship between income and value is to say that office buildings similar to the subject property sell for about 8.33 times their forecast annual NOIs. The process of directly dividing NOI by an R_o is called *direct capitalization using an overall rate.*

Building Capitalization Rates. Sometimes appraisers must estimate the values of buildings and land separately. Calculation of property and income taxes, for example, requires this separation. Also, the cost-less-depreciation approach requires a separate land value, and investors sometimes purchase either the land or building, but not both. When an appraiser estimates a building's value, he must divide the NOI between the land and building, and estimate a capitalization rate reflecting depreciation and a rate of return for the investor. As discussed in Chapter 16, capitalization rates have two components—a recapture of the investment over the building's expected life and a rate of return on investment; thus:

ROC (Recapture of capital) + ROI (Return on investment) = R_B (18–4)
(Building capitalization rate)

The ROI is also termed the discount rate or interest rate. It is usually the largest component of a capitalization rate. Appraisers derive it in the same way they derive R_os—by comparing ROIs for comparable properties.

The ROC represents the percentage annual return *of* the capital invested in the building. It is the percentage of the building's value that, if invested annually at the discount rate, would equal the building's value over the remaining economic life of the building.

Recall from Chapter 16 that we called an amount that, if invested at a discount rate, would equal $1 over a specified number of years a sinking-fund factor (SFF). Thus we can obtain the ROC rate in a building capitalization rate from Column 3 of the compound and discount interest tables or from a financial calculator as shown in Chapter 16. The discount rate plus the SFF equal the R_B.

Example. Assume that the appropriate discount rate for the Suburban Office Building is 11.0 percent, and that the building has an expected remaining economic life of 40 years. The R_B is:

ROI	.110
ROC (from Column 3, 11 percent annual table, 40 years)	$+ .002259$
R_B	.112259

If the building income portion of the NOI were $14,575, the indicated value of the building (V_B) would be

$$\$14,575/.112259 = \$124, 297, \text{ say } \$124,000$$

The R_B in this example is more generally known as an *annuity* or *level annuity* capitalization rate. An annuity is a series of payments, and a level annuity is a series of equal payments. Used in capitalizing the income of a building with a capitalization rate comprising a discount rate and an SFF, the calculation assumes a level income stream (annuity) for the period specified by the SFF. Column 6 of the compound and discount interest tables gives an annuity capitalization rate directly. Recall from Chapter 16 that this column is calculated by adding the SFF for each year to the discount rate shown at the top of the page.

Discount Rates. Discount rates are the largest component of most capitalization rates. As noted above, they represent the rate of return, or yield, on invested capital. The symbol for yield is y, and the symbols for the yield associated with properties or their components are:

y	=	General symbol for ROI, or yield
y_o	=	Overall yield on an entire property
y_B	=	Yield on a building
y_L	=	Yield on land
y_m	=	Yield on a mortgage (interest rate)
y_e	=	Yield on equity
y_{LF}	=	Yield on a leased fee
y_{LH}	=	Yield on a leasehold

Appraisers estimate yield rates by extracting yields on comparable properties and reconciling them to represent the yield of a subject property. This chapter's appendix shows a method of extracting yield rates from transactions. Nevertheless, yields on land and buildings, given varying levels of risk, generally fall in the ranges in Exhibit 18–6.

EXHIBIT 18–6
RISK LEVELS AND DISCOUNT RATES

Risk Level	Land	Buildings
Low	6–8	7–10
Medium	8–11	10–13
High	11–14	13–17
Speculative	14 up	17 up

Capital Recovery Rates.   A capital recovery rate represents the annual percentage of recapture of capital originally invested in a depreciating asset. To determine a capital recovery rate, an appraiser must estimate the asset's remaining economic life. Although the present authors conducted a major study[2] that investigated the typical economic lives of single-family residences, no studies have been done for income properties. Thus appraisers must rely on their experience and judgment in estimating remaining economic lives. Generally, however, buildings have total economic lives in the ranges shown in Exhibit 18–7.

EXHIBIT 18–7
TYPICAL ECONOMIC LIVES OF INCOME PROPERTIES

Type of Property	Total Economic Life in Years
Hotels and motels	15–30
Apartments	40–60
Warehouses	50–75
Banks	40–50
Offices	20–60
Stores	30–50
Shopping Centers	15–30
Restaurants	10–20
Garages and repair shops	40–60
Specialty properties	15–75

In order to estimate a building's remaining economic life, an appraiser must first estimate its total economic life. For example, if the building is an apartment building of average construction quality and well located, he might estimate its total economic life as 50 years. The appraiser then

---

[2]John B. Corgel and Halbert C. Smith, *The Concept and Estimation of Economic Life in the Residential Appraisal Process* (Chicago: Society of Real Estate Appraisers Foundation, 1981).

estimates the building's *effective age,* or chronological (actual) age adjusted up or down for worse-than-average or better-than-average maintenance. Suppose the apartment building being appraised is actually 15 years old, but has been maintained in much-better-than-average condition. The appraiser might estimate its effective age as 10 years. Its remaining economic life for appraisal purposes therefore would be 50 years − 10 years = 40 years. Note that *average* maintenance is assumed for the remaining term, since the future owners and future quality of maintenance are unknown.

If the appraiser estimates the discount rate as 11.0 percent and the building's remaining economic life as 40 years, the capital recovery rate would be an SFF of .001719. The annuity capitalization rate for the building income (R_B) would thus be .110 + .001719 = .111719.

Land Capitalization Rates.   Land capitalization rates are usually a special case of annuity capitalization rates. This is because land does not depreciate or wear out because of physical deterioration, as do buildings and other wasting assets, and may often increase in value. Thus in the absence of clear evidence that a parcel of land will lose or gain value, appraisers often make the constant value assumption. The effect of this assumption is that the capital recovery portion of R_L is zero. Thus, $R_L = y_L$. For example, if $y_L = .11$, $R_L = .11$

$$\text{ROI } (y_L) = .11$$
$$\text{ROC (SFF)} = \underline{\text{-0-}}$$
$$R_L = .11$$

Accountants assume the land does not depreciate, so it can produce income indefinitely, or to perpetuity. Thus, capitalizing income to land with an R_L in which ROC = 0 is called *capitalization to perpetuity.* Diagramatically, it means that land income appears as shown below.

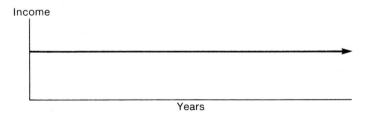

If the land portion of the Suburban Office Building Property produced $2,000 of the NOI, the value of the land (V_L) would be:

$$\$2,000/.11 = \$18,181, \text{ say } \$18,000.$$

The indicated value of the entire property (building value plus land value) would be $124,000 + $18,000 = $142,000.

R_os From Mortgage-Equity Analysis. Here we return to our discussion of overall rates (R_os), because they are the most important and widely used capitalization rates. We mentioned earlier that ideally appraisers can estimate R_os directly from recent transactions of similar income properties. Often, however, this procedure produces unreliable estimates of forecast NOI for the comparable properties. Also, the sale prices may reflect special considerations such as favorable financing or unusual income tax advantages. Thus, appraisers often must rely on other methods for estimating R_os. Perhaps the most useful such method derives from mortgage-equity analysis.

Mortgage-equity analysis recognizes that R_os include rates of return and capital recovery rates for both the equity portion and the debt (mortgage) portion of an investment. As in the separate valuations of land and buildings, the asset is divided into two parts—its debt and equity components. The appraiser weights the capitalization rates for the two parts by the proportion of each part of the total. He then adds the two weighted rates to obtain the R_o. Thus if he can obtain market terms for mortgage financing and equity dividend rates (R_e), R_o is the weighted average of R_m and R_e:

$$R_o = mR_m + (1 - m) R_e \qquad (18\text{--}5)$$

where

$$m = \text{loan-to-value (or mortgage) ratio}$$
$$1 - m = \text{equity-to-value ratio}$$

He obtains equity dividend rates (R_e) by dividing before-tax cash flow (BTCF) by the value of the equity (V_e):

$$R_e = \text{BTCF}/V_e \qquad (18\text{--}6)$$

where

$$\text{BTCF} = \text{NOI} - \text{ADS (annual debt service)}$$
$$V_e = \text{Sale price} - \text{Mortgage balance}$$

Example. An investor could obtain mortgage financing for the Suburban Office Building carrying a 10.5 percent interest rate (y_m) for 20

EXHIBIT 18–8
EQUITY DIVIDEND RATES

	Comparable		
	A	**B**	**C**
BTCF	9,500	7,800	8,250
V_e	77,500	65,000	70,000
R_e (BTCF/V_e)	.1226	.1200	.1179

years, with monthly payments. The R_m for these loan terms is $.009984^3 \times 12 = .119806$.

Equity dividend rates for three similar properties that sold recently are shown in Exhibit 18–8.

Thus, an R_e of .1200 is chosen, and R_o is calculated as follows:

$$R_o = .75 \,(.119806) + .25 \,(.12) \qquad\qquad (18\text{–}7)$$
$$= .119855, \text{ say } .12$$

The value of the property using this R_o would be:

$$\$16,575 \div .12 = \$138,125, \text{ say } \$138,000$$

General Formula for R_o. We can also view overall capitalization rates as containing two components—*ROI* and *ROC*. Since the ROC applies only to the building portion of the property's NOI, the ROC in the R_o must be an *effective ROC;* that is, the ROC for the depreciating portion of the property is weighted by the percentage of the total property that it represents. For example, if the ROC for a building were .02 and the building comprises about 80 percent of the total property value, the effective ROC in the R_o would be $.8 \times .02 = .016$. Such an effective rate, of course, would assume that the land portion of the property is expected to remain constant.

In the general formula for R_o, the appraiser multiplies the total percentage by which he expects the property to increase or decrease in value over a specified holding period by a sinking fund factor at the equity yield rate, and subtracts this percentage from the discount rate, thus:

$$R_o = y_o - \Delta_o \times \text{SFF} \qquad\qquad (18\text{–}8)$$

where

y_o = Discount rate, or yield
Δ_o = Expected percentage change in value over the holding period
SFF = Sinking fund factor at the equity yield rate for the holding period

This formula is more general and often more useful because discount rates (y_os) are often easier to obtain than R_es.[4] Since y_o does not include an allowance for capital recapture, Δ_o is added to it. Δ_o can reflect either appreciation or depreciation. Appreciation means that Δ_o is positive, whereas depreciation means a negative Δ_o. Since both expressions are

---

[3] Column 6 (monthly) at 10.5 percent for 20 years.
[4] We cover an extended form of mortgage-equity analysis that shows the relationship between yield rates, the discount rate, and R_o in the appendix at the end of this chapter. We also cover the Ellwood formulation there.

subtracted from y_o, the net result is that appreciation is subtracted, and depreciation is added to y_o:

$$R_o = y_o - (+\Delta_o) \text{ SFF (denotes appreciation)} \qquad (18\text{--}9)$$
$$R_o = y_o - (-\Delta_o) \text{ SFF (denotes depreciation)} \qquad (18\text{--}10)$$

Example: The appraiser obtains a discount rate (y_o) of 11 percent for the Suburban Office Building. He expects the property to decrease in value by 15 percent over the ten-year holding period. Equity yield rates for this type of investment are currently about .14. R_o is then calculated as:

$$R_o = .11 - (-.15) .0517$$
$$= .11 + .0078$$
$$= .1178$$

The value of the Suburban Office Building, using this R_o, would be

$$\$16,575/.1178 = \$140,705, \text{ say } \$140,500$$

Several Methods, But Only One R_o. The preceding sections show three methods for estimating R_o for a particular property in a given market, and Chapter 18's appendix contains three more. The questions that naturally arise are "Which one is correct?" or "Which should I use?" All are correct, of course; they are simply different methods of analyzing market data to find the same answer. Even so, the methods will not produce the same numerical results. Markets are not totally efficient, and different methods of analysis will not yield the same conclusions. Nevertheless, if accurate, reliable data are available for the various methods, the resulting R_os should be quite close.

The choice of method(s) depends on data availability and reliability. The preferred method *if* good price, income, and expense data are available for at least three (and preferably more) comparable properties is direct market extraction of R_o. We must remember, however, that prices should not reflect any nonmarket considerations such as unusual financing or other concessions. Also, we must place income and expense data in a reconstructed operating statement format and *forecast* income and expenses for the comparable properties to reflect the *same* future period as the subject property's forecast NOI. In other words, direct market extraction requires the same availability, reliability, and consistency of data and analysis for the comparable properties as for the subject property.

Mortgage-equity analysis and the general formula are substitute methods for deriving R_o. They are often used because appraisers cannot obtain accurate, reliable data for direct market extraction. Often, however, they are able to obtain typical mortgage financing data and equity dividend rates or discount rates. In these situations, one of the mortgage-equity methods is preferable to direct market extraction. We present three additional methods—two mortgage-equity methods and one based completely on financing terms—in this chapter's appendix.

SALES COMPARISON APPROACH

Gross-rent-multiplier (GRM) analysis is considered an application of the sales-comparison approach for the valuation of income properties. (Recall that GRM analysis is considered an application of the income-capitalization approach for the valuation of one- to-four-family residential properties.) In GRM analysis applied to income properties, appraisers compare sale prices of comparable properties on a unit basis—the dollar. Thus, the sale prices of comparable properties might be $5 or $6 for every dollar of annual gross income, as Exhibit 18–9 shows.

EXHIBIT 18–9
GRM ANALYSIS FOR SUBURBAN OFFICE BUILDING

	Comparable		
	A	B	C
Effective gross income	$ 32,500	$ 33,850	$ 35,300
Sale price	$130,000	$146,000	$145,000
GRM (sale price/EGI)	4.00	4.22	4.11

The appropriate GRM for Suburban Office Building is about 4.1, and the property's indicated value would thus be $35,400 × 4.1 = $145,140, say $145,000.

The same requirements for data consistency and applicability that we discussed for valuing small residential properties also apply in the valuation of income properties by this method.

Appraisers may also use other units of comparison to compare sale prices. Units of comparison adjust for size differences, and appraisers use them when properties are similar except for size. For example, if two apartment properties are similar except that one contains 200 units and the other 300, they could be compared on a price-per-apartment basis. If the 200-unit property sold for $10,000,000—a price of $50,000 per unit—it would indicate that the 300-unit property should sell for about $15,000,000. Exhibit 18–10 shows typical units of comparison that appraisers use for various types of income properties.

EXHIBIT 18–10
TYPICAL UNITS OF COMPARISON USED IN APPRAISING
INCOME PROPERTIES

Property Type	Unit(s) of Comparison
Rental housing	Square feet of living area
Rental stores	Square feet of gross leasable area
Office buildings	Square feet of net leasable area
Industrial buildings	Square feet of gross building area
Apartment buildings	Rooms; dwelling units
Hotels and motels	Beds
Hospitals and nursing homes	Beds
Restaurants, bars, and theatres	Seats
Factories	Finished units per day
Farms	Bushels per acre
Orchards and groves	Pounds per acre
Mines	Tons of ore per day

COST-LESS-DEPRECIATION APPROACH

Appraisers can also use the cost-less-depreciation approach in valuing income properties. They usually place less reliance on this approach, however, because of the difficulties in measuring costs and depreciation. Income is the most important characteristic for which these properties are purchased, and the greatest reliance is thus placed on the approach that converts income to present value. Nevertheless, appraisers use the cost-less-depreciation approach primarily as a check on the other approaches. Exhibit 18–11 shows the estimation of the value of the Suburban Office Building by this approach.

EXHIBIT 18–11
ESTIMATION OF VALUE OF SUBURBAN OFFICE BUILDING USING COST-LESS-DEPRECIATION APPROACH

Reproduction cost				$142,000
Less: Accrued depreciation				
Physical deterioration				
Curable		$ 2,200		
Incurable				
Short-lived	$ 2,700			
Long-lived	10,000	$12,700		
Total physical			$14,900	
Functional obsolescence				
Curable		$ 1,500		
Incurable		1,800		
Total functional			$ 3,000	
External obsolescence			1,800	
Total accrued depreciation				$ 20,000
Indicated building value				$112,000
Site value				$ 18,000
Indicated property value				$140,000

RECONCILIATION

Exhibit 18–12 summarizes the various indications of market value for the Suburban Office Building obtained in this chapter.

EXHIBIT 18–12
SUBURBAN OFFICE BUILDING, SUMMARY OF VALUE INDICATIONS

Approach	Indicated V_o
Income capitalization	
R_os derived by:	
Direct market extraction (M/E)	$138,000
Simple M/E analysis	138,000
General formula	140,500
Annuity capitalization	142,000
GRM analysis	145,000
Cost-less-depreciation	140,000

The appraiser obtains a final point estimate of value by reconciling these indications. Recall from our discussion of reconciliation in Chapter 17 that the appraiser must rely on experience, logic, and judgment to decide where, within the range of value indications, the final estimate of value should be placed. The range of indications for the Suburban Office Building is $145,000 − $138,000 = $7,000; the mean is $140,583.

In most income-property appraisals, the appraiser would not estimate R_o by three different methods. Normally, he would choose the one best method, based on availability and reliability of data. Nevertheless, in our Suburban Office Building example, we have estimated R_o by three methods that produce value indications that are quite close. The appraiser might average them to obtain an indicated value using R_o. The average (mean) of these three indications is $138,833.

The value indication produced by annuity capitalization is in the mid-range of the distribution. Recall that this method is based on an assumption about the amounts of NOI allocated to land and building. If this assumption is based on market evidence and is accurate, this method is highly appropriate for the property.

The value indications generated by GRM analysis and the cost-less-depreciation approach are less logically applicable to the appraisal of an income property than income capitalization. Thus we will weight each of these value indications 10 percent, and direct capitalization and annuity capitalization 40 percent each. The final estimate of value, $140,800, is the weighted average of these value indications, as Exhibit 18–13 shows.

EXHIBIT 18–13
SUBURBAN OFFICE BUILDING, RECONCILIATION OF VALUE INDICATIONS

Value Indication	Amount	Weight	Weighted Amount
Income capitalization using R_os	$138,833	40%	$ 55,533
Annuity capitalization	142,000	40	56,800
GRM analysis	145,000	10	14,500
Cost-less-depreciation	140,000	10	14,000
Final estimate of value			$140,833
		rounded off	$140,800

OVERVIEW

Appraisers evaluate income properties by one or more of the three approaches to value—sales comparison, cost-less-depreciation, and income capitalization. The sales-comparison approach often takes the form of GRM analysis in the appraisal of income properties. Income capitalization is the principal method for income properties, whereas the sales-comparison and cost-less-depreciation approaches are often accorded less weight or even omitted.

Income capitalization converts a property's net operating income (NOI) into a lump-sum, present value. The appraiser estimates NOI in the format of a reconstructed operating statement, usually based on market rents and expenses. For properties under long-term lease to financially reliable firms, contract rent may be appropriate if it differs from market rent.

There are several types of capitalization rates—overall rates, building rates, land rates, mortgage rates, equity rates, leased fee rates, and leasehold rates. An annuity-capitalization rate is a generic type of rate that can be applied to any depreciating asset. The capitalization rate is divided into the income produced by the property or into that portion for which the rate was developed.

Appraisers estimate overall rates by several methods—direct extraction from the market, simple mortgage-equity analysis, and the general formula, which recognizes that all capitalization rates have two components—return *on* investment and recapture *of* capital. Usually one method is best for a particular appraisal. If accurate income and sale price data are available from the market, appraisers prefer direct extraction. Otherwise, they use mortgage-equity analysis or the general formula.

Dividing an overall rate into a property's NOI gives an indication of a total property's value. Dividing a capitalization rate applicable to any portion of a property into the income from that portion produces an indication of the value of that portion (e.g., land, building, debt position, or equity position).

TEST YOURSELF

Explain the following terms and concepts presented in this chapter.

1. Net operating income.
2. Capitalization rate.
3. Yield or discount rate.
4. Mortgage-equity analysis.
5. Return of capital.
6. Annuity capitalization.
7. Capitalization to perpetuity.
8. Effective rate.

Answer the following multiple choice questions.

1. Which of the following expenses is not an operating expense?
    a. Utility.
    b. Reserve for replacements.
    c. Management.
    d. Mortgage payment.
    e. Advertising.

2. To estimate the value of the equity portion of a real estate investment, an appraiser divides the equity income (BTCF) by which of the following?
    a. Equity yield rate (y_e).
    b. Equity dividend rate (R_e).
    c. Overall capitalization rate (R_o).
    d. Mortgage constant (R_m).
    e. Discount rate (y_o).

3. What overall capitalization rate is indicated by the following characteristics of equity and debt in a transaction?

$$m = .80$$
$$R_m = .123432$$
$$R_e = .1400$$

    a. 14.00 percent.
    b. 12.00 percent.
    c. 12.68 percent.
    d. 13.25 percent.
    e. 12.50 percent.

4. An appraiser estimates a property to produce NOI of $25,000. The sales-comparison approach gives an estimate that the site is to be worth $20,000. The appraiser estimates that the building has a remaining economic life of 40 years, and that y_o is 11.0 percent. What is the total property value (unrounded)?
    a. $224,084.
    b. $227,273.
    c. $223,762.
    d. $243,762.
    e. $231,580.

5. An apartment property sold recently for $625,000. It produces NOI of about $60,000, indicating an R_o of 9.60 percent. If the y_o is 9.00 percent, and the building constitutes approximately 80 percent of the total property value, what is the *actual* capital recovery rate?
    a. 0.60 percent.
    b. 0.48 percent.
    c. 0.75 percent.
    d. 1.00 percent.
    e. 1.75 percent.

ADDITIONAL READINGS

American Institute of Real Estate Appraisers. *The Appraisal of Real Estate*, 8th ed. Chicago: AIREA, 1983.

Cohen, Arthur C. "Extracting Cap Rates 'From the Market': Beware!" *Appraisal Journal* 47, no. 3 (July 1979), pp. 370–73.

Friedman, Jack P., and Nicholas Ordway. *Income Property Appraisal and Analysis.* Reston, Va.: Reston Publishing, 1981.

Kinnard, William N., Jr. *Income Property Valuation.* Lexington, Mass.: D. C. Heath 1971.

Shenkel, William M. *Modern Real Estate Appraisal.* New York: McGraw-Hill, 1978.

Smith, Halbert C. and Jerry D. Belloit *Real Estate Appraisal,* 2d ed. Dayton, Ohio: Century 22, 1987.

APPENDIX: ADVANCED METHODS FOR ESTIMATING CAPITALIZATION RATES

We can use several other methods to estimate capitalization rates beyond those we discussed in this chapter. These methods are extensions of basic mortgage-quality analysis and include *extended mortgage-equity analysis,* the *Ellwood formulation,* and the *underwriter's method.*

Although we can use the methods to estimate R_os, perhaps the greatest value is in abstracting component parts of R_os. They break R_os into more components than the simple mortgage-equity method presented in the chapter, and thus are mechanically somewhat more difficult to use. Even so, they may not provide greater accuracy in estimating R_o than the simpler, more straightforward methods when relevant data are available. When reliable data for the simpler methods are not available, however, the more sophisticated methods may be used because the data requirements are different and are often more readily available.

EXTENDED MORTGAGE-EQUITY ANALYSIS

Extended mortgage-equity analysis is a development of the basic formula:

$$R_o = y_o - \Delta_o \text{SFF} \tag{18A-1}$$

Although y_o is not used in simple mortgage-equity analysis, we extract it from a mortgage capitalization rate R_m and an equity yield rate y_e in the extended method. We subtract the capital recovery portion of R_m from the weighted $R_m - y_e$ rate. We accomplish this step by subtracting the product of the debt ratio m, the percentage of principal paid off p, and the SFF. Thus, we calculate y_o as follows for the Suburban Office Building in which:

$$m = .75$$
$$y_m = .105$$
$$\text{term} = 20 \text{ yrs.}$$
$$\text{Amortization} = \text{monthly}$$
$$y_e = .14$$
$$p = .260103$$
$$HP = 10 \text{ yrs.}$$

$$m \times R_m = .75 \times .119806 = .0899$$
$$(1 - m) \times y_e = .25 \times .140000 = \underline{.0350}$$
$$\text{Weighted rate} = .1249$$
$$-m \times p \times \text{SFF} = .75 \times .2160103^{1} \times .0517 = \underline{.0101}$$
$$y_o = .1148$$

---

[1]We can obtain the value for p easily on a financial calculator, or one of several formulas can be used. On a financial calculator, calculate p by subtracting b (percentage of mortgage loan balance) from 1. The keystrokes for obtaining b are:

HP-12C Keystrokes for b   **Display**

| ON | f | REG / CLX | 0.0000

| 20 | g | n / 12x | 240.0000

| 10.5 | g | i / 12÷ | .8750

| 1 | CHS | PV | −1.0000

| PMT | .009984

10 (expired period of mortgage during

holding period) | g | n / 12x | FV | .739897 = b

BA-35 Keystrokes for b   **Display**

| 0
| ON/C | ON/C | 2nd | FIN | FIN
| 240
| 20 | × | 12 | = | N | FIN
| .875
| 10.5 | ÷ | 12 | = | %i | FIN
| 1
| 1 | PV | FIN
| .0099838
| CPT | PMT | ANNFIN
| 97
| 10 | × | 12 | = | N | CPT | FV | .739897 = b

Calculation for p

$p = 1 - b$
$= 1 - .739897$
$= .260103$

Next, the annualized change in the property's value that is expected over the holding period is subtracted from y_o.

$$
\begin{aligned}
y_o &= .1148 \\
-\Delta_o \text{ SFF} = -(-.15) \times .0517 &= +.0078 \\
R_o &= .1226
\end{aligned}
$$

The value of the Suburban Office Building, using this R_o would thus be:

$$\$15,230 \div .1226 = \$124,225, \text{ say } \$124,200$$

The procedure can be used in reverse to find y_o and R_m, if an appraiser can obtain R_o, Δ_o, y_e, and m from the market:

$$
\begin{aligned}
R_o &= .1226 \\
+\Delta_o \text{ SFF} &= -.0078 \\
y_o &= .1148 \\
\\
y_o &= .1148 \\
+mp \text{ SFF} &= +.0101 \\
\text{Weighted rate} &= .1249 \\
\text{Weighted rate} &= .1249 \\
-(1 - m)\, y_e &= -.0350 \\
m \times R_m &= .0899 \\
R_m &= .0899/.75 \\
&= .1199
\end{aligned}
$$

This procedure is thus a valuable tool for extracting y_os when R_os, Δ_os, and mortgage terms can be found in the market.

ELLWOOD FORMULATION

The Ellwood formulation is an algebraic presentation of extended mortgage-equity analysis. The basic formula and its components are

$$R_o = y_e - mc - \Delta_o \text{ SFF} \tag{18A–2}$$

where

$$c = y_e + p \times \text{SFF} - R_m \tag{18A–3}$$

We term c the mortgage coefficient. It is an adjustment for *leverage*—the use of debt financing. Thus, mc represents the *effect* of debt financing weighted by the *extent* of debt financing.

If we use the same data in the Ellwood formulation as in extended mortgage-equity analysis, we will obtain the same R_o:

$$R_o = .14 - .75 [.14 + (.2601 \times .0517) - .1198] + .15 (.0517)$$
$$= .14 - .75 [.14 \times .0134 - .1198] + .0078$$
$$= .14 - .75 [.0336] + .0078$$
$$= \underline{\underline{.1226}}$$

We can derive a useful formula for Δ_o from the basic Ellwood formula, thus:

$$R_o = y_e - mc - \Delta_o \text{ SFF}$$
$$R_o = y_o - \Delta_o \text{ SFF, where } y_o = y_e - mc$$
$$R_o - y_o = - \Delta_o \text{ SFF}$$
$$y_o - R_o = \Delta_o \text{ SFF}$$
$$\Delta_o = \frac{y_o - R_o}{\text{SFF}} \qquad (18A-4)$$

Thus, if we know y_o, R_o, and y_e, we can calculate Δ_o for one or more holding periods. Suppose that we know y_o for the Suburban Office Building is .1148, R_o is .1226, and y_e is .14; we can compute Δ_o for a 10-year holding period, thus:

$$\Delta_o = \frac{.1148 - .1226}{.10517}$$
$$= - .151$$

or depreciation of 15.1 percent.

For a five-year holding period, we first compute:

$$y_o = .14 - .75 (.0348)^*$$
$$= .1139$$
$$^*c = .14 + (.0968 \times .1513) - .1198$$
$$= .0348$$

Then,

$$\Delta_o = \frac{.1139 - .1226}{.1515}$$
$$= - .058$$

or depreciation of 5.8 percent.

If y_e were .16 instead of .14, Δ_o for the 10-year and 5-year holding periods would be as follows.

First, compute:

$$y_o = .16 - .75 (.0524)^*$$
$$= .1207$$
$$^*c = .16 + (.2601 \times .0469) - .1198$$
$$= .0524$$

Then,

$$\Delta_o = \frac{.1207 - .1226}{.049}$$
$$= - .041$$

or depreciation of 4.1 percent.

Again, we calculate:

$$y_o = .16 - .75 (.0543)^*$$
$$= .1193$$
$$^*c = .16 + (.0968 \times .1454) - .1198$$
$$= .0543$$

and plug it in to obtain $\Delta_o = \dfrac{.1193 - .1226}{.1454}$

$$= .023$$

or depreciation of 2.3 percent

The Δ_os can be shown in a table as follows, and graphed as Exhibit 18A–1 shows:

EXHIBIT 18A–1
ANALYSIS OF .1226 CAPITALIZATION RATE

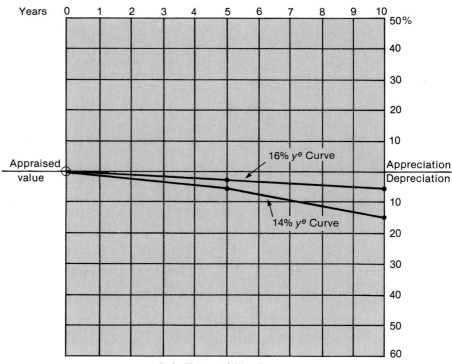

Scale: Horizontal 1″ = 2 years
Vertical   1″ = 20 percent

Prospects for yield in equity investment assuming purchase at appraised value 75 percent, financed by 20-year level payment loan at 10.5 percent interest.
Recommended graph form for use with Ellwood Tables.

| | | Holding Period | |
Equity Yield		5 years	10 years
14%		−5.8	−15.1
16%		−2.3	−4.1

The graph is useful for visual interpolation, either up and down the columns or across the rows. It shows, for example, that if the property depreciates 10 percent over 10 years, y_e will be approximately 15 percent. If it neither depreciates nor appreciates, y_e will be approximately 8 percent. It also shows that if the property depreciates 8 percent in seven years, y_e will be approximately 15 percent.

UNDERWRITER'S METHOD

Another technique that appraisers sometimes use to estimate R_o is the underwriter's method. Its name reflects the fact that it is based on financing terms. In other words, its use assumes that we know financing terms in the market and that R_e implied in the debt-service coverage ratio (DSCR) is consistent with equity requirements in the market.[2] The formula is

$$R_o = \text{DSCR} \times R_m \times m \qquad (18\text{--}5)$$

As an example, assume that a property can be financed as follows:

$$y_m = .1050$$
$$m = .75$$
$$\text{amort.} = \text{monthly for 20 years}$$
$$R_m = .1198$$
$$\text{DSCR} = 1.35$$

$$R_o = 1.35 \times .1198 \times .75$$
$$= \underline{\underline{.1213}}$$

Using this R_o, the indicated value of the Suburban Office Building is:

$$\$16,575/.1213 = \$136,645, \text{ say } \$136,600.$$

---

[2]This point is made in C. F. Sirmans and James R. Webb, "Mortgage-Equity Analysis, Again?!" *Appraisal Journal* 42, no. 1 (January 1979), pp. 44–52.

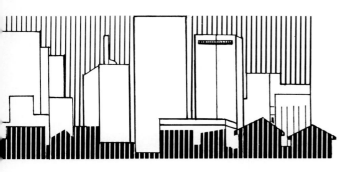

19
Residential Mortgage Financing

INTRODUCTION

When the Joneses decided to purchase the Johnsons' home (our "ongoing saga") they were faced with the problem of obtaining the funds to complete the purchase. Recall that the contract for sale contained a "financing contingency" clause, which made the sale conditional on the buyers' being able to obtain a $66,400, 30-year adjustable-rate mortgage loan, with the initial interest rate not to exceed 9.75 percent. The buyers specified these terms and the sellers agreed to them because both parties knew that a local lending institution (Last Federal Savings & Loan Association) was currently granting such loans to qualified buyers. Thus it seemed likely that the Joneses could obtain the necessary funds, and obtain them on acceptable terms.

Since a home is the largest single purchase that most families ever make, they usually do not have enough money to pay cash. They prefer to borrow most of the funds, rather than to wait many years before saving the full amount. By then, their children would not be able to use the home, and they themselves would either be dead or no longer need the space. Therefore a system of mortgage lending has developed, in which people with excess funds deposit them at interest in financial institutions, to be borrowed by people who need funds to buy houses.

What about families or individual persons who have enough to pay cash for a home? While some, such as wealthy families and older couples who have saved most of their lives, may have enough cash to buy a home, most choose to borrow because the interest rates and terms of borrowing on home loans tend to be relatively favorable. They can use the funds freed by the borrowing for other investments and, they hope, obtain *positive financial leverage*. As will be demonstrated in Chapter 20, this results when the rate of return from an investment is higher than the rate charged for the funds used to purchase the investment. Of course, they also run the risk of *negative financial leverage*, in which the rate of return is lower than the cost of funds.

471

For these reasons—lack of funds and the possibility of positive financial leverage—the vast majority of home buyers borrow most of the needed funds. Where can they borrow these funds, and what are the advantages and disadvantages associated with each source? More specifically, in our "ongoing saga," what sources of funds might the Joneses have considered in obtaining a mortgage loan to purchase the Johnsons' home?

SOURCES OF HOME MORTGAGE FINANCING

The major sources of home financing are financial institutions: savings and loan associations, commercial banks, mutual savings banks, and life insurance companies. Sometimes they are also called financial intermediaries because they stand between depositors and borrowers. They collect the deposits of many individuals, households, and organizations; they lend (invest) the funds to individuals, households, and organizations who need them. Mortgage companies and some individual investors also lend funds for home financing. They are not financial intermediaries, however, because they do not accept deposits. Mortgage companies use their own equity and borrowed capital to make (originate) loans, but usually sell the loans immediately in a secondary market. Individual investors more often lend small amounts to family members, secured by second mortgages. Exhibit 19–1 shows the general role of these lenders.

Savings and Loan Associations

During the past several years, savings and loan associations (S&Ls), because of government deregulation and competitive pressures, have evolved from highly specialized residential-mortgage-lending institutions to more general financial institutions. Today, in addition to home loans, most S&Ls make loans on commercial and industrial property, second mortgage loans, consumer loans, and commercial loans. They also offer many other services: credit cards, financial advice, real estate and stock brokerage services, safe deposit boxes, and travelers checks. Nevertheless, S&Ls still must invest at least 60 percent of their savings deposits in housing and housing-related loans and securities.

Thus, an S&L is a likely source of funds for the Joneses to purchase the Johnsons' home. They applied to Last Federal and were granted a loan equal to 80 percent of the sale price of the home. The loan carried a favorable 9.75 percent initial interest rate, had a 30-year term, and was amortized (paid off) monthly. The loan was an adjustable-rate mortgage (ARM), which means that Last Federal can adjust the interest rate, amor-

EXHIBIT 19–1
FLOW OF FUNDS TO FINANCIAL REAL ESTATE

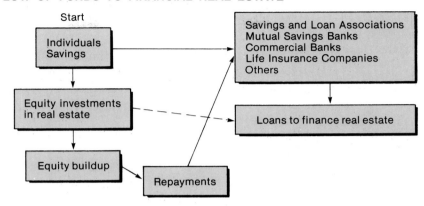

tization period, and monthly payment periodically to reflect changing interest rates in the economy.

The S&L could increase the interest rate on the Joneses' loan by a maximum of 2 percentage points per year or decrease it by any percentage, depending on an index of interest rates. Since the initial interest rate was about two percentage points below the index, it is likely that Last Federal will increase the Joneses' monthly payments at the beginning of the second and third years. Last Federal could increase the loan's 30-year amortization period up to 40 years to reflect higher interest rates. If interest rates in the economy decrease, Last Federal must decrease the interest rate on the Joneses' loan commensurately after it has reached the index level.

Last Federal also makes 30-year, fixed-interest-rate loans. The Joneses could have obtained such a loan, although the interest rate would have been at least 10.5 percent. To obtain the lower initial rate, they decided to accept the risk that rates would increase substantially over the life of their loan.

Mutual Savings Banks

Today, for all practical purposes, mutual savings banks (MSBs) are indistinguishable from S&Ls. In the past they had wider investment powers than S&Ls. MSBs are found primarily in the Northeast and started as depositories for working people; hence these banks have names such as Dime Savings Bank and Bowery Savings Bank.

Both federal and state governments charter mutual savings banks, like S&Ls. At the federal level the Federal Home Loan Bank Board charters and regulates MSBs and S&Ls. The Federal Savings and Loan Insurance Corporation insures deposits up to $100,000 in S&Ls and MSBs. For historical reasons, the Federal Deposit Insurance Corporation (FDIC) insures some MSB accounts. Mutual savings banks, like S&Ls, make all types of real estate loans, as well as consumer loans, commercial loans, and second-mortgage loans. They also sell life insurance and provide a wide variety of financial services similar to those offered by S&Ls.

Life Insurance Companies

Life Insurance companies (LICs) make mortgage loans, although they make relatively few loans directly to finance single-family homes. Laws or regulations do not require LICs to place any specified amount of funds in residential lending, unlike S&Ls. Thus LICs lend funds and buy securities that provide the highest yields at an acceptable risk level. Residential mortgages, while providing a relatively high level of safety, often do not provide high enough yields to attract LICs.

Another problem is size. Many LICs are extremely large financial institutions with millions of dollars to invest daily. Making loans directly to individual home buyers across the nation would require LICs to establish office facilities and personnel beyond their potential cost effectiveness.

However, many LICs provide funds for home mortgage finance by purchasing packages of loans from mortgage companies, which are also called mortgage bankers. The mortgage companies originate loans according to the LICs' criteria, group them into packages, and sell them to the LICs at—they hope—a small profit.

Life insurance companies also buy mortgage-backed securities in the secondary market—bonds issued by the Federal National Mortgage Association (FNMA), securities issued by approved lenders and backed by the Government National Mortgage Association (GNMA), and mortgage-participation certificates issued by the Federal Home Loan Mortgage Corporation (FHLMC). By buying these securities, LICs and other investors pump funds indirectly into the primary mortgage market—in which mortgages are originated—through the secondary mortgage market—where mortgage originators sell their loans. Thus LICs provide funds for home mortgage loans, although they are not a likely source of direct funding for the Joneses and other individual home buyers.

Commercial Banks

Commercial banks (CBs) primarily engage in the business of making short-term loans to businesses for inventory financing and other working capital needs. In addition, large CBs often make term loans (unsecured loans having terms of 5 to 15 years) and mortgage loans to corporations and other businesses. But, many CBs also make mortgage loans for homes as well as for businesses. The terms on such loans usually require shorter maturities (e.g., 20 rather than 30 years) and higher interest rates (e.g., 11 percent as opposed to 10 percent) than other mortgage lenders. Commercial banks usually require more stringent terms because the long-term loans must compete with the usually higher-yielding, more flexible short-term loans. Home mortgage loans tend to provide significantly lower yields than shorter-term loans especially during periods of high interest rates. During such times, CBs do not compete actively for home mortgage loans.

Commercial banks indirectly provide additional funds for the housing market in three ways. First, they buy secondary mortgage-market securities, as do LICs and other financial institutions. Second, they provide short-term funds to mortgage companies (as we will discuss in the following section) to enable them to originate mortgage loans and hold them until they can be sold to large financial institutions. This type of financing is termed *warehousing*, since the mortgage companies put up the loans as security for the bank financing and the loans are "stored" for a relatively short time. Third, CBs make short-term construction loans. These loans provide the funds for construction of buildings; builders must pay them off when the buildings are completed.

Mortgage Companies

Mortgage companies (MCs), as we noted above, originate mortgage loans almost exclusively for resale to institutional investors—primarily LICs and to a lesser extent MSBs. They usually have commitments from the institutional investors to buy a specified dollar amount of loans that meet certain criteria. Since the loans come from various parts of the country and the risk for each loan cannot be evaluated by the financial institution, the home loans are usually FHA loans (i.e., they are insured by the Federal Housing Administration). Such insurance relieves institutional investors of much of the default risk of home-mortgage loans.

Mortgage companies also originate mortgage loans to finance commercial properties such as apartments, office buildings, and small shopping centers. Borrowers usually negotiate extremely large loans (say, $10,000,000 and up) directly with institutional lenders.

TYPES OF MORTGAGE LOANS

Home-mortgage loans have a variety of characteristics and provisions, some of which are primary, or dominant. Thus, we may classify mortgage loans by the existence or absence of these key characteristics. Note that these classes are not mutually exclusive. A mortgage loan may be viewed in different ways: if it is government-insured, for example, it could also contain a graduated-payments feature. The type the Joneses obtained is a first-lien, conventional, adjustable-rate mortgage loan.

Priority of Lien

As we discussed in Chapter 5, we can classify mortgages by the priority of the lien they create against the property. A *first mortgage* usually has higher priority than—"is senior to"—a second or higher mortgage. Mortgages having lower priority are termed *junior mortgages*. In the event of foreclosure, their claims are paid only after mortgage holders that are senior to them are paid in full. The usual type of loan from financial institutions for a high percentage of the property's value is a first mortgage that carries the highest priority of lien except for tax liens.

Conventional versus Government-Underwritten Mortgages

Conventional Loans. Mortgage loans that do not enjoy government backing in the form of FHA insurance or a Veterans Administration (VA) guaranty are termed *conventional loans*. They are the dominant type of loan made by most financial institutions—over 80 percent of all mortgage loans in most periods—although, as we noted above, LICs tend to purchase FHA-insured loans from MCs. Local financial institutions generally prefer to make conventional loans because they can more easily tailor loans to fit the needs of the community and individual borrowers. Conventional loans are more flexible. Also, government-underwritten loans require more paper work and more adherence to regulations, and have substantially higher administrative costs.

FHA-Insured Loans. The FHA insures loans made by private lenders that meet FHA's property and credit-risk standards. The insurance protects the lenders against borrower default. If a borrower defaults, the FHA covers any lender loss after foreclosure and conveyance of title to the property to the U.S. Department of Housing and Urban Development. The borrower pays a one-time premium for the insurance, although the premium can be financed (included in the loan amount) and amortized over the life of the loan. On a 30-year loan of $67,500 (the normal maximum single-family loan) having a 10 percent interest rate, the mortgage insurance premium (MIP) is $2,565, of which $2,550 can be financed. Thus, the total amount borrowed would be $70,050, and the amount added to the monthly payments to amortize the MIP would be $22.38. The total monthly payment (including MIP) would be $614.74. The premiums are deposited in the Mutual Mortgage Insurance Fund, which reimburses lenders in case of foreclosure.

As we discussed in Chapter 12, the FHA has many programs to insure mortgages for various types of properties. Some of the programs, for example, insure loans for low-income housing, nursing homes, cooperative apartments, and condominiums. The most widely used FHA program insures single-family home mortgages and is authorized by Title II Section 203 of the National Housing Act. Thus they are often called *Section 203 loans*.

Generally, FHA-insured loans require lower down payments than conventional loans–3 percent of the first $50,000 of property value and 5 percent of amounts above $50,000 to the maximum amount allowed. Some borrowers who cannot qualify for a conventional loan can thus qualify for an FHA loan. Their monthly payments may be higher, however, because of the larger amounts borrowed due to the smaller down payment and because of the payments to amortize the insurance premium. Exhibit 19–2 shows an example of an FHA loan and foreclosure.

EXHIBIT 19–2
FHA-INSURED LOAN EXAMPLE

January. Buyers purchase a house appraised for $40,000.
Down payment: .03 × $40,000 = $1,200
Loan amount: $40,000 − $1,200 = $38,800

December. Borrowers default and lender forecloses.

Loan balance	$38,600
Foreclosure sale price	36,800
Loss	$ 1,800
Interest lost	500
Foreclosure costs	500
Total cost to lender reimbursed by FHA	$ 2,800

VA-Guaranteed Loans. The Veterans Administration (VA) is a government agency whose purpose is to help veterans with special problems (such as physical disability) and to readjust to civilian life. One way is helping veterans obtain home-mortgage loans for which they might not otherwise qualify. Usually, VA guarantees loans by private lending institutions to veterans up to a maximum loss of $27,500. Thus if a veteran defaults, the VA will reimburse the lender for any loss up to $27,500 after the property has been foreclosed and sold (see Exhibit 19–3).

The VA will guarantee loans to eligible veterans up to 100 percent of a property's value; zero down payments on VA loans are common. The VA also prohibits lenders from charging points (or discounts) to veterans for making a loan.[1] Sellers of properties however, may be willing to pay points in order for veterans to obtain loans to buy their properties. In areas where eligible veterans cannot obtain loans from financial institutions, the VA can make direct loans to them.

---

[1] We will discuss discount points later in this chapter.

EXHIBIT 19–3
VA-GUARANTEED LOAN EXAMPLE

January. Veteran purchases a house appraised for $40,000.

Down payment	=	–0–
Loan amount	=	$40,000

December. Veteran defaults and lender forecloses.

Loan balance	$39,500
Foreclosure sale price	34,500
Loss	$ 5,000
Interest lost	600
Foreclosure costs	750
Total cost to lender reimbursed by VA	$ 6,350*

*VA will reimburse the lender up to the amount of the guaranty. The maximum guaranty is $27,500 or 60 percent of the loan amount, whichever is less. In this example, therefore, the guaranty is $24,000 (.60 × $40,000), provided the veteran has not previously used any of his or her entitlement. If the loss to the lender exceeds the amount of the guaranty, the veteran may be sued for the excess.

Types of Amortization

Borrowers amortize (pay off) mortgage loans in three ways. First, they may pay off the loans completely in one repayment of principal. Second, they may amortize the loans in equal periodic payments (e.g., monthly payments) over the life of the loan. Third, they may partially amortize the loans, and pay a large, lump-sum payment on maturity. These types of amortization identify loans as *straight (or straight-term)* mortgages, *fully amortized* mortgages, or *partially amortized* mortgages, respectively.

Straight (or Straight-Term) Mortgages. Straight mortgages are repaid in full with one payment on maturity of the loan. During the life of the loan, however, borrowers make interest payments periodically (e.g., monthly or quarterly). Although such loans are used infrequently to finance single-family homes, they are used quite often in land transactions. Typically, developers purchase land with such loans, expecting to be able to repay the loans after development and sale of lots. During development they pay interest only.

Fully Amortizing Mortgages. Fully amortizing mortgages are paid off completely by periodic (usually monthly) payments. At maturity, the loan balance is zero. Most single-family residential loans are of this type, as are many loans for income-producing properties. As the loan is amortized, the owner's equity interest grows; this is termed *equity buildup*. When fully amortizing loans call for *equal* periodic payments they are known as *standard fixed-payment mortgages* (SFPMs). Before adjustable-rate mortgages were introduced, SFPMs were the dominant type of loan for home-mortgage financing. With adjustable-rate mortgages, however, monthly payments can change as interest rates vary, although the loans remain fully amortizing.

Partially Amortizing Mortgages. Partially amortizing mortgage loans require periodic payments but are not paid off completely by the payments. A balance remains on these loans at maturity that must be repaid in one relatively large lump sum. The balance is called a *balloon* and is satisfied by a *balloon payment*. These loans are seldom used to finance home purchases except in seller-provided second mortgages. Seller financing occurs frequently only during periods of high interest rates, when buyers cannot otherwise obtain adequate financing and sellers cannot sell without helping to finance buyers.

Payment or Yield Variability

Lenders have devised new forms of mortgages to increase their yields as interest rates rise or to enable young home buyers to afford loan payments that will rise as their incomes rise. The Joneses obtained such a loan from Last Federal Savings & Loan—an adjustable-rate mortgage loan. They also might have qualified for a graduated payment loan or a shared appreciation loan.

Adjustable Rate Mortgages. Adjustable-rate mortgages (ARMs) are offered by almost all lenders. They evolved from two other types of loans used previously to adjust lenders' yields—renegotiable-rate mortgages (RRMs, sometimes called *rollover mortgages*) and variable-rate mortgages (VRMs). The RRMs consisted of a series of short-maturity (e.g., three-year) loans. At each maturity the interest rate on the loan would be renegotiated according to current market rates. With VRMs, the lender could adjust the interest rate periodically (e.g., each year) according to an index of interest rates.

The Federal Home Loan Bank Board authorized ARMs for federal S&Ls in 1981 under the term *adjustable mortgage loan:*

> An adjustable mortgage loan (AML) permits adjustment of the interest rate, which may be implemented through changes in the payment amount, the outstanding principal loan balance, the loan term, or any combination of these variables.[2]

The interest rate on ARMs must be tied to an index of interest rates that is beyond the control of the lender. Examples of such indexes are (1)

---

[2]FHLBB Res. No. 81–206, 1981.

the FHLB District cost of funds of FSLIC-insured S&Ls, (2) the national average contract mortgage rate for the purchase of existing homes, (3) the monthly average of weekly auction rates on three- or six-month U.S. Treasury bills, and (4) the monthly average on U.S. Treasury securities adjusted to constant maturities of one, two, three, or five years. Either the *Federal Home Loan Bank Board* or the *Federal Reserve Bulletin* publish all of these indexes.

As with VRMs and RRMs, lenders must decrease interest rates on ARMs as the index declines, and of course they may increase them as the index rises. They must give notice of interest rate changes to borrowers at least 30 days in advance, and may not charge a prepayment penalty if the borrowers decide to pay off their loans.

Lenders may establish their own ARM plans within these regulations and guidelines. However, administrative costs, competition, and secondary market requirements place limits on most lenders' flexibility. Frequent adjustments are costly and may result in a loss of good will with borrowers. Competitors may place limits on the frequency and magnitude of adjustments. Lenders, for example, may place interest-rate caps on such loans. Such caps limit the total interest-rate increase to a maximum number of percentage points (e.g., five points). And secondary-market purchasers have limited the rate and payment adjustments for mortgages they will purchase (see Frame 19–1).

Frame 19–1

Fannie Mae Tightens Underwriting Standards

Tighter underwriting standards were announced this week by the Federal National Mortgage Association.

The changes, effective with commitments to purchase loans issued by Fannie Mae on and after October 15, 1985, will:

☐ Increase the required amount of income a borrower needs to qualify for mortgage loans with low down payments. Loans for sale to Fannie Mae with less than 10 percent down payments must be underwritten to 25 percent and 33 percent payment-to-income ratios. A borrower's monthly housing expenses will not be allowed to exceed 25 percent of gross monthly income, and housing expenses plus installment debt cannot exceed 33 percent. The ratio presently is 28 percent/36 percent. All outstanding installment debt must be included in the total obligations-to-income ratio, including that of less than 10 months' duration;

☐ Discontinue the purchase of any adjustable-rate mortgages (ARMs) that do not include an interest-rate cap or which have graduated-payment features;

☐ Limit contributions paid by any interested party to the transaction other than the home buyer (seller, builder, real estate agent, etc.) to 3 percent of the sales price or appraised value, whichever is less, on fixed-rate loans with less than 10 percent down. No contributions will be permitted on behalf of the home buyer on ARMs with less than 10 percent down. Buydowns will not be permitted on ARMs, regardless of down payment. When the buyer makes a down payment of 10 percent or more on a fixed-rate loan, contributions will be limited to 6 percent. Contributions are defined to include all financing costs, such as loan fees and buydowns, and other costs related to the transaction normally paid by the home buyer;

☐ Require that, when a borrower is aided by a co-borrower who contributes to the down payment, the co-borrower must take title and occupy the property if the down payment is less than 10 percent. If the down payment is 10 percent or more the co-borrower must be an immediate family member;

☐ Require a home buyer to make a minimum 5 percent cash down payment in addition to any funds received as a gift toward the purchase of a house; and

☐ Eliminate Fannie Mae's purchase of investor or second-home loans and of refinanced mortgages that include scheduled, or the potential for, negative amortization.

Fannie Mae plans to double its number of appraisal reviews, and will require mortgage originators to repurchase loans that have faulty appraisals.

Source: U.S. League of Savings Institutions. *Washington Notes* 39, no. 32 (August 9, 1985).

Exhibit 19–4 contains an example of a 30-year ARM. It assumes that the purchase price of a home was $40,000, with the buyers paying $4,000 down. Thus, the loan amount is $36,000, with a beginning interest rate of 10.0 percent (.100). The interest rate is tied to an index of the cost of funds at federally insured savings institutions, which was 8.5 percent (.085) when the loan was made. The interest rate and monthly payments can be changed for each six-month period, with a maximum annual change of 2 percentage points (.020). The maximum increase in the interest rate over the life of the loan is 5.0 percentage points (.050); thus, the highest possible rate is 15.0 percent.

Note that when the index goes up by two percentage points or less, the interest rate on the loan goes up by the same amount—unless the maximum increase has already been made in that year, as it had when the rate could not be increased at the beginning of the 31st month. Also, if an increase in the interest rate must be forgone by the lender, the amount forgone reduces the amount of any decrease in the next period.

It should be apparent that an ARM can contain a wide variety of provisions and their combinations. Borrowers should understand the essential characteristics of the loans they are considering, and they should calculate the payments in the most adverse situation. As a general rule, borrowers should always require loans with annual and overall caps on

EXHIBIT 19–4
ADJUSTABLE-RATE MORTGAGE

Time Period (Months)	Interest Rate	Monthly Payment	Cost of Funds Index	Remaining Balance at Beginning of Period
1–6	.100	315.96	.085	36,000.00
7–12	.105	329.22	.090	35,902.43
13–18	.125*	383.43	.115	35,810.01
19–24	.105†	329.52	.090	35,745.89
25–30	.125*	383.06	.130	35,643.19
31–36	.125‡	383.06	.130	35,570.65

*Maximum increase = 2.0 percent.
†Amount of decrease is reduced by amount of increase previously forgone.
‡Maximum increase for year has already been taken.

interest-rate adjustments. Also, they should avoid loans having negative amortization, for which the principal balance outstanding can increase.

Graduated-Payments Mortgages. In a graduated-payments mortgage (GPM), payments begin at a lower amount than in a comparable standard fixed-payment mortgage. They increase over several years (usually 5 to 10 years) to a level higher than the payments in a standard fixed-payment mortgage (see Exhibit 19–5). After the period for payment increases ends, the payments for the remaining term can be either fixed or adjustable.

EXHIBIT 19–5
PATTERN OF PAYMENTS

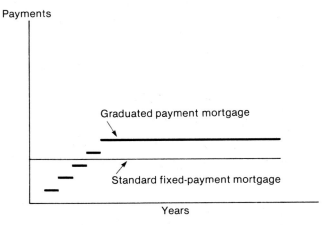

In the early years of a GPM, interest may accrue at a higher rate than is actually paid. The lender adds the unpaid interest to the principal balance, resulting in *negative amortization*. The remaining loan balance increases, rather than decreases, for this period.

The FHA has several plans for insuring GPMs under Section 245 of the National Housing Act. In an example of a five-year FHA-insured GPM, we can use the following factors to calculate the monthly payments for each $1,000 of loan amount of a 12.75 percent, 30-year loan:

Year	Factor
1	8.3983
2	9.0282
3	9.7053
4	10.4332
5	11.2157

The highest outstanding loan balance will occur in Year 6— $1,087.1331 per $1,000 of original loan amount.

We can compute the mortgage amount thus:

$$\frac{\text{Mortgage}}{\text{amount}} = \frac{\text{Sale price} \times .97}{\text{Highest outstanding balance per dollar}}$$

Therefore on a $60,000 home, the mortgage amount would be ($60,000 × .97)/1.0871331 = $53,535.30, compared with the $57,500 obtainable on a level-payment, FHA-insured loan. The payments for the first year with the GPM are 53.5353 × 8.3983 = $449.61, while the payments on the fixed-payment loan are $624.85. Payments from the sixth year to maturity on the GPM are higher at $645.47, however.

Note that negative amortization occurs with the GPM. The monthly interest would be .1275 × $53,535.30 = $568.81, while payments for the first year are $449.61. Thus, monthly negative amortization would be $658.81 − $449.61 = $119.20, the amount that the principal balance increases.

Shared-Appreciation Mortgages.   Shared-appreciation mortgages (SAMs) have gained favor with some lenders and borrowers during periods of high interest rates. Shared-appreciation mortgages usually carry lower rates than other mortgages because the lender shares in the property's sale proceeds when it is sold or at maturity of the loan. The share of a property's proceeds that an FHLBB-regulated lender (S&Ls and MSBs) can receive is limited to 40 percent. The maximum loan term permitted is 10 years, although the amortization period may be as long as 40 years.

The loan term is limited to 10 years so that inordinately large appreciation will not accumulate before settlement between lender and borrower. The amount of the proceeds that must be paid to the lender on sale or at maturity of the loan is termed *contingent deferred interest.* The lender must provide refinancing of a SAM at loan maturity if the property is not sold, and the refinancing must include an amount to cover the contingent deferred interest, as well as the remaining balance on the SAM. The term of a loan to refinance a SAM is limited to 30 years. The lender is prohibited from charging fees or prepayment penalties to refinance a SAM.

Before committing themselves to a SAM, borrowers should assess the probability of continuing high interest rates, the differential between the interest rate on the SAM and the rates on other types of loans, and the amount of possible appreciation in the property's value. On an $80,000 loan, a 2 percent interest rate differential over a 10-year term on a monthly payment, 40-year amortizing loan would be worth approximately $9,646,56 (discounted at 10 percent). Thus, if the property's value at the beginning of the 10-year period was $100,000 the property would need to increase to $165,284.09 for the lender's annual yield to equal 12 percent (see Exhibit 19–6). In other words, if the property were expected to increase in value by more than $65,284 over the 10-year period, the borrower would benefit in taking the higher-rate conventional loan.

EXHIBIT 19–6
COMPARISON OF A SAM WITH A FIXED-PAYMENT LOAN

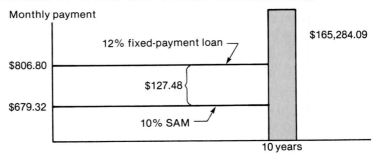

PV of $127.48 per month at 10% for 10 years = $9,646.56
PV of $(.40)($65,284.09) due in 10 years at 10% = $9,646.56

Function or Use

Mortgages can be used in different ways to accomplish different functions in a transaction. Thus we identify mortgages by the function they play in achieving certain objectives. Mortgages thus identified are termed *purchase money mortgages, blanket mortgages, package mortgages, participation mortgages,* and *reverse-annuity mortgages.*

Purchase Money Mortgages.   Whenever a seller lends all or part of the purchase price of a property to the purchaser, and the loan is secured by a mortgage on the property, the mortgage is termed a *purchase-money mortgage*. (PMM). Such mortgages are used fairly often in transactions involving single-family homes. Their function is to provide funds above the amount of the purchasers' equity and the funds they are able to borrow from an institutional lender.

Suppose the Browns want to sell their home for $100,000. The Greens want to buy it, but have only $10,000 in cash they can pay. They can borrow $80,000 on a first mortgage from Third Federal Savings and Loan, but they are still short $10,000. The Browns agree to lend them $10,000, with a second mortgage—a PMM—as security.

Purchase money mortgages are used to finance other types of real estate as well. Landowners often partially finance the sale of large tracts for development with a PMM. They take cash for a portion of the sale price but finance the remainder themselves. The PMM is paid off from the proceeds of lots as they are developed and sold. The landowner, in effect, is a partner of the developer.

Blanket Mortgages.   A mortgage secured by more than one property is termed a *blanket mortgage*. Such a mortgage creates security in one document for the financing of two or more—and often many—parcels of real estate. A blanket mortgage perhaps is used most often in financing large tracts of land, either developed or to be developed, into building lots. The mortgage covers all of the lots. Portions of the loan are paid off as the developer-owner sells the lot, and the lots are released from the mortgage. That is, they no longer secure the debt. Thus, blanket mortgages usually have a *release clause* that states that a lot will be released on payment of a specified amount. This amount is usually greater than the proportionate amount of the loan the lot secures. For example, if a developer has borrowed $1,000,000 to finance a tract to be developed into 100 lots, the proportionate amount of the loan per lot is $10,000. The release clause probably would require a payment of $12,000 or $15,000 for the release of one lot. Lenders use this requirement to increase the security on the remaining balance of the loan. They reason that the loan should be paid back from the early profits rather than from later profits.

Reverse-Annuity Mortgages.   Reverse-annuity mortgages (RAMs) provide income to homeowners who have a sizeable equity in their homes. Such homeowners are usually older persons who have paid off a substantial portion of their mortgages and have realized appreciation of their homes' values. In a RAM, a financial institution agrees to pay the homeowner a monthly payment, or annuity, and to be repaid from the homeowner's equity when she sells the home. The institution limits the annuity payments to a specified percentage of the homeowner's equity in the property. For example, the annuity payments might be based on a homeowner's 60 percent equity (say, $60,000) down to an equity ratio of 20 percent. The institution therefore would pay her annuity until her equity is reduced to $20,000 on a $100,000 property. The homeowner might then sell or refinance the property to pay off the debt to the annuity lender.

Some RAMs allow the homeowners to occupy the property until their deaths, with the annuity lender to be reimbursed then from the proceeds of the sale of the property.

Package Mortgages.   Package mortgages provide additional funds for home buyers. The mortgage includes home-related items of personal property such as a range, dishwasher, refrigerator, and furnishings. When these items are included in the mortgage, the lender can lend a larger amount, and the home buyer can amortize the equipment over a much longer period than if they were financed by a consumer loan.

QUALIFYING FOR A LOAN

A potential borrower first must apply for a mortgage loan, usually to a financial institution, and pay a mortgage application fee. Exhibit 19–7 illustrates a savings and loan association's residential loan application. Note that the form contains sections for the applicant to provide information about the property to be financed, personal information, projected income and housing expenses, judgments and other debts, assets, liabilities, and credit references. Using this information, the lender decides whether the applicant qualifies for a loan in the amount requested.

Ratios

Lenders use several standard ratios in seeing whether buyers are qualified for a loan. These ratios vary somewhat, depending on whether the loan is an FHA, VA, or conventional loan.

FHA Loans.   There are two qualification ratios for FHA-insured loans:

Total monthly housing expense ÷ Monthly net income[3] ≤ 38 percent

and

Total monthly obligations ÷ Monthly net income[3] ≤ 54 percent

---

[3]Gross income less income tax.

EXHIBIT 19–7

RESIDENTIAL LOAN APPLICATION

the BANK Empire of America FSA
Member FSLIC

MORTGAGE APPLIED FOR ➡	☐ Conventional ☐ FHA	Amount	Interest Rate	No. of Months	Monthly Payment Principal & Interest	Escrow/Impounds (to be collected monthly)
	☐ VA ☐ ____	$_____	____ %		$_____	☐ Taxes ☐ Hazard Ins. ☐ Mtg. Ins. ☐ _____

Prepayment Option Loan may be prepaid in part or in whole at any time without penalty.

SUBJECT PROPERTY

Property Street Address	City	County	State	Zip	No. Units

Legal Description (Attach description if necessary)	Year Built

Purpose of Loan: ☐ Purchase ☐ Construction-Permanent ☐ Construction ☐ Refinance ☐ Other (Explain)

Complete this line if Construction-Permanent or Construction Loan ➡	Lot Value Data	Original Cost	Present Value (a)	Cost of Imps (b)	Total (a + b)	Enter total as purchase price in details ◀ of purchase.
	Year Acquired ____	$_____	$_____	$_____	$_____	

Complete this line if a Refinance Loan

Year Acquired	Original Cost	Amt. Existing Liens	Purpose of Refinance	Describe Improvements ( ) made ( ) to be made	
$	$				Cost: $_____

Title Will Be Held in What Name(s)	Manner In Which Title Will Be Held

Source of Down Payment and Settlement Charges

This application is designed to be completed by the borrower(s) with the lender's assistance. The Co-Borrower Section and all other Co-Borrower questions must be completed and the appropriate box(es) checked if ☐ another person will be jointly obligated with the Borrower on the loan, or ☐ the Borrower is relying on income from alimony, child support or separate maintenance or on the income or assets of another person as a basis for repayment of the loan, or ☐ the Borrower is married and resides, or the property is located, in a community property state.

BORROWER	**CO-BORROWER**
Name	Name
Date of Birth: Age: School: ____ yrs.	Date of Birth: Age: School: ____ yrs.
Present Address No. Years ____ ☐ Own ☐ Rent	Present Address No. Years ____ ☐ Own ☐ Rent
Street	Street
City/State/Zip	City/State/Zip
Former Address if less than 2 years at present address	Former Address if less than 2 years at present address
Street	Street
City/State/Zip	City/State/Zip
Years at former address ☐ Own ☐ Rent	Years at former address ☐ Own ☐ Rent
Marital Status ☐ Married ☐ Separated ☐ Unmarried (incl. single, divorced, widowed) Deps. other than listed by Co-Borrower No. Ages	Marital Status ☐ Married ☐ Separated ☐ Unmarried (incl. single, divorced, widowed) Deps. other the listed by Borrower No. Ages
Name and Address of Employer Years employed in this line of work or profession? ____ years Years on this job ____ ☐ Self-Employed*	Name and Address of Employer Years employed in this line of work or profession? ____ years Years on this job ____ ☐ Self-Employed*
Position/Title Type of Business	Position/Title Type of Business
Social Security Number*** Home Phone Business Phone	Social Security Number*** Home Phone Business Phone

GROSS MONTHLY INCOME				**MONTHLY HOUSING EXPENSE****			**DETAILS OF PURCHASE**	
Item	Borrower	Co-Borrower	Total	Rent	PRESENT	PROPOSED	Do Not Complete If Refinance	
Base Empl Income	$	$	$	Rent	$		a. Purchase Price	$
Overtime				First Mortgage (P&I)		$	b. Total Closing Costs (Est.)	
Bonuses				Other Financing (P&I)			c. Prepaid Escrows (Est.)	
Commissions				Hazard Insurance			d. Total (a + b + c)	$
Dividends/Interest				Real Estate Taxes			e. Amount this Mortgage	( )
Net Rental Income				Mortgage Insurance			f. Other Financing	( )
Other† (before completing, see notice under Describe Other Income below.)				Homeowner Assn. Dues			g. Other Equity	( )
				Other:			h. Amount of Cash Deposit	( )
				Total Monthly Pmt.	$	$	i. Closing Costs Paid by Seller	( )
				Utilities			j. Cash Req. for Closing (Est)	$
Total	$	$	$	Total	$	$		

DESCRIBE OTHER INCOME

NOTICE: † Alimony, child support, or separate maintenance income need not be revealed if the Borrower or Co-Borrower does not choose to have it considered as a basis for repaying this loan.

➡ B - Borrower C - Co-Borrower

	Monthly Amount
	$

IF EMPLOYED IN CURRENT POSITION FOR LESS THAN TWO YEARS COMPLETE THE FOLLOWING

B/C	Previous Employer/School	City/State	Type of Business	Position/Title	Dates From/To	Monthly Amount
						$

THESE QUESTIONS APPLY TO BOTH BORROWER AND CO-BORROWER

If a "yes" answer is given to a question in this column, explain on an attached sheet.	Borrower Yes or No	Co-Borrower Yes or No	If applicable, explain Other Financing or Other Equity (provide addendum if more space is needed.)
Have you any outstanding judgments? In the last 7 years, have you been declared bankrupt?			
Have you had property foreclosed upon or given title or deed in lieu thereof?			
Are you a co-maker or endorser on a note?			
Are you a party in a law suit?			
Are you obligated to pay alimony, child support, or separate maintenance?			
Is any part of the down payment borrowed?			

* FHLMC/FNMA require business credit report, signed Federal Income Tax returns for last two years, and, if available, audited Profit and Loss Statement plus balance sheet for same period.
** All Present Monthly Housing Expenses of Borrower and Co-Borrower should be listed on a combined basis.
*** Neither FHLMC nor FNMA requires this information

FHLMC 65 (Rev. 8/78) L-AP-2 12 3/83

FNMA 1003 (Rev. 8/78)

EXHIBIT 19–7 *(concluded)*

This Statement and any applicable supporting schedules may be completed jointly by both married and unmarried co-borrowers if their assets and liabilities are sufficiently joined so that the Statement can be meaningfully and fairly presented on a combined basis; otherwise separate Statements and Schedules are required (FHLMC 65A/FNMA 1003A). If the co-borrower section was completed about a spouse, this Statement and supporting schedule must be completed about that spouse also.   ☐ Completed Jointly   ☐ Not Completed Jointly

ASSETS / LIABILITIES AND PLEDGED ASSETS

Indicate by ☒ those liabilities or pledged assets which will be satisfied upon sale of real estate owned or upon refinancing of subject property.

Description	Cash or Market Value	Creditors' Name, Address and Account Number	Acct. Name If Not Borrower's	Mo. Pmt. and Mos. left to pay	Unpaid Balance
Cash Deposit Toward Purchase Held By	$	Installment Debts (include ''revolving'' charge accts)		$ Pmt./Mos.	$
Checking and Savings Accounts (show Names of Institutions/Acct. No's.)				/	
				/	
				/	
Stocks and Bonds (No./Description)				/	
				/	
Life Insurance Net Cash Value Face Amount ($)		Other Debts Including Stock Pledges		/	
SUBTOTAL LIQUID ASSETS	$				
Real Estate Owned (Enter Market Value from Schedule of Real Estate Owned)		Real Estate Loans			
Vested Interest in Retirement Fund					
Net Worth of Business Owned (ATTACH FINANCIAL STATEMENT)					
Automobiles (Make and Year)		Automobile Loans		/	
Furniture and Personal Property		Alimony, Child Support and Separate Maintenance Payments Owed To		/	
Other Assets (Itemize)					
		TOTAL MONTHLY PAYMENTS		$	
TOTAL ASSETS	A $	NET WORTH (A minus B) $		TOTAL LIABILITIES	B $

SCHEDULE OF REAL ESTATE OWNED (If Additional Properties Owned Attach Separate Schedule)

Address of Property (Indicate S if Sold, PS if Pending Sale or R if Rental being held for income)	Type of Property	Present Market Value	Amount of Mortgages & Liens	Gross Rental Income	Mortgage Payments	Taxes, Ins. Maintenance and Misc.	Net Rental Income
		$	$	$	$	$	$
TOTALS ➤		$	$	$	$	$	$

LIST PREVIOUS CREDIT REFERENCES

➤ B-Borrower C-Co-Borrower	Creditor's Name & Address	Account Number	Purpose	Highest Balance	Date Paid
				$	

List any additional names under which credit has previously been received _____

AGREEMENT: The undersigned applies for the loan indicated in this application to be secured by a first mortgage or deed of trust on the property described herein, and represents that the property will not be used for any illegal or restricted purpose, and that all statements made in this application are true and are made for the purpose of obtaining the loan. Verification may be obtained from any source named in this application. The original or a copy of this application will be retained by the lender, even if the loan is not granted. The undersigned ☐ intend or ☐ do not intend to occupy the property as their primary residence.

I/We fully understand that it is a federal crime punishable by fine or imprisonment, or both, to knowingly make any false statements concerning any of the above facts as applicable under the provisions of Title 18, United States Code, Section 1014.

_____ Date _____   _____ Date _____
Borrower's Signature   Co-Borrower's Signature

INFORMATION FOR GOVERNMENT MONITORING PURPOSES

The following information is requested by the Federal Government if this loan is related to a dwelling, in order to monitor the lender's compliance with equal credit opportunity and fair housing laws. You are not required to furnish this information, but are encouraged to do so. The law provides that a lender may neither discriminate on the basis of this information, nor on whether you choose to furnish it. However, if you choose not to furnish it, under Federal regulations this lender is required to note race and sex on the basis of visual observation or surname. If you do not wish to furnish the above information, please initial below.

BORROWER. I do not wish to furnish this information (initials)_____   CO-BORROWER: I do not wish to furnish this information (initials)_____
RACE/ ☐ American Indian, Alaskan Native ☐ Asian, Pacific Islander   RACE/ ☐ American Indian, Alaskan Native ☐ Asian, Pacific Islander
NATIONAL ☐ Black ☐ Hispanic ☐ White   ☐ Female   NATIONAL ☐ Black ☐ Hispanic ☐ White   ☐ Female
ORIGIN ☐ Other (specify)_____ SEX ☐ Male   ORIGIN ☐ Other (specify)_____ SEX ☐ Male

FOR LENDER'S USE ONLY

(FNMA REQUIREMENT ONLY) This application was taken by ☐ face to face interview ☐ by mail ☐ by telephone

_____   EMPIRE OF AMERICA FSA
(Interviewer)   _____
                                             Name of Employer of Interviewer

Lot Size _____ Abstract _____ Title Ins. _____ Present Owner _____

Existing Lein _____ Held by _____ Address _____

Name and Address of Relative _____

FHLMC 65 (Rev. 8/78)   REVERSE   FNMA 1003 (Rev. 8/78)

From *The Wall Street Journal*, with permission of Cartoon Features Syndicate.

VA Loans.   These employ one principal ratio:

Total monthly housing expense ÷ Monthly net effective income[4]

$$\leq 54 \text{ percent}$$

Conventional Loans.   Private mortgage lenders use these qualification ratios:

Monthly housing expense ÷ Monthly gross income ≤ 25–30 percent

Total monthly obligations ÷ Monthly gross income ≤ 80–90 percent

The lender will have the property appraised, if the applicant meets these ratios and has an acceptable credit rating. The final loan amount, determined as a function of the property's appraised value (e.g., 80, 90, or 95 percent), will be established. The loan will then be ready to be closed, usually concurrently with the closing of the purchase of the property being purchased by the borrower.

Private Mortgage Insurance

Many lenders require private mortgage insurance (PMI) for conventional loans *over 80 percent* of the security property's value. Private mortgage

---

[4]Gross income less income tax, social security, and monthly obligations.

insurance companies provide such insurance, which usually covers the top 20 percent of loans. In other words, if a borrower defaults and the property is foreclosed and sold for less than the amount of the loan, the PMI will reimburse a loss up to 20 percent of the outstanding loan principal.

Suppose that a borrower purchased a $100,000 home with 5 percent cash and a $95,000 loan. He defaults after the loan has been paid down to $94,000, and the foreclosed property is sold for $90,000. The PMI will reimburse the lender for the $4,000 loss. Twenty percent of $94,000 is $18,800, which is the maximum the PMI would pay the lender; thus, the lender would bear any additional loss if the property sold below $75,200 ($94,000 − $18,800).

The PMI company, of course, charges a premium for such insurance coverage that the lender passes on to the borrower. Typically, the premium is a one-time payment of 2.5 percent of the loan amount or a payment of one percent of the loan amount for the first year and ¼ percent per year thereafter.

FINANCIAL ANALYSIS OF HOME FINANCING

When prospective buyers of single-family homes seek financing, they must consider several provisions of the mortgage contract that can affect the cost both of the financing and of the property. The interest rate is the most obvious such element of cost. In addition, the lender can charge a discount (or points) at the time of loan origination and later charge prepayment penalties when the loan is paid off before maturity. These charges can increase the borrower's financing cost. Developers' and builders' buydowns of the interest rate may lower the borrower's interest rate for a short period (such as one year) but may be more than offset by an increase in the price of the property. The following sections discuss the nature of these considerations and demonstrate the procedures for analyzing them.

The Interest Rate and Periodic Payments

The interest rate is the percentage that lenders charge for the use of borrowed funds. Normally the interest is due and payable at the end of the borrowing period, when the principal also must be repaid. For example, if you borrow $100 for one year at 10 percent interest, you would normally owe $110 at the end of the year—$100 to repay the loan plus $10 interest. If the $10 must be paid earlier, such as at the beginning of the loan period, your *true interest rate* will be higher than 10 percent because you have the use of only $90 for the year. Thus, your rate would be

$10/90 = .11, or about 11 percent. The interest rates on most first-mortgage loans for home financing are true rates in that the interest is payable at the end of the period in which the borrowed funds are used and is calculated only on the amount borrowed and used for the period.

Since most mortgage loans are amortized monthly, the interest is calculated and payable on a monthly basis. In addition to interest, a part of each month's payment also repays a portion of the loan principal. Thus in each succeeding month the interest must be recalculated on the outstanding balance of the loan. The vast majority of home-mortgage loans are level-payment loans, in which the repayment of principal increases each month by the amount that the interest payment decreases. Exhibit 19–8 shows the allocation to principal repayment and interest on an $80,000, 10 percent, 30-year, monthly payment loan for months 1, 2, and 12, and Exhibits 19–9 and 19–10 show the financial calculator keystrokes for computing the monthly payments, interest, principal, and remaining balance on the same loan.

EXHIBIT 19–8
TIME LINE OF MORTGAGE LOAN PAYMENTS

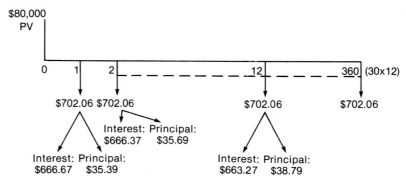

EXHIBIT 19–9
HP–12C KEYSTROKES FOR FINDING INTEREST, PRINCIPAL, AND REMAINING BALANCE

You borrow $80,000 to buy a house. The mortgage loan is amortized monthly for 30 years and carries an interest rate of 10.0 percent. What are the monthly payments, and how much of the first year's payments are applied to principal and interest? What is the balance remaining after one year?

Keystrokes	Display	Function
ON [f] REG/CLX	0.000000	Clears calculator

(continued)

EXHIBIT 19–9 *(concluded)*

Keystrokes	Display	Function
30 [g] [n / 12x]	360.000000	Enters n (number of months).
10 [g] [i / 12 ÷]	.833333	Enters i (monthly interest rate).
80,000 [PV]	80,000.00	Enters PV.
[PMT]	−702.057256	Calculates PMT (payment) with minus sign for cash paid out.
[g] [END]	−702.057256	Sets payment mode to end.
12 [f] [AMORT / n]	−7,979.984212	Portion of first year's payments (12 months) applied to interest.
[x≶y]	−444.702860	Portion of first year's payments applied to principal.
[RCL] [PV]	79,555.29715	Balance remaining after one year.
[RCL] [n]	12.000000	Total number of payments amortized.

To calculate the same information for the second year (the next 12 months) the following keystrokes are used:

Keystrokes	Display	Function
12 [f] [AMORT / n]	−7,933.418015	Portion of second year's payments applied to interest.
[x≶y]	−491.269057	Portion of second year's payments applied to principal.
[R↓] [R↓]	12.000000	Number of payments just amortized.
[RCL] [PV]	79,064.0281	Balance remaining after two years.
[RCL] [n]	24.000000	Total number of payments amortized.

EXHIBIT 19–10
BA-35 KEYSTROKES FOR FINDING INTEREST, PRINCIPAL, AND REMAINING BALANCE

Same Problem as Exhibit 19–9.

Keystrokes	Display	Function
[ON/C] [ON/C] [2nd] [FIN]	0 FIN	Clears calculator
80000 [STO] [PV]	80000 FIN	Enters initial mortgage amount and stores it

EXHIBIT 19–10 *(concluded)*

Keystrokes	Display	Function
30 × 12 = N	360 FIN	Enters total months of loan term
10 ÷ 12 = %i	.8333333 FIN	Enters monthly interest rate
CPT PMT	702.05725 FIN	Computes monthly payment
× 12 =	8424.687 ANN FIN	Computes annual payment
12 2nd BAL	79555.297 ANN FIN	Finds mortgage balance remaining after one year
EXC – RCL =	444.70281 ANN FIN	Finds portion of first year's payment applied to principal
+/– + 8424.687 = (note that the annual payment must be saved so that it can be recentered here)	7979.9842 ANN FIN	Portion of first year's payment applied to interest
12 × 2 = 2nd BAL	79064.028 ANN FIN	Balance remaining after two years
+/– + EXC =	491.26901 ANN FIN	Portion of second year's payments applied to principal
+/– + 8424.687 =	7933.418 ANN FIN	Portion of second year's payments applied to interest

Discount Points

As we noted above, most lenders charge borrowers a lump-sum amount (discount), or points, in addition to the interest rate when making mortgage loans. For example, lenders may quote an interest rate of nine percent and two or three points. A point equals one percent of the amount borrowed; therefore, two points on an $80,000 loan is $1,600, and three points is $2,400. Points decrease the net amount borrowed (i.e., the net amount available to the borrower is the original loan amount less $1,600 or $2,400, etc.) and increase the lender's yield on the loan. On FHA and conventional loans, lenders charge borrowers for the amount of the points. On VA loans, lenders by law may not charge borrowers points. *Sellers* may pay points, however, to induce a lender to grant a loan so the seller can sell the property.

Lenders charge points for two reasons. The first reason is that for tax accounting purposes, institutional lenders can include up to two points as income in the year the loan is made (any additional point income must be spread over the next 12 years). Most financial institutions, under severe pressure to generate more income (as has been the case in recent years), are eager to charge as many points as possible to increase their current year's income.

The second reason is to adjust the loan yield upward by relatively small amounts. It would be cumbersome to quote mortgage rates at 9.625 or 10.356 percent, but easier and less confusing to quote rates of 12.50 percent plus three points or 10.25 percent plus two points.

In addition to points, borrowers must usually also pay other loan fees and closing costs, such as a loan application fee, credit check fee, title charges, and an attorney's fee. These fees do not affect the lender's yield, however, as they presumably cover services provided.

Lender's Exact Yield.   As we noted, points reduce the amount of a loan available to the borrower. For example, in the loan the Joneses obtained to purchase the Johnsons' property, two points were charged, reducing the net loan proceeds to the Joneses by .02 × $66,400 = $1,328. Thus, the net loan proceeds were $66,400 − $1,328 = $65,072. We can calculate the lender's exact yield on a financial calculator by keying in the loan data, using the net proceeds instead of the loan amount, and solving for i; see Exhibits 19–11 and 19–12.

EXHIBIT 19–11
TIME LINE FOR JONESES' MORTGAGE LOAN (Assuming interest rate does not change)

```
              $570.48    $570.48                          $570.48
                 ↑          ↑                                ↑
   0 ┌──────────────────────────────────────────────────────────
     │         1          2 – – – – – – – – – – –  360
     ↓
  $65,072
($66,400 – $1,328)
```

EXHIBIT 19–12
KEYSTROKES FOR OBTAINING YIELD ON JONESES' LOAN

Keystrokes	Display	Function
HP-12C: ON f REG/CLX	0.000000	Clears calculator.
30 g n/12×	360.000000	Enters n.
$65,072 CHS PV	− 65,072.000000	Enters PV.
$570.48 PMT	570.480000	Enters PMT.

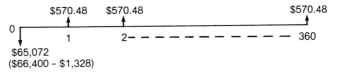

EXHIBIT 19–12 *(concluded)*

	Keystrokes				Display	Function
	i				0.832340	Calculates monthly *i*.
	12 ×				9.988074	Calculates annual *i*.
BA-35:	ON/C	ON/C	2nd	FIN	0 FIN	Clears calculator.
	30 × 12 =				360 FIN	Enters n.
	65.072 PV				67072 FIN	Enters PV.
	570.48 PMT				570.48 ANN FIN	Enters PMT.
	CPT %i				.8323395 ANN FIN	Calculates monthly *i*.
	× 12 =				9.9880742 ANN FIN	Calculates annual *i*.

Thus the lender's yield for the first year will be 9.99 percent, instead of the stated nominal interest rate of 9.75 percent. The yield would have to be recalculated each year as the interest rate, payments, and outstanding loan balance change.

Lender's Approximate Yield. Real estate practitioners often use an approximation to estimate the yield on mortgage loans: For each point, the yield on a loan is increased by $\frac{1}{8}$ percent. By this method, the Joneses loan would yield 10.00 percent to the lender, thus:

$$9.75 + \left(2 \times \frac{1}{8} \right) = 10.0$$

Obviously, the lender's yield is the effective rate that the borrower pays. Borrowers must be prepared to pay points, but should shop around and compare loan points and terms, as well as interest rates.

Buydowns

During periods of high interest rates and low demand, home builders often *buy down* the interest rate the first one to five years on a lender's loans to purchasers of homes in the new development. Buydowns enable builders to advertise a much lower interest rate for the first few years (see Frame 19–2). Buydowns attract some potential buyers who would otherwise be repelled by the interest rate. They also enable some buyers to qualify for a loan—based on the first few years' mortgage payments—

who otherwise would not qualify. Sometimes total mortgage payments are drastically reduced (see Frame 19–3). Builders may also advertise other sales incentives such as "free" swimming pool, furniture, bond, or vacation. The advertising of buydowns and other sales incentives have been an effective marketing device for builders in many areas; however, such plans have some important hazards for home-loan borrowers.

Payment Shock.   The first hazard of obtaining a loan with a buydown incentive is *payment shock.* Many borrowers seem unaware of or unconcerned about future payment increases after the buydown period elapses. These borrowers are not prepared when the payments later increase drastically, and often find themselves unable or unwilling to make the payments. They may attempt to sell their homes, or some may default and willingly allow the lender to foreclose and obtain title to the property.

Inflated Prices.   The second hazard of buydowns and other sales incentives is the likelihood that the property cannot be sold for as much as the owners paid. High interest rates dampen demand and keep prices down. To cover the cost of incentives, builders attempt to increase the sale prices of the homes. Although the lender requires the homes to be appraised, appraisers may use as comparables other similar properties in the same development that sold with similar incentives. Thus, a cycle is established in which a few inflated selling prices lead to higher appraised values, which then justify higher sale prices for all houses in the development. Then, when the homeowners experience payment shock and try to bail out, they find that new potential purchasers will not pay the inflated prices. They are saddled with financial commitments they cannot afford.

Valuing Buydowns.   Potential buyers must assume that the value of buydowns and other incentives is added to the price of a home to be financed. They can estimate relatively easily the values of such items as swimming pools, vacations, furniture, and bonds by obtaining the prices or costs of such items. Whatever their costs, they are not "free," and their values should be subtracted from a home's sale price to determine the home's value without the item.

Similarly, the value of a buydown should be subtracted from a home's price to estimate its resale value without the buydown. To do this, the difference between each buydown year's payments and the market level of payments must be obtained and capitalized at the market interest rate. Exhibit 19–13 shows these calculations for the buydown illustrated in Frame 19–2.

Home buyers should subtract the value of the buydown from the pur-

EXHIBIT 19–13
VALUE OF A BUYDOWN

Year	Payment	Difference between Payment and Fifth Year's Payment	Present Value of Difference at 13.65%	Discounted Present Values
1	$496	$285	$3,180	$3,180
2	574	207	2,310	$2,033
3	650	131	1,462	1,132
4	728	53	591	403
5	781	–0–	–0–	–0–
	Present value of the buydown			$6,748

chase price to obtain an estimate of the maximum resale price they could obtain from the property. This amount would be

$$\$65,000 - \$6,748 = \$58,252, \text{ say } \$58,000$$

Prepayment Penalties

Most modern home-mortgage loans do not contain a prepayment penalty provison. Nevertheless, a borrower sometimes encounters such a provision, and should be aware of its potential impact. A prepayment penalty provision requires a borrower to pay a specified amount when paying off the loan early. For home-mortgage loans, these provisions usually apply only during the early years of a loan (e.g., first three to five years) and require a relatively moderate amount, ranging from about .5 percent to 2 percent of the outstanding balance of the loan. Thus on a loan having an outstanding balance of $80,000, the prepayment penalty might range from $400 to $1,600.

While borrowers should be wary of a prepayment penalty provision, it may offset a higher interest rate. Therefore if borrowers believe there is a strong probability they will not sell the home and pay off the mortgage for three years or more, they may be willing to accept a prepayment penalty provision. The loan might carry a somewhat lower interest rate (e.g., .5 percent lower) than they could obtain on a loan without a prepayment penalty provision.

The Loan Balance

Analysis of real estate investment alternatives and financing plans often requires the calculation of a loan's outstanding balance. For example, questions about whether to sell a property and buy another or to refinance the property require that the loan balance be subtracted from the expected selling price to obtain the owner's equity. Calculation of an owner's rate of return also require that his equity be estimated.

Frame 19–2

Buydowns

NO CASH DOWN, 7.9% INTEREST, MOVE IN NOW.

NOW THERE'S NO EXCUSE TO RENT.

And no reason to wait! No down payment, no cash for closing costs, and 7.9% means you can move in to one of the roomiest condos around right now! 1, 2, and 3 bedrooms with all-new kitchens and wall-to-wall carpet, from $57,950. Take I-395 to Seminary Rd. West Exit. Left on North Beauregard, left on North Armistead, left to Sales Center. Open everyday, 11-6. Phone 941-7761.

13.65
annual percentage rate

INSIDE THE BELTWAY IN ALEXANDRIA!

saxony Square

BEATS THE HECK OUT OF RENTING!

Developed by Saxony Square Associates

	Payments	Increase	Buydown Amount
Yr 1	$496		$5,430
2	574	15%	2,484
3	659	13%	1,572
4	728	7.5%	636
5	781	7.5%	
			$6,084 (discounted)

Sales by
J.K. Robert Company
BROKERS WELCOME

Typical terms: Purchase price $65,000. Mortgage price $68,250. No money down. 12 equal monthly principal + interest payments of $496.00 at 7.9% (first year); $574 at 9.5% (second year); $650 at 11% (third year); $728 at 12.5% (fourth year); $781 at 13.5% (fifth year), annual percentage rate 13.65. Years 6-30 will be refinanced at current market rates. Based on the current rate of 13.5%, the monthly payment is estimated to be $781.

Source: *Washington Post*, January 14, 1984.

━━━━━━━━━━━━━━━━━━━━━━━━ *Frame 19–3* ━━━━━━━━━━━━━━━━━━━━━━━━

Condo Concessions

All manner of concessions are being offered by South Florida developers saddled with unsold luxury condo apartments. For instance, the developer of the Hamilton, a new 267-unit high-rise on Miami's Biscayne Bay, is offering to pick up half of a buyer's mortgage costs for three years. At the end of that time, the buyer has the option of picking up the full costs or returning the unit to the developer.

Calculation of the outstanding balance on an interest-only loan is, of course, quite simple. The outstanding balance is the original amount borrowed.

For fully amortizing, fixed-payment loans, it is important for borrowers to recognize that the outstanding balance on a loan is equal to the present value of all future mortgage payments.

$$b = \text{PV of future payments}$$
$$= \text{Monthly payment}/R_m$$

where R_m = the mortgage capitalization rate (mortgage constant) at the mortgage interest rate for the remaining number of months. R_ms may be obtained from compound and discount interest tables (Column 6), or from a financial calculator. The constant is the periodic payment on a loan of $1.00.

Example. A homeowner borrowed $80,000 on a 30-year, monthly payment, fully amortizing loan 5 ½ years ago. The loan carries an interest rate of 11.5 percent and monthly payments of $792.23. The homeowner wants to know her outstanding loan balance.

$$b = \$792.23/R_m$$
$$= \$792.23/.010201 \text{ (294 months at 11.5 percent)}$$
$$= \$77,661.99$$

The loan balance b may also be obtained directly from a financial calculator. For example, the following calculator keystrokes will calculate b:

	Keystrokes	Display
HP-12C:	ON f $\boxed{\frac{\text{REG}}{\text{CLX}}}$	0.000000
	30 g $\boxed{\frac{\text{n}}{12\times}}$	360

(continued)

	Keystrokes	Display
HP-12C (concluded):	11.5 [g] [i / 12÷]	.9583
	80,000 [CHS] [PV]	− 80,000
	[PMT]	792.23
	Balance after 5.5 years	
	5.5 [g] [n / 12×] [FV]	77,661.27
BA-35:	[ON/C] [ON/C] [2nd] [FIN]	0 FIN
	30 [×] 12 [=] [N]	360 FIN
	11.5 [÷] 12 [=] [%i]	.9583333 FIN
	80000 [PV]	80000 FIN
	[CPT] [PMT]	792.23 ANN FIN
	12 [×] 5.5 [=] [2nd] [BAL]	77661.266 ANN FIN

OVERVIEW

An elaborate system of financial institutions, legal instruments, and government support has evolved to enable people to purchase their own homes. Rather than waiting most of their lives until they save enough to pay cash for a home, purchasers can borrow most of the needed funds from an institutional lender—S&L, MSB, LIC, CB, or MC—and repay the loan over many years. The financial institutions obtain the funds from savers' deposits and sales of securities (stocks and bonds). They attempt to lend the funds at a higher interest rate than they have to pay to attract the funds. To protect themselves against the risk of default, the institutions require borrowers to guarantee personally to repay the loan by signing a note. They also require the borrowers to pledge the property as security by signing a mortgage.

Many different forms of mortgage loans have been created to serve various needs and purposes. Thus mortgages can be classified in several ways, which are not mutually exclusive. They can be categorized according to their priority of lien, whether they are government underwritten, by type of amortization, by payment or yield variability, and by function. Each category contains various types of mortgage loans.

To borrow funds to purchase a home, home buyers must meet certain financial standards. Their expected housing expenses and total obligations must be no more than a specified ratio to net or gross income. Credit references must also show an acceptable record of meeting other loan obligations.

Lenders make loans up to 80, 90, or 95 percent of the property's appraised value. On loans above 80 percent, lenders usually require the borrowers to pay for private mortgage insurance, which idemnifies the lenders for any losses up to 20 percent of the loan balance.

We can analyze the financial consequences of various mortgage features and plans to determine the relative desirability of alternatives. The key analytical tool is the mortgage constant, which is the percentage relationship between the periodic payment(s) and the amount of the loan. If we know the mortgage constant, we can calculate the periodic payments and analyze the effect of different interest rates and loan terms. Furthermore, the loan balance at any point during the term of the loan can be found. Discounts and buydowns are common in the mortgage market, and we can analyze their effects using the mortgage constant to determine how much they inflate the sale price.

TEST YOURSELF

Explain the following terms and concepts presented in this chapter.

1. Flow of funds to real estate.
2. Conventional mortgages.
3. Government-underwritten mortgages.
4. Adjustable-rate mortgages.
5. Shared-appreciation mortgages.
6. The loan constant.
7. Discount points.
8. Buydowns.
9. Equity build-up.
10. Graduated payments mortgage.

Answer the following multiple choice questions.

1. What is the annual mortgage constant (R_m) for a 27-year, monthly payment loan carrying an interest rate of 10.75 percent? (Note: Use a financial calculator.)

   a. .009486.
   b. .115451.
   c. .009621.
   d. .113829.
   e. .00114.

2. Dramatic and unexpected increases in mortgage payments often result in
   a. Buydowns.
   b. Loan payoffs.
   c. Lawsuits by borrowers.
   d. Payment shock.
   e. Prepayment penalties.

3. How much is the loan balance at the end of 15 months on an 18-year, monthly payment, $40,000 loan carrying an interest rate of 11.75 percent?
   a. $39,263.18.
   b. $39,126.23.
   c. $34,372.27.
   d. $31,864.23.
   e. $4,782.56.

4. What is the relationship between the annual debt service (ADS) on a monthly payment loan and on an annual payment loan having the same amount, interest rate, and maturity?
   a. Lower.
   b. Higher.
   c. Equal.
   d. Higher at the beginning, but lower at the end.
   e. Indeterminate.

5. What is the lender's exact yield in lending $125,000 for 20 years, with monthly amortization, an interest rate of 13.25 percent, and three discount points?
   a. 13.25 percent.
   b. 14.00 percent.
   c. 13.63 percent.
   d. 13.85 percent.
   e. 13.76 percent.

ADDITIONAL READINGS

Brueggeman, William B., and Leo D. Stone. *Real Estate Finance,* 7th ed. Homewood, Ill.: Richard D. Irwin, 1981.

Bloom, George F.; Arthur M. Weimer; and Jeffrey D. Fisher. *Real Estate,* 8th ed. New York: John Wiley & Sons, 1982, Chaps. 9–10.

Goebel, Paul R., and Normal G. Miller. *Handbook of Mortgage Mathematics.* Englewood Cliffs, N.J.: Prentice Hall, 1981.

Miller, Norman G., and Paul R. Goebel. *The Buyer Seller and Broker's Guide to Creative Home Finance.* Englewood Cliffs, N.J.: Prentice Hall, 1983.

Sirmans, C. F. *Real Estate Finance.* New York: McGraw-Hill, 1985.

Smith, Halbert C.; Carl J. Tschappat; and Ronald L. Racster. *Real Estate and Urban Development,* 3d. ed., Homewood, Ill.: Richard D. Irwin, 1981, Chaps. 16–17.

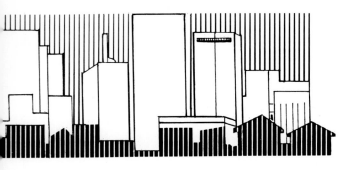

20
Income-Property Financing

OUTLINE

INTRODUCTION

LOAN DOCUMENTS AND PROVISIONS
The Note
The Mortgage

MOTIVATION OF BORROWERS
Lack of Funds
Positive Financial Leverage

EFFECT OF FINANCING

EQUITY PARTICIPATION
Adjustable-Rate Mortgage
Equity Kickers
Convertibility
Joint Venture
Sale-Leaseback

TYPES OF LOANS
Land Purchase and Development Financing
Construction Financing
Long-Term Permanent Financing
Interim Financing
Gap Financing

SEQUENCE OF FINANCING

REQUESTING A LOAN
Loan Submission Package
Channels of Submission

CASE: A LOAN REQUEST AND ALTERNATIVE LOAN PROPOSALS

OVERVIEW

TEST YOURSELF

ADDITIONAL READINGS

INTRODUCTION

Most income-producing properties require financing when they are bought and sold, as do single-family residential properties. Although the basic documents—the note and the mortgage—are the same in financing both, they must be tailored to meet the different property types and situations in financing income properties. Moreover, the same institutions that lend funds for small residential properties also finance large-scale income properties, although their roles are proportionately different. Life insurance companies play a much larger role in this market than in the single-family residential market. Savings and loan associations and mutual savings banks play a smaller but growing role. Commercial banks lend funds mainly for the short-term needs of developers and builders.

Another institutional lender that is gaining importance in income-property lending is pension funds. They hold vast sums for their participants' future retirement benefits, and typically invest 10–15 percent of their assets in real estate. Pension funds are not taxed and thus have no need to shelter income. Mortgage bankers also play an important role in originating and servicing large loans for institutional lenders.

Generally, there are fewer rules and other constraints governing loan terms and lender-borrower relationships for income-property financing than for single-family residential financing. Since both lenders and borrowers tend to be large, relatively sophisticated market participants, they do not need government protection from each other. Thus, whatever provisions that both parties agree to, govern lender-borrower obligations, rights, and relationships. Consequently every income-property financing arrangement is unique and many are creative in using unusual provisions or standard provisions in unusual combinations.

The term *income properties* covers a wide variety of property types. They include apartment buildings of more than four units, office buildings, commercial buildings, shopping centers, hotels, motels, warehouses, theatres, recreational properties (bowling alleys, golf courses, health clubs, tennis courts, amusement parks, etc.), restaurants, financial institutions, churches, funeral homes, cemeteries, farms, farm-service establishments (feed mills and stores, equipment dealers, grain elevators, etc.), manufacturing plants, assembly plants, other industrial plants, industrial parks, mobile-home parks, service stations, automobile dealerships, garages, developable land, and residential subdivisions. Since the income-producing characteristics of each of the types differ from the others, it is evident that the financing arrangements of individual properties within each type would vary greatly. Nevertheless, all is not chaos. Standard provisions are used frequently, and we can make generalizations about lenders' requirements and the abilities of different property types to generate income to cover debt service.

LOAN DOCUMENTS AND PROVISIONS

Many of the typical provisions in income-property loans are similar to those in residential financing. Lenders use the same basic types of documents, and many of the same standard clauses apply. These documents and provisions are described in the remainder of this section.[1]

The Note

As in residential financing, the note is the document that creates a debt when a loan is made to finance real estate. In residential property financing, the note is usually a relatively simple document. In income-property financing, however, the note is usually quite lengthy. It contains the terms of the loan and the provisions agreed to by each party. It presents in detail the borrower's obligations in various situations. The provisions typically deal with such matters as

1. Amounts and timing of periodic payments.
2. Calculation of payments above the basic level.
3. Record keeping.
4. Calculation of income.
5. Property maintenance.
6. Default.
7. Penalties.

---

[1]Chapter 5 provides more detailed explanations of mortgage-loan documents.

The Mortgage

The income-property mortgage creates security for the lender. As in a residential mortgage, it states that the lender can have the property sold to satisfy the debt, if the borrower defaults on any of the obligations in the note. The lender must follow foreclosure proceedings, just as in residential foreclosure.

MOTIVATION OF BORROWERS

Investors and developers of income properties usually borrow funds for the same two reasons that residential purchasers borrow funds:

1. They do not have sufficient funds to pay cash, or other resources to obtain an all-equity ownership position.
2. If they do have sufficient resources to avoid borrowing, they *desire* to borrow in the hope (or probability) of obtaining the benefits of positive financial leverage.[2]

Lack of Funds

This is relatively clear cut. If investors and developers had to accumulate the entire amount of funds to purchase or develop large income properties, most such purchases would not occur. Only a few large firms and wealthy persons would be able to purchase income properties. To increase access to the market of income properties, as well as of residential properties, several types of financial institutions have evolved. These institutions, by accumulating the savings of many small savers and investors, can provide the funds to finance large income properties as well as single-family homes.

All of the financial institutions discussed in Chapter 19 finance income properties: savings and loan associations, mutual savings banks, commercial banks, life insurance companies, and mortgage companies. Indeed, many of these institutions (including S&Ls, which were founded to finance home ownership) prefer to lend on income properties. Yields tend to be higher, and larger amounts can be invested with less overhead and administrative expenses than with a number of smaller loans adding

---

[2]As defined in Chapter 19, positive financial leverage results when the rate of return on an investment is higher than the rate charged for funds borrowed to purchase the investment. Thus, the net present value of the cash flows from the project is greater with a given level of financing than it is with a lower level of (or no) financing.

up to the same amount. Commercial banks generally prefer to make shorter-term loans to finance construction or to finance mortgage companies' operations.

Positive Financial Leverage

The second reason that income property investors and developers often prefer to borrow funds is less obvious. It involves the possibility that investors and developers can obtain a higher rate of return on their investment than the interest rate and other borrowing charges they must pay to borrow the funds. In other words, investors would receive a higher return on their equity after subtracting debt service. This phenomenon, termed *positive leverage* or *trading on the equity*, magnifies earnings. *Negative leverage*, on the other hand, works in the opposite direction. If the effective borrowing charges are higher than the rate of return earned on the property, the borrower's rate of return on the amount invested will be lower than otherwise would be the case. A simple example of positive leverage follows for an income property with a purchase price of $750,000 and a net operating income of $92,000.

The overall return, or capitalization rate (R_o) is calculated as the ratio of NOI to sale price, thus:

$$R_o = \frac{\$92,000}{\$750,000} = .12, \text{ or 12 percent}$$

If the property were purchased for cash, the rate of return to the equity owner would be equal to R_o, or 12 percent.

If a monthly amortizing loan could be obtained for 80 percent of the property's value (purchase price) at an interest rate of 10 percent for 25 years, the annual debt service (ADS) would be given by

$$\text{ADS} = (.009087^3 \times 12) \times (.80 \times \$750,000)$$
$$= \underline{\$65,426}$$

Of this amount, $60,000 is interest for the first year (10 percent × $600,000). The annual interest is subtracted from the property's NOI to obtain the return to the equity owner. This amount can then be divided by the amount of equity to obtain the rate of return on equity (ROE), thus:

$$\text{ROE} = \frac{\text{NOI} - \text{Annual interest}}{\text{Equity}}$$

---

[3]Monthly mortgage constant from 10 percent monthly table, Column 6, 300 periods.

$$= \frac{\$92{,}000 - 60{,}000}{\$750{,}000 - 600{,}000}$$

$$= \frac{\$32{,}000}{\$150{,}000}$$

$$= .213, \text{ or } 21.3 \text{ percent}$$

Thus positive financial leverage has increased the equity investor's return from 12 to 21.3 percent. Additionally, the investor has been able to purchase the property with only $150,000 in cash instead of $750,000. Of course, if NOI were lower than $92,000, the equity return would be below 21.3 percent. For example, if the NOI turned out to be $80,000 instead of $92,000, the equity return would be

$$\text{ROE} = \frac{\$80{,}000 - 60{,}000}{\$150{,}000}$$

$$= \frac{\$20{,}000}{\$150{,}000}$$

$$= .1333, \text{ or } 13.3 \text{ percent}$$

If the NOI fell below $60,000, the equity return would, of course, be negative.

EFFECT OF FINANCING

The preceding analysis demonstrates that financing can have a major impact on the desirability of a real estate investment. If investors or developers can own or control properties with only a 10 or 20 percent investment (or even less) of their own funds, and at the same time magnify their own rates of return, financing is highly desirable. In such cases, financial alternatives become a major factor in investment analysis. As demonstrated in Chapters 21 and 22, after-financing and after-tax cash flows are often divided by equity to obtain before-tax and after-tax equity return rates. The internal rate of return, net present value, and several simple ratios are criteria used to determine investment desirability.

From the investor-developer's standpoint, alternative financing plans affect the before-tax cash flow and the rate of return from the investment. The analysis of such effects is termed *financial sensitivity analysis,* as the following example illustrates.

Using the same property as in the previous example, suppose the potential buyers could obtain the four loans in Exhibit 20–1 to finance the property. How would the before-tax cash flow (BTCF) and the equity dividend rate (EDR) be affected? BTCF is NOI minus annual debt service,

EXHIBIT 20–1
LOAN SENSITIVITY ANALYSIS

Equity = $150,000
NOI = 92,000

	(a)	(b)	(c)	(d)	(e)	(f)	(g)	(h)	(i)
Loan Number	Loan to Value Ratio	Maturity	Interest Rate	Loan Amount	Required Equity	Annual Constant	Annual Debt Service	Before-Tax Cash Flow NOI-Col. *g*	Equity Dividend Rate Col. *h*/Col. *e*
1	80%	30 years	12.0	$600,000	$150,000	.123434	$74,060	$17,940	11.96%
2	80%	25 years	12.5	600,000	150,000	.130842	78,505	13,495	9.00%
3	75%	20 years	11.0	562,500	187,500	.123863	69,673	22,237	11.91%
4	70%	15 years	10.5	525,000	225,000	.132648	69,640	22,360	9.94%

and the EDR is BTCF divided by required equity. The EDR is discussed later in the chapter.

Note that the indicators of financial desirability conflict. Loan No. 1 would provide the highest EDR, but only the third-highest BTCF. Loan No. 4 would provide the highest BTCF, but the next-to-lowest EDR. It also would require the largest amount of equity funding ($225,000 compared with $150,000 for Loan Nos. 1 and 2). If the investors could invest only $150,000 of their own funds in the project, they would be limited to one of the first two plans; obviously, they would prefer No. 1 over No. 2. If they had the cash, they might prefer Loan No. 3, which provides almost as much BTCF as No. 4 and a considerably higher EDR.

It should also be noted from the sensitivity analysis in Exhibit 20–1 that three factors govern the BTCF and EDR. These factors for standard, fixed-payment loans are the loan-to-value ratio, the maturity, and the interest rate. Holding the other factors constant, monthly (and annual) payments rise as the loan-to-value ratio increases, as the maturity decreases, and as the interest rate increases. Thus, increases in maturity can sometimes offset higher interest rates or higher loan-to-value ratios. Investors should therefore seek the most advantageous terms among the available loan plans.

EQUITY PARTICIPATION

Many lenders increasingly want to share in the successful operation of properties they finance. This trend is because equity positions have been highly profitable. Lenders thus have come to believe that if they provide a high percentage of the funds to be invested in a property, they should receive more than a fixed amount of periodic interest. Several types of loan provisions are used to increase lenders' returns as economic conditions change, or as properties generate increased income or increase in value.

Adjustable-Rate Mortgage

Although not technically a device for participating in equity, the adjustable-rate mortgage enables lenders to increase their earnings if interest rates increase. The additional interest that must be paid if interest rates rise comes from the property's earnings that would otherwise accrue to the equity owners. In this sense the ARM may be regarded as a device for equity participation. ARMs are almost always used by income-property lenders, either instead of or in conjunction with other forms of equity participation.

Equity Kickers

Equity kickers require the borrowers to pay a specified amount or percentage of (usually) gross income above a specified level, in addition to the normal interest. For example, 60 percent of gross income above the amount produced in 1986 might be split on a 50–50 or 75–25 basis in future years; the 40 percent excluded is assumed to cover operating expenses. Disagreements over expenses are thus avoided. Occasionally, kickers are based on net income or gross income minus debt service.

Kickers also often call for splitting the proceeds from a sale of the property. For example, the net after-tax proceeds might be split on a 50–50 or 60–40 basis.

Convertibility

A convertible mortgage gives the lender an option to convert the debt to equity after a specified number of years. The option may allow the lender to purchase a specified percentage of the property by paying the market value of the portion converted. For example, a 60 percent convertibility feature might allow the lender to purchase a 60 percent equity position after five years by paying 60 percent of the property's market value at that time. Agreed-on appraiser(s) would determine the market value and the 60 percent would be paid by writing down (reducing) the loan balance.

Joint Venture

Large lenders sometimes prefer to go into partnership with a developer-investor, rather than enter a creditor-debtor relationship. The lender puts up all, or most of the funds, while the developer develops, constructs, and manages the property. They may split the net income from operation and/or sale equally, or in any other manner agreed. For example, the lender (say, a large insurance company) might obtain a specified percentage of gross or net proceeds first, after which any remaining proceeds would be split equally. Obviously, such arrangements require a complex partnership agreement to cover the rights and obligations of each party. The lender is particularly concerned about record keeping, payment of bills, and accurate income accounting.

Sale-Leaseback

A large financial institution may prefer to take a complete equity position, rather than a debt position. The institution may therefore agree to purchase an existing property or to underwrite all development and construction costs for a proposed property. The developer or operator of the property would be the lessee and would make lease payments to the financier (the lessor). From the developer's or operator's viewpoint, such an arrangement carries the advantages of 100 percent financing and the deductibility of lease payments for tax purposes. Appreciation in property value would, of course, accrue to the financier-owner, as would depreciation deductions for tax purposes. A sale-leaseback agreement could contain an option for the repurchase of the property, after a specified period and on specified terms, by the lessee.

TYPES OF LOANS

The development, construction, and operation of large income properties take time and different types of effort. Consequently, different financing requirements usually are involved in these different phases of a property's life, and several types of lending arrangements have evolved to serve these needs.

Land Purchase and Development Financing

A developer may need to finance the purchase of a parcel of land. Financial institutions may make such loans, although the developer's ability to obtain a construction loan would be affected by an existing land-purchase mortgage on the property. Thus, instead of borrowing funds to purchase land, developers often attempt to have the landowners finance the purchase. The landowners may become partners with the developer (thus taking an equity position in the development), or they may take a land-purchase mortgage but agree to subordinate the mortgage when other financing is needed.

Construction Financing

Construction lenders (such as banks, savings and loans, and insurance companies) almost always require that the loan to finance the construction of new buildings be a first lien on the property. Thus, the developer must already own the land free and clear, or must convince the land lender to subordinate his loan. The land lender may do this in exchange for an equity position in the project. Occasionally the developer will obtain the land under a long-term lease (50 to 99 years) from the owner. In these cases, the developer usually expects to be the permanent owner of the building.

Construction loans are short-term arrangements that allow the developer to obtain funds in "draws" after the completion of specified stages of the building. In this way, the lender is assured that adequate components of the property exist to secure the next draw on the loan in case the borrower defaults. For example, 20 percent of the loan might be payable after the footings, foundation, and floors are in place; 20 percent after the walls and roof are constructed; 20 percent on completion of plumbing and electrical work; and the remaining 40 percent after completion of the entire building. The construction loan is paid off from the proceeds of the sale of the property or by a long-term, permanent mortgage loan.

Long-Term Permanent Financing

A long-term mortgage loan usually must be obtained to provide the funds to retire the construction loan on completion of construction. It may contain many provisions relating to interest payments, maturity, options, legal obligations, property management, insurance, and equity participation, as we discussed previously. The proceeds of the permanent financing usually go to pay off the construction loan; the borrower-developer amortizes the loan over a relatively long term, usually 10–30 years.

Interim Financing

A typical developer often finances the land purchase by giving the landowner a mortgage as part or all of the purchase price. The developer must then borrow funds to develop the land and construct buildings. Since development and construction loans usually require a first lien, which cannot be obtained when there is already a first mortgage on the land, the landowner may be willing to subordinate the first mortgage to a development and/or construction loan. During the period of subordination, her lien is second in priority, and the interest rate on the land mortgage is usually increased. The financing for this period is termed *interim financing*.

Gap Financing

The builder of a large apartment project may only be able to obtain permanent financing on condition of a specified occupancy rate being achieved by time of loan closing. If occupancy falls short of the specified rate, the loan amount will be lower. Nevertheless, the builder must usually obtain a construction loan for a larger amount, which would normally be paid off by the permanent loan. The construction lender recognizes that the occupancy rate may not be achieved to obtain the full amount of the permanent financing, in which case the construction loan could not be paid off. Therefore, the construction lender typically will require the borrower to obtain a second-mortgage commitment to cover the potential gap between the construction and permanent financing. Because of the risk involved if the second mortgage is needed, both the commitment fees and the interest rates on gap loans are high.

SEQUENCE OF FINANCING

Financing of new income properties is not usually obtained in the same order that the work on the properties occurs. Landowners and lenders usually want some evidence that a development loan can be obtained to develop the land. The development lender wants to make certain that the building(s) will be constructed, and so she wants to see a loan commitment from a construction lender. The construction lender wants to be assured that long-term permanent financing will be available to pay off (or *take out*) the construction lender.

Developers thus must work backward through the chain of financing, as Exhibit 20–2 shows. They must convince a permanent lender to provide a loan commitment that is contingent, of course, on the building's being constructed. The permanent lender usually must be assured that the project is feasible by appropriate studies (such as market and feasibility analyses) and partial or total prelease of the proposed building.

With this commitment in hand, the developer can approach construction lenders, who then are usually willing to consider a short-term construction loan. After getting the construction-loan commitment, the developer can apply for a development and/or land-purchase loan. In short, each loan commitment shows project feasibility to the preceding lender.

Some lenders finance all phases of a project—development, construction, and operation. The developer's steps may thus be somewhat simplified and shortened. However, a single lender will demand the same or even greater assurances of feasibility as will multiple lenders. A single lender is also more likely to demand an equity position in the project to compensate for its increased exposure in totally financing the project.

EXHIBIT 20–2
SEQUENCE OF APPLICATIONS FOR FINANCING

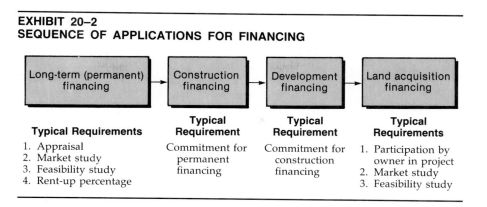

Long-term (permanent) financing	Construction financing	Development financing	Land acquisition financing
Typical Requirements	**Typical Requirement**	**Typical Requirement**	**Typical Requirements**
1. Appraisal 2. Market study 3. Feasibility study 4. Rent-up percentage	Commitment for permanent financing	Commitment for construction financing	1. Participation by owner in project 2. Market study 3. Feasibility study

REQUESTING A LOAN

Loan Submission Package

When seeking a long-term mortgage loan, developers or investors must provide prospective lenders with the relevant information the lenders need to make a decision. The information is usually presented in a number of documents, which are bound together as a *loan submission package.* Included in the loan submission package are the following items.

Loan Application.   This refers to the specific document or pages requesting funds in the package. It specifies the amount (or percentage of value) requested, the maturity of the loan, the interest rate, commitment terms, and identity of the borrower(s). It may also include the borrower's financial statements, credit reports, and experience with similar projects.

Property Description.   The property that will secure the loan usually must be described in considerable detail. Maps and photos of the area are usually included, as are surveys, plot plans, topographical maps, building plans, renderings, and specifications. Data on soil characteristics—from borings, drainage tests, and percolation tests—are normally required. The availability of utilities to the site is very important.

Legal Aspects.   Lenders require a precise description of the property and identification of any easements or encroachments. Information about property taxes, special assessments, and deed restrictions also must be included. Zoning is often a crucial matter, and prospective borrowers usually must demonstrate that proper zoning has been obtained. Other

land-use controls and environmental requirements such as flood plain restrictions and water runoff provisions must be discussed and compliance
demonstrated. Environmental-impact statements or other reports must be
included, as required.

Aspirant borrowers also provide a favorable title opinion or a commitment for title insurance. Lenders want to make certain that a long-
term mortgage loan will constitute a first lien on the property, and that
in the case of serious default the borrower's rights could be foreclosed,
the property sold, and the proceeds used to pay off the debt.

Appraisal Report.   The prospective lenders require an appraisal of the
property as an unbiased estimate of the market value of the property.
Their loans are often a percentage of the property's value, and some lenders are legally limited in the loan-to-value ratio of their loans. The borrower's appraisal firm must be acceptable to the lender, or the lender will
require another appraisal by a firm that is acceptable.

Feasibility Study.   Some lenders require a feasibility study for proposed
projects, although many believe that an appraisal report is sufficient, or
allow feasibility to be addressed in the appraisal report. A separate feasibility study is preferable for large projects, however, because it addresses
issues that appraisals usually do not. In-depth market analysis demonstrating the demand for the proposed property, along with existing and
projected supply, shows both the applicant and lenders the probability of
success.

Channels of Submission

A loan submission package may be presented directly to lenders or to a
mortgage company (banker). Prospective borrowers often submit loan requests directly to savings and loans, mutual savings banks, life insurance
companies, or pension funds. Such institutions often have commercial-
property lending units that are happy to consider such requests. Informal
discussions with loan officers in these firms will usually inform would-be
borrowers of the expected items in a loan submission package.

Another channel for loan requests is through mortgage companies.
Many of these firms enjoy close business relationships with large institutional lenders and may have ready access to several such lenders. A business relationship in which a large lender agrees to purchase loans or to
consider loan requests from a mortgage company is termed a *correspondent
relationship.* Many mortgage companies specialize in seeking loan opportunities and in putting together loan submission packages that meet the
requirements of large institutional lenders.

CASE: A LOAN REQUEST AND ALTERNATIVE LOAN PROPOSALS

This case of a loan submission package and alternative financing plans illustrates the procedures and analyses employed in the financing of income properties. The property to be financed is a proposed office building located in a medium-sized, growing U.S. city. The following sections contain excerpts from the loan submission package that was assembled by the Alluvial Mortgage Company. The package was submitted to three prospective permanent lenders—two life insurance companies and a pension fund management company. The name of the proposed office building is Turkey Run Plaza. Exhibit 20–3 contains the basic characteristics of the property. Exhibit 20–4 summarizes market characteristics and preleasing efforts. Exhibit 20–5 shows the project's development budget, and Exhibit 20–6 shows comparable sales.

EXHIBIT 20–3
PROPERTY DATA

Name of project	Turkey Run Plaza.
Address	8427 Prosperity Road
	Middle City, USA.
Location	The building will be located in a newly developed suburban office park. The park is well located in the major growth section of Middle City. An adjacent interstate highway and major arterial roads leading to the center of the city provide easy access to the park.
Physical description	One three-story building will be constructed of concrete, structural steel, and glass. It is designed in a contemporary architectural motif. The building will contain 156,000 square feet of gross area, with 146,000 square feet of net rentable area.
Parking	A total of 550 open-air parking spaces will be provided, a ratio of 3.77 spaces per 1,000 square feet of net rentable area.
Land	
Size	457,380 square feet, or 10.5 acres.
Purchase price	Purchased in October, 1986, for $175,000 per acre, or $4.02 per square foot.
Total construction cost	$13,300,000.
Time to construct building	14 months.
Sponsor	Diamond Development Company.
	Diamond is a second-tier developer that concentrates its efforts in the region of Middle City. The firm has successfully developed several previous office-building projects. It possesses the management and technical competence to be considered a good risk by investors.

EXHIBIT 20–4
MARKET DATA

Market conditions | Market performance of office buildings in the trade area has been quite good over the past several years. Four buildings totalling 500,000 square feet were completed in 1985 and 1986. All are 100 percent occupied. Four new office-building projects similar in quality and design have been announced. If all are built, a total of 650,000 square feet of office space will be coming on stream in the next 18 months. Absorption rates have been running about 350,000 square feet per year in the trade area.

Leasing conditions | Leases in the trade area typically run three to five years. Lease terms usually provide for a pass-through of expenses from the owner to the lessees above the first year's expenses or above a "stop" figure. Annual adjustments based on increases in the CPI are usually included.

Tenant improvements | Current market conditions require a landlord to allow tenants about $12 per square foot for improving their space.

Expenses | Comparable, recently built office buildings have operating expenses of about $4 per square foot of net rentable area.

Preleases | A total of 45,000 square feet have been preleased: 27,000 square feet on the first floor have been preleased for $17.50 per square foot, 3,000 square feet on the second floor have been preleased for $16.75 per square foot, and 15,000 square feet on the third floor have been preleased for $16.75 per square foot.

EXHIBIT 20–5
TURKEY RUN PLAZA DEVELOPMENT BUDGET

Cost Item	Project Total	Cost per Net Sq. Ft.
Land:		
Acquisition	$ 1,837,000	$12.58
Real estate tax	88,500	.61
Subtotal	1,925,500	13.19
Base building:		
Soil testing	5,450	.04
Shell construction	6,852,000	46.93
Architects	122,000	.84
Mechanical engineer	116,000	.79
Materials testing	10,000	.07
Permits & fees	55,000	.38
Survey	15,000	.10
Landscaping	100,000	.69
Developers overhead	200,000	1.37
Contingency	170,000	1.16
Subtotal	7,645,450	52.37
Tenant development:		
Tenant construction	1,752,000	12.00
Space planning	37,000	.25
Working drawings	15,000	.10
Developers overhead	75,000	.51
Contingency	45,000	.31
Subtotal	1,924,000	13.17

EXHIBIT 20–5 *(concluded)*

Cost Item	Project Total	Cost per Net Sq. Ft.
Financing:		
Construction lenders fee	179,550	1.23
Financing brokerage fee	133,000	.91
Construction lenders inspection fee	8,000	.06
Construction lenders legal fee	25,000	.17
Construction loan interest	837,000	5.37
Subtotal	1,183,050	8.10
Leasing/marketing:		
Leasing commissions	447,000	3.06
Advertising/PR	50,000	.35
Contingency	11,000	.07
Subtotal	508,000	3.48
General and administrative:		
Project legal	25,000	.17
Project audit	20,000	.14
Project insurance	34,000	.23
Title insurance	25,000	.17
Misc. expense	10,000	.07
Subtotal	114,000	.78
Total project cost	$13,330,000	$91.09

EXHIBIT 20–6
TURKEY RUN PLAZA COMPARABLE SALES

Date	Cap Rate	Sale Price	Price per Gross Sq. Ft.
September, 1985	9.0%	$ 4,000,000	$ 95.20
October, 1986	10.0%	17,000,000	100.24
June, 1986	9.5%	5,500,000	92.37
November, 1986	10.28%	5,500,000	84.62

Range of sales prices/sq. ft.: Low: $ 84.62
Mean: $ 93.11
High: $100.24

Based on the information provided in the loan submission package, the three large lending institutions made three different types of loan commitments. These loan commitments, and their principal terms and provisions, are summarized in the following sections.

Short Life Insurance Company (Loan Plan No. 1)

Type of loan	Fixed-rate mortgage
Amount	$11,620,000
	Will not exceed 75 percent of project's market value as determined by lender two weeks prior to closing. The amount was established such that the net rentals would provide a debt-service-coverage ratio of 1.15 times. Amount will be reduced if DSC falls below 1.05 times.
Equity required	$1,680,000

(continued)

Short Life Insurance Company (Loan Plan No. 1) *(concluded)*

Maturity	10 years
Amortization	30 years
Interest rate	Real estate department's best 10-year rate, as established two weeks prior to funding. Currently, it would be 12.5 percent.
Prepayment privilege	None
Letter of credit	Four times the amount of any shortfall between lease income and annual expenses plus debt service at time of funding must be covered by a letter of credit.*

Brokers Life of Wyoming (Loan Plan No. 2)

Type of loan	Adjustable-rate mortgage
Amount	$13,500,000 (project appraised at $18,000,000)
Equity required	−$200,000†
Maturity	15 years
Amortization	30 years
Interest rate	11.50 percent first year, adjusted quarterly thereafter to 175 percent of five-year Treasury note rate. There is an annual payment cap of ±107 ½ percent of prior year's payment.
Fees	Two points ($270,000) up front
Prepayment privilege	Full; no penalty

Smith, Jones, & Brown Pension Management, Inc. (Loan Plan No. 3)

Type of loan	Convertible mortgage
Amount	$14,000,000
Equity required	−$700,000
Maturity	15 years; call provision after 9 years, with 6 months' notice
Amortization	None (interest only)
Interest rate	10.5 percent
Participation interest	Seventy percent of the BTCF above actual 1987 BTCF
Fees	Two points ($280,000) up front
Prepayment privilege	None
Options for convertibility	*Option 1:* After seven years, lender has option to purchase 70 percent of the property for $14,000,000. *Option 2:* After Option 1 is exercised, lender may purchase remaining 30 percent of property for 30 percent times market value.

---

*A letter from a bank stating that Short Life Insurance Company can obtain payment on loan up to the amount specified.

†When a developer borrows as much or more as the cost of the project, the situation is termed *financing* or *mortgaging out*. The amount of borrowed funds above the development cost is sometimes called a *windfall*.

Obviously, there are many considerations in analyzing the three loans to determine which would be best for the developers of Turkey Run Plaza. The $1,680,000 of equity required under the fixed-rate loan proposal might eliminate that proposal from consideration, if the developer could not commit this amount to the project. The required equity might outweigh the desirability of a fixed-rate loan.

The adjustable-rate loan will require no equity contribution by the developer and has full prepayment privileges. The disadvantage, of course, is that the interest rate risk is borne by the borrowers through the adjustability mechanism. If relatively stable or declining interest rates are expected over the next several years, this loan would be quite attractive.

The convertible mortgage will put cash in the developer's pockets and carries a relatively low interest rate. If the property is successful and appreciates in value, however, the chances are great that the lender will exercise the options and purchase the property after the seventh year. Also, the increases in cash flows to the developer are limited by the provision allocating 70 percent of the increases to the lender. The prohibition against prepayments is another negative factor. Whether this loan is attractive depends upon whether the developer is more interested in cash up front and limited cash flow for seven years, or in the long-term cash flow and operation of the property.

While any of these considerations could be decisive in determining which loan plan the developer would prefer, more detailed analysis would be required if they were not decisive. For a more extensive analysis, we construct a cash-flow analysis and calculate various ratios. Exhibit 20–7 shows a summarized, six-year operating statement.

EXHIBIT 20–7
OPERATING STATEMENT, TURKEY RUN PLAZA

	Year 1	2	3	4	5	6
Potential gross income	$2,557,764	$2,651,260	$2,749,899	$2,958,280	$3,073,805	$3,330,284
Less: Vacancy and collection loss	84,997	53,803	56,762	63,013	66,479	71,600
Plus: Expense recovery	–0–	29,565	60,460	92,746	126,484	161,741
Effective gross income	2,472,767	2,627,022	2,753,597	2,988,013	3,133,810	3,420,425
Expenses (4 ½% increase)	657,000	686,565	717,460	749,746	783,484	818,741
Net operating income	$1,815,767	$1,940,457	$2,036,137	$2,238,267	$2,350,326	$2,601,684

For the fixed-rate loan, the before-tax cash flow (BTCF) is calculated in Exhibit 20–8.

EXHIBIT 20–8
BEFORE-TAX CASH FLOW—FIXED-RATE MORTGAGE (PLAN NO. 1)

	Year 1	2	3	4	5	6
Net operating income	$1,815,767	$1,940,457	$2,036,137	$2,238,267	$2,350,326	$2,601,684
Debt service	1,488,184	1,488,184	1,488,184	1,488,184	1,488,184	1,488,184
Before-tax cash flow	$ 327,583	$ 452,273	$ 547,953	$ 750,083	$ 862,142	$1,113,500

For the adjustable-rate loan, the BTCF is calculated in Exhibit 20–9, assuming an increase in the interest rate of .75 percent every two years.

EXHIBIT 20–9
BEFORE-TAX CASH FLOW—ADJUSTABLE-RATE MORTGAGE (PLAN NO. 2)

	Year					
	1	2	3	4	5	6
Net operating income	$1,815,767	$1,940,457	$2,036,137	$2,238,267	$2,350,326	$2,601,684
Annual debt service	1,604,272	1,604,272	1,695,438	1,695,438	1,785,485	1,785,485
Before-tax cash flow	$ 211,495	$ 336,185	$ 340,699	$ 542,829	$ 564,841	$ 816,199

The BTCF with the convertible mortgage is calculated in Exhibit 20–10.

EXHIBIT 20–10
BEFORE-TAX CASH FLOW—CONVERTIBLE MORTGAGE (PLAN NO. 3)

	Year					
	1	2	3	4	5	6
Net operating income	$1,815,767	$1,940,457	$2,036,137	$2,238,267	$2,350,326	$2,601,684
Annual debt service	1,470,000	1,470,000	1,470,000	1,470,000	1,470,000	1,470,000
Before-tax cash flow	$ 345,767	$ 470,457	$ 566,137	$ 768,267	$ 880,326	$1,131,684

PERFORMANCE MEASURES

To assess the relative desirability of various loan plans, both lenders and borrowers use several ratios and other indicators to enable them to compare certain key relationships. No single measure is sufficient to determine whether one loan is better than another, or how much should be loaned or borrowed. Usually loans have both advantages and disadvantages, and a number of ratios and other matters must be considered in deciding which plan is best. The most commonly used measures are given below and are calculated for the three loan alternatives for Turkey Run Plaza.

Debt Service Coverage Ratio

Lenders are particularly concerned about the DSCR. It shows whether and by how many times the net operating income (NOI) of the property will cover (equal or exceed) the annual debt service (ADS). The formula for this ratio is.

$$DSCR = \frac{NOI}{ADS}$$

It should be greater than one, and normally should be 1.2 or higher. A ratio lower than this indicates very little protection for the lender (and the borrower) in case the NOI should fall. The DSCRs for Turkey Run Plaza are shown for the three loan plans in Exhibit 20–11.

EXHIBIT 20–11
DEBT-SERVICE COVERAGE RATIOS, TURKEY RUN PLAZA

	Year					
	1	2	3	4	5	6
Loan Plan No. 1	1.22	1.30	1.37	1.50	1.58	1.75
Loan Plan No. 2	1.13	1.21	1.20	1.32	1.32	1.46
Loan Plan No. 3	1.24	1.32	1.39	1.52	1.60	1.77

Loan-to-Value Ratio

Loan-to-value is another ratio that lenders usually consider. Some have legal limits on the loans they can make relative to the value of the property being financed. The formula for this ratio, which has the symbol m, is

$$m = \frac{\text{Amount of loan}}{\text{Value of property}}$$

The ratio is normally calculated at only the beginning of the loan and depends on the appraised value of the property. The ratios for the three proposed loans are shown below, based on an appraised property value of $16,000,000.

$$\text{Loan Plan No. 1:} \quad m = \frac{\$11,620,000}{16,000,000} = 72.6\%$$

$$\text{Loan Plan No. 2:} \quad m = \frac{\$13,500,000}{16,000,000} = 84.4\%$$

$$\text{Loan Plan No. 3:} \quad m = \frac{\$14,000,000}{16,000,000} = 87.5\%$$

Breakeven Cash Ratio

This ratio indicates the percentage of occupancy required to guarantee sufficient income from a property to meet all cash outlays incurred for operating and financing the property. Generally, lower ratios are better than higher ratios; the property can be supported by fewer occupants. The normal range of this ratio is 70 to 90 percent.

The complement of this ratio (100% minus the ratio) is the percentage of income that can be lost to vacancies before the annual debt service and operating expenses cannot be met. Since the rental income of most income properties is the only source of funds for payment of debt service, lenders usually require that a minimum occupancy ratio be achieved before a loan commitment becomes effective. The formula for the breakeven cash ratio is

$$\text{B/ECR} = \frac{\text{Operating expenses} + \text{Debt service}}{\text{Potential gross income}}$$

The ratios for Turkey Run Plaza under the three loan plans are

Loan Plan No. 1: $\text{B/ECR} = \dfrac{\$657{,}000 + \$1{,}488{,}184}{\$2{,}557{,}764} = 83.9\%$

Loan Plan No. 2: $\text{B/ECR} = \dfrac{\$657{,}000 + \$1{,}604{,}272}{\$2{,}557{,}764} = 88.4\%$

Loan Plan No. 3: $\text{B/ECR} = \dfrac{\$657{,}000 + \$1{,}470{,}000}{\$2{,}557{,}764} = 83.2\%$

Equity Dividend Rate (Cash-on-Cash Return)

The equity dividend rate (sometimes called the cash-on-cash return) is the ratio of the before-tax cash flow to the amount of equity investment. In effect, EDR is a capitalization rate for the equity income, and thus another symbol sometimes used to represent EDR is R_e. The formula for the EDR is

$$\text{EDR} = \frac{\text{BTCF}}{\text{Equity}}$$

This ratio is customarily calculated for the first year of a series of expected cash flows; however, it is likely to change for each cash flow period, and could be calculated for each. For Turkey Run Plaza, the EDR for the first year's cash flow under Loan Plan No. 1 is

Loan Plan No. 1: $\text{EDR} = \dfrac{\$327{,}583}{\$1{,}680{,}000} = 19.5\%$

The EDR is not calculated for Loan Plan Nos. 2 and 3 because the equity is negative in both cases ($-\$200{,}000$ and $-\$700{,}000$, respectively) and would result in meaningless numbers for comparison purposes.

Internal Rate of Return

As we discussed in Chapter 16, the internal rate of return (IRR) is the yield rate that equates the cash flows from a property with the cash outlay required to obtain the property. It is the yield rate that makes NPV = 0. The IRR is based on the time value of money and can be calculated on a before- or after-tax basis. For illustrative purposes, the IRR for the equity investment in Turkey Run Plaza is calculated in Exhibit 20–12 under Loan Plan No. 1. The IRRs under Loan Plan Nos. 2 and 3 are not calculated, for the same reason that the EDRs are not calculated: The negative equity would produce meaningless IRRs.

EXHIBIT 20–12
CALCULATION OF IRR UNDER LOAN PLAN NO. 1, TURKEY RUN PLAZA

Equity investment = $1,680,000

Cash Flows		Before-tax cash proceeds on sale at end
Year 1	$ 327,583	of sixth year, assuming property is
Year 2	452,273	sold for $22,000,000: $22,000,000 −
Year 3	547,953	$11,303,466* = $10,696,534
Year 4	750,083	
Year 5	862,142	
Year 6	$1,113,500 + $10,696,534	
IRR = 53.8%†		

---

*Chapter 19 shows the calculator keystrokes for calculating b.
†Exhibit 16–5 shows the calculator keystrokes for calculating IRR.

The before-tax IRR for Loan Plan No. 1 is quite high, but not necessarily unreasonable or atypical. The IRR, of course, partially depends on the sale price obtained at the end of the holding period. If the sale price were $18,000,000 instead of the assumed $22,000,000, the IRR would be reduced to 46.7 percent. If the sale price were only $15,000,000, the IRR would be 39.6 percent. The after-tax IRRs would be substantially lower, but under any reasonable assumption on the sale price, the property should provide a relatively high rate of return to the development company under Loan Plan No. 1.

Net Present Value

As we discussed in Chapter 16, net present value (NPV) is the present value of the cash flows to the equity position, minus the amount of equity investment. The present value of the cash flows is obtained by discounting them at the equity investor's required, or specified, rate of return. Because of the negative equity under Loan Plan Nos. 2 and 3 in this example, the EDRs and IRRs cannot be calculated and used for comparison among the financing alternatives. We can calculate the NPVs, however, and use them in this situation. In these calculations, we assume that the developer's minimum required before-tax rate of return is 20 percent.

Exhibit 20–13 shows the calculation of the NPVs under the three fi-

EXHIBIT 20–13
CALCULATION OF NPVS UNDER ALTERNATIVE LOAN PLANS, TURKEY RUN PLAZA

	Loan Plan No. 1		Loan Plan No. 2		Loan Plan No. 3	
Year	Cash Flows	Present Value at 20%	Cash Flows	Present Value at 20%	Cash Flows	Present Value at 20%
1	$ 327,583	$ 272,986	$211,495	$ 176,246	$ 345,767	$ 288,139
2	452,273	314,078	336,185	233,462	470,457	326,706
3	547,953	317,102	340,699	197,164	566,137	327,626
4	750,083	361,730	542,829	261,781	768,267	370,499
5	862,142	346,476	564,841	226,997	880,326	353,783
6	1,113,500	372,909	816,199	273,343	1,131,684	378,999
	Total PV	$1,985,281		$1,368,993		$2,045,752
	Less: Equity Required	−1,600,000		−(−)200,000		−(−)700,000
NPV		$ 385,281		$1,568,993		$2,745,752

nancing plans. Loan Plan No. 3 produces the highest NPV, both because it produces the highest cash-flow PV and because it puts the largest equity windfall ($700,000) in the developer's pocket. Loan Plan No. 2 produces the second-highest NPV, although the PV of the cash flows is lower than with Loan Plan No. 1. The large difference in equity required ($1,600,000 versus −$200,000) more than makes up for the lower cash-flow PV. Since all NPVs are positive, the property will produce a before-tax rate of return well above the developer's required rate of 20 percent.

THE FINANCING DECISION

From the developer's viewpoint, all of the loan plans appear acceptable on the basis of their ratios and NPVs. Therefore, the decision among them must be based on the developer's objectives and the relative magnitudes of the various performance measures. In this case, the developer is very concerned with both long-term control of the property and obtaining a satisfactorily high rate of return (i.e., above 20 percent). The development company is not willing to maximize the rate of return at the cost of forgoing control, because it controls other land in the area and plans to implement a long-term development program. It expects the nature and quality of future developments to have a positive influence on the returns to Turkey Run Plaza, and vice versa.

Although Loan Plan No. 3 results in the highest NPV, stability, and return to the developer over the holding period, the developer undoubtedly will lose control after seven years if the property is successful. Loan Plan No. 1 has the advantages of safety, stability, and long-term control; however, the NPV is the lowest among the three alternatives. Loan Plan

No. 2 also provides for long-term control, although the developer may be faced with increasing rates and loan payments. However, the effect of this disadvantage can be reduced by hedging interest rates.[4] Also, the developer will not be required to risk any of its own equity funds in the project, and in fact will receive an equity windfall.

Therefore the developer chooses Loan Plan No. 2, the adjustable-rate mortgage from Brokers Life of Wyoming.

OVERVIEW

The financing of income properties is important for such properties as apartments, offices, commercial properties, shopping centers, entertainment and recreational properties, and industrial properties. Several types of loans are used in income property financing: land purchase and development loans, construction loans, long-term (permanent) loans, gap loans, and interim loans. Developers of new properties usually must obtain commitments for loans in the reverse order of their use. While the basic documents and provisions of income-property loans are similar to those used in single-family residential financing, additional terms and provisions make most income property loans quite complex. Such provisions include adjustability of the interest rate, participation in the property's income, participation in the proceeds on sale of the property, convertibility of the debt to equity, and the calculation of periodic payments on an amortization schedule that is much longer (e.g., 30 years) than the loan term (e.g., 10 or 15 years). Furthermore, some income-property loans allow prepayment, while others prohibit or penalize it. Almost all income-property loans require that substantial loan fees (usually 2 or 3 percent) and expenses be paid at closing of the loan.

Several performance measures can be used to analyze loans from both the lender's and borrower's points of view. The analysis of three loan proposals is illustrated in the case at the end of this chapter for a new office property, Turkey Run Plaza. Since the ratios and the NPVs are all basically acceptable in this case, the decision on which loan to take hinges on the basic nature of the financing plans relative to the developer's own objectives.

---

[4]Hedging is the process of purchasing or selling securities that will be affected by changing interest rates in the opposite direction from the investment or obligation being hedged. In this case the developer would buy securities for future delivery (GNMA futures). If interest rates increase, the value of the securities will go up, offsetting the higher mortgage loan payments.

TEST YOURSELF

Explain the following terms and concepts in this chapter.

1. Financial leverage.
2. Loan sensitivity analysis.
3. Equity participation.
4. Convertible mortgage.
5. Sale-leaseback.
6. Construction financing.
7. Interim financing.
8. Gap financing.
9. Loan submission package.
10. Debt service coverage ratio.

Answer the following multiple choice questions.

1. Lenders usually require a specified rent-up percentage as a condition for granting what type of loan?
   a. Construction loan.
   b. Land development loan.
   c. Long-term permanent loan.
   d. Gap loan.
   e. Land purchase loan.

2. When applying for a loan, developers usually submit all of the required and relevant information in what form?
   a. Loan submission package.
   b. Loan application.
   c. Correspondent submission.
   d. Feasibility study.
   e. Property promotion kit.

3. Financial leverage can result in a borrower's rate of return that holds what relationship to the rate of return that would be obtained without borrowing?
   a. Higher.
   b. Lower.
   c. Equal.
   d. Higher or lower.
   e. Higher and lower.

4. What type of mortgage loan gives the lender an option to purchase part or all of the property after a specified time has elapsed?
   a. Adjustable rate mortgage.
   b. Gap mortgage.
   c. Construction loan mortgage.
   d. Fixed-rate mortgage.
   e. Convertible mortgage.

5. What ratio indicates the percentage of occupancy required before the income from a property covers all cash outlays and vacancy losses?
   a. Equity dividend rate.
   b. Breakeven cash ratio.
   c. Debt-service-coverage ratio.
   d. Loan-to-value ratio.
   e. Internal rate of return.

ADDITIONAL READINGS

Bloom, George F.; Arthur M. Weimer; and Jeffrey Fisher. *Real Estate*, 8th ed. New York: John Wiley & Sons, 1982, Chaps. 9–10.

Brueggeman, William B., and Leo O. Stone. *Real Estate Finance*, 7th ed. Homewood, Ill.: Richard D. Irwin, 1981, Chaps. 11–12.

Epley, Donald R., and James A. Millar. *Basic Real Estate Finance and Investment*, 2d ed. New York: John Wiley & Sons, 1984, Chaps. 10–13.

Ferguson, Jerry T. *Fundamentals of Real Estate Investing.* Glenview, Ill.: Scott, Foresman, 1984, Chaps. 12–13.

Jaffee, Austin J., and C. F. Sirmans. *Real Estate Investment Decision Making.* Englewood Cliffs, N.J.: Prentice-Hall, 1982, Chaps. 10–11.

Smith, Halbert C.; Carl J. Tschappat; and Ronald L. Racster. *Real Estate and Urban Development,* 3d ed. Homewood, Ill.: Richard D. Irwin, 1981, Chaps. 16–17.

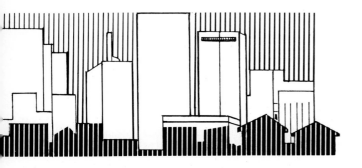

21
Real Estate Investment

INTRODUCTION

People, businesses (e.g., IBM), and institutions (e.g., pension funds), invest some portion of their incomes. Historically, Americans as individuals save and invest about 5 percent of their incomes.[1] This percentage, however, is usually much higher for businesses and especially institutions. Real estate is but one of several investment vehicles for these savings. Other important vehicles include stocks; corporate bonds; local, state, and U.S. government securities; tangibles such as gold, art, and antiques; savings accounts; certificates of deposit; individual retirement accounts; commercial paper; and so forth.

This chapter addresses some fundamental questions about individuals', businesses', and institutions' investments in real estate. First, we focus attention on the characteristics of real estate that offer investors higher returns than other investment opportunities and what those characteristics contribute to the relative *riskiness* of real estate investment. In other words, *why* (or *why not*) invest in real estate?

Also, we discuss in this chapter the various ways in which investors can commit funds to real estate. That is, *what* are the alternative investment opportunities in real estate? Finally, we outline the conceptual and analytical processes for making real estate investment decisions. This presentation answers the question of *how* investors should reach real estate investment decisions.

As in previous chapters, the emphasis here is on real property rights; specifically, we emphasize the extent of the rights received in exchange for invested funds. In accordance with the concept that the value of real estate is equal to its capitalized income, we assume the benefits of a real estate investment to be the income that the investment generates. Therefore the income generated by the real estate is evidence of the value of

---

[1]This savings rate is much lower than in most other industrialized nations.

the investor's property rights. Our perspective is that of the real estate investor who has a unique set of holding period, tax, and financing requirements, as well as expectations about the future. Thus, the objective in analyzing real estate investments is to compare the estimated investment value of the property rights to a prospective purchaser with the seller's asking price for those rights.

INVESTMENT CHARACTERISTICS OF REAL ESTATE

Real estate investors usually can earn returns on their investment from three potential sources. First, they can receive *before-tax cash flow* in a given period of operation. This results from the property's income (i.e., money received from selling or renting units) in excess of all of the property's expenses except federal income taxes. Second, real estate investors can receive returns through the federal and state *income tax benefits* of real property investment.[2] Finally, investors in real estate can benefit from *appreciation* in the value of real property over time.[3]

These three components of return in a real estate investment—cash flow, tax benefits, and appreciation—may vary with time. Any of these components, could be up next period and down the following period. The greater the fluctuation in returns, the greater the *risk* of the investment. Thus, the term *investment risk* is associated with variations in investment returns.[4]

The causes of risk are often external to the investment. Suppose an investor purchases an office building that is 95 percent occupied on the date of purchase. In the following year an economic recession bankrupts two of the tenants and they default on their leases. These vacancies have a devastating effect on cash flow: Less rent is coming in to cover the same level of fixed expenses. The source of this variation in returns is the general economic recession, which is *external* to the investment. Risk, or variation in returns, that originates in general economic conditions is known as *systematic risk.* Risk can also come from internal sources, of course. The cash flow of the office building in this example could suffer from a shortfall of lease renewals caused by an incompetent property manager or by failure to replace fixtures.

While risk is usually associated with "downside" movements in the returns due to external or internal factors, the "upside" potential also en-

---

[2]See Chapter 22 for detailed discussions of the tax regulations affecting real estate.

[3]In some real estate investments, such as raw land, appreciation is the only component of return.

[4]We discuss risk in more detail in Chapter 23.

ters into the *measurement* of risk. This is because up-and-down variation of returns is the conceptual basis for the measurement of risk. Accordingly, the *standard deviation of returns,* which measures variation around a mean or average return, is the most commonly accepted measure of the riskiness of real estate investment.

Basic Risk and Return Relationship

Using the *expected return* E[R] (i.e., forecast average rate of return) as a measure of the return from an investment and the standard deviation (σ) around E[R] as the measure of risk, Panel A of Exhibit 21–1 portrays the basic relationship between risk and return. This graphic represents two important ideas. First, the basic relationship between risk and return is positive: The more risk the investor is willing to take, the greater the rate of return she should expect. The risk, and therefore the expected return of investment B, are greater than those of Investment A.

EXHIBIT 21–1
RISK AND RETURN RELATIONSHIP

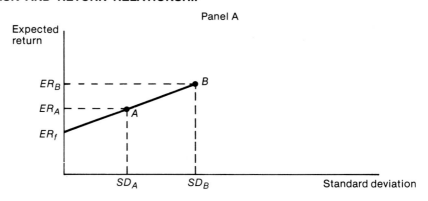

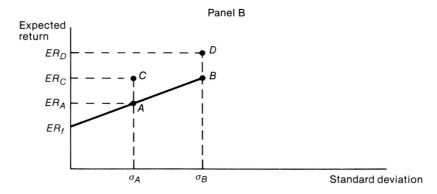

Second, some rate of return can be expected even if the investor is not taking any risk. According to interest rate theory, this *risk-free rate*, shown as ER_f, occurs because investors, even for an investment that carries no risk, will demand some rate of return to invest their funds instead of consuming them for food, clothing, etc.

Two new investments are introduced—Investments C and D—in Panel B. As the graph shows, Investment C has the same σ as investment A, but a higher expected rate of return. The same relationship exists between Investments B and D. Thus, Investments C and D *dominate* Investments A and B; any rational investor would choose an investment opportunity that offers higher returns for the same level of risk. This is termed the *dominance principle*.

Relative Rates of Return on Real Estate

One of the characteristics that attracts investors to real estate is the relatively high rate of return that can be earned on real estate investments. As we showed above, these higher returns come at the expense of higher risk. Therefore, unless real estate investments *dominate* other investments, there is no true advantage in rate of return. Several statistical studies have examined the relative investment performance of real estate and common stocks.[5] Their conclusion was that real estate dominates most other securities, particularly common stocks.

If real estate dominates other investments, then why do business and institutional investment portfolios usually contain less than 20 percent real estate? One common explanation for this disparity is that real estate markets are imperfect. As we discussed in Chapter 10, information on real properties is relatively poor in comparison to information on securities. It could also be argued that obtaining reliable data on returns and the calculation of standard deviations of returns to measure risks are more difficult for real estate investments. Therefore, suspicions may arise about the trustworthiness of statistical studies comparing returns on real estate to those of other investments. The relatively high rates of return from real estate and the reasons why business and institutional portfolios contain so little real estate are directly related to the investment characteristics of real estate that we discuss in the following sections.

Real Estate as an Inflation Hedge

Research on the investment performance of real estate during periods of high inflation shows that real estate, unlike some other securities, pro-

---

[5]See, for example, Stephen E. Roulac, "Can Real Estate Returns Outperform Common Stocks?," *Journal of Portfolio Management* (Winter 1976), pp. 26–43; Dennis G. Kelleher, "How Real Estate Stacks Up to the S&P 500," *Real Estate Review* (Summer 1976), pp. 60–65.

vides a hedge against inflation.[6] That is, the rate of appreciation in the value of real estate has been greater than the rate of inflation. Real estate investments can be a hedge against inflation because real estate is a *real asset*. This means that the incomes (i.e., rents) from real estate are not fixed, as are the incomes from bonds, for example, but can increase as inflation increases. Recall from the fundamental equation

$$V = \frac{I}{R} \tag{21-1}$$

that as the rate increases the value of the asset declines if income is fixed, as in the case of *financial assets* such as bonds. Inflation, which causes all interest rates to increase, does not have a negative effect on the values of real assets if the incomes from real estate increase at the rate of inflation or higher, because the demand for real estate has exceeded the supply. Moreover, most leases in commercial buildings today are *indexed* for inflation; rents are adjusted periodically (e.g., each quarter or year) in step with changes in the Consumer Price Index or other agreed indicators.

―――――――――――――――――― *Frame 21–1* ――――――――――――――――――

What Type of Real Estate Provides the Best Opportunity to Hedge Against Inflation?

Although most leases in office buildings, shopping centers, apartments, and industrial buildings are indexed for inflation, or extend no more than one year, they usually do not provide inflation protection on a day-to-day, week-to-week, or even month-to-month basis. The room rates in motels and hotels, however, can be adjusted on a daily basis and thus provide investors in hospitality properties the ultimate inflation-hedging opportunity among real estate investments.

Federal Tax Laws

The U.S. tax system has been structured to encourage private investment in real estate. There are two basic reasons for this bias toward real estate. First, good housing is deemed important for the social well-being of an advanced society. Special incentives in the past have been provided to encourage investment in apartments and especially in low-income rental housing. Perhaps the most generous provisions of the U.S. tax system, however, are for those who purchase and live in their own homes. Some

―――――――――――

[6]Frank K. Reilly, Raymond Marquardt, and Donald Price, "Real Estate as an Inflation Hedge," *Review of Business and Economic Research* 7 (Spring 1977), pp. 1–19.

believe a negative correlation exists between the rate of home ownership in a country and the country's crime rate.[7]

Second, real estate production is good for the economy. Construction is the single largest employer in the U.S. among industry groups. Also, real estate production stimulates activity in such other industries as building products, carpets, appliances, and furnishings.

As a result of favorable tax treatment, the tax-benefit component of the rate of return on real estate investment has been large in comparison to the tax benefits of other investment opportunities. Tax benefits have become very important to investors in recent years, as more and more investors have been pushed by inflation into the maximum tax bracket for earned income.[8]

Financial Leverage

Most real estate transactions involve large amounts of debt financing (i.e., mortgage loans). Many mortgages are structured so that debt service remains constant or increases rather modestly over time. This means that when the net income (rents minus operating expenses) from a real estate investment rises at a faster rate than the total debt service, the equity investor's returns are magnified. That is, the equity investor captures a relatively large portion of the growth in income and property value.[9] Usually financial leverage is positive (i.e., advantageous to the real estate investor) as long as the cost of borrowing is less than the investor's rate of return on investment.

Financial leverage also increases the risk of a real estate investment. Should the business cycle turn down properties with heavy debt-service loads are more susceptible to foreclosure than properties without such burdens. As vacancies rise in an economic recession, there is less income from the property to service the debt.[10]

Liquidity and Marketability

The *liquidity* of an investment means that an asset can be quickly sold for the *amount invested*. Marketability, in contrast, refers to the ability to sell

---

[7]One notable exception is Japan, which has both a low crime rate and a low rate of home ownership.

[8]We examine the details of federal tax provisions to aid real estate investment in Chapter 22.

[9]As we discussed in Chapter 20, mortgage lenders have become much more aggressive in recent years in capturing income growth and value appreciation by including *income* and *equity participation* features in loan agreements.

[10]See Chapter 23 for a discussion of this *financial risk.*

an asset for its *market value*. Much real estate is highly liquid, but relatively unmarketable. Stocks and bonds sold on an exchange are highly marketable, but illiquid. This characteristic of real estate is one of the main reasons why business and institutional investment portfolios are not devoted heavily to real estate, even though real estate returns tend to dominate other investments. The absence of an active trading market, such as that provided by securities exchanges, detracts greatly from real estate as an institutional outlet for investment funds.

Management

Another characteristic of real estate detracts from its investment appeal: management responsibility. When an investor invests in stocks or bonds, he or she receives dividends or interest payments on a regular basis without doing much more than opening his or her mail. For real estate investments, rents must be collected, expenses must be paid, and repair and maintenance must be performed. Real estate, therefore, is very management-intensive relative to most other investment opportunities.

Government Control

Zoning, land-use, and other government controls can result in significant expenditures on property improvements to conform to specific regulations. Such requirements may even result in a loss of opportunities to earn market rents. The owner of a shopping center, for example, might be forced to replace all advertising signs because of a new city sign ordinance, or the owner of an apartment house may lose the opportunity to raise rents to market levels because of a rent-control ordinance. These potential constraints on real estate investment are not present in competing investment opportunities.

REAL ESTATE INVESTMENT MODES

In the preceding section, we developed some answers to the questions of *why* or *why not* invest in real estate. Another major question of concern to real estate investors is *what* alternative investment opportunities are available in real estate. This can be examined from two perspectives. First, we consider the various *methods* for channeling investment funds into real estate. Second, we consider the various *types* of real properties that can serve as investments. The investment *mode*—the combination of method of investment and property type selected by the individual investor, business, or institution—depends on the investment strategy and objectives of that particular investor. Throughout this discussion of real estate investment, we stress the importance of having a well-established investment strategy and specific investment objectives.

Ways to Commit Funds to Real Estate

Because real estate offers investors opportunities for relatively high returns and because real estate is handicapped as an investment by non-marketability and management burdens, several alternative ways to commit funds to real estate have emerged in recent decades, ways that seek to provide the advantages of investing in real estate without the disadvantages. Currently, investors can invest in real estate through direct equity purchase, real estate investment trusts (REITs), public and private limited partnership syndications, and as lenders of mortgage money or purchasers of mortgage securities.

Direct Equity Purchase. An investor can commit funds (establish an equity position) directly through the purchase of property either alone or with other general partners. Taking a direct equity position offers the investor some recognizable benefits, but also has certain disadvantages. The greatest benefits come from the federal income tax provisions designed to encourage real estate investment, from having total management control over the asset underlying the investment, and from being able to manage the investment itself.[11]

On the other hand, direct equity investment may be undesirable for real estate investors, because

1. The investor is exposed to personal liability; if the property does not produce enough income to meet expenses, the investor's personal assets (e.g., stocks and bonds) can be attached by creditors.
2. Direct equity investment does not offer any way to improve liquidity as do some other methods of investing in real estate.
3. The investor may commit all available funds to one or possibly a very few properties and thus not benefit from diversification.[12]

Real Estate Investment Trusts (REITs). Real estate investment trusts have been described as mutual funds for real estate. An REIT raises equity through the sale of shares in the trust to the public and receives loans, usually from commercial banks. With these resources, the REIT

---

[11]We are distinguishing between *management of the investment* (i.e., when to buy, when to sell and what accounting system to use) and the *management of the asset*, which includes decisions such as how to structure leases.

[12]Diversification is an important concept for understanding how to analyze investment risks; we discuss it in Chapter 23.

either acquires properties directly (equity trusts) or makes mortgage loans (mortgage trusts). The REIT is not liable for federal income taxes if it satisfies specific requirements, including the distribution of 95 percent of its earnings to share holders. Since the shares of most REITs are traded on the over-the-counter stock markets, investors can sell their shares readily and receive returns from appreciation in the value.

The ability to liquidate one's real estate holdings in a reasonably short period is probably the major advantage of REITs as real estate investments. The investor also benefits from professional asset management and diversification, since REITs usually own many different types of properties in many different locations. In addition, investors have no personal liability if an REIT investment goes sour.

On the negative side, REITs, although tax exempt themselves, give their investors none of the tax benefits of direct ownership of real estate. This is a serious disadvantage, because many investors seek tax benefits. Finally, the investor who wishes to exercise management control over the asset would not choose the REIT method, since the REIT's assets are managed by professional managers.

Limited-Partnership Syndication. This method of investing in real estate has had such a dramatic impact on the real estate investment environment during the early 1980's that we have devoted an entire chapter to the subject.[13] There are several reasons why limited-partnership syndications have proliferated in recent years, but perhaps the foremost is that this method of investing in real estate provides most of the advantages of REIT investment—particularly avoidance of personal liability—and at the same time, offers income tax benefits to investors (although limited by recent tax legislation).

Limited-partnership syndications work very much like REITs in the sense that shares in a group of real properties are sold to investors. These shares, however, are not nearly as marketable as REIT shares, although marketability is improving every year.[14]

The substantial costs may offset the benefits of investing in real estate through a limited partnership syndication. The sponsor of the syndication—the general partner(s)—and professionals—lawyers, accountants, and real estate acquisition personnel—hired by the syndicator normally charge substantial fees to the limited partners for services to create and continue the partnership. These fees sometimes result in only 80 cents of every dollar paid by investors actually being invested in properties.

---

[13]See Chapter 27.

[14]Many stock brokerage houses are currently involved in marketing syndication shares, and are starting to make a secondary (i.e., resale) market in these shares.

Mortgage Loans and Mortgage Securities.   While not traditionally regarded as a method of investing in real estate, the mortgage lender and the purchaser of a security backed by mortgages are investing in real estate. The liquidity and marketability of mortgage investing is usually good, and the investor has no personal liability. This method, however, does not produce any significant tax benefits for the investor and often the investor in mortgages is not able to share in the growth of income or value of the property.[15]

Major Types of Real Estate Assets

In selecting the appropriate real estate investment mode, the investor should consider the advantages and disadvantages of investing in one or more of the various types of real estate as well as to the methods of investing in real estate. The advantages and disadvantages of these methods are summarized in Exhibit 21–2. The major types of real estate normally considered for investment include undeveloped land, residential rental real estate, office properties, shopping centers and other retail es-

---

EXHIBIT 21–2
A SUMMARY OF THE ADVANTAGES AND DISADVANTAGES OF REAL ESTATE INVESTMENT METHODS

Method of Investing in Real Estate	Main Advantages	Main Disadvantages
Direct equity purchase	Full tax benefits Asset management control	Personal liability Illiquidity Lack of marketability Little diversification
REIT	Marketability of shares Professional management Diversification No personal liability	No tax benefits No personal control
Limited partnership syndication	Tax benefits No personal liability Diversification opportunities Professional management Improving marketability	No personal control Large fees

Mortgage loans and mortgage
  securities
	Liquidity; marketability
	No personal liability
		No tax benefits
		Often no opportunity
		  to share in returns

---

[15]Sharing in the growth of income and value is often possible with mortgage loans on income properties, but is usually impossible in mortgage security investments.

tablishments, hospitality properties, and industrial and special-purpose properties.

Undeveloped Land. Undeveloped, or "raw" land is one of the riskier types of real estate investment opportunities. The investor in raw land is speculating that urban growth will produce increasing demands for undeveloped land for apartments, shopping centers, etc. The returns the investor receives from an investment in undeveloped land depend entirely on land value increases, since undeveloped land does not generate income unless put to some agricultural use. Sufficient increases in value may come soon, they may come years from now, or they may never come. Forecasting urban growth, must less its timing and direction, is a very inexact science, as we discussed in Chapter 11.

There are also unavoidable carrying costs in land investment. These include property taxes, insurance, and interest payments when the property is financed. In addition, the income tax features of such an investment are not favorable. Land cannot be depreciated for tax purposes, and there are certain limitations on interest deductability and capital losses on investments in undeveloped land.

The success of an undeveloped land investment depends on good location in relation to the pattern of growth and the following other considerations:

1. Access to major highways.
2. Proximity to political jurisdictions that provide public services, such as police and fire protection.
3. Proximity to utility service districts for the provision of water, sewer, gas, electricity, and telephone services.
4. Favorable topography (i.e., lack of slopes) and soil.
5. Favorable political climate for rezoning requests.

Investing in raw land, either through direct equity investment or through a raw land syndication, is often a highly speculative venture. The investor expects to realize large value increases within a few years or less. If such increases are not soon realized, the investor stands to lose considerable amounts of money as the result of paying carrying costs and incurring the opportunity costs of not having the capital invested in assets that generate income and income tax benefits.

Residential Rental Property. For a variety of reasons, residential rental property, including single-family homes, condominium units, duplexes, triplexes, fourplexes, and small and large apartment properties, is often the best type of real estate investment. First, the demand for good-quality housing has continued to be strong over the past few decades. This suggests that the opportunities for earning net income and obtaining appre-

Photo by Jack Corgel

Investment in undeveloped land may yield high returns through value increases but has several potential disadvantages.

Advantages:
Possibility of large increase in value
Low management responsibility

Disadvantages:
No or low income production
Considerable uncertainty about future development potential
Unavoidable carrying costs
No income tax benefits

Common investment methods: Direct equity participation (purchase) and raw-land syndications.

ciation are very good. Also, the demand for rental housing is usually not severely affected by downturns in the general economy, so vacancy rates in residential properties are generally lower than those for other types of rental property.

Second, the short-term lease contracts that normally exist between landlords (investors) and tenants in residential rental properties allow landlords to make frequent adjustments in rents up to market levels when the leases expire. This is especially important during periods of high inflation or rapidly increasing demand for rental housing.

Finally, residential rental real estate affords the small investor the opportunity to invest by taking a direct equity position with a very small down payment. Many people have gotten rich through the purchase of small residential rental properties. Sometimes the sellers of these properties help finance such purchases for investors.

A major drawback of investing directly in residential rental property is the heavy property management burden. Since leases are relatively short, tenant turnover can be rapid. Also, repairs and maintenance must be performed to keep rents up and to satisfy legal regulations involving the tenant-landlord relationship. This means large commitments of time for investors who decide to manage their own properties or a substantial commitment of funds (usually 5 to 8 percent of effective gross income) by investors who use professional property managers.

Office Properties. The growth of the service sector has created a tremendous demand for office space. High-rise office buildings in down-

Photo by Jack Corgel

Residential rental property may be the best type of real estate in which to invest.

Advantages:
Continuing strong demand and low
  vacancy risk from changes in general
  economic conditions
Good inflation protection
Opportunity for direct equity participation
  with small downpayments and good
  financing

Disadvantages:
Heavy management burden

Common investment methods: direct equity participation, REITs, syndications, and
  mortgages and mortgage securities.

town areas, low-rise buildings in suburban office parks, and office condominiums are proliferating in many urban areas. As investments, office buildings have some distinct advantages. First, long-term leases, when signed with quality corporate tenants, provide high security. Also, most office leases today are indexed for both inflation and sometimes for property expenses (e.g., property taxes). Second, office building investments are not subject to rent-control laws. Third, perhaps the single most important advantage is the strong demand for office space in many major urban areas. This strong demand is due to a conversion of the U.S. em-

Photo by John R. Disney

Office buildings are favored by many institutional investors (e.g., pension funds) because of the security provided by long-term leases.

Advantages:	Disadvantages:
Strong demand	Management and leasing require
Favorable lease contract features	considerable expertise
Absence of rent regulation	Success highly dependent on locations
Good financing opportunities	and linkages

Common investment methods: syndications, REITs, and direct equity participation.

ployment base from manufacturing to service jobs. Yet despite the strong demand for office space, office markets tend to become overbuilt as many lenders and developers simultaneously see good opportunities in the office market.

The disadvantages of office-property investments are related to the unique characteristics of office buildings. Office-property investments are riskier than residential-property investments because of the higher degree of expertise required to manage and lease office space. Management and leasing errors by inexperienced agents often have devastating effects on the cash flows from office buildings. Since prestige is important to the success of office developments, leasing to lower-quality tenants, for example, places a building in a lower quality category in the eyes of the market.

Location is another potential source of risk. The prestige of a building is often enhanced by its location. For suburban buildings, access to major highways and linkages with such places as restaurants, high-income residential areas, and shopping facilities are extremely important. The implication of this location sensitivity is that the land underlying office buildings is usually costly. High land costs affect depreciation allowances, as well as the overall return to the investor if occupancy is lower than expected or rents are depressed.

Shopping Centers and Other Retail Establishments. Retail establishments are found in a variety of forms. The simplest is a freestanding retail outlet (e.g., a fast food outlet). Many retail establishments today, however, are found in shopping centers. Shopping centers, more than freestanding establishments, have been popular with individual investors and institutions that invest in income-producing properties.

Before we discuss the advantages and disadvantages of shopping-center investments, we look at the various types of shopping centers.

1. *Neighborhood or "strip" center.* This type of center is located for the convenience of a close-by resident population. It contains retail establishments offering mostly convenience goods (e.g., groceries and drugs) and services (e.g., barber shop and dry cleaning). These centers are usually "anchored" by a large chain grocery store or drug store. The gross leasable area of the anchor(s) and nonanchored tenant space is usually about 50,000 square feet.
2. *Community center.* This is a larger version of a neighborhood center. Typically, this type of center is anchored by a discount department store and may include such outlets as clothing stores, banks, furniture stores, and professional offices (e.g., dentists). The gross leasable area is usually three times that of a neighborhood center.
3. *Regional and super-regional centers.* Regional centers usually have at least two anchor tenants, which are major department stores (e.g.,

Sears and Penneys), and 200,000 square feet of gross leasable area devoted to nonanchor tenants. These major department stores draw people from a much larger area than the neighborhood or community centers. The minor tenants are located between the anchor tenants to capture customers. In recent years, through expansion of regional centers and through new development, super-regional centers have emerged. These centers may have as many as five or six major tenants and hundreds of minor tenants. These centers are usually over a million square feet.

Shopping-center investment is probably the most complex of income property investments. Two factors are responsible for this. First, the market for shopping centers is extremely dynamic. On the demand side, the growth of an urban area can quickly alter market characteristics (e.g., family income and population density). On the supply side, competition for market areas is intense. The implication of these changing conditions is that the owners and managers of the center must be constantly aware of whether the tenant mix of the center is properly serving the market.

Second, the ownership arrangements and lease contracts between owners or managers and tenants are generally quite complicated.[16] Nonanchor tenants often make flat or indexed rental payments plus an additional payment based on some percentage of gross sales.[17] These *percentage leases* traditionally have been found in most centers, although recently they seem to be falling out of favor. Tenants also share in the payment of operating expenses of the center. Lease clauses to provide for adequate rent and operating-expense sharing are a source of risk to the investor. Nevertheless, when the economy is sound and the level of competition is not severe, shopping centers provide exceptional returns.

Hospitality Properties. Hospitality properties—hotels and motels— serve two distinct markets: the traveler (transient market) and the visitor or conventioneer (destination market). Both markets are highly susceptible to changes in general economic conditions and, because there are no leases in hospitality properties, these types of investments are riskier than other income-property investments. Yet with high risk comes the opportunity for high returns. Hospitality properties generate substantial returns when nightly occupancy consistently exceeds the break-even level (usually about 50 to 60 percent occupancy). The success of a hospitality property is also highly dependent on its management. A hotel is a business.

---

[16]Major tenants sometimes own their own buildings and lease the land under the building from the owner. Minor tenants almost always lease buildings and land.

[17]A minor tenant can be evicted from the center under some leases if gross sales are not high enough to provide a certain level of rent.

Property Profile: The Legendary Waldorf-Astoria*

Photos courtesy of the Waldorf-Astoria Hotel

The Waldorf-Astoria Hotel opened on New York City's Park Avenue during the Great Depression in 1931. At that time it was the largest hotel in the world, with 1,852 rooms. From the outset the Waldorf established itself as an elitist hotel. Until the early 1980s the Waldorf's management refused to advertise, relying solely on its clientele's references as a means of attracting new customers.

In more difficult and competitive times of the present, the Waldorf has managed to maintain its aura of elegance and distinction. Even in its attempt to serve the convention business, management insists that the Waldorf is not a "convention" hotel. It continues to provide customers with extravagant services. For example, if a guest informs the hotel's management that a relative is arriving that day for their first visit to New York, the hotel dispatches its limousine to pick up the relative and sends them a dozen roses and a box of candy. Management considers these services as vital to overturn the notion that "when you turn off the lights and the bed is comfortable, all hotels are the same."

The Waldorf remains the standard setter and innovator of the upper end of the hotel industry, just as it has since 1931. The Waldorf-Astoria is much more than simply another improvement on land—it is a truly unique *business*.

*Source: *U.S. News and World Report,* Feburary 13, 1984.

Photo by Jack Corgel

Due to the dynamics of the market for retail goods and highly complex lease provisions, shopping centers offer investors opportunities for high returns if they are willing to take on additional risks.

Advantages:
Possibilities for high returns
Good financing opportunities
Absence of rent regulations

Disadvantages:
Complex markets leading to a high level of risk
Complex lease provision that can alter returns dramatically
Heavy management burdens

Common investment methods: direct equity participation, REITs, and syndication.

═══════════════════════ Frame 21–3 ═══════════════════════

A "Super-Super" Regional Mall

The West Edmonton Mall in Edmonton, Alberta, Canada is listed in the *1986 Guinness Book of World Records* as the world's largest mall and also as having the world's largest parking lot—spaces for more than 30,000 cars. Here are some facts about this unique commercial center.

- ☐ 57 entrances.
- ☐ 836 stores (many regional malls have between 90–150).
- ☐ 2.5 acres artificial lake in the mall complete with submarines and live sharks and octopuses.
- ☐ an 18 hole miniature golf course in the mall.
- ☐ an ice rink in the mall where the Edmonton Oilers practice.
- ☐ five million square feet of retail space.
- ☐ 400,000 visitors on a typical fall weekend.
- ☐ one-mile-long shopping concourse.

Thus the manager should be versed in all aspects of this type of business, not just leasing and maintenance.

During periods of high inflation, the absence of leases is an advantage because rents can be adjusted on almost a daily basis. However, this is less of a comparative advantage with the advent of indexed leases in other income-property investments.

Industrial and Special-Use Properties.

Some investors, mainly institutions, invest funds in industrial properties and warehouses. Recently, special-use properties, such as mini-warehouses and research-and-development buildings, have become popular with noninstitutional investors. Because of their specialized designs for particular uses and users, these properties (especially industrial and research and development) are extremely risky. In other words, a property that is specially designed for the needs of one tenant may not be suitable for the next tenant and thus, substantial costs may be involved in readying the property for leasing.

In recent years much of the development of light-industrial and re-

Photo by Jack Corgel

One of the more recent innovations in hospitality property development is the suite hotel. These hotels offer the business traveler a greater degree of comfort and the ability to conduct business in the privacy of his or her own suite.

Advantages:
Potential high returns
Good financing opportunities
Good inflation protection

Disadvantages:
High susceptibility to general economic conditions
No lease contracts
Heavy management responsibility

Common investment methods: direct equity participation, REITs, and syndication.

The industrial park provides a quality working environment and the buildings are constructed for more generalized use than other industrial properties.

Advantages: Disadvantages:
Good financing opportunities   Substantial risk due to specialized nature of
Low management burden   these properties
Common investment methods: direct equity participation, REITs, and syndication.

search-and-development use has occurred in *industrial parks*. These resemble residential subdivisions, and offer a controlled environment with buildings that are designed to accommodate a wide variety of tenant needs.

One type of special-use property that has become extremely popular in recent years is mini-warehouses. Generally, these properties are located close to businesses and apartment units that have little space available for storage. In many areas, occupancy rates in mini-warehouses have been extremely high. Security is perhaps the most important consideration in the management of these facilities.

REAL ESTATE INVESTMENT ANALYSIS

We can divide the life of a real estate investment into three phases. The first involves the decision to acquire or not to buy the property. The second phase is the operation of the property during the investor's holding period. The final phase is the disposition of the property rights. In this section we are concerned with answering the question of how real estate investment decisions are made: the acquisition phase of a real estate investment. While the process and procedures we discuss pertain to investing through direct purchase and ownership, they apply generally to all methods and types of investments.

Investment Strategy

As Exhibit 21–3 shows, the formation of a general investment strategy is the starting point for investment analysis and establishes a plan that guides the investor. Do investors actually prepare strategies for investment, or is this simply a step found only in textbooks? In other words, is this what investors actually do or what they should be doing? The answer is that it is both. Most institutional investors draw up and follow a formal

EXHIBIT 21–3
GENERALIZED REAL ESTATE INVESTMENT PROCESS

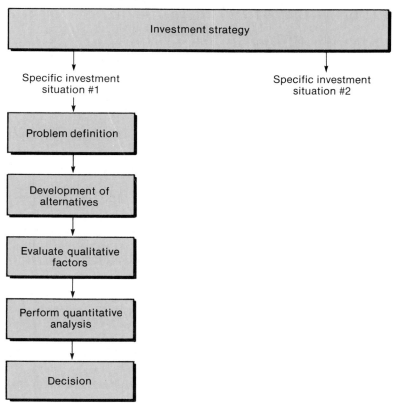

investment strategy. While most individual investors probably do not follow an explicit, pre-established investment strategy, individual investors *implicitly* know their investment objectives and the general course they plan to follow.

Why is an investment strategy so important? Although there is no statistical evidence to support the claim, many believe that the number and severity of investment errors can be reduced by following a pre-established strategy. Limiting such errors is critical in real estate for two reasons: there is usually much money at risk, and the investor's reputation or track record is crucial for obtaining financing.

The investment strategy can be separated into three components—investment philosophy, investment objectives, and investment policies.

Investment Philosophy. An investment philosophy outlines the activity the investor wants to perform with real estate investments: mainly, whether she will be *active* or *passive*. Active investment implies direct equity participation in which the investor takes an active role in finding, buying, and managing the real estate. A passive investor, in contrast, might elect to invest in real estate through an REIT or syndication, leaving the acquisition and property management to others—for a fee, of course.

The investment philosophy of individual, corporate, and institutional investors reflects the investor's preferences for risk and return. Some investors are highly risk-averse and therefore unwilling to invest in risky projects, such as new developments, even though high returns are possible.[18] The degree of risk aversion of the investor is related to the investor's wealth (i.e., usually the greater the wealth, the less risk-averse the investor) or to some institutional consideration.[19] Recognition of the investor's risk preferences is an important prerequisite to establishing investment objectives and policies.

Investment Objectives. Investor objectives should follow from investment philosophies, as well as from individual factors (e.g., tax status). The objective of preservation of capital, for example, follows from a philosophy of avoiding high risk. The objective of obtaining substantial tax shelter from real estate investments results from the investor's tax status. Thus, we may view objectives as general guidelines for choosing specific properties.

---

[18]New development projects are inherently more risky than existing property investments because they are not proven in the market.

[19]Pension fund managers, for example, can be held personally liable for their actions under the Employee Retirement Income Securities Act (ERISA) of 1974.

The following is a statement of the objectives of the Prudential Property Investment Separate Account (PRISA), one of the largest institutional investors in real estate:[20]

> The objective of PRISA is to obtain an attractive rate of *current income* from the property investments that offer prospects of long-term growth, in order to enhance the resources of participating pension plans to provide benefit payments. To fulfill that objective, Prudential invests PRISA funds primarily in the purchase of income-producing real property, including office and industrial buildings, shopping centers, other retail stores, apartments, hotels, and motels. Suitable *diversification* is maintained as to type of property and location. Particular attention is given to properties that are located in growth areas, may be leased on the basis of permitting suitable rent revisions, and are considered to have good *appreciation* potential.[21] (emphasis added)

This statement includes the specific objectives of earning current income, benefitting from appreciation, and diversifying across property types and locations. Other objectives, such as preserving capital, maximizing equity investment, and maximizing tax shelter, are not an explicit part of PRISA's statement of objectives.[22]

Investment Policies.   Investment policies create a profile of investments that satisfy the investor's objectives and are consistent with the investor's philosophy. As defined here, investment policies include financial criteria such as "property value appreciation of at least five percent," and nonfinancial criteria such as "the age of the buildings must not exceed ten years."

Investment policies also include special considerations such as investing only in small properties (e.g., "Apartment properties should have no more than 50 units" and "Office buildings should be no more than 50,000 square feet"), or "Investment only in the states of Florida and Texas." Therefore once the set of policies is drawn up, the investor has a profile of the desired investments.

The investment strategy serves as a preliminary screening device. Any potential property investment that is inconsistent with the investor's policies, objectives, or philosophy is rejected. As Exhibit 21–3 shows,

---

[20]PRISA, managed by Prudential Life Insurance Company, combines investible funds from several pension funds (mostly corporate) to buy real estate.

[21]"A New Dimension in Pension Funding: PRISA—The Prudential Property Investment Separate Account".

[22]Pension funds are exempt from federal income taxes and usually purchase real estate with all equity (i.e., without debt financing).

properties that are found to be generally consistent with the investor's investment strategy are evaluated further.[23]

Note to Students.   To help demonstrate the process of analyzing a specific real estate investment opportunity, we present the Prestige Products case.[24] Prestige Products wants to build an office building, mainly for its own use. The problems and issues in this case are typical of those facing large corporate investors, and the process for evaluating this investment opportunity is common to most real estate investment situations. The reader should examine this case before continuing.

PRESTIGE PRODUCTS CASE

In the winter of 1985 the executive committee of the Prestige Products Group faced the decision of what size of office building to build on the company's recently acquired site in Metropolis. Two alternatives were being considered. Under one, an 8-story building adequate for the company's current space needs would be constructed; the second, a 30-story building, would accommodate possible future expansion and permit the extra space to be leased to other firms. Exhibit 1 shows the Metropolis skyline with a rendering of the proposed 30-story building in the lower left. Exhibit 2 identifies the competitive office buildings shown in Exhibit 1. Exhibit 3 provides information on some of the characteristics of these buildings.

Prestige Products acquired the land for the proposed building for $1.5 million a year earlier. The firm has been headquartered in the Statler Center (Building 36 in Exhibit 2), but its lease expires at the end of 1989. While there is a renewal option, the decision is due by April 1, 1988, and the rent would increase from $10.00 to $15.00 per square foot. Management argued that this lease rate was excessive and that the company should investigate building its own office building.

Although Prestige had only 30,000 square feet in the Statler Center, in three other buildings it occupied another 100,000 square feet at rates from $8.75 to $10.90. On many occasions the executive committee had lamented the fact that the personnel of Prestige Products were spread out in four buildings. This did not present a problem for customer relations as it might have in other businesses, since Prestige Products does not have much direct contact with its customers, but it was argued that it affected employee morale. The executives realize, though, that few existing buildings could comfortably provide all of the company's space requirements. The staggered lease terms make the problem of scheduling such a consoli-

---

[23]Many investors today tie up properties at this point through contracts for sale with contingency clauses or letters of intent to insure that time is not wasted in evaluating properties that might be sold to someone else while an evaluation is being performed.

[24]Stephen E. Roulac, "What's Your Solution?" *Real Estate Today* 6 (August 1973), pp. 30–33; and J. Stephen E. Roulac, "A Case in Property Development," *Real Estate Today* 6 (October 1973), pp. 12–19. This case also appears in Stephen E. Roulac, *Cases in Property Development* (San Francisco: Property Press, 1973). This case has been updated and altered by the authors for use in this book.

EXHIBIT 1 The Metropolis skyline with a facsimile of the proposed 30-story building in the lower left.

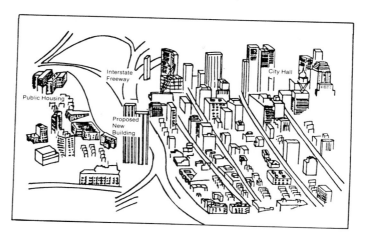

EXHIBIT 2 Identifies the competitive office buildings shown in Exhibit 1.

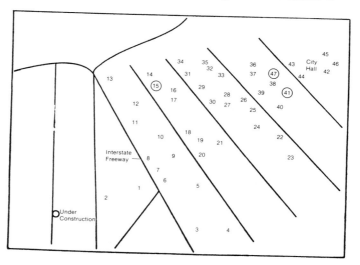

dation seem difficult. The marketing vice president is particularly enthusiastic about the proposal to build a new office building and suggests that the executive committee name the new facility "Prestige Plaza." This suggestion was well received and it was pointed out that the move would be consistent with the company's campaign to gain a greater following in the Metropolis business community.

EXHIBIT 3

Location	Building	Year Built	Floor Area (sq. ft.)	Approximate Occupancy Factor	Average Lease Rates
1	Prestige Plaza	(1987)	(600,000)	N/A	N/A
2	Havenstrite	1936	60,000	65	$ 8.60
3	Citizens Tower	1932	50,000	60	8.50
4	McArthur	1938	50,000	70	8.80
5	Rowan	1952	15,000	100	Owner occupied
6	Century	1946	18,000	80	9.00
7	Republican	1954	20,000	75	8.75
8	Democrat	1964	45,000	50	9.00
9	Golden West	1951	70,000	79	9.60
10	Argonaut	1973	190,000	96	10.90
11	Buckeye	1962	170,000	82	10.00
12	Workers Insurance	1947	225,000	94	9.80
13	Executive Towers	1970	150,000	96	10.75
14	National	1974	400,000	98	11.00
15	Second National Bank	(1987)	(800,000)	N/A	N/A
16	Midwest	1971	225,000	98	10.80
17	Waterworks	1974	100,000	99	11.00
18	American	1948	150,000	68	9.30
19	Continental	1953	180,000	80	9.55
20	Supreme	1955	55,000	76	9.80
21	Mercury	1951	100,000	75	9.50
22	Security	1934	80,000	60	8.50
23	First Montgomery	1926	60,000	50	8.30
24	Fidelity	1929	100,000	55	8.75
25	Patriot	1957	30,000	80	10.90
26	Park Place	1955	40,000	85	10.80
27	Union	1964	100,000	100	Owner occupied
28	Executive House	1969	120,000	93	10.85
29	Freedom Arms	1961	96,000	90	10.30
30	Hyman	1966	56,000	100	Owner occupied
31	Edison	1975	100,000	97	11.10
32	Sunkist	1977	120,000	99	11.30
33	Lincoln	1978	120,000	96	11.30
34	Embassy	1981	100,000	99	11.55
35	Madison	1983	600,000	97	11.85
36	Statler Center	1979	1,400,000	94	11.50
37	Pacific	1974	220,000	100	11.20
38	Atlantic	1975	100,000	95	11.00
39	Hayes	1971	90,000	100	Owner occupied
40	Washington	1968	35,000	100	10.90
41	Turner Towers	(1987)	(500,000)	N/A	N/A
42	The Metropolan	1952	500,000	100	9.50
43	Grey Building	1947	400,000	96	9.40
44	Thompson	1956	100,000	99	10.20
45	Veterans	1974	200,000	100	11.30
46	Central	1955	120,000	95	11.00
47	State Building	(1987)	(900,000)		

After the executive committee had tentatively agreed to the new Prestige Plaza, a local broker was contacted to identify possible sites. The management of Prestige Products told the broker that they wanted a site suitable for the distinctive building that they were planning. Because the company produced consumer goods, they wanted a location that would be easily visible. The management of Prestige Products was insistent that their building not be overshadowed by other competing structures. After several sites were rejected as unsuitable for the firm's objectives, the broker showed the executive committee the site identified as "1" in Exhibit 2. He pointed out that the proximity to the Interstate Freeway would insure considerable exposure. The broker emphasized the value of having Prestige Plaza seen by every person entering or leaving downtown Metropolis. When the architect's rendering of the proposed Prestige Plaza was superimposed on the skyline of Metropolis, all reluctance vanished. It was readily apparent that Prestige Plaza was the dominant structure in downtown Metropolis. This location, with its high visibility and ready access coupled with the excellence and distinctiveness of its modern architecture, made Prestige Plaza clearly superior to the competition.

The executive committee felt that it was an excellent time to build because of the strong occupancy factors in the more modern buildings constructed since 1965. Although there is still a good market for conservatively priced office space, many companies require newer and more modern facilities and are willing to pay the much higher rents. The expansion in economic activity over the last two decades has caused many companies seeking headquarters space, as well as service-related firms (e.g., law and public accounting firms), to move to downtown Metropolis.

The executive committee of Prestige Products felt a certain satisfaction that they were not alone in their optimistic assessment of the office market in Metropolis. The Turner Towers (Building 41 in Exhibit 2) would open sometime in late 1987 with 500,000 feet. The Second National Bank Building (Building 15 in Exhibit 2), with 800,000 feet, expected its first tenants to move in in late 1987. It was assumed that the State Building (Building 47 in Exhibit 2) would break ground during the next 12 months, with 900,000 feet to be ready for tenants in mid-1987. The sponsors of all of the new office buildings reported that active leasing programs were under way. The executive committee at Prestige Products realized that their construction costs are somewhat higher than the norm. They felt this was justified, however, because the usual two- or three-year construction period was being accelerated to only a year and a half so that the facility would be ready by the time the lease on the current space is up. Further, the distinctive architectural facade that has been specified necessitates additional expenditure. Preliminary estimates suggest that annual operating expenses of $4.00 per square foot could be anticipated, and because of the strong market, rental income is expected to grow at a slightly faster rate than operating expenses (i.e., approximately 4 percent as opposed to 3 percent for expenses). Prestige Products' long-range plan calls for all investments to return 14 percent after taxes. The improvement would be financed with a bond issue (85 percent) and from cash (15 percent).* Prestige Products currently has an excellent

---

*For the purposes of analyzing this case, the bond issue can be treated like a mortgage loan (i.e., full amortization of principal over the 30-year term, monthly payments).

Exhibit 4
SUMMARY OF THE SIGNIFICANT FINANCIAL DATA ON THE
TWO ALTERNATIVES

	Eight Stories	Thirty Stories
Square feet (20,000/floor)	160,000	600,000
Construction cost ($50/sq. ft.)	$8,000,000	$30,000,000
Land cost	1,500,000	1,500,000
	$9,500,000	$31,500,000

rating from the bond rating agencies. The issue would be ready within two months of any decision to build, would have 30-year maturities, and a rate of about 12 percent.

The most recent report from the architect suggests that the company must specify whether it plans to build 8 stories or 30 stories for its new Prestige Plaza (a summary of the costs of the two structures is in Exhibit 4). While a few members in the executive committee favor the more conservative approach because it involves a lesser commitment of funds, others argue that the object of creating the "aura of success" would be defeated by a restricted development. An 8-story building could hardly be called "Prestige Plaza," advocates of the 30-story structure pointed out. Both the marketing and financial vice presidents reminded the group that Prestige Products had announced that it would not build a new building limited only to the company's space requirements. Furthermore, these executives reminded the others that the company has had to move in the past because the need for space had outgrown the supply. The company should not allow itself to be placed in a similar bind in the future.

What is the best course for this firm to follow?
Additional assumptions to evaluate alternatives
    1. Corporate tax rate.
    2. Seven-year holding period.
    3. Straight-line depreciation.

Define the Problem

Problem definition is the first step toward decision making. This involves answering questions about what is to be accomplished, for example, and what are the key factors impeding a solution. But to analyze the Prestige Plaza case in accordance with the schematic in Exhibit 21–2, we should outline the firm's investment strategy before defining the specific investment problems. Prestige Products is not a firm that regularly deals in real estate investment. It is primarily a *user* of real estate. It wants appreciation and tax benefits from its real estate investments, but is unwilling to accept much risk.

Space requirements are an important part of the Prestige Plaza proposal and appear to be an essential element in the firm's investment strategy. Some managers contend that employee morale (although not customer relations) is suffering because the firm's employees are spread out over downtown Metropolis in several rental buildings. Also, rents are expected to increase sharply during the next renewal period, and the firm expects to expand its employment.

Notwithstanding, the key factors behind these proposals is the firm's corporate image—its prestige. Some officers of the firm are aggressively seeking the development of a "corporate monument" to enhance the firm's national exposure and its corporate reputation in Metropolis.

So, what must be accomplished in the analysis of this case is a decision regarding the proposal to construct a new building for Prestige Products. The key variable is said to be space needs but more likely it is corporate image.

Develop Alternatives

The evaluation of an investment opportunity should focus on a well-defined set of alternatives. In defining those alternatives, we should consider factors or constraints such as the relevancy, feasibility, and appropriateness of each alternative.

Since the Prestige Products case centers on the proposals for Prestige Plaza, two obvious alternatives are to construct a 30-story or an 8-story building. These are only two of many options available for improving employee morale, solving space needs, and improving the corporate image, but at this juncture they are the only alternatives that have been proposed. A third alternative, the "no-build" alternative, counterbalances these positive development proposals. Thus the decision in this case will be either to build the 30-story building, the eight-story building, or not to build on this site at this time.

Evaluate Qualitative Factors

We cannot overstate the importance of a thorough qualitative analysis of an investment opportunity. All too often real estate investment analysts plunge into the quantitative analysis (i.e., the "number-crunching" aspect of investment analysis) before carefully considering such qualitative factors as location, market conditions, consistency with investment strategy, and the ability of the proposal to solve the investor's problem(s). The qualitative analysis begins with a listing of the pros and cons of each alternative. The listing of specific qualitative factors uncovers the essential strengths and weaknesses of each alternative but perhaps more important, it provides critical inputs (e.g., rents and vacancy levels) to the quantitative analysis of the alternatives.

Exhibit 21–4 presents the *initial phase* of the qualitative analysis in the

EXHIBIT 21-4
QUALITATIVE ANALYSIS: PRESTIGE PRODUCTS CASE

Alternative	Pros	Cons
1. Do not build; continue to lease space.	1. Free-up $1.5 million from sale of land. 2. No large commitment of funds or increase in debt.	1. No consolidation of employees; thus morale problem unresolved. 2. Rent increase problem unresolved. 3. Prestige issue not addressed. 4. Does not take advantage of good timing to build speculative office space.
2. Build 8-story building.	1. Low-level commitment of funds. 2. Employees consolidated. 3. Prestige Plaza built as promised. 4. Good access to freeway.	1. Not prestigious enough. 2. Does not allow for growth. 3. Does not take advantage of good speculative market.
3. Build 30-story building.	1. All the advantages of eight story proposal. 2. Prestigious building. 3. Takes advantage of speculative market opportunities.	1. Large financial commitment.

Prestige Products case. The advantage seems to go to the 30-story construction alternative. However, much can be learned in the *second phase* of a qualitative analysis. This involves a critical re-evaluation and questioning of every aspect of the case or investment situation. Such re-evaluations are most successfully accomplished by persons with training and considerable experience in real estate investment-problem solving. The critical evaluation uncovers three key points.

1. The problem of space requirements by itself does not seem to warrant the construction of a 30-story building. Here, the firm's image is a strong motivating factor.
2. The idea of constructing a building with much more space than is currently needed for employees (only about 15 stories are needed for employees) is an ill-conceived idea for two reasons. First, the proposal runs contrary to the firm's investment strategy. This firm should not be in the real estate business. Second, the claim that the rental market for office space in the next two years will be good is not supported by the information supplied in the case. As shown in Exhibit 3 of the case, a tremendous amount of new office space is coming on the market within the next two years.
3. The location of the site sold to Prestige Products by the local real estate broker represents a potential disaster for the firm. While the

site is close to the expressway, thus affording good access and public exposure, the maps in Exhibit 21–5 indicate that the site is located too far from the prime office area of downtown Metropolis. The expressway is a barrier, the site is near public housing, vacancy rates are highest, the buildings are smallest (and oldest), and rents are lowest in the vicinity of the site. This site will not improve employee morale or afford rental opportunities to other tenants. It could even damage Prestige Product's image.

Perform Quantitative Analysis

Even though the critical evaluation of the Prestige Products site was unfavorable, the alternatives should still be analyzed quantitatively before a decision is reached. The quantitative analysis relies on the principle that the value of an investment is a function of the benefits received in the future. That is,

$$V = f \text{ (Future benefits)} \qquad (21\text{–}2)$$

These benefits come from (1) the cash flow received by the investor while operating the property[25] and (2) the proceeds from the sale of the property. The periodic cash flow is the result of deducting operating expenses, debt service, and income taxes from rental income each year and are termed *after-tax cash flows* (ATCFs).

The sale proceeds result from subtracting selling expenses, the remaining balance of the mortgage loan, and taxes from the future sale price of the property. These proceeds are termed the *after-tax reversion* (ATR). Thus, the valuation equation can be restated as

$$V = f \text{ (ATCF, ATR)} \qquad (21\text{–}3)$$

Since V represents the value in the present and the ATCFs and ATR are estimates of benefits in the future, the functional relationship represents an adjustment for time differences between the two sides of the equation. Thus f represents the process of discounting (i.e., taking the present value of) the future benefits. The key unknown in this relationship is the discount rate r (i.e., the interest rate used to take present values). Therefore there are three critical unknowns that must be estimated: ATCFs, ATR, and r, the discount rate. Good estimates of these unknowns will produce a good estimate of value.

When there is no debt financing, the value obtained directly by taking

---

[25]These cash flows include the cash generated by the property and the tax shelter benefits. Tax shelter provides cash flow in the form of tax savings. See Chapter 22.

EXHIBIT 21–5
**QUALITATIVE EVALUATION OF THE CHARACTERISTICS OF THE
PRESTIGE PRODUCTS SITE**

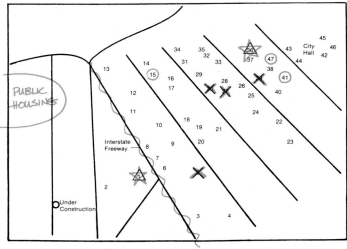

Mark "X" on all owner-occupied buildings (5, 27, 30, 39). Draw a jagged line down the
freeway—that is effectively a wall that isolates the Prestige Products site. Will other tenants
want to move to location 1? What other problems will the freeway cause? Draw in the
housing project. What effect is that likely to have? Put stars around Prestige Products' two
locations (1, 36).

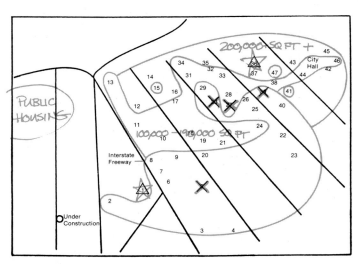

Enclose sites by floor area. Less than 100,000 sq. ft. (2-8, 25, 26, 40, 20, 22, 23, 9, 29, 30,
39); 100,000-190,000 (10, 11, 13, 17-19, 21, 24, 27, 28, 31-34, 38, 44, 46); 200,000 + (12,
14-16, 35-37, 41-43, 45, 47). Evaluate the appropriateness of a large building on location 1.

EXHIBIT 21–5 *(concluded)*

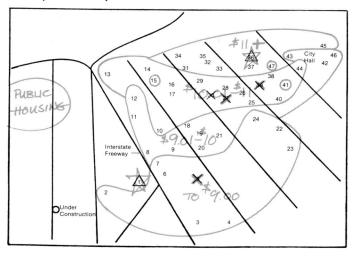

Next, enclose those sites with similar lease rates. To $9.00 (2-7, 22-24); $9.01-10.00 (8, 9, 11, 12, 18-21) (42, 43, 46); $10.01-11.00 (10, 13-17, 25-30, 38-41, 44); $11 + (31-37, 45, 47). How does location 1 look in terms of lease rates? Is there a relationship between occupancy and rate?

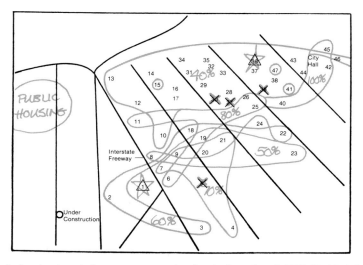

Enclose all sites having similar occupancy rates (excluding others). 50% (8, 23, 24); 60% (2, 3, 22, 18); 70% (4, 7, 5, 9, 20, 21); 80% (25, 26, 19, 6, 11); 90% (10, 12-17, 27-39, 41, 43, 44, 46, 47); 100% (40, 42, 45). How does location 1 look in terms of occupancy?

the present value of ATCFs and ATR is the property's *investment value.* That is,

$$\text{IV} = \text{Present value of ATCFs} + \text{Present value of ATR} \quad (21\text{--}4)$$

When there is debt financing, as is most often the case, the investment value equation is modified slightly to

$$\text{IV} = \text{PV of all ATCFs} + \text{PV of ATR} + \text{Original loan amount.} \quad (21\text{--}5)$$

Restructured Operating Statement. We must develop a restructured operating statement to estimate the ATCFs. Exhibit 21-6 shows the general form of the complete statement. There are two parts—the cash calculation and the tax calculation. The object of "restructuring" the operating statement is to sort out only the elements that directly affect the amount of *cash* coming to the investor.[26] Thus, the cash calculation is the main element of the restructured operating statement. The tax calculation simply provides an estimate of taxes for the calculation of ATCF; we discuss it in Chapter 22.

EXHIBIT 21-6
GENERAL FORM OF THE RESTRUCTURED OPERATING STATEMENT

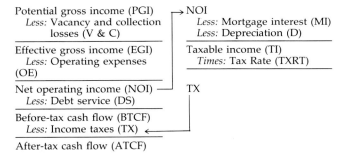

Cash Calculation	Tax Calculation
Potential gross income (PGI)	NOI
Less: Vacancy and collection losses (V & C)	*Less:* Mortgage interest (MI)
	Less: Depreciation (D)
Effective gross income (EGI)	Taxable income (TI)
Less: Operating expenses (OE)	*Times:* Tax Rate (TXRT)
Net operating income (NOI)	TX
Less: Debt service (DS)	
Before-tax cash flow (BTCF)	
Less: Income taxes (TX)	
After-tax cash flow (ATCF)	

The cash calculation begins with an estimate of the potential gross income (PGI) in a future period (e.g., next year). For a rental property, this is the maximum amount the property will generate, assuming that all units are rented and every tenant is paying on time. This figure should reflect the fact that not all units can be rented at market rental rates. Existing leases will affect rents in future periods for some units.

We must make an allowance for vacancy and collection losses. Due to market conditions and tenant turnover, some units undoubtedly will

---

[26]In accounting statements, depreciation is deducted as an operating expense but, since depreciation is a noncash item, it only appears in the tax calculation in the restructured statement.

go unrented during the next year. Also, some tenants may default on their leases or pay late. The expected vacancy and collection loss, therefore, must be deducted from PGI to obtain effective gross income (EGI), the amount of income actually received. Vacancy and collection losses normally run 3 to 12 percent of PGI for most types of rental properties.

Operating expenses (OE) include the periodic fixed outlays (e.g., property taxes, hazard insurance) and variable charges (e.g., maintenance, repairs, and supplies) needed to keep tenants from moving out.[27] These expenses usually account for 40 to 50 percent of EGI. The deduction of operating expenses gives net operating income (NOI). The deduction of debt service (DS) (i.e., the mortgage payments) yields before-tax cash flow (BTCF). After-tax cash flow is obtained by subtracting the expected tax liability (from the tax calculation) from BTCF.

The process of estimating ATCF by the restructured operating statement is repeated for every year of the holding period (usually 5 to 10 years). The analyst must be cognizant of changes in income (e.g., sales projections or lease renewal periods) and expenses over time.

After-Tax Reversion. In the final year of the holding period, a calculation is made of the expected after-tax reversion as well as of ATCF. The general form of this calculation is shown in Exhibit 21-7. The expected selling price (SP) of the property must be estimated first. This is usually done by assuming some growth rate in the price of property or by assuming some constant relationship between income and sale price (e.g., selling price is seven times EGI today; thus it, will be seven times EGI in the year of sale).

Net selling price (NSP) is obtained by subtracting selling expenses (SE) (e.g., brokerage fees, lawyer's fees) from the expected selling price. The mortgage lender or the bond holder, in the Prestige Products case, must also be paid the remaining balance (RMB) on the loan at the time of

EXHIBIT 21-7
GENERAL FORM OF THE CALCULATION OF AFTER-TAX REVERSION

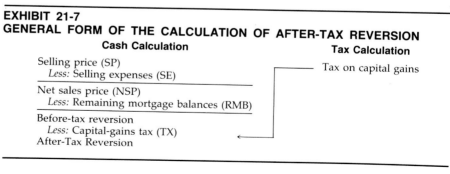

Cash Calculation	Tax Calculation
Selling price (SP) *Less:* Selling expenses (SE)	Tax on capital gains
Net sales price (NSP) *Less:* Remaining mortgage balances (RMB)	
Before-tax reversion *Less:* Capital-gains tax (TX) After-Tax Reversion	

[27]Variable means the expenses vary with the level of occupancy.

sale.[28] Finally, the sale of real estate results in a tax liability. The deduction of the expected tax on capital gain gives the after-tax reversion.

As with the restructured operating statement, the calculation of the after-tax reversion is separated into cash and tax components. The forms and details of the tax components are found in Chapter 22.

Discounted Cash-Flow Analysis. The term *discounted cash-flow analysis* refers to the process and procedures for estimating ATCFs, ATR, and the discount rate, and then using these inputs to generate meaningful summary information for the investor, such as the investment value of the property. While the ATCFs and ATR can be estimated directly after making assumptions about future events, estimation of the discount rate for a real estate investment is more subjective and indirect. The discount rate is the investor's *required rate of return* given the riskiness of ATCFs and ATR, the investor's preferences for risk, and the risk-free or real rate of return.

The traditional approach to estimating the appropriate discount rate is to begin with a risk-free rate (i.e., the current interest rate on a U.S. Treasury security) and then subjectively add risk premiums for projected risks of the real estate investment. We discuss this *risk-adjusted discount rate approach* further in Chapter 23.

Discounted cash-flow analysis has become the main financial analysis tool to evaluate the merits of real estate investments.[29] Although much of the effort in discounted cash-flow analysis goes into the estimation of the ATCFs, ATR, and discount rate, the summary measures of value and return are the bottom line concerns of investors: the investment value, the net present value, and the internal rate of return on equity.

The investor is keenly interested in the investment value of the property because it reflects her individualized inputs and because it can be compared directly to the asking price (or development cost) of the property. The investment value is the value of the equity investor's interest in, or claim against, income from the property plus the value of the mortgage lender's interest or claim.

$$IV = \text{Value of equity position } (V_e)$$
$$+ \text{Value of mortgage position } (V_m) \, m \, (LC) \quad (21\text{--}6)$$

[28]The mortgage term (e.g., 20 years) usually exceeds the investor's holding period (e.g., 5 to 10 years).

[29]In Edward J. Farragher, "Investment Decision-Making Practices of Equity Investors in Real Estate," *Real Estate Appraiser and Analyst* 48 (Summer 1982), pp. 36–41, the author found that over 60 percent of the investors questioned used discounted cash flow techniques as the primary tool for decision making.

where

$$V_e = \text{Present value of ATCFs} + \text{Present value of ATR}$$
$$V_m = \text{Loan amount}$$

Therefore if *IV* is greater than the asking price or development cost of the property, the investor should invest. This *decision rule* is straightforward and is probably the main reason why discounted cash-flow analysis is so well accepted today by real estate investors.

Return on the money invested (equity) is an essential concern of investors. The net present value of the equity (NPV$_e$), which is the difference between V_e and the original equity investment, yields an alternative decision rule to the *IV* rule:

- If NPV$_e$ is greater than or equal to 0, invest.
- If NPV$_e$ is less than 0, reject.

The internal rate of return on equity (IRR$_e$) is the discount rate that makes the value of the equity position equal to the initial equity invested.

Ratio Analysis.   Before the introduction of discounted cash-flow analysis, decisions on whether to invest in real estate were based on ratio analysis. Many investors and analysts today continue to believe that ratio analysis provides a sound basis for making investment decisions; it is frequently used in conjunction with discounted cash-flow analysis to make real estate investment decisions.

There are two arguments for using ratios instead of discounted cash-flow methods. First, ratios are much easier to calculate and more widely understood than NPV and IRR. Second, since discounted cash-flow analysis requires estimation of ATCFs and an ATR often many years in the future, some observers believe that the numbers can be easily manipulated to achieve any result the analyst desires.

Nevertheless, ratios are only single-period measures. They typically ignore such factors as tax effects and property appreciation, which are vitally important to investors. While ratios have their place in real estate investment analysis, the authors believe that the use of decision rules from a discounted cash-flow analysis is the best method of quantitative analysis of a real estate investment opportunity.

Exhibit 21–8 includes information about some of the more commonly used ratios in real estate investment analysis. Some have been discussed previously in conjunction with real estate appraisal and mortgage finance. Their application here is to real estate investment analysis. These ratios are usually intended to provide information about a specific aspect of the real estate investment analysis, are single-period in nature, are before-tax measures, and are void of decision rules. Their strength comes in isolat-

EXHIBIT 21–8
COMMON RATIOS USED IN REAL ESTATE INVESTMENT ANALYSIS

Ratio	Form	Use	Comment
Operating ratio	OE/EGI or OE/PGI	To determine the percentage of income used to pay operating expenses.	The normal range for this ratio varies by property type but is usually 40–50 percent of EGI.
Default point or breakeven	(OE + DS)/PGI	To determine how much vacancy can be tolerated before all income goes to paying OE and DS.	A default point of .90 suggests that a vacancy rate of ten percent or less could be tolerated.
Debt service coverage ratio	NOI/DS	By lenders to see how much room there is for a decrease in NOI before it will not cover the DS payment.	Lenders usually require a 1.20 to 1.30 coverage ratio but may vary their requirements when they are able to share in the income or property appreciation.
Mortgage constant	DS/V_m (loan amount)	To indicate the lender's rate of return and recapture of capital on investment.	Includes the return *on* capital investment and return of the capital investment.
Overall capitalization rate	NOI/Total Investment	To indicate the rate of return and recapture of capital on total investment (both lender and equity position).	The capitalization rate or overall rate is more commonly applied in appraisals.
Return on equity or equity dividend rate	BTCF/Equity Investment	To indicate the investor's one-period rate of return and recapture of capital.	This ratio accounts only for the income benefits; it ignores tax advantages and property appreciation.
Payback period	Equity/Average ATCF	To indicate the number of periods it will take to return the initial investment.	Averaging cash flows violates time-value-of-money principles.
Gross income multiplier	Total Investment/EGI	To indicate the relationship between income and total investment.	A quick method of comparing the income to total investment of one property to others sold in the market.

ing specific aspects of a property or investment and facilitating comparisons with similar investment opportunities. For example, an operating ratio of 70 percent says nothing about the acceptability of the investment, but when compared with similar properties having 40 percent operating ratios, it illuminates an undesirable feature of the investment.

The quantitative analysis, then, should be a combination of discounted cash-flow analysis and ratio analysis. These methods require considerable data, many assumptions, and much judgment. An essential consideration in satisfying the requirements for a successful quantitative analysis of a real state investment is applying what is learned from calculating the qualitative factors to the qualitative evaluation.

The Prestige Products case provides an excellent example of a situation where qualitative findings have a strong influence on the quantitative analysis. Since we have not discussed the tax aspects of a real estate investment, the qualitative analysis of the Prestige Products case is deferred to Chapter 22. There, we will combine all of the principles in this chapter with the tax considerations discussed in Chapter 22.

Make Decision

The most desirable course of action will seldom be clear cut. The final decision is often characterized by considerable uncertainty and unresolved conflict. It may even involve selecting the least-undesirable alternative. The Prestige Plaza proposal could be a case of this. Suppose that the quantitative analysis indicates that the 30-story building alternative will provide excellent returns to the investor. Then there would be a dilemma. The qualitative analysis suggests that the project should be aborted, whereas the quantitative analysis would indicate otherwise. We will see in Chapter 22 whether we must face this dilemma and if so, what to do about it.

OVERVIEW

Investment is one of the most interesting and important areas of study in the field of real estate. Whether the student is considering a career in a corporation or institution that invests in real state or is seeking knowledge in this area for personal investment reasons, several questions must be answered to make better-informed real estate investment decisions.

First, all investors should be concerned about answering the question of why invest in real estate. In other words, what are the potential returns and what are the potential risks? Partially because of the imperfect market for real estate, real estate investments have dominated other investments from a pure risk-return perspective. Federal tax-law changes over the past two decades have stimulated investment in real estate. Moreover, real estate has been a hedge against inflation and provides an opportunity for significant financial leverage.

Real estate investments have disadvantages as well. Illiquidity and lack of marketability is an ever-present problem. Also, real estate investments require considerable management in collecting rents and maintaining the property. Finally, real estate is often subject to government controls not found with other investments. For these reasons, many institutions have been hesitant to invest in real estate.

A second question facing a real estate investor is how to invest in real estate. Obviously, an investor can take a direct equity position, either by using the equity funds to borrow additional funds for a property purchase or through an all-cash direct investment in property. Other methods are also available to real estate investors, including limited partnership syndications, REITs, mortgage lending, and the purchase of mortgage securities.

The investment mode refers to the method of investment and the type of property invested in. Real estate investors have a wide range of choices in trying to decide on the appropriate property type(s). These include undeveloped land, residential rental properties, office properties, shopping centers and other retail properties, hotel properties, and industrial and special-use properties. Each has a unique set of risk and return characteristics, but due to the opportunity for small or large investment, advantageous tax features, and a stable market, many investors prefer residential rental properties.

The third and final question addressed in this chapter is how real estate investment opportunities are analyzed. The general process begins with the development of a formal investment strategy. This strategy screens out incompatible opportunities. It also helps the investor avoid very costly mistakes.

A case study (the Prestige Products case) is used to describe the decision framework for analyzing a specific investment. It begins with a definition of the investment problem and the development of alternative investment options. Next, each alternative is evaluated and critiqued qualitatively. Information from this important step is used in the quantitative analysis.

Much attention has been paid the quantitative analysis of real estate investments. In this chapter, we presented the accepted procedures for such an analysis. The Prestige Products case is a specific example of the use of these procedures and is presented in the next chapter. Real estate investment analysis involves discounted cash-flow techniques, specifically IRR and NPV, and performance ratios, including the operating ratio, debt-service coverage ratio, and break-even cash ratio. Discounted cash-flow techniques are preferred by the authors because they are multiperiod in nature, consider after-tax affects and all sources of return, and lead to useful decision rules. Performance ratios serve to provide additional information. Nevertheless, some investors and analysts prefer to use performance ratios as a primary tool for making real estate investment decisions because of their computational ease and the fact that they are easy to understand.

TEST YOURSELF

Explain the following terms and concepts presented in this chapter.

1. Risk and return relationship.
2. Financial leverage.
3. Liquidity versus marketability.
4. Investment strategy.
5. Qualitative analysis.
6. After-tax cash flows.
7. Investment value.
8. After-tax reversion.
9. Restructured operating statement.
10. Ratio analysis.

Answer the following multiple-choice questions.

1. Because real estate has been shown to produce greater returns than common stock with less risk, real estate is said to _____ common stocks.
   a. Be more liquid than.
   b. Be more marketable than.
   c. Hedge.
   d. Dominate.
   e. None of the above.

2. Of the following, which is *not* a typical way to invest funds in real estate?
   a. REIT.
   b. Direct equity purchase.
   c. Limited partnership syndications.
   d. Mutual funds.
   e. Mortgage lending.

3. One disadvantage of investing in rental residential real estate is
   a. No income tax benefits.
   b. No inflation protection.
   c. Low demand for residential rental space.
   d. Relatively large down payments are always required.
   e. None of the above.

4. As part of their investment philosophy, investors determine
   a. The level of diversification required.
   b. The required rate of return.
   c. Whether they want to be active or passive investors.
   d. Whether they want current income or appreciation.
   e. Their general plan for investment.

5. The operating expenses of a property plus the debt service divided by potential gross income is known as the
   a. Operating ratio.
   b. Default point.
   c. Debt-service coverage ratio.
   d. Overall capitalization rate.
   e. Payback period.

ADDITIONAL READINGS

Allen, Roger H. *Real Estate Investment and Taxation.* Cincinnati: Southwestern Publishing, 1984.

Epley, Donald R., and James A. Millar. *Basic Real Estate Finance and Investment.* New York: John Wiley & Sons, 1984, Chaps. 1, 16–23.

Ferguson, Jerry T. *Fundamentals of Real Estate Investing.* Glenview, Ill.: Scott, Foresman, 1984.

Pyhrr, Stephen A., and James R. Cooper. *Real Estate Investment.* Boston: Warren, Gorham & Lamont, 1982.

Sirmans, C. F., and Austin J. Jaffe. *The Complete Real Estate Investment Handbook.* Englewood Cliffs, N.J.: Prentice-Hall, 1984.

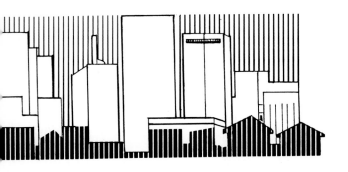

22
Income Tax Considerations in Real Estate Investment

OUTLINE

INTRODUCTION

Of the three major components of the return on investment from income-producing real estate—cash flow (i.e., income), tax benefits, and property value appreciation—the tax benefits of real estate probably increased the most in relative importance to investors during the 1970s and early 1980s.[1] But three things are inevitable: death, taxes, and tax law changes. In 1986, tax legislation enacted by Congress reversed the trend toward increasing tax benefits for real estate investors by eliminating or modifying some of the most favorable provisions. The effects of this legislation may not be fully realized until the early 1990s, but certainly the emphasis in coming years will be more on before-tax cash flow and property value appreciation and less on tax benefits.

This chapter presents the major provisions of the U.S. tax code affecting real estate investors and other owners of real estate, such as households who own their homes. The information we provide below should be considered as merely a foundation or starting point for learning about the tax benefits of owning real estate. Also, we will emphasize only federal income-tax policies and provisions. State income taxes can affect returns from real estate investments; however, many state tax provisions parallel the federal provisions, whereas other states have no income tax (e.g., Florida, Texas, Connecticut).[2]

---

[1] Some investors, such as pension funds and life insurance companies, because they are tax exempt or have special investment needs, invest in real estate for income and property value appreciation. They are not usually interested in tax benefits.

[2] States that have no income tax may still have state sales taxes on capital gains.

Objectives of U.S. Tax Law

The most obvious objective of U.S. tax law is to raise revenues for the operations of the federal government, preferably in an efficient and equitable manner. Yet there has been another objective that has led to favorable tax laws affecting real estate—to promote socially and economically desirable activities. Stimulating real estate investment has been viewed as economically desirable, since the construction industry is the single largest industrial employer of U.S. workers. Moreover, construction creates a demand for products and services for a vast number of other industries, such as the lumber, appliance, carpeting, and real estate service industries (e.g., appraisal and property management).

The Congress also designed the tax laws to promote certain socially desirable real estate-related activities. The most widespread is home ownership. The United States has one of the highest rates of home ownership in the world. Approximately 60 to 65 percent of U.S. households own their homes. The advantageous tax features of home ownership are an important reason for the high rate of home ownership.[3]

The tax code has also contained features to stimulate construction and rehabilitation of housing for low-income households as well as provisions to encourage the rehabilitation of nonresidential properties over 50 years old and the restoration of certified historical properties.

This chapter discusses the tax provisions intended to encourage both economically desirable activities—mainly investment in income-producing properties—and socially desirable activities, such as home ownership, investment in low-income housing, and property rehabilitation and restoration. We begin with a basic discussion of the U.S. tax system and how it treats real estate in general. Then specific tax provisions are analyzed as they affect real estate during the three phases of the ownership cycle: the *origination phase* when the investment is made, the *operation phase* when the property is held, and the *disposition phase* when the property is sold.

TAX BASICS

Before examining specific federal tax provisions affecting real estate, we review some basic elements of the U.S. tax system. These include the history and administration of the tax system, the types of income subject

---

[3]One study found that about 25 percent of the growth in the rate of homeownership in the United States since World War II can be attributed to advantageous federal tax provisions. See Harvey S. Rosen and Kenneth T. Rosen, "Federal Taxes and Homeownership: Evidence from Time Series," *Journal of Political Economy* 88 (February 1980), pp. 59–75.

to taxation, and the classifications of real estate under the current tax code. One important classification is *principal residences;* since the balance of the chapter focuses exclusively on income-producing properties, this section also discusses the tax advantages of owning a principal residence—the home you live in.

The U.S. Tax System: History and Administration

Exhibit 22–1 summarizes the historic milestones of the U.S. tax system. Probably the most important is the enactment of the modern income tax in 1913 under the authority of the 16th Amendment to the Constitution. The first tax code[4] was developed in 1939. The structure of the current Internal Revenue Code follows the code of 1954. Since then, there have been important amendments to the tax law which have necessitated revisions to the Internal Revenue Code. The recent tax-law changes are listed at the bottom of Exhibit 22–1. The most dramatic changes occurred

EXHIBIT 22–1
IMPORTANT EVENTS IN THE HISTORY OF THE U.S. TAX SYSTEM

Year	Event
1862	First income tax enacted to finance Civil War: a mildly progressive tax with rates of 1.5 to 5 percent.
1872	Tax of 1862 repealed.
1894	Second income tax enacted, with a flat rate of 2 percent on individual and corporate incomes.
1895	Supreme Court rules 1894 tax unconstitutional. Court held that the tax required apportionment among the states on the basis of population.
1909	Excise tax (1 percent) on corporate income enacted.
1909	Sixteenth Amendment to Constitution initiated. This amendment gives the Congress power to levy and collect taxes on income.
1913	Sixteenth Amendment ratified. Income tax enacted.
1916	Supreme Court upholds constitutionality of income tax.
1939	Income tax law of 1913 with its subsequent amendments brought together under a permanent code.
1954	Internal Revenue Code established; it is the present federal tax law with subsequent amendments.
1958, 1962, 1964, 1969, 1971, 1976, 1978	Major revisions made in code.
1981	Economic Recovery Tax Act (ERTA) creates the Accelerated Capital Cost Recovery System.
1982	Tax Equity and Fiscal Responsibility Act (TEFRA).
1984	Deficit Reduction Act.
1986	Tax Reform Act of 1986.

Source: Adapted from James B. Kan and C. F. Sirmans, *Tax Planning for Real Estate Investors* (Englewood Cliffs, N.J.: Prentice-Hall, 1982), p. 13.

---

[4]A code brings together existing laws in a single document.

as a result of the Economic Recovery Tax Act of 1981 and the Tax Reform Act of 1986.

Tax bills are originated in the House and passed by Congress; the president signs them into law. The Internal Revenue Service (IRS), an agency of the Treasury Department, is responsible for writing specific regulations to implement the law and for enforcing the law. Taxpayers who feel they have been unjustly treated by the IRS may appeal or seek other remedies.[5] Special tax courts handle disputes that cannot be resolved by negotiation between the taxpayer and the IRS. U.S. District and Appeals Courts and the Supreme Court also resolve disputes of a more substantive nature, such as test cases in particular areas of tax law.

Income Subject to Taxation and Tax Rates

Prior to the 1986 tax legislation, income subject to taxation under the Internal Revenue Code was divided into two general categories: ordinary income and capital gains. Taxable income from the sale of capital assets (i.e., capital gains) was taxed at rates lower than those applied to ordinary income. Thus, there was an incentive for investor-taxpayers to shift as much income to capital gains as possible. The 1986 tax act eliminated this difference in tax treatment of income. Capital gains are now considered ordinary income and, therefore, the incentive to shift income to capital gains treatment has been eliminated.

Ordinary Income. Income from wages and salaries, rent, dividends, interest, capital gains, and virtually all other sources is treated as ordinary income for federal income tax purposes. As Exhibit 22–2 shows there are

---

EXHIBIT 22–2
GENERALIZED INCOME TAX CALCULATION

Gross income (total income from wages, rents, interest, capital gains, etc.)
   Less: Adjustments to gross income (e.g., payments to certain retirement plans)
Adjusted gross income
   Less: Deductions (e.g., operating expenses from real estate, depreciation, and mortgage-interest payments)
Taxable income
   Times: Tax rate
Tax
   Less: Tax credits
Tax owed to IRS

---

[5]The Internal Revenue Service issues *letter rulings* on specific issues brought to it by taxpayers and *revenue rulings* to clarify issues settled in the courts.

EXHIBIT 22–3
TAX BRACKET COMPARISON—1986, 1987, AND 1988 AND BEYOND
(Married Taxpayer Filing Joint Return)

1986		1987		1988	
Taxable Income	Marginal Tax Rate	Taxable Income	Marginal Tax Rate	Taxable Income	Marginal Tax Rate
Less than $3,670	0%	$0–$3,000	11%	$0–$29,750	15%
$3,670–$5,930	11	$3,000–$28,000	15	Above $29,750	28
$5,930–$8,200	12	$28,000–$45,000	28		
$8,200–$12,840	14	$45,000–$90,000	35		
$12,840–$17,260	16	Above $90,000	38.5		
$17,260–$21,800	18				
$21,800–$26,540	22				
$26,540–$32,260	25				
$32,260–$37,980	28				
$37,980–$49,420	33				
$49,420–$64,740	38				
$64,740–$92,360	42				
$92,360–$118,040	45				
$118,040–$175,230	49				
$175,230 or more	50				

opportunities for reducing the income subject to taxes through adjustments and deductions. Thus the critical income measure for tax purposes is *taxable income*. The actual amount of tax owed also can be reduced through the use of tax credits.

Tax Rates. The 1986 tax legislation dramatically changed the tax rate structure for individual taxpayers. As shown in Exhibit 22–3, the tax rates for 1987 and 1988 and future years are less progressive (more flat) than 1986 tax rates.[6] While *marginal tax rates* were reduced for most taxpayers, *effective tax rates* will actually increase for many taxpayers. The tax rate applied to the next dollar of income is the marginal tax rate. In investment analysis, it is appropriate to treat an investment as an opportunity to earn *additional* income; therefore the marginal tax rate is the appropriate rate to use in investment analysis.

The effective tax rate in a given year is determined by the following equation:

$$\text{Effective tax rate} = \frac{\text{Total tax paid}}{\text{Gross income}}$$

---

[6]Progressivity in a tax system means that the higher the taxpayer's income, the higher the tax rate.

This equation yields an interesting number since it tells the taxpayer what percentage of income earned was paid in taxes. However, the effective tax rate should not be substituted for the marginal rate when analyzing real estate investments.

Marginal tax rates declined while effective tax rates remained fairly constant as a result of the 1986 tax legislation because many deductions and tax shelter opportunities were eliminated or substantially reduced. Several of these changes affected real estate investors, as we discuss later in this chapter. For corporations, the marginal tax rate was lowered in 1986 from a maximum rate of 46 percent to 34 percent. However, effective tax rates may not change for many firms because corporate deductions were also eliminated.

Classification of Real Estate

For purposes of federal income taxes, real estate is classified into four categories:

1. Real estate held as a *personal residence.*
2. Real estate held for sale to others, or *dealer property.*
3. Real estate held for use in a trade or business, or *trade* or *business property.*
4. Real estate held as an investment for the production of income, or *investment property.*

Income-producing real estate can be classified as dealer property, trade-or-business property, or investment property. The principal-residence classification applies strictly to property used as a taxpayer's home. Investors prefer not to have their income-producing property classified as dealer property (i.e., property held in inventory for sale to others) because dealer property cannot be depreciated the way trade or business property or investment property can. Many disputes between the IRS and taxpayers have arisen over whether property, such as developed residential lots, is dealer property or trade-or-business property.

There is at least one major difference between the treatment of trade or business property and investment property. When property is classified as investment property, there are limitations on the deduction of interest payments that do not exist when property is classified as trade or business property. This difference suggests that the trade or business property classification is slightly preferable. But, when is property classified as investment property, rather than trade or business property? This question is the subject of an ongoing debate in the tax courts. The following two property-holding situations, however, almost assuredly will result in the property's being deemed investment property:

1. When raw (undeveloped) land is held for speculation.
2. When income-producing property is operated under a triple-net lease.[7]

When they own income-producing real estate, taxpayers seek to avoid having it classified as dealer property or investment property as opposed to the less restrictive trade or business property.

Tax Advantages Afforded Owners of Principal Residences

As we mentioned earlier, housing has been treated with special favor in the tax code because it is deemed socially desirable to have citizens well housed. This is especially true when it comes to encouraging taxpayers to own their own homes instead of renting: the tax code provides a special set of tax advantages to homeowners, but not to renters. These advantages fall into two basic categories: deductions and avoidance of tax liabilities on capital-gains.

1. Although homeowners cannot take deductions for depreciation of their principal residences, they can take deductions for interest and property taxes paid on their homes. Also, expenses incurred in the sale of a principal residence are deductible in calculating tax liability on the sale.
2. An even stronger advantage of homeownership is the ability to avoid taxes on capital gains entirely during the period that a taxpayer is the owner of a principal residence. This is accomplished through the use of two special rules which apply only to principal residences. The first is the *residence replacement rule* or "rollover" rule that allows a taxpayer to avoid tax on capital gains from the sale of a principal residence if another principal residence is purchased within 24 months before or after the sale.[8]

   The second rule is the *over 55 rule* that allows a taxpayer who reaches the age of 55 to sell a principal residence and avoid paying taxes on the first $125,000 of capital gains.[9] Thus, a young family can purchase a home, trade up in the market without paying any

---

[7]A triple-net lease is one where the tenant pays all expenses in the three major property expense areas: repairs and maintenance, property taxes, and insurance.

[8]This may be done more than once in a lifetime. The taxpayer must have lived in the home at least 24 months before the sale.

[9]This provision can be used only once in a lifetime. The taxpayer must have lived in the home for at least three of the past five years.

tax, and finally, sell their principal residence when their children are grown and avoid all or a substantial part of the tax liability on the final sale.

Economists often cite one additional tax advantage of home ownership. Under the tax system in some countries, the amount of rent that a homeowner could receive if the property were rented to someone else is credited as income to the homeowner for tax purposes. This *imputed rent* can dramatically increase a taxpayer's income tax liability, although it does not increase actual, spendable income. Under the U.S. tax system, there is an *imputed rental exclusion* for homeowners, meaning that the rental income that could be realized from the principal residence's being rented to someone else is *not* credited to homeowners.

REAL ESTATE TAXATION
IN THE ORIGINATION PHASE

The origination phase is the period in which the real estate investment is made. This might include the period of construction for a new development project, the staging of capital contributions (i.e., investment funds) in a real estate syndication,[10] or the investing of funds for a direct equity purchase. Here we emphasize decisions investors make going into a real estate investment that can save them money by lowering their tax liabilities.

Specific opportunities to save on taxes during the origination phase have been eroded by tax-law changes during the past 10 years. For example, once it was possible to prepay property taxes and mortgage interest for future years and take tax deductions for such payments in the current year. Currently, the decisions involving tax savings during the origination phase are of a general nature and focus more on the choice of ownership form.

Ownership Forms and Income Taxes

The selection of an appropriate *ownership form* (e.g., corporate or partnership forms) for investing in real estate depends on both tax and nontax factors. The following is a list of criteria for selecting an appropriate form of ownership:

---

[10]This aspect of taxation at the origination phase is discussed in Chapter 27, which deals with real estate syndications.

1. *Avoidance of double taxation.* The form of ownership chosen should not offer the Internal Revenue Service an opportunity to tax the same income more than once.
2. *Avoidance of personal liability.* The form of ownership chosen should not open the investor to losing more than what is invested (by creating claims against personal assets, such as an automobile or securities).
3. *Provision of good liquidity of ownership interests.* The form of ownership chosen should allow the investor quickly and completely to liquidate (i.e., convert to cash) the ownership interest.
4. *Provision of maximum tax benefits.* The form of ownership chosen should allow the investor to share fully in tax deductions so that the investor can benefit from tax losses (i.e., negative taxable incomes) generated by the investment.

We discussed the alternative forms of ownership for investing in real estate in Chapter 2. They include the sole proprietorship, general partnership, limited partnership, regular corporation (C-corporation), S-corporation (formally, a "Subchapter S corporation"), and real estate investment trust. In Exhibit 22–4, we evaluate these forms of ownership with respect to how well they meet the four criteria above.

In terms of these criteria, there is no difference between sole proprietorships and general partnerships. Both have the advantages of avoiding double taxation and providing maximum tax benefits; however, both have low liquidity and expose investors to personal liability. The only disadvantage of real estate investment trusts is their failure to provide maximum tax benefits, a substantial disadvantage to tax-sensitive investors. C-corporations offer high liquidity and no personal liability, but have very poor tax features.

S-corporations and limited partnerships have the same basic advantages. Each allows the avoidance of double taxation and personal liability. Moreover, the liquidity of ownership shares in S-corporations and limited partnerships is better than other forms, such as sole proprietorships and general partnerships, and is continually improving, although it is not a true advantage of these ownership forms as yet. S-corporations have some advantages over limited partnerships, such as the ease with which shares can be transferred and the ease with which the legal entity can be formed.

Prior to the enactment of the 1986 tax legislation, limited partnerships and, to a lesser extent, S-corporations had a clear advantage over other ownership forms. Investors who adopted these forms of ownership could become involved passively (i.e., no management responsibility) in a real estate investment and obtain their pro rata share of tax benefits while not

EXHIBIT 22–4
EVALUATION OF OWNERSHIP FORMS FOR INVESTMENT IN REAL ESTATE

Criteria

1. Avoid double taxation
2. Avoid personal liability
3. Liquidity of ownership interests
4. Maximum tax benefits

Ownership forms

Sole proprietorship and general partnership

Pluses (+)	Minuses (−)
No double taxation	Low liquidity
Maximum tax benefits	Personal liability

Real estate investment trusts

Pluses (+)	Minuses (−)
No double taxation	Tax benefits not maximized
High liquidity	
No personal liability	

Regular corporation (C-corporation)

Pluses (+)	Minuses (−)
No personal liability	Double taxation
High liquidity	Tax benefits not maximized

S-corporation (formally subchapter S corporation)

Pluses (+)	Minuses (−)
No personal liability	Tax benefits not maximized
No double taxation	

Liquidity is neutral

Limited partnership

Pluses (+)	Minuses (−)
No double taxation	Tax benefits not maximized
No personal liability	

Liquidity is neutral

exposing themselves to personal liability. The 1986 legislation effectively put limited partnerships and S-corporations on a par with REITs. Because of their high liquidity, REITs should fare well in the coming years as a way to own real estate relative to other ownerships forms.

REAL ESTATE TAXATION IN THE OPERATION PHASE

Tax benefits can be generated during the period that investors hold and operate income-producing real estate. These benefits, which have been a major component of the returns on real estate investments in recent years, are often described under the general heading *tax shelter*. In addition opportunities exist in certain real estate investment situations to use *tax credits*.

What Is Tax Shelter?

Recall from Chapter 21 that the calculation of after-tax cash flow in the restructured operating statement requires two calculations: a cash calculation and a tax calculation. The formats for these are shown again in Exhibit 22–5. The sole purpose of the tax calculation is to estimate the expected income tax liability of the real estate investment in a given year. This requires an estimate of the income subject to tax. This *taxable income* is different from the actual or before-tax cash flow generated by the property.

EXHIBIT 22–5
RESTRUCTURED OPERATING STATEMENT: CASH CALCULATION AND TAX CALCULATION

Cash Calculation	Tax Calculation
Potential gross income (PGI)	PGI
Less: Vacancy and collection less (V&C)	*Less:* V&C
Effective gross income (EGI)	EGI
Less: Operating expenses (OE)	*Less:* OE
Net operating income (NOI)	NOI
Less: Mortgage interest (MI)*	*Less:* MI
Less: Principal amortization (PA)*	*Less:* Depreciation (DEP)
Before tax cash flow (BTCF)	Taxable income (TI)
Less: TX (from tax calculation)	*Times:* Tax rate (TXRT)
After-tax cash flow (ATCF)	Tax (TX)

*MI and PA together are the debt service (DS) on the loan.

As Exhibit 22–5 indicates, the difference between taxable income and before-tax cash flow is simply that amortization of the principal (PA) is subtracted from net operating income to get before-tax cash flow, and depreciation is subtracted from NOI to get taxable income. During the early years of the holding period PA is usually smaller (assuming a new loan has been taken out) than depreciation. This means that taxable income is less than before-tax cash flow and, therefore, *taxable income is less than the actual cash being received* (i.e., before-tax cash flow). This result is called a *partial tax shelter* since part of the cash received is sheltered from income tax.

Sometimes in a real estate investment, mortgage interest and depreciation are so large that taxable income is negative. The investor can utilize the negative taxable income from the real estate investment to offset positive taxable income from other sources, such as salary or bonds. Negative taxable income creates a *deep tax shelter*—a tax shelter that most investors find highly desirable.

Any negative taxable income from a real estate investment is a legitimate part of the return on investment and therefore must be included in the restructured operating statement. Suppose that a property in its first year of operation is expected to generate $20,000 in before-tax cash flow. The tax calculation yields a negative taxable income of $30,000 and the investor's marginal tax rate is 28 percent. The after-tax cash flow is shown below.

BTCF	$20,000	TI	$(30,000)
Less: TX	(8,400)	*Times:* TXRT	× .28
ATCF	$28,400	TX	$(8,400)

Since taxable income is negative, when it is multiplied by the tax rate the result is also negative. When the negative value for the tax is included in the calculation of after-tax cash flow, it becomes positive (i.e., a negative sign and a negative sign yield a positive sign). Therefore, after-tax cash flow is comprised of two components: cash flow and tax effect. This time the tax effect is positive due to the deep-tax-shelter benefit provided.

The measurement of the positive tax effect shown above is theoretically correct, since the investor's gain from having negative taxable income is the tax savings. Thus, if the investor has $30,000 in negative taxable income from a real estate investment, then $30,000 of other, positive taxable income is sheltered; for a 28 percent-bracket taxpayer, $8,400 is saved in taxes. This tax savings is a legitimate and important benefit from owning real estate.

Depreciation Rules

The logical conclusion about tax shelter from real estate investment is that it largely comes from depreciation, the noncash expense item in the tax calculation. The size of the depreciation deduction is largely prescribed by law and depends on three factors: the amount of the depreciable *base* or *basis*, the *life* of the asset, and the allowable *method* of depreciation.

Basis. Only properties held for use in trade or business or as investments are depreciable. Only the improvements to and on the land, both original and additions, are included in the basis for depreciation. Therefore, principal residences, dealer property, and land cannot be depreciated under current tax regulations.

The amount of the depreciable basis can be established in several ways. Perhaps the most accurate and defensible method (to the IRS) is to have an independent real estate appraiser estimate the value of the improvements. Usually, the value of the improvements is recorded for property-tax purposes as well, but if the assessment is not current it will be unfavorable to the investor, who wants to establish the highest possible depreciable basis. Sometimes the contract for sale of the property will contain a value for the land and improvements. As a general rule, the value of the improvements constitutes 80 to 85 percent of the total value of the property.

Life. The historical reason for depreciation is that depreciation allowances should provide for the replacement of the asset at the end of its economic life. For many years the IRS attempted to set and enforce economic-life standards for real estate (i.e., how long property would last in service). Under the Economic Recovery Tax Act of 1981, Congress created an entirely new system which prescribed, without reference to how long the property would be in service, depreciation lives and methods. The depreciation lives for most real estate, first 15 and later 18 years and 19 years, set by laws enacted in the early 1980s are much shorter than the economic lives of real estate, which could be as short as 35 years or as long as 200 years or more.

The 1986 tax legislation lengthened somewhat the statutory, depreciation lives of real estate, but like the previous standards, the current depreciation lives bear little resemblance to actual economic lives of real estate. This works to the advantage of the real estate investors because the shorter the depreciation life, the earlier that depreciation allowances can be deducted to compute taxable income. Currently, residential property (e.g., apartments) can be depreciated over 27½ years and nonresidential property (e.g., shopping centers), over 31½ years.

Method. Over the years, two basic methods of depreciating real estate have been allowed: the straight-line method and a variety of accelerated methods. Currently, only the straight-line method is permitted for the depreciation of real estate. Straight-line depreciation is less generous to investors than accelerated methods because accelerated methods result in greater depreciation allowances in the early years of the depreciation schedule than does straight-line depreciation.

The actual depreciation allowance for a given year is found by multiplying the appropriate base by the appropriate depreciation rate. The rate is a function of the life and the method. So, with a 27½-year life and the straight-line method, the rate is:

$$\text{Straight-line rate} = 1/\text{Life}$$
$$= 1/27.5$$
$$= .0363636$$

If the basis is $100,000, the depreciation allowance is $3,636.36 (.0363636 × $100,000) in the first and each of the 26½ subsequent years. With a 31½-year life the rate is .0317460, and the depreciation allowance, assuming a $100,000 basis, is $3,174.60.

Investment Tax Credits

The tax law allows investment tax credits—allowances that are deductible directly from the taxes otherwise owed by the taxpayer—for rehabilitation of older and historic structures and for construction and rehabilitation of low-income housing. These tax credits exist because policy makers believe that the private market will not provide for the rehabilitation of older and historic structures and will underproduce housing units for low-income households without tax incentive to developers.

The *rehabilitation investment tax credit* may be used by real estate investors who supply funds for the rehabilitation of older structures. This tax credit can be taken at one of two levels.

1. A *10 percent tax credit* can be taken on rehabilitation expenditures on structures that are for nonresidential use and were constructed before 1936.
2. A *20 percent tax credit* can be taken on rehabilitation expenditures on structures that are either residential or nonresidential and are on the National Register of Historic Places or nominated for placement on same.[11]

    Example: A developer buys a National Register property for $200,000 and spends $500,000 in 1987 on repairs and restoration approved by the Department of Interior. The developer's 1987 tax credit is $100,000 (.20 × $500,000). The $100,000 can be deducted from the developer's tax liability for 1987.

The rehabilitation investment tax credit is a subsidy feature of the tax code designed to encourage investment in the preservation of still-useful and historically significant structures. The historic-property tax credit (20 percent) regulations are highly restrictive with respect to the use of materials, construction methods, and building redesign to preserve the historic character of the structures. Thus, some redevelopers of nonresidential properties may instead opt for the 10 percent tax credit because of the less restrictive redevelopment provisions.

The 1986 tax legislation replaced all previous low-income housing tax incentives with the following three new tax credits:

---

[11]The National Register of Historic Places is a list of properties and areas or districts that are unique or have historical significance. The register is maintained by the U.S. Department of Interior. Placement on the register is made through nomination by a local historic-properties committee.

1. A *9 percent tax credit* (maximum) can be taken each year for new construction and rehabilitation expenditures on each unit of low-income housing.
2. A *4 percent tax credit* can be taken instead of the 9 percent tax credit if other federal subsidies are involved with the new construction or rehabilitation of low-income housing.
3. A *4 percent tax credit* can be taken by an investor who purchases existing housing for a low-income housing project.

The calculations of the tax credits for low-income housing expenditures are performed in the same way as those for rehabilitation of older and historic structures (see example above).

REAL ESTATE TAXATION IN THE DISPOSITION PHASE

As we discussed above, U.S. tax law provides beneficial treatment of capital gains at the time of sale of a principal residence. Some interesting and beneficial treatments of capital gains are also available to users of either trade-or-business or investment properties. The treatments of capital gains fall into two general categories: (1) an *ordinary sale* treatment in which gains are totally recognized and realized in the year of sale and (2) tax-deferred arrangements, including *installment sales* and *like-kind exchanges,* in which the proceeds from the sale and the capital gains are not realized until later periods.

Ordinary Sale

When a seller of property receives the full sale price in cash or its equivalent, the sale is usually treated as an ordinary sale. This means that the tax liability incurred on the sale must be paid in the year the sale occurs.

Tax on Capital Gain. The form of the calculation of the tax on capital gain from the sale of real estate is shown in Exhibit 22–6. The sale price (i.e., contract price) less the selling expenses (e.g., brokerage and lawyer's fees) give the net sale price. The capital gain is found by subtracting the adjusted basis in the property from net sale price; the calculation of adjusted basis is shown in the footnote to Exhibit 22–6. This calculation begins with the original basis, or the original purchase price of the property plus any capital improvements. To obtain the adjusted basis, the sum of all depreciation taken over the holding period is subtracted from the original basis.

Since the tax rate on capital gains is the same as the investor's marginal tax rate, the tax on capital gain is found by simply multiplying the

EXHIBIT 22–6
TAX CALCULATION ON CAPITAL GAIN FROM AN ORDINARY SALE

Sale price (SP) (amount stated in contract for sale)
  Less: Selling expenses (SE) (e.g., brokerage fees)

Net sale price (NSP) (also known as amount realized)
  Less: Adjusted basis (AB) (see calculation below)*

Capital gain (CG)
  Times: Ordinary tax rate (TXrt)

Tax on capital gain (Tx)

*Adjusted basis calculation
Original basis (price paid when purchased)
  Plus: Capital improvements (e.g., swimming pool)
  Less: Sum of depreciation (taken over the holding period)
Adjusted basis

capital gain by the marginal tax rate of the investor. The quantitative analysis of the Prestige Products case, presented in the final section of this chapter, provides a numerical example of the calculation of tax on capital gain.

Installment Sale

One important method for deferring capital-gains taxes is to sell property in installments. This means that the seller acts as a lender to the buyer and receives payments against the contract price over several years. Installment-sale reporting is *automatic,* meaning that a taxpayer must make a specific declaration that the sale is to be treated as an *ordinary* sale. Installment sales are quite easy for real estate investors to use. There are no binding restrictions on the amount the seller can receive in the year of sale or on the timing of payments in an installment sale.

The benefit to the investor of selling property as an installment sale is that taxes on capital gains are paid in the period in which the installment payments are actually received. This means that the investor is not liable for all taxes on capital gains in the year of the sale, as with ordinary sales.

To see how capital gains taxes are computed under installment sale treatment, assume the following situation:

Sale price	$100,000
Mortgage assumed by buyer	$ 5,000
Down payment	$ 10,000
Installment loan	$ 85,000
Terms of installment loan	10 percent/20 years/annual payments
Selling expenses	$2,000
Seller's adjusted basis	$20,000
Seller's ordinary income tax rate	28 percent

To calculate the tax liability on capital gains in the year of sale, a four-step process is followed.

Step 1: Calculate capital gain as under ordinary sale treatment (see Exhibit 22–6).

SP	$100,000
−SE	− 2,000
NSP	$ 98,000
−AB	−20,000
CG	$ 78,000

Step 2: Calculate contract price and capital gain-to-contract-price ratio.

SP	$100,000
−Mortgage assumed	− 5,000
Contract price	$ 95,000

The contract price represents the amount of money to be received by the seller, net of any mortgage assumption.

$$\text{Capital gain/Contract price} = \$78,000/\$95,000$$
$$= .82$$

This ratio establishes how much of each payment received by the seller is a capital gain (i.e., 82 percent).

Step 3: Calculate payments received in a given year (e.g., year of sale).

Down payment	$10,000
+Principal amortization portion of installment loan payment[12]	+ 1,484
Total payment in year of sale	$11,484

The mortgage interest portion of the installment loan payment is treated separately.

Step 4: Calculate capital gain and capital gains tax in a given year (e.g., year of sale).

Total payment	$11,484
× Ratio	× .82
Capital gain—year of sale	$ 9,416
× Tax rate	× .28
Tax on capital gain—year of sale	$ 2,636

Had the investor in this situation chosen an ordinary sale treatment, the capital-gains tax liability would have been $21,840 (.28 × $78,000) instead of $2,636. However, the investor would have received more money from the sale in that year. The next year's capital gains tax liability under installment sale treatment is calculated simply by repeating steps 3 and 4.

Installment-sale reporting offers the investor an opportunity to do considerable tax planning, as well as to defer payment of taxes. Suppose

---

[12]This amount is determined using the four-step process for separating mortgage interest and principal amortization, described later in this chapter.

an investor plans to retire from salaried employment in five years, but thinks the time to sell a particular property is now. Perhaps an installment-sale arrangement can be structured so that the investor receives most of the sale price after retirement, when the investor will be in a lower tax bracket. This strategy serves to lower the total tax on capital gains.

Like-Kind Exchanges

The second major option by which real estate investors can defer capital-gains taxes is the like-kind exchange. Under Section 1031 of the Internal Revenue Code, owners of real estate, under certain circumstances, can exchange their properties for other properties and avoid paying taxes on capital gains from the transaction. The primary motivation for a tax-deferred exchange is to change property ownership status and avoid capital gains taxes. Additionally, an exchange may be the best way to market property in a difficult market setting.

To enter into a tax-deferred exchange, the following requirements must be met:

1. The properties in an exchange must be *trade-or-business* or *investment properties.* This means that dealer properties and principal residences cannot be included in the tax-deferred part of an exchange. A trade-or-business property can be exchanged for an investment property and vice versa.
2. The properties in an exchange must be *like-kind properties.* Basically, to satisfy this requirement real estate cannot be exchanged for personal property such as mortgages, bonds, stocks, farm animals, etc.
3. Any cash or personal property (i.e., nonlike-kind property) used to equalize tax-deferred exchanges must be identified as *boot.* The existence of boot makes the exchange partly taxable.

Boot is present in most real estate exchanges, since the values of the two (or more) properties in the exchange are seldom equal. Thus, after it is determined that the exchange qualifies under the first two requirements of Section 1031, the partial capital-gains tax liabilities must be calculated for each of the exchanging parties. The concept of boot actually extends beyond the simple transfer of cash or nonlike-kind property to equalize an exchange. Boot also involves the relief from mortgage liability that one party in an exchange may gain. Thus, the party ending up with the lower mortgage balance in an exchange receives boot in the amount of the difference in the mortgage balances of the properties—the amount of mortgage relief.

The calculation of the tax incurred in conjunction with an exchange is somewhat complex. In a very general sense, the tax liability in an exchange is closely related to the tax on the boot received.

PRESTIGE PRODUCTS CASE: QUANTITATIVE ANALYSIS AND DECISION

In Chapter 21, we interrupted the analysis for the Prestige Products case because information critical to the quantitative analysis about the effects of federal income taxes had not yet been presented. Now that we have this information, we can proceed. In this section, the quantitative analysis of the 30-story proposal for the Prestige Plaza is described and a decision in the case is reached.

Estimation of After-Tax Cash Flows

Exhibit 22–7 presents the after-tax cash flows assuming a seven-year holding period for the 30-story building.[13] This investment opportunity is evaluated "at the market," which means that, even though approximately half of the building will be owner-occupied, we are assuming that the entire building will be rented out. The theory underlying this is that any new development venture that *could not* succeed in the market *should not* be built. Prestige Products could go bankrupt on the day after the completion of the building, and the stockholders might be left with an unmarketable property.

The inputs to the cash-flow analysis in Exhibit 22–7 are from the case information in Chapter 21. This set of inputs has been influenced heavily by the discovery, in the qualitative analysis, that the location of the site is poor. Thus, the potential gross income in the first year of operation[14] (1987) is estimated to be only $6,000,000, based on 600,000 square feet rented at $10 per square foot. As Exhibit 21–5 shows, rents in this area for *existing* office space are less than $9 per square foot. Vacancy and collection loss is expected to be 40 percent in the first year of operation due to the usual less-than-full lease-up in the early years of large office buildings and the current vacancy rates in this area (see Exhibit 21–5). Vacancy and collection losses are expected to decline to 35 percent in year two, 30 percent in year three, and 25 percent in years four through seven.

---

[13]We chose a 7-year holding period because most market investors tend to hold property between 5 and 10 years. The 30-story building alternative is evaluated because it proved more favorable following the qualitative analysis.

[14]Only the first seven full years of operation are evaluated. Usually the year(s) of construction cash flows are also considered, and partial-year cash flows are estimated.

EXHIBIT 22-7
AFTER-TAX CASH FLOWS: PRESTIGE PRODUCTS CASE

Cash Calculation	1987	1988	1989	1990	1991	1992	1993
Potential gross income	$ 6,000,000	$ 6,120,000	$ 6,242,400	$ 6,367,248	$ 6,494,593	$ 6,624,485	$ 6,756,975
Less: Vacancy and collection loss	−2,400,000	−2,142,000	−1,872,720	−1,591,812	−1,623,648	−1,656,121	−1,689,244
Effective gross income	3,600,000	3,978,000	4,369,680	4,775,436	4,870,945	4,968,364	5,067,731
Less: Operating expenses	−2,400,000	−2,472,000	−2,546,160	−2,622,545	−2,701,221	−2,782,258	−2,865,726
Net operating income	1,200,000	1,506,000	1,823,520	2,152,891	2,169,723	2,186,106	2,202,005
Less: Debt service	−3,147,555	−3,147,555	−3,147,555	−3,147,555	−3,147,555	−3,147,555	−3,147,555
Before-tax cash flow	(1,947,555)	(1,641,555)	(1,324,035)	(994,664)	(977,831)	(961,449)	(945,549)
Less: Tax	− (954,516)	− (846,486)	− (734,033)	− (616,980)	− (605,549)	− (599,666)	− (580,891)
After-tax cash flow	$ (993,039)	$ (795,069)	$ (590,002)	$ (377,684)	$ (372,282)	$ (361,783)	$ (364,658)

Tax Calculation	1987	1988	1989	1990	1991	1992	1993
Net operating income	$ 1,200,000	$ 1,506,000	$ 1,823,520	$ 2,152,891	$ 2,169,723	$ 2,186,106	$ 2,202,005
Less: Mortgage interest	−3,055,020	−3,043,285	−3,030,061	−3,015,159	−2,998,368	−2,997,448	−2,958,128
Less: Depreciation	− 952,381	− 952,381	− 952,381	− 952,381	− 952,381	− 952,381	− 952,381
Taxable income	(2,807,401)	(2,489,666)	(2,158,922)	(1,814,649)	(1,781,026)	(1,763,723)	(1,708,504)
Times: Tax rate	× .34	× .34	× .34	× .34	× .34	× .34	× .34
Tax	$ (954,516)	$ (846,486)	$ (734,033)	$ (616,980)	$ (605,549)	$ (599,666)	$ (580,891)

As the case states, operating expenses will be approximately $4 per square foot per year, or $2,400,000. This results in a net operating income of $1,200,000. Debt service is based on 85 percent of the cost of the building—$25,500,000—a 12 percent rate, a 30-year term, and monthly payments.[15] Subtracting the annual debt service of $3,147,555 from net operating income in 1987 yields a before-tax cash flow of ($1,947,555); parentheses indicate a negative amount.

The separate tax calculation begins with net operating income, since all expenses above net operating income (vacancy and collection losses and operating expenses) are tax deductible. Mortgage interest is calculated by the four-step process shown below.

Step 1: $\dfrac{R_m \text{ (entire term)}}{R_m \text{ (remaining term)}}$ = Percent of loan remaining

$\dfrac{.010286127^{16}}{.010323588}$ = .9964

Step 2: Percent of loan remaining × Loan amount = Dollar amount of loan remaining
.9964 × $25,500,000 = $25,407,465

Step 3: Loan amount − Dollar amount of loan remaining = Principal amortization in 1987
$25,500,000 − $25,407,465 = $92,535

Step 4: Debt service in 1987 − Principal amortization = Mortgage interest in 1987
$3,147,555 − $92,535 = $3,055,020

---

[15]Recall that the bond issue is treated like a fully amortizing mortgage loan in this case. The debt service payment is calculated as follows:

$$DS = \text{[Loan amount × Table factor (Col. 6, 12 percent, 360 months)] × 12}$$
$$= \text{[25,500,000 × .010286127] × 12}$$
$$= 3,147,555$$

or, using the financial calculator,

HP12C: $\boxed{\text{ON}}$ $\boxed{\text{f}}$ $\boxed{\dfrac{\text{REG}}{\text{CLX}}}$, 25,500,000 $\boxed{\text{CHS}}$ $\boxed{\text{PV}}$, 30 $\boxed{\text{g}}$ $\boxed{\dfrac{n}{12 \times}}$, 12 g $\boxed{\dfrac{i}{12 \div}}$,

PMT = 262,296.21, 12 $\boxed{\times}$ = 3,147,555

BA-35: $\boxed{\text{ON}/\text{C}}$ $\boxed{\text{ON}/\text{C}}$ $\boxed{\text{2nd}}$ $\boxed{\text{FIN}}$, 25500000 $\boxed{\text{PV}}$, 30 $\boxed{\times}$ 12

$\boxed{=}$ 360 $\boxed{\text{N}}$, 12 $\boxed{\div}$ 12 $\boxed{=}$ 1 $\boxed{\%\text{i}}$, $\boxed{\text{CPT}}$ $\boxed{\text{PMT}}$

= 262,296.21 $\boxed{\times}$ 12 $\boxed{=}$ 3147555.

[16]Usually, the six places as provided in the present value tables is sufficient.

The depreciation allowance is determined from the basis (the building cost of $30,000,000), the life (31½ years), and the method (straight line). The depreciation rate with the straight-line method is simply:

$$1/Life = 1/31.5 = .0317$$

Therefore, the depreciation allowance in 1987 and all subsequent years is

$$.0317 \times \$30,000,000 = \$952,381$$

Subtracting mortgage interest and depreciation from net operating income gives the amount of taxable income for 1987 of ($2,807,401). Since taxable income is negative, the tax effect is also negative in 1987. The tax is calculated by multiplying the assumed tax rate of 34 percent by the taxable income. This yields a negative tax effect of ($954,516). When this amount is subtracted from before-tax cash flow it becomes a positive tax effect (two negative signs make a positive sign) and, therefore, after-tax cash flow is increased. This investment is a deep tax shelter in 1987. Unfortunately, the positive tax effect does not offset the very large negative before-tax cash flow, so the resulting after-tax cash flow is *negative*.

Assuming the vacancy and collection expenses given above, a 2 percent growth rate in rental income, and a 3 percent growth rate in expenses, the remaining six years' after-tax cash flows can be estimated using the same approach. As Exhibit 22–7 shows, the expected after-tax cash flows from this investment remain negative through 1993.

Estimation of After-Tax Reversion

In 1993, at the end of the seventh year of the holding period, we assume that the property is sold. Exhibit 22–8 provides an estimation of the after-tax proceeds from the sale. The forecast selling price of $36,183,599 results from the assumption that the property value will increase by 2 percent per year. This compound growth rate is the same as that for rents and is quite conservative, due to the poor location of the project.

We assume selling expenses to be 4 percent of the selling price, or $1,447,344, for a net sale price of $34,736,255. The remaining mortgage balance is found through the use of Steps 1 and 2 in the four-step process for dividing principal and interest.[17] The before-tax reversion of $10,189,666 results from subtracting the remaining mortgage balance of $24,546,589 from the net sale price of $34,736,255.

---

17 $\dfrac{R_m \text{ Entire term}}{R_m \text{ Remaining term}} = \dfrac{.010286127}{.010685649} = .9626$

$.9626 \times 25,500,000 = \$24,546,589$

EXHIBIT 22–8
AFTER-TAX REVERSION: PRESTIGE PRODUCTS CASE

Cash Calculation (1993)

Selling price	$36,183,599
Less: Selling expenses	− 1,447,344
Net sale price	34,736,255
Less: Remaining mortgage balance	− 24,546,589
Before-tax reversion	10,189,666
Less: Tax on capital gain	− 3,366,993
After-tax reversion	$ 6,822,673

Tax Calculation (1993)

Net sale price	$34,736,255
Less: Adjusted basis*	− 24,833,333
Capital gain	9,902,922
Times: Tax rate	× .34
Tax on capital gain	$ 3,366,993

---

*The adjusted basis is found by taking the original purchase price or investment, $31,500,000, and subtracting the sum of the depreciation taken, $6,666,667 ($952,381 × 7).

The separate tax calculation in Exhibit 22–8 provides an estimate of the tax liability from this ordinary sale in 1993. The only tax liability is the tax on capital gains. The capital gain of $9,902,992 is found by subtracting the adjusted basis (explained in the footnote of Exhibit 22–8) from the net sale price. The tax is found by multiplying the tax rate of 34 percent by the capital gain, yielding a tax of $3,366,993.

The after-tax reversion is found by subtracting the capital gains tax from the before-tax reversion. The result is $6,822,673.

Application of Decision Rule

The investment value of this alternative is calculated by taking the sum of the present values of the after-tax cash flows and the after-tax reversion discounted at the required rate of return (i.e., the discount rate) and adding that amount to the original loan amount. Exhibit 22–9 shows the after-tax cash flows, including the after-tax reversion, and the equity investment required for this project of $6,000,000 (i.e., $31,500,000 − $25,500,000). The after-tax required rate of return of Prestige Products is 14 percent. Therefore, applying a Column 4 factor from the 14 percent annual table to each after-tax inflow gives a total of $123,191.

By adding $123,191 and the loan amount of $25,500,000, we obtain an investment value of $25,623,191. Since the total cost of this venture is $31,500,000, the cost of this alternative far outweighs the dollar value of its benefits.

The net present value of this project with respect to the equity in-

EXHIBIT 22–9
TIME-LINE REPRESENTATIONS OF THE CASH FLOWS: PRESTIGE PRODUCTS CASE

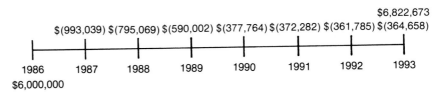

Year	ATCF		Col. 4 Factor	
1987	$ (993,539)	× .877193 =	$ (865,860)
1988	(795,069)	× .769468 =	(611,780)
1989	(590,082)	× .674972 =	(398,235)
1990	(377,684)	× .592080 =	(223,619)
1991	(372,282)	× .519369 =	(193,352)
1992	(361,785)	× .455587 =	(164,824)
1993	(364,658)	× .399637 =	(145,731)
1993	6,822,673	× .399637 =	2,726,592
Total			$ 123,191

vestment is found by subtracting the equity investment from the present value of the cash inflows.

$$NPV_{Equity} = \text{Present value (at the required rate) of cash inflows} - \text{Equity Investment}$$

$$\$(5,876,809) = \$123,191 - \$6,000,000$$

Since the net present value is negative, this investment opportunity should be rejected on quantitative grounds.

Decision

From both qualitative and quantitative standpoints, the Prestige Plaza proposals fail. The qualitative analysis indicates that the main reason the firm wants to construct Prestige Plaza is to enhance its image. Moreover, the location of the site chosen for the building is very poor. Using this information, inputs for the quantitative analysis are developed. Following an evaluation of the returns from the proposed venture and an application of quantitative decision rules, there is little doubt that the proposal to build Prestige Plaza should be rejected. Prestige Products has several remaining options. It could, for example, search for another site or for different ways to enhance the firm's image and improve employee morale.

This case is designed to demonstrate that there is more to real estate investment analysis than simply "crunching numbers." The qualitative and quantitative analyses of alternatives must be synchronized and conducted thoroughly to provide information for sound and defensible real estate investment decisions.

OVERVIEW

The U.S. income tax system is not only designed to raise revenues in an equitable manner, but also to promote socially and economically desirable activities. One of these activities is the production of improvements on land for housing (a socially desirable activity) and another is the production of income-producing real estate (an economically desirable activity). The current Internal Revenue Code has evolved through the enactment of tax laws since 1954—most recently the 1986 tax legislation. Some of the major provisions for promoting the production of owner-occupied housing involve lowering or eliminating the burden of capital gains taxes on homeowners (e.g., the residence-replacement rule and the over-55 rule).

Federal income taxes affect real estate decisions in all of the three major phases of the ownership cycle—origination, operation, and disposition. The principal decision to be made during the origination phase involves the selection of a form of ownership that offers both tax and nontax advantages (e.g., avoidance of personal liability).

Tax shelter benefits from the ownership of real estate are realized during the operation phase, mainly through the allowance for depreciation. Depreciation deductions, as a noncash expense, result in lower taxable income than before-tax cash flow and, therefore, save taxes. Sometimes taxable income is negative, which allows the investor to offset other positive taxable income (i.e., a deep tax shelter). Current depreciation rules prescribe a $27\frac{1}{2}$-year life for residential property and a $31\frac{1}{2}$-year life for commercial property.

For projects involving the rehabilitation of nonresidential structures that are at least 50 years old, rehabilitation investment tax credits may be taken. If the property has historical significance, 20 percent of all qualifying rehabilitation expenditures may be taken as a tax credit. Tax credits are also available to investors who invest in low-income housing.

Real estate investors have three basic options for tax treatment when they sell property—ordinary-sale treatment, installment-sale treatment, and like-kind exchange. With ordinary sale treatment, the investor generally receives all of the sale price in the year of the sale and must pay any tax liability from capital gains in that year. The capital gain is calculated by subtracting the adjusted basis from the net sale price. The taxable gain is multiplied by the ordinary income-tax rate to obtain the tax liability on the sale of the property.

Installment-sale treatment allows the investor to pay taxes when partial payments of the sale price are received in keeping with the installment sale agreement between the buyer and seller. Finally, real estate investors may exchange their properties for other real estate as long as the properties are in trade-or-business use or held as investments.

In the final section of this chapter, we conclude the quantitative analysis of the Prestige Products case from the previous chapter and discuss the decision on this case.

TEST YOURSELF

Explain the following key terms and concepts presented in this chapter.

1. Implications of the Tax Reform Act of 1986 to real estate investors.
2. Taxation of capital gains versus taxation of ordinary income.
3. Marginal tax rate.
4. Trade-or-business property versus investment property.
5. Tax shelter.
6. Basis for depreciation.
7. Rehabilitation tax credits.
8. Installment sale.
9. Like-kind exchange.
10. Tax credits for low-income housing.

Answer the following multiple-choice questions.

1. The only time taxes on the proceeds from the sale of property can be deferred is when the property is classified as
   a. A principal residence.
   b. Dealer property.
   c. Trade or business property.
   d. Investment property.
   e. Sale proceeds are always treated as capital gain.

2. The form of ownership that probably offers the most advantages for a real estate investor who does not want to take an active role in the management of the investment is
   a. Sole proprietorship.
   b. General partnership.
   c. Real estate investment trust.
   d. S-corporation.
   e. C-corporation.

3. A deep tax shelter from a real estate investment occurs when
   a. Before-tax cash flow is negative.
   b. Principal amortization is less than mortgage interest.
   c. Before-tax cash flow is greater than taxable income.
   d. Taxable income is negative.
   e. None of the above.

4. A residential property is placed in service in 1987. The property is valued at $150,000, whereas the land component of the property is valued at $50,000. What is the depreciation allowance for 1987?
   a. $1,111.11.
   b. $2,222.22.
   c. $3,636.36.
   d. $0.
   e. $13,333.34.

5. In an installment-sale tax treatment,
   a. All taxes on capital gains are due in the year of sale.
   b. Taxes on capital gains are determined as they are in a like-kind exchange.
   c. No taxes on capital gains are due on the sale.
   d. Capital gains are taxed as ordinary income.
   e. None of the above.

ADDITIONAL READINGS*

Epley, Donald R., and James A. Millar. *Basic Real Estate Finance and Investments.* New York: John Wiley & Sons, 1984, Chap. 18.

Faggen, Ivan, et al. of Arthur Andersen & Co. *Federal Taxes Affecting Real Estate.* Albany, N.Y.: Matthew Bender & Co., 1983.

Jeddeloh, James B., and Cheryl G. Perkins. *Real Estate Taxation.* Reston, Va.: Reston Publishing, 1982.

Kau, James B., and C. F. Sirmans. *Tax Planning for Real Estate Investors.* Englewood Cliffs, N.J.: Prentice-Hall, 1982.

Sirmans, C. F., and Austin J. Jaffe. *The Complete Real Estate Investment Handbook.* Englewood Cliffs, N.J.: Prentice-Hall, 1984, Chap. 8.

*Note: These books were published before the 1986 tax legislation. Only revised editions of these books should be consulted.

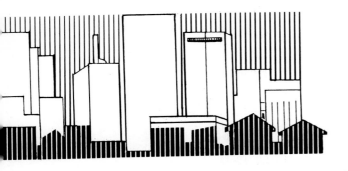

23
Risk and Real Estate Investment

INTRODUCTION

In the two preceding chapters we showed how to calculate the returns from a real estate investment. Investors are obviously interested in earning the maximum possible returns, but are also concerned with the risks they will be taking to obtain the high returns. This chapter is about the risks of real estate investment. Much of our discussion focuses on risk management, which entails measurement of risk. Unfortunately, risk measurement is not nearly as advanced as the measurement of returns, so it is difficult for real estate investors to evaluate effectively the trade off between risk and return.

The Concept of Variability

The riskiness of an investment is the degree of variability expected in the investment's future returns. When investors expect future returns to be highly variable, then these returns are said to be less certain. Thus, risk is linked to the *uncertainty* of future returns. After-tax reversions, for example, are inherently more risky than after-tax cash flows because they depend on highly uncertain future selling prices. Selling prices can *vary* widely from what was expected. As Exhibit 23–1 shows, two investment opportunities can have similar average returns, yet exhibit substantially different degrees of variability and thus uncertainty in their returns. The rational investor will choose Investment B over Investment A because Investment B offers the same expected level of return at less risk. This is simply a restatement of the dominance principle from Chapter 20.

Most investors are *risk-averse*. Even though Investment A in Exhibit 23–1 offers the possibility of very high returns, risk-averse investors view it as inferior to Investment B because it offers the possibility of very low returns as well. Risk-averse investors have a decided preference for avoiding exposure to losses even when opportunities for substantial gains

EXHIBIT 23–1
RISKS AND RETURNS OF TWO INVESTMENT OPPORTUNITIES

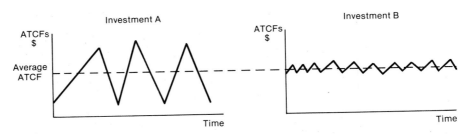

exist. The degree of risk aversion varies among investors, but is related to factors such as the age and wealth position of the investor.

Because the primary concern of investors is *downside risk* (i.e., risk of loss) the concept of variability, which allows for movement up and down, does not match up exactly with the concept of risk. Yet variability is easily measured by the standard deviation of returns,[1] and measurement of risk is essential for modern investment analysis, so the standard deviation is commonly used as a measure of risk. The standard deviation is a summary measure of the difference between each observation in a data series such as the after-tax cash flows, and the mean of that series. Thus for purposes of risk measurement and analysis, the *mean returns* and the *standard deviation of returns* are the relevant statistics.

Types of Risk

Risk is often categorized according to its sources. One source of risk is general economic conditions. This type of risk is known as *systematic* or *market risk*. When general economic conditions deteriorate fewer office condominiums are sold, less space is rented in shopping centers, and home purchasers postpone buying homes. Each type of property is affected by changes in general economic conditions to different degrees, but all are subject to some systematic risk.

The variability of returns on real estate investments also is affected by factors in the local economy and at the specific location. This local market and property-specific risk is labeled *unsystematic risk.*[2] As an example of unsystematic risk, the Houston and Denver real estate markets suffered

---

[1]The standard deviation is the square root of the variance. For a description of these measures of variability, see any statistics textbook.

[2]Local business conditions can be viewed as a source of systematic risk when only considering properties in one local market. However, if we take a national perspective, then local market conditions are a source of unsystematic risk.

high vacancy rates due to overbuilding during the mid-1980s, while the national real estate market continued to expand. Returns also can be adversely affected by unsystematic factors, such as poor property management that results in higher vacancies or by an unharmonious land use on an adjacent parcel (e.g., a noisy factory next to an office building).

We can also identify specific types of systematic and unsystematic risk. Some types of systematic risk are:

1. *External Business Risk.* This term is synonymous with systematic risk. It refers to variability resulting from forces external to the property from a local perspective, or outside the local economy from a national perspective.
2. *Financial Risk.* This exists only when the investment has debt in its capital structure. Specifically, it is the risk that changes in general business conditions will force net operating income below the level needed to pay debt service, and thus increase the possibility of foreclosure.
3. *Interest-Rate Risk.* When an investor enters into a variable-rate mortgage contract, the possibility that interest rates will change is called interest-rate risk. A rise would cause monthly payments to increase and might cause the value of the property to decline. Another form of interest-rate risk results from the fact that an investor might be forced to borrow funds on a short-term basis when general business conditions adversely affect income to the point where borrowing is the only means of paying property expenses.

The term *internal business risk* is synonymous with unsystematic risk in much the same way external business risk is synonymous with systematic risk. Internal business risk refers to management errors and inefficiencies that may result in losses of property income.

Risk-Adjusted Discount Rate

Economist Irving Fisher, writing in the late 1800s and early 1900s, propounded a theory of interest rates that has withstood the test of time. His theory held that the nominal interest rate r_n (the rate observed in the market) is comprised of two components: a real rate of return r_r, which compensates investors for investing rather than consuming; and a premium for expected inflation i_e, which compensates investors for anticipated losses in the purchasing power of their invested capital. This premium for inflation is a premium for *purchasing-power risk,* a form of systematic risk. In symbols, the Fisher theory may be expressed as

$$r_n = r_r + i_e \qquad (23\text{--}1)$$

Recall that real estate investment analysis using the discounted cash-flow methodology requires specification of three major items: the after-tax cash flows in each period, the after-tax reversion when the property is sold, and the discount rate. We described objective analytical techniques for estimating after-tax cash flows and the after-tax reversion in the preceding two chapters. What remains to be specified is the discount rate.

Traditionally, real estate investment analysts have relied on a *risk-adjusted* discount-rate approach for specifying the rate at which returns are discounted (i.e., the rate used to calculate the present value of the after-tax cash flows and after-tax reversion). This approach is simply an extension of the Fisher equation. The analyst estimates the future returns, then makes a judgment about how risky the returns are in relation to other comparable investment opportunities and, finally, assigns a risk premium, r_{rp}, to the *nominal rate,* also called the *risk-free rate.* The risk-free rate is often represented by the U.S. Treasury bill (short term), note, (intermediate term) or bond rate (long term). Thus, the term *risk-free* in this context means default-free, since Treasury securities are void of any risk premiums other than those for purchasing-power risk.

The equation for the discount rate following a risk-adjusted discount-rate approach is

$$r_n = r_r + i_e + r_{rp} \tag{23-2}$$

Some analysts believe premiums should also be added for investment management and nonmarketability, since real estate, in comparison to other investments, is more management-intensive and less marketable. This practice is not generally followed.

Because the returns are subject to variation over time, there is no question that risk premiums should be a part of the discount rate. A major problem with the risk-adjusted discount-rate approach is that the specification of the risk premium is entirely subjective, relying exclusively on the analyst's judgment. Therefore it is not aided by the use of objective quantitative models or techniques. This subjectivity of the discount rate specification is the Achilles heel of the discounted cash-flow model. Later in this chapter we consider some methods for objectively specifying the discount rate.

PROCESS FOR INCORPORATING RISK ANALYSIS

As we noted above, the tools for analyzing real estate investment risks are not nearly as well developed as those for analyzing investment returns. One survey of professional real estate investment analysts revealed that 62 percent of the respondents never use even the simplest of risk analysis techniques, and over 90 percent never use the more advanced techniques.[3] Nevertheless, 10 years earlier similar surveys found that discounted cash-flow methods were being used (or *not* used) to about the same extent. Today, the majority of real estate investment analysts use discounted cash-flow methods.[4]

We can attribute the low rate of professional use of risk-analysis methods to the fact that these techniques are not thoroughly developed and the user must have a certain level of statistical and corporate-finance training. Risk analysis, however, does provide important information for making real estate investment decisions. Therefore a well-defined process should be established for combining the analysis of investment risks with the analysis of real estate investment returns. This process, as part of the general process for making real estate investment decisions described in Chapter 21, includes the specification of investor preferences for risk, the identification of the major risks from making the investment, measurement of risk, and making a decision.

Specification of Investor Risk Preferences

A critical element of the investor's investment strategy is a determination of the investor's preferences for risk. The risk preferences cannot be ignored in the development of investment philosophy, objectives, and policies. As Panel A of Exhibit 23–2 shows, three generalized states of the relationship between risk and return can exist. The *risk-loving* investor is willing to accept exponentially lower returns for taking on greater risks. This response to risk is irrational and, therefore, unrealistic. The *risk-neutral* investor requires the same return regardless of the risk incurred. Again, most investors do not behave in this manner. The *risk-averse* investor requires returns that increase exponentially as the level of investment risk increases.

Virtually all investors are risk-averse. The key question in formulating an investment strategy is, How risk averse is this particular investor? Panel B of Exhibit 23–2 presents the risk-preference functions for two individual investors. Aunt Jane is a retired school teacher on a fixed income, with investment capital limited to only a few thousand dollars of her life's savings. She is highly risk-averse and willing to accept risk beyond risk level *a* only if the returns on investment are infinite. In contrast, Dr. Jones is a successful young professional with substantial investment capital. He will accept lower returns than Aunt Jane for the same level of risk and is willing to take on far greater levels of risk.

---

[3]See Edward J. Farragher, "Investment Decision-Making Practices of Equity Investors in Real Estate," *Real Estate Appraiser and Analyst* 48 (Summer 1982), pp. 36–41.
[4]Ibid.

EXHIBIT 23–2
INVESTOR RISK PREFERENCES

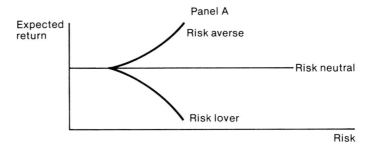

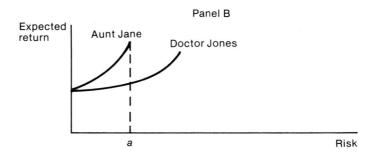

Specifying an investor's risk preferences is entirely subjective. There are no easily applied objective measures of risk aversion. Using their best judgment, analysts identify the investor's degree of risk aversion and then attempt to find investment opportunities with risk and return characteristics that are consistent with the investor's overall investment strategy. As we noted, for individual investors, the degree of risk aversion is usually related to their ages and wealth, as it is in the cases of Aunt Jane and Dr. Jones. Among institutional investors, the degree of risk aversion is often related to the importance of preserving capital and the extent to which the institution's investment managers are personally liable for their actions. For example, life insurance companies place a high premium on preserving capital because they *must* pay claims, and pension fund managers are legally personally liable for their actions as investment managers.

Identification of Major Investment Risks

Part of the problem of matching the real estate investor with the real estate investment is the identification of the major risks likely to be encountered in the investment. In terms of the process established in Chapter 21, risk identification is part of the *qualitative analysis* conducted for each investment alternative.

As with other qualitative aspects, the identification of major investment risks is subjective. The analyst should consider each of the various forms of systematic and unsystematic risk in the evaluation of an alternative by asking such questions as, Will the returns from this investment alternative be highly susceptible to changes in general economic conditions? Do the returns depend strongly on property management?

Risk Management

Risk management is a general term that refers to two separate activities: the transfer of investment risks and the measurement and analysis of risks. One important element of the qualitative analysis of a real estate investment is the determination of which risks associated with each alternative can be transferred to others. We can cite two examples of transferring real estate investment risks. First, most investors buy insurance against losses due to fire and natural hazards.[5] The purchase of a relatively inexpensive insurance policy enables investors to transfer to others the risk of losses of returns due to fire and natural hazards. Second, the risk of interest-rate movements resulting from adjustable- or variable-rate mortgage contracts are transferable to speculators in the financial-futures markets by hedging in those markets. While the topic of financial futures is beyond the scope of this book, suffice it that financial futures are playing an ever-increasing role in the risk management of real estate investments.

The measurement and analysis of real estate investment risks is an intricate part of the quantitative analysis; we devote the remaining sections of this chapter to these topics. They are discussed with respect to measuring and analyzing the risk of a single investment—the *project-in-isolation view*—and a collection of investments—the *portfolio view*.

Decision

With the proper consideration and incorporation of risk, the decision on the investment of funds in a particular real estate venture reduces to a single question: Do the returns from this investment compensate the investor for the risks taken, given the investor's overall investment strategy and preference for risk?

---

[5]While mortgage lenders generally require that such insurance be purchased, most investors would purchase fire and hazard insurance anyway, since the cost of this insurance is low relative to the potential loss.

PROJECT-IN-ISOLATION RISK ANALYSIS

Project-in-isolation risk analysis requires that the investor or investment analyst concentrate entirely on the riskiness of a *single* real estate investment. This is the most direct approach to analyzing investment risks and is well-grounded in tradition. In this section we discuss traditional methods of risk analysis and more modern techniques. The major difference between the two approaches is the concern in the modern approach for quantifying risks.

Traditional Approaches to Risk Measurement

The advantages of traditional approaches to risk analysis are ease of application and simplicity. These are more than offset by the fact that traditional methods are unsystematic, nonquantitative, and thus highly subjective. The absence of quantitative measurement of risks leads to three potential problems. First, differences in the risk levels of two investment opportunities cannot be evaluated unless risks are quantitatively measured. Second, the investment analyst cannot adequately convey to investors the level of risk of a given investment opportunity unless risks are quantitatively measured. Third, when risks are measured subjectively there is a possibility that analysts will enter their *own* risk preferences into the analysis, thus leading to a biased assessment.

The subjective manipulation of an investment measure known as the *payback period* is a good example of traditional risk analysis. The payback period is defined as[6]

$$\text{Payback period} = \frac{\text{Equity investment}}{\text{Average after-tax cash flow}} \qquad (23\text{--}3)$$

If an investor contributes $50,000 of equity funds to an investment and expects an average annual after-tax cash flow of $10,000 over the holding period, the payback period is

$$\text{Payback period} = \frac{\$50,000}{\$10,000}$$
$$= 5 \text{ years}$$

For an investor with a minimum policy requirement of five years for payback, this investment is acceptable.

---

[6]The payback period has two critical flaws as a tool for real estate investment decision making. First, averaging ATCFs is in violation of the principles of time value of money. Secondly, the payback-period approach ignores money flows occurring after the payback period, especially the reversion.

Now assume that the investment is perceived as being riskier than the average investment opportunity encountered by the investor. To compensate, the investor might adjust the minimum acceptable payback period downward to four years, leading to rejection of the project. The adjustment of one year for risk is entirely subjective. No attempt is made to measure the riskiness of the investment and to match the risk level with the size of the risk adjustment.

The risk-adjusted discount-rate approach to specifying a discount rate is another example of a traditional approach. Adding risk premiums to the real rate of return and expected inflation rate to account for the expected variability in returns is a *subjective* method of arriving at an estimate of a discount rate. Seldom do investors or analysts using the risk-adjusted discount-rate approach attempt to measure the riskiness of the investment and quantitatively link riskiness to the risk premiums added to the risk-free rate. The discount rate clearly must contain risk premiums to compensate the investor for taking risks; the issue is how one estimates a risk-adjusted discount rate *objectively* rather than subjectively.

The Use of Subjective Probabilities

The challenge to modern approaches for analyzing real estate investment risk lies in the measurement of risks. The ideal process is to collect data from recent periods on the returns for the property under evaluation. Then the analyst would calculate the mean and standard deviation of returns as the measure of risk. Even if past returns were not available for the subject property—for example, if it were a new venture—data on returns from comparable properties could be gathered. This approach is essentially the way risk analysis is done for stock and bond investments.

Unfortunately, data on past returns for subject properties and comparables usually are not available. Unlike stocks and bonds, one simply cannot leaf through back issues of the *Wall Street Journal* to obtain past data on returns from shopping centers in Kansas, for example. Moreover, real estate markets are not nearly as active as securities markets, and therefore data on sales (i.e., reversions) are not available.

These data constraints mandate that the analysis of real estate investment risks follow alternative—and not altogether satisfactory—courses. One course involves the use of *subjective probabilities*. The example that follows demonstrates a very simple application of subjective probabilities.

Suppose economic forecasts for next year suggest a 20 percent chance for a mild recession, a 50 percent chance for a stable economy, and a 30 percent chance for moderate economic expansion. Given these three possible states of the economy and the *subjective* assignment of *probabilities* of their occurrence, we can develop after-tax cash flows for two alternative rental-property investments, Option X and Option Y. Exhibit 23–3 Panel A, presents these estimates. The differences between after-tax cash flows for the different states of the economy for each alternative are attributable to differences in rental-income-growth rates and vacancy rates. Thus rental growth would be the lowest and vacancy the highest in a mild recession.

EXHIBIT 23–3
SUBJECTIVE PROBABILITY DISTRIBUTIONS FOR TWO ALTERNATIVE INVESTMENT OPTIONS

Panel A

State of the Economy	Probability	ATCF Option X	ATCF Option Y
Expansion	.30	$60,000	$60,000
Stability	.50	$40,000	$30,000
Recession	.20	–0–	$20,000
	1.00		

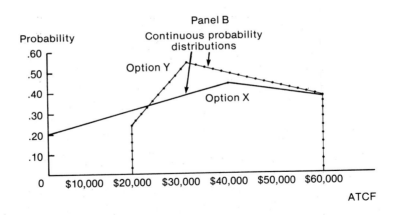

Panel B
Continuous probability distributions

Panel B of Exhibit 23–3 shows the continuous probability distributions for the two options as derived from the data in Panel A. Which option is preferred, given that these are the only cash flows?

We require some additional calculations to ascertain the relative risk and return relationships of these two investment alternatives. Suffice it that their variability of returns, assuming a simple one-year return, has been brought out through the use of subjective probabilities. Some investment analysts believe that the assignment of probabilites in this manner is too subjective to be of any use. Others, however, feel that the use of subjective probabilities is the only way in many cases to quantify the risks of real estate investments; the alternative is to do no risk analysis at all.

Calculating the Mean and Standard Deviation

We require further analysis to evaluate the risk and return relationships of the two investment alternatives. This entails a calculation of the expected return, or mean, and the standard deviation of returns for each option. The expected after-tax cash flow E(ATCF), is calculated as follows

HP-12C: Mean → $\boxed{\text{ON}}$ $\boxed{\text{f}}$ $\boxed{\frac{\Sigma}{\text{SST}}}$, 60000 $\boxed{\text{ENTER}}$ .3 $\boxed{\Sigma+}$

40000 $\boxed{\text{ENTER}}$ .5 $\boxed{\Sigma+}$, 0 $\boxed{\text{ENTER}}$ .2 $\boxed{\Sigma+}$, $\boxed{\text{g}}$ $\boxed{\frac{6}{\bar{x}w}}$

= 38,000

Standard Deviation → Keystrokes for standard deviation calculation can be found in the HP-12C *Solutions Handbook.*

Mean → $\boxed{\text{ON}}$ $\boxed{\text{f}}$ $\boxed{\frac{\Sigma}{\text{SST}}}$, 60000 $\boxed{\text{ENTER}}$ .3 $\boxed{\Sigma+}$

30000 $\boxed{\text{ENTER}}$ .5 $\boxed{\Sigma+}$, 20000 $\boxed{\text{ENTER}}$ .2 $\boxed{\Sigma+}$,

$\boxed{\text{g}}$ $\boxed{\frac{6}{\bar{x}w}}$ = 37,000

Standard Deviation → Keystrokes for the standard deviation calculation can be found in the HP-12C *Solutions Handbook.*

BA-35: Mean → $\boxed{\text{ON/C}}$ $\boxed{\text{ON/C}}$ $\boxed{\text{2nd}}$ $\boxed{\text{STAT}}$, 60000 $\boxed{\text{FRQ}}$

30 $\boxed{\Sigma+}$, 40000 $\boxed{\text{FRQ}}$ 50 $\boxed{\Sigma+}$, 0 $\boxed{\text{FRQ}}$ 20 $\boxed{\Sigma+}$ $\boxed{\bar{x}}$ = 38000

Standard Deviation → $\boxed{\sigma n}$ = 20881

Mean → $\boxed{\text{ON/C}}$ $\boxed{\text{ON/C}}$ $\boxed{\text{2nd}}$ $\boxed{\text{STAT}}$, 60000 $\boxed{\text{FRQ}}$

30 $\boxed{\Sigma+}$, 30000 $\boxed{\text{FRQ}}$ 50 $\boxed{\Sigma+}$, 20000 $\boxed{\text{FRQ}}$

20 $\boxed{\Sigma+}$ $\boxed{\bar{x}}$ = 37000

Standard Deviation → $\boxed{\sigma n}$ = 14866

Interpretation of Investment Risk

While the expected returns from Options X and Y are quite similar, their standard deviations indicate that Option X is about 40 percent more risky than Option Y ([20,881 − 14,866]/14,886 = .4027). By assuming that the distributions of ATCFs from the two options coincide with the *normal dis-*

tribution, additional interpretations are possible. The relevant properties of the normal distribution are:

1. Sixty-eight percent of the area under the normal curve falls between plus and minus one standard deviation from the mean.
2. Approximately 95 percent of the area falls between plus and minus two standard deviations from the mean.

This means that the interval produced by adding to and subtracting from the mean two times the standard deviation is one in which the analyst can be 95 percent confident that next year's after-tax cash flow will fall.

Exhibit 23–4 presents normal distributions for the two investment alternatives. With Option X, there is a 95 percent chance that the actual ATCF for next year will be between ($3,762) and $79,762. For Option Y, the 95 percent interval is $7,248 to $66,772. As we mentioned previously, investors are risk-averse and thus have a greater desire to avoid losses than to realize greater gains. Since Option X represents substantially greater downside risk, most investors would likely prefer Option Y. Had the mean returns been significantly different, additional analysis of the return and risk relationships would have been required.

This example is a very simple demonstration of the analysis of real estate investment risk for a single investment. Extensions are possible in several directions. The next logical step is to consider the riskiness of the after-tax cash flows in Years 2, 3, and so on, and the riskiness of the reversion. We can convert these results into distributions of investment value, net present value, or internal rate of return. Futher interpretations of the results are possible; however, they are *not* susceptible to decision rules such as those available for determining whether to accept or reject an investment.

Sensitivity and Simulation

Sensitivity analysis and simulation are perhaps the two most widely known and utilized techniques for analyzing real estate investment risk. Both techniques are project-in-isolation approaches, and are deeply rooted in the philosophy that risk should be quantified.

Sensitivity analysis is used to answer simple "what if" questions. For example, suppose after-tax cash flows from an investment are estimated on the basis of a 5 percent vacancy rate throughout the holding period. To evaluate the systematic risk of the investment, we determine the *sensitivity* of changes in the vacancy rate on after-tax cash flows. This might entail re-estimating the after-tax cash flows with a 10 percent vacancy rate during the first three years of the holding period. With this procedure, the analyst is asking, What if vacancy rates exceed expectations? What is the effect on returns? What is the variation in returns from this new assumption? What is the risk from increased vacancy? Sensitivity analysis

EXHIBIT 23-4
NORMAL DISTRIBUTIONS FOR TWO ALTERNATIVE
INVESTMENT OPTIONS

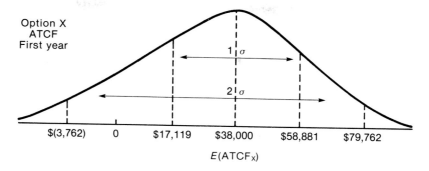

Option X
ATCF
First year

1σ

2σ

$(3,762) \quad 0 \quad \$17,119 \quad \$38,000 \quad \$58,881 \quad \$79,762$

$E(\text{ATCF}_X)$

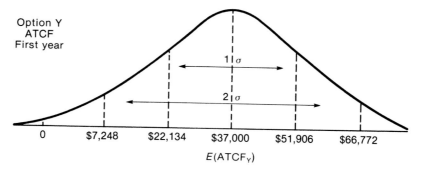

Option Y
ATCF
First year

1σ

2σ

$0 \quad \$7,248 \quad \$22,134 \quad \$37,000 \quad \$51,906 \quad \$66,772$

$E(\text{ATCF}_Y)$

can be extended to any probablistic input in the discounted cash-flow model such as growth rates in rents and mortgage interest rates. It is a simple technique that is well understood by most analysts and many investors.

Simulation can be described as a sophisticated version of sensitivity analysis. The idea behind simulation is to evaluate the effects on returns caused by changes in several inputs simultaneously. In many types of simulations (e.g., the Monte Carlo method), subjective probability distributions are specified for risky inputs such as vacancy rates and growth rates in rents and value. Then the discounted cash-flow model is run perhaps 100 to 250 times, each time with a different input from the subjective probability distributions. This produces a set of observations for such outputs as investment value, from which means and standard deviations are calculated.

Simulation is not as well understood by analysts as sensitivity analysis. It requires the use of specialized computer programs to be cost effective, but is potentially a powerful tool for real estate investment risk analysis.

THE CONCEPT OF PORTFOLIO RISK

Even before project-in-isolation techniques became well integrated into the applied world of real estate risk analysis, the portfolio concept of risk had begun to emerge. The portfolio concept is broader in scope than the project-in-isolation concept. Essentially, it involves answering the question, How does the investment in a given asset affect the total risk of the investor's portfolio or collection of assets? This is quite different from simply analyzing the riskiness of a single asset.

The portfolio concept of risk embodies some special properties that lead to a lowering of total portfolio risk through *asset diversification*. Moreover, the portfolio concept extends to *capital market theory*, in which modeling techniques are used to estimate discount rates objectively. Although larger institutional investors are the primary users of portfolio techniques today, the portfolio concept of risk underlies techniques that have unlimited potential for objective risk analysis of real estate investments at all levels.

Diversification

Diversification is an essential element of the portfolio concept of risk. Early portfolio theorists showed that, through the selection of just a few assets at random, virtually all of the *unsystematic risk* of the portfolio of assets can be eliminated (i.e., diversified away). This occurs because the specific characteristics of individual assets that cause returns to move up or down tend to cancel each other when the assets are grouped into a portfolio. Since a portfolio can be fully diversified in the sense that its unsystematic risk is eliminated by choosing perhaps as few as 15 assets at random, this type of diversification is often termed *naive diversification*. Assets can be selected on the basis of their relative riskiness as well as at random. For example, an asset that is quite risky can be combined in a portfolio with a risk-free asset to reduce the overall risk of the portfolio. This so-called *smart diversification* has two implications. First, it is possible to reduce the unsystematic risk in a portfolio to zero with fewer assets under a smart diversification strategy than under a naive strategy. Second, smart diversification can reduce somewhat, the systematic risk in a portfolio, although it cannot eliminate portfolio risk entirely. In practice, portfolio analysis uses smart diversification.

From a technical standpoint, portfolio models require past data on returns, since the measurement of portfolio risk and diversification relies on the calculation of *covariances* among the returns from the different assets in the portfolio.[7]

---

[7]A covariance is like variance or standard deviation, except it measures the variation between two series of data (e.g., return from two assets) instead of variation within one series.

Herein lies the problem of applying portfolio models in the analysis of real estate investment risk. As we mentioned earlier, in conjunction with estimating standard deviations for project-in-isolation risk analysis, past data on returns from real estate assets are usually not available. Only large institutions with a large number of properties already in their portfolios can use portfolio models for real estate investment analysis.[8] Even then, institutions must have their properties appraised, usually on a quarterly basis, to obtain an estimate of the value of the reversion component of return. The one encouraging note is that much work is now in progress to assemble large data bases of properties for public use. These data bases eventually will overcome most of the data problems currently restricting the application of portfolio models to real estate.

Capital Asset Pricing Model (CAPM)

Suppose an investor has the ability to use portfolio models to diversify away the unsystematic risk of her real estate portfolio. In analyzing the riskiness of her next real estate investment opportunity, she therefore would be interested only in the amount of systematic risk this new investment brings to her portfolio. The unsystematic risk is of no concern, since it can be eliminated through diversification.

The ability to diversify has some important implications in establishing the discount rate to be applied to the cash flows of any new investment. Because unsystematic risk is irrelevant, risk premiums are not required to compensate the investor for taking on such risk. Thus, the discount rate can be expressed as

$$r = f(r_f, r_{psr}) \tag{23-4}$$

This equation reads: "The required rate of return or discount rate (r) is a function of the risk-free rate (r_f) and a risk premium for systematic risk (r_{psr}).

This functional relationship leads to a very important model in finance and real estate known as the *capital asset pricing model.* The form of this model is

$$r = r_f + (r_m - r_f)\,\beta \tag{23-5}$$

The discount rate is calculated as the sum of the risk-free rate and the difference between the return on a market index r_m and the risk-free rate times a fixed parameter $\beta(beta)$. The r_m is a measure of the return that would be available to an investor who owns the entire market of real estate investments and securities. The β relates the premium of r_m over r_f to the specific asset under evaluation. If $\beta = 1$, then the returns on the asset move exactly as the market moves. If $\beta = 2$, the returns are twice

---

[8] See Robert H. Zerbst and Barbara R. Cambon, "Real Estate: Historical Returns and Risks," *Journal of Portfolio Management* (Spring 1984), pp. 5–20.

as volatile as the market returns. Therefore, β is a measure of systematic risk.

Suppose that r_f = .05 (i.e., 5 percent), r_m = .14, and β = 1. The appropriate discount rate using the capital asset pricing model is therefore

$$r = .05 + (.14 - .05) \times 1$$
$$= .14$$

If β = 1.5, then the discount rate is

$$r = .05 + (.14 - .05) \times 1.5$$
$$= .185$$

and .185 would be used to discount the returns from the investment.

Like the application of portfolio models, the application of the capital asset pricing model to real estate investments is not easily accomplished. First, r_m is difficult to estimate, since there is currently no composite market index of real estate returns or index such as the Standard and Poors 500 in the stock market, that covers real estate. Second, to obtain β, past data on r_m and the returns on the specific property are needed. This is because β is ordinarily estimated with these past data through a statistical technique known as regression analysis. Nevertheless analysts should try to fulfill the data requirements of the capital asset pricing model because it represents a theoretically sound and objective way to estimate discount rates. As we mentioned earlier, the subjective specification of discount rates is probably the greatest weakness of the discounted cash-flow methodology.

OVERVIEW

The term risk is synonymous with variability. Thus the more variable the returns on an asset such as a real estate investment, the more risky the asset. Risk in real estate investments can be divided into two broad categories. Systematic risk is the variation in returns caused by general market conditions; unsystematic risk is the variation caused by property-specific sources such as management. In the traditional method for specifying discount rates known as the risk-adjusted discount-rate approach, risk premiums for systematic and unsystematic risk are subjectively added to a risk-free rate to account for the variation in returns. These risk premiums are included in the discount rate to compensate the investor for taking on the systematic and unsystematic risks of the investment.

The incorporation of risk analysis into the overall decision-making process for real estate investments includes the specification of investor risk preferences, identification of major investment risks, and risk management. The most crucial of these elements is risk management because it involves measurement of risk. Risk measurement is guided by two alternative perspectives—project-in-isolation risk analysis and portfolio risk analysis.

Project-in-isolation risk analysis focuses on measuring the riskiness of one investment at a time. Since past data are rarely available to calculate the standard deviations of returns, the analysis of risk depends on the use of subjective probability techniques. These techniques allow the analyst to estimate means and standard deviations of returns and thus to interpret the riskiness of an investment. Sensitivity analysis and simulation are popular forms of project-in-isolation risk analysis. Simulation relies heavily on subjective probability assignments. Sensitivity analysis looks at the effects on returns of changes in one input.

The portfolio concept of risk considers the riskiness of various assets taken together and is a more encompassing framework for risk analysis. Two implications arise from the portfolio concept. First, it allows for virtual elimination of unsystematic risk through asset diversification (naive diversification) and may lead to a lowering of systematic risk (smart diversification). Second, it allows the analyst to estimate discount rates objectively through the use of the capital asset pricing model. This extension is of great importance, since the subjective specification of discount rates is perhaps a major shortcoming of real estate investment analysis using discounted cash-flow methods.

TEST YOURSELF

Explain the following terms and concepts presented in this chapter.

1. Risk, variability, and uncertainty of returns.
2. Systematic versus unsystematic risk.
3. Risk-adjusted discount rate.
4. Risk aversion.
5. Risk management.
6. Subjective probabilities.
7. Sensitivity analysis and simulation.
8. Diversification.
9. Capital asset pricing model.
10. Beta.

Answer the following multiple choice questions.

1. If the expected rate of inflation is 6 percent, the real rate of return is 4 percent, and the required rate of return (or discount rate) is 15 percent, what risk premium is assumed?
   a. Twenty-five percent.
   b. Five percent.
   c. Eight percent.
   d. Fifteen percent.
   e. Cannot be determined from information given.

2. A property with an 80 percent loan-to-value ratio is expected to have more _____ than a property purchased with all equity funds.
   a. Internal business risk.
   b. External business risk.
   c. Unsystematic risk.
   d. Systematic risk.
   e. Beta risk.

3. Combining assets in a portfolio so that the risk of the portfolio is less than the sum of the risks of each individual asset is called
    a. Subjective probability analysis.
    b. Risk measurements.
    c. Risk aversion.
    d. Diversification.
    e. Capital asset pricing.

4. Risk management includes all of the following *except*
    a. Transferring risks.
    b. Measuring risks.
    c. Diversification.
    d. Purchasing insurance against fire, floods, etc.
    e. Risk management includes all of the above.

5. The main function of the capital asset pricing model is
    a. To estimate the discount rate or required rate of return.
    b. To diversify the portfolio.
    c. To measure the degree of risk aversion.
    d. To find the value of an asset.
    e. To find the mean of a distribution of returns from real estate.

ADDITIONAL READINGS

Epley, Donald R., and James A. Millar. *Basic Real Estate Finance and Investment.* New York: John Wiley & Sons, 1984, Chap. 22.

Martin, William B. "A Risk Analysis Rate of Return Model for Evaluating Income-Producing Real Estate Investments." *Appraisal Journal* 46 (July 1978), pp. 424–42.

Montgomery, J. Thomas. "Real Estate Investment Risk—Basic Concepts." *Appraisal Journal* 44 (January 1976), pp. 9–22.

Pyhrr, Stephen A., and James R. Cooper. *Real Estate Investment.* Boston: Warren, Gorham & Lamont, 1982, Chap. 12.

Young, Michael S. "Evaluating the Risk of Investment Real Estate." *Real Estate Appraiser and Analyst* 43 (October, 1977), pp. 39–45.

Part Four

The Business Perspective

Since many businesses deal with real estate directly—brokerage, property management, development construction, appraisal, consulting, financing and syndication—it is important to look at real estate from a business perspective in an introductory real estate course. The five chapters that comprise this section are devoted to the *business* of real estate. These chapters come at the end of this book not because the business perspective is less important than other perspectives, but because business people in real estate draw extensively on legal, economic, and financial principles in their daily work, and, therefore, students of real estate should be well grounded in these principles before taking on the finer points of the real estate business.

People in the real estate business view themselves as the creators, distributors, and financiers of products and services that are used by nearly everyone in society. These products and services provide the housing, offices, factories, schools, recreation facilities, and other real estate that people use every day. When real estate production enhances society's welfare, it is worth more than the sum of the values of its parts and is said to be *productive*. Chapter 24, the first chapter in this section, is devoted to the features of real estate that make it productive.

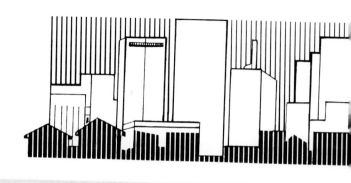

In addition to having an intellectual foundation in the law, economics, and finance, real estate businesspeople should be well versed in marketing and management. Chapter 25 demonstrates how some of the more important theories and techniques of marketing and management are applied to the problems often faced by real estate businesspeople. Many of these problems are encountered, for example, when raw land is improved by real estate developers. In Chapter 26, we discuss the legal, economic, financial, marketing, and management aspects of real estate development.

Two of the more important trends in the real estate business in recent years have been real estate syndication as a method of financing projects, and technical innovation in building design and business operations. Chapter 27 contains a comprehensive survey of the real estate syndication business, including an analysis of federal and state regulations. In Chapter 28, we explore how new technologies are enhancing real estate productivity and how increased productivity affects the way real estate people operate in today's business environment. ∎

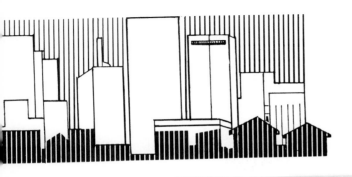

24
Real Estate Productivity

INTRODUCTION

The ultimate source of all real estate value is the productivity of real estate. *Productivity* means the ability of a person, good, commodity, or product to enhance people's quality of life or to add value to other products and services. In particular, real estate is productive because it provides shelter and comfort to people, as well as a base for the production of goods, products, and services that contribute to people's quality of life. As examples, factories provide a base for the manufacture of automobiles and school buildings provide a base for educational services.

The term productivity, however, implies more than just shelter, comfort, and a base for the production of other goods and services. It implies the creation of values that are greater than the costs of production. The concept of productivity thus involves a relationship in which the value of outputs is greater than the value of inputs.

Consider the production of a single-family house. Various materials (such as lumber, plaster, nails, pipes, and wires), labor, and management talent are combined with land to produce a residential unit. The land and materials are puchased, and laborers and managers are paid wages or salaries. Yet the home builder may end up with a surplus (profit) above all costs. The profit is created because the whole (the house) is worth more than the sum of its parts (land, labor, and materials).

Because real estate is productive, its owners are entitled to a return just as laborers, suppliers of capital, and entrepreneurs are entitled to their returns.[1] The returns produced by real estate cause it to have value and to be traded in its own markets. Therefore, the value of real estate is not derived from, or determined by, the prices of other goods, as the classical economists believed. Land and real estate are regarded as equal

---

[1]The return to labor is called wages, the return to capital is called interest, the return to entrepreneurship is called profit, and the return to land is called rent.

in importance to labor, capital, and entrepreneurship; the return to real estate is not dependent on, nor is it residual to, other returns.

━━━━ *Frame 24–1* ━━━━

The Negative Image of Landlords and Landladies

The modern theory of land (real estate) value contrasts with the classical theory of land value in which the return to land was regarded as an unearned surplus. Land was regarded as different from the other factors of production because it was God-given and fixed in location. The owners of all but the poorest land received an "unearned increment" and were looked on as exploiters of a resource that they did not create. Is it any wonder that landlords and landladies are sometimes even today regarded with a certain degree of contempt?

The Profit Motive

Real estate investment and financing decisions—buying, selling, rehabilitating, refinancing—are made continually. As noted in Part Three of this book, profitability is usually a major objective of real estate investors and business firms. They purchase or lease real estate to provide shelter and facilities for business operations from which profit is generated. For example, developers and builders create new real estate resources (housing, commercial properties, industrial properties, etc.) and attempt to sell them for a price greater than the total cost of producing them. Financial institutions accumulate funds and seek to make loans providing a higher yield than the rate they must pay to attract the funds. And various types of real estate specialty firms (e.g., appraisal, brokerage, and property management firms) sell their services for more than the cost of providing them.

In their search for profits, real estate investors and business firms must identify products and services that consumers (users) of real estate need and want. If they can identify these opportunities and can provide the products and services efficiently, real estate investors and business firms will earn profits. Profits enable firms to expand and their owners and investors to purchase more goods and services than they otherwise could; therefore the profit motive is a powerful incentive for exploiting the productivity of real estate.

The Satisfaction Motive

Household and business firms need the shelter and basic services provided by real estate. More important in today's world, however, is the satisfaction derived from the additional services, conveniences, and prestige provided by many properties. The physical features that increase the utility of a property are termed *amenties:* built-in appliances, air conditioning, carpeting, swimming pools, multiple bathrooms, attractive designs, large rooms, and scenic views. Beyond the increased livability provided by such features, they may also increase the status of the owner-users. Both types of benefits contribute to the overall utility, or satisfaction, provided by a property.

It should be noted that amenities are important to many businesses and government agencies, as well as households. Executives of large businesses and government agencies often want amenity-laden offices, prestigious addresses, and distinctive buildings. The architectural landscapes of many large U.S. cities are dominated by the buildings of such firms as General Motors, U.S. Steel, Gulf Oil, Prudential Insurance, John Hancock Insurance, Atlantic Richfield, Georgia-Pacific, Seagram Distilleries, Sears Roebuck, Equitable Insurance, and Union Oil. And government bureaucrats typically have offices that reflect the rank of their positions.

Real estate therefore is purchased for its ability to satisfy people's emotional needs, as well as its ability to produce profits. Even if such benefits are not measurable quantitatively as profits are, they must be regarded as similar to profits in their relationship to real estate productivity. Both the profit motive and the satisfaction motive cause households, firms, and government agencies to purchase real estate to enhance their well being.

Since people invest in real estate because they expect it to be productive, several questions naturally come to mind: "Why is real estate productive? What characteristics cause it to be useful and desirable? In what basic ways does it contribute to the production of other goods and services?" We answer these questions by contending that the productivity of real estate is derived from its physical, locational, legal, and environmental characteristics. The following sections discuss each of these sources of productivity.

PHYSICAL CHARACTERISTICS

The physical characteristics of real estate are very important determinants of the ability of a parcel of real estate to perform a particular function. For example, the fertility of land determines its usefulness for growing crops. The number and sizes of rooms determine the usefulness of a single-family house for residential occupancy. And the number and size of rooms determine how useful a suite of offices may be for a professional or business firm.

Sites

The physical characteristics of sites include the chemical, mineral, and textural qualities of the soil, the terrain, the flora and fauna on the site, and its amenities such as its view. These determine whether a site can be used for mining, for the construction of buildings, or for agriculture.

Improvements *to* the site—man-made alterations—are also considered physical characteristics and may alter the usefulness of a site. A site may have been leveled and graded, be served by storm and sanitary sewers, have paved driveways and walkways, and be landscaped. Such improvements are termed *on-site improvements* in contrast to *off-site improvements* or *infrastructure.*

Off-site improvements include the streets, sewer system, lighting system, sidewalks, and even public parks. They represent the expenditure of capital to create and preserve the values of all sites in a constituent area, and constitute the difference between raw land and developed land. Because almost all land has been altered by both on-site and off-site improvements, land has been called a *manufactured product.*[2] This term emphasizes the inseparable bond of land, labor, capital, and entrepreneurship in real estate.

The analysis of a site's physical characteristics must be related to its expected use. For example, if the site is to be used for farming, the analysis would concentrate on such factors as drainage, percolation (seepage of water through the soil), size, shape, and fertility. However, if the site is to be used for construction of a large office building, the analysis would focus on the size, shape, terrain, and subsurface characteristics. While almost all sites can be built upon, construction on some sites is much more costly than on others. A high water table or quicksand may require much more expensive construction techniques. On sites where rock outcroppings are on or close to the surface, additional costs will be required for excavation and subsurface utilities.

Surface Characteristics.   These are important to most developed properties. They include such features as size, shape, terrain, vegetation, exposure, and fertility. Sites that are oddly shaped or too small may preclude desirable development. Similarly, steep slopes or large rock formations may also preclude development or increase costs. Vegetation can either enhance or detract from the desirability of sites. Trees, for example, may be desirable and contribute to the value of residential sites but be detrimental to commercial or industrial sites.

Exposure means proximity or access to positive or negative off-site

---

[2]Richard U. Ratcliff, *Real Estate Analysis* (New York: McGraw-Hill, 1961), pp. 1, 43, and 54–55.

influences.[3] Positive influences include pleasant views (e.g., ocean, mountains, woods, or a stream), an attractive neighborhood, and freedom from unpleasant odors and noises.

Fertility is obviously an important consideration when land is to be used for agriculture. Soil characteristics are usually better suited for growing some crops than others. Proper fertilization depends on analysis of the soil's chemical and mineral composition. Agronomists should be consulted for these types of analysis.

Subsurface Characteristics. These include porosity, stability, bearing strength, and mineral composition. Porosity determines the ability of water to seep through the soil. Clay is very dense and tends to retain moisture, so water accumulates at the surface of clay soils, causing problems for most uses of the land. Adequate drainage may solve this problem for agricultural uses, but does not solve the problem of instability that may be caused by or worsened by clay subsoil.

Unstable subsoils shift, causing structural problems in buildings that are built on them. The instability may be caused by the presence of clay and quicksand, by volcanic activity, or by earthquakes. Clay or quicksand can be detected by soil borings at a site. Either usually must be removed to preclude future structural damage. The possibility of volcanic activity or earthquakes requires that special construction techniques be employed so that buildings can absorb the shocks. All of these factors add considerable cost to the development and construction of buildings.

Off-Site Improvements. The adequacy of off-site improvements must be considered in relation to the use of the site. For example, commercial or industrial uses usually require wider streets, more parking, more lighting, and different modes of transportation than does residential use. Residential uses, however, need good streets, curbs, gutters, sewers, and lighting. They also require adequate commercial establishments, schools, recreational facilities, churches, and libraries. The analysis of off-site improvements requires that they be identified and their quantity and quality compared with those provided for similar developments.

Improvements

The physical characteristics of improvements include the size, shape, quality, condition, and components of major improvements *on* sites. Major improvements are usually structures such as houses or apartment,

---

[3]Although sometimes regarded as a locational characteristic, exposure does not involve transportation or transfer; thus, it is more properly regarded as a physical characteristic. See Edgar M. Hoover, *The Location of Economic Activity* (New York: McGraw-Hill, 1963), p. 91.

office, commercial, or industrial buildings. However, they could also include paving for a parking lot, golf courses, tennis courts, and other types of nonbuilding improvements. Secondary or support improvements include such structures as garages, barns, sheds, other agricultural buildings, shelters, and so on. Their physical characteristics also help determine the usefulness of a parcel of real estate.

An investor or owner-user of real estate should analyze the improvements for their ability to perform the functions for which they are intended. The analysis usually includes an evaluation of the architectural style, quality and types of construction, distribution of space, condition, and adequacy of building systems (e.g., elevators, heating, cooling, electrical, and plumbing). Even for single-family homes, experts may be required to evaluate the adequacy and condition of these items. In general, a building's physical characteristics must be evaluated with respect to (1) quality and condition and (2) functionality.

Quality and Condition.   A building's roof, walls, foundation, floors, ceilings, and service systems (air conditioning, heating, electrical, plumbing, elevators, etc.) can be evaluated for their quality and condition. Architects usually are employed to assure adequate quality in the construction of new buildings. Engineers may be required to evaluate the quality and condition of an existing or proposed building and its components. Although nonprofessionals' visual inspections of interior walls, ceilings, and floors may be adequate, the fees for professional analyses of nonvisible components, machinery, equipment, and systems are usually funds well spent.

Functionality.   The ability of a building to serve the purpose for which it was constructed is the essence of this characteristic. Older buildings must compete with newer buildings that have better designs, more modern styles, new equipment, and increased efficiency. New buildings must have the most appropriate designs, materials, and equipment, or other new buildings will be preferred. For example, a new hotel in a large western city experienced financial difficulties because it did not contain meeting rooms and convention facilities that two other hotels in the city had. Since much of the hotel business was for convention purposes, the hotel's occupancy rate was well below financial breakeven. The hotel's creditors foreclosed and sold it to a hotel chain at a loss of several million dollars. The new owners operated the hotel successfully by lowering room rates.

LOCATIONAL CHARACTERISTICS

As we discussed in Chapter 10, the locational characteristics of a property include the time-distance relationships between the property and the common destinations of typical users. The time-distance relationships are termed *linkages,* and the sum of all its linkages compared with the sums of all linkages of competing properties, determines whether a property's location is desirable.

The concept of location and the nature of linkages are also discussed in this chapter for two reasons: to emphasize the nature of location as an element of real estate productivity; and to present a general procedure for analyzing a property's locational characteristics.

Location as an Element of Productivity

The role of location in real estate productivity is unique. Location is inherent to real estate and applies to no other good, product, or service. As Ratcliff stated:

> The essence of location derives from one of the elemental physical facts of life, the reality of space. We cannot conceive of existence without space; if there were no such thing, all objects and all life would have to be at one spot. If this happened to be the case, real estate would have no such quality as location; all real estate would be in the same place, equally convenient to every other piece of real estate and to every human activity and establishment. But under the physical laws of the universe, each bit of matter—each atom, molecule, stone, dog, house, and man—takes up space at or near the surface of the earth. As a result, no two objects can be at the same place at the same time. Necessarily, then, all people, animals, and objects are distributed in a spatial pattern.[4]

This description implies that the essence of location is transfer—the movement of people, goods, products, services, and communications among parcels of real estate. Thus, good locations have relatively low costs of transfer, and poor locations have relatively high costs of transfer. Transfer costs are all of the costs associated with overcoming the *friction of space* and include transportation costs (vehicle depreciation, gasoline, oil, electricity, and maintenance), time, and ease of movement.

Analyzing a Property's Locational Characteristics

The analysis of a property's locational characteristics requires identifying important *linkages,* ranking the importance of the linkages, and comparing the linkages with the linkages of other competing properties. The analysis of locational characteristics for residential properties is usually straightforward and easily accomplished; the analysis for commercial and industrial properties may be more involved. Such analysis often involves identification of input and output markets and various sites' transporta-

---

[4]Ratcliff, *Real EstateAnalysis,* p. 62.

tion costs to and from the markets. A favorable location can determine the desirability of a residential property and the success or failure of a business property.

Identify Linkages. The primary linkages for residential properties are usually with employment centers, schools, shopping, churches, professional services (e.g., doctors and lawyers), and recreational facilities (see Chapter 17). All important destinations should be identified, and distances and walking or driving times should be measured. A chart, as shown in Exhibit 24–1, and a map or schematic diagram can be used to record and visually evaluate the location.

The primary linkages for professional offices and commercial properties are with consumers—those who use the services and purchase the goods. To determine the important linkages, an analyst must first identify and delineate the relevant market. For convenience goods, the relevant market may be delineated by a radius of five or ten minutes' driving time around the site. Exhibit 24–1 illustrates the linkages for a potential shopping center site.

The market for professional services and shopping goods, for which people will spend time and travel several miles, may be the entire community or an even larger area. Regional shopping centers and hospitals, for example, may draw customers from several counties or states. Whatever the market area, the consumers' economic and social characteristics in that area must be analyzed to estimate the demand for the goods and services to be supplied. Other suppliers serving the same market area must be identified to determine whether any surplus or scarcity exists for the good or service. Finally, the capture rate for the commercial or professional activity must be estimated (see Chapter 11).

Measure the Costs of Linkages. After the linkages are identified, their costs must be estimated. Driving or walking times must be measured, and aggravation, hazards, and the potential for unusual delays considered. The effective cost of a linkage can be represented by the length of the line drawn on a map to represent the linkage or by the driving time weighted by other factors. For the shopping center site depicted in Exhibit 24–1, the lengths of the lines represent driving times adjusted for faster- or slower-than-average conditions.

Often the most important linkage for properties that serve families with children is with schools. Convenient and safe walking routes to school (particularly grade schools) are often a primary consideration when these families seek housing. Older households without young children often find convenience to work, shopping, and recreation to be more important.

EXHIBIT 24–1
LOCATIONAL CHARACTERISTICS POTENTIAL SHOPPING CENTER SITE

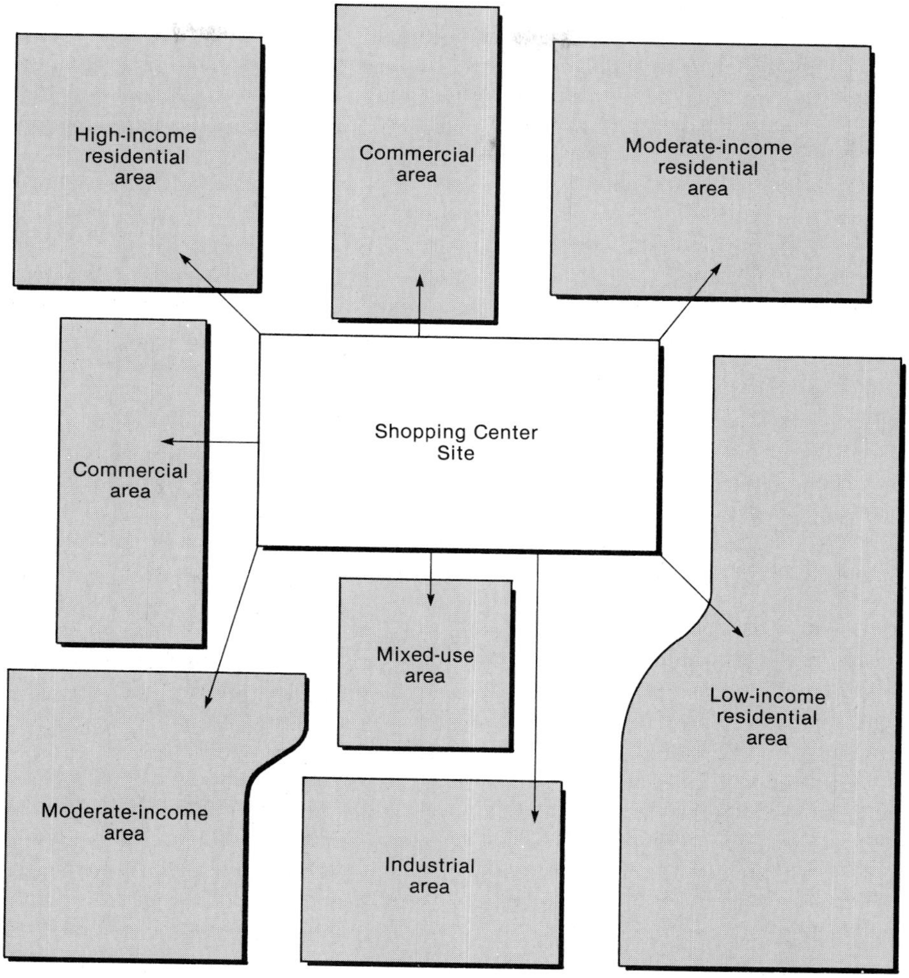

For industrial properties, dollar costs of linkages with both input and output markets often must be measured. As Chapter 10 shows, the optimal location for an industrial plant is the point between the two markets where total transfer costs are minimized. This point tends to be close to the input market for some products (e.g., steel, automobiles, and rubber) and close to the output market for others (e.g., milk, beer, and home building).

═══════════════ *Frame 24–2* ═══════════════

Locational or Physical Characteristics?

In the early part of the 20th Century, William Randolph Hearst, the newspaper magnate, constructed one of the grandest private residences in the world. The estate consisted of four castles, 240,000 acres of land, and 50 miles of frontage on the Pacific Ocean at San Simeon, California. The main castle overlooked the ocean and contained priceless collections of art, antiques, and Oriental rugs. It was many miles from work centers, shopping, churches, and schools. Obviously, the primary value-generating productivity determinant was physical in nature. The magnificent view, the grand structures, and the inaccessibility were much more important than accessibility, or location.

Compare Total Transfer Costs.   After identifying and measuring the transfer costs of a particular location, they can be estimated for other locations and compared with the subject location. The transfer costs for residential properties usually will not vary greatly among properties in a neighborhood, or perhaps even in an entire section of a community. Thus buyers in residential markets tend to identify neighborhoods or sectors within which all properties have acceptable locations. The decision on which property to purchase is thus based on other variables such as physical characteristics; in effect, location is held constant.

For commercial and industrial properties, the total transfer costs in dollars of various locations can be compared. If other factors are equal, the location having the lowest total transfer costs would be the location chosen.

LEGAL CHARACTERISTICS

The legal characteristics of a property are all of the rights, obligations, and restrictions concomitant with the ownership of the property. They include the quantity and quality of the estate (interest) in the property, public land use restrictions, private restrictions (deed and subdivision covenants), environmental laws and regulations, and tax laws and regulations affecting the property. Such laws and regulations may create advantages for a property as compared with other similar properties, or they may restrict the use of the property unfavorably, thus adversely affecting the property's productivity.

Estates

Chapter 2 presented the types of estates, or interests, in real property. Estates can range from fee simple to short-term leaseholds. They can be estates in possession or estates at some future time (reversions and remainders). Furthermore, they can be estates in severalty (single ownership) or joint estates (joint tenancy and tenancy in common). They can be life estates, determinable fee estates, or leaseholds. And leaseholds can range from long-term (99 years) to tenancy at sufferance. Obviously, the type of estate held by a property owner determines how productive the property is to him or her.

Public Restrictions

Zoning is the principal type of public restriction on land use. In Chapter 14 we noted that properties are often used to the maximum intensity permitted by the zoning ordinance. Thus, zoning tends to establish the upper limit on a property's productivity. While market forces might enable some properties to be used more intensively, such use might detract from the productivity of surrounding properties. Thus, zoning laws are imposed under the premise that the sum of the productivities of all properties in an area is greater with zoning than it would be with no restrictions. In other words, zoning laws attempt to prevent or reduce the effects of negative externalities and thereby to maximize overall productivity.

Private Restrictions

Restrictions imposed on a property by previous owners can affect the potential uses of real estate. As we explained in Chapter 2, restrictions imposed in deeds or subdivision recordings are valid, if they are reasonable and are not against public policy. Examples of such restrictions are limitations on the size of a building that can be constructed on a site, limitations on the specific uses of a property (such as single-family occupancy or educational activities), limitations on ownership (such as a particular church), and limitations on architectural style of buildings. Obviously, private restrictions, like public restrictions, may limit a property's productivity.

Environmental Laws and Regulations

All levels of government have enacted laws to help preserve the environment. Many of these laws have imposed restrictions and additional costs upon both the developers and users of real estate. While federal laws generally have been concerned with pollution standards and control, laws at the state and local levels have more directly affected land use. Important federal laws include the Water Pollution Control Act, the Clean Air Act, the Noise Control Act, the Safe Drinking Water Act, the River and Harbors Act, the Fish and Wildlife Act, the Marine Protection and Sanctuaries Act, and the National Environmental Policy Act.

A number of states, particularly the fastest-growing states, have passed laws protecting environmentally endangered lands, laws requiring analysis of the environmental impact of large developments, and laws requiring adequate planning and zoning by local jurisdictions. Properties in designated environmentally sensitive areas may be subject to severe development regulations and restrictions. And the preparation of environmental impact statements can add substantially to the cost of large developments.

Tax Laws and Regulations

Local taxation of property and federal taxation of income produced by property can greatly enhance some uses of a property and impede other uses. Such matters as depreciation deductions, interest expense and other deductions, and capital-gains treatment make some properties more productive than others. For example, large depreciation deductions have been allowed in the past on low-income residential properties. Such deductions lower taxable income, making these properties more productive than they otherwise would be. By treating some properties differently for tax purposes, the government often attempts to effect social policy. In the example above, the policy is to encourage the construction of more low-income housing. Another application of differential tax treatment to effect social policy can be seen in the proposal for enterprise zones (see Frame 24–3).

State and local property taxes can result in different levels of productivity for properties in different jurisdictions. Tax burdens vary greatly among states, and sometimes among counties within states (see Exhibit 24–2). Also, communities sometimes agree to reduce property taxes for industries which they recruit from other communities. They hope that the reduced property-tax burden will increase the firms' productivity sufficiently to convince firms to move to one community rather than other communities.

━━━━━━━━━━━━━━━━━━━━━━━ *Frame 24–3* ━━━━━━━━━━━━━━━━━━━━━━━

Enterprise Zones: A Proposal to Increase Real Estate Productivity in Depressed Areas of Our Cities

The concept of enterprise zones has been championed by two members of Congress, Rep. Robert Garcia (D–NY) and Rep. Jack Kemp (R–NY). Basically, the proposal is designed to make depressed areas of cities more attractive as business locations by providing a generous package of federal tax incentives to any business that locates in one of the designated zones. The following are among the many proposed incentives:

1. *Capital incentives to businesses locating in enterprise zones*
   □ Investment tax credits

□ Elimination of capital gain taxes on the sale of qualified zone property
□ Availability of Industrial Revenue Bonds for financing
2. *Labor incentives to businesses locating in Enterprise Zones*
   □ 10 percent tax credit for wages paid to zone employees
   □ An additional credit for wages paid to disadvantaged employees
   □ 5 percent tax credit could be claimed by employees for income earned in the zone

This plan has several advantages. First, it is national in scope and therefore does not foster regional competition for federal dollars. Second, it targets labor-intensive businesses to create more jobs where they are most needed. Finally, it does not require subsidies from the local areas being assisted by the program. At the time of this writing there is considerable uncertainty about the passage of this bill. It does represent a significant departure from the way cities have been helped by the federal government in the past.

Sources: R. Garcie, "Enterprise Zones: Restoring Economic Vitality to Inner Cities," *USA Today* (November 1982) pp. 50–53, and J. Kemp, "A Case for Enterprise Zones," *Nation's Business* (November 1982), pp. 54–56.

EXHIBIT 24–2
STATE AND LOCAL PER CAPITA TAX BURDEN IN FISCAL 1983–1984

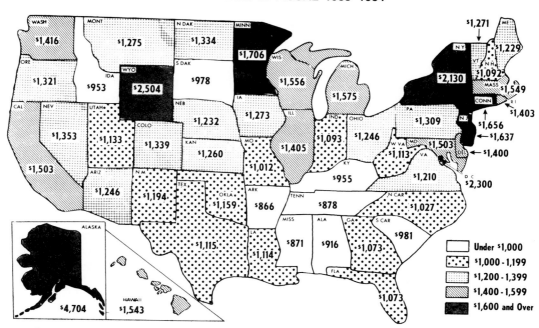

Source: Reproduced with permission of the publisher and copyright holder, Commerce Clearing House, Inc., Chicago, Illinois 60646.

ENVIRONMENTAL CHARACTERISTICS

A property's surroundings help determine its productivity. This includes the immediate neighborhood or district, the community, the region, and the nation. Positive or negative forces at each level affect the property in ways that make it more or less productive and desirable relative to other properties.

Neighborhood or District

This level of impact is the most direct and obvious. A property's physical environment is extremely important, but its economic and social environments must not be overlooked. The physical aspects of a neighborhood or district include size of structures, density of structures, width of streets, presence or absence of curbs and gutters, terrain, vegetation, quality and maintenance of private properties and public facilities, and the area's general attractiveness. Economic aspects include the income levels of residents or business firms and the value of properties. Social aspects include the residents' occupations; their educational levels; and their religious, ethnic, and racial characteristics. Moderate diversity in each category is usually desirable for maximum productivity. Homogeneity or wide diversity usually result in less-than-optimal values, especially in residential neighborhoods.

Community

At the community level, a property's productivity is usually determined by the availability of services (fire and police protection, garbage removal, and social services), the availability of facilities (schools, churches, shopping, and recreational and cultural facilities), the tax structure, and the political organization. An optimal combination of these results in a good "quality of life"—a general characteristic for which many communities strive (see Frame 24–4).

The availability of services and facilities is obviously necessary for maximum property values in communities. The impacts of the tax structure and political organization are not so evident. The tax structure must be fair and consistent with tax burdens imposed in similar communities. Tax burdens that are significantly heavier than those in other communities will tend to discourage new businesses and residents from coming to the community, and they may tend to drive existing residents and businesses away. On the other hand, low tax burdens usually reflect a low level of services and facilities, resulting in a lower quality of life than is available in other communities. Obviously, an optimal tax structure that will finance the optimal level of services and facilities is the goal toward which elected taxing officials must continually strive.

The political organization refers to the type of government in the community and its relative efficiency. Generally, elected officials should establish policy, and appointed managers should administer operations to carry out policy. Inefficiencies usually occur when policy makers attempt to administer and administrators attempt to set policy.

Overlapping governments and jurisdictions is another problem faced by many communities. County and city governments frequently have conflicting goals, policies, and laws that affect the same residents. There may be duplication of services and variations of service between city and noncity residents. Strains resulting from differing philosophies, policies, and procedures may appear among employees as well as among elected officials. The net result for residents is inefficiency and higher taxes than would otherwise be the case.

━━━━━━━━━━━━━━━ *Frame 24–4* ━━━━━━━━━━━━━━━

Best and Worst U.S. Cities

Rand McNally's 1985 edition of its *Places Rated Almanac* rates the 329 metropolitan areas in the United States as places in which to live. While highly controversial, the ratings attempt to measure the overall effect of such factors as climate, housing, health care, crime, transportation, education, culture, and economics. The 10 best and 10 worst metropolitan areas, according to these rankings, are:

Ten Best	Ten Worst
1. Pittsburgh, Pa.	1. Anderson, Ind.
2. Boston, Mass.	2. Rockford, Ill.
3. Raleigh-Durham, N.C.	3. Casper, Wyo.
4. San Francisco, Calif.	4. Gadsden, Ala.
5. Philadelphia, Pa.	5. Benton, Harbor, Mich.
6. Nassau-Suffolk, N.Y.	6. Albany, Ga.
7. St. Louis, Mo.	7. Dothan, Ala.
8. Louisville, Ky.	8. Modesto, Calif.
9. Norwalk, Conn.	9. Pine Bluff, Ark.
10. Seattle, Wash.	10. Yuba City, Calif.

Region

Trends and developments at the regional level can affect a property's productivity. A region is usually regarded as a state or a group of states. At this level, the availability of resources (e.g., coal, oil or gas), favorable climate or terrain, or interstate cooperation (such as regional banking laws) may affect the general desirability of properties in the region. Also, as we noted previously, tax burdens among states can vary substantially (again, see Exhibit 24–2).

Regional trends and their effects on property values can be dramatic. For example, in the 1950s and 1960s Appalachia was depressed because of the shift away from coal as the principal fuel. With the Arab oil embargo of 1973 the region became vibrant for a few years, only to lose much of its economic vibrancy in the 1980s as coal again lost out to oil. The migration of people to the Sunbelt is another regional phenomenon largely related to climate. Texas and Louisiana experienced great economic growth during the 1970s and early 1980s when oil and gas were in short supply. As supplies increased during the mid-1980s, however, the rate of economic growth declined. Properties in these regions increased in value faster than the rate of inflation when oil was in short supply, but fell behind the rate of inflation when oil prices dropped.

Nation

Many developments and trends at the national level have profound effects on property productivity and value. Monetary policy, fiscal policy, debt-management policy, and special-assistance policy provide the influence at the national level. Monetary policy deals with the availability and cost of credit. Restrictive monetary policy probably affects real estate more than any other economic good because of real estate's reliance on credit. An ample supply of funds at moderate cost is usually necessary for real estate to be a productive and desirable asset.

Fiscal policy involves the taxation and spending policies of the government. Real estate has long enjoyed certain tax benefits that have made it more productive and valuable than it otherwise would be (see Chapter 22). Shifts in tax policy can have dramatic effects on real estate. The government's spending plans can also have important effects on real estate. Housing subsidies, highway construction, defense spending, farm subsidies, and national parks are only a few of the programs where government spending affects real estate. One of the most dramatic efforts was the construction of interstate highways during the 1960s and 1970s that opened up vast new areas of the country for development. The impact upon property productivity and values in much of the country was incalculable.

REAL ESTATE PRODUCTIVITY AND BUSINESS FUNCTIONS

As we noted, real estate is productive, and therefore it has value and is bought and sold in the market. Households, businesses, institutions, and government agencies need and want various types of real estate. Developers produce new real estate and those who demand properties purchase it and existing real estate. The needs of real estate users change: Families grow, divide, and disappear. Business firms, institutions, and government agencies expand or contract. Thus whereas some people and organizations demand real estate, others need to sell it. Real estate also must be managed for efficient operation. Owners manage their own properties or hire managers. Finally, real estate usually must be financed, and one of the newest and most popular methods of financing is syndication.

Businesses are formed to market, manage, develop, construct, and finance real estate. In performing these functions, businesses both create and exploit the productivity of real estate. They create new real estate that is productive, and they perform such services as marketing, financing, and management that help owners to exploit the productivity of real estate. The existence of all real estate businesses depends on the physical, locational, legal, and environmental aspects of real estate—the sources of its productivity. The following sections provide a brief overview of these major types of real estate businesses. We describe them in greater depth in Chapters 25–27.

Real Estate Marketing and Management

Marketing is the business function that "greases the wheels" of real estate buying and selling. Professionals perform marketing to attempt to match those who demand real estate with the supply provided by developers, builders, and owners. Management is the operation of real estate to achieve its maximum efficiency and thus its greatest productivity.

Both the marketing and management functions may be performed by owners and their employees or by hired firms that specialize in these areas. An owner who attempts to sell her own home and a construction company that attempts to sell its inventory of homes are examples of owners' performing the marketing function. Homeowners and large industrial companies are examples of owners that usually manage their own properties. In contrast, many sellers employ real estate brokerage firms to market their properties, and many owners of apartment and commercial properties employ property-management firms to manage their properties.

The objective of marketing is to identify, create, and sell real estate having the optimal productivity characteristics to those who need those characteristics. Similarly, the objective of management is to maximize the operating productivity of properties to meet owners' objectives most efficiently. Thus, both functions are intended to maximize real estate productivity. The businesses themselves are successful if they add productivity sufficient to induce owners to employ the firms.

Real Estate Development and Construction

There is a continuous need for new real estate. Old properties wear out—both physically and locationally—and must be replaced. Population continues to expand; more people require housing and the services and products provided by commercial and industrial properties. People's needs for various types of real estate shift with changing technology, customs, traditions, and social mores. And people's demand shifts upward as incomes increase and the country's wealth expands.

For all of these reasons, the business of developing and constructing new properties is a response to the need for productive real estate. The importance of the function of providing new real estate is attested by the fact that the development and construction industry is the single largest industry in the United States. It provides employment for some six to seven million persons, and it accounts for roughly 10 percent of the country's gross national product.

Real Estate Syndication

As we pointed out previously, marketing and financing are important functions in distributing the benefits of real estate to those who need them. *Syndication* contains aspects of both functions. It involves a division of property ownership among a number of investors, either by a corporate, limited-partnership, or trust arrangement. By dividing and marketing ownership interests, the investment benefits of real estate are distributed more widely. And, by bringing together a number of investors to purchase shares or interests in properties, syndicators provide the financing for many real estate projects that otherwise probably could not be produced.

Syndication has become very popular in recent years. Many properties are too large for single investors, even large institutions that usually seek asset diversification as well as yield.

Innovations to Enhance Real Estate Productivity

Technological and organizational innovations continually increase the productivity of real estate and the ability of investors to evaluate that productivity. Advances in construction techniques have virtually eliminated physical height restrictions on buildings and have greatly increased the usable space in buildings. Computerized controls for heating and cooling systems have dramatically improved building efficiency. Computer models have resulted in a whole range of investment analysis techniques for real estate. Even hand-held calculators enable investors to perform analyses that only the largest computers could perform as recently as 15 years ago.

Telecommunications is another area of innovation that is expected to have dramatic effects on real estate productivity. Many face-to-face meetings will be replaced by "image-to-image" discussions and conferences via long-distance electronic hookups. The time and costs of travel may be greatly reduced, allowing real estate investors and professionals to spend this time more productively. Advanced telecommunications systems are beginning to be installed in modern office buildings, giving lessees more efficient communications and lessors another source of productivity and profits.

Finally, organizational innovations are occurring and will continue to occur in real estate businesses. Trends are leading both to greater vertical and horizontal integration of real estate operations.[5] Vertically, a number of brokerage firms have recently merged with financing and development firms. And some appraisal firms have combined with brokerage and financing firms. The goal of many firms such as Sears, Roebuck and Company, Bank of America, Prudential Insurance Co., and Empire of America, is to provide a "department store" of real estate and financial services.

Many real estate firms are expanding horizontally through merger and franchise operations. Nationwide chains of brokerage and financing firms are now common, and the trend is likely to continue. Both vertical and horizontal trends probably will go on, as large firms attempt to provide integrated real estate and financial services and to expand their operations nationwide.

OVERVIEW

Real estate is productive and has value because of its physical, locational, legal, and environmental characteristics. As a combination of the four factors of production (land, labor, capital, and enterpreneurship), real estate serves fundamental needs of people (shelter, convenience, and comfort), and thus its owners are entitled to a return. Physical characteristics pertain to both the site and improvements and include such matters as size, shape, soil fertility, quality of construction, condition, and functional adequacy. Location is concerned with the time-distance relationships be-

---

[5]Vertical integration refers to a combining of firms that perform different functions in the provision of real estate services, while horizontal integration refers to a combining of firms that perform the same real estate function.

tween a property and common destinations of people who occupy the property or the points of origin of people who come to the property.

Legal characteristics involve the types of estates that may be owned, public and private restrictions, and other laws and regulations governing the use of property. By determining the division of benefits and responsibilities for owners and users (lessees) of a property, the legal characteristics enhance or diminish a property's total productivity. Generally, the greater the owners' legal interest and the fewer the restrictions, the more productive a property is to its owners or users.

Because real estate is fixed in location, it is subject to environmental (external) influences. Such influences can be analyzed at the neighborhood, community, regional, and national levels. Physical, economic, social, and legal-governmental conditions and trends at each level help determine a property's productivity. As properties are operated in this multitiered environment, real estate owners and analysts must be aware of shifts among investment vehicles, geographic areas, and property types that raise or lower property productivity.

Finally, we discuss the role of productivity in creating various business functions. Because real estate is productive, it is created, financed, bought, sold, operated, and analyzed. The business activities of marketing, management, development, construction, and syndication create and exploit real estate productivity. Simultaneously, technological and organizational innovations are occurring that will change both the nature of the product and real estate businesses. The roles of the computer and telecommunications, the vertical integration of real estate functions, and the horizontal integration of real estate firms are some of the innovations that are expected to enhance real estate productivity.

TEST YOURSELF

Explain the following terms and concepts presented in this chapter.

1. Productivity.
2. Amenities.
3. On-site improvements.
4. Off-site improvements.
5. Location.
6. Transfer costs.
7. Legal characteristics.
8. Environmental characteristics.
9. Linkage.
10. Physical characteristics.

Answer the following multiple choice questions.

1. When real estate analysts compare linkages among properties, they are concerned with
   a. Environmental characteristics.
   b. Physical characteristics.
   c. Legal characteristics.
   d. Financial characteristics.
   e. Location.

2. The size, shape, vegetation, and terrain of a site being considered for development of a shopping center are types of
   a. Environmental characteristics.
   b. Physical characteristics.
   c. Legal characteristics.
   d. Financial characteristics.
   e. Location.

3. The productivity of real estate results in values that hold what relationship to the costs of real estate?
   a. Higher.
   b. Lower.
   c. Equal.
   d. Higher and lower.
   e. Indeterminate.

4. A well-managed commercial property that is physically appropriate, well constructed, and attractive might fail due to?
   a. Poor management
   b. Inappropriate zoning.
   c. Competition.
   d. Poor location.
   e. Inadequate physical characteristics.

5. A view of the ocean from a seaside condominium would be regarded as a(n)
   a. Locational characteristic.
   b. Physical characteristic.
   c. Legal characteristic.
   d. Environmental characteristic.
   e. Financial characteristic.

ADDITIONAL READINGS

Barlowe, Raleigh. *Land Resource Economics*, 3rd. ed. Englewood Cliffs, N.J., Prentice-Hall, 1978, Chap. 9.

Haggett, Peter. *Locational Analysis in Human Geography*. New York: St. Martin's Press, 1966.

Hoover, Edgar M. *The Location of Economic Activity*. New York: McGraw-Hill, 1963.

Lawrence, Richard L. *The Selection of Retail Locations*. New York: McGraw-Hill, 1958.

Ratcliff, Richard U. *Real Estate Analysis*. New York: McGraw-Hill, 1961, Chaps. 3–4.

Ratcliff, Richard U. *Urban Land Economics*. New York: McGraw-Hill, 1949, Chap. 12.

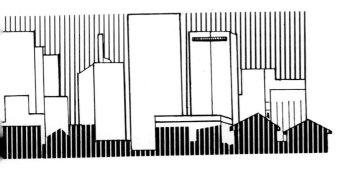

25
Real Estate Marketing and Management

INTRODUCTION

Real estate businesses are organized and operated to create, expand, and exploit the productivity of real estate. In this chapter we focus on two important types of real estate businesses—marketing and management. Marketing businesses or departments primarily advertise, promote, and distribute various types of real estate to those who need them, while management businesses or departments operate real estate efficiently to extract its maximum productivity. Although owners sometimes perform both the marketing and management functions, specialized knowledge and abilities are required to perform them efficiently—especially for larger properties. Thus they are usually performed by specialized real estate firms or by subsidiaries of large, multifaceted firms such as AmeriFirst Management (a subsidiary of AmeriFirst Federal Savings and Loan) or BA Management (a subsidiary of Bank of America).

Marketing and management are pervasive functions. Marketing must be performed by real estate brokerage firms, land developers, builders, and owners of properties. Real estate brokerage firms specialize in the marketing function, primarily serving owners and purchasers of existing properties. They also may serve developers and builders in identifying market needs and finding purchasers of their products—developed land and improved properties. Nevertheless, development and construction firms often have their own marketing departments, and owners sometimes sell (or attempt to sell) their own properties.

Similarly, management must be performed for all existing properties, although some require much less than others. Vacant land, for example, requires much less management than a large apartment building. But even for vacant land debt must be managed, taxes must be paid, and a program of use or sale must be designed and operated. Although owners often manage small properties, most larger income-producing properties are managed by professional property-management firms.

======================================= Frame 25–1 =======================================

Professional Organizations and Designations

Several professional organizations serve the marketing and management functions of real estate. They are all affiliated with the National Association of REALTORS® and award professional designations to those members who complete educational and training programs and attain substantial experience in the field. These organizations and their professional designations are:

> *REALTORS National Marketing Institute (RNMI)*
>   Professional designations:
>   CRB (Certified Residential Broker)
>   CCIM (Certified Commercial-Investment Member)
> *Society of Industrial REALTORS (SIR)*
>   Professional designation:
>   SIR (Senior Industrial REALTOR)
> *Institute of Real Estate Management (IREM)*
>   Professional designations:
>   CPM (Certified Property Manager)
>   ARM (Accredited Resident Manager)
>   AMO (Accredited Management Organization)

See Frame 17–1 for a listing of professional designations in appraisal.

Nature of the Marketing and Management Functions

Marketing is more than selling, and management is more than collecting rents. Marketing includes the identification of needs for various types of real estate (market analysis), devising ways of meeting those needs, publicizing their availability through advertising and promotion, bringing together the suppliers of real estate with those who need it, effecting transactions, and providing post-purchase education and comfort to new owners. Real estate marketing thus is much broader in scope than real estate *brokerage,* which connotes primarily the handling of legal arrangements involved in transactions. It is also much broader than advertising, promotion, or selling—all of which are important functions within the marketing concept.

The property management function is the process of meeting owners' objectives through the efficient operation of real property. Usually this process requires the manager to maximize a property's net income while maintaining and preserving the long-term usefulness of the property. The long-term utility must be preserved in order to maximize the value of the property for resale at the end of the ownership cycle. To accomplish these objectives, a property manager plans, organizes, and controls the operation and maintenance of a property.

Need for Specialized Marketing and Management Firms

While owners (including developers and builders) can perform the marketing and property management functions, they usually are not primarily interested in or trained in these functions. The specialized knowledge and effort required to perform these functions efficiently and effectively usually means that professional marketers and managers can perform them better and more cheaply. Some of the specific forces and trends leading to this reality are:

1. Technological Advancements. Specialized knowledge is needed for both functions. Many buildings contain complex systems for heating, air conditioning, and security. Computerized access to market listings, record-keeping, tax reporting, and systems control require considerable technical knowledge. Even more important, legal rights and obligations exist between owners and tenants, and a manager must always be aware of potential legal problems. Procedures for dealing with tenants' complaints must be efficient and fair. Tenant relations must be developed professionally and consistently within the constraints of the legal requirements. Buyers and sellers must be brought together, and transactions must be effected within the framework of the legal rights and obligations created by the contract for sale. Marketing professionals usually understand the legal and psychological aspects involved in buying and selling.

2. Absentee Ownership. Many income-producing properties are owned by people or firms who rarely see the properties. The management must be hired, and professional marketing firms must be employed when the property is sold. Although many individual investors own properties away from their own communities, the more important types of absentee owner are, of course, large institutions and investor groups. Life insurance companies, pension funds, real estate investment trusts, and syndicates own properties and require the services of professional marketing and management firms.

3. Urbanization. As the population of the country has grown, it has become increasingly concentrated in urban areas. The rural population continues to decline as a percentage of total population, and even the rural population has taken on the values and attitudes of the urbanites. These trends have caused the development, construction, marketing, and management of all types of urban properties to become necessary and profitable. The increasing complexity of real estate markets, legal requirements, social relationships, and technological innovations have greatly expanded the need for professional assistance in marketing and managing urban properties.

DEVELOPING A MARKETING STRATEGY

The Market Model of Monopolistic Competition

Real estate markets are perhaps best characterized by the monopolistic-competition model of market behavior (see Chapter 10). This model recognizes that firms and properties are different from each other, yet compete vigorously with each other. To the extent that a property or a firm is different from other properties and firms, it contains some element of monopoly. For example, only one property can occupy a particular location, or only one firm may be known as the oldest, most stable firm in a city. Yet the property or the firm is in competition with other properties and firms.

This competition tends to focus on nonprice matters. A property has a better location or is better able to perform a particular function than other properties that may be purchased for similar prices. Similarly, a real estate marketing firm may claim to be able to sell a property faster or more efficiently than other firms, although they all charge similar commission rates.

The model of monopolistic competition suggests that real estate marketing firms should develop a marketing strategy, and that they should be aware of the monopolistic elements in the properties they attempt to market. The strategy should focus on the needs of those in the market and should employ the principles of market segmentation and specialization. Also included in the strategy should be the development of an image for the firm and procedures for attaining competitive advantage.

Identifying Market Needs

Professional marketers identify market needs by segregating potential buyers into various categories. For example, potential home buyers may be divided into age groups, family size, income class, and social status. Each category or subcategory (e.g., high-income, small-family, ages 30–40) is then analyzed in depth to determine what factors are considered important to purchasers of housing. Exhibit 25–1 shows a two-dimensional market grid for identifying market needs. A three- or four-dimensional grid would allow an even more detailed analysis of buyer needs.

EXHIBIT 25-1
MARKET GRID OF HOUSING NEEDS

Characteristics of Potential Buyers	Needs						
	Good Location	Prestige	Space for Entertainment	Work Arrangement	Sense of Excitement	Space for Children	Quietness
Age group:							
20–30	L	L	L	L	L	L	L
30–40	M	H	M	L	L	L	L
40–50	H	H	H	M	H	H	L
Over 50	H	M	H	L	H	H	M
Family size:							
1. Single person	H	L	L	M	M	L	M
2. Married couple	H	M	M	H	M	L	M
3. One parent and children	H	M	M	L	H	M	H
4. Two parents and children	M	H	M	L	H	H	L
Income class:							
$20,000–40,000	H	L	L	L	L	H	L
$40,000–60,000	M	M	M	H	M	H	L
$60,000–80,000	L	H	M	H	H	M	M
Above $80,000	L	H	H	L	H	M	H
Social status:							
Low	M	L	L	L	M	M	L
Medium	H	M	M	H	M	H	M
High	L	H	H	L	H	L	H

Legend: High (H), Medium (M), Low (L)

Meeting Market Needs

Note that the market grid does not focus on ways of meeting needs; there may be several ways to meet a need. For example, the need for a good location might be met by an apartment downtown within walking distance of stores, schools, churches, and theaters. Or it might be met by proximity to shopping centers, bus lines, or by the provision of a private transportation system. Prestige might be created by proximity to a high-income area, unusual design, attractive grounds, or exclusivity. Space for work at home could be provided by a separate room, a convertible bedroom, or a desk in the master bedroom. Quietness could be obtained by isolation, thick insulation, concrete dividing walls, room arrangement, and other design characteristics (such as placement of bedrooms away from common walls). A sense of excitement could be created by landscaped grounds, by design features such as vaulted ceilings, or by proximity to such recreational facilities as a golf course, swimming pool, or tennis courts.

The objective of such analysis is to identify needs in the market so ways can be devised to meet those needs. It must be recognized, of course, that a marketing firm cannot begin to meet all needs, and so must focus on some segment of the market. By concentrating on one or a few segments, the specialized firm should be able to serve that part of the market better than other firms. In effect, the firm will create for itself an area of competitive advantage.

Developing the Firm's Image

Real estate firms tend to be perceived by the public in ways that may or may not contribute to their business success. Some perceptions may be negative and contribute to a firm's failure or poor performance. As part of the marketing strategy, a firm's management should determine as precisely as possible the firm's public perceptions. The actual image may then be compared with the desired image, and ways of achieving the latter can be formulated.

It should, of course, be emphasized that an image cannot replace substance. If a firm does not provide superior service, it cannot convince the public that it is a service-oriented firm. Similarly, a firm that does not participate in or contribute to community activities cannot hope to create the image of a community-oriented firm.

What are some desirable types of images that firms have created and used successfully? In a community one or two firms usually have an image of being old, reliable, and stable. They have been in business for many years and have survived recessions, and grown in prosperous times. The firm enjoys a relationship of trust with community leaders and major investors.

Another image is that of the young, fast-growing, dynamic firm. The firm usually advertises heavily, provides a variety of services, and has young managers. It may attempt to specialize by serving a younger-than-average clientele, a particular income group, or particular property types, such as moderately priced detached houses and condominiums.

In attempting to create a particular image, a firm can use several approaches. Participation in community activities by employees or associates, advertising, qualifications and competence of employees and associates, their personal appearance and dress, appearance and location of the office, and the ability to serve customers' needs and resolve their problems—all determine how the public regards the firm. The use of a logo or an easily-remembered name helps in keeping the firm in the public's mind.

Developing a Marketing Speciality

In segmenting real estate markets to identify the needs of various subgroups, marketing firms often recognize opportunities to specialize by concentrating on specific property types. Although these specialties may be identified as accommodating specific needs, we should understand that a subcategory of potential purchasers may find new ways to fill their needs. For example, a real estate marketer who specializes in small medical office buildings may find doctors shifting to multiunit buildings in medical office parks. Nevertheless, a focus on ways of meeting needs, rather than the needs themselves, may help identify the existing approaches to need satisfaction. We present below the various property types in which some real estate marketing firms specialize. These, of course, are broad categories and may comprise a number of subcategories.

1. *Residential properties:* Many marketing firms specialize in selling small residential properties. These include single-family detached houses; duplexes, triplexes, and quadraplexes; condominiums; attached housing units; and cooperative apartments. Marketing specialists in this area attempt to match the desires, needs, and financial capabilities of people seeking housing with the inventory of properties for sale.

2. *Commercial properties:* This includes most income-producing properties such as office buildings, apartments, shopping centers, motels, hotels, restaurants, stores, and specialty properties. Commercial-property specialists are aware of the availability of such properties and match them with investors or firms that may need them.

3. *Industrial properties:* Warehouses, factories, assembly plants, processing plants, and industrial parks and land fall into this category. These properties are typically used by their owners and not leased. Industrial marketing firms must be knowledgeable about the requirements of different types of industrial firms and the availability of industrial properties or industrially zoned land.

4. *Agricultural properties:* Some marketing firms specialize in farms, ranches, orchards, groves, grain elevators, feed mills, and other types of agricultural properties. The geographic scope of their business is usually larger than that of other types of real estate marketing operations. Obviously, considerable technical knowledge about the type of agricultural properties in which they specialize is important to a successful marketing effort.

5. *Land:* In this context, land means undeveloped and unimproved land that is ripe, or shortly will become ripe, for development.

Although such land currently may be used for agriculture, its value is determined by its potential for development. Some firms purchase land for development, develop the land into buildable sites, and then sell the sites to builders. Other firms purchase such land for long-term investment or speculation. They may obtain the zoning required for development, hold the land, and sell it to developers when the time is right. Land-marketing firms must be particularly cognizant of city growth trends and the political and legal requirements for development.

ANALYZING THE BUYING PROCESS

Buyers go through several stages leading to a major purchase decision. Real estate marketing specialists must know these steps and be able to identify the stage in which a buyer may be. Although a marketing strategy is important in directing the marketing effort of real estate firms, it is not sufficient to guarantee success. Effective coordination of buyers' needs and available properties can be achieved most efficiently by analyzing the buying process and tailoring the marketing effort to the steps in the process.

Steps in the Buying Process

Kotler identifies five steps in the buying process for a major purchase.[1] Each step may be long or short, quite complex or relatively simple. A marketing specialist must be prepared to help a buyer through each step by resolving factual and emotional issues (see Exhibit 25–2).

Problem Recognition. In this step, buyers become aware of a need. Apartment dwellers may want a detached home, or current homeowners may develop a need for a larger or more expensive home because of the birth of a child or an increase in income. Similarly, empty nesters[2] may decide they need smaller quarters in attached housing or a condominium. Business firms, educational institutions, or government agencies may need larger or different quarters because of increased business or an impending move. Whatever its source, the need creates tension in the prospective buyer, a tension that can be relieved only by fulfillment of the need.

---

[1]Philip Kotler, *Marketing Management: Analysis, Planning, and Control*, 5th ed. (Englewood Cliffs, N.J.: Prentice-Hall, 1984), chap. 4.

[2]Empty-nesters are parents whose children are grown and have left home.

EXHIBIT 25–2
STEPS IN THE BUYING PROCESS

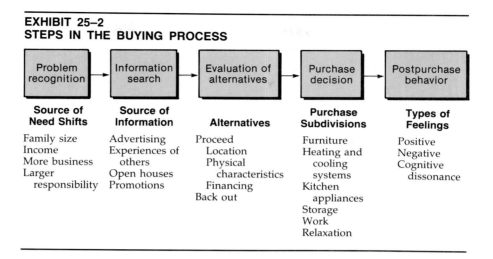

Problem recognition	Information search	Evaluation of alternatives	Purchase decision	Postpurchase behavior
Source of Need Shifts	**Source of Information**	**Alternatives**	**Purchase Subdivisions**	**Types of Feelings**
Family size	Advertising	Proceed	Furniture	Positive
Income	Experiences of	Location	Heating and	Negative
More business	others	Physical	cooling	Cognitive
Larger	Open houses	characteristics	systems	dissonance
responsibility	Promotions	Financing	Kitchen	
		Back out	appliances	
			Storage	
			Work	
			Relaxation	

Information Search.   After buyers acknowledge a need, they begin to seek information about alternative solutions. They become aware of real estate advertising, experiences of others, news, and educational opportunities that provide information. For example, a family who never reads the classified real estate ads will probably begin doing so when they decide to seek new or different housing.

During this step a real estate marketer should provide information about available properties and about the buying process itself. The purchase of a home or a major investment is often a traumatic experience for buyers, and the more information they receive, the better they are able to deal with their questions and fears.

Activities during this stage usually produce a sequence of changes in a buyer's mind from perceived need to purchase conviction. The information search leads to awareness of alternatives, preference for one alternative over others, and the conviction that one alternative is the best solution.

Evaluation of Alternatives.   After potential buyers have conducted an information search, they proceed with a purchase or back out entirely. In most cases, the buyers will proceed with the purchase alternative that best meets their perceived needs, within their financial constraints. One possibility, however, is that the buyers will decide the risk of financial strain more than offsets the benefits of the purchase. Thus, the purchase decision is a function of the perceived risk—the possibilities that the purchase is financially unwise or that the best alternative will not meet the perceived needs.

In evaluating alternatives, buyers usually identify the characteristics of the product that are most important to them (such as location, number of bedrooms, quality of construction, and attractive lot). They evaluate the benefits that they expect to be provided by the characteristics of each alternative property and balance the benefits against the price and ease of purchase. Most buyers are faced with a financial constraint, and they must usually trade off some less desirable characteristics for favorable characteristics that are more important to them. For example, a family with school-age children may be willing to give up a highly modern kitchen in favor of a location convenient to schools.

Purchase Decision. After evaluating alternatives, buyers decide whether to proceed with a purchase. They may decide to go no further in the buying process—to stick with what they have. None of the alternatives may be sufficiently better to justify the higher price. And the increased risk of not being able to meet higher financing costs may cause the buyers to reevaluate their problem. They may, however, decide to proceed with the transaction by making the purchase decision.

The purchase decision is the manifestation of favorable prepurchase activity. The buyers have gathered information and evaluated the alternatives; they now decide which is the best alternative. A commitment is made to purchase. The significance of this step is that it may open new areas for decisions by the buyers. These decisions, which are derived from the primary decision, are termed *secondary decisions.*

The purchase of a new or different home often requires several secondary decisions. For example, buyers often must obtain financing, buy new furnishings and decorations, and arrange for remodeling or rehabilitation work. They must now go through the buying process for each of these items. The real estate marketer can help solidify the home purchase decision by providing information and helping the buyers evaluate the alternatives. He can, for example, explain the financing options offered by major lenders, suggest furnishing arrangements and stores where furnishings can be purchased, and identify remodeling and rehabilitation firms. By doing these things, the marketer keeps the buyers from becoming overwhelmed by secondary decisions and thus agreeable to completion of the transaction.

Postpurchase Behavior. Although buyers perceive needs, they must also incur a cost—for real estate, a heavy cost—to have those needs satisfied. Thus the purchase of a major asset is seen both positively and negatively: positively, as a resolution of a problem or need; negatively, as a cost and punishment. Most purchasers question whether they purchased the right home, whether they should have stayed where they were, whether they should have taken on so much debt, whether they paid too much, and whether the house will hold its value. They may question whether their problem has been solved and feel they are being punished for a bad decision. This anxiety has been termed *cognitive dissonance*—awareness of mixed emotions.

Previous clients, both sellers and buyers, are often a real estate marketer's best source of advertising. They also can provide much repeat business and recommendations to other prospective clients. Therefore it is highly important for real estate marketers to ensure that buyers are satisfied both with their new purchase and with the marketing service. To accomplish this objective, real estate marketers should practice good *follow-up procedures.* They can visit new purchasers in their homes, introduce them to neighbors, point out what a good (low) price they paid, remark on the attractiveness of the house, and review other favorable aspects of the purchase decision. The objective is to create satisfied customers who will employ the marketing firm again when they wish to sell the house and purchase another one. Since a large part of the business of most real estate marketing firms comes from referrals, smart firms attempt to develop customers who will report a favorable experience and relationship to other homeowners and prospective purchasers.

Roles in the Buying Process

A real estate marketer should carefully analyze the role that each person plays in a buying group such as a family or a business. One member of a family may dominate the decision-making process, whereas another may influence the decision and a third member may actually purchase the property and be the principal user. When a business purchases a property, a senior vice-president may be the decision maker, lower staff may be influencers, the president may sign the papers, and workmen may be the principal users. Kotler identifies the roles as those of initiators, influencers, deciders, buyers, and users.[3]

Initiators.   Initiators originate the purchase idea. They first feel a need and express it to others. For example, a pregnant wife may be the first member of a family to realize that a small apartment will not be adequate for a larger family. Or a company vice-president may first see that the firm's plant should be expanded. Such realizations then are expressed to other group members for consideration.

Influencers.   Influencers stimulate, suggest, persuade, or provide information to the decision maker(s). In a family, some members may be influencers rather than decision makers. The husband or wife in some fam-

---

[3]Kotler, *Marketing Management*, chap. 4.

ilies may be the decision maker, while the other spouse and children are influencers. In other families, the decision-making process may be a joint and equal effort between both husband and wife or among all family members. In firms, important decisions may be made by one person (say, the president), by a senior management group, or by a board of directors.

Influencers may also be outsiders. Sales representatives, friends, advertising media, and promotional efforts may be important influencers. Such influencers may work indirectly through other influencers, as when advertising depicting an efficient or pleasant kitchen convinces a wife to influence her husband to buy a certain house.

Real estate marketers should attempt to determine the important influences and influencers in any buying situation. Children, friends, husband, wife, or business colleagues should not be overlooked. The proper types of sales efforts directed at influencers may yield large dividends.

Deciders.   These may be husbands or wives in families, or presidents or general managers of firms. In some families, the entire family may make decisions democratically. In business firms, some types of decisions are not made by a single person but by the board of directors or a management team. Real estate marketers should attempt to identify the decision maker(s) and direct appropriate marketing efforts toward them.

Buyers.   Buyers actually consummate the transaction. They may or may not be deciders. For example, the wife in a family may be the decider, while the husband may handle the purchase. Or the board of directors of a business firm may decide to purchase a new office building, but the president implements the decision.

Users.   People who use a purchased service, product, or property are termed *users*. In the purchase of most homes, the entire family uses it, although the wife and children may use it to a greater extent than the husband. In a manufacturing firm, the factory is used by the workers, although they did not make the decision to purchase it. They may also be influences, however, in convincing management that new or better facilities are needed.

Objectives of Buying-Process Analysis

The primary objective of buying-process analysis is to serve the needs of customers better. This analysis by professional real estate marketers helps marketers perform a better service in enabling both buyers and sellers to realize their objectives.

Identification of the step of the buying process that a buyer is in enables the marketer to direct the appropriate type of information to the prospect. For example, if the prospect is in the prepurchase activity step, the marketer should provide information relevant to that step. The marketer will probably lose the sale if she attempts to force a decision and close the sale at this point. Similarly, identification of the roles played by various participants can enable her to direct the appropriate sales messages to them.

MANAGING PROPERTIES

Planning is the primary concern of the real estate manager. Effective planning and decision making stem from careful analysis of data about the situation. The first task of a newly appointed property manager should be the development of a comprehensive economic analysis of the property to be supervised. The analysis (or survey) should encompass the entire operation; it is vital to the success of decisions made about any phase of the enterprise. The data collected help the manager develop a marketing program, an appropriate accounting system, and an inventory of the property's current physical condition and future maintenance requirements.

The Management Survey

The Institute of Real Estate Management defines the management survey as a comprehensive analysis of an income property. An important purpose of the survey is to evaluate the physical condition of the property. Another aim is to determine the property's relationship to its neighborhood and to the market in general. Finally, an analysis of income, expenses, and alternative uses of the property allows the manager to recommend a plan of action to the owner. The following topics are typically covered in the management survey.

Inventory of Physical Real Property.   Both the interior and exterior of the property are inventoried with regard to their condition and functionality. Suggested repairs and improvements are noted, along with their estimated cost. The physical inventory data will ultimately provide the cost information needed when income projections are prepared.

Neighborhood Analysis.   This portion of the survey describes the long-range desirability of the property's location and indicates the current stage of the neighborhood's life cycle. Is the area growing, stable or declining? What important forces are determining the neighborhood's trends? This information helps set rental schedules. The following items also should be considered:

1. Traffic patterns.
2. Transportation facilities.
3. Age and condition of other neighborhood buildings.
4. Area land uses and zoning.
5. Population characteristics/trends.
6. Access to shopping.
7. Quality and location of educational facilities.
8. Direct competition in the neighborhood.

Market/Tenant Analysis. This deals with past tenant history and the various sources of tenant income. Each lease is examined to determine its date of termination, renewal options, and current rental income. What is the vacancy rate for the complex, and how does that rate compare with other similar properties? Have tenants made timely rent payments? Not only are leases analyzed, but part of this research also deals with tenants' incomes. What is the main source of present and future tenants' income? With an understanding of local rents and tenants' income sources, the manager can make appropriate decisions.

Gross Income Analysis. The survey should include the calculation of gross income per unit and per square foot of rentable area. These data are compared to competitive properties to develop an appropriate rent schedule. Some allowance should be made for variations in services provided by different buildings. Items such as parking, tenant services, extra storage, swimming pools, and utilities affect the reported gross income level. Recommendations depend on the current rental market and the competition for tenants.

Operating-Expense Analysis. Due to the competitive situation, it is often impossible for a complex to produce higher rents. A careful investigation of a property's operating expenses may reveal potential savings. Beginning with an operating statement prepared for income tax purposes, the manager develops a forecast operating statement. A statement of current expenses does not indicate the true cost of earning gross income, since some expenses may be deferred, whereas others are incurred only as repairs are made or items are replaced. For this reason, a stabilized expense statement that includes an annual sum to cover the replacement of short-lived items should be constructed. This statement outlines the projected expenses and indicates the true annual cost of earning annual gross income. From this a stabilized net-operating-income report can be prepared.

It is also recommended that each item on the operating statement be calculated as a percentage of gross income so that the manager can see the relative importance of each. This often reveals problem areas more readily than the traditional income statement.

Alternative Plans.   Based on the research above, the property management team may recommend a program of modernization, rehabilitation, or conversion to some other use. The recommended actions are based on a capital budgeting decision. Using investment-analysis techniques (internal rate of return and net present value), the risks and rewards associated with each alternative are analyzed and the profit-maximizing option is recommended.[4] This portion of the management survey may not be requested or expected by the client, but it is potentially the most important aspect of the analysis. To sum up, the management survey begins with a study of the local market, and concludes with a plan for adapting the property to meet current needs while generating maximum profits for the owner.

Marketing Rental Space

Most successful management firms combine space merchandizing with their management activities. Even though the rental of commercial space differs in many respects from the rental of residential space, both require several common steps—analysis of effective demand at various rent levels, the skillful use of selling techniques, credit and financial analysis of prospective tenants, and economic analysis of the profitability from potential tenants. Much of this information is provided by the market survey discussed in the preceding section. Often the most likely tenants are those of nearby buildings. The marketing program is designed to rent building space efficiently so that the owner receives maximum gross income as soon as possible. To achieve this objective in a short period, advertising, publicity, and sales promotion must be coordinated to reach the target markets effectively.

Thematic Image.   With all of the previous research conducted in the market survey, the property manager should have a good understanding of the property and who the prospective tenants are. Often, however, for commercial property little thought is given to naming a property and building or creating a thematic image around which all promotion is geared. A thematic image is essential for promotion to be effective. It can be achieved by capitalizing on the complex's name or its unique architectural style, or by maintaining consistency in the use of logo types, signs,

---

[4]See Chapters 21–23.

or colors in the promotional materials and activities designed to lure prospective clients to the site. It is often useful for the marketing manager to find out who the decision maker is in the firm and what his favorite activity or sport may be. By discussing the activity, or by capitalizing on it in other ways, the manager may develop a personal rapport that will yield him an advantage over alternative properties. Obviously, the time and budget constraints of a promotional program will vary depending on the size, type, and location of the property. Regardless of the type of property, the manager should develop a carefully conceived and implemented merchandizing strategy.

Promotional Program.   After the thematic image has been established, the property manager should develop a promotional program that emphasizes the theme. Signs and advertising are the most important elements of promotion; however, brochures and other traffic-building measures are also helpful. A budget of 3–5 percent of effective gross income is a guideline for overall promotional activities.

1. *Signs:* It is estimated that signs account for 50–75 percent of property merchandizing. Signs for the property should inform, promote, direct, identify, and correctly portray the thematic image. Additionally, signs must be well maintained and updated as needed.
2. *Advertising:* The marketing manager should develop a data base of all tenants in the area for direct mail advertising. Names can often be obtained by photographing the directories in the lobbies of other buildings in the market area. Also, studies indicate that more than 50 percent of those who sign leases do so because they received a favorable impression when driving by the property. Therefore, the best advertisement is a well-maintained property with a vacancy sign on the premises. Projects in remote locations need advertising to build prospect traffic. The amount spent for advertising will depend on the current vacancy rate, the size of the project, and how well established the thematic image is in the market area. Advertising media include television, newspapers, radio, direct mail, classified ads, yellow pages, and billboards. The appropriate media should be carefully selected to attract the targeted prospective clients. When prospects contact the property manager, an effort to determine how they heard about the complex will facilitate effective allocation of future advertising expenditures.
3. *Other traffic builders:* There may be other promotional techniques that are well suited to a specific project. Other potential traffic builders include handbills, apartment guides, newsletters, airport displays, apartment locator services, and brokers.

Showing the Property.   Showing the complex is one of the most important aspects of property merchandizing, because clients do not usually rent units without first inspecting them. The professional property manager should teach good showing techniques to the resident manager and office personnel. Otherwise, the money spent to attract prospects to the property will be wasted because the prospects cannot be sold after their arrival.

Important features should be highlighted and superflous remarks should be avoided. Additionally, the amenities of the building and the caliber of the tenants should be stressed. The apartment, office, store, or industrial space being shown should be rehabilitated, decorated and clean. Public areas should also be attractive.

Tenant Administration

Tenants are the foundation of income property management and therefore are the owner's greatest asset. A well-developed, tenant-oriented policy is required to ensure profit maximization. First, a tenant selection policy is needed to ensure that leases are signed only by acceptable applicants. Additionally, an ongoing tenant-relations program is required to keep existing tenants satisfied and to encourage them to renew their leases. Finally, a rent-collection program is necessary to ensure that tenants pay their rent promptly. Tenant administration on this basis should reduce vacancies and tenant turnover, lead to a compatible group of tenants, and lower rent-collection expenses.

Tenant Selection.   While the specific nature of the selection criteria varies from residential to commercial and retail tenants, every effort must be made to select tenants who are responsible and suited to the particular property. This task requires the skills of a credit manager, a personnel manager, and a psychologist. Some general guidelines to be used in evaluating the quality of prospective tenants include:

1. *Creditworthiness:* Ideally, before selecting any tenant, the property manager should obtain a credit report on the prospective tenant. This report, of course, will reflect the tenant's capacity to pay. Employment, sales volume, and other income should be substantiated.
2. *Tenant compatibility:* Selection of new tenants should also be based on compatibility with existing tenants. Retail and commercial prospects should be considered only if they complement businesses already occupying space. The same rationale should be applied to the selection of residential tenants.
3. *Permanence potential:* By carefully evaluating the staying power of

prospects, vacancy rates can be lowered and other administrative costs can be avoided. Apartment application forms can reveal frequency of moves, job changes, and other indications of nomadic tendencies. Bank references and business associates can provide the necessary information on commercial/industrial prospects.

Tenant Relations.   In the real estate management business, dissatisfied tenants present serious problems. Conflicts between landlords and tenants frequently are avoidable when sound management practices are employed. In most cases, a poor relationship between the two parties stems from misunderstanding. The first step in correcting this should be taken during the original negotiation stage. As often as possible, the results of these negotiations should be in written form (the lease) and the contents reviewed with the tenant when the discussions are completed.

In addition to a written statement covering the fundamental points of the agreement, the manager should explain rent collection policies, review the operating regulations of the property, discuss the methods of enforcing them, and be certain that the tenant understands maintenance policies and how responsibilities are divided between the owner and tenant. These policies and procedures ideally should be outlined in a tenant brochure.

There is no substitute for frankness and honesty in human relations. Most problems center on service requests; when such a request is made, the tenant should be told immediately whether it will be granted. If the manager accepts a request and procrastinates, the tenant's respect will be lost, and possibly the tenant will vacate the property as soon as possible. Efficient management realizes that good tenants are a valuable asset. They remain in residence and eliminate expensive turnover; they protect the owner's property, which lowers maintenance costs; and they advertise the reputation of the complex, which reduces vacancy losses and promotional expenses.

Rental Collection Policy.   It is a nearly universal practice to collect rents once a month, usually on the first day of each month. In a well-run real estate management office, more than 75 percent of all rents due on the first day of each month are paid on that date, and more than 95 percent of all rentals due on the first are paid before the fifth day of the month. Tenants will pay their rents as promptly as the efficiency, effectiveness, and reasonableness of the property manager's collection policy permits.

If tenants do not fulfill their financial obligations as prescribed in the lease, prompt action is required. If the property manager does not act immediately, the tenant loses a sense of responsibility and becomes slack in rent payments. The only sound policy is to collect promptly or initiate legal action. Procedures should be developed for taking action against tenants who fail to meet their rental obligations. This action usually entails sending reminder notices to all delinquents and if no response is received, initiating legal action for eviction.

The Lease Document[5]

A lease is a contract between one person (the landlord or lessor) and another (the tenant or lessee) for the use or possession of real property for a specified time, in exchange for rent. The contract is usually written and is legally binding with respect to the commitments given by the signatories. The standard-form leases developed by local owner/manager associations are a good beginning when choosing a lease that is appropriate to the real estate product. These leases often have passed the test of local litigation.

Accounting, Recordkeeping, and Insurance

The most important fiscal items of concern to the property manager are the annual budget and the monthly operating statement. The property manager must be able to prepare a meaningful annual budget that includes all anticipated income and expense items for the property. Once the budget has been approved, care should be taken to operate within it. Monthly operating statements include all operating income from such sources as unit rents, parking, swimming pool, washing machines, dryers, and vending machines. The operating statement also includes all operating expenses and debt service. It allows the owner to see how the property is working on a cash basis. The statement can also include the yearly budget and the percentage of the budget that has been spent to date, thus providing budgetary control as well as cash control.

Carefully maintained records for the following items will also be required:

1. Lease contracts and tenant files.
2. Building code violations.
3. Occupational Safety and Health Act requirements.
4. Anti-discrimination laws.
5. Mandatory licenses and notices.
6. Correspondence concerning the property.

If the property manager is hired to procure insurance or monitor its adequacy in protecting the property or owner, those duties should be carefully specified. Duties and authority to be considered include:

1. Obtaining recommendations on required insurance protection.

---

[5]We discuss leases in depth in Chapter 8.

2. Selecting suitable insurance companies.
3. Procuring and paying for necessary coverage.
4. Supplying the owner with proof of coverage.
5. Investigating accidents or claims for damage.
6. Filing reports with insurers and cooperating with them.

Maintenance

A maintenance program provides the services and repairs that are necessary to preserve a property owner's investment while satisfying and providing for the well being of tenants. While it is not necessary for him to be proficient in performing maintenance tasks, the manager must be able to identify the various types of maintenance required and plan for their performance. A complete maintenance program incorporates four types of maintenance activities:

Physical Integrity.   The property manager is responsible for ensuring that each element of the physical structure functions as it should. These structural elements require attention: walks, driveways, parking areas, foundations, exterior walls, stairways, roofs, interior walls, and gutters.

Functional Performance.   One of the building manager's major responsibilities is to assure the functioning of the property's mechanical equipment. This equipment usually demands maintenance attention: heating, ventilating, and air-conditioning (HVAC) systems; plumbing; electrical systems; elevators; locks and security systems; laundries; storage areas; and swimming pools and other recreational amenities.

Housekeeping and Cleanliness.   Even if a building's physical equipment is well maintained, it is poorly operated if it is not clean. Similarly, the readiness and capability of the maintenance staff in responding to tenant requests for service affect a building's reputation. The building's janitorial and maintenance crews and the tenants should share the responsibility for cleanliness and good housekeeping.

Merchandising.   Since an investment property's success depends on the marketing of its space, it follows that certain maintenance operations are performed solely for merchandising reasons. When spending the client's money in the operation of any property, the manager must recognize the desirability of creating the maximum beautification and functionality per dollar. Items such as a carpeted lobby, well-landscaped grounds, and the use of color inside and outside of buildings may not create greater functionality, but may increase marketability.

Beyond understanding the types of maintenance, the property manager also must assign someone to perform the specific tasks associated with each type. These tasks may be assigned in one of three ways:

1. The manager may contract with a service agency or individual maintenance engineers.
2. The management agency may form a maintenance department, which then contracts with the property manager.
3. On-site personnel may be hired to service the property.

To assure that quality maintenance is being performed, the property manager also must establish a schedule of regular inspections.

The Resident Manager

The resident or on-site manager has the overall responsibility for a property's daily operations. Special emphasis is placed on the general administration and maintenance of the complex and the supervision of its personnel and resources. These responsibilities may be divided into three categories:

Marketing and Public Relations. The on-site representative is often the first point of contact for prospective tenants and other visitors. His job is to create a favorable image for the property and to qualify prospective tenants, that is, to learn what a prospect's needs and financial capabilities are. For example, the on-site representative may find that a prospect has a large family that could not fit into small apartments in the project. Or, he may learn that a prospect cannot pay the rents charged in the project. Such prospects can be referred to other projects that may serve their needs better. Proper greeting and qualifying of rental prospects are among the main marketing responsibilities of the resident manager. The importance of properly trained and well-mannered resident managers cannot be overstressed.

Rent Collections and Recordkeeping. The resident manager typically collects rents, handles delinquent accounts, maintains proper records of each tenant, and keeps other required records.

Operational Supervision. In organizing and supervising operations, the on-site manager must follow a monthly maintenance calendar, initiate purchase-order requests, and maintain employee work records.

Selecting a Property Manager

The choice of a manager requires careful consideration by an owner. The latter naturally desires the services of a management firm or agent that will produce the best results with the property. The success of the property manager's work is shown not only by the size of the net income resulting but also by the condition of the property. When selecting a property management company, the owner should consider the firm's professional qualifications, the responsibilities and authority of the manager, and the compensation required for management services.

Duties and Authority.   As an agent, the manager owes loyalty to the owner. The manager exercises his best judgement as a general agent or fiduciary of the owner, and must use his best efforts to further the legitimate interests of the principal in lease negotiation, rent collection, tax payments, and maintenance and repair of the property. The manager's authority and the scope and nature of the services to be performed should be carefully specified. In the interest of a trouble-free owner-manager relationship, a detailed contract should be drawn that delineates both the duties and the authority of the property manager. This management contract is a personal agreement and is not binding on a subsequent purchaser of the property.

The standard form, suggested by the Institute of Real Estate Management, covers the following crucial items:

1. Exclusive agency agreement.
2. Terms of renewal and termination.
3. Renting and lease negotiations.
4. Monthly statements to the owner.
5. Separation of owner and manager funds.
6. Bonding of employees.
7. The agent's authority.
   a. Repairs and remodeling.
   b. Management of employees.
   c. Management of service contracts.
8. Limitation of agent liability by owner.
9. Owner payment to agent for services rendered.

Management Fees.   The types of compensation that a property manager may receive can vary from a fixed salary or fee to a variable commission or percentage of income, with living expenses and fringe benefits. Usually the range of management fees is 5–8 percent of a property's effective gross income, depending on local custom. Information on appropriate fees and commissions is usually available through local lenders, appraisers, and other property owners; however, a manager should expect to negotiate compensation, since uniform fee schedules are a violation of the antitrust laws. In negotiating the form of compensation, the owner and property manager should consider the type of compensation to be paid for each specific service rendered. When the service requires a fixed expenditure of time and money, or an incentive for extraordinary effort is not necessary, compensation in the form of a fixed salary or fee may be appropriate and desirable for both parties. When the service requires a variable amount of time or money, or when additional incentive for special effort is appropriate, variable compensation in the form of a commission or a percentage of rent may be best. Additionally, as the relationship progresses, the duties and responsibilities often change so that previous forms of compensation are no longer appropriate and do not provide sufficient incentive for proficient performance.

Evaluating a Property Manager's Performance. Management accounting permits the use of financial measurements for judging managerial performance. Scrutiny of the budgets and actual expenditures per account from year to year and month to month can indicate the relative performance of management personnel on a building or project basis. The management agreement should also specify that certain other reports be furnished by the manager, such as:

1. Vacancy and bad-debt ratios.
2. Competitive properties.
3. Physical conditions and maintenance problems.
4. Forecast tenant demand.
5. Showings-to-rentals ratio.
6. Changes in tenant profiles.
7. Recommendations for capital improvements, replacements, refinancing, or selling.

The owner should also inspect the property on a regular basis.

OVERVIEW

The productivity of a property generates its value. A property's value, however, can be enhanced or diminished by the manner in which the marketing and management functions are performed for the property. A successful marketing program attempts to enhance productivity, make known the property's availability, and distribute it to those who need it. A successful management program seeks to enhance productivity by conserving and maximizing a property's operating efficiency.

A marketing program requires a marketing strategy. Such a strategy involves identification of markets or submarkets of needs and publicizing the availability of properties that meet those needs. The buying process itself can be analyzed in terms of the steps that a purchaser goes through and the roles that participants in a transaction play. By knowing which step a buyer may be in and what roles are played, a real estate marketer can direct the proper message to the relevant party at the correct time.

The difference between profit and loss in any real estate investment frequently depends upon skilled property management. Larger buildings, the increasing complexity of maintenance and repair, and the trend toward absentee ownership have made property management a full-time profession. Owners are increasingly turning to property managers who can direct, control, or operate real estate for a fee. The property manager's main task is to secure the highest net income over the useful life of a property. Management activity concentrates on four major areas: (1) developing a management survey, (2) marketing, (3) operation and maintenance, and (4) recordkeeping and rent collection.

TEST YOURSELF

Explain the following concepts and procedures presented in this chapter.

1. The marketing and management functions.
2. Marketing strategy.
3. Monopolistic competition.
4. Market grid.
5. The buying process—steps and roles.
6. Cognitive dissonance.
7. The management survey.
8. Thematic image.
9. Promotional program.
10. Tenant administration.

Answer the following multiple choice questions.

1. A market grid focuses on
   a. Need.
   b. Buyer-group characteristics.
   c. Ways of meeting needs.
   d. Inventory characteristics.
   e. Models of market behavior.

2. In which buying-process step can home buyers be expected to be susceptible to advertising and attend open houses?
   a. Problem recognition.
   b. Information search.
   c. Evaluation of alternatives.
   d. Purchase decision.
   e. Postpurchase behavior.

3. Which role in the buying process is played by someone who provides information or an advertising message to a prospective home buyer?
   a. Initiator.
   b. Influencer.
   c. Decider.
   d. Buyer.
   e. User.

4. What promotional aspect can be developed through a property's name, a unique architectural style, or consistency in the use of logos, signs, and colors?
   a. Goodwill.
   b. Name.
   c. Tenant relations.
   d. Profitability.
   e. Thematic image.

5. Tenant administration does *not* involve which of the following activities or elements?
   a. Tenant selection.
   b. Tenant relations.
   c. Rent collection.
   d. Maintenance.
   e. Tenant policy.

ADDITIONAL READINGS

Case, Fred E. *Real Estate Brokerage: A Systems Approach,* 2nd ed. Englewood Cliffs, N.J.: Prentice-Hall, 1982.

Downs, James C., Jr. *Principles of Real Estate Management,* 12th ed. Chicago: Institute of Real Estate Management, 1980.

Kotler, Phillip. *Marketing Management: Analysis, Planning, and Control,* 5th ed. Englewood Cliffs, N.J.: Prentice-Hall, 1984.

Lindeman, Bruce. *Real Estate Brokerage Management.* Reston, Va.: Reston Publishing, 1981.

National Association of REALTORS. *Profile of Real Estate Firms.* Chicago, 1983.

Shenkel, William L. *Marketing Real Estate.* Englewood Cliffs, N.J.: Prentice-Hall, 1980.

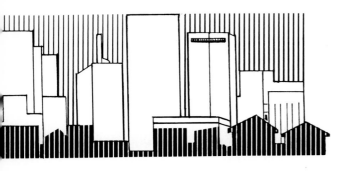

26
Real Estate Development and Construction

OUTLINE

INTRODUCTION

The development of land and the construction of improvements *on* land are the essential activities in the production of real estate. *Land development* is the process of changing raw land to a developed state. This includes the installation of improvements *to* land (e.g., streets and utilities) as well as the activities necessary for land acquisition and zoning changes. The *construction* of improvements (usually buildings) *on* land is the process of bringing a developed parcel to an *improved* state (i.e., land with buildings).

The term *real estate developer* usually applies to a person or firm that develops land and constructs improvements on developed parcels. In the strictest sense, however, the developer is someone who only develops land, and *builder* refers to an individual or firm that constructs improvements on developed land. The division of labor between those who only develop land and builders is most often found in the production of single-family residential real estate. The development of a residential subdivision frequently involves two parties. The developer (first party) acquires a large parcel of land, obtains zoning approval, subdivides the parcel into smaller lots, adds improvements to the land, and finally sells the developed lots either to a builder (second party) or a person who wants to have a home built. For income-producing properties, land development and construction are usually performed by one party: the developer.

Developers and builders are businesspersons. From an economic perspective, developers and builders combine their entrepreneurial skills with land and labor to produce capital (i.e., buildings and land improvements). From a business perspective, developers and builders are managers who plan, organize, and control the process of development and construction through the important marketing phase. We devote this chapter, in accordance with the business perspective of Part Four of this book, primarily to the business of real estate development and construction.

Macroeconomic Importance of Real Estate Production

By almost any measure, the production of real estate is one of the most important business activities in the U.S. economy. Of the $637.8 billion of new investment in the United States in 1984, $150.4 billion, or 23.6 percent of the total, was for nonresidential construction and another $148.8 billion, or 23.3 percent, was for residential construction.[1] Thus nearly half the new investment in recent years has been for the production of real estate.[2] Total employment in the United States now exceeds 100 million persons. Of this total, over four percent are employed in the construction industry while another 2 to 3 percent are employed in real estate services, including real estate development.[3] Although tax law provisions designed to encourage real estate investment have been changed, the production and servicing of real estate in the United States should continue to be important throughout the 1980s, unless the economy turns down severely.

THE PARTICIPANTS

We may view land development and construction as activities that alter the bundle of physical and legal property rights that accompany land parcels. Development and construction activities may also affect the property rights of others who own adjacent and nearby parcels. The altering of property rights through development and construction involves an intricate set of relationships that facilitate the successful completion and operation of the project as well as protecting the property rights of all members of society. Exhibit 26–1 portrays these relationships. One set is between major groups: the *space-production group*, the *space-consumption group*, and the *infrastructure group*. The second set is within the space-production group, and involves interactions between the developer or builder and those supplying financial capital, materials, and labor for the project. In the following sections we will describe major group relationships and production group relationships by examining the roles of the various participants in the development and construction process.

---

[1]U.S. Department of Commerce, *Survey of Current Business* 67, no. 8 (August 1985), p. 5.

[2]Some economists argue that the United States has overinvested in structures, especially residential structures, and instead should be investing more in equipment and research.

[3]U.S. Department of Labor, *Employment and Earnings.*

EXHIBIT 26–1
RELATIONSHIPS IN THE REAL ESTATE DEVELOPMENT
AND CONSTRUCTION PROCESS

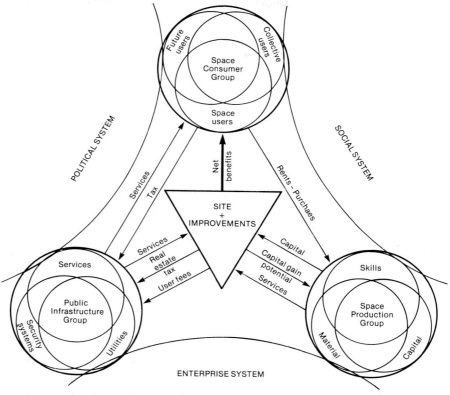

Source: Adapted from James A. Graaskamp, *Fundamentals of Real Estate Development*, Development Component Series (Washington, D.C.: Urban Land Institute, 1981), p. 4.

Major Group Relationships

The production group, headed by the developer, interacts with two other major groups. Developers have a business and a social relationship with space consumers: persons and firms who purchase or rent space. The essence of the business relationship between developers and space consumers is the marketing function. As Chapter 25 describes, the selling and leasing of space is much like the marketing of other products.

There is a more delicate relationship between developers and the public infrastructure group. Broadly defined, this group includes public and quasi-public agencies that provide basic service (e.g., garbage collection), security (e.g., police), utilities (e.g., electric power), and regulation (i.e., building codes, housing codes, land-use controls, and zoning). Public regulation of development and construction protects public health and safety (e.g., building codes) and prevents negative externalities (e.g., protects the property rights of those who might be affected by development.)

Developers sometimes say that the two keys to a successful development are "sewage and finance." Including sewage in this elite set of prerequisites underscores the importance of the developer's establishing good relationships with those in the public infrastructure group who supply services and utilities. Nevertheless, the developer's biggest obstacle in many instances is the existing land-use and zoning regulations. Such issues are particularly sensitive, since they have the potential of creating conflict among all three of the major groups. Developers usually commit substantial resources to ensure that zoning changes proceed swiftly—time is money in the construction and development business!

Production Group Relationships

From a business perspective, the developer is both an entrepreneur who commits time and capital for uncertain returns and a manager who assembles and administers the skills necessary to ensure the success of the project. Yet the developer is much more than an entrepreneur and manager. Developers are investors and originators of ideas. Each real estate project begins with two components—land and an idea. The developer is the sole supplier of ideas, along with the initiative to carry them out.

Implementing ideas requires business expertise. Exhibit 26–2 shows the various business relationships among the developer and other parties in the production group. These relationships are divided into two categories—relationships with suppliers of financial capital and relationships with suppliers of labor and materials.

Suppliers of Financial Capital.   Development and construction projects, like most real estate investment opportunities, have a capital structure comprising equity and debt. Usually, the developer supplies part of the equity contribution to the project and equity partners provide part. Limited-partnership syndication, in which the developer serves as the general partner, is a popular form of equity partnership, as we will examine in Chapter 27.

Developers must establish good relationships with construction lenders and permanent lenders to secure debt financing. Debt usually constitutes 60 to 70 percent of the total capital structure of development projects. This relationship is much like the relationship between a novelist and a publisher. The first loan, or book contract advance, is extremely

EXHIBIT 26–2
PRODUCTION GROUP RELATIONSHIPS

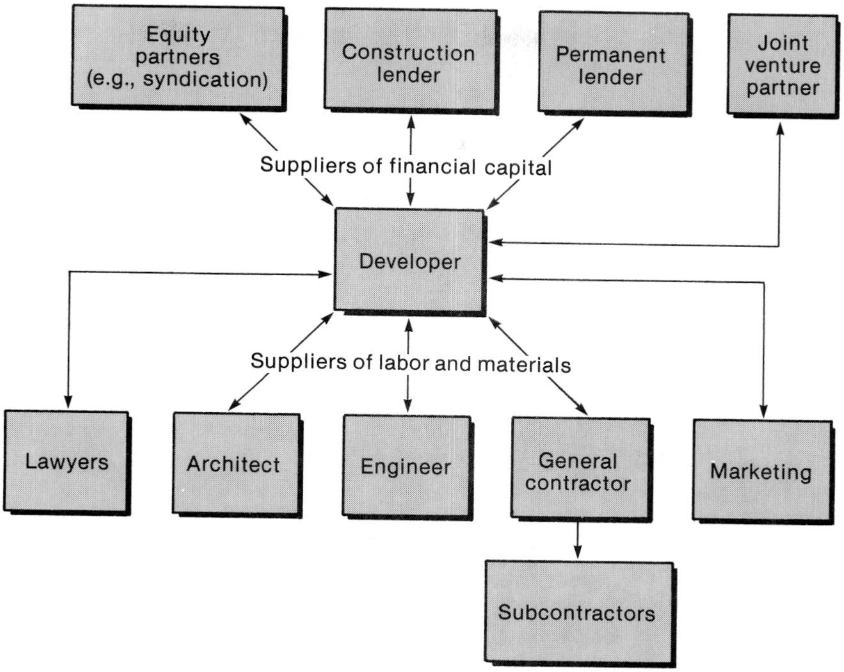

difficult to get, but once the developer or novelist establishes a good track record, the loans and book contract advances are routinely provided. (It also may help in dealing with lenders to have a respectable golf game!)

Joint venture arrangements are also frequent today. Lenders in joint ventures supply all funds necessary to advance the project, while the developer supplies the ideas and managerial skills. Lenders have been more willing to act as equity partners in development projects in recent years. In such arrangements, the lender receives debt service and a sizeable portion of before-tax cash flow. The developer receives a smaller share of BTCF and some or all of the tax benefits as compensation for services rendered.

Suppliers of Labor and Materials. The bottom part of Exhibit 26–2 shows the relationship between the developer and suppliers of labor and materials. The relationship between the developer and the *real estate lawyer* begins when the rights to land are first acquired and continues through the signing of leases or sales contracts at the end of the project. In between, the real estate lawyer is involved in every phase of the project, including preparing the limited-partnership agreement; reviewing and sometimes modifying loan contracts; and preparing employment contracts with architects, engineers, and contractors.

Architects (including landscape architects) and *engineers* provide essential services during the early phases of the project. Architects translate the ideas of the developer, along with their own ideas, into architectural renderings and plans. Engineers work with architects to ensure that the architectural plans will result in structurally sound buildings. The relationship between architects, engineers, and the developer continues throughout the project. Architects and engineers often serve as the agents of the developer on technical matters in the developer's dealings with the general contractor.

When the developer does not have in-house expertise in land preparation and construction, a contractual relationship is established with a *general contractor*. The general contractor manages the physical implementation of the project (i.e., land preparation and construction of improvements). Usually, subcontractors assemble labor and materials to complete specific tasks in the project such as plumbing, painting, and carpeting. The general contractor hires and supervises the various subcontractors required for a project.

Finally, the marketing agents are retained to lease or sell the space the developer produced. This occurs before the actual completion of the project so that as much space as possible can be *presold* or *preleased*. In the case of rental properties, the amount of money received by the developer from lenders at the time of completion often depends on the proportion of the space that is preleased. Thus the success of the project frequently depends on the developer's having a relationship with good marketing agents.

THE DEVELOPMENT PROCESS

A real estate development and construction project should proceed according to a logical sequence of events. However, the development process in the real world is often unlike textbook examples. The process outlined in this section and graphically displayed in Exhibit 26–3, therefore, is a normative (what should be) representation of the steps involved in taking an undeveloped parcel of land to a fully developed state. This exhibit is designed to show how the various participants interact in the course of a typical development project. Since each development project is unique and a great deal of innovation and creativity are involved in a project, the development process described herein should not be construed as the only model for success. Many variations on this theme are possible.

EXHIBIT 26–3
STAGES IN A TYPICAL DEVELOPMENT AND CONSTRUCTION PROJECT

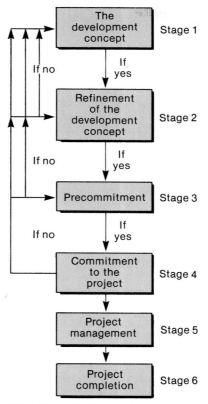

Source: Adapted from Mike E. Miles, "A Conceptual and Computer Model for the Analysis and Management of Risk in Real Property Development," Ph.D. dissertation, University of Texas, 1976.

Stage 1: The Development Concept ("The Idea")

Every real estate development project begins with an idea or *development concept*. The development concept embodies the developer's preconceptions about a particular project, its size and location, and the types of tenants or buyers. It also embodies such questions as the financial structuring and preliminary feasibility of the project. For example, a developer might envision a project to develop a suite hotel of 50 to 100 rooms near an emerging office center. The developer believes that a limited-partnership syndication could be used to finance the project.

Although many people can come up with a sound development concept, the developer is the person or firm who advances the concept to the stage where a decision can be made about making improvements to land. Therefore, moving to the next stage in the process—where the development concept is refined—is a crucial step. It requires the developer to take specific action and make a certain level of commitment to the concept.

Stage 2: Refinement of the Development Concept ("The Site")

The most important activities during the concept-refinement stage are site location, site analysis, and the acquisition of development rights. The developer's concept for the project sets the initial parameters for site location. In the example of the suite hotel, the location parameters suggest a site near an emerging office center that is large enough to accommodate a 50–100 room hotel with amenities (e.g., pool and tennis courts). The analysis of the site, once located, includes investigations into legal ownership (not only of the specific parcel but also of adjacent parcels), current zoning and opportunities for rezoning (when appropriate), soil conditions, topography, visibility, and access. Close coordination between the developer, the engineer, and the architect (for layout feasibility) is required at this stage.

If the project is to advance further, the developer must contact the owner of the property to acquire the development rights to the site. Three of the most popular forms for acquiring development rights are the *option contract*, the *letter of intent*, and the *contract for sale with contingencies*. Option contracts and contracts for sale with contingencies[4] tie up the property for a specified period in return for the payment of a fee (e.g., the option price or an earnest-money deposit). A letter of intent does not tie up the property. The owner could still sell the property to another party while the developer is studying the market feasibility or trying to obtain financing. Thus the letter of intent is more risky but is less costly, because an earnest-money deposit is usually not required.

Several other crucial activities should be initiated during the concept-refinement stage. These include determining the availability of the general contractor, and initial discussions with prospective major tenants (when appropriate) and with lenders and syndicators (when appropriate).

---

[4]For example, the contract might be written so the developer is not obligated to purchase the parcel if the market study indicates that there is no market for that use at that location. The developer would forfeit any deposits, however. Other contingencies include those for obtaining financing at current market rates, title problems, and physical inspection of the property.

Stage 3: Precommitment ("Project Feasibility")

During the concept-refinement stage, the developer can return to the development-concept stage to reevaluate the project. One important reason to halt progress on a project is the unavailability of an acceptable site. If, however, site location, site analysis, and acquisition activities proceed smoothly, the developer is able to advance the project to the precommitment stage.

Probably the most crucial element at the precommitment stage is the preparation of the market and financial feasibilitiy study (see Chapter 11). The information derived from the market component of the feasibility study helps the architect make preliminary drawings and the engineer develop cost estimates.

The feasibility study, architectural drawings, and cost estimates, along with an appraisal, comprise a major portion of the loan submission package that is needed for specific discussions with construction and permanent lenders. If the feasibility study is not positive, or favorable financing is not available, the project is recycled to an earlier stage or discontinued outright. But if all essential elements of the project are in place, the developer is ready to commit to completing the project.

Stage 4: Commitment ("The Contracts")

The decision to commit to the project is a decision to enter into contracts with additional members of the production group and members of other major groups. At this stage, the developer obtains formal commitments from lenders, obtains building permits, signs contracts with the general contractor, signs leases with major tenants, and enters into partnership agreements with limited partners. The developer is now ready to initiate development and construction.

Stage 5: Project Management ("The Improvements")

The developer has two major concerns during this stage, when improvements to land are produced. First, he wants to make certain that the project proceeds in a timely manner. Time is money during this stage. For every month the project is not completed, the developer pays interest on the unpaid balance of the development or construction loan. Thus, to ensure timely progress, the developer works closely during this period with the suppliers of labor and materials, including the general contractor, engineer, and architect.

The second major concern is marketing. Actually, leasing activities for rental properties, and sales activities for salable properties such as residential condominiums begin before the project management stage. The objective of the marketing group is to pre-lease or pre-sell as much of "the product" as possible. Usually, most of the marketing force's work is done during actual development and construction and immediately thereafter.

Marketing is a major concern of the developer because the success of the project ultimately depends on the timing and the absorption of the project into the market. Developers are often undercapitalized (they especially lack equity funds), and cost overruns on projects are common. This suggests that early leases or sales will preclude the need to raise additional capital (e.g., short-term borrowing), which is often extremely expensive. Perhaps more important, permanent-loan commitments for rental properties contain rental-achievement clauses that restrict the amount of funds available to repay the construction loan unless the property is pre-leased to a prescribed level (e.g., 80 percent) by the end of construction. For salable properties, marketing is also important because financing contracts usually preclude developers from receiving their required rates of return until the last, say, 20 percent of the properties are sold.

Stage 6: Project Completion ("On to the Next Project")

The project is technically complete when all of the physical elements of the improvements are in place. This officially ends the relationship between the developer, engineer, and architect. Also, the relationship between the developer and the construction lender is terminated, since the permanent loan is closed at this stage. The equity owners (e.g., partnership) take control of the property at this point, or a sale is negotiated in the case of a salable property.

The marketing people are probably the most active members of the production group during the completion stage. Pre-opening advertising and promotion must be initiated and any opening events planned. Tenants sometimes require assistance to help them move in, and sales or leasing activities usually must continue past the opening. Since developers are exclusively in the business of developing real estate and constructing improvements on land, the developer at this stage is looking forward to his next project or to the completion of another ongoing project.

RISKS AND RETURNS

Real estate development is probably the most glamorous occupation in the field of real estate. Many developers are national figures (e.g., Donald Trump and James Rouse), and a number own professional sports teams (e.g., Jack Kent Cooke owner of the Washington Redskins). Obviously, many developers have made a lot of money, but as we have argued in previous chapters, high returns from real estate usually come because sizable risks have been taken. The returns from real estate development and construction are indeed high, and more often than not, so are the risks. Given this fact, a discussion of the returns from development would be incomplete without a discussion of the risks that can cause reduced returns or investment losses.

The Risks of Real Estate Development

New development and construction projects are inherently risky because they involve the assembly of labor, land, and materials into a finished product—the property. Once assembly is complete, the finished product is in a form that can be offered in the market. If the project is successful, the developer earns a reasonable return on investment. But if the project is not completed for any reason, little value may have been added from assembly and thus the project is merely worth the resale value of the land and materials. Exhibit 26–4 presents the relationship between risk, time until completion, and value. As we can see, the risk usually remains high and the value does not increase significantly until the project nears completion.

The sources of development and construction risk include cost overruns caused by labor disputes and other reasons, land-use and zoning problems, high interest rates, poor weather, poor cost estimation, and changes in demand caused by a variety of market factors. As in the case of existing property investments, the risks of development and construction projects can be classified as either systematic (market related) or unsystematic (project specific).

EXHIBIT 26–4
RELATIONSHIPS BETWEEN THE RISK OF A DEVELOPMENT OR CONSTRUCTION PROJECT, TIME TOWARD COMPLETION, AND THE VALUE OF THE PROPERTY

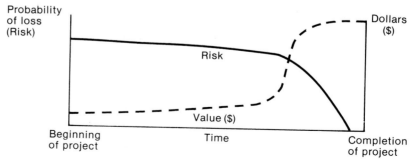

Systematic Risk. Changes in general economic conditions—the source of systematic risk—can have a variety of adverse effects on development and construction projects. First, since interest rates on construction and development loans usually fluctuate with market rates and interest is paid on the outstanding balance of the loan, a rise in interest rates will increase developers' risk and may result in financial distress.[5]

Second, changes in general economic conditions that result in changed demand for space can have dire consequences for developers. Recall that the fundamental equation relates the value of a property to its income (i.e., rents or sale prices). When an economic downturn occurs, the demand for space decreases and developers have a more difficult time leasing or selling space. This decreased demand in turn depresses value. An investor might be able to ride out an economic downturn, but developers, as we pointed out above, are in the business of *producing* improvements to and on land. Therefore, developers often sell the rental properties they are developing near the end of the development period. If preleasing is poor, the developer loses money on the sale.

Market studies (see Chapter 11) tend to reduce the systematic risk of development and construction projects. Although the study does not predict the actual level of general economic activity in the future, it presents information on expected leasing and sales activity under various economic scenarios. For example, the market study for a downtown hotel should tell the developer the level of occupancy expected in a moderate economic recession.

Unsystematic Risk. Through the use of interest-rate futures and market research, systematic risk can be managed reasonably. For all but the very large developer, however, unsystematic risk (project-specific risk) is difficult to manage. Large-scale developers can diversify away the unsystematic risk of their portfolio of development projects by working simultaneously on projects in different parts of the United States or by developing different types of properties. Developers without the capacity to diversify must incur the endemic risks of each project.

The unsystematic risks of development and construction projects emanate from problems with the relationships between the developer and members of the production group on one hand, and with the members of other major groups on the other. Unsystematic risk may come from changes in local market conditions that are unrelated to changes in the general economy (e.g., factory closings).

---

[5]The financial futures market gives the developer an opportunity to hedge interest-rate risk. For example, see Edward W. Schwartz, *How to Use Interest Rate Futures Contracts* (Homewood, Ill.: Dow Jones-Irwin, 1979).

Problems of poor weather, labor strikes, design mistakes, cost-estimation mistakes, and materials shortages can disrupt relationships between the developer and the general contractor, architect, and engineer, and result in severe cost overruns. Developers have a difficult time protecting themselves against such risks. Sometimes general contractors are willing to sign contracts with developers in which the cost is guaranteed not to exceed a fixed amount. Also, some contractors are bonded, so if the project is not completed at the estimated cost, the bonding agency pays the difference between the actual cost and the contract cost, similar to having an insurance policy. In a competitive market for services, the cost of guaranteed contracts and bonding would be included in the initial cost estimate. Therefore the developer may not be much better off with such provisions.

Developers have an even more difficult time protecting themselves against risk from their relationships with public agencies that regulate land use and provide infrastructure (e.g., roads and sewers). Obtaining approvals, permits, and extensions of services from public agencies is inherently expensive and uncertain. For example, zoning approval for a multimillion-dollar project might hinge on the wills and whims of a small group of local homeowners. Some communities require that developers pay the full cost of extending services to new development projects, whereas others require developers to donate land from each project for open space. The costs of these local rules and regulations are difficult to estimate at the beginning of a project and are virtually impossible to manage.

Finally, local economic conditions not linked to the general economy may contribute to the unsystematic risk of development and construction projects.[6] For example, a manufacturing plant that moves to another city may have devastating effects on the demand for housing in both communities. The move may not be related at all to changes in general economic conditions. To some extent market studies can help supply information to assist the developer in understanding these local market risks.

The Returns from Real Estate Development

As with investments in existing property, returns from the production of real estate come from the sale or rental of space. To illustrate how returns

---

[6]If we take a local perspective, these risks are mostly systematic because the developer only has projects in one area. If we take a national perspective, these risks are mostly unsystematic.

from a development project are estimated, we will examine how those of a typical land development project are determined.

The Smith & Corgel Development Company (SCDC) is in the business of buying raw land and developing it into residential lots. These lots are usually sold to people who want to build new homes. (Sometimes a builder will purchase all or some of the developed lots and build homes on them for sale to the general public. When homes are constructed without previously being sold, they are called *spec*—for speculation—*homes*.)

Recently, SCDC discovered a 50-acre tract on the outskirts of a rapidly growing metropolitan area in the western United States. The tract will soon be placed on the market for $1,000,000, or $20,000 per acre. Zoning is currently agricultural, but the planning and zoning commission in the county where this tract is located has been receptive during the past year to rezoning proposals for quality residential development. The commission has recently allowed densities of 2.5 homes per acre, so the 50 acres could be developed into 125 lots if zoning approval is granted.

Smith & Corgel Development Company analysts estimate that a developed lot would sell for $16,000 to $18,000 in the current market. Development costs are expected to be approximately $6,200 per lot. Exhibit 26–5 presents the cost estimates for this project. Costs are divided into four major groups: land acquisition, hard costs (i.e., the costs of the physical improvement), soft costs (i.e., the costs of services supporting the project), and miscellaneous expenses.

EXHIBIT 26–5
PROJECT COST ESTIMATES—SMITH & CORGEL DEVELOPMENT COMPANY PROJECT

Land Acquisition		$1,000,000
Hard costs:		
Development costs—grading, streets, and subsurface improvements	$600,000	
Soft costs:		
Engineering support	40,000	
General and administrative expenses	120,000	
Miscellaneous	20,000	
Total development cost [Cost per lot ($780,000/125 lots = $6,240)].		780,000
Total project cost		$1,780,000

An *acquisition and development loan* has been secured through a local bank in the form of a line of credit for 75 percent of the total project cost. This means that part of the loan will be *drawn down* each period as needed. Thus the loan amount is $1,335,000 (.75 × $1,780,000) and the equity contribution of SCDC is $445,000 (.25 × $1,780,000). As each lot is sold, the lender will receive 80 percent of the price until the balance of the loan is repaid plus 10 percent interest on the unpaid balance. The amount the lender receives (i.e., 80 percent of each sale) is often called the *release price* because the lender releases individual lots from the mortgage contract once the lot is sold and the 80 percent is paid.

Real estate taxes are expected to be 3 percent of the raw land value (adjusted for sales each year); SCDC is in the 50 percent tax bracket and has a required rate of return of 18 percent on its development projects. The vice president for marketing estimates that the project will sell out in four years, so approximately 32 lots will be sold in each of the next four years.

EXHIBIT 26–6
SCDC LAND DEVELOPMENT PROJECT—CASH FLOW ESTIMATION FORMAT

	Closing	Year 1 . . . Year n	
Inflows:			
Sales		$	$
Loan draws	$	$	$
Total inflow	$	$	$
Outflows:			
Land purchase	$		
Closing fees	$		
Loan repayment		$	$
Land development costs		$	$
Title and surveys		$	$
Brokerage commissions		$	$
Real estate taxes		$	$
Federal income taxes		$	$
Total outflow	$	$	$
Net after-tax cash flow	$	$	$

Exhibit 26–6 shows the form of the cash-flow statement for estimating the profitability of this project.[7] The inflows come from the sale of lots (i.e., 32 lots sold per year times $18,000 per lot) and from loan draws (i.e., 75 percent of land acquisition and development costs). The outflows go to payments for acquisition of the land and the closing costs (at closing only), to loan repayment (i.e., 80 percent of the sales revenue for this project), title and surveys, brokerage fees, real estate taxes, and federal income taxes. The analysts calculate net after-tax cash flows for each year and compute net present value and internal rate of return to determine whether to go forward with the project.

---

[7]Due to the complexity of this type of analysis, only the form of the cash-flow statement is presented. A complete presentation of a typical land development project is found in William B. Brueggeman and Jeffrey D. Fisher, *Real Estate Finance* (Homewood, Ill.: Richard D. Irwin, forthcoming).

Estimates for the SCDC project (not shown) indicate that the developers would earn over 18 percent on their investment if sales projections are realized. The major risk of this project is the uncertainty about future sales—just as it is with most development projects.

Frame 26-1

The First Master's Degree Program in Real Estate Development May Be the Best Ever

In 1982 Charles Spaulding, retired president of the Massachusetts-based development firm of Spaulding and Slye, approached the Massachusetts Institute of Technology (MIT) with an idea for starting a professional school of real estate development. Contributions from Spaulding and approximately 65 other developers and corporations, including IBM and Citicorp Real Estate, Inc., provided the funding to inaugurate MIT's new Center for Real Estate Development, which grants a master's degree in real estate development.

During the fall of 1984, 35 students were selected from 225 applicants to form the first class. Members of the class are an average of 30 years old, and all have previous real estate experience with large firms or have run their own businesses. The curriculum includes courses in real estate finance, market analysis, design, construction, and community politics. As Charles Spaulding confesses: "You can't teach a person to be an entrepreneur. You either have it or you don't"; however, MIT, with one of the finest and most diverse faculties in the country, may provide the best possible opportunity to overcome such business-related birth defects.

Source: *Fortune*, February 4, 1985, p. 49.

OVERVIEW

The developer (broadly defined to include builders) is a business person. He brings together labor, capital, land, and his own entrepreneurial skills to produce improvements to and on land. For the successful completion of a project, the developer must also be a competent manager and must rely on other business disciplines, especially marketing. The activities of real estate developers have tremendous macroeconomic significance, since nearly one half of the new investment in the United States each year involves the production of real estate.

Developers must establish good relationships with members of the space-production group (*e.g.,* engineers, architects, and the marketing force), space consumers, and members of the public infrastructure group. The developer's relationship with the public infrastructure group is especially delicate, since there is a possibility for serious conflicts between public regulators, consumers, and the developer over such issues as re-zoning. The most important relationships, however, are within the space-production group. These may be divided into two categories: relations with suppliers of financial capital (e.g., lenders) and with suppliers of labor and materials (e.g., attorneys and the general contractor).

Following a well-designed process for the completion of a development and construction project is another important element of success. This begins with an idea or concept for the improvement of a parcel of land. The developer refines and advances the idea to the point where a decision can be made regarding whether to proceed. This involves the acquisition of development rights to the parcel and a project feasibility study. Once a commitment is made to the project, the developer's role is one of negotiating contracts and managing the project efficiently.

The returns to the developer from a successful construction and development project can be tremendous, but so can the risks. Developers incur both systematic risk and unsystematic risk. National economic events, such as a rise in interest rates, can have a great impact on developer returns by reducing sales or leasing below expected levels. Local and project-specific events, such as a factory closing or a labor strike, can have similar effects and also cause severe project delays leading to cost overruns. Thus, the returns on investment by a developer are very uncertain and extremely difficult to forecast with certainty; that is, they are *risky*.

TEST YOURSELF

Explain the following terms and concepts presented in this chapter.

1. Differences and similarities between a builder and a developer.
2. Importance of a developer's track record.
3. General contractor.
4. Development concept.
5. Letter of intent versus a contract for sale with contingencies.
6. Development risks.
7. Sources of returns from real estate development.
8. Release price.
9. Hard costs.
10. Soft costs.

Answer the following multiple-choice questions.

1. All of the following are members of the production group in a real estate development *except*
   a. Lawyers.
   b. Engineers.
   c. Zoning board.
   d. Equity partners.
   e. Construction lender.

2. The role of the architect in the development and construction process is
   a. To translate the ideas of the developer into plans and renderings.
   b. To advise the developer on technical matters pertaining to the development and construction of the project.

c. To work closely with engineers to see that the plans are followed during development and construction.

d. Only *a* and *b*.

e. All of the above (*a*, *b*, and *c*).

3. During the concept-refinement stage of the development process

a. The feasibility study is prepared.

b. Development rights are acquired.

c. The site is located and analyzed.

d. Only *b* and *c*.

e. All of the above (*a*, *b*, and *c*).

4. The risks of a development and construction project

a. Are greater toward the end of the project.

b. Can be managed if they are mostly systematic risks.

c. Are frequently related to land-use and zoning problems.

d. Are totally unmanageable.

e. None of the above.

5. Which of the following costs of a development project would be considered "hard costs"?

a. Administrative expenses.

b. Engineering fees.

c. Land acquisition.

d. Grading.

e. Developer profit.

ADDITIONAL READINGS

Graaskamp, James A. *Fundamentals of Real Estate Development*, Development Component Series. Washington, D.C.: Urban Land Institute, 1981.

Lochmoeller, Donald C.; Dorothy A. Muney; Oakleigh J. Thorne; and Mark A. Veits. *Industrial Development Handbook*, Community Builders Handbook Series. Washington, D.C.: Urband Land Institute, 1975.

McKeever, Ross J., and Nathaniel M. Griffin. *Shopping Center Development Handbook*, Community Builders Handbook Series. Washington, D.C.: Urban Land Institute, 1977.

McMahan, John. *Property Development*. New York: John Wiley & Sons, 1976.

O'Mara, Paul W. *Office Development Handbook*, Community Builders Handbook Series. Washington, D.C.: Urban Land Institute, 1982.

————. *Residential Development Handbook*, Community Builders Handbook Series (Washington, D.C.: Urban Land Institute, 1978).

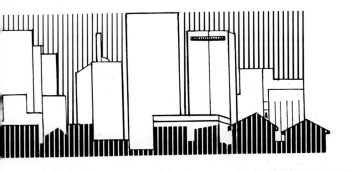

27
Real Estate Syndication

OUTLINE

INTRODUCTION

Like the real estate developer, the real estate syndicator is a businessperson or firm involved in increasing the productivity of real estate. A syndicate is generally defined as "a group of persons or legal entities who come together to carry out a particular activity." A real estate syndicate therefore is a group organized to develop a parcel of land, buy an office building, purchase an entire portfolio of properties, make mortgage loans, or perform other activities. The syndicator organizes such groups and manages the activities it is organized to carry out. Much of the syndicator's work is raising money. The other members of the real estate syndicate are usually money partners or investors. The productivity of real estate is enhanced by syndicators because without their efforts and organizational skills, fewer new development projects would be initiated, fewer existing property transactions would occur,[1] and fewer mortgage loans would be made.

Real estate syndicates traditionally have been legally organized as limited partnerships. The real estate syndicator therefore is the general partner in a limited-partnership syndication, and the other members are limited partners. The limited partners in real estate syndicates cannot participate in the syndicate's business activities beyond their initial investment of funds, or they will lose their limited-partnership status for tax purposes. In this chapter, we take the perspective of both the syndicator (general partner) and the investors (limited partners) in an examination of real estate syndication.

---

[1]Such transactions free capital for new investment.

Types of Real Estate Syndication

Real estate syndications can be classified in several ways; for example, they are often described as either *public offerings* or *private offerings*. This classification refers to the manner in which the syndication is structured for purposes of state and federal securities regulations. In general, public offerings are larger than private offerings both in terms of the money raised from real estate investors and in terms of the number of investors in the syndicate. Moreover, public offerings, unlike private offerings, involve general solicitation (e.g., brokers calling potential investors at random over the phone)[2] and advertising the offering in the media. As we discuss later in this chapter, large public offerings must be fully registered with federal and state securities regulators, whereas smaller private placements can be exempt from full registration and disclosure regulations.

Another way to classify real estate syndications is by the amount of the syndicate's business activity that has been carried out at the time the offering is made to investors. A *fully-specified fund* is an offering in which the syndicator has acquired or developed all of the properties (or mortgage loans) that the syndicate could purchase with available contributions from investors. In other words, all the money that could be spent on real estate or loans has already been spent by the syndicator. The offering *prospectus* is the document presented to potential investors in the syndication. It describes various aspects of the offering, and usually contains information on the operating performance of properties acquired. Thus the future returns from the fully-specified fund can be estimated by potential investors.

Exhibit 27–1 shows the front cover of a prospectus for a fully-specified *private* offering. Note that this is only the front cover of a document that has over 100 pages. The cover provides an abstract of some of the more important information about the offering, including the name, affiliation, and address of the general partner; the objectives of the partnership; the amount of money to be raised; and information about the property to be acquired with the funds raised.

Prospectuses for other types of offerings describe funds in which only a portion of the money available to invest has been used to purchase rights to real estate. This type of syndication is known as a *partially-specified fund*. Finally, some syndication offering documents provide the investor with only a description of the type and nature of the real estate investments that will be made. These *unspecified* or "blind" funds are the most difficult for the investor to analyze and have come under the closest scrutiny from securities regulators. Exhibit 27–2 shows the front cover of

---

[2]For a private offering, a broker might contact only a few selected investors.

**EXHIBIT 27–1
PROSPECTUS (FRONT COVER) FOR A FULLY-SPECIFIED PRIVATE
SYNDICATION OFFERING**

PROSPECTUS

HERITAGE LIMITED

675 LIMITED PARTNERSHIP INTERESTS ("UNITS")

Heritage Limited (the "Partnership") is a Georgia Limited Partnership with Richard R. Felker and RFC Realty, Inc. as General Partners, formed for the purpose of acquiring, operating and holding for investment 460 apartment units in Cobb County, Georgia known as Heritage Apartments. The purchase of a Unit requires an initial investment of $9,900 payable $3,300 in cash and $6,600 by means of the investor's non-interest bearing promissory note payable in two (2) equal installments of $3,300 each, the first installment being due and payable on or before October 15, 1985, and the second on or before October 15, 1986. Certain additional contributions may thereafter be required from time to time, although the General Partners do not presently anticipate that this will prove necessary.

THESE ARE SPECULATIVE SECURITIES. THEY ARE SUBJECT TO CERTAIN RESTRICTIONS ON TRANSFER, WILL NOT BE READILY MARKETABLE AND INVOLVE A HIGHLY LEVERAGED TRANSACTION. INDEBTEDNESS SECURED BY THE PROPERTY WILL REQUIRE A BALLOON PAYMENT OF $11,518,000 ON THE TENTH ANNIVERSARY OF THE FIRST DAY OF THE MONTH FOLLOWING THE ACQUISITION OF THE PROPERTY. SEE "FACTORS TO BE CONSIDERED."

	Price to Purchaser (1)*	Underwriting Commissions (2)*	Proceeds to Partnership (3)*
Per Unit	$ 9,900	-0-	$ 9,900
Total	$6,682,500	-0-	$6,682,500

*See footnotes on first inside page of this Prospectus.

THESE SECURITIES ARE OFFERED THROUGH RFC EQUITIES, INC. ONLY TO PERSONS WHO ARE BONA FIDE RESIDENTS OF THE STATE OF GEORGIA AND WHO PURCHASE FOR THE PURPOSE OF INVESTMENT AND NOT FOR RESALE. BECAUSE THESE SECURITIES ARE BELIEVED EXEMPT FROM REGISTRATION UNDER FEDERAL LAWS, THEY HAVE NOT BEEN REGISTERED WITH THE UNITED STATES SECURITIES AND EXCHANGE COMMISSION AND HAVE NOT BEEN APPROVED OR DISAPPROVED BY SUCH COMMISSION.

CERTAIN OF THE SECURITIES OFFERED HEREBY MAY BE OFFERED OR SOLD IN TRANSACTIONS BELIEVED TO BE EXEMPT FROM REGISTRATION UNDER THE GEORGIA SECURITES ACT OF 1973, AS AMENDED, PURSUANT TO THE EXEMPTION PROVIDED IN SECTION 10-5-9(13) THEREOF. THESE SECURITIES HAVE BEEN REGISTERED WITH THE SECURITIES COMMISSIONER OF THE STATE OF GEORGIA. THE SECURITIES COMMISSIONER, BY ACCEPTING REGISTRATION, DOES NOT IN ANY WAY ENDORSE OR RECOMMEND THE PURCHASE OF ANY OF THESE SECURITIES.

THE DATE OF THIS PROSPECTUS IS SEPTEMBER 14, 1984.

**RICHARD R. FELKER
INDIVIDUAL GENERAL PARTNER**

**2427 THE EQUITABLE BUILDING
ATLANTA, GEORGIA 30303**

a prospectus for a large *public* offering. Note Item No. 2 under the title "This Offering Involves Certain Risk Factors." It indicates that this is an unspecified, or blind, fund.

Real estate syndicates are also classified somewhat more informally as (1) leveraged (i.e., using mortgage loans as well as investor funds to purchase real estate) or unleveraged offerings, and (2) according to how much tax shelter is provided (e.g., two for one, three for one). The degrees of leverage and tax shelter in a syndication have a direct effect on the risks and returns of the investors. These aspects of syndicates are discussed later in this chapter.

EXHIBIT 27–2
PROSPECTUS (FRONT COVER) FOR AN UNSPECIFIED PUBLIC SYNDICATION OFFERING

PROSPECTUS

$50,000,000

PREFERRED PROPERTIES FUND 82

50,000 Limited Partnership Units
(with General Partner's right to increase to 60,000 Units)
$1,000 Per Unit – Minimum Investment – 5 Units ($5,000)
(Or 2 Units ($2,000) for an Individual Retirement Account or Keogh Plan)

Preferred Properties Fund 82 (the "Partnership") is a California limited partnership of which Montgomery Realty Company-80, a California limited partnership, is the General Partner. The Partnership has been formed with the intention of acquiring, directly or through joint ventures, hotels and other lodging facilities. The Partnership intends to acquire properties that are completed, although it may expand or renovate such properties.

The Partnership's investment objectives are to invest in properties which will (i) preserve and protect the Partnership's invested capital; (ii) provide capital gains through potential appreciation; (iii) provide cash distributions from operations; (iv) provide federal income tax deductions so that during the early years of property operations all or a portion of cash distributions may be treated as a return of capital for tax purposes and, therefore, may not represent taxable income to the Limited Partnership Unit Holders; and (v) build up equity through the reduction of mortgage loans. There is no assurance that such objectives will be attained. (See "Investment Objectives and Policies," p. 98.)

THIS OFFERING INVOLVES CERTAIN RISK FACTORS

Prospective investors should carefully consider that:
(1) There are tax risks associated with this offering. (See "Risk Factors," p. 15, "Investment Objectives and Policies," p. 98 and "Tax Consequences," p. 118.)
(2) The Partnership owns no property nor, other than as described in "Proposed Real Property Investments" appearing in the supplement to this Prospectus, has it identified any property that there is a reasonable probability it will acquire. Therefore, investors will not have an opportunity to evaluate all properties to be acquired by the Partnership. During the offering period, this Prospectus will be supplemented to include a description of any specific property which, in the opinion of the General Partner as of the date of such supplement, there is a reasonable probability that the Partnership will acquire. (See "Acquisition Policies and Procedures," p. 104.)
(3) This offering involves the payment of substantial fees to the General Partner and Affiliates, including Acquisition Fees in an amount not to exceed, in the aggregate, 10.5 percent of Gross Offering Proceeds. None of such fees was determined by arm's length negotiations. (See "Summary of Management Compensation," p. 8.)
(4) The General Partner and Affiliates will be subject to various conflicts of interest in managing the Partnership. (See "Conflicts of Interest," p. 11.)
(5) The operations of the Partnership will be affected by general economic conditions, including economic cycles, availability of financing and fluctuations in mortgage interest rates. (See "Risk Factors," p. 15.)
(6) No market for Limited Partnership Units exists nor is one expected to develop. Investors may not be able to liquidate their investment in the event of an emergency or for any other reason. The sale of Limited Partnership Units by a Limited Partnership Unit Holder may result in substantial adverse federal income tax consequences. (See "Risk Factors," p. 15, and "Tax Consequences," p. 118.)

THESE SECURITIES HAVE NOT BEEN APPROVED OR DISAPPROVED BY THE SECURITIES AND EXCHANGE COMMISSION NOR HAS THE COMMISSION PASSED UPON THE ACCURACY OR ADEQUACY OF THIS PROSPECTUS. ANY REPRESENTATION TO THE CONTRARY IS A CRIMINAL OFFENSE.
NEITHER THE ATTORNEY GENERAL OF THE STATE OF NEW YORK OR NEW JERSEY NOR THE BUREAU OF SECURITIES OF THE STATE OF NEW JERSEY HAS PASSED ON OR ENDORSED THE MERITS OF THIS OFFERING. ANY REPRESENTATION TO THE CONTRARY IS UNLAWFUL.

	Price to Public(A)	Selling Commission (B) (C)	Proceeds to Partnership (D) (E)
Per Limited Partnership Unit	$ 1,000	$ 95	$ 905
Total Minimum	1,200,000	114,000	1,086,000
Total Maximum	50,000,000	4,750,000	45,250,000
Total Maximum with Additional Right(F)	60,000,000	5,700,000	54,300,000

(Cover page continued on following page.)   (Footnotes on page 2)

The date of this Prospectus is July 9, 1982
and as thereafter supplemented on the date of each Supplement.

Supplemental Information—For information on matters occurring since the date of this Prospectus, and for information on properties acquired or to be acquired by the Partnership, see the Supplement contained in the inside back cover of the Prospectus.

FOX & CARSKADON SECURITIES CORPORATION

History and Current Business Environment

The first partnership syndicates for real estate appeared in New York City during the 1950s. However, the origins of modern real estate syndicates are the raw land syndicates that were organized in California during the 1960s. Syndication of real estate spread to many different property types and situations during the early 1970s, but was limited primarily to California until only the last decade. In 1975 the Real Estate Securities and Syndication Institute (RESSI) was formed under the auspices of the National Association of REALTORS® (see Chapter 13). The creation of RESSI, which provides educational seminars, confers a professional designation, and publishes a professional journal, represented a significant step in the development of real estate syndication as a separate industry.

The "real estate syndication explosion" did not occur until the early 1980s. Sales of public real estate syndication offerings in 1977 were less than $500 million. By 1979, revenues had grown to about $750 million. In 1981, sales were approximately $1.75 billion but by 1985 they topped $8 billion. Exhibit 27–3 presents data on the sales of all public limited-partnership offerings in 1985. Seventy percent of these offerings are for real estate investments. Among those making real estate offerings, many syndicates diversify by property type by making investments in both residential and commercial properties. The fastest growing segment is syndications set up as REITs. In 1983 this segment only constituted three percent

EXHIBIT 27–3
1985 SALES OF LIMITED PARTNERSHIP INTERESTS IN PUBLIC SYNDICATIONS (millions of dollars)

	Value	Percent of Total
By type of investment:		
Real estate syndications	$8,061.7	70.0%
Oil and gas syndications	1,827.6	15.9
Equipment leasing	(556.7)	4.8
Other	1,074.3	9.3
Total	$11,520.3	100.0%
By type of real estate investment:		
Both commercial and residential property	$2,525.7	31.3%
Commercial property only	1,382.2	17.1
Residential property only	311.6	3.9
Mortgage loans	1,901.6	23.6
Commercial net leases	303.5	3.8
Subsidized housing	98.6	1.2
Set up as REITs	948.3	11.8
All others	610.3	2.6
Total	$8,061.7*	100.0%*

*Differences in totals due to rounding errors.
Source: Robert A. Stanger and Company, P.O. Box 8, Fair Haven, NJ 07701. *Real Estate Review* publishes these data in a special section of each issue.

of the total as compared to 11.7 percent in 1985. The reasons for this trend are given later in this chapter.

What caused this explosive growth during the early 1980s? Most observers agree that two factors were at work. First, rapid inflation, rising real incomes of white collar workers, and more working women during the late 1970s pushed many households into the maximum federal income tax brackets. Second, the Economic Recovery Tax Act of 1981 with the creation of the accelerated capital cost recovery system (See Chapter 22) greatly enhanced the tax shelter benefits of real estate.[3] Therefore more taxpayers needed tax shelter, and real estate syndicates provided a means of accessing the newly created tax benefits of real estate.

The 1986 tax act substantially reduced the tax benefits available to limited partners in real estate syndicates by not allowing investors to fully utilize tax losses from these partnerships to offset other income, such as wages and salaries. As discussed in Chapter 22, these changes are subject to phase-in rules so their full effect on the real estate syndication business will not be known until the early 1990s.

The Role of the Syndicator

Who are real estate syndicators and exactly what do they do? Since the risks and returns from real estate syndications are difficult for investors to evaluate, the success of public and private offerings often depends on the reputation and track record of the syndicator. Today's private syndicator is a businessperson who usually is well known in the local business community. Typically, the private syndicator has a background in real estate, most often brokerage. Public syndicators, in contrast, are large national firms in which syndication is one of several real estate-related services the firm offers. Exhibit 27–4 lists the largest public syndicators of real estate in 1982. These same firms continue to dominate the public syndication industry. Each of these firms relies heavily on its reputation, most are involved in other activities, such as mortgage brokerage (e.g., Consolidated Capital), some are grounded in real estate brokerage (e.g., JMB Realty), and, given the history of syndications, many are based in California.

Syndicators organize, manage, and control the syndicate from origination through completion (e.g., a ten-year period). As shown in Exhibit 27–5, the syndicator's role in the syndication process is most important during origination. Much of the syndicator's work in this phase involves coordination with lawyers on the preparation of the offering documents,

---

[3]The major change was in lowering the number of years over which a taxpayer could depreciate real estate from an average of 50 years before 1981 to 15 years. The shorter the depreciable life, the larger the depreciation allowance in each year of the investment, and therefore the greater the tax shelter.

EXHIBIT 27–4
THE LARGEST PUBLIC SYNDICATORS OF REAL ESTATE (1982)

Firm/Location	Dollars Raised
JMB Realty (Chicago)	$673 million
Integrated Resources (New York)	$516 million
Fox and Corskadon (San Mateo, Calif.)	$443 million
Robert A. McNeil Corp. (San Mateo, Calif.)	$440 million
Consolidated Capital Equity Corp. (Emeryville, Calif.)	$339 million
Balcor Co. (Skokie, Ill.)	$273 million

Source: Gaylon E. Greer and Michael D. Farrell, *Investment Analysis for Real Estate Decisions* (Hinsdale, Ill.: Dryden Press, 1983), p. 439.

EXHIBIT 27–5
SYNDICATION PROCESS: THE ROLE OF THE SYNDICATOR

Origination Phase ⟶	Operation Phase ⟶	Completion Phase
The syndicator . . .	The syndicator . . .	The syndicator . . .
☐ develops the concept for the syndication	☐ manages the syndication	☐ prepares the properties for sale
☐ organizes the legal entity (e.g., limited partnership).	☐ manages the property (frequently)	☐ sells the properties (frequently)
☐ has the offering memorandums drafted		☐ dissolves the syndication or resyndicates
☐ markets the ownership interests to investors		
☐ acquires the real estate		

with accountants to set up the syndicate's accounting system, with marketing agents (e.g., a financial services firm like Merrill Lynch) to market the syndication shares to investors, and with real estate brokers to acquire the property or properties. These activities may be done in-house or with the aid of outside professionals. Real estate brokerage, for example, is typically handled in-house and legal counsel typically comes from outside law firms.

During the operations phase the syndicator manages the syndicate and, frequently, the property. Managing the syndicate involves making sure that all investors receive their cash distributions and statements of tax losses, typically on a quarterly basis. Most syndicators have an in-house property-management division. Finally, the completion phase involves the sale of the property and dissolution of the syndicate. The syndicator either performs these activities or *resyndicates* the property, which involves a sale to another group of investors that the syndicator has organized.

REGULATION

Real estate syndications are heavily regulated by state and federal governments. As we discussed in Chapter 13, government regulation is usually rationalized by the argument that markets will fail and innocent consumers will be hurt without the intervention of a disinterested third party. The general argument for regulating limited-partnership syndications is that investors require information to make rational investment decisions; therefore, without government regulation requiring syndicators to *disclose* and *disseminate information,* the market would not operate efficiently. Stricter regulation that prohibits certain sponsors from operating has been justified on the grounds that it is needed to protect the public against unscrupulous syndicators. Interestingly, while syndications have proliferated in recent years, the trend is for government regulators to take less rigid positions toward sponsors.

What Is a Security?

The Federal Securities Acts of 1933 and 1934 established the Securities and Exchange Commission (SEC) and the structure for most of the federal security regulations in existence today. This act required registration of securities with SEC and disclosure of information to investors for all securities, including *investment contracts.* Whether an investment is a security is determined primarily by the manner in which it is marketed and managed, and not necessarily by the nature of the underlying asset. In the 1946 case of *SEC* vs. *W.J. Howey Co.,* the U.S. Supreme Court ruled that real estate investment contracts are securities and thus fall under the requirements of the 1933 act. An investment contract exists when three conditions are satisfied:

1. Several investors invest in a common enterprise.
2. Investors expect profits from their investments.
3. Profits from the investment are generated *through the efforts of others.*

Item 3 is especially important in deeming real estate investment contracts through syndications as securities under federal law. The states have adopted similar philosophies about the dependence of investors' profits on the efforts of others, as exemplified by the following quotation from a 1974 opinion by the attorney general of Georgia:

> A real estate syndication, whatever its legal form, will be a security under the Georgia Securities Act of 1973 if, as a matter of economic reality, the investor's return is essentially *dependent upon the efforts of the syndicator or an affiliate* (emphasis added).

All real estate syndication offerings, public or private, specified or unspecified, leveraged or unleveraged, are *subject* to all federal and state securities laws. Because certain exemptions exist, however, not all offerings must satisfy every requirement of these laws.

Federal Regulation

The SEC has responsibility for administering federal securities laws. This includes insuring that all offerings are registered or covered by some registration exemption, and that information is properly disclosed to potential investors. In addition, as taxes have become more and more important in real estate syndications, the Internal Revenue Service (IRS) has played a larger role in the regulation of syndications. Limited partnerships file a tax return every year but pay no taxes. Taxes are paid by the partners individually. To maintain this status, partnerships must follow closely the federal income tax rules prescribed by Congress and IRS. These rules have had an increasingly important impact on the financial structure and operation of real estate syndicates in recent years, as we discuss later in this chapter.

Full registration of securities with the SEC is a lengthy and expensive process. One can expect that an SEC review will take as long as nine months, and over $30,000 could be spent in fees for such professionals as lawyers and accountants to complete full registration. Syndicators, therefore, seek to avoid full registration whenever possible. An exemption from full registration does not mean, however, that a syndicator can avoid the responsibilities of disclosing information to investors about the nature of the offering and about the periodic performance of the syndicate's investments during its operation. For most registration exemptions, the syndicator continues to have disclosure responsibilities.

Exhibit 27–6 presents the two major types of exemptions that syndicators of public offerings can apply for to avoid full registration. Regulation "A" registrations are for relatively small offerings of $1.5 million or less. This type of registration results in only a partial exemption, since the syndicator must still file a "short form" with the regional SEC office. Nevertheless, much time and money are saved compared to full registration. Rule 147 Registration is for public intrastate offerings. Since it is difficult to prove that all activities in a public offering will be carried out within the boundaries of a single state, Rule 147 exemptions are relatively difficult to obtain, and thus are uncommon.

To consolidate and simplify the various security regulations governing private placements, SEC adopted Regulation "D" in 1982. This regulation sets forth several rules under which a private-placement syndicator can qualify for exemption from full registration. The most important rules are Rules 504, 505, and 506.

EXHIBIT 27–6
SECURITIES AND EXCHANGE COMMISSION REGISTRATION OF REAL ESTATE SYNDICATIONS*

Type of Registration	Type of Offering	Main Qualifications	Main Exemptions
Full registration	Public or private	No exemption allowed	N/A
Regulation "A" registration exemption	Public	☐ Less than $1.5 million raised from investors. ☐ No limit on the number of investors.	☐ "Short-form" registration. Less time less money needs to be committed to registration. ☐ Registration can be handled at SEC regional office.
Rule 147 registration exemption	Public	☐ Property, sponsor, and investors are all located in the same state.	☐ Full exemption from SEC registration, but difficult to prove that all activity is intrastate.
Regulation "D" Rule 504 exemption	Private	☐ Less than $500,000 raised. ☐ No advertising or general solicitation. ☐ No investor qualification. ☐ Sales to out-of-state residents allowed.	☐ Full exemption. ☐ No specific disclosure requirements.
Rule 505 exemption	Private	☐ Less than $5 million raised. ☐ No advertising or general solicitation. ☐ No investor qualifications. ☐ No more than 35 investors. ☐ Sales to out-of-state residents allowed.	☐ Full exemption. ☐ Some disclosure requirements must be satisfied.
Rule 506 exemption	Private	☐ No limit on amount of money raised. ☐ No more than 35 investors. ☐ No advertisement or general solicitation. ☐ Investor qualification required.	☐ Full exemption. ☐ Full disclosure.

*For detailed explanation of federal securities laws, see Theodore S. Lynn and Harry F. Goldberg, *Real Estate Limited Partnerships* (New York: John Wiley & Sons, 1983), chap. 8.

Rule 504 provides an exemption for small (less than $500,000) private offerings. The syndicator is not only exempt from full registration under this rule but also need not satisfy any particular set of disclosure requirements. If less than $5 million is being raised in a private offering and no more than 35 investors are involved, the offering may qualify for an exemption under Rule 505. This rule offers full exemption, but not complete immunity from disclosure requirements, as in the case of Rule 504. Finally, an exemption from full registration, but not from disclosure, for a private offering can be obtained, regardless of the size of the offering, under Rule 506 of Regulation "D." Under this rule, no more than 35 investors can be involved, and investors must be *qualified* (or accredited). This means that for an investor to participate in the syndication, certain income and net worth requirements must be satisfied. In theory investors who meet the minimum income and wealth requirements are financially able to withstand losses and sophisticated enough to make their own decisions about syndication investment. Therefore they do not need full protection under federal securities laws.

State Regulation

Every state has securities laws.[4] These laws are commonly referred to as "blue sky" laws, since their aim is to prevent "speculative schemes which have no more basis than so many feet of blue sky."[5] While many blue-sky laws are modeled after the Uniform Securities Act developed in 1932, considerable variation among top states exists today in both the intent and the letter of these laws. The blue-sky laws of a particular state, for example, might focus on the following three major areas while other states might have a somewhat different focus.

1. Registration of offerings with a state official charged with responsibility for reviewing offering documents (e.g., secretary of state).
2. Provision for injunctive relief to stop fraudulent or unregistered offerings from being sold in the state.
3. Provisions for civil liberties (i.e., standings in courts of law) for investors who purchase prohibited offerings.

One major difference among the state securities laws is the theory under which state officials operate in evaluating syndications. In so called "merit" states, which are mostly located in the Midwest, state securities officials carefully analyze each offering to determine whether it is *fair* from the perspective of potential investors. If the offering is deemed unfair, then it cannot be sold in the state. Other states, typically in the South, are termed "full disclosure" states. Securities officials in these states review syndication offering documents to determine whether the syndicator is providing sufficient information so that investors can deter-

---

[4]In addition to their securities laws, some states (e.g., New Jersey and New York) have laws specifically related to real estate syndications.

[5]*Hall* v. *Geiger-Jones Co.*, 242 U.S. 539, 550 (1917).

mine the potential for returns from the offering. The laws in merit states, therefore, are based on a strong public-protection philosophy, whereas the laws in full-disclosure states are based on a *caveat emptor* (let the buyer beware) philosophy, provided that investors have adequate and accurate information about the securities sold in those states.

The granting of exemptions for state securities registration has also been a point of difference among the states. Recently, however, several states have adopted, either in whole or in part, the exemption provisions provided in federal Regulation "D." This trend is important in bringing greater uniformity to state and federal securities regulation.

Limited Partnership Laws. States also have limited-partnership statutes that affect the behavior (especially with respect to taxes) of real estate investors and syndicators. While state blue-sky laws are concerned mainly with the relationship between the syndicator and the general public (potential investors), state laws governing limited partnerships are concerned specifically with the internal relationships between general and limited partners (actual investors). Nearly every state has enacted the provisions of the Uniform Limited Partnership Act developed in 1916, and at least 15 states have adopted the 1976 revisions to the act.[6] Some of the more important features of the act are:

1. General rights (including rights to profits and tax losses) and responsibilities of general and limited partners are specified.
2. Legal relationships with third parties are defined.
3. Limited partners are given the right to inspect the books of the partnership.
4. Limited partners are given the right to vote on removal of the general partner, sale of partnership assets, and amendments to the partnership agreement.

A *certificate of limited partnership* must be filed with the designated state office to establish a limited partnership. If the partnership agreement is not approved by state officials or if the certificate is not filed, the partnership will be treated as a general partnership and, therefore, all partners will be taxed as general partners and have personal liability for the debts of the partnership.

NASAA Statement of Policy. The North American Securities Administrators Association (NASAA) is a national organization of state securities

---

[6]A detailed discussion of the provisions of this model statute as well·as a copy of it can be found in Theodore S. Lynn and Harry E. Goldberg, *Real Estate Limited Partnerships* (New York: John Wiley & Sons, 1983).

officials.[7] Recognizing the need for specific and uniform guidelines for states to follow in evaluating real estate syndication, NASAA developed its *Statement of Policy Regarding Real Estate Programs* in 1980 (revised in 1984).[8] Most states have adopted many or all of the provisions in these guidelines. Consequently, there has been much greater uniformity in the state evaluations of real estate syndications in recent years.

The NASAA statement of policy addresses some very difficult issues facing state regulators of real estate syndications. One such issue, which is especially critical in merit-state reviews of real estate offerings, is the setting of acceptable levels for sponsor (i.e., general partner) compensation. The concern of state regulators is that unscrupulous sponsors of real estate syndications may extract excessive fees and other compensation from the money the offering raised and from the cash generated by the properties the syndicate owns. Thus, NASAA sponsor-compensation policies seek to set reasonable levels for such fees and other compensation so that the investing public will not be overcharged.

Exhibit 27–7 provides a table of NASAA sponsor-compensation policies. At the origination phase, the sponsor is allowed to divert up to 33 percent of the proceeds from the offering for the payment of expenses to individuals and firms outside the control of the syndicator (e.g., payment to outside law firms for the preparation of offering documents) and *fees* for activities performed by those in the control of the syndicator (e.g., a fee to the syndicator for acquiring properties). Thus, investors are certain that at least 67 cents of every dollar they invest will be used for the purchase of rights of real estate.

During the operation phase of the syndicate, the sponsor, under NASSA policy, is allowed to receive a fee not to exceed 6 percent of gross income for managing syndicate properties. Property management is an activity that syndicators often perform themselves to earn additional fees. The sponsor is also limited on the amount that can be received from the annual income generated from the syndicate's properties. This limit is 10 percent of cash available for distribution, usually defined as before-tax cash flow (BTCF).

When the syndication is dissolved the sponsor may earn brokerage fees and may participate in the proceeds from the sale of syndicate properties. However, neither the brokerage commission (usually 3 percent) nor the incentive distribution on sale (15 percent of the before-tax reversion) can be taken until the investors have received a return of their cap-

---

[7]All states, except California, belong to NASAA.

[8]These guidelines may be purchased from NASAA, 151 Burns Lane, Suite 103, Springfield, Ill. 62702.

EXHIBIT 27–7
SPONSOR COMPENSATION PROVISIONS OF NASAA STATEMENT OF POLICY

Phase in Syndication Process	Compensation Item	NASAA Policy*
Origination (formation of the syndicate).	Front-end fees and expenses†.	Not to exceed 33 percent of the gross proceeds from the offering.
Operation (during the life of the syndicate).	Management fee.	Not to exceed 6 percent of gross income where the sponsor is involved in leasing.
	Incentive distributions for sponsor.	Not to exceed 10 percent of cash flow available for distribution (BTCF).
Disposition (when the syndicate is dissolved).	Real estate brokerage commission.	Not to exceed one half of 6 percent of contract price subordinated to return of capital contributions plus 6 percent return.‡
	Incentive distribution for sponsor.	Not to exceed 15 percent of net proceeds from the sale (BTR) subordinated to return of capital contributions plus 6 percent return.‡

*These are limits placed on the amounts sponsors can extract from the offering at the various phases of the syndication. The NASAA statement of policy typically offers more than one alternative guideline. The guidelines shown are the most commonly used.

†Fees are amounts paid to the syndicator. Expenses are amounts paid to third parties (e.g., lawyer in outside law firm). Thus, the policy covers both types of payments out of the funds raised.

‡For these payments to be allowed, the limited partners must first have received their initial investment back plus a 6 percent return.

ital invested plus a 6 percent cumulative return over the life of the syndicate.[9]

In addition to proper compensation for syndicators, the NASAA policy addresses a host of other issues. One such issue, which has been almost as controversial as the sponsor-compensation issue, pertains to syndicators' economic forecasts of the returns from syndicated properties. State regulators have been concerned for some time about the use of overly optimistic forecasts of rents, occupancy, and sale prices to bolster sales of partnership shares. The NASAA policy states specifically how such forecasts are to be handled and disclosed in the offering prospectuses.

---

[9]A cumulative 6 percent return means that if the dollar amount needed to give investors a 6 percent return in one year is not adequate, then the deficit is made up the next year plus the normal 6 percent return for that year.

Economic forecasts, for example, are not permitted for blind pools or raw-land syndications. For specified funds, economic forecasts as discussed in the prospectus must be accompanied by a statement that the forecasts have been reviewed by a certified public accountant (CPA), usually a large CPA firm. In addition, the discussion of these forecasts must focus on such things as tax effects on investors and the methods of depreciation to be used, terms of financing, holding-period assumptions, and the components of the return to the investor. The NASAA policy has done much to defuse the issue of overly optimistic economic forecasts by real estate syndicators.

RISKS AND RETURNS

The analysis of the risks and returns of sponsors and investors in real estate syndications is performed much as the analyses of other real estate investment opportunities are performed. The current approach, as discussed in Chapters 21 and 22, is to estimate the ATCFs and ATR to each partner and then calculate the present value of these estimates of future benefits by a discount rate that reflects the riskiness of the cash flows. This section of the chapter discusses some of the unique aspects of real estate syndications that affect the analysis of risks and return.

The Sponsor

Sponsors (syndicators or general partners) of real estate syndications receive compensation for their involvement from front-end fees paid from money raised through the initial offering, from other fees for services rendered during the life of the syndication (e.g., property management), and from property return. Because of fears that sponsors were earning excessive fees and returns on investment, states have limited sponsor compensation by using the NASAA policy or some other set of guidelines. In the past two to three years the real estate syndication business has become highly competitive. The combined effects of a highly competitive market and state-imposed ceilings on fees suggests, at least in theory, that sponsor fees are currently not excessive for the risks that sponsors are incurring.[10] Moreover, one might argue that sponsors are taking substantial business risks. If, for example, the offering does not produce sufficient capital to purchase properties, the syndicator may lose substantial purchase-option payments and loan-commitment fees.

But for offerings that do sell out, the returns on investment of sponsor

---

[10] Unfortunately no studies exist to verify or refute this claim.

funds can be quite high. General partners frequently have very little of their own capital invested in the partnership. Thus, incentive distributions can produce extremely high returns on the amount of their capital at risk. Yet recall from Chapter 21 that general partners have personal liability; their personal assets are exposed to the syndicate's creditors. And much of a sponsor's return comes at a disposition stage, after the investors have received their returns.

Advantages of Syndication Investment

For the investor (or limited partner), there are several distinct advantages of investing in real estate through a real estate syndicate. First, syndicate investment is extremely simple in comparison to investing directly in property. Second, for a relatively small capital outlay (e.g., $1,000 to $5,000), an investor can buy rights to the income from a large property or perhaps a diversified portfolio of large properties. Third, the investor benefits from professional management of the investment and the property. This means that the sponsor provides quarterly (usually) reports on the amount of cash flow and tax loss generated from the investor's ownership in the syndicate, and the distractions of managing properties are handled without involving the investor.

Real estate syndications also offer investors staying power because the funds of many investors support the offering. Investors also are protected by state and federal securities laws against unscrupulous syndicators. Nevertheless, "There is no free lunch!" The fees and expenses for all of these benefits sometimes result in less than 75 cents of each dollar invested actually being spent on real estate. Much higher proportions are attainable by investing directly in real estate but, of course, without the advantages offered by the syndication arrangement.

The Investor

Who are these investors in real estate syndications who are willing to pay large fees and expenses to avoid the responsibilities of direct property ownership? Until 1987 they were predominantly high-income investors demanding investments offering tax shelter that could not afford to spend their own time searching for and acquiring real estate.[11] This suggests that, of the three major components of return on real estate investment (cash flow from operations, tax effects from operations, and cash proceeds from sale), tax effects played a dominant role in syndications during the first half of the 1980s.

---

[11]That is, they could afford to pay the high fees and expenses of syndicate ownership because the tax shelter benefits were important to them.

Two events during the past few years have changed the emphasis of real estate syndications from providing positive tax effect to providing economic returns (i.e., cash flow and sale proceeds). First, in 1985, the IRS tightened the rules that allow investors to take generous write-offs from real estate limited partnerships. These changes may be responsible for much of the growth in REIT syndications during 1985 discussed earlier. The REITs do not give investors the opportunity to use tax losses (i.e., negative taxable incomes) from the real estate owned by the syndication. Thus, the emphasis in REIT investment is entirely on economic returns.

Second, changes in the tax law enacted in 1986 phased out the opportunities investors had to use tax losses to offset their ordinary incomes. Tax losses from real estate limited partnerships can still be used to offset positive taxable income from other investments, such as partnerships that generate positive taxable income. This change in the tax law will undoubtedly have an effect on the nature of real estate syndications in the coming years, but the extent of the effect will not be known for some time. Presumably, syndicates in the future will offer investors mostly economic returns.

Why have these changes occurred? Most observers believe that the historically high vacancy rates in certain segments (e.g., office markets) of the real estate market in many metropolitan areas were caused by overbuilding in response to overly generous tax advantages for real estate investors. The actions of the IRS and Congress, therefore, are designed to make real estate investment decisions rely more on the economics of properties and less on their favorable tax aspects.

Creating Tax Shelter. Syndicators of real estate seeking to fulfill the demand for tax shelter must construct offerings that provide maximum tax effects (i.e., large negative taxable income).[12] The term *two-for-one write-offs* is frequently used to describe the tax shelter from an investment. A two-for-one write-off means that for every dollar invested the investor gets $2 back in the same year in negative taxable income. Recall from Chapter 22 that $2 of negative TI offsets $2 of the investor's positive TI, which saves the investor in the 50 percent tax bracket $1 in taxes. This means that for every dollar invested in a given year, the investor gets one dollar back in tax savings.

One scheme for achieving two-for-one write-offs is to have investors contribute funds a little at a time. For example, an investor might invest $5,000 each year for the next five years, instead of $25,000 all in the first year. This makes it easier for syndicators to provide two-for-one write-offs, since less money is invested each year, and therefore less money in

---

[12]See Chapter 22 for a review.

tax savings needs to be generated in any year. Another devise is to pay more than the market value for syndicated properties (see Frame 27–1). This increases the depreciation base, and thus the depreciation charge each year, which increases negative taxable income.

Investor Returns. Although investors have been somewhat preoccupied with the tax shelter aspects of real estate syndicates, this does not mean that they ignore total rates of return on investment. It is irrational for an investor to want to earn high returns from the tax shelter component and, in the same investment, incur large losses when the partnership shares are sold. Thus, we are interested in how investors in real estate syndicates have fared in their total rates of return.

On this score, the results are mixed. One set of results, shown in Exhibit 27–8, indicates that returns from public syndications have been quite strong, ranging from 12.6 percent to 25.2 percent (averaging 17.3

Frame 27–1

Have Sponsors of Real Estate Syndications Been "Ripping Off" Investors? The Results From the Infamous Forbes Article

In its December 19, 1983, issue, *Forbes* carried an article critical of real estate syndicators that sent shock waves through the syndication industry. *Forbes* essentially makes the following three points:

1. Syndicators and real estate brokers take too much, sometimes 20 percent, of the investor's investment in fees.
2. Investments are often poorly chosen.
3. Many syndicators pay too much for properties.

As far as the third point is concerned, one recent statistical study shows that syndicators pay no more for properties than other investors.* Also, there is no evidence to support the claim that syndicators consistently choose poorer properties to syndicate than other investors invest in.

The first claim, however, is somewhat more difficult to support or refute. One study found that investors in syndications did not fare well, perhaps because of excessive fees.† Other estimates indicate that rates of return are substantially higher for syndicated property investments. To conclude, the syndication market has become very competitive in recent years, and fees have declined on average. This competitiveness has probably made the value of syndicators' services just about equal to the fees syndicators charge.

---

*William Beaton and C. F. Sirmans, "Do Syndications Pay More for Real Estate?" *AREUEA Journal,* 14 (Summer 1986), pp. 206–15.

†Ronald C. Rogers and James E. Owers, "The Investment Performance of Public Real Estate Limited Partnerships," *AREUEA Journal* 13 (Summer 1985), pp. 153–66.

EXHIBIT 27–8
RATES OF RETURN ON SELECTED PUBLIC SYNDICATIONS

Syndication	Time Period	Rate of Return, Tax Exempt Investor (e.g., Pension Fund)	Rate of Return, Investor in 50 Percent Bracket
Pacific Plan Investors Fund No. 1 (The Robert A. McNeil Corp.)	9/70–8/79	14.6%	17.5%
SB Partners (Smith Barney Real Estate Corp.)	4/71–12/79	11.8	12.6
Carlyle—71 (JMB Realty Corp.)	12/71–12/84	15.6	18.5
Real Properties Ltd.—1971 (Angeles Corp.)	7/71–12/82	13.2	15.7
California Realty Fund (Consolidated Capital Equities Corp.)	12/70–12/85	12.3	13.3
Pacific Plan Investors Fund No. 2 (The Robert A. McNeil Corp.)	6/71–12/84	16.5	25.2
Real Properties Ltd.–1972 (Angeles Corp.)	3/72–8/84	<u>15.8</u>	<u>18.9</u>
Average Rate of Return		14.2%	17.3%

Source: Derived from Exhibit 7, Robert H. Zerbst and Barbara R. Cambon, "Real Estate: Historical Returns and Risks," *Journal of Portfolio Management*, Spring 1984, pp. 5–20.

percent) for an investor in the highest tax bracket. Another study found that the rates of return on real estate limited partnerships have been in the range of 8.44 percent to 10.49 percent in recent years.[13] Finally, an article in *Forbes* (December 19, 1983, p. 243) suggests that the rate of return for investors in real estate limited partnerships was about 11 percent at a time when rates of return on other investments exceeded 11 percent (see Frame 27–1).

The returns to limited partners in real estate syndications are difficult to calculate because the shares are *not* bought and sold in an active secondary market, like the stock exchanges. However, the relevant question is whether the returns compensate investors for the risks they take. From the estimates of returns obtained to date, some preliminary conclusions can be reached. In general, there is reasonable doubt that the returns from real estate syndications are sufficient to compensate for investment risks. Moreover, substantial risk looms on the horizon, as many real estate markets remain overbuilt and tax law changes are likely to reduce incentives to invest in real estate.

---

[13]Ronald C. Rogers and James E. Owers, "The Investment Performance of Public Real Estate Limited Partnerships," *AREUEA Journal* 14 (Summer 1985), pp. 153–66.

OVERVIEW

Syndicators of real estate have been an important force in increasing the economic productivity of real estate during the early 1980s. Most syndicates have been organized as limited partnerships and are most often categorized as private (no general solicitation or advertising) or public offerings. Another way to classify syndicates is by how much property has been acquired at the time of the offering. In a specified fund all the property has been acquired, whereas in an unspecified, or blind, fund none of the property has been purchased.

Syndicators are primarily promoters. Thus, most of their involvement occurs in the origination phase, including developing the concept for the syndicate, having the offering memoranda (e.g., the prospectus) prepared, and marketing the offering. During the operation phase the syndicator manages the investment and the property. The syndicator also helps dissolve the syndicate when the properties are sold.

Syndications are heavily regulated both at the state and federal levels. Under federal securities laws which apply to real estate syndications, the syndicator must complete an expensive and time-consuming registration process for each offering unless the offering qualifies for an exemption. Regardless of whether the issue must be fully registered or is exempt, the syndicator must follow certain rules on the disclosure of information to potential investors. Many states have adopted many of the federal rules for exempting private offerings from full registration.

In regulating real estate syndications, the states also follow the policy statement of the North American Securities Administrators Association (NASAA). These guidelines specify, for example, the amount of compensation a sponsor of a syndication can earn and rules for making economic forecasts.

Much attention has been focused recently on the rates of return investors in real estate syndicates earn, in addition to how much the sponsor earns. The evidence on investor rates of return is mixed; yet some data suggest that limited partners have not earned high returns even though tax-shelter benefits have been high in recent years. The future of real estate syndication is highly uncertain. Tax law changes reduce the tax shelter benefits to investors. Thus, more emphasis will be placed on the economic productivity of real estate owned by syndicates.

TEST YOURSELF

Explain the following terms and concepts.

1. Private versus public offering.
2. Prospectus.
3. "Blind" fund or pool.
4. RESSI.
5. Registration and disclosure.
6. Investment contract.
7. Regulation "D."

8. Qualified investor.
9. NASAA policy.
10. Two-for-one write-offs.

Answer the following multiple choice questions.

1. What factor(s) were responsible for the explosive growth in real estate syndications during the early 1980s?
   a. RESSI.
   b. Economic Recovery Tax Act of 1981 provisions.
   c. Rapid Inflation.
   d. Both *(b)* and *(c)*.
   e. None of the above.

2. State and federal courts agree that the primary determinant that makes an investment contract a security for regulatory purposes is
   a. The existence of a contract.
   b. Parties come together to earn profits.
   c. Parties come together to invest in real estate.
   d. Profits of investors depend on efforts of others.
   e. None of the above.

3. Which is *not* an exemption from full registration under current SEC rules?
   a. Regulation D.
   b. Rule 147.
   c. Rule X.
   d. Rule 504.
   e. All are exemptions.

4. In "merit" states
   a. Each syndication offering is analyzed to determine whether it is fair to investors.
   b. The syndicator need only disclose to investors all relevant information.
   c. The syndicator may earn only merit fees.
   d. Securities are regulated by a merit board.
   e. Syndicators are limited to fees that do not exceed the average level of fees by more than 20 percent.

5. Under the NASAA Statement of Policy Regarding Real Estate Programs the sponsor
   a. May not use more than 20 cents per dollar raised from investors for up-front fees and expenses.
   b. May receive only 5 percent as an incentive distribution during the life of the syndication.
   c. Must have all economic forecasts reviewed by a REALTOR.®
   d. Cannot share in the proceeds from the sale of syndicate properties.
   e. Must have the marketing program approved by NASAA.

ADDITIONAL READINGS

Bricker, Ruth Baker. *Getting Rich in Real Estate Partnerships*. New York: Warner Books, 1982.

Brueggeman, William B., and Jeffrey D. Fisher. *Real Estate Finance*. Homewood, Ill.: Richard D. Irwin, forthcoming.

Dawson, Peter. "How to Compare Real Estate Private Placements Using IRR." *Financial Planner*, August 1983, pp. 63–66.

Eber, Alan R. "Real Estate Programs: The Key Questions to Ask." *Financial Planner*, August 1983, pp. 54–62.

Greer, Gaylon E., and Michael D. Farrell. *Investment Analysis for Real Estate Decisions*. Hinsdale, Ill.: Dryden Press, 1983, chap. 23.

Lerman, Terry A., and Stephen P. Jarchow. "The King of Syndication." *Real Estate Review* 13 Winter 1984, pp. 26–30.

Lynn, Theodore S., and Harry E. Goldberg. *Real Estate Limited Partnerships*. New York: John Wiley & Sons, 1983.

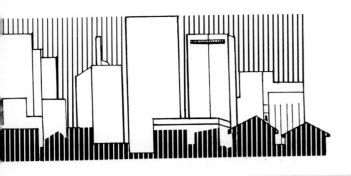

28
Innovations to Enhance Real Estate Productivity

OUTLINE

INTRODUCTION

TECHNOLOGICAL INNOVATIONS
Computers
Telecommunications
Building Design

INNOVATIONS IN THE BUSINESS ENVIRONMENT
Vertical Integration
Horizontal Integration

OVERVIEW

INTRODUCTION

Traditionally, introductory texts in real estate have contained a final chapter offering rather general forecasts of the future of real estate and the future of the real estate industry. Instead of this, we believe that students should be challenged to consider factors that are changing the use of real estate and the real estate industry, in order to gain an understanding of *why* trends may occur. For example, what factors may cause real estate to become more valuable relative to other goods? Why will the real estate industry have more or fewer employees during the next decade?

Some of the factors that will cause change in the coming years, such as new tax laws and future rates of inflation, are inherently unpredictable. Other forces, however, are more predictable; they are already at work, altering future real estate uses and real estate's future role in the economy. These include recent innovations that will continue to increase the *productivity* of real estate and real estate services. In this chapter, we discuss two major types of innovations destined for productivity enhancement. These are technological innovations and innovations in the business environment.

TECHNOLOGICAL INNOVATIONS

Advances in technology result in higher productivity for all firms in an industry. Supppose that a new machine is introduced in the widget manufacturing industry. This machine produces widgets at a rate that is twice as fast as the old machine and requires only one employee to operate it, instead of the two employees needed for the old machine. Also, the new machine costs the same as a replacement for the old machine. Widget manufacturers using the new machines are able to produce twice as many

713

widgets as before in the same amount of time. Moreover, they are able to save on the production costs of widgets because one fewer employee is needed to operate each machine.

Thus productivity increases resulting from the introduction of new technology come in the form of increased output at the same or less cost in the same or less amount of time. Economists call this the *substitution* of a cheaper factor of production for a more expensive one. Often during the past few decades productivity gains from new technology have occurred because capital (machines) has been substituted for labor (employees). This is analagous to the substitution of cheaper capital (buildings) for more expensive land at prime locations, as we discussed in Chapter 10.

The real estate industry, like all other industries that have flourished during the latter half of the 20th Century, has and will continue to enjoy productivity gains from technological innovation. Some of the future gains will come from the more productive use of real estate per se; others will come from greater productivity in real estate services (e.g., brokerage, appraisal, and development). The potential technological sources of higher productivity in the real estate industry are numerous. Three of the most important are computers, telecommunications, and building design.

Computers

Computers are the classic example of a technological innovation that increases productivity by saving time. The real magic of computers lies in the speed with which they can perform tasks. Calculations and analyses that previously took hours or days can now be done in a matter of seconds. And although wage rates have increased dramatically in recent years, the prices of smaller and increasingly more powerful computers have declined. These trends have important implications for firms offering such real estate services as brokerage, appraisal, property management, mortgage banking, development, and consulting services. First, firms in the real estate industry almost certainly will rely less on human capital and more on computer technology (perhaps including robots) in the future. Unfortunately, no detailed studies have been performed to verify that the substitution of computers for people has led to productivity gains in the real estate industry. One observer suggests that computers may increase the volume of real estate business in the future and, therefore, more employees in real estate service firms will be needed.[1]

---

[1]James R. Follain, "A Look at Long-Term Trends That Affect the Real Estate Brokerage Industry," working paper, Office of Real Estate Research, University of Illinois, Champaign-Urbana.

Second, regardless of whether more or fewer employees will be needed, students and other aspiring employees in the real estate industry *must* obtain substantial computer skills to be competitive in the job market.

Computers are revolutionizing many areas of the real estate business. For example, financial analysis involving discounted cash-flow calculations have traditionally been performed with computers using relatively inflexible fixed-format programs. Today, most financial analysis is conducted with highly flexible spreadsheet programs, such as Lotus 1–2–3. Enhancements to this software in the coming years will undoubtedly make appraisers and investment analysts more productive.

Yet perhaps the greatest contribution computers will make during the next ten years will be in helping to supply data on the operation of real estate markets. The absence of such data has been a tremendous hindrance to productivity in the real estate industry; curing that shortcoming will help make real estate markets more efficient (see Frame 28–1). Perhaps in ten years, because of computerized information systems, daily prices of properties in various geographic areas will be reported in the *Wall Street Journal,* just as the prices of securities are reported today.

Frame 28–1

A Nationwide Housing Market

As reported by the *Wall Street Journal,* some major changes have been occurring recently in the housing market, and even bigger changes are yet to come. Looking 30 years down the road, housing experts see a national housing market rather than the traditional local market. They predict that computers will offer information about homes nationwide and that computer processing will put a house in its new owner's hands in as few as one or two days—down from the usual six to eight weeks. Along the way, financial-services networks will mushroom until the real-estate agent and the banker meld into one, providing home buyers with one-stop shopping.

Source: *The Wall Street Journal,* January 25, 1984.

Telecommunications

With the markets for goods and services, including real estate and real estate services, becoming more nationwide, the need to have branch offices and to conduct business in various parts of the country has become increasingly important. While there is no perfect substitute for face-to-face contact with members of the same firm and with clients in other parts of the country, rising salaries for business executives and increasing travel costs have created a strong demand for substitutes for face-to-face meetings.

Telecommunications is the science of long-distance communication of sound, images, and data. Recently, for the reasons mentioned above, telecommunications has emerged as an important technological innovation in the real estate business.

The advantages of telecommunications systems should be examined in terms of augmented productivity. An employee of a firm located in New York, for example, who conducts the same business in her offices via telecommunications that she would have conducted during a trip to San Francisco will be able to use the time otherwise spent in travel more productively. The costs of airfare, local transportation, food, and lodging beyond the cost of the telecommunications system would also be saved.

"Smart" Buildings. Developers of "smart" buildings, which include some of the newest office buildings and hotels, are attempting to satisfy the communication needs of tenants as well as their space needs. The advantages to the developer of introducing telecommunications innovations, such as sophisticated telephone switchboards (PBXs), satellite antennas, and data transmission cables in their buildings include gaining a comparative advantage in several areas. These include leasing, generating additional revenues from the operation of the systems, and lowering the cost of incorporating other computerized systems (e.g., energy-control,

Frame 28–2

The First of the "Smart" Buildings

Over 50 buildings in the United States currently have telecommunications systems installed. Some examples are:

1. Lincoln Plaza in Dallas, Texas, in which Lincoln Property Co. (a large commercial property developer) is offering telecommunications systems to some of its tenants. This service will be extended to at least 17 other buildings developed by the firm.
2. 49 Tower in midtown Manhattan.
3. Texas Plaza, an office complex in Irving, Texas. Tenants share a computerized telephone system and a satellite broadcasting room.
4. International developer Olympia and York plans to install shared communications in buildings the firm owns in 40 cities.

Source: *The Mortgage and Real Estate Executives Report* (New York: Warren, Gorham, & Lamont, 1984).

security, and fire protection systems) into their buildings. The advantage to the tenant is increased productivity and lower cost of leasehold improvements, since the PBX and data network are already installed.

Video Conferencing. The cornerstone of the real estate telecommunication revolution is video conferencing. Video conferencing has two basic formats. *Interactive videoconferencing* involves the traditional two-way audio and video interaction between two or more people or two or more groups of people. A more recent innovation is known as *participative videoconferencing*. This format involves a lecture presentation in one location and listening groups in one or more other locations. The listening group is able to interact with the lecturer through the system as if he were in front of the group.

Videoconferencing could dramatically change the way business is conducted. Real estate developers who provide the facilities for future business operations are currently facing a bewildering set of choices. Should videoconferencing become the accepted mode of business "travel," the hotel industry will undergo substantial changes. Less travel means less demand for hotel rooms. However, hotels are a logical place for interactive videoconferencing among small groups and participative videoconferencing among larger groups. The implications of the video-conferencing revolution for the hotel industry might include fewer guest rooms and more and larger meeting rooms, equipped with telecommunications equipment.

Technological innovations in telecommunication will have a dramatic impact on the demand for both residential and business space, as well as the way in which such space is used. Less travel by employees to their offices because of enhanced telecommunication ("telecommuting") will allow households more freedom in choosing residential locations and result in less dense cities. The demand for office space may decrease, while the demand for homes with offices may increase. Retailers may undergo redesign to allow for fewer walk-in customers and more viewing of products through telecommunication networks. These are just a few of many possible implications of the widespread innovations in telecommunications. Others can be found simply by letting one's imagination take over.

Building Design

Building design and materials have improved continually over the last 100 years and undoubtedly will continue to do so. The Monadnock Building, constructed in 1891, is regarded as the highest wall-bearing structure in Chicago. Constructed of solid masonry (stone load-bearing walls), the building is 16 stories tall and is still being used. Beginning in the early 1900s, the use of steel-frame construction allowed buildings to be constructed to much greater heights. Many skyscrapers were erected in the 1920s and early 1930s, including such famous buildings as the Flatiron Building, Empire State Building, and Chrysler Building in New York City and the Board of Trade Building, Wrigley Building, and Tribune Tower in Chicago.

An indicator of the improvement of building-design efficiency over about 40 years is the ratio of usable space to total space in the Empire State Building compared with the World Trade Center. The World Trade Center, completed in 1971 in lower Manhattan and consisting of twin 110-story towers, has an 85 percent ratio of usable space to total space. The Empire State Building has a ratio of about 58 percent. A much higher percentage of space in the older building was required for structural beams, elevators, mechanical equipment, and public areas.

While such dramatic increases in usable space ratios are unlikely in the future, continued improvements are probable in such areas as building equipment, heating and cooling efficiency, structural design and materials, and architectural style. In modern buildings, computers monitor and control the major mechanical equipment, such as elevators and HVAC systems, for maximum efficiency. They allow operation only of the number of elevators actually needed, instead of allowing, for example, an elevator for each person during slack periods. HVAC systems are zoned and operate only as needed to achieve the desired temperature. And computerized diagnostic systems warn managers of equipment failure or inefficient operation.

Architectural styles are becoming more varied and imaginative. Unusual designs and spatial concepts are being incorporated in buildings, especially in the newer Sunbelt cities such as Atlanta, Houston, Miami, Dallas, and Phoenix. A variety of exterior materials; pleasant vistas; and dramatic, glass-enclosed areas are being included in many buildings. Many new hotels such as the Hyatt-Regencies in Atlanta, Chicago, Dallas, and San Francisco have as their trademark dramatic, open, multistory atriums.

Although building economics may limit the future height of buildings, engineering considerations will not. Over 50 years ago the famous architect Frank Lloyd Wright proposed a mile-high building for Chicago. More recent proposals have also been advanced for super skyscrapers, but have not been considered economical (see Exhibit 28–1). Much like supersonic jet transports, super skyscrapers to date have become technically but not economically feasible.

Housing designs are also changing. An increasing proportion of apartments, condominiums, and attached houses are being constructed. And the character of the single-family, detached home is changing. In general, smaller houses are being built on smaller lots than a few years ago as construction costs have skyrocketed. Families have decreased in

EXHIBIT 28–1
HEIGHTS OF SOME OF THE WORLD'S TALLEST OFFICE BUILDINGS

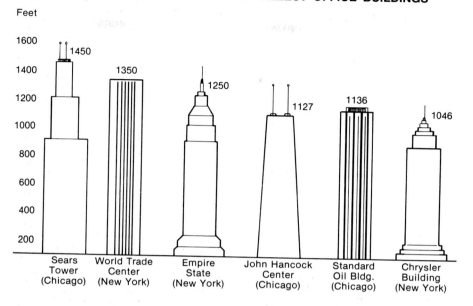

size, and there is more emphasis on efficiency in heating, cooling, and general living. Labor-saving devices such as dishwashers, microwave ovens, and waste disposals have become the norm, even in moderately priced new housing.

What does the future hold for housing and other types of buildings? Undoubtedly, the trend toward greater efficiency will continue. The operation of large buildings will become ever more computerized, and single-family homes will become increasingly energy-efficient and economical in the use of space. New homes will become more amenable to computerized operation for controlling heating, cooling, lights, appliances, and security systems. More and more, consumers will obtain information, shop, and carry out financial transactions through home computers. The emphasis on convenience and security may lead to less urban sprawl than otherwise would occur, as households seek to limit commuting time and to live close to police and fire protection.

INNOVATIONS IN THE BUSINESS ENVIRONMENT

Just as in technology, innovations occur continually in the organization and management of real estate businesses. Entrepreneurs, managers, and executives try to develop new ways of organizing business functions, new managerial concepts and techniques, and new products and services to attract consumers' dollars. Some of the main trends that are occurring, and undoubtedly will continue to occur, generally fall into two categories—vertical integration and horizontal integration.

Vertical Integration

Economists have long been aware of the propensity of successful business firms in a capitalistic society to become larger. They attempt to grow either through internal expansion (by reinvestment of profits, or retained earnings) or through external expansion (by merging with other firms). In some industries expansion has led to domination by one or a few firms, which in turn has led to the enactment of antimonopoly and pro-competition laws. Such laws prohibit business combinations and trade practices that would enable one or a few firms to monopolize a market or to restrain competition.

Until recently, the vertical expansion of real estate firms did not seem economically viable. Most real estate businesses were local in ownership and control, and they performed only one or possibly two functions (such as building and marketing their own products). In very few cases did they attempt to develop, construct, market, finance, and appraise even for their own inventory. Recently, however, real estate firms have begun to combine functions. This process is known as *vertical integration*.

The impetus for vertical integration has come mainly from large non-real estate firms such as Sears, Roebuck and Company; Merrill Lynch, Pierce, Fenner, and Smith; Bank of America; and other large financial services firms. As noted in Chapter 24, these firms are attempting to become "department stores" for financial services, including real estate brokerage (such as Sears' Coldwell-Banker Division and Merrill Lynch's Merrill Lynch Realty), mortgage financing (such as Sears' American Savings and Loan), mortgage insurance (such as Sears' PMI Mortgage Insurance Division), and appraisal (such as Bank of America's BA Appraisals Co.). Many large banks and savings associations such as Empire of America, AmeriFirst Federal Savings and Loan Association, and Gold Dome Savings Bank have real estate development, brokerage, mortgage banking, and appraisal subsidiaries.

With large firms leading the way toward the vertical integration of real estate and financial services, it is likely the trend will continue. To remain competitive, other large firms will probably follow the lead of these giants. And smaller firms at the local level also will have to provide a greater variety of services to attract customers. More and more consumers will be encouraged to take care of all of their financial and real estate needs with a single firm.

Horizontal Integration

The tendency for external expansion also includes the merger of firms performing similar functions. While real estate firms have long been characterized by small size and local ownership, there is an evolving trend toward regional and national affiliation among brokerage firms. The principal type of affiliation is by franchising.

Franchised brokerage firms include Century 21, ERA (Electronic Realty Associates), Red Carpet, Better Homes and Gardens, and Gallery of Homes. While the firms in most cases continue to be owned individually, they contract with the franchisors for their organizational and marketing services and their expertise. Affiliated firms may also share listings and customers when customers move between cities. This increases their productivity and improves market efficiency.

As we noted previously, some brokerage chains are owned by a single, large company. For example, Merrill Lynch Realty owns offices across the country. It seems likely that the trend will continue toward national brokerage chains, either through franchise or direct corporate ownership.

What does the future hold for the horizontal integration of other types of real estate firms? Certainly the mortgage-financing function is being performed by every large financial institution of national scope. Will the trend extend to development, construction, and appraisal? To date, these functions remain largely the domain of relatively small, local firms. Some inroads have begun, however, with such firms as Landauer and Associates, Lincoln Property Company, and Olympia and York. The future holds exciting potential for innovations in organization and managerial techniques to increase productivity and provide better services for consumers.

OVERVIEW

Real estate productivity increases continually through technological, organizational, and managerial innovations. This chapter discusses trends in these areas, with the objective of stimulating readers to consider how these trends may affect the productivity of real estate and real estate businesses in the future. Computers and telecommunications are two major technological innovations that are likely to affect real estate productivity for many years. Computers have become part of our lives; in real estate they are becoming ever more useful in the analysis of financial and investment decisions, the storage and retrieval of transaction data, and the control of buildings. Telecommunications are increasingly being used as a substitute for personal travel and face-to-face contact. Through direct communication and videoconferencing, executives' time will be spent on more productive activities than travel. Both computers and telecommunications have important implications for land use and city functions.

Technological innovations are also changing some important characteristics of buildings. They are becoming more efficient, both in the use of space and of power and fuel. Designs are shifting to reflect human needs and architectural diversity.

Finally, we noted the innovations occurring in the business environment of real estate. Real estate firms are being merged vertically and horizontally into multifunction "department stores" of financial services covering, in some cases, the entire country. These trends are likely to continue, resulting in increasing numbers of consumers' obtaining real estate services in one large, nationwide firm. Real estate entrepreneurs can be expected to devise many variations on these basic trends.

Appendix

Annual and Monthly Compound Interest Tables for Various Rates*

*Reprinted from Paul Wendt and Alan R. Cerf, *Tables for Investment Analysis*, (Berkeley Calif.: Center for Real Estate and Urban Economics, Institute of Urban and Regional Development, University of California, 1966).

8.00%   ANNUAL COMPOUND INTEREST TABLES   8.00%
                               EFFECTIVE RATE 8.00

	1 AMOUNT OF $1 AT COMPOUND INTEREST	2 ACCUMULATION OF $1 PER PERIOD	3 SINKING FUND FACTOR	4 PRESENT VALUE REVERSION OF $1	5 PRESENT VALUE ORD. ANNUITY $1 PER PERIOD	6 INSTALMENT TO AMORTIZE $1
YEARS						
1	1.080000	1.000000	1.000000	0.925926	0.925926	1.080000
2	1.166400	2.080000	0.480769	0.857339	1.783265	0.560769
3	1.259712	3.246400	0.308034	0.793832	2.577097	0.388034
4	1.360489	4.506112	0.221921	0.735030	3.312127	0.301921
5	1.469328	5.866601	0.170456	0.680583	3.992710	0.250456
6	1.586874	7.335929	0.136315	0.630170	4.622880	0.216315
7	1.713824	8.922803	0.112072	0.583490	5.206370	0.192072
8	1.850930	10.636628	0.094015	0.540269	5.746639	0.174015
9	1.999005	12.487558	0.080080	0.500249	6.246888	0.160080
10	2.158925	14.486562	0.069029	0.463193	6.710081	0.149029
11	2.331639	16.645487	0.060076	0.428883	7.138964	0.140076
12	2.518170	18.977126	0.052695	0.397114	7.536078	0.132695
13	2.719624	21.495297	0.046522	0.367698	7.903776	0.126522
14	2.937194	24.214920	0.041297	0.340461	8.244237	0.121297
15	3.172169	27.152114	0.036830	0.315242	8.559479	0.116830
16	3.425943	30.324283	0.032977	0.291890	8.851369	0.112977
17	3.700018	33.750226	0.029629	0.270269	9.121638	0.109629
18	3.996019	37.450244	0.026702	0.250249	9.371887	0.106702
19	4.315701	41.446263	0.024128	0.231712	9.603599	0.104128
20	4.660957	45.761964	0.021852	0.214548	9.818147	0.101852
21	5.033834	50.422921	0.019832	0.198656	10.016803	0.099832
22	5.436540	55.456755	0.018032	0.183941	10.200744	0.098032
23	5.871464	60.893296	0.016422	0.170315	10.371059	0.096422
24	6.341181	66.764759	0.014978	0.157699	10.528758	0.094978
25	6.848475	73.105940	0.013679	0.146018	10.674776	0.093679
26	7.396353	79.954415	0.012507	0.135202	10.809978	0.092507
27	7.988061	87.350768	0.011448	0.125187	10.935165	0.091448
28	8.627106	95.338830	0.010489	0.115914	11.051078	0.090489
29	9.317275	103.965936	0.009619	0.107328	11.158406	0.089619
30	10.062657	113.283211	0.008827	0.099377	11.257783	0.088827
31	10.867669	123.345868	0.008107	0.092016	11.349799	0.088107
32	11.737083	134.213537	0.007451	0.085200	11.434999	0.087451
33	12.676050	145.950620	0.006852	0.078889	11.513888	0.086852
34	13.690134	158.626670	0.006304	0.073045	11.586934	0.086304
35	14.785344	172.316804	0.005803	0.067635	11.654568	0.085803
36	15.968172	187.102148	0.005345	0.062625	11.717193	0.085345
37	17.245626	203.070320	0.004924	0.057986	11.775179	0.084924
38	18.625276	220.315945	0.004539	0.053690	11.828869	0.084539
39	20.115298	238.941221	0.004185	0.049713	11.878582	0.084185
40	21.724521	259.056519	0.003860	0.046031	11.924613	0.083860
41	23.462483	280.781040	0.003561	0.042621	11.967235	0.083561
42	25.339482	304.243523	0.003287	0.039464	12.006699	0.083287
43	27.366640	329.583005	0.003034	0.036541	12.043240	0.083034
44	29.555972	356.949646	0.002802	0.033834	12.077074	0.082802
45	31.920449	386.505617	0.002587	0.031328	12.108402	0.082587
46	34.474085	418.426067	0.002390	0.029007	12.137409	0.082390
47	37.232012	452.900152	0.002208	0.026859	12.164267	0.082208
48	40.210573	490.132164	0.002040	0.024869	12.189136	0.082040
49	43.427419	530.342737	0.001886	0.023027	12.212163	0.081886
50	46.901613	573.770156	0.001743	0.021321	12.233485	0.081743

8.00% MONTHLY COMPOUND INTEREST TABLES 8.00%
EFFECTIVE RATE 0.667

	1	2	3	4	5	6	
	AMOUNT OF $1 AT COMPOUND INTEREST	ACCUMULATION OF $1 PER PERIOD	SINKING FUND FACTOR	PRESENT VALUE REVERSION OF $1	PRESENT VALUE ORD. ANNUITY $1 PER PERIOD	INSTALMENT TO AMORTIZE $1	
MONTHS							
1	1.006667	1.000000	1.000000	0.993377	0.993377	1.006667	
2	1.013378	2.006667	0.498339	0.986799	1.980176	0.505006	
3	1.020134	3.020044	0.331121	0.980264	2.960440	0.337788	
4	1.026935	4.040178	0.247514	0.973772	3.934212	0.254181	
5	1.033781	5.067113	0.197351	0.967323	4.901535	0.204018	
6	1.040673	6.100893	0.163910	0.960917	5.862452	0.170577	
7	1.047610	7.141566	0.140025	0.954553	6.817005	0.146692	
8	1.054595	8.189176	0.122112	0.948232	7.765237	0.128779	
9	1.061625	9.243771	0.108181	0.941952	8.707189	0.114848	
10	1.068703	10.305396	0.097037	0.935714	9.642903	0.103703	
11	1.075827	11.374099	0.087919	0.929517	10.572420	0.094586	
12	1.083000	12.449926	0.080322	0.923361	11.495782	0.086988	
YEARS							MONTHS
1	1.083000	12.449926	0.080322	0.923361	11.495782	0.086988	12
2	1.172888	25.933190	0.038561	0.852596	22.110544	0.045227	24
3	1.270237	40.535558	0.024670	0.787255	31.911806	0.031336	36
4	1.375666	56.349915	0.017746	0.726921	40.961913	0.024413	48
5	1.489846	73.476856	0.013610	0.671210	49.318433	0.020276	60
6	1.613502	92.025325	0.010867	0.619770	57.034522	0.017533	72
7	1.747422	112.113308	0.008920	0.572272	64.159261	0.015586	84
8	1.892457	133.868583	0.007470	0.528414	70.737970	0.014137	96
9	2.049530	157.429535	0.006352	0.487917	76.812497	0.013019	108
10	2.219640	182.946035	0.005466	0.450523	82.421481	0.012133	120
11	2.403869	210.580392	0.004749	0.415996	87.600600	0.011415	132
12	2.603389	240.508387	0.004158	0.384115	92.382800	0.010825	144
13	2.819469	272.920390	0.003664	0.354677	96.798498	0.010331	156
14	3.053484	308.022574	0.003247	0.327495	100.875784	0.009913	168
15	3.306921	346.038222	0.002890	0.302396	104.640592	0.009557	180
16	3.581394	387.209149	0.002583	0.279221	108.116871	0.009249	192
17	3.878648	431.797244	0.002316	0.257822	111.326733	0.008983	204
18	4.200574	480.086128	0.002083	0.238063	114.290596	0.008750	216
19	4.549220	532.382966	0.001878	0.219818	117.027313	0.008545	228
20	4.926803	589.020416	0.001698	0.202971	119.554292	0.008364	240
21	5.335725	650.358746	0.001538	0.187416	121.887606	0.008204	252
22	5.778588	716.788127	0.001395	0.173053	124.042099	0.008062	264
23	6.258207	788.731114	0.001268	0.159790	126.031475	0.007935	276
24	6.777636	866.645333	0.001154	0.147544	127.868388	0.007821	288
25	7.340176	951.026395	0.001051	0.136237	129.564523	0.007718	300
26	7.949407	1042.411042	0.000959	0.125796	131.130668	0.007626	312
27	8.609204	1141.380571	0.000876	0.116155	132.576786	0.007543	324
28	9.323763	1248.564521	0.000800	0.107253	133.912076	0.007468	336
29	10.097631	1364.644687	0.000733	0.099033	135.145031	0.007399	348
30	10.935730	1490.359449	0.000671	0.091443	136.283494	0.007338	360
31	11.843390	1626.508474	0.000615	0.084435	137.334707	0.007281	372
32	12.826385	1773.957801	0.000564	0.077964	138.305357	0.007230	384
33	13.890969	1933.645350	0.000517	0.071989	139.201617	0.007184	396
34	15.043913	2106.586886	0.000475	0.066472	140.029190	0.007141	408
35	16.292550	2293.882485	0.000436	0.061378	140.793338	0.007103	420
36	17.644824	2496.723526	0.000401	0.056674	141.498923	0.007067	432
37	19.109335	2716.400273	0.000368	0.052330	142.150433	0.007035	444
38	20.695401	2954.310082	0.000338	0.048320	142.752013	0.007005	456
39	22.413109	3211.966288	0.000311	0.044617	143.307488	0.006978	468
40	24.273386	3491.007831	0.000286	0.041197	143.820392	0.006953	480

9.00%   ANNUAL COMPOUND INTEREST TABLES   9.00%
                                         EFFECTIVE RATE 9.00

	1	2	3	4	5	6
	AMOUNT OF $1 AT COMPOUND INTEREST	ACCUMULATION OF $1 PER PERIOD	SINKING FUND FACTOR	PRESENT VALUE REVERSION OF $1	PRESENT VALUE ORD. ANNUITY $1 PER PERIOD	INSTALMENT TO AMORTIZE $1
YEARS						
1	1.090000	1.000000	1.000000	0.917431	0.917431	1.090000
2	1.188100	2.090000	0.478469	0.841680	1.759111	0.568469
3	1.295029	3.278100	0.305055	0.772183	2.531295	0.395055
4	1.411582	4.573129	0.218669	0.708425	3.239720	0.308669
5	1.538624	5.984711	0.167092	0.649931	3.889651	0.257092
6	1.677100	7.523335	0.132920	0.596267	4.485919	0.222920
7	1.828039	9.200435	0.108691	0.547034	5.032953	0.198691
8	1.992563	11.028474	0.090674	0.501866	5.534819	0.180674
9	2.171893	13.021036	0.076799	0.460428	5.995247	0.166799
10	2.367364	15.192930	0.065820	0.422411	6.417658	0.155820
11	2.580426	17.560293	0.056947	0.387533	6.805191	0.146947
12	2.812665	20.140720	0.049651	0.355535	7.160725	0.139651
13	3.065805	22.953385	0.043567	0.326179	7.486904	0.133567
14	3.341727	26.019189	0.038433	0.299246	7.786150	0.128433
15	3.642482	29.360916	0.034059	0.274538	8.060688	0.124059
16	3.970306	33.003399	0.030300	0.251870	8.312558	0.120300
17	4.327633	36.973705	0.027046	0.231073	8.543631	0.117046
18	4.717120	41.301338	0.024212	0.211994	8.755625	0.114212
19	5.141661	46.018458	0.021730	0.194490	8.950115	0.111730
20	5.604411	51.160120	0.019546	0.178431	9.128546	0.109546
21	6.108808	56.764530	0.017617	0.163698	9.292244	0.107617
22	6.658600	62.873338	0.015905	0.150182	9.442425	0.105905
23	7.257874	69.531939	0.014382	0.137781	9.580207	0.104382
24	7.911083	76.789813	0.013023	0.126405	9.706612	0.103023
25	8.623081	84.700896	0.011806	0.115968	9.822580	0.101806
26	9.399158	93.323977	0.010715	0.106393	9.928972	0.100715
27	10.245082	102.723135	0.009735	0.097608	10.026580	0.099735
28	11.167140	112.968217	0.008852	0.089548	10.116128	0.098852
29	12.172182	124.135356	0.008056	0.082155	10.198283	0.098056
30	13.267678	136.307539	0.007336	0.075371	10.273654	0.097336
31	14.461770	149.575217	0.006686	0.069148	10.342802	0.096686
32	15.763329	164.036987	0.006096	0.063438	10.406240	0.096096
33	17.182028	179.800315	0.005562	0.058200	10.464441	0.095562
34	18.728411	196.982344	0.005077	0.053395	10.517835	0.095077
35	20.413968	215.710755	0.004636	0.048986	10.566821	0.094636
36	22.251225	236.124723	0.004235	0.044941	10.611763	0.094235
37	24.253835	258.375948	0.003870	0.041231	10.652993	0.093870
38	26.436680	282.629783	0.003538	0.037826	10.690820	0.093538
39	28.815982	309.066463	0.003236	0.034703	10.725523	0.093236
40	31.409420	337.882445	0.002960	0.031838	10.757360	0.092960
41	34.236268	369.291865	0.002708	0.029209	10.786569	0.092708
42	37.317532	403.528133	0.002478	0.026797	10.813366	0.092478
43	40.676110	440.845665	0.002268	0.024584	10.837950	0.092268
44	44.336960	481.521775	0.002077	0.022555	10.860505	0.092077
45	48.327286	525.858734	0.001902	0.020692	10.881197	0.091902
46	52.676742	574.186021	0.001742	0.018984	10.900181	0.091742
47	57.417649	626.862762	0.001595	0.017416	10.917597	0.091595
48	62.585237	684.280411	0.001461	0.015978	10.933575	0.091461
49	68.217908	746.865648	0.001339	0.014659	10.948234	0.091339
50	74.357520	815.083556	0.001227	0.013449	10.961683	0.091227

9.00%   MONTHLY COMPOUND INTEREST TABLES   9.00%
                           EFFECTIVE RATE 0.750

	1 AMOUNT OF $1 AT COMPOUND INTEREST	2 ACCUMULATION OF $1 PER PERIOD	3 SINKING FUND FACTOR	4 PRESENT VALUE REVERSION OF $1	5 PRESENT VALUE ORD. ANNUITY $1 PER PERIOD	6 INSTALMENT TO AMORTIZE $1	
MONTHS							
1	1.007500	1.000000	1.000000	0.992556	0.992556	1.007500	
2	1.015056	2.007500	0.498132	0.985167	1.977723	0.505632	
3	1.022669	3.022556	0.330846	0.977833	2.955556	0.338346	
4	1.030339	4.045225	0.247205	0.970554	3.926110	0.254705	
5	1.038067	5.075565	0.197022	0.963329	4.889440	0.204522	
6	1.045852	6.113631	0.163569	0.956158	5.845598	0.171069	
7	1.053696	7.159484	0.139675	0.949040	6.794638	0.147175	
8	1.061599	8.213180	0.121756	0.941975	7.736613	0.129256	
9	1.069561	9.274779	0.107819	0.934963	8.671576	0.115319	
10	1.077583	10.344339	0.096671	0.928003	9.599580	0.104171	
11	1.085664	11.421922	0.087551	0.921095	10.520675	0.095051	
12	1.093807	12.507586	0.079951	0.914238	11.434913	0.087451	
YEARS							MONTHS
1	1.093807	12.507586	0.079951	0.914238	11.434913	0.087451	12
2	1.196414	26.188471	0.038185	0.835831	21.889146	0.045685	24
3	1.308645	41.152716	0.024300	0.764149	31.446805	0.031800	36
4	1.431405	57.520711	0.017385	0.698614	40.184782	0.024885	48
5	1.565681	75.424137	0.013258	0.638700	48.173374	0.020758	60
6	1.712553	95.007028	0.010526	0.583924	55.476849	0.018026	72
7	1.873202	116.426928	0.008589	0.533845	62.153965	0.016089	84
8	2.048921	139.856164	0.007150	0.488062	68.258439	0.014650	96
9	2.241124	165.483223	0.006043	0.446205	73.839382	0.013543	108
10	2.451357	193.514277	0.005168	0.407937	78.941693	0.012668	120
11	2.681311	224.174837	0.004461	0.372952	83.606420	0.011961	132
12	2.932637	257.711570	0.003880	0.340967	87.871092	0.011380	144
13	3.207957	294.394279	0.003397	0.311725	91.770018	0.010897	156
14	3.508886	334.518079	0.002989	0.284991	95.334564	0.010489	168
15	3.838043	378.405769	0.002643	0.260549	98.593409	0.010143	180
16	4.198078	426.410427	0.002345	0.238204	101.572769	0.009845	192
17	4.591887	478.918252	0.002088	0.217775	104.296613	0.009588	204
18	5.022638	536.351674	0.001864	0.199099	106.786856	0.009364	216
19	5.493796	599.172747	0.001669	0.182024	109.063531	0.009169	228
20	6.009152	667.886870	0.001497	0.166413	111.144954	0.008997	240
21	6.572851	743.046852	0.001346	0.152141	113.047870	0.008846	252
22	7.189430	825.257358	0.001212	0.139093	114.787589	0.008712	264
23	7.863846	915.179777	0.001093	0.127164	116.378106	0.008593	276
24	8.601532	1013.537539	0.000987	0.116258	117.832218	0.008487	288
25	9.408415	1121.121937	0.000892	0.106288	119.161622	0.008392	300
26	10.290989	1238.798494	0.000807	0.097172	120.377014	0.008307	312
27	11.256354	1367.513924	0.000731	0.088839	121.488172	0.008231	324
28	12.312278	1508.303750	0.000663	0.081220	122.504035	0.008163	336
29	13.467255	1662.300631	0.000602	0.074254	123.432776	0.008102	348
30	14.730576	1830.743483	0.000546	0.067886	124.281866	0.008046	360
31	16.112406	2014.987436	0.000496	0.062064	125.058136	0.007996	372
32	17.623861	2216.514743	0.000451	0.056741	125.767832	0.007951	384
33	19.277100	2436.946701	0.000410	0.051875	126.416664	0.007910	396
34	21.085425	2678.056697	0.000373	0.047426	127.009850	0.007873	408
35	23.063384	2941.784473	0.000340	0.043359	127.552164	0.007840	420
36	25.226888	3230.251735	0.000310	0.039640	128.047967	0.007810	432
37	27.593344	3545.779215	0.000282	0.036241	128.501250	0.007782	444
38	30.181790	3890.905350	0.000257	0.033133	128.915659	0.007757	456
39	33.013050	4268.406696	0.000234	0.030291	129.294526	0.007734	468
40	36.109902	4681.320272	0.000214	0.027693	129.640902	0.007714	480

10.00%   ANNUAL COMPOUND INTEREST TABLES   10.00%
                              EFFECTIVE RATE 10.00

	1 AMOUNT OF $1 AT COMPOUND INTEREST	2 ACCUMULATION OF $1 PER PERIOD	3 SINKING FUND FACTOR	4 PRESENT VALUE REVERSION OF $1	5 PRESENT VALUE ORD. ANNUITY $1 PER PERIOD	6 INSTALMENT TO AMORTIZE $1
YEARS						
1	1.100000	1.000000	1.000000	0.909091	0.909091	1.100000
2	1.210000	2.100000	0.476190	0.826446	1.735537	0.576190
3	1.331000	3.310000	0.302115	0.751315	2.486852	0.402115
4	1.464100	4.641000	0.215471	0.683013	3.169865	0.315471
5	1.610510	6.105100	0.163797	0.620921	3.790787	0.263797
6	1.771561	7.715610	0.129607	0.564474	4.355261	0.229607
7	1.948717	9.487171	0.105405	0.513158	4.868419	0.205405
8	2.143589	11.435888	0.087444	0.466507	5.334926	0.187444
9	2.357948	13.579477	0.073641	0.424098	5.759024	0.173641
10	2.593742	15.937425	0.062745	0.385543	6.144567	0.162745
11	2.853117	18.531167	0.053963	0.350494	6.495061	0.153963
12	3.138428	21.384284	0.046763	0.318631	6.813692	0.146763
13	3.452271	24.522712	0.040779	0.289664	7.103356	0.140779
14	3.797498	27.974983	0.035746	0.263331	7.366687	0.135746
15	4.177248	31.772482	0.031474	0.239392	7.606080	0.131474
16	4.594973	35.949730	0.027817	0.217629	7.823709	0.127817
17	5.054470	40.544703	0.024664	0.197845	8.021553	0.124664
18	5.559917	45.599173	0.021930	0.179859	8.201412	0.121930
19	6.115909	51.159090	0.019547	0.163508	8.364920	0.119547
20	6.727500	57.274999	0.017460	0.148644	8.513564	0.117460
21	7.400250	64.002499	0.015624	0.135131	8.648694	0.115624
22	8.140275	71.402749	0.014005	0.122846	8.771540	0.114005
23	8.954302	79.543024	0.012572	0.111678	8.883218	0.112572
24	9.849733	88.497327	0.011300	0.101526	8.984744	0.111300
25	10.834706	98.347059	0.010168	0.092296	9.077040	0.110168
26	11.918177	109.181765	0.009159	0.083905	9.160945	0.109159
27	13.109994	121.099942	0.008258	0.076278	9.237223	0.108258
28	14.420994	134.209936	0.007451	0.069343	9.306567	0.107451
29	15.863093	148.630930	0.006728	0.063039	9.369606	0.106728
30	17.449402	164.494023	0.006079	0.057309	9.426914	0.106079
31	19.194342	181.943425	0.005496	0.052099	9.479013	0.105496
32	21.113777	201.137767	0.004972	0.047362	9.526376	0.104972
33	23.225154	222.251544	0.004499	0.043057	9.569432	0.104499
34	25.547670	245.476699	0.004074	0.039143	9.608575	0.104074
35	28.102437	271.024368	0.003690	0.035584	9.644159	0.103690
36	30.912681	299.126805	0.003343	0.032349	9.676508	0.103343
37	34.003949	330.039486	0.003030	0.029408	9.705917	0.103030
38	37.404343	364.043434	0.002747	0.026735	9.732651	0.102747
39	41.144778	401.447778	0.002491	0.024304	9.756956	0.102491
40	45.259256	442.592556	0.002259	0.022095	9.779051	0.102259
41	49.785181	487.851811	0.002050	0.020086	9.799137	0.102050
42	54.763699	537.636992	0.001860	0.018260	9.817397	0.101860
43	60.240069	592.400692	0.001688	0.016600	9.833998	0.101688
44	66.264076	652.640761	0.001532	0.015091	9.849089	0.101532
45	72.890484	718.904837	0.001391	0.013719	9.862808	0.101391
46	80.179532	791.795321	0.001263	0.012472	9.875280	0.101263
47	88.197485	871.974853	0.001147	0.011338	9.886618	0.101147
48	97.017234	960.172338	0.001041	0.010307	9.896926	0.101041
49	106.718957	1057.189572	0.000946	0.009370	9.906296	0.100946
50	117.390853	1163.908529	0.000859	0.008519	9.914814	0.100859

10.00%

MONTHLY COMPOUND INTEREST TABLES
EFFECTIVE RATE 0.833

10.00%

	1 AMOUNT OF $1 AT COMPOUND INTEREST	2 ACCUMULATION OF $1 PER PERIOD	3 SINKING FUND FACTOR	4 PRESENT VALUE REVERSION OF $1	5 PRESENT VALUE ORD. ANNUITY $1 PER PERIOD	6 INSTALMENT TO AMORTIZE $1	
MONTHS							
1	1.008333	1.000000	1.000000	0.991736	0.991736	1.008333	
2	1.016736	2.008333	0.497925	0.983539	1.975275	0.506259	
3	1.025209	3.025069	0.330571	0.975411	2.950686	0.338904	
4	1.033752	4.050278	0.246897	0.967350	3.918036	0.255230	
5	1.042367	5.084031	0.196694	0.959355	4.877391	0.205028	
6	1.051053	6.126398	0.163228	0.951427	5.828817	0.171561	
7	1.059812	7.177451	0.139325	0.943563	6.772381	0.147659	
8	1.068644	8.237263	0.121400	0.935765	7.708146	0.129733	
9	1.077549	9.305907	0.107459	0.928032	8.636178	0.115792	
10	1.086529	10.383456	0.096307	0.920362	9.556540	0.104640	
11	1.095583	11.469985	0.087184	0.912756	10.469296	0.095517	
12	1.104713	12.565568	0.079583	0.905212	11.374508	0.087916	
YEARS							MONTHS
1	1.104713	12.565568	0.079583	0.905212	11.374508	0.087916	12
2	1.220391	26.446915	0.037812	0.819410	21.670855	0.046145	24
3	1.348182	41.781821	0.023934	0.741740	30.991236	0.032267	36
4	1.489354	58.722492	0.017029	0.671432	39.428160	0.025363	48
5	1.645309	77.437072	0.012914	0.607789	47.065369	0.021247	60
6	1.817594	98.111314	0.010193	0.550178	53.978665	0.018526	72
7	2.007920	120.950418	0.008268	0.498028	60.236667	0.016601	84
8	2.218176	146.181076	0.006841	0.450821	65.901488	0.015174	96
9	2.450448	174.053713	0.005745	0.408089	71.029355	0.014079	108
10	2.707041	204.844979	0.004882	0.369407	75.671163	0.013215	120
11	2.990504	238.860493	0.004187	0.334392	79.872986	0.012520	132
12	3.303649	276.437876	0.003617	0.302696	83.676528	0.011951	144
13	3.649584	317.950102	0.003145	0.274004	87.119542	0.011478	156
14	4.031743	363.809201	0.002749	0.248032	90.236201	0.011082	168
15	4.453920	414.470346	0.002413	0.224521	93.057439	0.010746	180
16	4.920303	470.436376	0.002126	0.203240	95.611259	0.010459	192
17	5.435523	532.262780	0.001879	0.183975	97.923008	0.010212	204
18	6.004693	600.563216	0.001665	0.166536	100.015633	0.009998	216
19	6.633463	676.015601	0.001479	0.150751	101.909902	0.009813	228
20	7.328074	759.368836	0.001317	0.136462	103.624619	0.009650	240
21	8.095419	851.450244	0.001174	0.123527	105.176801	0.009508	252
22	8.943115	953.173779	0.001049	0.111818	106.581656	0.009382	264
23	9.879576	1065.549097	0.000938	0.101219	107.853730	0.009272	276
24	10.914097	1189.691580	0.000841	0.091625	109.005045	0.009174	288
25	12.056945	1326.833403	0.000754	0.082940	110.047230	0.009087	300
26	13.319465	1478.335767	0.000676	0.075078	110.990629	0.009010	312
27	14.714187	1645.702407	0.000608	0.067962	111.844605	0.008941	324
28	16.254954	1830.594523	0.000546	0.061520	112.617635	0.008880	336
29	17.957060	2034.847259	0.000491	0.055688	113.317392	0.008825	348
30	19.837399	2260.487925	0.000442	0.050410	113.950820	0.008776	360
31	21.914634	2509.756117	0.000398	0.045632	114.524207	0.008732	372
32	24.209383	2785.125947	0.000359	0.041306	115.043244	0.008692	384
33	26.744422	3089.330596	0.000324	0.037391	115.513083	0.008657	396
34	29.544912	3425.389448	0.000292	0.033847	115.938387	0.008625	408
35	32.638650	3796.638052	0.000263	0.030639	116.323377	0.008597	420
36	36.056344	4206.761236	0.000238	0.027734	116.671876	0.008571	432
37	39.831914	4659.829677	0.000215	0.025105	116.987340	0.008548	444
38	44.002836	5160.340305	0.000194	0.022726	117.272903	0.008527	456
39	48.610508	5713.260935	0.000175	0.020572	117.531398	0.008508	468
40	53.700663	6324.079581	0.000158	0.018622	117.765391	0.008491	480

11.00%   ANNUAL COMPOUND INTEREST TABLES   11.00%
                                     EFFECTIVE RATE 11.00

	1	2	3	4	5	6
	AMOUNT OF $1 AT COMPOUND INTEREST	ACCUMULATION OF $1 PER PERIOD	SINKING FUND FACTOR	PRESENT VALUE REVERSION OF $1	PRESENT VALUE ORD. ANNUITY $1 PER PERIOD	INSTALMENT TO AMORTIZE $1
YEARS						
1	1.110000	1.000000	1.000000	0.900901	0.900901	1.110000
2	1.232100	2.110000	0.473934	0.811622	1.712523	0.583934
3	1.367631	3.342100	0.299213	0.731191	2.443715	0.409213
4	1.518070	4.709731	0.212326	0.658731	3.102446	0.322326
5	1.685058	6.227801	0.160570	0.593451	3.695897	0.270570
6	1.870415	7.912860	0.126377	0.534641	4.230538	0.236377
7	2.076160	9.783274	0.102215	0.481658	4.712196	0.212215
8	2.304538	11.859434	0.084321	0.433926	5.146123	0.194321
9	2.558037	14.163972	0.070602	0.390925	5.537048	0.180602
10	2.839421	16.722009	0.059801	0.352184	5.889232	0.169801
11	3.151757	19.561430	0.051121	0.317283	6.206515	0.161121
12	3.498451	22.713187	0.044027	0.285841	6.492356	0.154027
13	3.883280	26.211638	0.038151	0.257514	6.749870	0.148151
14	4.310441	30.094918	0.033228	0.231995	6.981865	0.143228
15	4.784589	34.405359	0.029065	0.209004	7.190870	0.139065
16	5.310894	39.189948	0.025517	0.188292	7.379162	0.135517
17	5.895093	44.500843	0.022471	0.169633	7.548794	0.132471
18	6.543553	50.395936	0.019843	0.152822	7.701617	0.129843
19	7.263344	56.939488	0.017563	0.137678	7.839294	0.127563
20	8.062312	64.202832	0.015576	0.124034	7.963328	0.125576
21	8.949166	72.265144	0.013838	0.111742	8.075070	0.123838
22	9.933574	81.214309	0.012313	0.100669	8.175739	0.122313
23	11.026267	91.147884	0.010971	0.090693	8.266432	0.120971
24	12.239157	102.174151	0.009787	0.081705	8.348137	0.119787
25	13.585464	114.413307	0.008740	0.073608	8.421745	0.118740
26	15.079865	127.998771	0.007813	0.066314	8.488058	0.117813
27	16.738650	143.078636	0.006989	0.059742	8.547800	0.116989
28	18.579901	159.817286	0.006257	0.053822	8.601622	0.116257
29	20.623691	178.397187	0.005605	0.048488	8.650110	0.115605
30	22.892297	199.020878	0.005025	0.043683	8.693793	0.115025
31	25.410449	221.913174	0.004506	0.039354	8.733146	0.114506
32	28.205599	247.323624	0.004043	0.035454	8.768600	0.114043
33	31.308214	275.529222	0.003629	0.031940	8.800541	0.113629
34	34.752118	306.837437	0.003259	0.028775	8.829316	0.113259
35	38.574851	341.589555	0.002927	0.025924	8.855240	0.112927
36	42.818085	380.164406	0.002630	0.023355	8.878594	0.112630
37	47.528074	422.982490	0.002364	0.021040	8.899635	0.112364
38	52.756162	470.510564	0.002125	0.018955	8.918590	0.112125
39	58.559340	523.266726	0.001911	0.017077	8.935666	0.111911
40	65.000867	581.826066	0.001719	0.015384	8.951051	0.111719
41	72.150963	646.826934	0.001546	0.013860	8.964911	0.111546
42	80.087569	718.977896	0.001391	0.012486	8.977397	0.111391
43	88.897201	799.065465	0.001251	0.011249	8.988646	0.111251
44	98.675893	887.962666	0.001126	0.010134	8.998780	0.111126
45	109.530242	986.638559	0.001014	0.009130	9.007910	0.111014
46	121.578568	1096.168801	0.000912	0.008225	9.016135	0.110912
47	134.952211	1217.747369	0.000821	0.007410	9.023545	0.110821
48	149.796954	1352.699580	0.000739	0.006676	9.030221	0.110739
49	166.274619	1502.496534	0.000666	0.006014	9.036235	0.110666
50	184.564827	1668.771152	0.000599	0.005418	9.041653	0.110599

11.00% MONTHLY COMPOUND INTEREST TABLES 11.00%
EFFECTIVE RATE 0.917

	1 AMOUNT OF $1 AT COMPOUND INTEREST	2 ACCUMULATION OF $1 PER PERIOD	3 SINKING FUND FACTOR	4 PRESENT VALUE REVERSION OF $1	5 PRESENT VALUE ORD. ANNUITY $1 PER PERIOD	6 INSTALMENT TO AMORTIZE $1	
MONTHS							
1	1.009167	1.000000	1.000000	0.990917	0.990917	1.009167	
2	1.018417	2.009167	0.497719	0.981916	1.972832	0.506885	
3	1.027753	3.027584	0.330296	0.972997	2.945829	0.339463	
4	1.037174	4.055337	0.246589	0.964158	3.909987	0.255755	
5	1.046681	5.092511	0.196367	0.955401	4.865388	0.205533	
6	1.056276	6.139192	0.162888	0.946722	5.812110	0.172055	
7	1.065958	7.195468	0.138976	0.938123	6.750233	0.148143	
8	1.075730	8.261427	0.121044	0.929602	7.679835	0.130211	
9	1.085591	9.337156	0.107099	0.921158	8.600992	0.116266	
10	1.095542	10.422747	0.095944	0.912790	9.513783	0.105111	
11	1.105584	11.518289	0.086818	0.904499	10.418282	0.095985	
12	1.115719	12.623873	0.079215	0.896283	11.314565	0.088382	
YEARS							MONTHS
1	1.115719	12.623873	0.079215	0.896283	11.314565	0.088382	12
2	1.244829	26.708566	0.037441	0.803323	21.455619	0.046608	24
3	1.388879	42.423123	0.023572	0.720005	30.544874	0.032739	36
4	1.549598	59.956151	0.016679	0.645329	38.691421	0.025846	48
5	1.728916	79.518080	0.012576	0.578397	45.993034	0.021742	60
6	1.928984	101.343692	0.009867	0.518408	52.537346	0.019034	72
7	2.152204	125.694940	0.007956	0.464640	58.402903	0.017122	84
8	2.401254	152.864085	0.006542	0.416449	63.660103	0.015708	96
9	2.679124	183.177212	0.005459	0.373256	68.372043	0.014626	108
10	2.989150	216.998139	0.004608	0.334543	72.595275	0.013775	120
11	3.335051	254.732784	0.003926	0.299846	76.380487	0.013092	132
12	3.720979	296.834038	0.003369	0.268747	79.773109	0.012536	144
13	4.151566	343.807200	0.002909	0.240873	82.813859	0.012075	156
14	4.631980	396.216042	0.002524	0.215890	85.539231	0.011691	168
15	5.167988	454.689575	0.002199	0.193499	87.981937	0.011366	180
16	5.766021	519.929596	0.001923	0.173430	90.171293	0.011090	192
17	6.433259	592.719117	0.001687	0.155442	92.133576	0.010854	204
18	7.177708	673.931757	0.001484	0.139320	93.892337	0.010650	216
19	8.008304	764.542228	0.001308	0.124870	95.468685	0.010475	228
20	8.935015	865.638038	0.001155	0.111919	96.881539	0.010322	240
21	9.968965	978.432537	0.001022	0.100311	98.147856	0.010189	252
22	11.122562	1104.279485	0.000906	0.089907	99.282835	0.010072	264
23	12.409652	1244.689295	0.000803	0.080582	100.300098	0.009970	276
24	13.845682	1401.347165	0.000714	0.072225	101.211853	0.009880	288
25	15.447889	1576.133301	0.000634	0.064734	102.029044	0.009801	300
26	17.235500	1771.145485	0.000565	0.058020	102.761478	0.009731	312
27	19.229972	1988.724252	0.000503	0.052002	103.417947	0.009670	324
28	21.455242	2231.480981	0.000448	0.046609	104.006328	0.009615	336
29	23.938018	2502.329236	0.000400	0.041775	104.533685	0.009566	348
30	26.708098	2804.519736	0.000357	0.037442	105.006346	0.009523	360
31	29.798728	3141.679369	0.000318	0.033558	105.429984	0.009485	372
32	33.247002	3517.854723	0.000284	0.030078	105.809684	0.009451	384
33	37.094306	3937.560650	0.000254	0.026958	106.150002	0.009421	396
34	41.386816	4405.834459	0.000227	0.024162	106.455024	0.009394	408
35	46.176050	4928.296368	0.000203	0.021656	106.728409	0.009370	420
36	51.519489	5511.216961	0.000181	0.019410	106.973440	0.009348	432
37	57.481264	6161.592447	0.000162	0.017397	107.193057	0.009329	444
38	64.132929	6887.228627	0.000145	0.015593	107.389897	0.009312	456
39	71.554317	7696.834582	0.000130	0.013975	107.566320	0.009297	468
40	79.834499	8600.127195	0.000116	0.012526	107.724446	0.009283	480

12.00%   ANNUAL COMPOUND INTEREST TABLES   12.00%
                              EFFECTIVE RATE 12.00

	1 AMOUNT OF $1 AT COMPOUND INTEREST	2 ACCUMULATION OF $1 PER PERIOD	3 SINKING FUND FACTOR	4 PRESENT VALUE REVERSION OF $1	5 PRESENT VALUE ORD. ANNUITY $1 PER PERIOD	6 INSTALMENT TO AMORTIZE $1
YEARS						
1	1.120000	1.000000	1.000000	0.892857	0.892857	1.120000
2	1.254400	2.120000	0.471698	0.797194	1.690051	0.591698
3	1.404928	3.374400	0.296349	0.711780	2.401831	0.416349
4	1.573519	4.779328	0.209234	0.635518	3.037349	0.329234
5	1.762342	6.352847	0.157410	0.567427	3.604776	0.277410
6	1.973823	8.115189	0.123226	0.506631	4.111407	0.243226
7	2.210681	10.089012	0.099118	0.452349	4.563757	0.219118
8	2.475963	12.299693	0.081303	0.403883	4.967640	0.201303
9	2.773079	14.775656	0.067679	0.360610	5.328250	0.187679
10	3.105848	17.548735	0.056984	0.321973	5.650223	0.176984
11	3.478550	20.654583	0.048415	0.287476	5.937699	0.168415
12	3.895976	24.133133	0.041437	0.256675	6.194374	0.161437
13	4.363493	28.029109	0.035677	0.229174	6.423548	0.155677
14	4.887112	32.392602	0.030871	0.204620	6.628168	0.150871
15	5.473566	37.279715	0.026824	0.182696	6.810864	0.146824
16	6.130394	42.753280	0.023390	0.163122	6.973986	0.143390
17	6.866041	48.883674	0.020457	0.145644	7.119630	0.140457
18	7.689966	55.749715	0.017937	0.130040	7.249670	0.137937
19	8.612762	63.439681	0.015763	0.116107	7.365777	0.135763
20	9.646293	72.052442	0.013879	0.103667	7.469444	0.133879
21	10.803848	81.698736	0.012240	0.092560	7.562003	0.132240
22	12.100310	92.502584	0.010811	0.082643	7.644646	0.130811
23	13.552347	104.602894	0.009560	0.073788	7.718434	0.129560
24	15.178629	118.155241	0.008463	0.065882	7.784316	0.128463
25	17.000064	133.333870	0.007500	0.058823	7.843139	0.127500
26	19.040072	150.333934	0.006652	0.052521	7.895660	0.126652
27	21.324881	169.374007	0.005904	0.046894	7.942554	0.125904
28	23.883866	190.698887	0.005244	0.041869	7.984423	0.125244
29	26.749930	214.582754	0.004660	0.037383	8.021806	0.124660
30	29.959922	241.332684	0.004144	0.033378	8.055184	0.124144
31	33.555113	271.292606	0.003686	0.029802	8.084986	0.123686
32	37.581726	304.847719	0.003280	0.026609	8.111594	0.123280
33	42.091533	342.429446	0.002920	0.023758	8.135352	0.122920
34	47.142517	384.520979	0.002601	0.021212	8.156564	0.122601
35	52.799620	431.663496	0.002317	0.018940	8.175504	0.122317
36	59.135574	484.463116	0.002064	0.016910	8.192414	0.122064
37	66.231843	543.598690	0.001840	0.015098	8.207513	0.121840
38	74.179664	609.830533	0.001640	0.013481	8.220993	0.121640
39	83.081224	684.010197	0.001462	0.012036	8.233030	0.121462
40	93.050970	767.091420	0.001304	0.010747	8.243777	0.121304
41	104.217087	860.142391	0.001163	0.009595	8.253372	0.121163
42	116.723137	964.359478	0.001037	0.008567	8.261939	0.121037
43	130.729914	1081.082615	0.000925	0.007649	8.269589	0.120925
44	146.417503	1211.812529	0.000825	0.006830	8.276418	0.120825
45	163.987604	1358.230032	0.000736	0.006098	8.282516	0.120736
46	183.666116	1522.217636	0.000657	0.005445	8.287961	0.120657
47	205.706050	1705.883752	0.000586	0.004861	8.292822	0.120586
48	230.390776	1911.589803	0.000523	0.004340	8.297163	0.120523
49	258.037669	2141.980579	0.000467	0.003875	8.301038	0.120467
50	289.002190	2400.018249	0.000417	0.003460	8.304498	0.120417

12.00%   MONTHLY COMPOUND INTEREST TABLES   12.00%
                        EFFECTIVE RATE 1.000

	1 AMOUNT OF $1 AT COMPOUND INTEREST	2 ACCUMULATION OF $1 PER PERIOD	3 SINKING FUND FACTOR	4 PRESENT VALUE REVERSION OF $1	5 PRESENT VALUE ORD. ANNUITY $1 PER PERIOD	6 INSTALMENT TO AMORTIZE $1	
MONTHS							
1	1.010000	1.000000	1.000000	0.990099	0.990099	1.010000	
2	1.020100	2.010000	0.497512	0.980296	1.970395	0.507512	
3	1.030301	3.030100	0.330022	0.970590	2.940985	0.340022	
4	1.040604	4.060401	0.246281	0.960980	3.901966	0.256281	
5	1.051010	5.101005	0.196040	0.951466	4.853431	0.206040	
6	1.061520	6.152015	0.162548	0.942045	5.795476	0.172548	
7	1.072135	7.213535	0.138628	0.932718	6.728195	0.148628	
8	1.082857	8.285671	0.120690	0.923483	7.651678	0.130690	
9	1.093685	9.368527	0.106740	0.914340	8.566018	0.116740	
10	1.104622	10.462213	0.095582	0.905287	9.471305	0.105582	
11	1.115668	11.566835	0.086454	0.896324	10.367628	0.096454	
12	1.126825	12.682503	0.078849	0.887449	11.255077	0.088849	
YEARS							MONTHS
1	1.126825	12.682503	0.078849	0.887449	11.255077	0.088849	12
2	1.269735	26.973465	0.037073	0.787566	21.243387	0.047073	24
3	1.430769	43.076878	0.023214	0.698925	30.107505	0.033214	36
4	1.612226	61.222608	0.016334	0.620260	37.973959	0.026334	48
5	1.816697	81.669670	0.012244	0.550450	44.955038	0.022244	60
6	2.047099	104.709931	0.009550	0.488496	51.150391	0.019550	72
7	2.306723	130.672274	0.007653	0.433515	56.648453	0.017653	84
8	2.599273	159.927293	0.006253	0.384723	61.527703	0.016253	96
9	2.928926	192.892579	0.005184	0.341422	65.857790	0.015184	108
10	3.300387	230.038689	0.004347	0.302995	69.700522	0.014347	120
11	3.718959	271.895856	0.003678	0.268892	73.110752	0.013678	132
12	4.190616	319.061559	0.003134	0.238628	76.137157	0.013134	144
13	4.722091	372.209054	0.002687	0.211771	78.822939	0.012687	156
14	5.320970	432.096982	0.002314	0.187936	81.206434	0.012314	168
15	5.995802	499.580198	0.002002	0.166783	83.321664	0.012002	180
16	6.756220	575.621974	0.001737	0.148012	85.198824	0.011737	192
17	7.613078	661.307751	0.001512	0.131353	86.864707	0.011512	204
18	8.578606	757.860630	0.001320	0.116569	88.343095	0.011320	216
19	9.666588	866.658830	0.001154	0.103449	89.655089	0.011154	228
20	10.892554	989.255365	0.001011	0.091806	90.819416	0.011011	240
21	12.274002	1127.400210	0.000887	0.081473	91.852698	0.010887	252
22	13.830653	1283.065278	0.000779	0.072303	92.769683	0.010779	264
23	15.584726	1458.472574	0.000686	0.064165	93.583461	0.010686	276
24	17.561259	1656.125905	0.000604	0.056944	94.305647	0.010604	288
25	19.788466	1878.846626	0.000532	0.050534	94.946551	0.010532	300
26	22.298139	2129.813909	0.000470	0.044847	95.515321	0.010470	312
27	25.126101	2412.610125	0.000414	0.039799	96.020075	0.010414	324
28	28.312720	2731.271980	0.000366	0.035320	96.468019	0.010366	336
29	31.903481	3090.348134	0.000324	0.031345	96.865546	0.010324	348
30	35.949641	3494.964133	0.000286	0.027817	97.218331	0.010286	360
31	40.508956	3950.895567	0.000253	0.024686	97.531410	0.010253	372
32	45.646505	4464.650519	0.000224	0.021907	97.809252	0.010224	384
33	51.435625	5043.562459	0.000198	0.019442	98.055822	0.010198	396
34	57.958949	5695.894923	0.000176	0.017254	98.274641	0.010176	408
35	65.309595	6430.959471	0.000155	0.015312	98.468831	0.010155	420
36	73.592486	7259.248603	0.000138	0.013588	98.641166	0.010138	432
37	82.925855	8192.585529	0.000122	0.012059	98.794103	0.010122	444
38	93.442929	9244.292938	0.000108	0.010702	98.929828	0.010108	456
39	105.293832	10429.383172	0.000096	0.009497	99.050277	0.010096	468
40	118.647725	11764.772510	0.000085	0.008428	99.157169	0.010085	480

	1	2	3	4	5	6
	AMOUNT OF $1 AT COMPOUND INTEREST	ACCUMULATION OF $1 PER PERIOD	SINKING FUND FACTOR	PRESENT VALUE REVERSION OF $1	PRESENT VALUE ORD. ANNUITY $1 PER PERIOD	INSTALMENT TO AMORTIZE $1
YEARS						
1	1.130000	1.000000	1.000000	0.884956	0.884956	1.130000
2	1.276900	2.130000	0.469484	0.783147	1.668102	0.599484
3	1.442897	3.406900	0.293522	0.693050	2.361153	0.423522
4	1.630474	4.849797	0.206194	0.613319	2.974471	0.336194
5	1.842435	6.480271	0.154315	0.542760	3.517231	0.284315
6	2.081952	8.322706	0.120153	0.480319	3.997550	0.250153
7	2.352605	10.404658	0.096111	0.425061	4.422610	0.226111
8	2.658444	12.757263	0.078387	0.376160	4.798770	0.208387
9	3.004042	15.415707	0.064869	0.332885	5.131655	0.194869
10	3.394567	18.419749	0.054290	0.294588	5.426243	0.184290
11	3.835861	21.814317	0.045841	0.260698	5.686941	0.175841
12	4.334523	25.650178	0.038986	0.230706	5.917647	0.168986
13	4.898011	29.984701	0.033350	0.204165	6.121812	0.163350
14	5.534753	34.882712	0.028667	0.180677	6.302488	0.158667
15	6.254270	40.417464	0.024742	0.159891	6.462379	0.154742
16	7.067326	46.671735	0.021426	0.141496	6.603875	0.151426
17	7.986078	53.739060	0.018608	0.125218	6.729093	0.148608
18	9.024268	61.725138	0.016201	0.110812	6.839905	0.146201
19	10.197423	70.749406	0.014134	0.098064	6.937969	0.144134
20	11.523088	80.946829	0.012354	0.086782	7.024752	0.142354
21	13.021089	92.469917	0.010814	0.076798	7.101550	0.140814
22	14.713831	105.491006	0.009479	0.067963	7.169513	0.139479
23	16.626629	120.204837	0.008319	0.060144	7.229658	0.138319
24	18.788091	136.831465	0.007308	0.053225	7.282883	0.137308
25	21.230542	155.619556	0.006426	0.047102	7.329985	0.136426
26	23.990513	176.850098	0.005655	0.041683	7.371668	0.135655
27	27.109279	200.840611	0.004979	0.036888	7.408556	0.134979
28	30.633486	227.949890	0.004387	0.032644	7.441200	0.134387
29	34.615839	258.583376	0.003867	0.028889	7.470088	0.133867
30	39.115898	293.199215	0.003411	0.025565	7.495653	0.133411
31	44.200965	332.315113	0.003009	0.022624	7.518277	0.133009
32	49.947090	376.516078	0.002656	0.020021	7.538299	0.132656
33	56.440212	426.463168	0.002345	0.017718	7.556016	0.132345
34	63.777439	482.903380	0.002071	0.015680	7.571696	0.132071
35	72.068506	546.680819	0.001829	0.013876	7.585572	0.131829
36	81.437412	618.749325	0.001616	0.012279	7.597851	0.131616
37	92.024276	700.186738	0.001428	0.010867	7.608718	0.131428
38	103.987432	792.211014	0.001262	0.009617	7.618334	0.131262
39	117.505798	896.198445	0.001116	0.008510	7.626844	0.131116
40	132.781552	1013.704243	0.000986	0.007531	7.634376	0.130986
41	150.043153	1146.485795	0.000872	0.006665	7.641040	0.130872
42	169.548763	1296.528948	0.000771	0.005898	7.646938	0.130771
43	191.590103	1466.077712	0.000682	0.005219	7.652158	0.130682
44	216.496816	1657.667814	0.000603	0.004619	7.656777	0.130603
45	244.641402	1874.164630	0.000534	0.004088	7.660864	0.130534
46	276.444784	2118.806032	0.000472	0.003617	7.664482	0.130472
47	312.382606	2395.250816	0.000417	0.003201	7.667683	0.130417
48	352.992345	2707.633422	0.000369	0.002833	7.670516	0.130369
49	398.881350	3060.625767	0.000327	0.002507	7.673023	0.130327
50	450.735925	3459.507117	0.000289	0.002219	7.675242	0.130289

13.00%   MONTHLY COMPOUND INTEREST TABLES   13.00%
                                EFFECTIVE RATE 1.083

	1 AMOUNT OF $1 AT COMPOUND INTEREST	2 ACCUMULATION OF $1 PER PERIOD	3 SINKING FUND FACTOR	4 PRESENT VALUE REVERSION OF $1	5 PRESENT VALUE ORD. ANNUITY $1 PER PERIOD	6 INSTALMENT TO AMORTIZE $1	
MONTHS							
1	1.010833	1.000000	1.000000	0.989283	0.989283	1.010833	
2	1.021784	2.010833	0.497306	0.978680	1.967963	0.508140	
3	1.032853	3.032617	0.329748	0.968192	2.936155	0.340581	
4	1.044043	4.065471	0.245974	0.957815	3.893970	0.256807	
5	1.055353	5.109513	0.195713	0.947550	4.841520	0.206547	
6	1.066786	6.164866	0.162210	0.937395	5.778915	0.173043	
7	1.078343	7.231652	0.138281	0.927349	6.706264	0.149114	
8	1.090025	8.309995	0.120337	0.917410	7.623674	0.131170	
9	1.101834	9.400020	0.106383	0.907578	8.531253	0.117216	
10	1.113770	10.501854	0.095221	0.897851	9.429104	0.106055	
11	1.125836	11.615624	0.086091	0.888229	10.317333	0.096924	
12	1.138032	12.741460	0.078484	0.878710	11.196042	0.089317	
YEARS							MONTHS
1	1.138032	12.741460	0.078484	0.878710	11.196042	0.089317	12
2	1.295118	27.241655	0.036708	0.772130	21.034112	0.047542	24
3	1.473886	43.743348	0.022861	0.678478	29.678917	0.033694	36
4	1.677330	62.522811	0.015994	0.596185	37.275190	0.026827	48
5	1.908857	83.894449	0.011920	0.523874	43.950107	0.022753	60
6	2.172341	108.216068	0.009241	0.460333	49.815421	0.020074	72
7	2.472194	135.894861	0.007359	0.404499	54.969328	0.018192	84
8	2.813437	167.394225	0.005974	0.355437	59.498115	0.016807	96
9	3.201783	203.241525	0.004920	0.312326	63.477604	0.015754	108
10	3.643733	244.036917	0.004098	0.274444	66.974419	0.014931	120
11	4.146687	290.463399	0.003443	0.241156	70.047103	0.014276	132
12	4.719064	343.298242	0.002913	0.211906	72.747100	0.013746	144
13	5.370448	403.426010	0.002479	0.186204	75.119613	0.013312	156
14	6.111745	471.853363	0.002119	0.163619	77.204363	0.012953	168
15	6.955364	549.725914	0.001819	0.143774	79.036253	0.012652	180
16	7.915430	638.347406	0.001567	0.126336	80.645952	0.012400	192
17	9.008017	739.201542	0.001353	0.111012	82.060410	0.012186	204
18	10.251416	853.976825	0.001171	0.097548	83.303307	0.012004	216
19	11.666444	984.594826	0.001016	0.085716	84.395453	0.011849	228
20	13.276792	1133.242353	0.000882	0.075319	85.355132	0.011716	240
21	15.109421	1302.408067	0.000768	0.066184	86.198412	0.011601	252
22	17.195012	1494.924144	0.000669	0.058156	86.939409	0.011502	264
23	19.568482	1714.013694	0.000583	0.051103	87.590531	0.011417	276
24	22.269568	1963.344717	0.000509	0.044904	88.162677	0.011343	288
25	25.343491	2247.091520	0.000445	0.039458	88.665428	0.011278	300
26	28.841716	2570.004599	0.000389	0.034672	89.107200	0.011222	312
27	32.822810	2937.490172	0.000340	0.030467	89.495389	0.011174	324
28	37.353424	3355.700690	0.000298	0.026771	89.836495	0.011131	336
29	42.509410	3831.637843	0.000261	0.023524	90.136227	0.011094	348
30	48.377089	4373.269783	0.000229	0.020671	90.399605	0.011062	360
31	55.054699	4989.664524	0.000200	0.018164	90.631038	0.011034	372
32	62.654036	5691.141761	0.000176	0.015961	90.834400	0.011009	384
33	71.302328	6489.445641	0.000154	0.014025	91.013097	0.010987	396
34	81.144365	7397.941387	0.000135	0.012324	91.170119	0.010969	408
35	92.344923	8431.839055	0.000119	0.010829	91.308095	0.010952	420
36	105.091522	9608.448184	0.000104	0.009516	91.429337	0.010937	432
37	119.597566	10947.467591	0.000091	0.008361	91.535873	0.010925	444
38	136.105914	12471.315170	0.000080	0.007347	91.629487	0.010914	456
39	154.892951	14205.503212	0.000070	0.006456	91.711747	0.010904	468
40	176.273210	16179.065533	0.000062	0.005673	91.784030	0.010895	480

14.00%   ANNUAL COMPOUND INTEREST TABLES   14.00%
                                   EFFECTIVE RATE 14.00

----

	1 AMOUNT OF $1 AT COMPOUND INTEREST	2 ACCUMULATION OF $1 PER PERIOD	3 SINKING FUND FACTOR	4 PRESENT VALUE REVERSION OF $1	5 PRESENT VALUE ORD. ANNUITY $1 PER PERIOD	6 INSTALMENT TO AMORTIZE $1
YEARS						
1	1.140000	1.000000	1.000000	0.877193	0.877193	1.140000
2	1.299600	2.140000	0.467290	0.769468	1.646661	0.607290
3	1.481544	3.439600	0.290731	0.674972	2.321632	0.430731
4	1.688960	4.921144	0.203205	0.592080	2.913712	0.343205
5	1.925415	6.610104	0.151284	0.519369	3.433081	0.291284
6	2.194973	8.535519	0.117157	0.455587	3.888668	0.257157
7	2.502269	10.730491	0.093192	0.399637	4.288305	0.233192
8	2.852586	13.232760	0.075570	0.350559	4.638864	0.215570
9	3.251949	16.085347	0.062168	0.307508	4.946372	0.202168
10	3.707221	19.337295	0.051714	0.269744	5.216116	0.191714
11	4.226232	23.044516	0.043394	0.236617	5.452733	0.183394
12	4.817905	27.270749	0.036669	0.207559	5.660292	0.176669
13	5.492411	32.088654	0.031164	0.182069	5.842362	0.171164
14	6.261349	37.581065	0.026609	0.159710	6.002072	0.166609
15	7.137938	43.842414	0.022809	0.140096	6.142168	0.162809
16	8.137249	50.980352	0.019615	0.122892	6.265060	0.159615
17	9.276464	59.117601	0.016915	0.107800	6.372859	0.156915
18	10.575169	68.394066	0.014621	0.094561	6.467420	0.154621
19	12.055693	78.969235	0.012663	0.082948	6.550369	0.152663
20	13.743490	91.024928	0.010986	0.072762	6.623131	0.150986
21	15.667578	104.768418	0.009545	0.063826	6.686957	0.149545
22	17.861039	120.435996	0.008303	0.055988	6.742944	0.148303
23	20.361585	138.297035	0.007231	0.049112	6.792056	0.147231
24	23.212207	158.658620	0.006303	0.043081	6.835137	0.146303
25	26.461916	181.870827	0.005498	0.037790	6.872927	0.145498
26	30.166584	208.332743	0.004800	0.033149	6.906077	0.144800
27	34.389906	238.499327	0.004193	0.029078	6.935155	0.144193
28	39.204493	272.889233	0.003664	0.025507	6.960662	0.143664
29	44.693122	312.093725	0.003204	0.022375	6.983037	0.143204
30	50.950159	356.786847	0.002803	0.019627	7.002664	0.142803
31	58.083181	407.737006	0.002453	0.017217	7.019881	0.142453
32	66.214826	465.820186	0.002147	0.015102	7.034983	0.142147
33	75.484902	532.035012	0.001880	0.013248	7.048231	0.141880
34	86.052788	607.519914	0.001646	0.011621	7.059852	0.141646
35	98.100178	693.572702	0.001442	0.010194	7.070045	0.141442
36	111.834203	791.672881	0.001263	0.008942	7.078987	0.141263
37	127.490992	903.507084	0.001107	0.007844	7.086831	0.141107
38	145.339731	1030.998076	0.000970	0.006880	7.093711	0.140970
39	165.687293	1176.337806	0.000850	0.006035	7.099747	0.140850
40	188.883514	1342.025099	0.000745	0.005294	7.105041	0.140745
41	215.327206	1530.908613	0.000653	0.004644	7.109685	0.140653
42	245.473015	1746.235819	0.000573	0.004074	7.113759	0.140573
43	279.839237	1991.708833	0.000502	0.003573	7.117332	0.140502
44	319.016730	2271.548070	0.000440	0.003135	7.120467	0.140440
45	363.679072	2590.564800	0.000386	0.002750	7.123217	0.140386
46	414.594142	2954.243872	0.000338	0.002412	7.125629	0.140338
47	472.637322	3368.838014	0.000297	0.002116	7.127744	0.140297
48	538.806547	3841.475336	0.000260	0.001856	7.129600	0.140260
49	614.239464	4380.281883	0.000228	0.001628	7.131228	0.140228
50	700.232988	4994.521346	0.000200	0.001428	7.132656	0.140200

14.00%   MONTHLY COMPOUND INTEREST TABLES   14.00%
EFFECTIVE RATE 1.167

	1 AMOUNT OF $1 AT COMPOUND INTEREST	2 ACCUMULATION OF $1 PER PERIOD	3 SINKING FUND FACTOR	4 PRESENT VALUE REVERSION OF $1	5 PRESENT VALUE ORD. ANNUITY $1 PER PERIOD	6 INSTALMENT TO AMORTIZE $1	
MONTHS							
1	1.011667	1.000000	1.000000	0.988468	0.988468	1.011667	
2	1.023469	2.011667	0.497100	0.977069	1.965537	0.508767	
3	1.035410	3.035136	0.329475	0.965801	2.931338	0.341141	
4	1.047490	4.070546	0.245667	0.954663	3.886001	0.257334	
5	1.059710	5.118036	0.195387	0.943654	4.829655	0.207054	
6	1.072074	6.177746	0.161871	0.932772	5.762427	0.173538	
7	1.084581	7.249820	0.137934	0.922015	6.684442	0.149601	
8	1.097235	8.334401	0.119985	0.911382	7.595824	0.131651	
9	1.110036	9.431636	0.106026	0.900872	8.496696	0.117693	
10	1.122986	10.541672	0.094862	0.890483	9.387178	0.106528	
11	1.136088	11.664658	0.085729	0.880214	10.267392	0.097396	
12	1.149342	12.800745	0.078120	0.870063	11.137455	0.089787	
YEARS							**MONTHS**
1	1.149342	12.800745	0.078120	0.870063	11.137455	0.089787	12
2	1.320987	27.513180	0.036346	0.757010	20.827743	0.048013	24
3	1.518266	44.422800	0.022511	0.658646	29.258904	0.034178	36
4	1.745007	63.857736	0.015660	0.573064	36.594546	0.027326	48
5	2.005610	86.195125	0.011602	0.498601	42.977016	0.023268	60
6	2.305132	111.868425	0.008939	0.433815	48.530168	0.020606	72
7	2.649385	141.375828	0.007073	0.377446	53.361760	0.018740	84
8	3.045049	175.289927	0.005705	0.328402	57.565549	0.017372	96
9	3.499803	214.268826	0.004667	0.285730	61.223111	0.016334	108
10	4.022471	259.068912	0.003860	0.248603	64.405420	0.015527	120
11	4.623195	310.559535	0.003220	0.216301	67.174230	0.014887	132
12	5.313632	369.739871	0.002705	0.188195	69.583269	0.014371	144
13	6.107180	437.758319	0.002284	0.163742	71.679284	0.013951	156
14	7.019239	515.934780	0.001938	0.142466	73.502950	0.013605	168
15	8.067507	605.786272	0.001651	0.123954	75.089654	0.013317	180
16	9.272324	709.056369	0.001410	0.107848	76.470187	0.013077	192
17	10.657072	827.749031	0.001208	0.093834	77.671337	0.012875	204
18	12.248621	964.167496	0.001037	0.081642	78.716413	0.012704	216
19	14.077855	1120.958972	0.000892	0.071034	79.625696	0.012559	228
20	16.180270	1301.166005	0.000769	0.061804	80.416829	0.012435	240
21	18.596664	1508.285522	0.000663	0.053773	81.105164	0.012330	252
22	21.373928	1746.336688	0.000573	0.046786	81.704060	0.012239	264
23	24.565954	2019.938898	0.000495	0.040707	82.225136	0.012162	276
24	28.234683	2334.401417	0.000428	0.035417	82.678506	0.012095	288
25	32.451308	2695.826407	0.000371	0.030815	83.072966	0.012038	300
26	37.297652	3111.227338	0.000321	0.026811	83.416171	0.011988	312
27	42.867759	3588.665088	0.000279	0.023328	83.714781	0.011945	324
28	49.269718	4137.404360	0.000242	0.020296	83.974591	0.011908	336
29	56.627757	4768.093468	0.000210	0.017659	84.200641	0.011876	348
30	65.084661	5492.970967	0.000182	0.015365	84.397320	0.011849	360
31	74.804537	6326.103143	0.000158	0.013368	84.568442	0.011825	372
32	85.975998	7283.656968	0.000137	0.011631	84.717330	0.011804	384
33	98.815828	8384.213826	0.000119	0.010120	84.846871	0.011786	396
34	113.573184	9649.130077	0.000104	0.008805	84.959580	0.011770	408
35	130.534434	11102.951488	0.000090	0.007661	85.057645	0.011757	420
36	150.028711	12773.889539	0.000078	0.006665	85.142966	0.011745	432
37	172.434303	14694.368869	0.000068	0.005799	85.217202	0.011735	444
38	198.185992	16901.656479	0.000059	0.005046	85.281792	0.011726	456
39	227.783490	19438.584900	0.000051	0.004390	85.337989	0.011718	468
40	261.801139	22354.383359	0.000045	0.003820	85.386883	0.011711	480

15.00%   ANNUAL COMPOUND INTEREST TABLES   15.00%
                                      EFFECTIVE RATE 15.00

	1 AMOUNT OF $1 AT COMPOUND INTEREST	2 ACCUMULATION OF $1 PER PERIOD	3 SINKING FUND FACTOR	4 PRESENT VALUE REVERSION OF $1	5 PRESENT VALUE ORD. ANNUITY $1 PER PERIOD	6 INSTALMENT TO AMORTIZE $1
YEARS						
1	1.150000	1.000000	1.000000	0.869565	0.869565	1.150000
2	1.322500	2.150000	0.465116	0.756144	1.625709	0.615116
3	1.520875	3.472500	0.287977	0.657516	2.283225	0.437977
4	1.749006	4.993375	0.200265	0.571753	2.854978	0.350265
5	2.011357	6.742381	0.148316	0.497177	3.352155	0.298316
6	2.313061	8.753738	0.114237	0.432328	3.784483	0.264237
7	2.660020	11.066799	0.090360	0.375937	4.160420	0.240360
8	3.059023	13.726819	0.072850	0.326902	4.487322	0.222850
9	3.517876	16.785842	0.059574	0.284262	4.771584	0.209574
10	4.045558	20.303718	0.049252	0.247185	5.018769	0.199252
11	4.652391	24.349276	0.041069	0.214943	5.233712	0.191069
12	5.350250	29.001667	0.034481	0.186907	5.420619	0.184481
13	6.152788	34.351917	0.029110	0.162528	5.583147	0.179110
14	7.075706	40.504705	0.024688	0.141329	5.724476	0.174688
15	8.137062	47.580411	0.021017	0.122894	5.847370	0.171017
16	9.357621	55.717472	0.017948	0.106865	5.954235	0.167948
17	10.761264	65.075093	0.015367	0.092926	6.047161	0.165367
18	12.375454	75.836357	0.013186	0.080805	6.127966	0.163186
19	14.231772	88.211811	0.011336	0.070265	6.198231	0.161336
20	16.366537	102.443583	0.009761	0.061100	6.259331	0.159761
21	18.821518	118.810120	0.008417	0.053131	6.312462	0.158417
22	21.644746	137.631638	0.007266	0.046201	6.358663	0.157266
23	24.891458	159.276384	0.006278	0.040174	6.398837	0.156278
24	28.625176	184.167841	0.005430	0.034934	6.433771	0.155430
25	32.918953	212.793017	0.004699	0.030378	6.464149	0.154699
26	37.856796	245.711970	0.004070	0.026415	6.490564	0.154070
27	43.535315	283.568766	0.003526	0.022970	6.513534	0.153526
28	50.065612	327.104080	0.003057	0.019974	6.533508	0.153057
29	57.575454	377.169693	0.002651	0.017369	6.550877	0.152651
30	66.211772	434.745146	0.002300	0.015103	6.565980	0.152300
31	76.143538	500.956918	0.001996	0.013133	6.579113	0.151996
32	87.565068	577.100456	0.001733	0.011420	6.590533	0.151733
33	100.699829	664.665525	0.001505	0.009931	6.600463	0.151505
34	115.804803	765.365353	0.001307	0.008635	6.609099	0.151307
35	133.175523	881.170156	0.001135	0.007509	6.616607	0.151135
36	153.151852	1014.345680	0.000986	0.006529	6.623137	0.150986
37	176.124630	1167.497532	0.000857	0.005678	6.628815	0.150857
38	202.543324	1343.622161	0.000744	0.004937	6.633752	0.150744
39	232.924823	1546.165485	0.000647	0.004293	6.638045	0.150647
40	267.863546	1779.090308	0.000562	0.003733	6.641778	0.150562
41	308.043078	2046.953854	0.000489	0.003246	6.645025	0.150489
42	354.249540	2354.996933	0.000425	0.002823	6.647848	0.150425
43	407.386971	2709.246473	0.000369	0.002455	6.650302	0.150369
44	468.495017	3116.633443	0.000321	0.002134	6.652437	0.150321
45	538.769269	3585.128460	0.000279	0.001856	6.654293	0.150279
46	619.584659	4123.897729	0.000242	0.001614	6.655907	0.150242
47	712.522358	4743.482388	0.000211	0.001403	6.657310	0.150211
48	819.400712	5456.004746	0.000183	0.001220	6.658531	0.150183
49	942.310819	6275.405458	0.000159	0.001061	6.659592	0.150159
50	1083.657442	7217.716277	0.000139	0.000923	6.660515	0.150139

15.00%

MONTHLY COMPOUND INTEREST TABLES
EFFECTIVE RATE 1.250

15.00%

	1 AMOUNT OF $1 AT COMPOUND INTEREST	2 ACCUMULATION OF $1 PER PERIOD	3 SINKING FUND FACTOR	4 PRESENT VALUE REVERSION OF $1	5 PRESENT VALUE ORD. ANNUITY $1 PER PERIOD	6 INSTALMENT TO AMORTIZE $1	
MONTHS							
1	1.012500	1.000000	1.000000	0.987654	0.987654	1.012500	
2	1.025156	2.012500	0.496894	0.975461	1.963115	0.509394	
3	1.037971	3.037656	0.329201	0.963418	2.926534	0.341701	
4	1.050945	4.075627	0.245361	0.951524	3.878058	0.257861	
5	1.064082	5.126572	0.195062	0.939777	4.817835	0.207562	
6	1.077383	6.190654	0.161534	0.928175	5.746010	0.174034	
7	1.090850	7.268038	0.137589	0.916716	6.662726	0.150089	
8	1.104486	8.358888	0.119633	0.905398	7.568124	0.132133	
9	1.118292	9.463374	0.105671	0.894221	8.462345	0.118171	
10	1.132271	10.581666	0.094503	0.883181	9.345526	0.107003	
11	1.146424	11.713937	0.085368	0.872277	10.217803	0.097868	
12	1.160755	12.860361	0.077758	0.861509	11.079312	0.090258	
YEARS							**MONTHS**
1	1.160755	12.860361	0.077758	0.861509	11.079312	0.090258	12
2	1.347351	27.788084	0.035987	0.742197	20.624235	0.048487	24
3	1.563944	45.115506	0.022165	0.639409	28.847267	0.034665	36
4	1.815355	65.228388	0.015331	0.550856	35.931481	0.027831	48
5	2.107181	88.574508	0.011290	0.474568	42.034592	0.023790	60
6	2.445920	115.673621	0.008645	0.408844	47.292474	0.021145	72
7	2.839113	147.129040	0.006797	0.352223	51.822185	0.019297	84
8	3.295513	183.641059	0.005445	0.303443	55.724570	0.017945	96
9	3.825282	226.022551	0.004424	0.261419	59.086509	0.016924	108
10	4.440213	275.217058	0.003633	0.225214	61.982847	0.016133	120
11	5.153998	332.319805	0.003009	0.194024	64.478068	0.015509	132
12	5.982526	398.602077	0.002509	0.167153	66.627722	0.015009	144
13	6.944244	475.539523	0.002103	0.144004	68.479668	0.014603	156
14	8.060563	564.845011	0.001770	0.124061	70.075134	0.014270	168
15	9.356334	668.506759	0.001496	0.106879	71.449643	0.013996	180
16	10.860408	788.832603	0.001268	0.092078	72.633794	0.013768	192
17	12.606267	928.501369	0.001077	0.079326	73.653950	0.013577	204
18	14.632781	1090.622520	0.000917	0.068340	74.532823	0.013417	216
19	16.985067	1278.805378	0.000782	0.058875	75.289980	0.013282	228
20	19.715494	1497.239481	0.000668	0.050722	75.942278	0.013168	240
21	22.884848	1750.787854	0.000571	0.043697	76.504237	0.013071	252
22	26.563691	2045.095272	0.000489	0.037645	76.988370	0.012989	264
23	30.833924	2386.713938	0.000419	0.032432	77.405455	0.012919	276
24	35.790617	2783.249347	0.000359	0.027940	77.764777	0.012859	288
25	41.544120	3243.529615	0.000308	0.024071	78.074336	0.012808	300
26	48.222525	3777.802015	0.000265	0.020737	78.341024	0.012765	312
27	55.974514	4397.961118	0.000227	0.017865	78.570778	0.012727	324
28	64.972670	5117.813598	0.000195	0.015391	78.768713	0.012695	336
29	75.417320	5953.385616	0.000168	0.013260	78.939236	0.012668	348
30	87.540995	6923.279611	0.000144	0.011423	79.086142	0.012644	360
31	101.613606	8049.088447	0.000124	0.009841	79.212704	0.012624	372
32	117.948452	9355.876140	0.000107	0.008478	79.321738	0.012607	384
33	136.909198	10872.735858	0.000092	0.007304	79.415671	0.012592	396
34	158.917970	12633.437629	0.000079	0.006293	79.496596	0.012579	408
35	184.464752	14677.180163	0.000068	0.005421	79.566313	0.012568	420
36	214.118294	17049.463544	0.000059	0.004670	79.626375	0.012559	432
37	248.538777	19803.102194	0.000050	0.004024	79.678119	0.012550	444
38	288.492509	22999.400698	0.000043	0.003466	79.722696	0.012543	456
39	334.868983	26709.518627	0.000037	0.002986	79.761101	0.012537	468
40	388.700685	31016.054774	0.000032	0.002573	79.794186	0.012532	480

20.00%   ANNUAL COMPOUND INTEREST TABLES   20.00%
                                    EFFECTIVE RATE 20.00

	1 AMOUNT OF $1 AT COMPOUND INTEREST	2 ACCUMULATION OF $1 PER PERIOD	3 SINKING FUND FACTOR	4 PRESENT VALUE REVERSION OF $1	5 PRESENT VALUE ORD. ANNUITY $1 PER PERIOD	6 INSTALMENT TO AMORTIZE $1
YEARS						
1	1.200000	1.000000	1.000000	0.833333	0.833333	1.200000
2	1.440000	2.200000	0.454545	0.694444	1.527778	0.654545
3	1.728000	3.640000	0.274725	0.578704	2.106481	0.474725
4	2.073600	5.368000	0.186289	0.482253	2.588735	0.386289
5	2.488320	7.441600	0.134380	0.401878	2.990612	0.334380
6	2.985984	9.929920	0.100706	0.334898	3.325510	0.300706
7	3.583181	12.915904	0.077424	0.279082	3.604592	0.277424
8	4.299817	16.499085	0.060609	0.232568	3.837160	0.260609
9	5.159780	20.798902	0.048079	0.193807	4.030967	0.248079
10	6.191736	25.958682	0.038523	0.161506	4.192472	0.238523
11	7.430084	32.150419	0.031104	0.134588	4.327060	0.231104
12	8.916100	39.580502	0.025265	0.112157	4.439217	0.225265
13	10.699321	48.496603	0.020620	0.093464	4.532681	0.220620
14	12.839185	59.195923	0.016893	0.077887	4.610567	0.216893
15	15.407022	72.035108	0.013882	0.064905	4.675473	0.213882
16	18.488426	87.442129	0.011436	0.054088	4.729561	0.211436
17	22.186111	105.930555	0.009440	0.045073	4.774634	0.209440
18	26.623333	128.116666	0.007805	0.037561	4.812195	0.207805
19	31.948000	154.740000	0.006462	0.031301	4.843496	0.206462
20	38.337600	186.688000	0.005357	0.026084	4.869580	0.205357
21	46.005120	225.025600	0.004444	0.021737	4.891316	0.204444
22	55.206144	271.030719	0.003690	0.018114	4.909430	0.203690
23	66.247373	326.236863	0.003065	0.015095	4.924525	0.203065
24	79.496847	392.484236	0.002548	0.012579	4.937104	0.202548
25	95.396217	471.981083	0.002119	0.010483	4.947587	0.202119
26	114.475460	567.377300	0.001762	0.008735	4.956323	0.201762
27	137.370552	681.852760	0.001467	0.007280	4.963602	0.201467
28	164.844662	819.223312	0.001221	0.006066	4.969668	0.201221
29	197.813595	984.067974	0.001016	0.005055	4.974724	0.201016
30	237.376314	1181.881569	0.000846	0.004213	4.978936	0.200846
31	284.851577	1419.257883	0.000705	0.003511	4.982447	0.200705
32	341.821892	1704.109459	0.000587	0.002926	4.985372	0.200587
33	410.186270	2045.931351	0.000489	0.002438	4.987810	0.200489
34	492.223524	2456.117621	0.000407	0.002032	4.989842	0.200407
35	590.668229	2948.341146	0.000339	0.001693	4.991535	0.200339
36	708.801875	3539.009375	0.000283	0.001411	4.992946	0.200283
37	850.562250	4247.811250	0.000235	0.001176	4.994122	0.200235
38	1020.674700	5098.373500	0.000196	0.000980	4.995101	0.200196
39	1224.809640	6119.048200	0.000163	0.000816	4.995918	0.200163
40	1469.771568	7343.857840	0.000136	0.000680	4.996598	0.200136
41	1763.725882	8813.629408	0.000113	0.000567	4.997165	0.200113
42	2116.471058	10577.355290	0.000095	0.000472	4.997638	0.200095
43	2539.765269	12693.826348	0.000079	0.000394	4.998031	0.200079
44	3047.718323	15233.591617	0.000066	0.000328	4.998359	0.200066
45	3657.261988	18281.309940	0.000055	0.000273	4.998633	0.200055
46	4388.714386	21938.571928	0.000046	0.000228	4.998861	0.200046
47	5266.457263	26327.286314	0.000038	0.000190	4.999051	0.200038
48	6319.748715	31593.743577	0.000032	0.000158	4.999209	0.200032
49	7583.698458	37913.492292	0.000026	0.000132	4.999341	0.200026
50	9100.438150	45497.190751	0.000022	0.000110	4.999451	0.200022

20.00%   MONTHLY COMPOUND INTEREST TABLES   20.00%
                    EFFECTIVE RATE 1.667

	1 AMOUNT OF $1 AT COMPOUND INTEREST	2 ACCUMULATION OF $1 PER PERIOD	3 SINKING FUND FACTOR	4 PRESENT VALUE REVERSION OF $1	5 PRESENT VALUE ORD. ANNUITY $1 PER PERIOD	6 INSTALMENT TO AMORTIZE $1	
MONTHS							
1	1.016667	1.000000	1.000000	0.983607	0.983607	1.016667	
2	1.033611	2.016667	0.495868	0.967482	1.951088	0.512534	
3	1.050838	3.050278	0.327839	0.951622	2.902710	0.344506	
4	1.068352	4.101116	0.243836	0.936021	3.838731	0.260503	
5	1.086158	5.169468	0.193444	0.920677	4.759408	0.210110	
6	1.104260	6.255625	0.159856	0.905583	5.664991	0.176523	
7	1.122665	7.359886	0.135872	0.890738	6.555729	0.152538	
8	1.141376	8.482551	0.117889	0.876136	7.431865	0.134556	
9	1.160399	9.623926	0.103908	0.861773	8.293637	0.120574	
10	1.179739	10.784325	0.092727	0.847645	9.141283	0.109394	
11	1.199401	11.964064	0.083584	0.833749	9.975032	0.100250	
12	1.219391	13.163465	0.075968	0.820081	10.795113	0.092635	
YEARS							**MONTHS**
1	1.219391	13.163465	0.075968	0.820081	10.795113	0.092635	12
2	1.486915	29.214877	0.034229	0.672534	19.647986	0.050896	24
3	1.813130	48.787826	0.020497	0.551532	26.908062	0.037164	36
4	2.210915	72.654905	0.013764	0.452301	32.861916	0.030430	48
5	2.695970	101.758208	0.009827	0.370924	37.744561	0.026494	60
6	3.287442	137.246517	0.007286	0.304188	41.748727	0.023953	72
7	4.008677	180.520645	0.005540	0.249459	45.032470	0.022206	84
8	4.888145	233.288730	0.004287	0.204577	47.725406	0.020953	96
9	5.960561	297.633662	0.003360	0.167769	49.933833	0.020027	108
10	7.268255	376.095300	0.002659	0.137585	51.744924	0.019326	120
11	8.862845	471.770720	0.002120	0.112831	53.230165	0.018786	132
12	10.807275	588.436476	0.001699	0.092530	54.448184	0.018366	144
13	13.178294	730.697658	0.001369	0.075882	55.447059	0.018035	156
14	16.069495	904.169675	0.001106	0.062230	56.266217	0.017773	168
15	19.594998	1115.699905	0.000896	0.051033	56.937994	0.017563	180
16	23.893966	1373.637983	0.000728	0.041852	57.488906	0.017395	192
17	29.136090	1688.165376	0.000592	0.034322	57.940698	0.017259	204
18	35.528288	2071.697274	0.000483	0.028147	58.311205	0.017149	216
19	43.322878	2539.372652	0.000394	0.023082	58.615050	0.017060	228
20	52.827531	3109.651838	0.000322	0.018930	58.864229	0.016988	240
21	64.417420	3805.045193	0.000263	0.015524	59.068575	0.016929	252
22	78.550028	4653.001652	0.000215	0.012731	59.236156	0.016882	264
23	95.783203	5686.992197	0.000176	0.010440	59.373585	0.016843	276
24	116.797184	6947.831050	0.000144	0.008562	59.486289	0.016811	288
25	142.421445	8485.286707	0.000118	0.007021	59.578715	0.016785	300
26	173.667440	10360.046428	0.000097	0.005758	59.654512	0.016763	312
27	211.768529	12646.111719	0.000079	0.004722	59.716672	0.016746	324
28	258.228656	15433.719354	0.000065	0.003873	59.767648	0.016731	336
29	314.881721	18832.903252	0.000053	0.003176	59.809452	0.016720	348
30	383.963963	22977.837794	0.000044	0.002604	59.843735	0.016710	360
31	468.202234	28032.134021	0.000036	0.002136	59.871850	0.016702	372
32	570.921630	34195.297781	0.000029	0.001752	59.894907	0.016696	384
33	696.176745	41710.604725	0.000024	0.001436	59.913815	0.016691	396
34	848.911717	50874.703013	0.000020	0.001178	59.929321	0.016686	408
35	1035.155379	62049.322767	0.000016	0.000966	59.942038	0.016683	420
36	1262.259241	75675.554472	0.000013	0.000792	59.952466	0.016680	432
37	1539.187666	92291.259934	0.000011	0.000650	59.961018	0.016678	444
38	1876.871717	112552.303044	0.000009	0.000533	59.968032	0.016676	456
39	2288.640640	137258.438382	0.000007	0.000437	59.973784	0.016674	468
40	2790.747993	167384.879554	0.000006	0.000358	59.978500	0.016673	480

Glossary of Terms

A

Absorption rate Estimated rate at which property for sale or lease can be marketed.

Abstract of title Historical summary of documents affecting title to real property.

Accelerated Cost Recovery System (ACRS) Depreciation schedule allowed by the Economic Recovery Tax Act of 1981 in which a property may be depreciated on an accelerated basis over 15 years.

Acceleration clause Mortgage contract clause that makes all payments due immediately if a scheduled payment is missed.

Accretion Growth in size, especially by addition or accumulation; the addition of soil to land by gradual, natural deposits.

Ad valorem Latin for "according to value."

Adjustable rate mortgage Mortgage loan on which the interest rate rises or falls with changes in market rates.

Adverse possession Acquisition of title to real property by action of law through fulfilling certain statutory requirements.

Agency Law governing the relationship between employers and their agents.

Air rights Right to occupy and use the airspace above the surface of a parcel of land.

Amortization Systematic apportionment of costs, loan principal, or other input to discrete periods of time such as months, years, and so on.

Annual percentage rate (APR) Term used in the Truth in Lending Act that describes simple annual interest charged to the borrower, including points and other charges.

Assessed value Dollar amount assigned to taxable property for tax purposes by the assessor or county property appraiser. It is usually a statutory percentage of market value.

Assignment Transfer of one person's rights under a contract to another.

Avulsion Sudden transference of a piece of land from one person's property to another's without change of ownership, as by a change in the course of a stream.

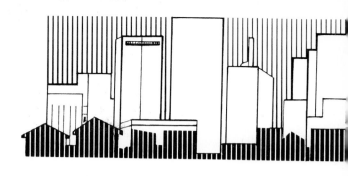

B

Balloon payment Amount of loan principal remaining unamortized and outstanding at the end of the mortgage term.

Band of investment approach Method of finding a capitalization rate for appraisal purposes by developing a weighted average of the mortgage rate and the required return on equity.

Bargain and sale deed Deed that conveys the land itself rather than the ownership interest.

Base line East/west line in the rectangular survey system from which land lying north or south is described in rows of townships.

Beta coefficient A measure of systematic risk in the capital asset pricing model.

Bid rent curve Graph that maps rent per square foot to distance from a central business district.

Bilateral contract Contract that involves the exchange of one promise for another promise.

Blanket mortgage Mortgage lien secured by several land parcels.

Blue-sky laws State laws to protect persons from buying into dubious investment schemes.

Boot Cash or other non-real-estate assets exchanged for real property

Breakeven cash ratio Ratio of debt service and operating expenses to gross income. Interpreted as the occupancy level that must be achieved to break even.

Broker In real estate, a person licensed to buy, sell, lease, rent, exchange, auction, or appraise real property as an agent for another, for compensation.

Building code Local and state laws that set minimum construction standards.

Buy-down Cash payment to a lender to reduce the borrower's interest rate and payment.

C

Capital improvement Expenditures that slow deterioration of property or add new improvements and appreciably prolong its economic life. Repairs merely maintain property in an efficient operating condition.

Capitalization Process of estimating value by discounting stabilized net operating income by an appropriate rate (i.e., converting an income flow to a capital stock).

Capitalization rate   Rate used to discount future income to estimate value.

CAPM   Capital asset pricing model. Theory that all assets are priced on the basis of expected return and the risk associated with receiving the expected return.

Cash inflow (outflow)   In investment analysis, all cash received (paid out) in connection with the investment. Outflows are the amount of equity in the investment.

Certificate of Occupacy   Governmentally (locally) issued document stating that a structure meets local zoning and building code requirements and is ready for use.

Certificate of title   Opinion by an attorney as to who owns a parcel of land or a Torrens certificate that shows ownership as recognized by a court of law.

Chain of title   Linkage of property ownership that connects the present owner to the original source of the title.

Closing   Event at which title to real estate is transferred.

Collateral   Assets that are pledged to secure or guarantee the discharge of an obligation.

Commission   Payment the broker receives for services rendered, usually expressed as a percentage of the property sale price.

Comparable properties   In the sales comparison approach, other properties to which the subject property can be compared in order to estimate market value.

Condemnation   Declaration that property is legally appropriated for public use; also, a declaration that something is unfit for use or service (e.g., the condemnation of a slum tenement).

Condominium   Arrangement under which tenants in an apartment building or in a complex or multiunit dwellings hold full title to their own units and joint ownership in the common grounds.

Consideration   Anything of value given to induce another party to enter into a contract.

Contract for deed   Agreement under which the buyer does not receive title to property until certain conditions are met.

Contract for sale   Legal document between the buyer and seller that states the purchase price and the manner in which ownership rights are to be transferred.

Contract rent   Rental fixed by agreement among parties which may or may not be comparable to rentals of similar properties.

Conventional mortgage   Mortgage not insured or guaranteed by a public or private agency.

Cooperative   Ownership form in which a single property is divided into several portions, with each user owning stock in a corporation that owns the property.

Cost-depreciation approach   Property value is estimated by subtracting accrued depreciation from reproduction cost new and then adding the value of the land.

Cost of capital   Charge that must be paid to attract money into an investment project.

CPM   Certified Property Manager.

Curable deterioration or obsolescence Cost to correct the item of physical deterioration or functional obsolescence is equal to or greater than the value added to the property.

D

Dealer Person or entity who cannot depreciate real estate held because the properties are the person's or entity's stock in trade.

Debt capital Borrowed money.

Debt service Mortgage payment.

Debt service coverage Requirement imposed by lender that earnings be a percentage or dollar sum higher than debt service.

Deed Document transferring title to real property.

Deed convenants Warranties made by a seller of property to protect the buyer against items such as liens, encumbrances, or title defects.

Deed of trust Document which transfers of ownership interest to a trustee acting on behalf of a money lender. The trustee is usually instructed to supervise collection of the debt and return the trust deed to the borrower upon retirement of the debt.

Deed restrictions Land-use constraints imposed in the deed passed from seller to buyer. These constraints then pass with the property in future transfers.

Default Failure to perform or carry out the terms of a contract.

Defeasance clause Prevents the mortgagee from foreclosing so long as the debtor fulfills the conditions of the mortgage.

Deficiency judgment Personal judgment against a borrower if the sale of foreclosed property does not bring enough to pay the loan balance.

Delinquent loan Loan in which the borrower is behind in his or her payments.

Depreciable basis Portion of original tax basis representing value or cost of improvements.

Depreciation (economic) Loss in property value due to physical, functional, and locational problems.

Depreciation (tax) Deductible expense for investment or business property that reflects the presumed wasting of the asset. Land and principal residences may not be depreciated.

Descent Transfer of ownership upon death by action of law as stated in the state's Statute of Descent.

Development of regional impact (DRI) In Florida, any proposed development large enough to have a measurable effect on the economy, environment, or public services of more than one county.

Devise Transfer of ownership by means of a will.

Direct capitalization Processing net operating income into value by dividing by an overall capitalization rate.

Direct sales comparison Value estimation methodology utilizing the sales prices of comparable properties to which adjustments are made to reflect value-creating differences between the property under appraisal and the comparables.

Discount Additional interest taken by a lender by lending less actual cash than the mortgage loan principal.

Discount points Charges imposed by lenders to adjust the effective interest rate on loans.

Discount rate   Relationship between dollars transmitted from the lender to a borrower and dollars that must be repaid by the borrower. If a lender advances $960 and the borrower must repay $1,000, the discount rate is $40/$1,000 = 4 percent.

Discounting   Process of converting any cash flow into present value at a selected rate of return. Based on the idea that one would pay less than $1 today for the right to receive $1 at a future date.

Dower   The right of a property owner's widow to obtain a life estate in her deceased husband's real estate.

Downzoning   Changing the zoning classification of property from a higher use to a lower use (e.g., from commercial to residential).

Due on sale clause   Clause in a mortgage or deed of trust requiring the balance to be paid in full when the property is sold.

E

Earnest money   Money paid to evidence good faith when a contract of purchase is submitted to a property owner by a prospective purchaser.

Easement   Right or privilege that a person may have to use another's land.

Easement appurtenant   Easement that is attached to a parcel of land and passes with the land when sold to a subsequent owner.

Easement by necessity   Easement created when land is subdivided or separated into more than one parcel without a provision for ingress and egress.

Easement by prescription   Easement created by adverse use, openly and continuous for a specified (by state law) period of time.

Easement in gross   Easement that is not attached to any parcel of land but is merely a personal right to use the land of another.

Economic base analysis   Study of a community's employment and income to forecast population changes and to plan for future expansion of basic and service employment.

Economic good   Any material or immaterial thing that satisfies human desire and that is relatively scarce, so it commands a price in market exchange.

Economic life   Length of time improvements (usually buildings) will produce a competitive return; land may have an infinite economic life.

Effective yield   Return on investment calculation that considers the price paid, the time held, and the interest rate.

Elastic demand   Phenomenon of a large response in quantity demanded due to a small change in price.

Elasticity   Ability of supply of real estate to respond to price increases over a short period of time.

Ellwood technique   Mortgage-equity income capitalization methodology for estimating an overall capitalization rate.

Embargo   Action by one government prohibiting trade with another country.

Eminent domain   Right of a government or agency thereof to take private property for a public purpose. Just compensation must be paid to the owner whose property is taken.

Encroachment   Unauthorized intrusion of a building or other improvement onto another's property.

Encumbrance Claim against title, such as a mortgage, tax lien, or mechanic's lien.

Environmental impact report (EIR) A detailed analysis of a project's potential effect on an area's environmental subsystems, such as air, water, sewer, and transportation.

Environmental Protection Agency (EPA) Federal agency set up to protect the health and welfare of Americans by controlling environmental pollution hazards.

Equity Share of property possessed by owners after allowing for borrowed funds.

Equity build-up Increase in an investor's equity in an investment due to loan balance reduction.

Equity-dividend rate Cash flow divided by initial equity investment. May be before or after taxes.

Equity kickers Provision in the loan terms that guarantees the lender a percentage of property appreciation over some specified time and/or a percentage of income from the property.

Equity of redemption Borrower's right prior to foreclosure to repay the balance due on a delinquent mortgage loan.

Escalator clause Permits a lender to vary the mortgage interest rate unilaterally, usually upward. Adjustment is not tied to an index.

Escheat Revision of real property to the government when the owner dies without a will or heirs.

Escrow Real estate transactions are accomplished in escrow when the deed is delivered to a third party (escrow agent) for delivery to the buyer on performance of a condition. The condition may be that title is made clear in the buyer. Escrow also refers to earmarked bank accounts in which are kept earnest money or other funds designated for a particular use.

Escrow agreement Establishment of a fiduciary who holds documents, cash, or both until all elements of a transaction can be completed.

Estate Quantity, duration, or extent of interest in real property.

Estate at sufferance Rights of a tenant after the lease expires whereby tenant stays without special permission from the landlord.

Estate at will Interest in property that arises when the owner leases the property to another and the duration of the lease is at the will of the owner or the tenant.

Estate for years Leasehold interest in real property that terminates after a fixed period of time.

Estate from period to period Leasehold interest of a tenant that automatically renews for the period specified in the original lease, until terminated by either tenant or owner.

Estopped certificate Document in which the borrower verifies the remaining amount owed and interest rate of a loan.

Exchange Ownership of like-kind properties are transferred between two or more owners; can result in postponement of part or all of the tax for one or more of the parties to the exchange.

Exclusive listing Agreement between seller of property and broker in which the seller agrees to pay a commission to the broker if the seller's property is sold by anyone other than the seller.

Exclusive right of sale listing Agreement between seller of property and broker in which the broker is assured a commission if the property is sold by the broker or anyone else, including the owner.

Exculpatory clause Clause in the mortgage that relieves the borrower of personal liability to repay the loan.

Expected value Weighted average of values of an experiment's outcome. This is a measure of central tendency.

F

FDIC Federal Deposit Insurance Corporation.

Feasibility analysis Study of the cash flow, profitability potential, and overall desirability of a project.

Fee simple absolute Entire bundle of rights to use and control of real property.

FHA Federal Housing Administration. A division of the U.S. Department of Housing and Urban Development that insures mortgage loans.

FHLBB Federal Home Loan Bank Board. The administrative agency that charters federal savings institutions and regulates the members of the Federal Home Loan Bank System.

FHLBS Federal Home Loan Bank System. The Federal Home Loan Bank Board, Federal Home Loan Banks, and member financial institutions.

FHLMC Federal Home Loan Mortgage Corporation. Referred to as "Freddie Mac" and supervised by the Federal Home Loan Bank Board, the FHLMC creates a secondary mortgage market for conventional loans.

FNMA Federal National Mortgage Association. Referred to as "Fannie Mae," the FNMA is a privately owned, government-sponsored agency that buys and sells FHA-insured, VA-guaranteed, and conventional mortgage loans.

FSLIC Federal Savings and Loan Insurance Corporation. Insures deposits of members of FHLBs.

Fiduciary One who the law regards as having a duty toward another by reason of a relationship of trust and confidence.

Fiduciary relationship Relationship between an agent and principal in that the agent has the duty of acting for the benefit of the principal.

Filtering Movement of people of one income group into homes that have recently dropped in price and that were previously occupied by persons in the next higher income group.

Financial risk Possibility of losses caused by borrowing.

Fixture Fittings or components of a property attached to a building which legally are considered to be a part of the real estate.

Flat lease Equal rental payments are made over the term of the lease.

Foreclosure Act of depriving a borrower of the right to redeem a mortgage when regular payments have not been kept up.

Freehold estate Estate in land held for life or with the right to pass it on through inheritance.

Functional obsolescence Decline in value of property caused by changes in technology or by defects in design, layout, or size of building. Loss of a building's ability to perform its function.

G

General partnership Form of co-ownership for business purposes wherein all partners have a voice in the management and unlimited liability for its debts.

General warranty deed Highest form of deed a granter can give a grantee in that the grantor is liable for any title defects that were created during his period of ownership and all previous owners.

Gentrification Process in which rising prices and condominium conversions squeeze out low-income tenants in central cities in favor of high-income tenants.

H

HVAC Heating, ventilation, and air conditioning.

Highest and best use Vacant site—that use of the site which results in maximum productivity and return on investment. Improved property—the type of occupancy that maximizes the return to the total property.

Historic preservation Restoration of a property to its original form.

Homestead Primary domicile, as declared by the head of a family and filed with county clerk of courts. Purpose is to exempt homestead from claims of creditors.

Homestead exemption Deduction from assessed value for purposes of real estate tax calculation, granted by state laws to the head of a family on property designated as his or her homestead.

Hospitality facility Facility offering lodging accommodations to the general public and usually providing a wide range of additional services, including restaurants, meeting rooms, and a swimming pool; a hotel or motel.

HUD U.S. Department of Housing and Urban Development.

Hundred percent commission Arrangement whereby the salesperson receives 100% of sales commissions and pays for office overhead directly, rather than splitting commission income with the broker.

I

IAAO International Association of Assessing Officials.

Implied agency Agency relationship created by circumstances that give the agent justified reasons for believing the principal had created an agency.

Implied contract Contract created by the actions of the parties involved.

Implied easement Right of access to a property that is created by conveyance of the property in such a manner that it would not be accessible, e.g., if it were landlocked by the grantor's property.

Incurable deterioration or obsolescence Cost to correct the item of physical deterioration or functional obsolescence exceeds the value added to the property.

Inelastic demand Situation in which a change in price produces a proportionately smaller change in quality demanded.

Ingress   Place or means of entering; entrance.

Installment sale   Disposition of a property that permits deferral of taxes over time provided certain rules are observed.

Insured loan   Loan which is insured by the FHA or a private mortgage insurance company.

Insured mortgage   Mortgage insured by the Federal Housing Administration or a private insurance agency such as Mortgage Guaranty Insurance Corporation.

Interest rate risk   Risk of an investment's price change in reaction to interest rate changes.

Internal rate of return   Interest rate that discounts future cash flows and cash reversion from a project equal to the initial investment.

Intestate   Without a last will and testament.

Inverse condemnation   Loss of property rights by government action, such as downzoning.

Investment holding period   Length of time that the investor is assumed to hold a property before sale or exchange.

Investment property   Asset owned for the purpose of earning an investment return as opposed to one held as stock in trade or one held for operation in the ordinary course of business.

Investment value   Value to investors based on their particular requirements.

IREM   Institute of Real Estate Management.

J

Joint tenancy   Special ownership situation in which two or more owners hold equal shares, acquire shares concurrently, and have equal rights of possession. The rights of one owner pass to the other owner upon the one's death.

Joint venture   Association of two or more persons or firms in order to carry out a single business project.

Junior mortgage   Any mortgage on a property that is subordinate to a senior mortgage in priority.

L

Land contract   Method of conveying title to real property in which legal title does not pass to the buyer until the contract for deed is fulfilled. The contract for deed usually requires the purchase price to be paid in installments.

Lease   Contract providing for the transfer of a right to use real estate.

Leaseholds   Less-than-freehold estates that are usually considered to be personal property.

Leverage   Use of money borrowed at a fixed rate of interest in an investment project with the expectation of obtaining a higher rate of return on the equity investment as a result.

License   Formal permission to do some specified activity, especially some activity authorized by law; also, a document, permit, and so on, indicating such permission has been granted.

Lien Claim against property whereby the property is security for a debt. The holder of the lien is entitled to have the property sold to satisfy the debt.

Lien theory State law permitting lenders to secure a lien against property as collateral for a loan.

Limited partnership Ownership form in which a general partner performs all management functions and assumes all operating liabilities on behalf of passive investors known as limited partners.

Linkage Time and distance relationship between a subject site and an important location such as a school, a shopping area, or a place of employment.

Liquidity Relationship between a speedy sale price and the total number of dollars invested in a property.

Liquidity risk Risk that an asset cannot be sold quickly for an amount equal to or above the amount invested.

Loan-to-value ratio Amount of money a lender will loan on a property divided by the value of the property.

Locational obsolescence Decline in value of property caused by deterioration in the quality of its neighborhood; also known as external obsolescence.

M

Management survey Comprehensive analysis of an income property, including its physical condition, its market, its alternative potential uses, and its income and expense potential.

Marginal Last unit or increment of change.

Marginal cost Increased cost resulting from the production of one additional item or unit of items.

Marginal rate of return Return on investment resulting from the production of an additional item or unit of items.

Marginal revenue Increased income resulting from the production of an additional item or unit of items.

Marginal tax rate Percentage of an additional dollar of taxable income paid in income taxes.

Market Interaction of suppliers (sellers) and demanders (buyers) of a particular good or product that establishes the price for the good or product.

Market analysis Study of a market to determine the type of real estate needed.

Market rent Rental level determined by rents for similar properties in a selected market area.

Market risk Possibility that downward market trends will cause a loss in market value. Also known as systematic or nondiversifiable risk.

Market segmentation Identification and delineation of a submarket.

Market value Price a property should bring in a competitive market when there has been a normal offering time, no coercion, arms-length bargaining, typical financing, and informed buyer and sellers; exchange value.

Marketability Relationship between a speedy sale price and the current market value of a property.

Marketer Person engaged in marketing of a product or service; one who deals with the satisfaction of human needs on a broad scale.

Mechanic's lien Right to have a property sold by those who perform labor, services, or furnished materials in the improvement of real property.

Metes and bounds Method of legally decribing real estate in which a mete is a unit of measure (foot, mile) and a bound is a boundary marker.

Metropolitan Statistical Area (MSA) Areas defined by the Bureau of the Census as a group of counties with a high degree of economic and social integration. MSAs must include at least one city with 50,000 or more inhabitants or a Census Bureau defined urbanized area of at least 50,000 inhabitants and a total MSA population of at least 100,000. Current MSA standards were adopted in January 1980, and the term was officially changed from Standard Metropolitan Statistical Area (SMSA) to MSA in 1983.

Millage rate Tax rate expressed as dollars payable per $1,000 of assessed property value; for example 15 mills means $15 tax on each $1,000 of assessed property value.

Monopolistic competition Control of a market by a number of sellers who differentiate their services on some basis other than price (such as quality or service).

Monopoly Control of a market by one seller.

Monument Permanent marker indicating a corner of a parcel of land. A method of legally describing real estate.

Mortgage Written evidence of the right of a creditor to have property of a debtor sold upon default, with the proceeds applied to the debt.

Mortgage-backed securities Securities whose income is derived from a pool of mortgages whose payments have been guaranteed by a secondary mortgage market institution such as GNMA or FHLMC.

Mortgage bankers Real estate financial specialists who serve as agents of lenders in originating and servicing loans.

Mortgage constant Percentage of original loan balance represented by the periodic mortgage payment. A payment of $100,000 per year on a $1 million mortgage results in a mortgage constant of 10 percent.

Mortgage equity analysis Estimating a property's value by estimating the values separately of the debt and equity, and then summing them.

Mortgagee Lender who receives a mortgage from a borrower as security for a promissory note.

Mortgagor Borrower who conveys a mortgage interest to a lender as security for a promissory note.

Multiple listing Sharing of property sales listings by a number of real estate brokers with an agreement as to how costs and commissions are to be shared.

Mutual savings banks Financial institutions in which the depositors are the owners. Mutual savings banks are a primary source of home mortgage funds.

N

NAR (National Association of REALTORS®) An organization of real estate professionals within which there are several institutes, societies, and councils that sponsor educational, research, and political lobbying activities in their areas of expertise.

Net lease Lease agreement under which lessee pays all taxes, insurance, maintenance, utilities, and other expenses.

Net listing Type of contract in which the seller specifies the amount he or she will accept from the sale of his or her property, with the broker keeping all proceeds in excess of that amount.

Net operating income (NOI) Potential gross income less an allowance for vacancies and collection losses, minus operating expenses, and minus reserves for replacement.

Net present value Difference between the value of the cash flow and the property reversion (discounted at the investor's required rate of return) and the initial equity investment.

Nominal rate of return Rate of return on investment unadjusted for inflation or other risk.

Nonconforming use Existing improvement that could no longer be constructed on a site because of a change in zoning.

Nonmarketable securities Usually notes taken in an installment or deferred payment sale containing restrictive clauses that hinder their marketability. This hindrance may be designed to reduce the seller's income tax liability.

Note (promissory) Document evidencing a debt and describing the terms by which the debt is to be repaid.

O

Obsolescence Process of becoming less useful and losing value.

Occupancy Period during which a house or other real estate is kept in possession; in law, the taking possession of a previously unowned object, thus establishing ownership.

Officer's deed Document that transfers property from a public official to an auction purchaser, with the ownership rights of the foreclosed owner being cut off after a stated redemption period. No warranties are made.

Oligopoly Control of a market by a small number of suppliers.

Open-end mortgage A mortgage that provides for the borrowing of additional sums.

Open listing Agreement between the seller of property and a broker which provides for the broker to receive a commission if he or she sells the property. No exclusive protection is provided the broker.

Operating expense ratio Relationship between operating expenses and a property's effective gross income.

Operating expenses Periodic outlays of up to one year's duration required to maintain and operate a property.

Option Contract given by a landowner to another person, giving the latter the right to buy (lease) the property at a certain price within a specified time.

Original tax basis Cost of acquisition of the real estate or cost of construction of improvements, plus the acquisition cost of the site.

P

Package mortgage Debt secured by the pledge of both real property and personal property (range, refrigerator, and so on).

Paired sales analysis Estimating the value of property components or characteristics by comparing sale prices of properties that are similar in most respects but differ with respect to the component or characteristic whose value is sought.

Participation mortgage   Loan in which the lender receives profits or ownership of the property as well as contract interest.

Partnership   Form of business organization in which two or more people join together to operate a business. No federal income taxes must be paid by the partnership; all profits and losses are allocated to the partners according to their contributions to the partnership. Each partner then is liable for taxes on income received.

Pass-through security   Mortgage-backed security in which all principal and interest payments received by the servicing agent are passed along to investors in the securities.

Patent   Special type of deed that conveys title to land owned by the federal government to a private party.

Payback period   Length of time required for the cash flow from a project to equal the amount of money invested.

Periodic tenancy   Leasehold estate that is automatically extended from period to period unless lessee or lessor gives appropriate notice. Also called a tenancy from period to period.

Personal property (personalty)   Chattels; items of property that are not land or permanently attached to land.

Physical characteristics   Nonlocational and nonlegal characteristics of a property and its immediate surroundings.

Physical deterioration   Wearing out of a property.

Planned unit development (PUD)   Land development project involving a mixture of land uses and densities not available with separate zoning for each land use. It is allowed because the entire development is viewed as an integrated whole.

Plat   Drawing that shows boundaries, shape, and size of a parcel of land.

Plottage value   Value added to land by assembling small parcels into large tracts.

Points   Additional interest charged by a lender at origination of a loan; one point equals 1 percent of the mortgage loan principal.

Police power   Constitutional authority of government to limit the exercise of private property rights as necessary to protect the health, safety, and welfare of all citizens. It constitutes the legal basis for zoning.

Portfolio   Collection of investments.

Prepayment privilege   Mortgage contract clause permitting the borrower to make loan payments in advance of their due dates without penalty.

Prescription   Right of one who uses the land of another for a period of time stated by law to obtain an easement to the subject land.

Present value   Today's value derived by measuring all future benefits of an investment and converting those benefits into a lump-sum amount.

Price-level adjusted mortgage   Loan in which the outstanding balance is adjusted periodically to reflect changes in a price level index.

Primary mortgage market   Market in which real estate loans are originated.

Principal   In brokerage, the person giving authority to an agent; in finance, the amount borrowed and owed on a loan.

Principal meridian   Main north-south reference line used in a rectangular survey description.

Prisoner's dilemma   Situation in which an individual owner's desire for action is restrained by surrounding owners' inaction, as in the case of neighborhood deterioration.

Private mortgage insurance   Insurance plan that protects a lender from financial loss in case of default by the borrower. Usually covers only a portion of the total loan amount.

Private grant   Conveyance of property from one private owner to another private owner.

Productivity   Relationship between the value of outputs in the production process and the value of all inputs.

Profit   Amount received for goods, products, or services that exceeds the total cost of producing them.

Promissory note   Document containing the promise of a borrower to pay a lender a sum or sums of money at specified times at a particular interest rate.

Property   Interests or rights in physical assets.

Property management   Process of operating a parcel of real estate.

Property residual technique   Income capitalization methodology that discounts net operating income and the site reversion to present value without separating NOI into income attributable to the building and the site.

Proration   Allocation of costs and revenues between buyer and seller of real property at closing, based on the time of ownership by each party.

Public goods   Products and services that are consumed collectively by society.

Public grant   Conveyance of property from the government to a private owner.

Public planning   Process followed by a public agency to prepare communitywide comprehensive plans.

Purchase money mortgage   Mortgage taken by the seller of property as part of the purchase price. For example, a buyer might pay $20,000 cash and give the seller an $80,000 mortgage to purchase a $100,000 property.

Purchasing power risk   Devaluation of assets due to inflation and the decreasing purchasing power of a dollar.

Q

Quantity survey   Method of estimating building reproduction or replacement cost in which all elements of labor, materials, and overhead are priced and totaled to obtain building cost.

Quitclaim deed   Deed that passes property rights without guarantees.

R

Range line   North/south line parallel to a principal meridian from which land lying east or west is described in columns of townships.

Rapid write-off (accelerated) depreciation   All tax depreciation methods that permit taking depreciation expense greater than what would be taken using straight-line depreciation.

Real estate   Land including the buildings or improvements on the land. Also included are the airspace above the land and the contents below the surface.

Real estate investment trust (REIT)   Passive investment vehicle whose distributed earnings are taxed only to investors who receive them. It is similar to a corporation except for the permitted avoidance of double taxation of dividends.

Real Estate Settlement Procedures Act (RESPA) 1973 federal law requiring advance disclosure of settlement practices and costs and restricting practices that may increase settlement costs.

Real property Legal rights to possession, use, and disposition of real estate.

REALTOR® Registered trademark reserved for members of the National Association of Realtors; Realtors subscribe to an idealistic code of ethics that sets standards for conduct and integrity in all business dealings.

Reappraisal lease Lease having a clause calling for periodic rent adjustments based on changes in property value, as determined by appraisals.

Recapture (depreciation) Disallowance of a portion of rapid depreciation income tax deductions when accumulated rapid depreciation exceeds the amount of depreciation that would have been taken during the holding period if straight-line depreciation had been used.

Reconciliation Process of evaluating data, conclusions, or value indications to reach a single answer.

Reconstructed operating statement Statement of income and expenses for a property in a form relevent to appraisal.

Recording Filing a document with the appropriate public official in order to provide constructive notice.

Rectangular survey system Grid arrangement for legally describing land based on principal meridians and base lines.

Redemption Right of a defaulting borrower to pay principal and interest owed on a mortgaged property prior to foreclosure and to regain unclouded title.

Redlining Delineation of geographic areas in which a lender does not make real property loans or in which loans are made on terms less favorable than those found in preferred areas.

Regressive tax Tax that takes a higher percentage of lower-income taxpayers' incomes than higher-income taxpayers' incomes.

Rehabilitation Restoration of a property to satisfactory condition without changing the plan, form, or style of a structure.

Reliction Receding water boundary that leaves dry land to be added to the title holder's property.

Remainder Right held by someone other than the grantor to receive title to a property upon termination of an intervening interest, such as a life estate.

Remainderman Person who holds a remainder.

Remodeling Renovation of a property that changes the plan, form, or style of a structure to remove physical deterioration and functional obsolescence.

Renegotiable rate mortgage Short-term mortgage with payments calculated over a normal 25- to 30-year period but renewed at 3- to 5-year intervals with possible interest rate adjustments.

Rent Consideration given for a leasehold estate; in economic theory, unearned or surplus income.

Replacement cost Cost of constructing an improvement with utility similar to a subject property.

Reproduction cost Cost at current prices of constructing a replica of an existing building.

Reserve for replacements   Account deducted from effective gross income which prorates the cost of replacing short-lived items over their useful lives.

Residual techniques   Assignment of a portion of income to part of an asset, with the remainder (or residual) flowing automatically to the rest of the asset. Also, the assignment of part of the income to cover debt payments with the balance accruing to the equity.

Restrictive covenant   Limitation on the use of real property created by a clause in the deed at the time a property is conveyed from one owner to another. Also called a deed restriction.

Return on investment (ROI)   Percentage relationship between the stream of income dollars obtained from an investment and the price paid by an investor.

Reverse annuity mortgage   Loan to a homeowner that is paid as an annuity, with interest accumulating on the increasing balance. The loan is paid back in a lump sum, usually from the sale or refinancing of the property.

Reversion   Return of an estate to a grantor after the period of grant is over or at the end of an investment holding period.

Reversion value   Worth of the site at a time when improvements value is zero (end of their economic life); worth of the property (improvements and site) at the end of an investment holding period.

Right of survivorship   Right of cotenants to receive all rights in the co-owned property of a deceased cotenant.

Right-of-way   Right of passage over another's property; also, land over which a public road, an electric power line, or other public utility passes.

Riparian rights   Property rights obtained by the movement of a body of water.

Risk   Potential variance in estimates of a project's income, expenses, or cash flow.

Risk-adjusted discount rate   A rate of return which has been increased to reflect the riskiness of the investment.

Risk averse   Category of investors who try to avoid risks.

S

Sales comparison approach   Method for estimating the market value of real estate in which adjustments are made to the sale prices of comparable properties to reflect the characteristics of a subject property.

Salesperson   Person who performs the acts of a broker through association with a licensed broker.

Salvage value   Estimated market value of improvements or other depreciable assets at the end of their useful life.

Sandwich lease   Lease by which a lessee sublets a leasehold estate.

Secondary financing market   Market composed of purchasers of mortgages from institutions that originate mortgage loans to individual borrowers. The principal entities in the secondary home loan market are the Federal National Mortgage Association (FNMA), the Federal Home Loan Mortgage Corporation (FHLMC), and the Government National Mortgage Association (GNMA).

Section   Area of land one mile square containing 640 acres. In the rectangular survey systems, 36 sections comprise a township.

Section 8 program Program of rent supplements established in 1975 by HUD and allocated to local governments.

Sensitivity analysis Changes in selected dependent variables (aftertax internal rate of return, etc.) resulting from a given change in one or more independent variables (rents, vacancy levels, mortgage terms, etc.).

Servient estate Property over which the owners of another property have an easement.

Sequential analysis Estimating the rate of change in the prices of the same property over time.

Settlement Final accounting in a real estate transaction which shows amounts owed by seller and buyer and to whom payable; closing.

Shared appreciation mortgage Mortgage loan made at below market rates in return for the lender's participating in any appreciation in the property's value when it is sold.

Simulation Computer-assisted investment analysis which assigns probabilities of occurrence to variables such as rents, vacancy rates, and operating expenses in order to observe the resulting distributions of dependent variables (rates of return, property values).

Site Parcel of land that is developed to a point that it is ready for construction of a building or other improvements.

Site residual technique Income capitalization method in which building cost is assumed to equal building value. Net operating income is allocated between building income and site income, which is capitalized into site value and added to building value (cost) to obtain market value of the property.

Smart buildings Buildings that have sophisticated communications systems built in and available for tenants' use.

Social class Group of people delineated by selected social characteristics.

Special agent Agent with authority to perform only a specific act or function on behalf of a principal. Real estate brokers usually act as special agents.

Special assessment Charge made by local government against properties to defray costs of public improvements which directly benefit the properties assessed.

Special warranty deed Deed in which the grantors covenant only against claims arising from the time during which they owned the property.

Specifications Requirements about the quantity and quality of materials and components used in a construction project.

Standard deviation Measure of dispersion about a central value; mathematically, the square root of the variance.

Statement of consideration Statement in a deed that the purchaser actually paid something for the property.

Statutes of descent and distribution State laws specifying who receives the property of a deceased person who dies intestate.

Statute of frauds Legal requirement that all matters affecting title to real estate must be in writing to be enforced by a court of law.

Statutory redemption Right of a mortgagor to redeem a property after foreclosure for a specified time. This right exists only in some states.

Straight-line capitalization Process of discounting future income into present value given the assumption that the investment in improvements is recaptured in equal annual amounts that are not reinvested.

Straight-term loan Loan in which there is no repayment of the principal until the due date.

Subdividing Separation of a parcel of land into smaller parcels. Selling more than five parcels in a single year can cause investors to become dealers in real property.

Submarket (housing) Collection of housing units considered to be close substitutes by a relatively homogeneous group of households; similar housing units that provide equal utility or satisfaction.

Subordination Lowering of a claimholder's priority to a position below an otherwise lower claimholder's position.

Surcharge Additional amount added to the usual charge.

Survey Process of accurately establishing the boundaries of a parcel of real estate.

Syndicate Group of individuals, corporations, trusts, or a combination of these who pool money to undertake economic ventures. The syndicate can take the form of a corporation, a trust, a partnership, a tenancy in common, or any other legal ownership form.

Syndication Formation of a group of individuals, trusts, corporations, or combination of these to carry out a financial venture.

Systematic risk Undiversifiable risk in a portfolio. It is the same as market risk.

T

Tandem plan Process in which GNMA subsidizes socially desirable loans by buying them at face value and selling them at a discount to FNMA.

Tax abatement Reduction in property tax for particular properties, usually intended to promote development.

Tax base Taxable value to which a tax rate is applied to calculate tax liability.

Tax credit Allowable reduction in the amount of income tax owed.

Tax deferral Postponement of a tax bill.

Tax deferred exchange Trade of like-kind property that does not trigger recognition of taxable gain at the time of the exchange.

Tax exempt Category of properties that are not subject to the property tax.

Tax lien Right of a taxing jurisdiction to have property sold for the nonpayment of taxes.

Tax preference Sources of income that are taxed, if not already included in the tax calculation.

Tax shelter Net loss that can be deducted from other income for tax purposes.

Tax shelters Legally permissible methods of reducing or postponing the burden of the federal income tax, including accelerated depreciation, capital gains, exchanges, and so on.

Taxable income Rent collections minus operating expenses, depreciation, and interest paid on borrowed funds.

Technical efficiency Producing a good or product for the lowest cost.

Telecommunications Methods of communicating over long distances.

Tenancy Right to possession and use of real property and the conditions relating to those rights.

Tenancy at sufferance Status a tenant occupies when the leasehold no longer exists and the tenant still occupies the property without the owner's permission.

Tenancy at will   Leasehold estate that continues for an indefinite period until notice is given by either lessee or lessor.

Tenancy by the entirety   Joint tenancy ownership by a husband and wife with right of survivorship.

Tenancy for a fixed or definite term   Leasehold estate of specified duration, such as a year, that automatically terminates at the end of that period.

Tenancy in common   Joint ownership in which each owner has an undivided interest in the property. There is no right of survivorship among the owners.

Tenancy in partnership   Ownership of real estate by a partnership. Interests among the partners are equal and may not be conveyed without the consent of all partners.

Testate   The status of dying with a valid will.

Thematic image   Conceptual view of a property developed around a central theme.

Tier   Row of townships either north or south of the base line.

Time line   Graphic depiction of money inflows and outflows over time.

Time value of money   Concept that the value of money depends on when it is received, with money at or nearer the present time worth more than the same amount received in a later period.

Title   Right of ownership, especially of real estate.

Title examination   Attorney's review of all recorded documents relating to a particular property to determine the nature of interests in the property.

Title insurance   Insurance paying monetary damages for loss of property from superior legal claims not excepted in the policy.

Title opinion   Attorney's opinion of the quality of title following a title examination.

Title theory   State law which recognizes that lenders obtain title to property in a mortgage as collateral for a loan.

Torrens system   Method of providing evidence of ownership to real property by means of a single document or certificate.

Township   In the rectangular survey system, an area six miles square containing 36 sections.

Trade fixtures   Items of personal property owned by tenants which, unlike fixtures, can be removed by the tenants.

Trading on the equity   Using borrowed funds for which the interest rate is lower than the return on a property or project; synonymous with leverage.

Transfer characteristics   Relative ease of movement of goods, persons, and messages among geographically separated sites and establishments; location or locational characteristics.

Transfer costs   Costs of overcoming the friction of space.

Transfer payments   Redistribution of private sector income via government taxes and subsidies to citizens or groups in an attempt to achieve equity.

Transfer tax   Tax levied on deeds, usually based on the purchase price and payable at the time the deed is recorded.

Transferable development rights   Rights to develop which cannot be used at one site but can be sold and used at another site.

Trust deed Conveyance of contingent title to a trustee who holds it as security for a lender; used in some states in lieu of a mortgage.

Trustee Person who administers property held in trust for another.

U

Undivided interest Partial interest by a joint owner in an entire parcel of real estate rather than total interest in a physically divided portion of the parcel.

Unfavorable exposure Environmental influence that reduces the desirability of a site.

Unilateral contract Agreement in which one party agrees to act in return for a promise by the other party.

Unit-in-place costs Method of estimating building reproduction or replacement cost in which materials and labor are costed on an installed basis and summed to obtain building cost.

Usury laws State laws limiting the maximum interest rate that can be charged on loans.

Unsystematic risk Diversifiable risk in a portfolio of investments; risk that is not related to market changes.

Urban renewal Process of renovation or rehabilitation of deteriorated areas within a city.

Useful life Period of time permitted by the Internal Revenue Service for computing annual depreciation expense.

V

VA Veterans Administration.

VA loan Loan guaranteed by the Veterans Administration.

Valuable consideration Consideration in the form of money, promises, or property.

Valuation Appraisal of the market value of real estate.

Value Ratio at which goods exchange; the relative worth of an object, usually measured in money terms.

Value in exchange Price an asset is expected to bring based on comparable market transactions; price which people in general expect to pay. It is distinguished from value in use, which is usually a higher price to an atypical owner or user.

Value in use Price an owner or investor would pay based on his or her personal assessment of the asset's merit; it usually implies a higher price than value.

Variance In statistics, a measure of dispersion about a central value; in zoning, a permitted deviation for a particular property from the zoning category for the property.

Vertical equity Fairness among people in different income groups.

Vertical integration Performance of different economic functions by one firm.

Vested remainder Remainder in which the remainderman can be identified.

Videoconferencing Two-way telecommunications conferences in which participants can both see and hear each other.

W

Warehousing (loans)   Lending funds to a mortgage banker with existing loans as security so that he or she may increase the inventory of mortgage loans. Typically a commercial bank does the warehousing.

Warranty deed   The most desirable type of deed from a buyer's viewpoint because it provides certain warranties or guarantees. Warranties include the covenant of seizin, covenant against encumbrances, and covenant for quiet enjoyment.

Wraparound mortgage   Junior lien on a property that enables the borrower to increase the amount of borrowing without paying off the original loan or paying the higher interest rates or other types of secondary financing.

Will   Document executed during a person's lifetime that conveys the person's property at death.

Y

Yield   Relationship between income or cash received from an investment and the value of the capital producing the income or cash; synonymous with internal rate of return.

Z

Zoning   Regulation of land use, population density, and building size by district. May be viewed as a phase of comprehensive planning in which the plan's implementation is enforced through police power.

Index

This book has been set in 10 and 9 point Palatino, leaded 2 points. Part and chapter numbers are 30 point Helvetica Bold; part and chapter titles are 24 point Helvetica Regular. The size of the type page is 36 by 47 picas.